Modern Scandals

1904-2008

Modern Scandals

1904-2008

Volume 3
1998-2008
Appendixes
Indexes

Editor
Carl L. Bankston III
Tulane University

SALEM PRESS
Pasadena, California   Hackensack, New Jersey

Editor in Chief: Dawn P. Dawson

Editorial Director: Christina J. Moose   *Research Supervisor:* Jeffry Jensen
Development Editor: R. Kent Rasmussen   *Design and Graphics:* James Hutson
Project Editor: Desiree Dreeuws   *Layout:* William Zimmerman
Acquisitions Editor: Mark Rehn   *Research Assistant:* Keli Trousdale
Production Editor: Andrea E. Miller   *Editorial Assistant:* Dana Garey
Photo Editor: Cynthia Breslin Beres

Cover photos (pictured clockwise, from top left): (The Granger Collection, New York); Duke and Duchess of Windsor. (Hulton Archive/Getty Images); (The Granger Collection, New York); Jean-Bédel Bokassa. (AP/Wide World Photos); (AP/Wide World Photos); (©iStockphoto.com/Mark Sauerwein)

Library of Congress Cataloging-in-Publication Data

Great events from history. Modern scandals / editor, Carl L. Bankston III.
    v.   cm. — (Great events from history)
    Includes bibliographical references and indexes.
    ISBN 978-1-58765-468-8 (set : alk. paper) — ISBN 978-1-58765-469-5 (v. 1: alk. paper) — ISBN 978-1-58765-470-1 (v. 2 : alk. paper) — ISBN 978-1-58765-471-8 (v. 3 : alk. paper)
1. Scandals—History—20th century. 2. Scandals—History—21st century. 3. Scandals—United States—History—20th century. 4. Scandals—United States—History—21st century. 5. History, Modern—20th century—Anecdotes. 6. History, Modern—21st century—Anecdotes. 7. United States—History—20th century—Anecdotes. 8. United States—History—21st century—Anecdotes. I. Bankston, Carl L. (Carl Leon), 1952- II. Title: Modern scandals.

D422.G74 2009
909.82—dc22

                                                                                    2008054757

First Printing

CONTENTS

Keyword List of Contents lxxi

1990's *(continued)*

April, 1998, Scottish Historian Is Charged with Plagiarism 879
April 7, 1998, Pop Singer George Michael Is Arrested for Lewd Conduct 881
May, 1998, Police Corruption Is Revealed in Los Angeles's Rampart Division 884
May 11, 1998, Journalist Stephen Glass Is Exposed as a Fraud 887
December 23, 1998, Prominent Belgians Are Sentenced in Agusta-Dassault
   Corruption Scandal 889
March 4, 1999, Quebec Offers Support for Abused Duplessis Orphans 892
May, 1999, Civil Rights Leader Jesse Jackson Fathers a Child Out of Wedlock 895
May 7, 1999-March 2, 2001, Ethics Counselor Exonerates Canadian Prime Minister
   Jean Chrétien 898

2000's

January 28, 2000, John Spano Is Sentenced for Fraudulent Purchase of Ice Hockey Team 901
May 2, 2000, New York Mayor Rudy Giuliani's Extramarital Affair Is Revealed 904
May 9, 2000, Former Louisiana Governor Edwin Edwards Is Convicted on
   Corruption Charges 907
September, 2000, American Scientists Are Accused of Starting a Measles Epidemic
   in the Amazon 910
September 19, 2000, Ex-gay Leader John Paulk Is Photographed Leaving a Gay Bar 913
September 26, 2000, Gymnast Andreea Răducan Loses Her Olympic Gold Medal
   Because of Drugs 916
November 5, 2000, Japanese Amateur Archaeologist's "Discoveries" Are Proven Fakes 919
December, 2000, Sexual Abuse of Children in France Leads to the Outreau Affair 922
2001, Clearstream Financial Clearinghouse Is Accused of Fraud and Money Laundering 925
January 30, 2001, Liverpool Children's Hospital Collects Body Parts Without Authorization . . . 927
February 18, 2001, CIA Agent Robert Hanssen Is Arrested for Spying for the Russians 931
April 30, 2001, Washington Intern Chandra Levy Disappears 933
June 18, 2001, Award-Winning Historian Joseph J. Ellis Is Accused of Lying 936
June 30, 2001, Korean Religious Teacher Jung Myung Seok Is Charged with Rape 939
August 27, 2001, Little League Baseball Star Danny Almonte Is Found to Be Overage 942
December 2, 2001, Enron Bankruptcy Reveals Massive Financial Fraud 945
December 14, 2001, Notre Dame Football Coach Resigns for Falsifying His Résumé 948
January 4, 2002, Historian Stephen E. Ambrose Is Accused of Plagiarism 951
January 6, 2002, *Boston Globe* Reports on Child Sexual Abuse by Roman Catholic Priests 954

January 18, 2002, Historian Doris Kearns Goodwin Is Accused of Plagiarism 959
February 11, 2002, French Judge Admits Favoring Russian Figure Skaters in
Winter Olympics 962
February 17, 2002, Rotting Human Bodies Are Found at Georgia Crematory 964
March 27, 2002, Georgia Basketball Coach Jim Harrick, Sr., Resigns over
Fraud Allegations 968
June 25, 2002, Internal Corruption Forces Adelphia Communications to
Declare Bankruptcy 971
July, 2002, Journalist Alleges Release of Genetically Modified Corn Seeds
in New Zealand 974
August, 2002, Immunologist Resigns After Being Accused of Falsifying Research 977
September 25, 2002, Inquiry Reveals That Physicist Jan Hendrik Schön Faked
His Research. 980
September 28, 2002, British Politician Reveals Her Affair with Prime Minister
John Major. 983
October 25, 2002, Historian Michael A. Bellesiles Resigns After Academic
Fraud Accusations. 985
December 5, 2002, Senator Trent Lott Praises Strom Thurmond's 1948 Presidential Campaign 988
January 2, 2003, E-mail Message Prompts Inquiry into Air Force Academy Sexual Assaults 991
March 2, 2003, U.S. National Security Agency Is Found to Have Spied on U.N. Officials. 995
April 29, 2003, *New York Times* Reporter Jayson Blair Is Exposed as a Fraud 998
May 3, 2003, University of Alabama Fires New Football Coach in Sex Scandal 1002
May 21, 2003, Sexually Provocative Film *The Brown Bunny* Premieres at
Cannes Film Festival. 1004
July 1, 2003, Basketball Star Kobe Bryant Is Accused of Rape 1008
July 14, 2003, Columnist Robert Novak Leaks the Name of CIA Operative Valerie Plame. 1010
September 3, 2003, Mutual Fund Companies Are Implicated in Shady Trading Practices 1013
October 2, 2003, Newspaper Claims That Arnold Schwarzenegger Groped Women 1016
Early November, 2003, Paris Hilton Sex-Tape Appears on the Web. 1019
December 17, 2003, Senator Strom Thurmond's Biracial Daughter Is Revealed 1022
December 18, 2003, Pop Star Michael Jackson Is Charged with Child Molestation 1025
March 4, 2004, Former United Way Charity Chief Pleads Guilty to Embezzlement. 1028
March 5, 2004, Martha Stewart Is Convicted in Insider-Trading Scandal 1031
April 28, 2004, CBS Broadcasts Photos of Abused and Tortured Prisoners at Abu Ghraib 1034
June 2, 2004, U.N. Report Reveals That Secretary-General Kofi Annan Dismissed
Sexual Harassment Charges 1039
August 19, 2004, Blog "Outs" Antigay Congressman Edward Schrock 1041
September 8, 2004, *60 Minutes II* Reports on George W. Bush's Evasion of Wartime Duty 1044
October 13, 2004, Television Producer Files Sex Harassment Suit Against Bill O'Reilly. 1047
October 14, 2004, Insurance Brokerage Marsh & McLennan Is Charged with Fraud 1050
January 15, 2005, Iqbal Riza Resigns from the United Nations in Oil-for-Food Scandal 1053
January 27, 2005, German Soccer Referee Admits to Fixing Games for Money. 1055
March 17, 2005, Former Baseball Star Mark McGwire Evades Congressional Questions
on Steroid Use 1058
June 22, 2005, U.S. Air Force Investigates Religious Intolerance at Its Academy. 1062
July 1, 2005, Federal Agents Raid Congressman Randall Cunningham's Home. 1064

CONTENTS

Beginning August 29, 2005, Government Incompetence Mars Hurricane Katrina
Relief Efforts. 1068

September 12, 2005, Westar Energy Executives Are Found Guilty of Looting
Their Company. 1072

September 30, 2005, Danish Newspaper's Prophet Muhammad Cartoons Stir
Violent Protests 1075

November 17, 2005, Liberian Workers Sue Bridgestone Firestone over Slave Labor 1078

December 6, 2005, Spokane, Washington, Mayor Recalled in Gay-Sex Scandal 1081

January 21, 2006, British Politician Resigns After Gay-Sex Orgy 1084

March 14, 2006, Duke Lacrosse Players Are Accused of Gang Rape 1086

April 26, 2006, Britain's Deputy Prime Minister Admits Affair with Secretary 1089

May 4, 2006, Media Uncover Match-Fixing in Italian Soccer 1092

May 12, 2006, Scientist Is Indicted for Faking His Research on Creating Stem Cells 1094

Summer, 2006-March 16, 2007, Manufacturer Recalls Pet Food That Killed Thousands
of American Pets. 1097

July 14, 2006, *New York Times* Exposes Grading Scandal at Auburn University 1101

July 26, 2006, Tour de France Is Hit with a Doping Scandal. 1103

July 28, 2006, Actor Mel Gibson Is Caught Making Anti-Semitic Remarks. 1106

August 12, 2006, Novelist Günter Grass Admits to Youthful Nazi Ties 1109

September 17, 2006, New Zealand Prime Minister's Husband Is "Outed" as Gay. 1112

September 18, 2006, *Newsweek* Reveals That Hewlett-Packard Spied on Its Own Board 1114

September 29, 2006, Congressman Mark Foley Resigns in Sex Scandal Involving
a Teenage Page. 1118

October 22, 2006, Chilean Politicians Use Community Funds for Personal Campaigns. 1121

November 2, 2006, Evangelist Kent Hovind Is Convicted of Federal Tax Violations 1123

November 2, 2006, Male Escort Reveals Sexual Liaisons with Evangelist Ted Haggard 1126

November 20, 2006, News Corp Abandons Plan to Publish O. J. Simpson's Book 1129

November 23, 2006, Former Russian Security Service Officer Dies from Radiation Poisoning. . . . 1132

Early 2007, Subprime Mortgage Industry Begins to Collapse 1134

February 18, 2007, *Washington Post* Exposes Decline of Walter Reed Army Hospital 1138

April 11, 2007, Shock Jock Don Imus Loses His Radio Show over Sexist and
Racist Remarks. 1142

May 28, 2007, Japanese Politician Charged with Corruption Hangs Himself 1145

June 4, 2007, Congressman William J. Jefferson Is Indicted for Corruption. 1147

July 9, 2007, Senator David Vitter's Name Is Found in D.C. Madam's Address Book 1150

July 11, 2007, Florida Politician Is Arrested for Soliciting an Undercover Male Police Officer. . . . 1153

July 24, 2007, University of Colorado Fires Professor for Plagiarism and
Research Falsification 1155

August 20, 2007, Football Star Michael Vick Pleads Guilty to Financing a Dogfighting Ring 1158

September 13, 2007, New England Patriots Football Team Is Fined for Spying on
Other Teams 1161

October 5, 2007, Olympic Champion Marion Jones Admits Steroid Use 1164

March 12, 2008, New York Governor Eliot Spitzer Resigns in Prostitution Scandal 1167

June 13, 2008, Singer R. Kelly Is Acquitted on Child Pornography Charges 1170

July 29, 2008, NBA Referee Tim Donaghy Is Sentenced to Prison for Betting on Games. 1172

September 7, 2008, Financial Institutions and Markets Begin to Collapse 1175

Appendixes

Bibliography. 1183
Chronological List of Entries 1189
Geographical Index 1200
Category Index 1216

Indexes

Personages Index. III
Subject Index XVII

KEYWORD LIST OF CONTENTS

Abdicates, Belgium's Disgraced King
Leopold III (July 16, 1951). 276

Abdicates to Marry an American Divorcée,
King Edward VIII (Dec. 10, 1936). 187

Abu Ghraib, CBS Broadcasts Photos of Abused
and Tortured Prisoners at (Apr. 28,
2004) 1034

Acting Career, Director Taylor's Murder Ruins
Mabel Normand's (Feb. 1, 1922) 73

Actor Carole Landis Commits Suicide During
Affair with Rex Harrison (July 5, 1948) 245

Actor Charles Chaplin Cannot Reenter the
United States (Sept. 19, 1952) 283

Actor Charles Chaplin Is Sued for Paternity
(June 4, 1943). 220

Actor Claudine Longet Kills Ski Champion
Vladimir Sabich (Mar. 21, 1976). 485

Actor Errol Flynn Was a Nazi Spy, Biographer
Claims (1980). 559

Actor Is Suspected of Falsely Claiming to Be
an American Indian (1928-1929). 130

Actor Joan Crawford's Daughter Publishes
Damning Memoir, *Mommie Dearest*
(1978). 517

Actor Lana Turner's Daughter Kills Turner's
Gangster Lover (Apr. 4, 1958) 317

Actor Lee Marvin Is Ordered to Pay Palimony
to Former Lover (Apr. 18, 1979). 540

Actor Mel Gibson Is Caught Making Anti-
Semitic Remarks (July 28, 2006) 1106

Actor Rita Hayworth Marries Aly Khan After
Adulterous Affair (May 27, 1949) 254

Actor Rob Lowe Videotapes His Sexual
Encounter with a Minor (July 18, 1988) 717

Actor Rory Calhoun's Criminal Past, Scandal
Magazine Reveals (May, 1955) 295

Actor Wallace Reid's Death in Drug Rehab
Shakes Film Industry (Jan. 18, 1923) 86

Adelphia Communications to Declare
Bankruptcy, Internal Corruption Forces
(June 25, 2002). 971

Âge d'or Provokes French Rioting, Surrealist
Film *L'* (Dec. 3, 1930). 147

Agnew Resigns Vice Presidency in Disgrace,
Spiro T. (Oct. 10, 1973) 447

Agusta-Dassault Corruption Scandal,
Prominent Belgians Are Sentenced in
(Dec. 23, 1998) 889

Air Force Academy Sexual Assaults, E-mail
Message Prompts Inquiry into (Jan. 2,
2003) 991

Air Force Investigates Religious Intolerance at
Its Academy, U.S. (June 22, 2005) 1062

Air Force Prosecution of Female Officer for
Adultery Reveals Double Standard
(May 20, 1997) 855

Airbus Scandal, Former Canadian Premier
Brian Mulroney Is Exposed in (Nov. 18,
1995) 830

Airmail Routes Creates a Scandal, Postmaster's
Division of (May, 1930) 144

Albanian Government to Fall, Pyramid
Investment Schemes Cause (Jan., 1997) 846

Albert Is Tried for Sexual Assault, Sportscaster
Marv (Sept. 22, 1997) 865

Allen Has Affair with Lover Mia Farrow's
Adopted Daughter, Woody (Jan. 13,
1992) 773

Almonte Is Found to Be Overage, Little League
Baseball Star Danny (Aug. 27, 2001) 942

Amazon, American Scientists Are Accused of
Starting a Measles Epidemic in the (Sept.,
2000) 910

Ambrose Is Accused of Plagiarism, Historian
Stephen E. (Jan. 4, 2002). 951

Andrews and Blake Edwards Deny Being Gay,
Julie (Dec., 1982). 612

Annan Dismissed Sexual Harassment Charges,
U.N. Report Reveals That Secretary-General
Kofi (June 2, 2004) 1039

Anti-Semitic Remarks, Actor Mel Gibson Is
Caught Making (July 28, 2006) 1106

Anti-Semitic Writings Are Revealed, Yale
Scholar's Wartime (Dec. 1, 1987) 705

Aquino Is Assassinated on Return Home,
Filipino Opposition Leader (Aug. 21, 1983) . . 628

Arbuckle Is Acquitted of Manslaughter, Film
Star Fatty (Apr. 12, 1922) 79

Archaeologist's "Discoveries" Are Proven
Fakes, Japanese Amateur (Nov. 5, 2000). . . . 919

Archer Wins Libel Trial Against the *Daily Star*,
Novelist-Politician Jeffrey (July 25, 1987) . . . 696

Armory Modern Art Show Scandalizes the
Public (Feb. 17-Mar. 15, 1913) 49

Armstrong Excommunicates His Own Son,
Evangelist Herbert W. (June 27, 1978) 525

Art Show Scandalizes the Public, Armory
Modern (Feb. 17-Mar. 15, 1913) 49

Assassinated on Return Home, Filipino
Opposition Leader Aquino Is (Aug. 21,
1983) 628

Astor's Diary Becomes a Public Sensation, Film
Star Mary (Summer, 1936) 184

Atherton Report Exposes San Francisco Police
Corruption (Mar. 17, 1937) 191

Bakker Resigns as Head of PTL Television
Network, Jim (Mar. 19, 1987) 690

"Bananagate" Bribery Scandal Leads to
Executive's Suicide, Honduras's (Feb. 3,
1975) 471

Banco Ambrosiano Collapses Amid Criminal
Accusations (Aug. 6, 1982) 606

Banks Admit to Holding Accounts of Holocaust
Victims, Swiss (June 25, 1997) 858

Banque Oustric et Cie Failure Prompts French
Inquiry (Nov., 1929) 139

Barry Is Arrested for Drug Use, Washington,
D.C., Mayor Marion (Jan. 18, 1990) 748

Baseball Commissioner Peter Ueberroth
Suspends Players for Cocaine Use (Feb. 28,
1986) 666

Baseball Commissioner Suspends Mickey
Mantle and Willie Mays for Casino Ties
(Nov. 29, 1979, and Jan. 31, 1983) 556

Baseball for Betting on Games, Pete Rose Is
Banned from (Aug. 24, 1989) 735

Baseball Games, Ty Cobb and Tris Speaker Are
Accused of Fixing (Dec. 26, 1926) 118

Baseball Manager Leo Durocher Is Suspended
for Gambling Ties (Spring, 1947) 242

Baseball Players Are Implicated in Game Fixing,
Japanese (Fall, 1969-Winter, 1971) 398

Baseball Star Danny Almonte Is Found to Be
Overage, Little League (Aug. 27, 2001) . . . 942

Baseball Star Mark McGwire Evades
Congressional Questions on Steroid Use,
Former (Mar. 17, 2005) 1058

Baseball Star Steve Garvey's Marital Problems,
Magazine Reveals (July 28, 1980) 574

Basketball Coach Jim Harrick, Sr., Resigns over
Fraud Allegations, Georgia (Mar. 27,
2002) 968

Basketball Players, Mobster's Arrest Reveals
Point Shaving by Boston College (Apr. 27,
1980) 568

Basketball Players Begin Shaving Points for
Money, College (Jan. 17, 1951) 274

Basketball Star Kobe Bryant Is Accused of Rape
(July 1, 2003) 1008

Bauman Is Arrested for Liaison with Teenage
Boy, Congressman (Sept. 3, 1980) 577

Beck Is Convicted of Tax Fraud, Teamsters
Leader Dave (May, 1959) 323

Bedaux Is Arrested for Nazi Collaboration,
Industrialist Charles (Dec. 5, 1942) 212

Begelman Is Found to Have Forged Checks,
Film Producer David (Feb. 25, 1977) 509

Bellesiles Resigns After Academic Fraud
Accusations, Historian Michael A. (Oct. 25,
2002) 985

Ben Barka Disappears in Paris, Moroccan
Politician Mehdi (Oct. 29, 1965) 374

Bendix Executive Resigns Amid Rumors of an
Affair (Oct. 9, 1980) 580

Bergman Has a Child Out of Wedlock, Swedish
Film Star Ingrid (Feb. 7, 1950) 263

Biden's Presidential Campaign, Plagiarism
Charges End Joe (Sept. 23, 1987) 698

"Black Sox" Scandal, White Sox Players
Conspire to Lose World Series in (Sept. 21,
1919) 66

Blair Is Exposed as a Fraud, *New York Times*
Reporter Jayson (Apr. 29, 2003) 998

Bobbitt Severs Her Husband's Penis, Lorena
(June 23, 1993) 795

Boston Globe Reports on Child Sexual Abuse
by Roman Catholic Priests (Jan. 6, 2002) . . . 954

Bowles Is Taped, Prince Charles's Intimate
Phone Conversation with Camilla Parker
(Dec. 18, 1989) 745

Boxer Jack Johnson Is Imprisoned for Abetting
Prostitution (May 13, 1913) 52

Breuning Pleads Guilty to Medical Research
Fraud, Stephen (Sept. 19, 1988) 720

Bribe, French President Giscard d'Estaing Is
Accused of Taking a (Oct. 10, 1979) 550

Bribery, Senator Joseph R. Burton Is Convicted
of (Jan. 23, 1904) 4

Bribery, Supreme Court Justice Abe Fortas Is
Accused of (May 9, 1969) 391

Bribery and Fraud, Police Arrest Architect John
Poulson for (June 22, 1972) 431

Bribery Scandal Leads to Executive's Suicide,
Honduras's "Bananagate" (Feb. 3, 1975). . . . 471

Bribes, Federal Tax Official Resigns After
Accepting (Nov. 16, 1951) 279

Bribing Foreign Officials, Lockheed Is
Implicated in (Feb. 4, 1976) 482

Bridgestone Firestone over Slave Labor,
Liberian Workers Sue (Nov. 17, 2005) 1078

British Cabinet Member Resigns After
Fathering a Child Out of Wedlock (Jan. 5,
1994) 798

Brown Bunny Premieres at Cannes Film Festival,
Sexually Provocative Film The (May 21,
2003) 1004

Brown Is Murdered by Lover, Former U.S.
Senator Arthur (Dec. 8, 1906) 22

Brownlee, Sex Scandal Forces Resignation of
Alberta Premier (July 10, 1934) 176

Bryant Campaigns Against Lesbian and Gay
Rights, Singer Anita (Jan., 1977). 506

Bryant Is Accused of Rape, Basketball Star
Kobe (July 1, 2003) 1008

Buddhist Teacher Orders His Students to
Remove Their Clothes (Oct. 31, 1975). . . . 474

Buddhists, Madame Nhu Derides Self-Immolation
of (Aug. 14, 1963) 362

Buñuel's Un Chien Andalou Shocks Parisian
Audience, Luis (June 6, 1929) 136

Burton Is Convicted of Bribery, Senator Joseph R.
(Jan. 23, 1904). 4

Bush Is Investigated for Insider Trading,
George W. (Apr. 5, 1991) 762

Bush's Evasion of Wartime Duty, 60 Minutes II
Reports on George W. (Sept. 8, 2004) 1044

Butcher Pleads Guilty to Fraud, Banker Jake
(May 7, 1985). 648

Buttafuoco, Amy Fisher Shoots Mary Jo
(May 19, 1992) 781

Butz Resigns After Making Obscene Joke,
Agriculture Secretary Earl (Oct. 4, 1976) . . . 500

Calhoun's Criminal Past, Scandal Magazine
Reveals Actor Rory (May, 1955). 295

Carter, Registers as a Paid Agent for Libya,
President's Brother, Billy (Late July, 1980) . . 571

Carter Admits Committing Adultery in His Heart,
Jimmy (Sept., 1976) 497

Carter Cabinet Member Resigns over Ethics
Violations (Sept. 21, 1977) 511

Cartoons Stir Violent Protests, Danish
Newspaper's Prophet Muhammad (Sept. 30,
2005) 1075

Casey's Romantic Affair Leads to His
Resignation, Irish Bishop Eamonn (May 6,
1992) 779

Catholic Priests, Boston Globe Reports on
Child Sexual Abuse by Roman (Jan. 6,
2002) 954

Chaplin Cannot Reenter the United States,
Actor Charles (Sept. 19, 1952) 283

Chaplin Is Sued for Paternity, Actor Charles
(June 4, 1943). 220

Charles's Intimate Phone Conversation with
Camilla Parker Bowles Is Taped, Prince
(Dec. 18, 1989) 745

Chavis, Sex Scandal Forces Dismissal of NAACP
Chief Benjamin (Aug. 21, 1994) 821

Cheating, U.S. Naval Academy Expels
Midshipmen for (Apr. 28, 1994) 800

Cheating on Exams, West Point Cadets Are
Caught (Apr. 4, 1976) 488

Cheating Scandal Shocks Soap Box Derby
(Aug. 19, 1973). 444

Chicago Sun-Times Reports That Cardinal
Cody Diverted Church Funds (Sept. 10,
1981) 597

Chien Andalou Shocks Parisian Audience,
Luis Buñuel's Un (June 6, 1929). 136

Child-Abuse Case, McMartin Preschool Is
Embroiled in (Aug. 12, 1983-July 27,
1990) 624

Child Molestation, Pop Star Michael Jackson
Is Charged with (Dec. 18, 2003) 1025

Child Sexual Abuse by Roman Catholic
Priests, Boston Globe Reports on (Jan. 6,
2002) 954

Children, Psychoanalyst Ernest Jones Is Accused
of Molesting Mentally Disabled (Mar. 2,
1906) 12

Children in France Leads to the Outreau Affair,
Sexual Abuse of (Dec., 2000) 922

Chilean Politicians Use Community Funds for Personal Campaigns (Oct. 22, 2006) 1121

Chrétien, Ethics Counselor Exonerates Canadian Prime Minister Jean (May 7, 1999-Mar. 2, 2001) 898

CIA Operative Valerie Plame, Columnist Robert Novak Leaks the Name of (July 14, 2003) 1010

Cisneros Is Indicted for Lying to Federal Agents, HUD Secretary Henry (Dec. 11, 1997). . . . 872

Clearstream Financial Clearinghouse Is Accused of Fraud and Money Laundering (2001) 925

Clinton Denies Sexual Affair with a White House Intern, President Bill (Jan. 17, 1998) 874

Cobb and Tris Speaker Are Accused of Fixing Baseball Games, Ty (Dec. 26, 1926) 118

Cocaine Use, Baseball Commissioner Peter Ueberroth Suspends Players for (Feb. 28, 1986) 666

Cody Diverted Church Funds, *Chicago Sun-Times* Reports That Cardinal (Sept. 10, 1981) 597

"Cold Fusion" Claims Cannot Be Verified, Scientists' (Mar. 23, 1989) 723

College Basketball Players, Mobster's Arrest Reveals Point Shaving by Boston (Apr. 27, 1980) 568

College Basketball Players Begin Shaving Points for Money (Jan. 17, 1951) 274

Communist Letter Brings Down British Government, Forged (Oct. 25, 1924) 105

Communist Witch Hunt, U.S. Senator Joseph McCarthy Launches (Feb. 9, 1950) 266

Congo Free State from King Leopold II, Belgium Confiscates (Nov. 15, 1908) 31

Cooke Admits Fabricating Her Pulitzer Prize-Winning Feature, Janet (Apr. 15, 1981) 585

Corruption Charges, Former Louisiana Governor Edwin Edwards Is Convicted on (May 9, 2000) 907

Corruption in Turkey, Car Crash Reveals Depth of Government (Nov. 3, 1996) 843

Corruption Scandal, Prominent Belgians Are Sentenced in Agusta-Dassault (Dec. 23, 1998) 889

Crawford's Daughter Publishes Damning Memoir, *Mommie Dearest*, Actor Joan (1978) 517

Crematory, Rotting Human Bodies Are Found at Georgia (Feb. 17, 2002) 964

Crime Connection, Italian Justice Minister Resigns Because of (May 23, 1981) 591

Crime Connections, Vice President Lyndon B. Johnson Aide Resigns over (Oct. 7, 1963) . . . 365

Curie Has Affair with Physicist Paul Langevin, Nobelist Marie (1910) 37

Dalkon Shield Contraceptive Is Removed from the Market (Summer, 1974) 459

Daniélou Dies in a Prostitute's House, French Cardinal (May 20, 1974) 456

Daugherty's Aide Commits Suicide, U.S. Attorney General Harry M. (May 30, 1923) . . . 92

Defects to East Germany, West German Counterintelligence Chief (Aug. 19, 1985). . . 657

De Lorean Is Arrested in a Drug Sting, Car Manufacturer John (Oct. 19, 1982) 609

Diana Dies in a Car Crash, Princess (Aug. 31, 1997) 861

Diana's Phone Conversation with Her Lover Is Made Public, Princess (Aug. 23, 1992) 789

"Diary of a Mad Congresswife" Scandalizes Washington, Rita Jenrette's (Dec. 7, 1980) 582

Dines, Film Star Mabel Normand's Chauffeur Shoots Millionaire Courtland S. (Jan. 1, 1924) 100

Dodd Is Censured for Misappropriating Funds, Senator Thomas J. (June 23, 1967) 384

Doerfer Resigns for Accepting Gifts from Networks, FCC Chairman John C. (Mar. 14, 1960) 335

Dogfighting Ring, Football Star Michael Vick Pleads Guilty to Financing a (Aug. 20, 2007). 1158

Donaghy Is Sentenced to Prison for Betting on Games, NBA Referee Tim (July 29, 2008). 1172

Doping Scandal, Tour de France Is Hit with a (July 26, 2006). 1103

Dracula Copyright, *Nosferatu* Is Found to Have Violated (July, 1925) 111

Dreyfus Innocent of Treason, French Court Declares Alfred (July 12, 1906) 19

Drug Possession, Film Star Robert Mitchum Is Arrested for (Aug. 31, 1948) 251

Drug Sting, Car Manufacturer John De Lorean Is Arrested in a (Oct. 19, 1982) 609

Drug Use, Washington, D.C., Mayor Marion Barry Is Arrested for (Jan. 18, 1990) 748

Drugs, Gymnast Andreea Răducan Loses Her Olympic Gold Medal Because of (Sept. 26, 2000). 916

Duke and Duchess of Windsor Visit Nazi Germany (Oct. 11-22, 1937) 196

Duke Lacrosse Players Are Accused of Gang Rape (Mar. 14, 2006) 1086

Duncan Begins Affair with Millionaire Heir, Dancer Isadora (1909-1916) 34

Duplessis Orphans, Quebec Offers Support for Abused (Mar. 4, 1999) 892

Durocher Is Suspended for Gambling Ties, Baseball Manager Leo (Spring, 1947) 242

E. F. Hutton Executives Plead Guilty to Fraud (May 2, 1984). 636

Eagleton Withdraws from Vice Presidential Race, Thomas F. (July 31, 1972) 440

Edward VIII Abdicates to Marry an American Divorcée, King (Dec. 10, 1936) 187

Edwards Deny Being Gay, Julie Andrews and Blake (Dec., 1982) 612

Edwards Is Convicted on Corruption Charges, Former Louisiana Governor Edwin (May 9, 2000) 907

Eisenhower's Chief of Staff Resigns for Influence Selling, President (Sept. 22, 1958) 320

Ellis Is Accused of Lying, Award-Winning Historian Joseph J. (June 18, 2001) 936

Embezzlement, Former United Way Charity Chief Pleads Guilty to (Mar. 4, 2004). 1028

Enron Bankruptcy Reveals Massive Financial Fraud (Dec. 2, 2001) 945

Environmental Protection Agency Chief for Contempt, Congress Cites (Dec. 16, 1982). . . 615

Estes Is Arrested for Corporate Fraud, Billie Sol (Mar. 29, 1962). 341

Exstase, Hedy Lamarr Appears Nude in the Czech Film (Jan. 20, 1933). 163

Extortion, San Francisco Mayor Schmitz Is Found Guilty of (June 13, 1907). 28

Faked Hitler Diaries, German Magazine Publishes (Apr. 25, 1983) 618

Fakes, Japanese Amateur Archaeologist's "Discoveries" Are Proven (Nov. 5, 2000) . . . 919

Faking His Research on Creating Stem Cells, Scientist Is Indicted for (May 12, 2006) . . . 1094

Faking Howard Hughes Memoirs, Clifford Irving Admits (Jan. 28, 1972) 422

Falsifying Research, Immunologist Resigns After Being Accused of (Aug., 2002) 977

Farmer Is Jailed and Institutionalized, Film Star Frances (Jan. 14, 1943) 214

Farrow's Adopted Daughter, Woody Allen Has Affair with Lover Mia (Jan. 13, 1992) 773

FBI Sting Implicating Dozens of Lawmakers, Media Uncover (Feb. 2, 1980) 561

Figure Skaters in Winter Olympics, French Judge Admits Favoring Russian (Feb. 11, 2002) 962

Film Producer Thomas H. Ince Dies After Weekend on Hearst's Yacht (Nov. 19, 1924) 108

Film Star Errol Flynn Is Acquitted of Rape (Feb. 6, 1942). 202

Film Star Fatty Arbuckle Is Acquitted of Manslaughter (Apr. 12, 1922) 79

Film Star Frances Farmer Is Jailed and Institutionalized (Jan. 14, 1943) 214

Film Star Hugh Grant Is Arrested for Lewd Conduct (June 27, 1995) 827

Film Star Ingrid Bergman Has a Child Out of Wedlock, Swedish (Feb. 7, 1950) 263

FIlm Star Jean Harlow's Husband Is an Apparent Suicide (Sept. 4, 1932) 160

Film Star Mabel Normand's Chauffeur Shoots Millionaire Courtland S. Dines (Jan. 1, 1924) 100

Film Star Mary Astor's Diary Becomes a Public Sensation (Summer, 1936) 184

Film Star Robert Mitchum Is Arrested for Drug Possession (Aug. 31, 1948). 251

Film Star Thelma Todd's Death Cannot Be Explained (Dec. 16, 1935) 178

Film The Brown Bunny Premieres at Cannes Film Festival, Sexually Provocative (May 21, 2003) 1004

Financial Institutions and Markets Begin to Collapse (Sept. 7, 2008). 1175

Financier Michael Milken Is Indicted for Racketeering and Fraud (Mar. 29, 1989). . . . 726

Fire, Nearly 150 Workers Die in Triangle Shirtwaist Factory (Mar. 25, 1911) 40

Fire Kills Thirty-five Girls, Irish Orphan School
(Feb. 23, 1943) 217

Firestone Recalls Millions of Defective Car Tires
(Oct. 20, 1978) 534

Fisher Shoots Mary Jo Buttafuoco, Amy
(May 19, 1992) 781

Florida Politician Is Arrested for Soliciting an
Undercover Male Police Officer (July 11,
2007). 1153

Flynn Is Acquitted of Rape, Film Star Errol
(Feb. 6, 1942) 202

Flynn Was a Nazi Spy, Biographer Claims Actor
Errol (1980). 559

Foley Resigns in Sex Scandal Involving a
Teenage Page, Congressman Mark
(Sept. 29, 2006) 1118

Fonda's Visit to North Vietnam Outrages Many
Americans, Jane (July 8-22, 1972) 434

Football, NCAA Imposes "Death Penalty" on
Southern Methodist University (Feb. 25,
1987) 687

Football Coach in Sex Scandal, University of
Alabama Fires New (May 3, 2003) 1002

Football Coach Resigns for Falsifying His
Résumé, Notre Dame (Dec. 14, 2001) 948

Football Star Michael Vick Pleads Guilty to
Financing a Dogfighting Ring (Aug. 20,
2007). 1158

Football Team Is Fined for Spying on Other
Teams, New England Patriots (Sept. 13,
2007). 1161

Ford Ignored Pinto's Safety Problems, Court
Finds That (May 29, 1981) 594

Forged Checks, Film Producer David Begelman
Is Found to Have (Feb. 25, 1977) 509

Forged Communist Letter Brings Down British
Government (Oct. 25, 1924) 105

Fortas Is Accused of Bribery, Supreme Court
Justice Abe (May 9, 1969) 391

Fraud, Banker Jake Butcher Pleads Guilty to
(May 7, 1985). 648

Fraud, Billie Sol Estes Is Arrested for Corporate
(Mar. 29, 1962) 341

Fraud, Boston Alderman Is Reelected While in
Jail for (Dec., 1904) 6

Fraud, E. F. Hutton Executives Plead Guilty to
(May 2, 1984). 636

Fraud, Enron Bankruptcy Reveals Massive
Financial (Dec. 2, 2001) 945

Fraud, Faith Healer Peter Popoff Is Exposed as
a (Apr. 22, 1986) 673

Fraud, Financier Michael Milken Is Indicted
for Racketeering and (Mar. 29, 1989) 726

Fraud, Guinness Four Are Found Guilty of
Share-Trading (Aug. 27, 1990) 753

Fraud, Guru Bhagwan Shree Rajneesh Is Indicted
for Immigration (Oct. 23, 1985) 662

Fraud, Insurance Brokerage Marsh & McLennan
Is Charged with (Oct. 14, 2004). 1050

Fraud, Journalist Stephen Glass Is Exposed as a
(May 11, 1998) 887

Fraud, New York Times Reporter Jayson Blair Is
Exposed as a (Apr. 29, 2003). 998

Fraud, Police Arrest Architect John Poulson for
Bribery and (June 22, 1972) 431

Fraud, Prize-Winning Aborigine Novelist
Revealed as a (Mar. 12, 1997) 852

Fraud, Stephen Breuning Pleads Guilty to
Medical Research (Sept. 19, 1988). 720

Fraud, U.S. Senate Investigates Veterans Bureau
Chief for (Mar. 2, 1923) 89

Fraud Accusations, Historian Michael A.
Bellesiles Resigns After Academic
(Oct. 25, 2002) 985

Fraud Allegations, Georgia Basketball Coach
Jim Harrick, Sr., Resigns over (Mar. 27,
2002) 968

Fraud and Money Laundering, Clearstream
Financial Clearinghouse Is Accused of
(2001). 925

Fraud Charges, ZZZZ Best Founder Is Indicted
on Federal (Jan. 15, 1988) 708

Fraud Upsets Belmont Park Raceway, Horse-
Swapping (Sept. 23, 1977) 514

Frauds, Ponzi Schemes Are Revealed as
Investment (1919-1920) 63

Fraudulent Article, Physicist Publishes a
Deliberately (Spring, 1996). 837

Fraudulent Purchase of Ice Hockey Team, John
Spano Is Sentenced for (Jan. 28, 2000). . . . 901

Fraudulent Schemes Rock French Government,
Stavisky's (Jan. 8, 1934-Jan. 17, 1936) 170

Garvey's Marital Problems, Magazine Reveals
Baseball Star Steve (July 28, 1980) 574

Gay, Julie Andrews and Blake Edwards Deny
Being (Dec., 1982) 612

Gay Bar, Ex-gay Leader John Paulk Is Photographed Leaving a (Sept. 19, 2000) . . . 913

Gay Congressman Edward Schrock, Blog "Outs" Anti- (Aug. 19, 2004) 1041

Gay Rights, Singer Anita Bryant Campaigns Against Lesbian and (Jan., 1977) 506

Gay Sex Leads to Ethics Scandal, Study of Anonymous (1970) 407

Gay-Sex Orgy, British Politician Resigns After (Jan. 21, 2006). 1084

Gay-Sex Scandal, Evangelist Billy James Hargis Resigns College Presidency During (Oct. 25, 1974) 465

Gay-Sex Scandal, Spokane, Washington, Mayor Recalled in (Dec. 6, 2005). 1081

Gay-Sex Sting, President Lyndon Johnson's Aide Is Arrested in (Oct. 7, 1964) 371

Gays Is Banned on Broadway, Mae West's Play About (1927) 122

Geisha, Japanese Prime Minister Sosuke Resigns After Affair with a (Aug. 10, 1989) 733

Genetically Modified Corn Seeds in New Zealand, Journalist Alleges Release of (July, 2002) 974

Genovese Dies as Her Cries for Help Are Ignored, Kitty (Mar. 13, 1964) 369

Georgia Crematory, Rotting Human Bodies Are Found at (Feb. 17, 2002) 964

Gibson Is Caught Making Anti-Semitic Remarks, Actor Mel (July 28, 2006). 1106

Giscard d'Estaing Is Accused of Taking a Bribe, French President (Oct. 10, 1979) 550

Giuliani's Extramarital Affair Is Revealed, New York Mayor Rudy (May 2, 2000) 904

Glass Is Exposed as a Fraud, Journalist Stephen (May 11, 1998) 887

Glyn's Novel Three Weeks Shocks Readers, Elinor (1907). 25

Goetz Shoots Four Black Youths, Subway Vigilante Bernhard (Dec. 22, 1984) 641

Goodwin Is Accused of Plagiarism, Historian Doris Kearns (Jan. 18, 2002) 959

Grading Scandal at Auburn University, New York Times Exposes (July 14, 2006) 1101

Grant Is Arrested for Lewd Conduct, Film Star Hugh (June 27, 1995). 827

Grass Admits to Youthful Nazi Ties, Novelist Günter (Aug. 12, 2006) 1109

Greenpeace Ship Rainbow Warrior, French Secret Service Sinks the (July 10, 1985) 651

Guinness Four Are Found Guilty of Share-Trading Fraud (Aug. 27, 1990) 753

Haggard, Male Escort Reveals Sexual Liaisons with Evangelist Ted (Nov. 2, 2006) 1126

Haley Is Sued for Plagiarism, Roots Author Alex (1978) 520

Hamsun Is Arrested for Treason, Norwegian Writer Knut (May 26, 1945) 229

Hanssen Is Arrested for Spying for the Russians, CIA Agent Robert (Feb. 18, 2001) 931

Harding Is Banned from Skating After Attack on Rival, Tonya (June 30, 1994). 812

Harding's Lover Publishes Tell-All Memoir, President Warren G. (1927) 124

Hargis Resigns College Presidency During Gay-Sex Scandal, Evangelist Billy James (Oct. 25, 1974) 465

Harlow's Husband Is an Apparent Suicide, Film Star Jean (Sept. 4, 1932) 160

Harrick, Sr., Resigns over Fraud Allegations, Georgia Basketball Coach Jim (Mar. 27, 2002) 968

Harrison Loses Plagiarism Lawsuit, Former Beatle George (Sept. 1, 1976) 494

Hays's Affair, Washington Post Exposes Congressman Wayne L. (May 23, 1976) 491

Hayworth Marries Aly Khan After Adulterous Affair, Actor Rita (May 27, 1949) 254

Hearst Helps Rob a Bank, Kidnapped Heir Patty (Apr. 15, 1974) 450

Hearst's Yacht, Film Producer Thomas H. Ince Dies After Weekend on (Nov. 19, 1924) 108

Helmsley Enters Prison for Tax Evasion, Hotel Tycoon Leona (Apr. 15, 1992) 776

Herman Is Arrested for Public Indecency, Comedian Pee-wee (July 26, 1991) 765

Hewlett-Packard Spied on Its Own Board, Newsweek Reveals That (Sept. 18, 2006) . . . 1114

Hilton Sex-Tape Appears on the Web, Paris (Early Nov., 2003) 1019

Hindemith's Opera Sancta Susanna Depicts a Nun's Sexual Desires (Mar. 26, 1922). 76

Hiss Is Convicted of Perjury, Alger (Jan. 21, 1950) 259

Hitler Diaries, German Magazine Publishes Faked (Apr. 25, 1983) 618

Hoax, Piltdown Man Is Revealed to Be a
(Nov. 21, 1953) 292

Holocaust, Play Accuses Pope Pius XII of
Complicity in the (Feb. 23, 1963) 353

Holocaust Victims, Swiss Banks Admit to
Holding Accounts of (June 25, 1997) 858

Homosexual "Circle" Scandalizes Germany,
Emperor William II's (1906-1909) 9

Homosexuality Investigation, U.S. Senate
Rebukes Navy in (July 19, 1921) 70

Horse-Swapping Fraud Upsets Belmont Park
Raceway (Sept. 23, 1977) 514

House Post Office Scandal, Congressman Dan
Rostenkowski Is Indicted in (June 1, 1994) . . 803

Hovind Is Convicted of Federal Tax Violations,
Evangelist Kent (Nov. 2, 2006) 1123

Hughes Memoirs, Clifford Irving Admits
Faking Howard (Jan. 28, 1972) 422

Hurricane Katrina Relief Efforts, Government
Incompetence Mars (Beginning August 29,
2005) 1068

Husband Is "Outed" as Gay, New Zealand Prime
Minister's (Sept. 17, 2006) 1112

"Hymietown," Jesse Jackson Calls New York
City (Jan. 25, 1984) 633

Ice Hockey Team, John Spano Is Sentenced for
Fraudulent Purchase of (Jan. 28, 2000) 901

Imus Loses His Radio Show over Sexist and
Racist Remarks, Shock Jock Don (Apr. 11,
2007) 1142

Ince Dies After Weekend on Hearst's Yacht,
Film Producer Thomas H. (Nov. 19,
1924) 108

Insider Trading, British Prime Minister's Staff
Is Investigated for (Jan., 1913) 43

Insider Trading, George W. Bush Is Investigated
for (Apr. 5, 1991) 762

Insider-Trading Scandal, Martha Stewart Is
Convicted in (Mar. 5, 2004) 1031

Insider-Trading Scandal Rocks Japanese
Government (June, 1988-June, 1989) 714

Insull Utilities Trusts Collapse Prompts New
Federal Regulation (1932) 154

Internment of Japanese Americans, President
Roosevelt Orders (Feb. 19, 1942) 205

Iran-Contra Weapons Scandal Taints Reagan's
Administration (Nov. 13, 1986-May 4,
1989) 676

Irving Admits Faking Howard Hughes
Memoirs, Clifford (Jan. 28, 1972) 422

Italian Justice Minister Resigns Because of
Crime Connection (May 23, 1981) 591

Jackson Calls New York City "Hymietown,"
Jesse (Jan. 25, 1984) 633

Jackson Fathers a Child Out of Wedlock, Civil
Rights Leader Jesse (May, 1999) 895

Jackson Is Charged with Child Molestation, Pop
Star Michael (Dec. 18, 2003) 1025

Japanese Americans, President Roosevelt Orders
Internment of (Feb. 19, 1942) 205

Japanese Politician Charged with Corruption
Hangs Himself (May 28, 2007) 1145

Jefferson Is Indicted for Corruption,
Congressman William J. (June 4, 2007) . . . 1147

Jenrette's "Diary of a Mad Congresswife"
Scandalizes Washington, Rita (Dec. 7,
1980) 582

Johnson Aide Resigns over Crime Connections,
Vice President Lyndon B. (Oct. 7, 1963) . . . 365

Johnson Is Imprisoned for Abetting Prostitution,
Boxer Jack (May 13, 1913) 52

Johnson's Aide Is Arrested in Gay-Sex Sting,
President Lyndon (Oct. 7, 1964) 371

Jones Admits Steroid Use, Olympic Champion
Marion (Oct. 5, 2007) 1164

Jones Is Accused of Molesting Mentally
Disabled Children, Psychoanalyst Ernest
(Mar. 2, 1906) 12

Jorgensen Becomes Christine Jorgensen, George
(Dec. 1, 1952) 289

Jung Myung Seok Is Charged with Rape, Korean
Religious Teacher (June 30, 2001) 939

Katrina Relief Efforts, Government Incompetence
Mars Hurricane (Beginning August 29,
2005) 1068

Kelly Is Acquitted on Child Pornography Charges,
Singer R. (June 13, 2008) 1170

Kennan Proves Russian Sisson Documents Are
Fakes, George F. (June, 1956) 307

Kennedy Begins an Affair with Gloria Swanson,
Joseph P. (Early 1928) 127

Kennedy's Driving Accident Kills Mary Jo
Kopechne, Senator Edward (July 18,
1969) 394

Kennedy's Romantic Affair Links Him to Organized Crime, President (Feb. 7, 1960) 329

Kent State Students, National Guardsmen Kill Protesting (May 4, 1970) 410

Kidnapped Heir Patty Hearst Helps Rob a Bank (Apr. 15, 1974) 450

King Is Sued for Palimony, Tennis Star Billie Jean (Apr. 28, 1981) 588

King, Jr.'s, Doctoral-Thesis Plagiarism Is Revealed, Martin Luther (Dec. 3, 1989) 739

Kopechne, Senator Edward Kennedy's Driving Accident Kills Mary Jo (July 18, 1969) 394

Koreagate Scandal, U.S. Congress Members Are Implicated in (1976-1977) 479

Lacrosse Players Are Accused of Gang Rape, Duke (Mar. 14, 2006) 1086

Lamarr Appears Nude in the Czech Film *Exstase*, Hedy (Jan. 20, 1933) 163

Landis Commits Suicide During Affair with Rex Harrison, Actor Carole (July 5, 1948) 245

Langevin, Nobelist Marie Curie Has Affair with Physicist Paul (1910) 37

Langley Is Convicted of Violating the Volstead Act, Kentucky Congressman John W. (May 12, 1924) 103

Laval Wants Germany to Win World War II, French Prime Minister Pierre (Apr. 22, 1942) 209

Leak, British Cabinet Member Resigns After Budget Information (May 20, 1936) 181

Leopold II, Belgium Confiscates Congo Free State from King (Nov. 15, 1908) 31

Leopold III Abdicates, Belgium's Disgraced King (July 16, 1951) 276

Lesbian and Gay Rights, Singer Anita Bryant Campaigns Against (Jan., 1977) 506

Letourneau Is Arrested for Statutory Rape, Teacher Mary Kay (Feb. 26, 1997) 849

Levy Disappears, Washington Intern Chandra (Apr. 30, 2001) 933

Lewis Marries Thirteen-Year-Old Cousin, Rock Star Jerry Lee (Dec. 12, 1957) 313

Libel, General Douglas MacArthur Sues Newspaper Columnist for (May 16, 1934) . . . 173

Libel Trial Against the *Daily Star*, Novelist-Politician Jeffrey Archer Wins (July 25, 1987) 696

Literary Hoax, Australian Poets Claim Responsibility for a (June 5, 1944) 223

Liverpool Children's Hospital Collects Body Parts Without Authorization (Jan. 30, 2001) 927

Lloyd George Is Accused of Selling Honors, British Prime Minister David (June 22, 1922) 83

Lockheed Is Implicated in Bribing Foreign Officials (Feb. 4, 1976) 482

Longet Kills Ski Champion Vladimir Sabich, Actor Claudine (Mar. 21, 1976) 485

Lott Praises Strom Thurmond's 1948 Presidential Campaign, Senator Trent (Dec. 5, 2002) 988

Love Canal Residents Sue Chemical Company (Sept. 26, 1979) 546

Lowe Videotapes His Sexual Encounter with a Minor, Actor Rob (July 18, 1988) 717

Lying, Award-Winning Historian Joseph J. Ellis Is Accused of (June 18, 2001) 936

Lying to Federal Agents, HUD Secretary Henry Cisneros Is Indicted for (Dec. 11, 1997) 872

MacArthur Sues Newspaper Columnist for Libel, General Douglas (May 16, 1934) 173

McCarthy Launches Communist Witch Hunt, U.S. Senator Joseph (Feb. 9, 1950) 266

McGwire Evades Congressional Questions on Steroid Use, Former Baseball Star Mark (Mar. 17, 2005) 1058

McMartin Preschool Is Embroiled in Child-Abuse Case (Aug. 12, 1983-July 27, 1990) 624

McPherson Claims She Was Kidnapped, Evangelist Aimee Semple (May-June, 1926) 115

Major, British Politician Reveals Her Affair with Prime Minister John (Sept. 28, 2002) . . . 983

Mantle and Willie Mays for Casino Ties, Baseball Commissioner Suspends Mickey (Nov. 29, 1979, and Jan. 31, 1983) 556

Maradona Is Expelled from World Cup, Soccer Star Diego (July 1, 1994) 815

Marcos Forces the Entire Supreme Court to Resign, Philippine President (May 11, 1982) 600

Marsh & McLennan Is Charged with Fraud, Insurance Brokerage (Oct. 14, 2004) 1050

Marvin Is Ordered to Pay Palimony to Former
Lover, Actor Lee (Apr. 18, 1979) 540

Mau Mau Rebellion Are Revealed, British
Atrocities in Kenya's (Late 1955) 298

Mayflower Madam Pleads Guilty to Promoting
Prostitution (July 19, 1985). 654

Mays for Casino Ties, Baseball Commissioner
Suspends Mickey Mantle and Willie
(Nov. 29, 1979, and Jan. 31, 1983). 556

Measles Epidemic in the Amazon, American
Scientists Are Accused of Starting a (Sept.,
2000) 910

Media Allege Canadian Officials Allowed Sale
of Rancid Tuna (Sept. 17, 1985) 660

Mellor Resigns over Romantic Affair, British
Cabinet Member David (Sept. 24, 1992). . . . 792

Menendez Brothers Are Arrested for Murdering
Their Parents (Mar., 1990) 750

Michael Is Arrested for Lewd Conduct, Pop
Singer George (Apr. 7, 1998). 881

Michael Milken Is Indicted for Racketeering
and Fraud, Financier (Mar. 29, 1989) 726

Milgram Begins Obedience-to-Authority
Experiments, Psychologist Stanley (July,
1961) 338

Military Setbacks, British Government Falls
Because of Munitions Shortages and (May,
1915). 58

Milken Is Indicted for Racketeering and Fraud,
Financier Michael (Mar. 29, 1989). 726

Milli Vanilli Lose Grammy Award, Lip-Synching
Duo (Nov. 19, 1990) 756

Mills's Stripper Affair Leads to His Downfall,
Congressman Wilbur D. (Oct. 7, 1974) 462

Miss America to Resign, Vanessa Williams Is the
First (July 23, 1984) 638

Mitchum Is Arrested for Drug Possession, Film
Star Robert (Aug. 31, 1948) 251

Mommie Dearest, Actor Joan Crawford's
Daughter Publishes Damning Memoir
(1978). 517

Money Laundering, Clearstream Financial
Clearinghouse Is Accused of Fraud and
(2001). 925

Money Laundering, Senate Denounces
Herman E. Talmadge for (Oct. 11, 1979) . . . 553

Monroe Sings "Happy Birthday, Mr. President,"
Marilyn (May 19, 1962) 344

Muhammad Cartoons Stir Violent Protests,
Danish Newspaper's Prophet (Sept. 30,
2005) 1075

Muhammad Is Sued for Paternity, Muslim
Leader Elijah (July 2, 1963) 359

Muldergate Scandal, South African President
B. J. Vorster Resigns in (June 4, 1979). . . . 543

Mulroney Is Exposed in Airbus Scandal, Former
Canadian Premier Brian (Nov. 18, 1995) . . . 830

Munsinger Sex and Spy Scandal Rocks Canada
(Mar. 4, 1966) 377

Murder, British Politician Jeremy Thorpe Is
Charged with Attempted (Aug. 4, 1978) 531

Murder, Former Mexican President Carlos
Salinas's Brother Is Arrested for (Feb. 28,
1995) 824

Murder Case, Belgian Media Reveal How Police
Bungled Serial (Aug. 16, 1996) 840

Murder Leads to Sensational O. J. Simpson Trial,
Double (June 12, 1994). 806

Murder of Volunteer in Tonga, Peace Corps
Conceals (1976) 476

Murder Ruins Mabel Normand's Acting Career,
Director Taylor's (Feb. 1, 1922). 73

Murdered, United Mine Workers Leader Joseph
Yablonski Is (Dec. 30, 1969). 404

Murdered by His Grandson, Utah Millionaire Is
(July 23, 1978) 528

Murdered by Lover, Former U.S. Senator Arthur
Brown Is (Dec. 8, 1906) 22

Murdering Their Parents, Menendez Brothers
Are Arrested for (Mar., 1990) 750

Murders Architect Stanford White, Millionaire
Heir (June 25, 1906) 16

Music Industry, U.S. Congress Investigates Payola
in Pop (Feb. 8, 1960) 332

Mutual Fund Companies Are Implicated in
Shady Trading Practices (Sept. 3, 2003) . . . 1013

My Lai Is Revealed, American Massacre of
Vietnamese Civilians at (Nov. 13, 1969). . . . 401

Myerson Resigns as New York Commissioner of
Cultural Affairs, Bess (Apr. 9, 1987). 693

NAACP Chief Benjamin Chavis, Sex Scandal
Forces Dismissal of (Aug. 21, 1994) 821

Naval Academy Expels Midshipmen for
Cheating, U.S. (Apr. 28, 1994). 800

Navy in Homosexuality Investigation, U.S.
Senate Rebukes (July 19, 1921) 70

Nazi Collaboration, French War Hero Pétain Is
  Convicted of (Aug. 14, 1945) 232
Nazi Collaboration, Industrialist Charles Bedaux
  Is Arrested for (Dec. 5, 1942) 212
Nazi Collaboration, Norwegian Politician Quisling
  Is Arrested for (May 9, 1945) 226
Nazi Germany, Duke and Duchess of Windsor
  Visit (Oct. 11-22, 1937) 196
Nazi Past Is Revealed, Former U.N. Secretary-
  General Kurt Waldheim's (Mar. 3, 1986) . . . 669
Nazi Pilot, German Generals Must Retire for
  Supporting a Neo- (Nov. 9, 1976) 503
Nazi Spy, Biographer Claims Actor Errol Flynn
  Was a (1980) 559
Nazi Ties, Novelist Günter Grass Admits to
  Youthful (Aug. 12, 2006) 1109
NBA Referee Tim Donaghy Is Sentenced to
  Prison for Betting on Games (July 29,
  2008). 1172
New York Times Exposes Grading Scandal at
  Auburn University (July 14, 2006) 1101
New York Times Publishes the Pentagon Papers
  (June 13, 1971) 416
New York Times Reporter Denies Reports of a
  Soviet Famine (Mar. 31, 1933). 167
New York Times Reporter Jayson Blair Is Exposed
  as a Fraud (Apr. 29, 2003) 998
Nhu Derides Self-Immolation of Vietnamese
  Buddhists, Madame (Aug. 14, 1963). 362
Nixon Denies Taking Illegal Campaign
  Contributions, Richard (Sept. 23, 1952) 286
Nixons Received Jewelry Gifts, *Washington Post*
  Reveals That the (May 14, 1974). 453
Nixon's Resignation, Watergate Break-in Leads to
  President (June 17, 1972-Aug. 9, 1974) 425
Normand's Acting Career, Director Taylor's
  Murder Ruins Mabel (Feb. 1, 1922) 73
Normand's Chauffeur Shoots Millionaire
  Courtland S. Dines, Film Star Mabel
  (Jan. 1, 1924) 100
Nosferatu Is Found to Have Violated *Dracula*
  Copyright (July, 1925) 111
Novak Leaks the Name of CIA Operative Valerie
  Plame, Columnist Robert (July 14, 2003). . . 1010

Oil-for-Food Scandal, Iqbal Riza Resigns from
  the United Nations in (Jan. 15, 2005) 1053
Olympic Champion Marion Jones Admits
  Steroid Use (Oct. 5, 2007). 1164

Olympic Gold Medal Because of Drugs,
  Gymnast Andreea Răducan Loses
  Her (Sept. 26, 2000) 916
Olympics, French Judge Admits Favoring Russian
  Figure Skaters in Winter (Feb. 11, 2002). . . . 962
O'Reilly, Television Producer Files Sex
  Harassment Suit Against Bill (Oct. 13,
  2004) 1047
Organized Crime, President Kennedy's Romantic
  Affair Links Him to (Feb. 7, 1960). 329
Organized Crime, U.S. Senate Committee Begins
  Investigating (May 3, 1950) 270
Outreau Affair, Sexual Abuse of Children in
  France Leads to the (Dec., 2000) 922

Palimony, Tennis Star Billie Jean King Is Sued
  for (Apr. 28, 1981) 588
Palimony to Former Lover, Actor Lee Marvin Is
  Ordered to Pay (Apr. 18, 1979). 540
Parkinson Resigns After His Secretary Becomes
  Pregnant, British Cabinet Secretary (Oct. 14,
  1983) 631
Paternity, Actor Charles Chaplin Is Sued for
  (June 4, 1943). 220
Paternity, Muslim Leader Elijah Is Sued for
  (July 2, 1963). 359
Paulk Is Photographed Leaving a Gay Bar,
  Ex-gay Leader John (Sept. 19, 2000). 913
Payola in Pop Music Industry, U.S. Congress
  Investigates (Feb. 8, 1960) 332
Peace Corps Conceals Murder of Volunteer in
  Tonga (1976) 476
Pearson Exposes Congressman's Corruption,
  Columnist Drew (Aug. 4, 1948) 248
Pee-wee Herman Is Arrested for Public
  Indecency, Comedian (July 26, 1991) 765
Pendergast Pleads Guilty to Income Tax Evasion,
  Kansas City's Boss (May 22, 1939) 199
Pentagon Papers, *New York Times* Publishes the
  (June 13, 1971) 416
Perjury, Alger Hiss Is Convicted of (Jan. 21,
  1950) 259
Pet Food That Killed Thousands of American
  Pets, Manufacturer Recalls (Summer, 2006-
  Mar. 16, 2007). 1097
Pétain Is Convicted of Nazi Collaboration,
  French War Hero (Aug. 14, 1945) 232
Physicist Publishes a Deliberately Fraudulent
  Article (Spring, 1996) 837

Piltdown Man Is Revealed to Be a Hoax (Nov. 21, 1953) 292

Pinto's Safety Problems, Court Finds That Ford Ignored (May 29, 1981) 594

Pius XII of Complicity in the Holocaust, Play Accuses Pope (Feb. 23, 1963) 353

Plagiarism, Historian Doris Kearns Goodwin Is Accused of (Jan. 18, 2002) 959

Plagiarism, Historian Stephen E. Ambrose Is Accused of (Jan. 4, 2002). 951

Plagiarism, *Roots* Author Alex Haley Is Sued for (1978). 520

Plagiarism, Scottish Historian Is Charged with (Apr., 1998). 879

Plagiarism Charges End Joe Biden's Presidential Campaign (Sept. 23, 1987) 698

Plagiarism Is Revealed, Martin Luther King, Jr.'s, Doctoral-Thesis (Dec. 3, 1989). 739

Plagiarism Lawsuit, Former Beatle George Harrison Loses (Sept. 1, 1976) 494

Plame, Columnist Robert Novak Leaks the Name of CIA Operative Valerie (July 14, 2003). . . 1010

Poisoning, Former Russian Security Service Officer Dies from Radiation (Nov. 23, 2006). 1132

Polanski Flees the United States to Avoid Rape Trial, Roman (Feb. 1, 1978) 522

Police Bungled Serial Murder Case, Belgian Media Reveal How (Aug. 16, 1996) 840

Police Corruption, Atherton Report Exposes San Francisco (Mar. 17, 1937) 191

Police Corruption, Media Reports Spark Investigation of Australian (Jan. 12 and May 11, 1987) 681

Police Corruption Is Revealed in Los Angeles's Rampart Division (May, 1998). 884

Ponzi Schemes Are Revealed as Investment Frauds (1919-1920) 63

Popoff Is Exposed as a Fraud, Faith Healer Peter (Apr. 22, 1986) 673

Pornography, British Conductor-Composer Is Arrested for Possessing (Mar. 9, 1956). . . . 304

Pornography Charges, Singer R. Kelly Is Acquitted on Child (June 13, 2008). 1170

Postmaster's Division of Airmail Routes Creates a Scandal (May, 1930) 144

Poulson for Bribery and Fraud, Police Arrest Architect John (June 22, 1972) 431

Pound Is Charged with Treason and Institutionalized, Poet Ezra (Dec. 14, 1945) 236

Powell, Jr., Is Excluded from Congress, Adam Clayton (Mar. 1, 1967) 380

Prescription Elixir Causes More than One Hundred Deaths (Sept.-Oct., 1937). 193

Profumo Affair Rocks British Government, John (Mar. 2-Sept. 25, 1963). 355

Prostitute's House, French Cardinal Daniélou Dies in a (May 20, 1974) 456

Prostitution, Boxer Jack Johnson Is Imprisoned for Abetting (May 13, 1913). 52

Prostitution, Mayflower Madam Pleads Guilty to Promoting (July 19, 1985) 654

Prostitution Scandal, New York Governor Eliot Spitzer Resigns in (Mar. 12, 2008) 1167

PTL Television Network, Jim Bakker Resigns as Head of (Mar. 19, 1987) 690

Pulitzer Prize-Winning Feature, Janet Cooke Admits Fabricating Her (Apr. 15, 1981) 585

Pyramid Investment Schemes Cause Albanian Government to Fall (Jan., 1997) 846

Quisling Is Arrested for Nazi Collaboration, Norwegian Politician (May 9, 1945) 226

Quiz Show, Charles Van Doren Admits to Being Fed Answers on Television (Nov. 2, 1959) 326

Racketeering and Fraud, Financier Michael Milken Is Indicted for (Mar. 29, 1989) 726

Radiation Poisoning, Former Russian Security Service Officer Dies from (Nov. 23, 2006) . . 1132

Răducan Loses Her Olympic Gold Medal Because of Drugs, Gymnast Andreea (Sept. 26, 2000). 916

Rainbow Warrior, French Secret Service Sinks the Greenpeace Ship (July 10, 1985) 651

Rajneesh Is Indicted for Immigration Fraud, Guru Bhagwan Shree (Oct. 23, 1985) 662

Randall Cunningham's Home, Federal Agents Raid Congressman (July 1, 2005). 1064

Rape, Basketball Star Kobe Bryant Is Accused of (July 1, 2003). 1008

Rape, Duke Lacrosse Players Are Accused of Gang (Mar. 14, 2006) 1086

Rape, Film Star Errol Flynn Is Acquitted of (Feb. 6, 1942). 202

Rape, Korean Religious Teacher Jung Myung Seok Is Charged with (June 30, 2001) 939

Rape, Teacher Mary Kay Letourneau Is Arrested for Statutory (Feb. 26, 1997) 849

Rape, William Kennedy Smith Is Accused of (Mar. 30, 1991) 759

Rape Trials, "Scottsboro Boys" Are Railroaded Through (Mar. 30, 1931) 150

Raped by Police Officers, Black Teenager Claims to Have Been Gang- (Nov. 28, 1987) 702

Reagan's Administration, Iran-Contra Weapons Scandal Taints (Nov. 13, 1986-May 4, 1989) 676

Reid's Death in Drug Rehab Shakes Film Industry, Actor Wallace (Jan. 18, 1923) 86

Riza Resigns from the United Nations in Oil-for-Food Scandal, Iqbal (Jan. 15, 2005) 1053

Rockefeller Dies Mysteriously, Former Vice President Nelson (Jan. 26, 1979) 537

Romanian Revolution, Harassment of a Christian Minister Sparks the (Dec. 15-25, 1989) 742

Roosevelt Is Accused of Accepting Corporate Funds, Theodore (1904) 1

Roosevelt Orders Internment of Japanese Americans, President (Feb. 19, 1942) 205

Rose Is Banned from Baseball for Betting on Games, Pete (Aug. 24, 1989) 735

Rostenkowski Is Indicted in House Post Office Scandal, Congressman Dan (June 1, 1994). . . 803

Sabich, Actor Claudine Longet Kills Ski Champion Vladimir (Mar. 21, 1976) 485

Salinas's Brother Is Arrested for Murder, Former Mexican President Carlos (Feb. 28, 1995) . . . 824

Sancta Susanna Depicts a Nun's Sexual Desires, Hindemith's Opera (Mar. 26, 1922) 76

Scarsdale Diet Doctor Is Killed by His Lover (Mar. 10, 1980) 565

Schmitz Is Found Guilty of Extortion, San Francisco Mayor (June 13, 1907) 28

Schmitz Is Found to Have Children Out of Wedlock, Conservative Politician John G. (July 20, 1982) 603

Schön Faked His Research, Inquiry Reveals That Physicist Jan Hendrik (Sept. 25, 2002) 980

Schwarzenegger Groped Women, Newspaper Claims That Arnold (Oct. 2, 2003) 1016

"Scottsboro Boys" Are Railroaded Through Rape Trials (Mar. 30, 1931) 150

Sex and Spy Scandal Rocks Canada, Munsinger (Mar. 4, 1966) 377

Sex Harassment Suit Against Bill O'Reilly, Television Producer Files (Oct. 13, 2004) . . 1047

Sex Scandal, Congress Members Censured in House-Page (July 20, 1983) 621

Sex Scandal, University of Alabama Fires New Football Coach in (May 3, 2003) 1002

Sex Scandal Forces Dismissal of NAACP Chief Benjamin Chavis (Aug. 21, 1994) 821

Sex Scandal Forces Resignation of Alberta Premier Brownlee (July 10, 1934) 176

Sex Scandal Involving a Teenage Page, Congressman Mark Foley Resigns in (Sept. 29, 2006) 1118

Sex-Tape Appears on the Web, Paris Hilton (Early Nov., 2003) 1019

Sexual Abuse by Roman Catholic Priests, Boston Globe Reports on Child (Jan. 6, 2002) 954

Sexual Abuse of Children in France Leads to the Outreau Affair (Dec., 2000) 922

Sexual Affair with a White House Intern, President Bill Clinton Denies (Jan. 17, 1998) 874

Sexual Assault, Sportscaster Marv Albert Is Tried for (Sept. 22, 1997) 865

Sexual Assaults, E-mail Message Prompts Inquiry into Air Force Academy (Jan. 2, 2003) 991

Sexual Encounter with a Minor, Actor Rob Lowe Videotapes His (July 18, 1988) 717

Sexual Liaisons with Evangelist Ted Haggard, Male Escort Reveals (Nov. 2, 2006) 1126

Simpson Photo, Time Magazine Cover Uses Altered O. J. (June 24, 1994) 810

Simpson Trial, Double Murder Leads to Sensational O. J. (June 12, 1994) 806

Simpson's Book, News Corp Abandons Plan to Publish O. J. (Nov. 20, 2006) 1129

Sisson Documents Are Fakes, George F. Kennan Proves Russian (June, 1956) 307

Skating After Attack on Rival, Tonya Harding Is Banned from (June 30, 1994) 812

Slave Labor, Liberian Workers Sue Bridgestone Firestone over (Nov. 17, 2005) 1078

Slavery, Liberia Is Accused of Selling Its Own Citizens into (1930) 142

Smith Is Accused of Rape, William Kennedy (Mar. 30, 1991) 759

Soap Box Derby, Cheating Scandal Shocks
(Aug. 19, 1973). 444

Soccer, Media Uncover Match-Fixing in Italian
(May 4, 2006) 1092

Soccer Match, Players Fix Liverpool-Manchester
United (Apr. 2, 1915) 55

Soccer Referee Admits to Fixing Games for
Money, German (Jan. 27, 2005) 1055

Soccer Star Diego Maradona Is Expelled from
World Cup (July 1, 1994) 815

Sosuke Resigns After Affair with a Geisha,
Japanese Prime Minister (Aug. 10, 1989) . . . 733

Soviet Famine, *New York Times* Reporter Denies
Reports of a (Mar. 31, 1933) 167

Spano Is Sentenced for Fraudulent Purchase of
Ice Hockey Team, John (Jan. 28, 2000) 901

Speaker Are Accused of Fixing Baseball Games,
Ty Cobb and Tris (Dec. 26, 1926) 118

Spiegel Magazine Offices, West German Police
Raid *Der* (Oct. 26, 1962) 349

Spitzer Resigns in Prostitution Scandal, New
York Governor Eliot (Mar. 12, 2008). 1167

Spy, Biographer Claims Actor Errol Flynn Was a
Nazi (1980). 559

Spy Scandal Rocks Canada, Munsinger Sex and
(Mar. 4, 1966) 377

Spying, British Civil Servant Is Arrested for
(Sept. 12, 1962). 347

Spying for the Russians, CIA Agent Robert
Hanssen Is Arrested for (Feb. 18, 2001) 931

Spying on Other Teams, New England Patriots
Football Team Is Fined for (Sept. 13,
2007). 1161

Stanford Prison Experiment, Abusive Role-
Playing Ends (Aug. 20, 1971) 420

Starr Is Appointed to the Whitewater
Investigation, Kenneth (Aug. 5, 1994) 818

Stavisky's Fraudulent Schemes Rock French
Government (Jan. 8, 1934-Jan. 17, 1936) . . . 170

Stem Cells, Scientist Is Indicted for Faking His
Research on Creating (May 12, 2006) 1094

Sterilizes Thousands Deemed Genetically and
Mentally Unfit, Alberta Government
(Mar. 21, 1928) 133

Steroid Use, Former Baseball Star Mark McGwire
Evades Congressional Questions on (Mar. 17,
2005) 1058

Steroid Use, Olympic Champion Marion Jones
Admits (Oct. 5, 2007) 1164

Stewart Is Convicted in Insider-Trading Scandal,
Martha (Mar. 5, 2004). 1031

Stonehouse Fakes His Suicide, British Politician
John (Nov. 20, 1974) 468

Subprime Mortgage Industry Begins to Collapse
(Early 2007). 1134

Suicide, British Politician John Stonehouse Fakes
His (Nov. 20, 1974). 468

Suicide, Film Star Jean Harlow's Husband Is an
Apparent (Sept. 4, 1932) 160

Suicide, U.S. Attorney General Harry M.
Daugherty's Aide Commits (May 30,
1923) 92

Suicide During Affair with Rex Harrison, Actor
Carole Landis Commits (July 5, 1948) 245

Swaggart Tearfully Confesses His Adultery,
Evangelist Jimmy (Feb. 21, 1988) 711

Swanson, Joseph P. Kennedy Begins an Affair
with Gloria (Early 1928) 127

Syphilis Study, Newspaper Breaks Story of
Abuses in Tuskegee (July 25, 1972) 437

Tailhook Sexual Assault Scandal, U.S. Navy
Secretary Resigns in the Wake of (June 26,
1992) 784

Tainted Blood, Canadian Health Commissioner
Releases Report on (Nov. 26, 1997) 868

Talmadge for Money Laundering, Senate
Denounces Herman E. (Oct. 11, 1979) 553

Tax Conspiracy, President Truman's
Appointments Secretary Is Convicted of
(June 25, 1956) 310

Tax Evasion, Hotel Tycoon Leona Helmsley
Enters Prison for (Apr. 15, 1992). 776

Tax Evasion, Kansas City's Boss Pendergast
Pleads Guilty to Income (May 22, 1939) . . . 199

Tax Fraud, Teamsters Leader Dave Beck Is
Convicted of (May, 1959) 323

Tax Official Resigns After Accepting Bribes,
Federal (Nov. 16, 1951) 279

Tax Violations, Evangelist Kent Hovind Is
Convicted of Federal (Nov. 2, 2006) 1123

Taylor's Murder Ruins Mabel Normand's Acting
Career, Director (Feb. 1, 1922) 73

Teamsters Leader Dave Beck Is Convicted of Tax
Fraud (May, 1959) 323

Teapot Dome Oil Leases, U.S. Senate Begins
Hearings on (Oct. 22, 1923) 95

Television Quiz Show, Charles Van Doren Admits to Being Fed Answers on (Nov. 2, 1959) . . . 326

Tennis Star Bill Tilden Is Arrested for Lewd Behavior with a Minor (Nov. 23, 1946) 239

Tennis Star Billie Jean King Is Sued for Palimony (Apr. 28, 1981) 588

Thalidomide Causes Widespread Birth Disorders, Prescription (1956-1962) 301

Thatcher's Government, Westland Affair Shakes Prime Minister (1985-1986) 645

Thomas's Confirmation Hearings Create a Scandal, Justice Clarence (Oct. 11-13, 1991) 768

Thorpe Is Charged with Attempted Murder, British Politician Jeremy (Aug. 4, 1978) 531

Three Weeks Shocks Readers, Elinor Glyn's Novel (1907) 25

Thurmond's Biracial Daughter Is Revealed, Senator Strom (Dec. 17, 2003) 1022

Thurmond's 1948 Presidential Campaign, Senator Trent Lott Praises Strom (Dec. 5, 2002) 988

Tilden Is Arrested for Lewd Behavior with a Minor, Tennis Star Bill (Nov. 23, 1946) 239

Time Magazine Cover Uses Altered O. J. Simpson Photo (June 24, 1994) 810

Tires, Firestone Recalls Millions of Defective Car (Oct. 20, 1978) 534

Tobacco Industry Corruption, Whistle-Blower Reveals (Feb. 4, 1996) 833

Todd's Death Cannot Be Explained, Film Star Thelma (Dec. 16, 1935) 178

Tour de France Is Hit with a Doping Scandal (July 26, 2006). 1103

Trading Practices, Mutual Fund Companies Are Implicated in Shady (Sept. 3, 2003). 1013

Treason, French Court Declares Alfred Dreyfus Innocent of (July 12, 1906) 19

Treason, Norwegian Writer Knut Hamsun Is Arrested for (May 26, 1945) 229

Treason and Institutionalized, Poet Ezra Pound Is Charged with (Dec. 14, 1945) 236

Triangle Shirtwaist Factory Fire, Nearly 150 Workers Die in (Mar. 25, 1911) 40

Truman's Appointments Secretary Is Convicted of Tax Conspiracy, President (June 25, 1956) 310

Tuna, Media Allege Canadian Officials Allowed Sale of Rancid (Sept. 17, 1985) 660

Turkey, Car Crash Reveals Depth of Government Corruption in (Nov. 3, 1996) 843

Turner's Daughter Kills Turner's Gangster Lover, Actor Lana (Apr. 4, 1958) 317

Tuskegee Syphilis Study, Newspaper Breaks Story of Abuses in (July 25, 1972) 437

Ueberroth Suspends Players for Cocaine Use, Baseball Commissioner Peter (Feb. 28, 1986) 666

U.N. Officials, U.S. National Security Agency Is Found to Have Spied on (Mar. 2, 2003) 995

U.N. Report Reveals That Secretary-General Kofi Annan Dismissed Sexual Harassment Charges (June 2, 2004) 1039

United Way Charity Chief Pleads Guilty to Embezzlement, Former (Mar. 4, 2004) 1028

U.S. National Security Agency Is Found to Have Spied on U.N. Officials (Mar. 2, 2003). 995

Van Doren Admits to Being Fed Answers on Television Quiz Show, Charles (Nov. 2, 1959) 326

Vick Pleads Guilty to Financing a Dogfighting Ring, Football Star Michael (Aug. 20, 2007). 1158

Viet Minh Broadcasts French General's Damaging Report (Aug. 26, 1949) 257

Vietnamese Buddhists, Madame Nhu Derides Self-Immolation of (Aug. 14, 1963) 362

Vigilante Bernhard Goetz Shoots Four Black Youths, Subway (Dec. 22, 1984) 641

Vitter's Name Is Found in D.C. Madam's Address Book, Senator David (July 9, 2007). 1150

Volstead Act, Kentucky Congressman John W. Langley Is Convicted of Violating the (May 12, 1924) 103

Vorster Resigns in Muldergate Scandal, South African President B. J. (June 4, 1979) 543

Wakeman Shoots Her Politician-Husband, Socialite Nancy (Sept. 5, 1967) 386

Waldheim's Nazi Past Is Revealed, Former U.N. Secretary-General Kurt (Mar. 3, 1986). 669

Walter Reed Army Hospital, *Washington Post* Exposes Decline of (Feb. 18, 2007) 1138

Washington Post Exposes Congressman Wayne L. Hays's Affair (May 23, 1976) 491

Washington Post Reveals That the Nixons Received Jewelry Gifts (May 14, 1974) 453

Watergate Break-in Leads to President Nixon's
Resignation (June 17, 1972-Aug. 9, 1974) . . . 425

Weapons, Irish Politicians Are Tried for
Conspiring to Import (May 28, 1970) 413

Wedlock, British Cabinet Member Resigns After
Fathering a Child Out of (Jan. 5, 1994) 798

Wedlock, Civil Rights Leader Jesse Jackson
Fathers a Child Out of (May, 1999) 895

Wedlock, Conservative Politician John G. Schmitz
Is Found to Have Children Out of (July 20,
1982) 603

Wedlock, Swedish Film Star Ingrid Bergman Has
a Child Out of (Feb. 7, 1950). 263

West Point Cadets Are Caught Cheating on
Exams (Apr. 4, 1976). 488

Westar Energy Executives Are Found Guilty of
Looting Their Company (Sept. 12, 2005). . . 1072

West's Play About Gays Is Banned on Broadway,
Mae (1927) 122

Westland Affair Shakes Prime Minister
Thatcher's Government (1985-1986). 645

Whistle-Blower Reveals Tobacco Industry
Corruption (Feb. 4, 1996) 833

White, Millionaire Heir Murders Architect
Stanford (June 25, 1906). 16

White Sox Players Conspire to Lose World Series
in "Black Sox" Scandal (Sept. 21, 1919) 66

Whitewater Investigation, Kenneth Starr Is
Appointed to the (Aug. 5, 1994) 818

William II's Homosexual "Circle" Scandalizes
Germany, Emperor (1906-1909) 9

Williams Is the First Miss America to Resign,
Vanessa (July 23, 1984) 638

Windsor Visit Nazi Germany, Duke and Duchess
of (Oct. 11-22, 1937) 196

Wolfson Is Convicted of Selling Stock Illegally,
Investor Louis (Nov. 28, 1967). 389

World Series in "Black Sox" Scandal, White Sox
Players Conspire to Lose (Sept. 21, 1919). . . . 66

World War I Veterans from Washington, U.S.
Troops Drive (July 28, 1932). 156

World War II, French Prime Minister Pierre
Laval Wants Germany to Win (Apr. 22,
1942) 209

Wright Resigns in Ethics Scandal, Speaker of
the House Jim (May 31, 1989) 730

Yablonski Is Murdered, United Mine Workers
Leader Joseph (Dec. 30, 1969) 404

ZZZZ Best Founder Is Indicted on Federal Fraud
Charges (Jan. 15, 1988). 708

Modern Scandals

1904-2008

April, 1998
SCOTTISH HISTORIAN IS CHARGED WITH PLAGIARISM

Scottish historian and biographer James A.
Mackay was first accused of plagiarizing the
works of others for his noted biography Alexander
Graham Bell *(1997). Further plagiarism charges*
were leveled against other works, including his
biographies of John Paul Jones, Andrew
Carnegie, William Wallace, and Mary, Queen of
Scots. The long string of fraud allegations marred
his reputation as a scholar and, in effect, ended
his career as a writer.

LOCALE: Glasgow, Scotland

CATEGORIES: Cultural and intellectual history;
hoaxes, frauds, and charlatanism; publishing
and journalism; plagiarism; public morals;
ethics

KEY FIGURES

James A. Mackay (1936-2007), Scottish historian
and biographer
Robert V. Bruce (b. 1923), professor emeritus,
Boston University

SUMMARY OF EVENT

James A. Mackay became a renowned historian and
biographer through his studies of stamps and coins,
his scholarship on poet Robert Burns, and his 1996
biography *Michael Collins: A Life*. In 1997, he published the biography *Alexander Graham Bell: A
Life*, which had marketable success. Mackay then
faced a stunning accusation from Robert V. Bruce,
a professor emeritus at Boston University. In April,
1998, Bruce accused Mackay of plagiarizing his
work and the work of others in writing the Bell biography.

Bruce detailed the questionable passages, some
of which were multiple pages in length, which were
taken from his biography *Bell: Alexander Graham
Bell and the Conquest of Solitude* (1973). The passages in Mackay's book retained a remarkable simi-
larity—some even identical. Bruce found 285
pages (of Mackay's 297) with lifted material. Fur-

thermore, he noted that Mackay, in the biography,
acknowledged and thanked the Bell Collection archives of the National Geographic Society (NGS),
archives that had been relocated to the Library of
Congress during the mid-1970's. Mackay published his book more than twenty years after the
Bell archives at the NGS was moved. More charges
of plagiarism were leveled against Mackay, charges
related to his other biographies.

While Bruce's accusation against Mackay was
the opening salvo, another scholar, Graeme Morton, a lecturer in economic and social history at the
University of Edinburgh in Scotland, wrote in a
journal article that Mackay's biography *William
Wallace: Brave Heart* (1995) was strikingly reminiscent of Sir James Fergusson's 1938 biography of
the thirteenth century Scottish patriot William
Wallace. Morton found lifted arguments, structure,
and even entire paragraphs. Mackay's *William
Wallace* was reprinted nonetheless.

Mackay's career began as an assistant keeper at
the British Museum, and he also worked as a columnist for the *Financial Times*. He went on to research
stamps and coins and produced *History of Scottish
Postmarks, 1693-1978* (1978), a landmark work on
Scottish stamps. He received the distinguished
Saltire Award in 1992 for his work on Burns and
had been a well-respected historian and scholar of
Scottish history. He had received an honorary doctorate in literature from Glasgow University in
1993. His name accompanies more than two hundred books and ten thousand articles, and he edited
The Burns Chronicle for several years. He published six biographies in three years and had plans
for more. Prior to his notorious work on Bell,
Mackay was known for his histories of Scottish figures, including Allan Pinkerton, Andrew Carnegie,
and Sir Thomas Lipton.

In 1998, Mackay's biography on Bell was published in an American edition, and *The New Yorker*
magazine and *The New York Times* praised the work
in reviews. It was about this time that Bruce, whose

1990's

biography of Bell was a runner up for a Pulitzer Prize in 1974, first began to pay attention to Mackay's book, finding that Mackay had duplicated letters between Bell and his wife that were included in his 1973 biography, and that Mackay did so without attribution. This revelation was the main trigger in the scandal, leading Bruce to inspect more of Mackay's biography. What he found led him to contact Mackay's American publisher, John Wiley & Sons, to alert them to the plagiarism. To avoid being sued by Bruce, Wiley agreed to destroy all American editions of the book that were still with distributors and booksellers.

Another Mackay work is the formidable biography of Mary, Queen of Scots. That book, *In My End Is My Beginning* (1998), was found to be reminiscent—or, in some places, more like a carbon copy—of Antonia Fraser's monumental and bestselling work *Mary, Queen of Scots* (1969). Mackay's biography of John Paul Jones, *I Have Not Yet Begun to Fight: A Life of John Paul Jones*, was dissected upon its publication in 1999. Journalists and scholars investigated the book carefully, even comparing it to *John Paul Jones: A Sailor's Biography* (1959) by Samuel Eliot Morison. Once again, a pattern emerged. Entire passages matched Morison's words, and in those instances in which the words did not match, Mackay used similar sentence structure and made comparable use of sources.

Mackay was adamant throughout the string of accusations that he had not plagiarized. Instead, he argued, he had used similar sources but never consciously copied material from previous biographers. The only charge to which he acquiesced was his use of the letters between Bell and his wife, which Mackay had assumed were in the public domain. He later apologized to Bruce for using the letters.

IMPACT

Following the accusations of plagiarism, Mackay's British publisher, Mainstream, terminated all pending contracts with the author and did not seek any further work from him. His books on Bell and Jones, and on Mary, Queen of Scots, were removed from circulation in the United States by his American publishers. His work on Carnegie was removed from the shelves of British booksellers in 1999 after he was accused of plagiarizing parts of that work as well.

Also receiving greater scrutiny after the 1998 scandal was the work for which Mackay received great accolades and was awarded the Saltire Prize in 1993: the biography of Burns. Andrew Noble, a senior lecturer at the University of Strathclyde and coeditor of *The Canongate Burns* (2001), revealed that Mackay's biography of Burns contained similar passages from a little-known nineteenth century work, *The Life and Works of Robert Burns* (1852), edited by Robert Chambers. Given this new round of accusations, it seemed that Mackay would never write again, or get published. His name and reputation had been permanently marred. However, he still maintained some degree of credibility because of his earlier work on Burns and still was accepted as a foremost authority on the early Scottish poet.

—*Meredith A. Holladay*

FURTHER READING

Hauptman, Robert. *Documentation: A History and Critique of Attribution, Commentary, Glosses, Marginalia, Notes, Bibliographies, Works-cited Lists, and Citation Indexing and Analysis*. Jefferson, N.C.: McFarland, 2008. A study of scholarly documentation. This unique work "examines and critiques the history, use, and abuse of various literary documentation systems" including those systems used in the humanities and sciences.

Hoffer, Peter Charles. *Past Imperfect: Facts, Fictions, and Fraud—American History from Bancroft and Parkman to Ambrose, Bellesiles, Ellis, and Goodwin*. New York: PublicAffairs, 2007. Examination of the key controversies in the historical profession as the culmination of the tensions between New Left scholars and traditional historians.

Mackay, James A. *Alexander Graham Bell: A Life*. New York: John Wiley & Sons, 1998. The controversial biography of Bell, which initiated the series of plagiarism allegations against Mackay. First published in Great Britain in 1997.

Wiener, Jon. *Historians in Trouble: Plagiarism, Fraud, and Politics in the Ivory Tower.* New York: New Press, 2005. A detailed analysis of the fraud and plagiarism scandals of historians and other scholars. Good for background material on the subject of academic fraud.

SEE ALSO: June 5, 1944: Australian Poets Claim Responsibility for a Literary Hoax; Jan. 28, 1972: Clifford Irving Admits Faking Howard Hughes Memoirs; 1978: *Roots* Author Alex Haley Is Sued for Plagiarism; Dec. 3, 1989: Martin Luther King, Jr.'s, Doctoral-Thesis Plagiarism Is Revealed; May 11, 1998: Journalist Stephen Glass Is Exposed as a Fraud; June 18, 2001: Historian Joseph J. Ellis Is Accused of Lying; Jan. 4, 2002: Historian Stephen E. Ambrose Is Accused of Plagiarism; Jan. 18, 2002: Historian Doris Kearns Goodwin Is Accused of Plagiarism; Oct. 25, 2002: Historian Michael A. Bellesiles Resigns After Academic Fraud Accusations; July 24, 2007: University of Colorado Fires Professor for Plagiarism and Research Falsification.

April 7, 1998
POP SINGER GEORGE MICHAEL IS ARRESTED FOR LEWD CONDUCT

In 1998, pop singer George Michael was arrested by an undercover Beverly Hills police officer for engaging in a lewd act in a public restroom. Michael, who paid a fine and did community service, incorporated the incident into a song and music video. His arresting officer sued him for slander because of the song and video, but lost his case. After the arrest, Michael also came out as gay.

LOCALE: Beverly Hills, California

CATEGORIES: Drugs; law and the courts; music and performing arts; popular culture; public morals; publishing and journalism; sex crimes

KEY FIGURES

George Michael (Georgios Kyriacos Panayiotou; b. 1963), British pop singer

Marcelo Rodriguez (fl. 1990's), Beverly Hills police officer

SUMMARY OF EVENT

The 1980's brought the British pop duo Wham! out of its native Great Britain and into the forefront of the American music scene. Singing peppy tunes such as "Wake Me Up Before You Go Go" and sad ballads such as "Careless Whisper," the duo, made up of George Michael and Andrew Ridgeley, attracted a fairly broad audience. Flashy singer Michael drew much press attention for his alleged relationships with a variety of celebrities, ranging from Whoopi Goldberg to Brooke Shields. However, Michael knew he was gay from a relatively young age and had been out to much of his family, including one sister, by the time he was nineteen years old.

By the end of 1986, Wham! disbanded, and Michael launched his own career. He had a number of hits, including "Faith" and "I Want Your Sex," and a hit duet with R&B singer Aretha Franklin called "I Knew You Were Waiting for Me." While he was touring in 1991, he met and fell in love with Anselmo Feleppa, a Brazilian fashion designer, who died in 1993 from AIDS-related complications. Michael's 1996 single "Jesus to a Child" and his album *Older*, from the same year, are both dedicated to Feleppa. Michael wrote *Older* under the influence of marijuana and developed a habit for the drug. In 1998, he claimed he was outing himself to his fans with *Older* and with "Jesus to a Child," and he had already been out to his family and friends for several years. One family member he was not out to was his mother, who died in 1997.

George Michael, left, with Wham! partner Andrew Ridgeley in 1984. (PA Photos/Landov)

Michael's career by this point had moved almost entirely to Britain, and he had little popularity with American fans. However, while in California in 1998, his sexuality became tabloid fodder. On April 7, he was followed into a park's public restroom by undercover Beverly Hills police officer Marcelo Rodriguez. Michael exposed himself and was arrested as he left the restroom for his car. The arrest was not a surprise to the media, and it failed as a major news story in either the United States or Great Britain.

The arrest did trigger some publicity, however, and Michael took quick steps to address the matter. He came out as gay while interviewed by Jim Moret on CNN's *NewsNight*. Michael had not intended to discuss his sexual orientation with the press, but he wanted to discuss the circumstances that led up to his arrest. In an MTV interview in November, Michael said that being oversexed was the issue, not his homosexuality. In later interviews, he said

he thought he had been set up by the Beverly Hills Police Department with help from the London paparazzi, but he could not prove his accusations. In 2005, he said that gay celebrities did what they could to desexualize themselves so as to appear nonthreatening to their fans. Michael said he felt no need to maintain such a low profile, and he admitted to enjoying public gay sex.

During his *NewsNight* interview, Michael said he had been embarrassed by his arrest, suggesting he had behaved in the same manner before. He was, in fact, involved in a monogamous relationship with Kenny Goss, an American clothing executive, at the time of his arrest. Michael told MTV the relationship was not open, but that Goss had forgiven him. However, he told other news sources that the relationship indeed was open. Years later, in 2007, he admitted that the actions that led to his arrest were unconsciously deliberate, that he wanted to get caught. He said it was difficult for him to be closeted publicly but out privately. He had kept his sexuality secret before 1998, largely for the sake of his mother, whom, he believed, would have suffered from worrying about his chances of HIV infection or of developing AIDS.

Michael pleaded no contest at his criminal trial for lewd conduct. He received a light fine (approximately eight hundred dollars) and was ordered to perform community service.

IMPACT

The consummate entertainer, Michael immediately capitalized on his arrest and conviction with his next single, "Outside," which mocked and condemned police persecution of public sex between men. The video for the single, released in November, 1998, depicts dancers in police uniforms kissing in a men's restroom transformed into a dance club.

In 1999, the scandal reemerged when the arresting police officer, Rodriguez, sued Michael, claiming he was maligned by his video, song, and interviews with the media. Rodriguez said the video was intended to mock him specifically and that Michael had slandered him in interviews. He filed a ten-million-dollar civil suit in a California court, demanding compensation for emotional distress. The case was dismissed but reinstated on appeal. The court determined that because Rodriguez was a public servant, he was ineligible to recover monies for emotional damages. The media suggested, indirectly, that the suit was nothing more than an attempt to get a chunk of Michael's roughly $100 million estate.

Michael's career was unaffected by the scandal. His greatest hits album *Twentyfive* debuted at the top of the British charts in November, 1998, just months after his arrest. Scandal is often an intrinsic part of celebrity life, and Michael's arrest was accepted in stride by his fans. Furthermore, his coming out as gay had no apparent negative effect on his career.

—Jessie Bishop Powell

FURTHER READING

Gill, John. *Queer Noises: Male and Female Homosexuality in Twentieth Century Music.* Minneapolis: University of Minnesota Press, 1995. Analyzes the music industry's shift from repression to general acceptance of homosexuality beginning during the early part of the twentieth century with the blues and through the age of rock during the 1990's.

Jovanovic, Rob. *George Michael: The Biography.* London: Portrait, 2007. Critical biography of Michael, incorporating much discussion of his sexuality and his pop-music career.

Leap, William L., ed. *Public Sex/Gay Space.* New York: Columbia University Press, 1999. A collection of studies that explore the intersections of gay sex and public sex and how these acts coalesce to form a type of gay space. Good background material.

Michael, George. *George Michael: In His Own Words.* London: Omnibus, 1999. Michael discusses his homosexuality and his admittedly oversexed personality.

Newton, Michael, and John L. French. *Celebrities and Crime.* New York: Chelsea House, 2008. Written especially for younger readers, this book examines the intersection of celebrity and crime. Discusses how law enforcement handles celebrities accused of criminal acts and celebrities victimized by crime.

Wapshott, Nicholas, and Tim Wapshott. *Older: The Unauthorized Biography of George Michael.* London: Sidgwick & Jackson, 1998. Published in the same year as the scandal. A critical examination of Michael's life and career.

SEE ALSO: July 19, 1921: U.S. Senate Rebukes Navy in Homosexuality Investigation; Jan. 14, 1943: Film Star Frances Farmer Is Jailed and Institutionalized; Nov. 23, 1946: Tennis Star Bill Tilden Is Arrested for Lewd Behavior with a Minor; 1970: Study of Anonymous Gay Sex Leads to Ethics Scandal; Dec., 1982: Julie Andrews and Blake Edwards Deny Being Gay; July 18, 1988: Actor Rob Lowe Videotapes Sexual Tryst with a Minor; July 26, 1991: Comedian Pee-wee Herman Is Arrested for Public Indecency; June 27, 1995: Film Star Hugh Grant Is Arrested for Lewd Conduct; Sept. 22, 1997: Sportscaster Marv Albert Is Tried for Sexual Assault; Early Nov., 2003: Paris Hilton Sex-Tape Appears on the Web; Dec. 18, 2003: Pop Star Michael Jackson Is Charged with Child Molestation; June 13, 2008: Singer R. Kelly Is Acquitted on Child Pornography Charges.

1990's

May, 1998

POLICE CORRUPTION IS REVEALED IN LOS ANGELES'S RAMPART DIVISION

The Los Angeles Police Department was rocked by scandal when the investigation into the road-rage murder of black police officer Kevin Gaines by white officer Frank Lyga revealed a web of corrupt officers in an antigang unit called CRASH, many of whom were affiliated with a notorious street gang. The name of the LAPD division where the officers had worked, Rampart, is now synonymous with police corruption.

ALSO KNOWN AS: Rampart scandal
LOCALE: Los Angeles, California
CATEGORIES: Corruption; racism; murder and suicide; law and the courts; government; violence

KEY FIGURES

Kevin Gaines (1966-1997), LAPD officer
Frank Lyga (fl. 1990's), LAPD officer
David Anthony Mack (b. 1960), LAPD officer
Rafael Antonio Perez (b. 1967), LAPD officer
Bernard Parks (b. 1943), LAPD chief, 1997-2002
Suge Knight (b. 1965), owner of Death Row Records

SUMMARY OF EVENT

According to witness testimony, at approximately 4:00 P.M. on March 18, 1997, off-duty Los Angeles Police Department (LAPD) officer Kevin Gaines pulled his green sport utility vehicle (SUV) next to a Buick at a stop light. Behind the wheel of the Buick was off-duty LAPD officer Frank Lyga, who was dressed casually in jeans and a Hawaiian shirt, his long black hair pulled back in a pony tail. Gaines looked at Lyga in a threatening way; Lyga asked if Gaines needed assistance. Lyga sped away when the light turned green. Gaines sped after him and pulled out his handgun.

Pulling up to a stop light, Gaines threatened Lyga once again. Witnesses reported seeing Gaines extend his arm toward the window of his vehicle, as if

he was about to brandish a gun. Fearing for his life, Lyga fired two shots into the SUV and mortally wounded Gaines. A gunshot entered Gaines's armpit, but he managed to make a U-turn and pull into a convenience store parking lot. Lyga followed moments later.

Two California Highway Patrol (CHP) officers had been on a coffee break behind the store when they heard the gunshots. They drove their patrol cars around the building and saw Lyga pointing his handgun at Gaines, who was slumped forward in the front seat of his SUV. The officers ordered Lyga to drop his weapon. He shouted back that he was a police officer and showed his badge. Lyga revealed that he was an undercover narcotics officer who was just returning home from duty when the road-rage incident began.

Gaines died at the scene. By the time detectives from the LAPD's robbery-homicide division arrived, Gaines's identity was established. The shooting of a black police officer by a white police officer became a media sensation and brought cries of racism from the residents of Los Angeles, a metropolis that was recovering from the Rodney King beating and uprising of 1992. The shooting also caused a deep divide between black and white officers of the Rampart division, where Gaines was stationed.

Detective Russell Poole was assigned to the case. In the days following the shooting, he learned that two dozen off-duty black police officers canvassed the neighborhood around the shooting to look for witnesses to counter Lyga's testimony. Lyga's version of events, however, was supported by the evidence. In addition, witness statements corroborated Lyga's account. The LAPD discovered that Gaines had been involved in similar road-rage incidents prior to his fatal encounter with Lyga. It was also revealed that he was associated with the record label Death Row Records and its owner, convicted felon Suge Knight. Knight was a controversial figure, claiming ties to a Los Angeles street gang, the

Bloods, and hiring off-duty police officers, including Gaines, for his security detail. Also, at the time of his death, Gaines had been living with Knight's estranged wife.

By the spring of 1998, LAPD leadership began to question these associations with Death Row Records and Knight. To investigate, it established the Rampart Corruption Task Force in May. The task force confirmed that several Rampart officers, including Gaines, David Mack, and Rafael Perez, were on the payroll of Death Row Records. All three, among others, were soon implicated in a wide range of crimes. (In November, 1997, Mack had participated in one of the largest bank robberies in Los Angeles history. He was convicted and sentenced to fourteen years in prison.) With the creation of the task force, the scandal came to light.

Rampart officer Perez, who would turn out to be the major figure uncovering the widespread CRASH unit corruption, was arrested on August 25 for stealing six pounds of cocaine a few months earlier from the Rampart division property room. The cocaine had been booked into evidence following an arrest made by Lyga. In September, 1999, Perez, who admitted that he stole the cocaine in retaliation for Gaines's shooting, agreed to cooperate with investigators in exchange for leniency and provided extensive details into the misdeeds of the elite Community Resources Against Street Hoodlums unit, or CRASH.

The goal of the antigang CRASH unit was to arrest as many gang members as possible, to do so by any means necessary, and to gain convictions. Its corruption included unprovoked shootings by officers on unarmed civilians, planting evidence, false arrests, beatings, and false testimony. Perez claimed that 90 percent of CRASH officers framed innocent people and perjured themselves on the witness stand to gain convictions. He also claimed that his superiors, including at least one police lieutenant at Rampart, actively supported and even encouraged the misconduct.

The investigation by the task force revealed widespread corruption within the rank and file

of the Rampart division. More than seventy officers from CRASH were implicated in the scandal, making Rampart one of the most widespread cases of police misconduct in American history.

IMPACT

The Rampart scandal forced the city of Los Angeles to answer to more than 140 lawsuits against the LAPD and the city itself. One case involved an unarmed gang member named Javier Ovando who had been shot by Rampart division officers Nino Durden and Perez and then framed for a crime he did not commit. Ovando, who had been paralyzed by the shooting, was awarded the largest Rampart-related judgment against the LAPD: more than fifteen million dollars. Also, more than one hundred cases in which persons were convicted with evidence obtained illegally by implicated Rampart officers or because of the testimony of these same officers were overturned by the courts.

Bernard Parks, who was in charge of the department's Internal Affairs division during the years of

Former LAPD officer Rafael Perez in court in 2001. Perez, a key informant in the Rampart corruption scandal, was released from prison after serving nearly three years of a five-year sentence for stealing cocaine from the Rampart division's evidence room in 1998. (AP/Wide World Photos)

misconduct and corruption at Rampart, was alleged to have obstructed justice in the investigation. Many claimed that Parks, who would become chief of police in August, 1997, had protected Gaines and other officers by suppressing reports and instructing investigators not to pursue their inquiries. In September, 1999, Parks formed a board of inquiry to look into the corruption. The board focused not only on corrupt officers but also the failures of management in handling the crisis. In March, 2000, Parks disbanded the CRASH unit, just days after the board released its final report.

On September, 19, 2000, the Los Angeles City Council voted 10-2 to accept a federal consent decree allowing the U.S. Department of Justice to oversee and monitor recommended reforms within the LAPD for a five-year period. On September 26, Detective Poole filed a federal civil rights lawsuit against the city of Los Angeles and Parks. Poole claimed in his suit that Parks shut down his efforts to fully investigate the corruption within the department and suppressed critical information. Parks was not rehired by Los Angeles mayor James Hahn. As a result, Hahn lost support with the African American community in Los Angeles.

In 2005, a wrongful death lawsuit was filed against several former LAPD officers for the March 9, 1997, murder of rap-music star Christopher Wallace, also known as Notorious B.I.G. Among the many acts of criminal misconduct uncovered by Detective Poole was a link between Wallace's murder and corrupt Rampart officers, most notably Perez and Mack. Poole learned that Perez and Mack arranged for the hit on Wallace at Knight's order. Furthermore, Poole found links between Death Row Records, CRASH-unit officers on Death Row Records' payroll, and the killing of another rap star—Tupac Shakur—six months prior to Wallace's murder.

—Jesus F. Gonzalez

FURTHER READING

Boyer, Peter J. "Bad Cops." *The New Yorker*, May 21, 2001. A thorough report on the Rampart scandal and its aftermath. This article was used as the basis for a special Public Broadcasting Service *Frontline* news feature at pbs.org/frontline.

Juarez, Juan Antonio. *Brotherhood of Corruption: A Cop Breaks the Silence on Police Abuse, Brutality and Racial Profiling*. Chicago: Chicago Review Press, 2004. Written by a former Chicago police officer, this work provides an insider's view into the behind-the-scenes actions of some police officers and how a "wall of silence" can perpetuate problems and hide police corruption and misconduct.

Katz, Charles M. *The Police in America: An Introduction*. 5th ed. New York: McGraw-Hill, 2005. General textbook on police work that covers the history of American police forces, their organization and functions, and issues such as corruption.

Scott, Cathy. *The Murder of Biggie Smalls*. New York: St. Martin's Press, 2000. Examines the Christopher Wallace killing and covers the corruption at LAPD's Rampart station.

Sullivan, Randall. *Labyrinth: A Detective Investigates the Murders of Tupac Shakur and Notorious B.I.G., the Implication of Death Row Records' Suge Knight, and the Origins of the Los Angeles Police Scandal*. New York: Atlantic Monthly Press, 2002. A fascinating account of the Rampart scandal, tying the murders of Tupac Shakur and Christopher Wallace with Suge Knight and the Rampart CRASH division of the LAPD.

_____. "The Unsolved Mystery of the Notorious B.I.G." *Rolling Stone*, December 4, 2005. A follow-up to his 2002 book *Labryinth*, Sullivan examines the aftermath of an FBI investigation into the Rampart scandal and cover-up.

SEE ALSO: Mar. 17, 1937: Atherton Report Exposes San Francisco Police Corruption; May 3, 1950: U.S. Senate Committee Begins Investigating Organized Crime; Jan. 12 and May 11, 1987: Media Reports Spark Investigation of Australian Police Corruption; Feb. 18, 2001: CIA Agent Robert Hanssen Is Arrested for Spying for the Russians.

May 11, 1998
JOURNALIST STEPHEN GLASS IS EXPOSED AS A FRAUD

Stephen Glass, an up-and-coming reporter and associate editor with The New Republic *magazine, was fired after Adam Penenberg, a Forbes.com reporter, found inconsistencies and factual errors in Glass's 1998 article "Hack Heaven." The story, about a large company that hired a teenage computer hacker as an information security consultant after being extorted by the hacker, turned out to be fabricated. After investigating the accusations,* The New Republic *editors found that Glass had partly or wholly fabricated many of his other published stories as well.*

LOCALE: Washington, D.C.

CATEGORIES: Hoaxes, frauds, and charlatanism; publishing and journalism; communications and media; corruption

KEY FIGURES

Stephen Glass (b. 1972), reporter and associate editor of *The New Republic*

Charles Lane (fl. 1990's), executive editor of *The New Republic*

Adam Penenberg (b. 1962), reporter for Forbes.com

SUMMARY OF EVENT

Stephen Glass was born and raised in the Chicago suburb of Highland Park. He began his journalism career as the editor of his college newspaper, *The Daily Pennsylvanian*, at the University of Pennsylvania. After his graduation in 1995, he was hired as an editorial assistant at *The New Republic*, a well-known and respected national magazine of social and political commentary. He quickly rose through the ranks, eventually achieving the position of associate editor.

Glass was writing his own articles for the prestigious publication by the age of twenty-three. He became known for his eagerness to please and his industrious research habits. His stories, which were characterized by their intriguing characters and colorful anecdotes and quotations, began attracting widespread attention. While he wrote mainly for *The New Republic*, his work also appeared in other magazines, including *Rolling Stone*, *George*, and *Harper's*.

Glass's career quickly came to an end in 1998. His article "Hack Heaven," which was published in the May 18 edition of *The New Republic*, centered on a fifteen-year-old computer hacker named Ian Restil who had hacked into the computer system of a California software firm called Jukt Micronics. Glass wrote that Restil, who "looks like an even more adolescent version of Bill Gates," then extorted the company executives at a meeting at a Hyatt Hotel in Bethesda, Maryland. The company then hired the hacker as a computer security consultant. The article also detailed a convention of computer whizzes from the National Assembly of Hackers being held near the hotel where Restil and Jukt representatives met. Glass's article gained reader interest as another intriguing tale of a larger-than-life character.

Intrigued by Glass's story, which includes the names of official-sounding organizations such as the "Center for Interstate Online Investigations" and the "Computer Security Center" and mentions federal legislation called the "Uniform Computer Security Act," a reporter for Forbes Digital Tool (now Forbes.com) began researching "Hacker Heaven" for a follow-up article. The reporter, Adam Penenberg, could not verify any fact from Glass's article, leading him to question its truthfulness and prompting him to notify his editors about the matter. *Forbes* magazine editors then contacted Charles Lane, executive editor of *The New Republic*, and told him about Penenberg's findings. Penenberg's brief exposé, "Lies, Damn Lies and Fiction" (Forbes.com, May 11, 1998), an account of his findings, accused Glass of perpetrating a hoax, and the scandal was born.

Glass had faced earlier accusations of misrepresentation or fabrication, claims not uncommon in journalism, by various organizations, including the College Republican National Committee, the American Conservative Union, the Drug Abuse Resistance Education (D.A.R.E.) program, the Center for Science in the Public Interest, and Hofstra University. With each accusation *The New Republic* supported its reporter. The questions from *Forbes*, however, elicited a different response from Glass's editors.

Lane began investigating the accusations, and he ultimately revealed that Glass had fabricated the entire article and fabricated evidence, such as voice mail, e-mails from Restil, a Web site for Jukt Micronics, and a newsletter for the fictitious National Assembly of Hackers, in an attempt to thwart the investigation. Glass even had his brother pose as Jukt executive George Sims in a phone call. *The New Republic* then expanded its investigation to include all of the forty-one articles Glass had written for them since December, 1995, articles published under three different editors—Andrew Sullivan, Michael Kelly, and Lane.

The fabrications ranged from inserted quotations in legitimate stories to entire articles. Most articles proved to be a blend of fact and fiction. Some of the more colorful fabrications included a political memorabilia convention in which Monica Lewinsky items were available and a church dedicated to the worship of George H. W. Bush. Glass was able to escape the magazine's fact-checking process through the creation of elaborate notes, voice mails, e-mails, faxes, business cards, and other evidence. Glass's dishonesty also led many to question the truthfulness of his other work.

Glass was fired, bringing an end to a promising journalism career. He later published an article, "Canada's Pot Revolution," in the September, 2003, edition of *Rolling Stone*. D.A.R.E. sued Glass for libel for one of his articles on the organization, a case in which Glass settled. At the time the scandal broke, he was enrolled as a law student at Georgetown University, where he continued his studies. He earned his law degree, passed the New York State bar exam, but was not admitted to the bar. He became a national figure, arousing public curiosity about his motives and how he had been able to get away with the lies for so long.

GLASS'S FABRICATION

Writer Stephen Glass presented as fact the story of a fifteen-year-old computer whiz named Ian Restil, but the story was a fabrication. The New Republic *magazine had published the article, "Hacker Heaven," in its May 18, 1998, issue, not knowing the story was a fake. The article's first paragraph includes the following:*

Over and over again, the boy, who is wearing a frayed Cal Ripken Jr. T-shirt, is shouting his demands. Across the table, executives from a California software firm called Jukt Micronics are listening.

In 2003, Steve Kroft interviewed Glass for the CBS News program *60 Minutes*, and Glass was the subject of a major motion picture, *Shattered Glass* (2003), starring Hayden Christensen as Glass and Peter Sarsgaard as Lane. Glass also wrote a fictional account of his story, *The Fabulist* (2003), featuring a protagonist sharing his name.

IMPACT

In the immediate aftermath of the Glass scandal, many publications began to reevaluate their fact-checking policies and procedures. Until this time, fact checking worked well to catch honest mistakes but had not been equipped to deal with deliberate fabrications on such a large scale. The closer scrutiny led to the uncovering of similar scandals, most notoriously the 2003 case of *New York Times* reporter Jayson Blair, who was found to have plagiarized quotations and fabricated material in more than thirty-five articles he wrote for the paper. Journalists feared that these scandals could further distance editors and reporters, who already shared some professional animosity, and the profession feared that the scandal could further erode relations with a public already distrustful of journalists.

—Marcella Bush Trevino

FURTHER READING

Cowan, Coleman, and Melissa Castro. "After the Falls (Currents): Unethical Practices of Some Journalists, and Their Repercussions." *Columbia Journalism Review* 46, no. 1 (May-June,

2007). Examines the details of Glass's fabricated article and the consequences of his actions. Also discusses other well-known episodes of unethical reporting in journalism.

Dowd, Ann Reilly. "The Great Pretender: How a Writer Fooled His Readers (Writer Stephen Glass)." *Columbia Journalism Review* 37, no. 2 (July-August, 1998). Discusses the key question of how Glass was able to pass off as true not only fictional quotations but also entire events.

Glass, Stephen. *The Fabulist: A Novel.* New York: Simon & Schuster, 2003. Although this version of Glass's story about his hoax is fictional, it provides a valuable perspective into the writer's point of view.

Iggers, Jeremy. *Good News, Bad News: Journalism Ethics and the Public Interest.* Boulder, Colo.: Westview Press, 1998. A study of journalistic ethics and the media's responsibility to get the story right in the interest of its audience and readership.

Mnookin, Seth. "Total Fiction." *Newsweek*, May 19, 2003. Provides Glass's account of the scandal five years later. Includes discussion of how he came to write a fictional tale—*The Fabulist*—of his experience with the scandal.

SEE ALSO: Apr. 15, 1981: Janet Cooke Admits Fabricating Her Pulitzer Prize-Winning Feature; Apr., 1998: Scottish Historian Is Charged with Plagiarism; June 18, 2001: Historian Joseph J. Ellis Is Accused of Lying; Jan. 4, 2002: Historian Stephen E. Ambrose Is Accused of Plagiarism; Jan. 18, 2002: Historian Doris Kearns Goodwin Is Accused of Plagiarism; Apr. 29, 2003: *New York Times* Reporter Jayson Blair Is Exposed as a Fraud; July 24, 2007: University of Colorado Fires Professor for Plagiarism and Research Falsification.

December 23, 1998
PROMINENT BELGIANS ARE SENTENCED IN AGUSTA-DASSAULT CORRUPTION SCANDAL

An inquiry into the 1991 assassination of Belgian Socialist Party politician André Cools showed that Cools had knowledge of suspicious dealings in the purchases of helicopters and fighter planes for the Belgian military. The Agusta and Dassault manufacturing companies had bribed a number of politicians and other ranking officials to get the contracts.

ALSO KNOWN AS: Agusta scandal
LOCALE: Liegè, Belgium
CATEGORIES: Law and the courts; corruption; government; murder and suicide; organized crime and racketeering; business; politics

KEY FIGURES
André Cools (1927-1991), Belgian Socialist Party politician and former government minister, 1968-1985, 1988-1990

Willy Claes (b. 1938), Belgian foreign minister, 1992-1994, and secretary-general of NATO, 1994-1995
Serge Dassault (b. 1925), French businessman and politician
Raffaello Teti (fl. 1990's), Italian business executive
Véronique Ancia (fl. 1990's), Belgian magistrate

SUMMARY OF EVENT
On December 23, 1998, the Belgian court of cassation, Belgium's highest court, issued verdicts in the Agusta and Dassault case against several prominent Belgians. The verdicts were the result of the largest scandal in Belgium in modern times. The criminal activity originated in bribes paid by the Italian company Agusta and the French company Dassault to numerous Belgian politicians to obtain lucrative military manufacturing contracts. Over the course

1990's

of the scandal, one government minister had been assassinated, another committed suicide, others were forced to resign, and Belgian political parties were disgraced.

Despite its formidable international reputation as the headquarters of the European Union (EU) and the North American Treaty Organization (NATO), Belgium has had a tempestuous domestic history. Belgium is a single country made up of two distinct nationalities. The Dutch-speaking Flemish live largely in the north and the French-speaking Walloons live largely in the south. Rivalries between these two populations have often made for unstable, contentious domestic politics. Political parties, such as the Socialist Party, are divided along Dutch- and French-speaking lines. Over the course of the 1970's and 1980's, Belgian life had been marked by political corruption and organized crime.

On July 18, 1991, the prominent Walloon politician André Cools was assassinated in the industrial city of Liegè, which had been tarred by a climate of crime and corruption. The killing of its leading politician, however, could not be overlooked. The sixty-four-year-old Cools had served as a minister in several governments, as head of the Walloon Socialist Party, and as one of the more powerful and controversial Liegè politicians. Cools was shot in a parking lot near the apartment of his alleged mistress. Pursuant to article 56 of the Belgian constitution, the federal Parliament exercised its right of inquiry and launched an investigation into the murder. The inquiry was headed by Magistrate Véronique Ancia. In her investigation, Ancia uncovered widespread corruption of Belgian officials.

Of particular significance during the 1980's was the competition among the manufacturing firms Agusta (based in Milan, Italy), Aerospatiale (based in France), and MBK (of Germany). The three companies were vying for lucrative military helicopter contracts with the Belgian government. Likewise, the Dassault Electronique Aviation company of France was competing with an American company, Litton Industries, for contracts involving Belgian air-force fighter planes. The Belgian army had recommended purchase of Aerospatiale's helicopter, but on December 8, 1988, Defense Minister Guy

Coëme announced that the government would purchase forty-six military helicopters (eighteen for reconnaissance and twenty-eight antitank) from Agusta for 11.97 billion Belgian francs. Similarly, Dassault was awarded a 6.5-billion-franc contract to re-equip Belgian air force F-16 fighter planes with new electronic warfare systems. Cools was killed a few years after these contracts were awarded.

The first big break in the investigation into Cool's killing came with the February, 1993, arrest of Agusta trade representative Georges Cywie. With the statements of Cywie and other witnesses, Magistrate Ancia was able to put together a ten-thousand-page report detailing extensive bribes and kickbacks the Agusta and the Dassault companies had paid to several Socialist parties of Belgium and to Belgian politicians. It was alleged that Cools had been assassinated in connection with these kickbacks.

In July, 1994, three Belgian politicians under investigation in the scandal—Coëme, Guy Mathot, and Guy Spitaels—were compelled to resign from their government posts. The minister of foreign affairs and another government official resigned soon after. On March 5, 1995, a Belgian air force general who was being questioned about the Agusta and Dassault bribes committed suicide. On April 7, the Belgian parliament voted to suspend diplomatic immunity from criminal investigation and prosecution of the highest level suspect, Willy Claes, who had been minister of economic affairs during the 1980's and became general-secretary of the North Atlantic Treaty Organization (NATO) in 1994. Agusta's former chief executive, Raffaello Teti, who had met with Claes several times to discuss the military contracts, was arrested on October 18 on charges of fraud and corruption. Claes resigned as NATO general-secretary two days later.

The trial of the twelve suspects began in August, 1998, in the court of cassation in Brussels with a fifteen-judge panel. Chief prosecutor Eliane Lienkedael presented evidence that Claes had received payments of $60,000 in 1988 and $125,000 in 1992 directly to his personal bank accounts, although Claes alleged the payments had been received from his wife's savings. On December 23, 1998, the court handed down its verdict, convicting all twelve defendants. The court affirmed that Agusta and Dassault had paid a total of 110 million Belgian francs ($3.188 million U.S.) to the Socialist parties to acquire military contracts.

Claes was given a three-year suspended sentence for passive corruption and fined 60,000 Belgian francs and barred from politics for five years. Coëme and Spitaels both received two-year suspended sentences for passive corruption, were fined 60,000 francs, and also were barred from politics for five years. Serge Dassault, head of Dassault, was convicted of active criminal corruption and sentenced to two years (suspended) and fined 60,000 francs. The eight other defendants, who had been aides to the above-named politicians and Socialist Party officials, also were convicted of passive corruption and received similar sentences. The Socialist parties were fined millions of francs. In 2005, the European Convention on Human Rights affirmed the verdicts against the defendants.

In June, 1998, two Tunisian gangsters were convicted by a Tunisian court for the murder of Cools and sentenced to twenty years in prison. Investigators found that the hit men had been hired by a Liegè mafioso for $12,000 to assassinate Cools. In January, 2004, a Liegè court sentenced two persons linked to Socialist minister Alain van der Biest to twenty years' imprisonment for complicity in the murder of Cools. Van der Biest had committed suicide while under investigation. Other defendants who were found to have assisted in the assassination plan received prison sentences ranging from five to twenty years.

IMPACT

The 1980's was a troubled decade for Belgian politics. The nation was plagued by corruption and organized crime, while internal rivalries between Walloon and Flemish parties prevented the efficient administration of justice. Charges against Belgian politicians quickly deteriorated into squabbles over bias based on nationality and over allegations that set one group against another. The Nivelles gang atrocities of the early 1980's, in which twenty-eight people were killed in a string of armed robberies by a well-organized gang with political associations, represented an escalating viciousness in Belgian public life.

The Agusta-Dassault scandal epitomized both the corruption of Belgian politics and a determination to restore order to the country. The cold-blooded assassination of Cools was too much for the country to ignore. In her closing summary of the prosecution case at trial, chief prosecutor Lienkedael condemned the pervasive corruption. Because private contributions to Belgian political parties had been legal until 1989, the case against the twelve defendants had not been an easy one. Only with evidence of money wired to Swiss bank accounts and payments for villas on the Riviera was the prosecution able to show that the payments were bribes, not gifts, and secure convictions for passive corruption. The resolve of the prosecution was echoed by Belgian voters who punished the Socialist Party at the polls and threatened its position in the ruling coalition.

—Howard Bromberg

FURTHER READING

Braembussche, Antoon van den. "The Silence of Belgium: Taboo and Trauma in Belgian Memory." In *Belgian Memories*, edited by Catherine Labio. New Haven, Conn.: Yale University Press, 2002. In this work, van den Braembussche argues that Belgians suppress memories of their nation's history of corruption, including the Agusta-Dassault scandal.

Cook, Bernard A. *Belgium: A History*. New York: Peter Lang, 2002. A short survey of Belgian history, emphasizing its tensions as a country with two major nationalities, Dutch and French.

Judt, Tony. *Postwar: A History of Europe*. New York: Penguin, 2005. In surveying corruption in modern Europe, Judt blames the Agusta-Dassault scandal on divisions in Belgian society, leading to a weakening of constitutional authority and the justice system.

Schmidt, Oliver. *The Intelligence Files: Today's Secrets, Tomorrow's Scandals*. Atlanta: Clarity Press, 2005. A publication of the French organi-

1990's

zation ADI (Association for the Right to Information), with a chapter on the Agusta-Dassault scandal by Michael Quilligan.

SEE ALSO: Feb. 4, 1976: Lockheed Is Implicated in Bribing Foreign Officials; Oct. 10, 1979: French President Giscard d'Estaing Is Accused of Taking a Bribe; Feb. 2, 1980: Media Uncover FBI Sting Implicating Dozens of Lawmakers; 1985-1986: Westland Affair Shakes Prime Minister Thatcher's Government; Jan. 12 and May 11, 1987: Media Reports Spark Investigation of Australian Police Corruption; Feb. 28, 1995: Former Mexican President Carlos Salinas's Brother Is Arrested for Murder; Aug. 16, 1996: Belgian Media Reveal How Police Bungled Serial Murder Case; Nov. 3, 1996: Car Crash Reveals Depth of Government Corruption in Turkey; Jan., 1997: Pyramid Investment Schemes Cause Albanian Government to Fall; 2001: Clearstream Financial Clearinghouse Is Accused of Fraud and Money Laundering.

March 4, 1999
QUEBEC OFFERS SUPPORT FOR ABUSED DUPLESSIS ORPHANS

Beginning during the mid-1930's, thousands of children in the care of Roman Catholic orphanages were labeled mentally deficient and sent to psychiatric hospitals, where they suffered years of abuse and neglect. Adult survivors organized as the Duplessis Orphans' Committee and demanded an official investigation, apology, and compensation. In 1999, the Quebec government and Church officials separately created funds to support the orphans' efforts at rehabilitation, but both institutions refused to compensate the orphans individually for their suffering.

LOCALE: Quebec, Canada
CATEGORIES: Government; families and children; psychology and psychiatry; human rights; corruption; religion

KEY FIGURES
Lucien Bouchard (b. 1938), premier of Quebec, 1996-2001
Maurice Duplessis (1890-1959), premier of Quebec, 1936-1939 and 1944-1959
Jean-Claude Turcotte (b. 1936), Roman Catholic cardinal, archbishop of Montreal

Pierre Morissette (b. 1944), Roman Catholic bishop and president of the Assembly of Quebec Catholic Bishops

SUMMARY OF EVENT
In 1999, the premier of the Canadian province of Quebec, Lucien Bouchard, announced that his administration would establish a fund to provide social services to the surviving children of Duplessis, also known as the Duplessis orphans. Thousands of children in Quebec, in the state's care because they had been born out of wedlock or into poverty, were wrongly diagnosed and institutionalized in Catholic hospitals, raised in Church-run orphanages, and educated in Church schools.

The children were victims of a scheme devised under the administration of Premier Maurice Duplessis beginning during the mid-1930's to label the children as mentally disabled so that they could be moved into psychiatric hospitals. Duplessis's administration saved millions of dollars by shifting the cost of the children's care to the Church, and the Church, in turn, received twice as much federal funding for institutionalizing children who were classified as mental patients rather than as orphans. The children were released from care by 1964.

Religious orders received subsidies from the Canadian government for the care and education of children in need. Given that the subsidy for mental patients was more than double that for healthy children, the Duplessis government persuaded Catholic organizations to declare children mentally deficient or psychotic and move them to psychiatric institutions. Some orphanages and schools were converted suddenly to psychiatric hospitals, and the children were classed as mental patients literally overnight. The Church received more federal funds for running hospitals than for orphanages and schools, while Quebec province saved millions of dollars that would have gone toward childcare and education.

Investigations beginning during the early 1960's revealed that thousands of children had been diagnosed improperly and that the orphans were unprepared for life outside institutional settings. The orphans reported they were used as slave labor in hospitals and on local farms. Nuns and other hospital employees routinely placed them in straitjackets and subjected them to beatings and sexual abuse. They were not educated and many remained illiterate, and some had become unstable after years of living among true mental patients. They had no families or support systems outside the institutions, lacked basic skills for living in society, and received no job training. They did not have their original birth certificates and struggled to establish legal identities, and their medical records indicated they were mentally deficient or ill.

During the late 1990's, approximately three thousand survivors organized the group Duplessis Orphans' Committee, calling for an official investigation and compensation from the government of Quebec and the Church. The orphans also were seeking formal apologies. In March, 1997, Premier Bouchard said his government would examine the orphans' claims and respond within a month to their demands. A year passed without further word from Bouchard. His representatives later said Quebec might apologize, but there would be no compensation and the government could do nothing to correct the orphans' medical records.

On March 4, 1999, the Quebec government announced the establishment of a three-million-dollar

Maurice Duplessis in 1937. (Hulton Archive/Getty Images)

fund—about one thousand dollars per surviving orphan—to support survivors' efforts to correct their medical records, obtain their original birth certificates, and seek job training. Bouchard apologized for how they were treated but said Quebec would not conduct a public inquiry nor compensate individuals for their suffering. Also, the government did not intend to hold anyone legally responsible. Bouchard indicated Catholic nuns and others had taken on a thankless task in raising large numbers of unwanted children, and they should not be blamed if the results were not always ideal.

Unsurprisingly, the Duplessis Orphans rejected Bouchard's offer. They had not been informed in advance of his announcement, found his comments insulting, and took the limited plan for financial assistance as a further attempt to dismiss their claims. Speaking for Quebec's Liberal Party opposition, Madeline Boulanger suggested the Duplessis Orphans should instead be known as "the orphans of Lucien Bouchard."

In September, 1999, Cardinal Jean-Claude Turcotte and Bishop Pierre Morissette, president of the Assembly of Quebec Catholic Bishops, publicly refused to apologize to the orphans or to compensate them. The Church, they said, would provide counseling and social support to the orphans. Turcotte indicated the Duplessis orphans should be thankful to have been housed during their childhoods, as they would have been homeless without the Church. Morissette added that the Church "has already given a lot" to the orphans "and continues to give generally." In response to the official Church statement, the orphans called upon Catholics to stop tithing at church and instead give their money to Centraide, a charity serving the Montreal area.

In 2004, the Duplessis orphans came forward with new allegations that they had been given experimental drugs and shock treatments and were subjected to lobotomies. They called for the exhumation of orphans who had died in psychiatric institutions and were still buried in unmarked graves. Surviving orphans believed autopsies and forensic testing on these bodies would confirm many deaths resulted from medical experimentation.

IMPACT

Bouchard's refusal to compensate individual orphans and his qualified apology made headlines in the United States, tarnishing Canada's image in the national press. Bouchard's response was considered inadequate and lacking in compassion, considering the Duplessis administration's horrifying and deliberate mistreatment of thousands of children for its financial gain.

Following Bouchard's resignation, Quebec premier Bernard Landry and his Parti Québécois established the National Program of Reconciliation with the Duplessis Orphans. On June 30, 2001, the Duplessis Orphans' Committee, on behalf of the approximately fifteen hundred orphans who qualified for compensation, accepted the government's newest apology and agreed to individual "fault-free" payments of ten thousand dollars plus one thousand dollars for each year spent in institutions. The totals

averaged twenty-five thousand dollars per person. On December 21, 2006, under Premier Jean Charest, the government announced it would increase the orphans' compensation to twenty-six million dollars, provided the orphans waive any legal action against the Catholic Church. The Church, in turn, refused once again to apologize to the orphans.

Also in 2006, an estimated seventeen hundred people received twenty-five thousand dollars each in compensation under the National Reconciliation Program for Duplessis Orphans Who Were Residents of Certain Institutions. These survivors, called forgotten orphans, had not been declared mentally disabled but had suffered abuses similar to that of the Duplessis Orphans in nonpsychiatric institutions. In return for compensation, they agreed to make no further claims against Quebec or the Church.

The indifference of the Church to the suffering of children further damaged its already tarnished public image. The Church's once-pervasive influence over life in Quebec had been fading for years. The shocking alliance of the government with Church authorities and the medical profession to use children as a means of revenue forever linked Bouchard with the memory of Duplessis's administration, nicknamed La Grande Noirceur, or Great Darkness.

—*Maureen Puffer-Rothenberg*

FURTHER READING

Black, Conrad. *Render unto Caesar: The Life and Legacy of Maurice Duplessis.* Toronto, Ont.: Key Porter Books, 1998. Considered the definitive biography of Duplessis. Balances his controversial political style with the long-term positive impact of his policies in Quebec.

DePalma, Anthony. "Orphans Who Weren't Recall Care That Wasn't." *The New York Times*, March 5, 1999. Looks at the role of the Roman Catholic Church in the Duplessis orphans' scandal in the context of the Church's waning influence throughout Quebec.

Pearlstein, Steven. "Abandoned and Abused: Children Locked Up in Quebec Mental Wards Now Seek Redress for Suffering, Decades Lost." *The Washington Post*, April 7, 2000. Two surviving

Duplessis orphans recount the abuse they suffered while institutionalized. Physician Denis Lazure explains the hospital conditions that may have led to abuse. Includes photographs.

Perry, J. Christopher et al. "Seven Institutionalized Children and Their Adaptation in Late Adulthood: The Children of Duplessis (Les Enfants de Duplessis)." *Psychiatry* 69, no. 4 (Winter, 2006): 283-301. A study of several Duplessis orphans that examined their ability or inability to adapt to society as adults, primarily older adults. Presents seven life studies. For advanced readers.

SEE ALSO: Mar. 2, 1906: Psychoanalyst Ernest Jones Is Accused of Molesting Mentally Disabled Children; Mar. 21, 1928: Alberta Government Sterilizes Thousands Deemed Genetically and Mentally Unfit; Feb. 23, 1943: Irish Orphan School Fire Kills Thirty-five Girls; 1956-1962: Prescription Thalidomide Causes Widespread Birth Disorders; Nov. 26, 1997: Canadian Health Commissioner Releases Report on Tainted Blood; Dec., 2000: Sexual Abuse of Children in France Leads to the Outreau Affair; Jan. 30, 2001: Liverpool Children's Hospital Collects Body Parts Without Authorization; Jan. 6, 2002: *Boston Globe* Reports on Child Sexual Abuse by Roman Catholic Priests; Aug., 2002: Immunologist Resigns After Being Accused of Falsifying Research.

May, 1999
CIVIL RIGHTS LEADER JESSE JACKSON FATHERS A CHILD OUT OF WEDLOCK

Ashley Jackson was born to Jesse Jackson's staff assistant, Karin Stanford. Financial records show that Jesse Jackson had paid Stanford substantial amounts of money from his nonprofit Rainbow/PUSH Coalition prior to his admitting publicly in January, 2001, that he was Ashley's father. This news was particularly significant as Jesse Jackson had been a spiritual adviser to President Bill Clinton during the Monica Lewinsky scandal.

LOCALE: United States
CATEGORIES: Families and children; politics; sex; public morals; ethics

KEY FIGURES
Jesse Jackson (b. 1941), civil rights leader, Baptist minister, and Democratic candidate for U.S. president, 1984 and 1988
Karin Stanford (b. 1962), former director of the Rainbow/PUSH bureau in Washington, D.C., writer, and university professor
Ashley Jackson (b. 1999), Stanford and Jackson's daughter

SUMMARY OF EVENT
Jesse Jackson has been an important figure in the American Civil Rights movement and in American politics since the late 1960's. He was born in 1941 in segregated Greenville, South Carolina, to a seventeen-year-old single mother. His father was at the time married to another woman and had almost no involvement in his life. He was later adopted by his stepfather, Charles Henry Jackson, who adopted the young Jackson, and Jackson adopted his surname.

On January 18, 2001, Jackson, who at the time was fifty-nine years old, issued a statement in anticipation of a story by the tabloid the *National Enquirer* that he had fathered a child out of wedlock with Karin Stanford, who was twenty years younger. Their child, Ashley Jackson, was born in May, 1999.

Jackson had been a successful athlete and student at a segregated high school and received a football scholarship to the University of Illinois. He left Illinois after one year and transferred to North Carolina A&T. While completing his undergraduate

1990's

895

degree, he married Jacqueline Lavinia Davis, and they had five children.

Jackson attended seminary from 1964 to 1966 but left before completing a degree to pursue civil rights activism. He led the Southern Christian Leadership Conference (SCLC) project in Chicago known as Operation Breadbasket in 1966-1967. He was with Martin Luther King, Jr., on April 4, 1968, in Memphis, Tennessee, when King was assassinated. He remained with SCLC until 1971, at which time he formed Operation PUSH (People United to Save Humanity). King ran for the Democratic nomination for president in 1984 and 1988. He also founded, in 1984, the National Rainbow Coalition, which merged with Operation PUSH in 1996. He has also been engaged in diplomatic efforts.

During Bill Clinton's presidency, Jackson served as a political adviser and as a special envoy to Africa for the promotion of democracy. In 1998, when it was revealed that President Clinton had an inappropriate sexual relationship with former White House intern Monica Lewinsky, Jackson became publicly identified as a moral and spiritual adviser to Clinton.

Mainstream news organizations had heard rumors about Jackson having had an illegitimate child but either did not pursue the story or did not pursue the story with the intensity of the *National Enquirer*. Patricia Shipp of the *National Enquirer* defended the story, in a television interview on CNN, stating that "it's a legitimate news story, not only because he's head of Rainbow" Coalition but also because of "the woman [sic] of his child [who] worked under him." Moreover, Shipp said that Jackson "was at one time the spiritual adviser to the president of the United States." The *National Enquirer*, which also claimed that the story was not given to them by political opponents of Jackson, published a photograph of Jackson with Stanford, appearing with President Clinton on December 3, 1998—which was approximately five months before the child was born.

In his public statement, Jackson said that "this is no time for evasions, denials or alibis." He continued,

I fully accept responsibility, and I am truly sorry for my actions. As her mother does, I love this child very much and have assumed responsibility for her emotional and financial support since she was born. I was born of these circumstances, and I know the importance of growing up in a nurturing, supportive and protected environment, so I am determined to give my daughter and her mother the privacy they both deserve.

Jackson also said that he would be "taking some time off to revive my spirit and reconnect with my family." At the time, a spokesperson for Jackson said that the reverend would keep immediate commitments but would scale back on his activities.

The New York Times reported on January 20, 2001, that Jackson had been paying Stanford three thousand dollars per month to support Ashley and that Stanford had been given about thirty-five thousand dollars to help with expenses in moving from Washington, D.C., to Los Angeles. The news story said the Rainbow/PUSH Coalition had called the funds a "severance package." The *National Enquirer* first reported that the money had been paid through accounts of the Rainbow/PUSH Coalition, and that this information had been confirmed by staff members of Rainbow/PUSH. A *Washington Post* report on February 1, 2001, told of a source that said Jackson's Citizenship Education Fund approved a "draw" of forty thousand dollars against future consulting fees and also indicated that the money would be used to help purchase real estate. On February 2, 2001, a copy of the source's statement (in letter form) appeared in the *National Enquirer*.

Jackson had first met Stanford when she was an assistant professor of political science and African American studies at the University of Georgia. Jackson offered Stanford the job as the director of the Washington bureau of the Rainbow/PUSH Coalition. Stanford, who had degrees from California State University, Chico, the University of Southern California, and Howard University, published a book on Jackson's foreign policy impact, *Beyond the Boundaries: Reverend Jesse Jackson and International Affairs* (1997), which won the National

Conference of Black Political Scientists' Outstanding Book Award in 1998.

Stanford gave no interviews in January, 2001, but she did have a lengthy interview with Connie Chung, which was televised on ABC's *20/20* in August. In the interview, Stanford stated that her relationship with Jackson had become strained in the last year and that the frequency of his visits to see his child had decreased. In the first year of Ashley's life, Stanford said that Jackson saw Ashley frequently, but he only saw her once in the first seven months of 2001.

Stanford also confirmed that Jackson had been paying her several thousand dollars per month in child support and that she had taken Jackson to court to formalize the agreement. Stanford also stated in the interview that she did not immediately inform him that he was the father of her child, but after she did inform him, he decided not to run for U.S. president in 2000.

Stanford also stated that lawyers representing Jackson had asked her to sign a confidentiality agreement, but she did not sign the agreement. Stanford added that she did not regret having Ashley, even though her birth caused pain for others. The story faded from public attention after 2001.

IMPACT

Jackson's credibility as a political figure was undermined in the short term. Even if he had not fathered a child with Stanford, it is likely he would not have run for the presidency of the United States. He had limited visibility in 2001, but soon regained public prominence. Jackson spoke in London in 2003 to nearly one million people at an antiwar rally. He also continued to join protests and make public appearances at racially charged events.

Stanford worked with the Los Angeles bureau of Rainbow/PUSH, then as a consultant for a supermarket chain with stores located mostly in city neighborhoods. She returned to college teaching and also wrote the book *Breaking the Silence: Inspirational Stories of Black Cancer Survivors* (2005).

—*Michael Coulter*

FURTHER READING

Bruns, Roger. *Jesse Jackson: A Biography*. Westport, Conn.: Greenwood Press, 2005. A balanced and short biography of Jackson that also provides an excellent description of the Civil Rights movement. Written especially for high school students.

Frady, Marshall. *Jesse: The Life and Pilgrimage of Jesse Jackson*. 1996. New ed. New York: Simon & Schuster, 2006. A balanced biography of Jackson that shows his penchant for egomania and discusses his moral leadership abilities.

Stanford, Karin. *Breaking the Silence: Inspirational Stories of Black Cancer Survivors*. Chicago: Hilton, 2005. Stanford explores the words of African Americans who have lived through cancer. Stanford is a breast cancer survivor.

Timmerman, Kenneth R. *Shakedown: Exposing the Real Jesse Jackson*. Washington, D.C.: Regnery, 2004. A critical biography of Jackson that seeks to show that he has not measured up to his own ideals.

SEE ALSO: June 4, 1943: Actor Charles Chaplin Is Sued for Paternity; Feb. 7, 1950: Swedish Film Star Ingrid Bergman Has a Child Out of Wedlock; July 2, 1963: Muslim Leader Elijah Muhammad Is Sued for Paternity; July 28, 1980: Magazine Reveals Baseball Star Steve Garvey's Marital Problems; July 20, 1982: Conservative Politician John G. Schmitz Is Found to Have Children Out of Wedlock; Oct. 14, 1983: British Cabinet Secretary Parkinson Resigns After His Secretary Becomes Pregnant; Jan. 25, 1984: Jesse Jackson Calls New York City "Hymietown"; May 6, 1992: Irish Bishop Eamonn Casey's Romantic Affair Leads to His Resignation; Jan. 5, 1994: British Cabinet Member Resigns After Fathering a Child Out of Wedlock; Aug. 21, 1994: Sex Scandal Forces Dismissal of NAACP Chief Benjamin Chavis; Dec. 17, 2003: Senator Strom Thurmond's Biracial Daughter Is Revealed.

1990's

Ethics Counselor Exonerates Canadian Prime Minister Jean Chrétien

Despite three exonerations by the federal ethics counselor, Canadian prime minister Jean Chrétien continued to face allegations that he had improperly used his influence on behalf of a government-backed loan involving a potential conflict of interest. The issue of illicit gain was often overshadowed by credible evidence that he made misleading statements about his efforts on behalf of the loan.

Also known as: Auberge Grand-Mère scandal; Shawinigate

Locale: Canada

Categories: Government; politics; ethics; corruption; banking and finance

Key Figures

Jean Chrétien (b. 1934), prime minister of Canada, 1993-2003

Yvon Duhaime (fl. late twentieth century), member of the Liberal Party and Chrétien's close friend

Howard Wilson (fl. late twentieth century), Canadian government ethics counselor

Joe Clark (b. 1939), leader of the Conservative Party

François Beaudoin (fl. late twentieth century), president of the Business Development Bank of Canada

Summary of Event

In 1988, Jean Chrétien and two business associates purchased the Auberge Grand-Mère, a large hotel near Chrétien's hometown of Shawinigan, Quebec, Canada. The group also purchased the golf course adjacent to the hotel. In the elections of 1993, the Liberal Party, with Chrétien as its candidate for prime minister, issued a campaign platform that promised to "govern with integrity" and overcome "cynicism about public institutions."

After winning the election, Chrétien attempted to reorganize his private business affairs to avoid a possible conflict of interest. He and his associates sold their shares in the hotel to his longtime friend and fellow Liberal, Yvon Duhaime. Shortly thereafter, the associates entered into an agreement to sell the golf course to Jonas Prince, a Toronto businessman. Unknown to Chrétien, however, Prince backed out of the deal, claiming that he had only agreed to a nonbinding option to purchase the property.

In deciding what to do with his various investments, Chrétien sought the advice of Howard Wilson, the federal ethics councilor responsible for upholding the code of conduct among federal officials in Canada. In accordance with Wilson's recommendations, Chrétien put all of his investments into a blind trust. Because the golf course had not been sold, his share of the property, which had an estimated value of $275,000, was included as part of the trust. In 1996, Chrétien finally learned that he continued to be part owner of the golf club, and he informed Wilson about the matter.

About this time, Duhaime, the new owner of the Auberge Grand-Mère, wanted to expand and improve the building. He attempted to borrow $2 million, but private institutions refused the loan, saying that it was too risky. Duhaime then asked his friend Chrétien for assistance to obtain a loan from the Business Development Bank of Canada (BDC), a federal government enterprise. Chrétien agreed, and on April, 1996, he telephoned BDC president François Beaudoin on behalf of Duhaime. Even after a second appeal by the prime minister, however, the BDC rejected the loan application as too risky. In early 1997, Duhaime applied to the BDC for a smaller loan of $616,000, and he also applied for a grant of $164,000 from the Canadian Human Resources Department (HRD). This time, after additional encouragement from Chrétien, both the loan and the grant were approved.

In early 1999, an investigative journalist working for the *National Post* learned that Duhaime had obtained the BDC loan and the HRD grant. Many observers suspected that the federally supported aid was a conflict of interest. Because the expansion of the hotel increased the monetary value of the golf course shares, the loan indirectly, and to a minor extent, advanced the net worth of the prime minister. Leaders of rival political parties, including Reform leader Preston Manning and Progressive Conservative leader Joe Clark, called for a full investigation into the affair.

Ethics counselor Wilson conducted a relatively superficial inquiry. On May 7, he ruled that Chrétien had not violated any conflict-of-interest rules in regard to the Duhaime loan, although at this time Wilson did not know that Chrétien had personally intervened to help secure the loan. Chrétien's critics pointed out that Wilson reported to the prime minister alone. The next month, Reform leader Manning and another member of Parliament alleged that Chrétien had benefited from deals with businessman Claude Gauthier, who had purchased land next to the golf course. Chrétien threatened to sue the two men, but then dropped the threat, saying that he did not want to stifle debate. A few months later, Chrétien's shares in the golf course were finally sold to a prosperous Montreal investor.

Meanwhile, the financial situation of the Auberge Grand-Mère deteriorated significantly, and in April, 1999, BDC president Beaudoin recommended that the loan be recalled. Within a few weeks, Beaudoin's responsibilities were sharply reduced, and he resigned in September with an annual pension plus a severance payment of $245,000. In December, however, the BDC repealed both the severance agreement and pension. Beaudoin initiated a wrongful-discharge lawsuit, alleging that he had been forced to resign and had lost his severance package because he had dared to question the Grand-Mère loan. BDC officials claimed that Beaudoin had been incompetent and violated bank policies.

Beaudoin's suit revealed the details of Chrétien's personal appeals to the BDC. While Chrétien admitted that he had helped Duhaime secure the mortgage, he argued that it was appropriate for a member of Parliament to help promote the eco-

nomic growth of his or her parliamentary riding. Wilson conducted a second inquiry into the matter, and on November 21, 2000, he ruled that Chrétien's telephone calls did not violate the federal ethics code.

Because federal elections were about to take place, however, the revelations were very embarrassing to both Chrétien and the Liberal Party. The leaders of the four major political parties insisted that there was a need for an independent inquiry, perhaps even a criminal investigation by the Royal Canadian Mounted Police (RCMP). The leaders suggested that Wilson, who had been appointed by the prime minister, might have a conflict of interest himself. The leader of the Canadian Alliance went so far as to call Chrétien a criminal. The New Democratic Party leader called Chrétien "morally bankrupt." The leader of the Bloc Québécois Party

Jean Chrétien casting his ballot in a 1995 election. (AP/ Wide World Photos)

remarked that the bank loan "still smells like something." Conservative leader Clark declared that Chrétien should apologize to Canadian citizens for his abuse of power.

In the parliamentary elections of November 27, despite the bad publicity about the Grand-Mère loan, the Liberal Party won the majority of seats, thereby making Chrétien the first prime minister in half a century to win three consecutive majorities. On February 19, 2001, the RCMP announced that there was no basis for a criminal investigation into the loan. Clark, nevertheless, vowed to continue asking questions about the loan, and the next day he accused Chrétien of making false statements in the House of Commons. As evidence, he produced a 1999 memo indicating that Chrétien's former assistant had recommended the loan to the BDC, which appeared to contradict Chrétien's earlier claim that his assistants had not played any role in the affair. The prime minister's office explained that Chrétien had meant that his assistants had nothing to do with the approval of the loan. Accusing Clark of conducting a witch hunt, Chrétien declared, "He started as Joe Who and now he's perhaps Joe McCarthy."

On March 2, Wilson's office cleared Chrétien for the third time. However, because Chrétien announced Wilson's ruling in the House of Commons ninety minutes before Wilson released the report, the opposition asserted that the relationship between the prime minister and the ethics counselor was too cozy. Meanwhile, news reports about Beaudoin's lawsuit kept the Shawinigate affair, as the scandal came to be called, in the news media. On March 23, Clark insisted on an independent investigation into the controversy and that Chrétien should step down as prime minister until the investigation's conclusion. On March 26, Chrétien tried to limit criticism by agreeing to release all documents relating to the Grand-Mère affair, pending the consent of those persons involved in the loan.

IMPACT

In early 2002, Chrétien finally endorsed a bill that included an independent ethics commissioner who would report directly to the House of Commons

rather than to the prime minister. Although the House quickly passed the bill, it was stalled in the Senate.

The Shawinigate scandal continued to have a negative impact on Chrétien's popularity, and it contributed to the Liberal Party leaders' decision to replace him with his rival, Paul Martin. In Chrétien's farewell address of November, 2003, the integrity agenda was not on his list of achievements. On December 12, the same day that Martin was sworn in as prime minister, Martin announced that one of his priorities was to obtain passage of the ethics bill, and he achieved this goal within a few months. If such legislation had been in place at the beginning of the Chrétien era, it is entirely possible that Shawinigate as well as other scandals might have been avoided.

Even after Chrétien left office, stories relating to the Shawinigate scandal continued to appear in Canadian newspapers. On February 6, 2004, Beaudoin won his lawsuit against the BDC and the judge ordered the restoration of his annual pension and severance payment. In addition, the financial situation of the Auberge Grand-Mère continued to deteriorate, forcing taxpayers to absorb a significant loss. The complex was badly damaged by fire in February, and Duhaime was charged with the crime.

—Thomas Tandy Lewis

FURTHER READING

Chrétien, Jean. *My Years as Prime Minister*. Toronto, Ont.: Knopf Canada, 2007. Describes Shawinigate as a politically motivated witch hunt and puts much of the blame for the scandal on Conrad Black, owner of the *National Post*.

Glor, Eleanor, and Ian Greene. "The Government of Canada's Approach to Ethics: The Evolution of Ethical Government." *Public Integrity* 5 (2002): 41-67. A useful summary of the state of Canadian standards at the end of Chrétien's term as prime minister.

Greene, Ian. "The Chrétien Ethics Legacy." In *The Chrétien Legacy*, edited by Louis Harder and Steve Patten. Montreal: McGill-Queen's University Press, 2006. Summarizing Shawinigate and ten other scandals during Chrétien's premiership, Greene concludes that his record was "mediocre" but better than that of predecessor Brian Mulroney.

Martin, Lawrence. *Iron Man: The Defiant Reign of Jean Chrétien*. Toronto, Ont.: Penguin Canada, 2003. A critical biography of Chrétien written by one of Canada's most outstanding journalists.

Tuns, Paul. *Jean Chrétien: A Legacy of Scandal*. London: Freedom Press, 2004. A rather extreme and one-sided attack on Chrétien's ethical record

as prime minister, written by a conservative journalist.

SEE ALSO: July 10, 1934: Sex Scandal Forces Resignation of Alberta Premier Brownlee; Mar. 4, 1966: Munsinger Sex and Spy Scandal Rocks Canada; Sept. 17, 1985: Media Allege Canadian Officials Allowed Sale of Rancid Tuna; Nov. 18, 1995: Former Canadian Premier Brian Mulroney Is Exposed in Airbus Scandal.

January 28, 2000
JOHN SPANO IS SENTENCED FOR FRAUDULENT PURCHASE OF ICE HOCKEY TEAM

Businessman John A. Spano began negotiations in 1996 to purchase the New York Islanders ice hockey team. He represented himself as the owner of a large company and as an inheritor of substantial wealth. When Spano failed to pay for the club he just bought, investigators found that his company was much smaller than claimed to be and that he had no inherited wealth. Spano was convicted of fraud and forgery.

LOCALE: Long Island, New York
CATEGORIES: Banking and finance; corruption; forgery; hoaxes, frauds, and charlatanism; law and the courts; sports

KEY FIGURES

John A. Spano, Jr. (b. 1964), owner of a Dallas equipment-leasing company
Gary Bettman (b. 1952), commissioner of the National Hockey League
John O. Pickett (fl. twenty-first century), owner of the New York Islanders

SUMMARY OF EVENT

The New York Islanders, one of the newest teams in the National Hockey League (NHL), served as a standout franchise in its first decade-plus. The team originated in 1972 and soon surpassed its fabled

neighbors, the New York Rangers, by winning a Stanley Cup in 1979. Unfortunately, the team's on-ice success did not bring enough money into the coffers of owner Roy Boe. Suffering from financial woes associated with the startup of his hockey team and the expenses of his National Basketball Association team, Boe sold the Islanders to John O. Pickett, one of the team's limited partners, in 1979.

By 1983, the Islanders had won three more Stanley Cups and seemed on the verge of establishing a dynasty. The team remained competitive for the rest of the decade, but Pickett kept the money from the team's cable television contract rather than reinvest it in the club. The lack of money reduced the competitiveness of the Islanders as departing stars were replaced by less expensive players. The Islanders had their first losing season in 1988-1989. After the season, Pickett retired to Florida and turned over operation of the team to four people who had purchased minor stakes in the club. Chaos in the front office resulted in losses on the ice and a poor showing at the box office. Pickett put the team up for sale amid talk that the club would leave Long Island, New York.

At this point, John A. Spano appeared on the scene. The owner of the Bison Group, a Dallas equipment-leasing company, Spano had tried to purchase the hockey teams the Dallas Stars in 1995

2000's

John Spano holds up a team jersey after purchasing the New York Islanders hockey club in 1997. (Hulton Archive/Getty Images)

and the Florida Panthers in 1996. The deals collapsed partly due to financing difficulties. Nevertheless, NHL commissioner Gary Bettman called Spano, who bought the Islanders in February, 1997, a savior. Spano promised to keep the Islanders in Long Island and end Pickett's penny-pinching ways. Spano claimed to be worth $230 million. A person later described by stunned colleagues as very engaging and likable, Spano charmed the public. Islanders fans began to dream of a winning season, or even another Stanley Cup. Pickett sold the team and its cable television rights to Spano for $165 million.

Spano defaulted on his first payment for $16.8 million to Pickett on April 7, 1997, when a wire transfer of the money failed to deposit the funds into Pickett's account. Spano then stopped payment on one check for $16.8 million, bounced another for $17 million, wired $5,000 instead of $5 million, and

then wired $1,700 instead of $17 million. Pickett's attorneys asked the NHL to take the team back from Spano on grounds of fraud. The media had a field day with the affair.

As his name was increasingly muddied, Spano vehemently denied that he lied, cheated, or stole anything. He continued to claim that he had the money to purchase the Islanders. Spano accused Pickett of undermining him in an attempt to get the team back and sell it at a higher price. Bettman forced Spano to return control of the team to Pickett on April 11, and the NHL voided Spano's purchase.

Bettman came under heavy attack for approving the sale of the Islanders to Spano. He claimed due diligence, arguing that six banks had checked on Spano's finances. The NHL hired the firm of Ernst & Young as well as Arnold Burns, a former deputy U.S. attorney general, to review bank procedures. Amid rumors of pending charges, Spano traveled to the Cayman Islands to meet with bank officials. He returned to the United States after three days. On July 23, he surrendered to U.S. authorities in Uniondale, Long Island, to face bank and wire fraud charges.

A U.S. Postal Service investigation revealed that Spano was accused of making fraudulent claims to obtain an $80 million loan from Fleet Bank, a loan he used to buy the Islanders. He misrepresented his net worth. He only had about $1.2 million in assets yet claimed in a statement of financial worth that he had $107 million in a trust, $52 million in a bank account, and $39 million in a certificate of deposit. A trustee hired by Spano could not verify the existence of the trust, nor could he verify the existence of any money. The trustee said that Spano failed to provide him with information about the trust that would allow him to perform his duties with due diligence.

Furthermore, Spano forged signatures and letters to imply that he had the money to buy the Islanders. The prosecutor described the documents that Spano mailed to Pickett, the NHL, and Fleet Bank as nothing more than faxed "cut-and-paste jobs," which also included the misspelled names of foreign bank officials. The postal investigators looked at the letter to Pickett from Comerica Bank in Dallas that attested to Spano's net worth. They discovered that a bank executive admitted that the sum was based upon unverified documents from Spano and that the banker had no personal knowledge of Spano's net worth. Spano forged another letter from Comerica Bank, certifying that the bank held enough funds in his account to cover the bounced $17 million check. The bank executive who purportedly signed the letter denied any knowledge of that letter. The postal investigators described the letter as an obvious forgery. It had a fax machine mark virtually identical to the one used by Spano's Bison Group. A fax sent to Pickett from the brokerage firm of Donaldson, Lufkin & Jenrette that claimed Spano had U.S. Treasury bill holdings of $27 million also had the Bison Group fax mark.

Spano also was accused of spending $220,000 of the Islanders's money in undocumented expenses after fraudulently assuming ownership. Additionally, his equipment-leasing firm in Dallas was virtually bankrupt. He bounced a July 10, 1997, check for more than $85,000 to pay property taxes on a $2.5 million home in the University Park section of Dallas. When his attorney claimed in court that all of Spano's taxes and mortgage payments were current, the prosecutor produced the bounced check. The bad check showed that Spano's promises were empty, leading the judge to set the bail amount high at $3 million.

On October 7, 1999, Spano pleaded guilty to federal charges of mail and wire fraud in Long Island and bank and wire fraud in Texas. He subsequently pleaded guilty to one count of bank fraud in Boston. All other charges and potential charges were dropped. His wife divorced him and sold their Dallas home. Spano moved into a condominium in Philadelphia and developed a drug addiction. When he tried to pay his rent with a bad credit card, bad checks, and bad wire transfers, his $3 million bail was revoked for continued criminal conduct. Spano was sentenced on January 28, 2000, to six years and $11.9 million in restitution. He left prison in 2004.

IMPACT

Pickett did not lose any money from the Spano affair. Indeed, in July, 1997, he regained control of the Islanders. He then sold the team and its cable television rights to Howard Milstein for $195 million. Milstein initially poured money into the franchise but, without victories, essentially gave up on the team by adopting an austere budget. In 2000, he sold the team to Charles Wang. The Fleet Bank executive who approved the $80 million loan to Spano resigned in August, 1997. Pickett repaid the loan after it was restructured.

Wang, the newest majority owner of the Islanders, reinvigorated the team with an infusion of money. The Islanders won more points in the 2001-2002 season than they had earned in any of the previous eighteen seasons. The victories sent ticket sales and fan interest skyrocketing, and the Islanders became one of the premier clubs in professional hockey in the United States.

—*Caryn E. Neumann*

FURTHER READING

Botte, Peter, and Alan Hahn. *Fish Sticks: The Fall and Rise of the New York Islanders.* Champaign, Ill.: Sports Publishing, 2005. A good general history of the New York Islanders hockey club. Includes some discussion of the Spano scandal.

Fried, Gil, Steven Shapiro, and Timothy D. Deschriver. *Sport Finance.* Champaign, Ill.: Human Kinetics, 2007. Explains the complex financing involved in modern professional sports. Useful as a primer for understanding Spano's dealings with the NHL.

Wolf, Alexander. "Busted: John Spano's Giddy Run as an NHL Owner Ended Quickly Amid Charges of Fraud and Deceit." *Sports Illustrated*, August 4, 1997. An account of Spano's fraudulent dealings with the NHL, his purchase and loss of the Islanders, and the scandal's fallout.

SEE ALSO: Mar. 29, 1962: Billie Sol Estes Is Arrested for Corporate Fraud; Jan. 15, 1988: ZZZZ Best Founder Is Indicted on Federal Fraud Charges; Mar. 29, 1989: Financier Michael Milken Is Indicted for Racketeering and Fraud; May 9, 2000: Former Louisiana Governor Edwin Edwards Is Convicted on Corruption Charges; Mar. 27, 2002: Georgia Basketball Coach Jim Harrick, Sr., Resigns over Fraud Allegations.

2000's

May 2, 2000
NEW YORK MAYOR RUDY GIULIANI'S EXTRAMARITAL AFFAIR IS REVEALED

Rudy Giuliani was married to Donna Hanover when he began an extramarital affair with Judith Nathan. The media's exposure of the affair set off a firestorm of coverage by New York City's tabloid press and television stations. After a public and very contentious divorce, Giuliani married Nathan.

LOCALE: New York, New York

CATEGORIES: Politics; public morals; sex; families and children

KEY FIGURES

Rudy Giuliani (b. 1944), mayor of New York, 1994-2001

Judith Nathan Giuliani (b. 1954), pharmaceutical sales manager and Giuliani's third wife

Donna Hanover Giuliani (b. 1950), actor and television news anchor-reporter, who was Giuliani's second wife

Cristyne Lategano (fl. twenty-first century), Giuliani's press secretary

SUMMARY OF EVENT

During four weeks in early 2000, New York mayor Rudy Giuliani experienced a stunning reversal of fortune. In mid-April, he was the Republican candidate for a vacant U.S. Senate seat; was promised financial help from people across the country who disliked his opponent, Hillary Rodham Clinton; and was supported by many New Yorkers. Less than one month later, he was fighting cancer, his marital difficulties were headline news, his reputation for morality was shattered, and he abandoned any hope of election to the Senate.

Giuliani's announcement on April 27 that he was suffering from prostate cancer brought forth an outpouring of get-well wishes. The public was unaware of, and newspapers chose not to comment on, his most recent sexual adventure until a *New York*

Daily News gossip columnist on May 2 noted that Giuliani and a friend (not identified) frequently dined together. The next day the *New York Post* published three pictures of the mayor and his friend that it had been holding back, identifying the woman as Judith Nathan. When questioned, Giuliani said Nathan was "a very good friend," stimulating the two tabloids, New York City television stations, and national scandal magazines to tell their readers how good a friend.

Giuliani had been so open about the relationship it seemed as though he wanted to be caught. Newspapers now reported how frequently the two had dined together in posh New York restaurants, noted how often Giuliani was accompanied by Nathan rather than his wife at public events, and described his practice of arriving, escorted by two carloads of New York City police officers, for summer weekends at Nathan's condominium in the Hamptons. Reporters had known about his behavior, but never mentioned it until the *Daily News* gossip columnist broke the silence.

Follow-up stories disclosed an extensive pattern of womanizing that did not fit Giuliani's carefully cultivated reputation as defender of public morality, including condemning profane or licentious museum exhibits. When living alone in Washington, D.C., and estranged from his first wife, Giuliani had been actively dating other women. Even before his 1982 divorce, Giuliani and television reporter Donna Hanover began living together.

Giuliani and Hanover married in 1984. The two had an openly warm and mutually supportive relationship, and Hanover played a major role in Giuliani's mayoral campaigns in 1989 and 1993. The closeness ended in 1995 when Giuliani began to spend most of his time with his press secretary, Cristyne Lategano. In its August, 1997, issue, *Vanity Fair* magazine asserted the two were intimate, but both denied the accusation. Hanover concentrated on her increasingly successful career as an actor, anchor on television news, and host of television cooking programs. She rarely accompanied Giuliani at public or social occasions and asked to be addressed by her professional name, Donna Hanover, rather than Mrs. Giuliani or Donna Giuliani.

On May 10, 2000, Giuliani called a morning press conference that was covered live by New York City television news stations. He announced his decision to separate from Hanover and hoped to reach a formal agreement with her. He praised Nathan, a registered nurse and sales representative for a drug company, for the support she had given him, which he expected would be even more valuable as he fought his own cancer.

Giuliani had not told his wife he intended to publicly call for a separation. Hanover learned of his plans when a friend phoned and told her to turn on her television. She was furious and arranged a press conference of her own for that afternoon. Standing in front of Gracie Mansion, the official mayoral residence, with tears in her eyes, she stated that she had tried to keep the marriage together but that Giuliani had not cooperated. Hanover asserted she had been unable to take part in his political life for years because of his relationship with one of his staff members—a reference to Lategano that newspapers gleefully explained to their readers. Now, she would reluctantly discuss a legal separation with her husband.

Defiantly, Giuliani issued a press release on May 12 that informed the media where he and Nathan planned to dine that evening. After dinner, Giuliani escorted her back to her apartment, ten blocks from the restaurant. They were followed by photojournalists and television camera operators.

New York State's Republican leaders grew increasing

concerned and impatient as the media circus over Giuliani's sex life continued. They expected the contest between Giuliani, who cleaned up New York City, and the controversial former first lady of the United States, Hillary Rodham Clinton, to generate voter excitement that would help their candidates for state office. Republican leaders urged Giuliani to end his garish behavior and concentrate on preparing for the U.S. Senate election less than six months away.

Giuliani vacillated. Doctors assured him he would recover sufficiently in a month or two to return to active campaigning. However, he could not be sure how badly his chances of election had been damaged by his public reputation as an immoral adulterer. On May 19, less than four weeks after his shocking announcement that he had cancer, Giuliani withdrew his Senate candidacy, claiming he needed to concentrate on his health in the coming months.

Giuliani filed for divorce in October. Acrimonious public battles broke out between spokespersons for both parties. Hanover continued to live in Gracie Mansion and secured a court order barring her estranged husband from entering the house or meet-

Donna Hanover Giuliani and Rudy Giuliani in 1994. (Hulton Archive/Getty Images)

ing his children before the divorce became final. The case dragged on until June, 2002, six months after the end of Giuliani's term as mayor. The court awarded Hanover full custody of their two children and $6.8 million.

Giuliani and Nathan were married in Gracie Mansion by Mayor Michael Bloomberg on May 24, 2003. This was the third marriage for both Giuliani and Nathan. Hanover, after her divorce from Giuliani, reunited with her high school sweetheart, whom she had not seen for twenty years. The two were married in 2003, her third marriage as well.

IMPACT

After the nasty public breakup of his marriage and the venomous rancor of the divorce proceedings, pundits predicted that Giuliani's political career was over because of the divorce scandal. However, everything changed on September 11, 2001. Giuliani's calm demeanor in response to the destruction of the World Trade Center and the murder of close to three thousand people turned him into a hero whose peccadilloes were forgiven. However, term limits set by the city charter prevented him from running for reelection. After leaving office, Giuliani opened a security consulting firm whose profits, along with hefty speaking fees, made him a multimillionaire.

In 2006, Giuliani began exploring the possibility of running for president of the United States. He formally announced his candidacy for the Republican nomination in February, 2007. September polls indicated he was the front runner, but by the time Florida voted on January 29, 2008, the competition had narrowed to an exciting two-person contest between John McCain and Mitt Romney. Giuliani withdrew from the race the next day.

—*Milton Berman*

FURTHER READING

Apostolidis, Paul, and Juliet A. Williams, eds. *Public Affairs: Politics in the Age of Sex Scandals.* Durham, N.C.: Duke University Press, 2004. A study of politics and political culture in the context of sex scandals.

Barrett, Wayne, with Adam Fifield. *RUDY! An Investigative Biography of Rudolph Giuliani.* New York: Basic Books, 2000. A biography of Giuliani that attacks his character and treats him as a trickster and fraud.

Kirtzman, Andrew. *Rudy Giuliani: Emperor of the City.* New York: William Morrow, 2000. Praises what Giuliani accomplished for New York City but regrets the effect of his abrasiveness and egotism on his reputation.

Polner, Robert, ed. *America's Mayor, America's President? The Strange Career of Rudy Giuliani.* Brooklyn, N.Y.: Soft Skull Press, 2007. Nineteen essays by New York journalists and academics that negatively assess Giuliani's behavior and character, arguing that he is unfit to be president of the United States.

Siegal, Frederick, with Harry Siegal. *The Prince of the City: Giuliani, New York, and the Genius of American Life.* San Francisco, Calif.: Encounter Books, 2005. An admirer of Giuliani praises his achievements as mayor of New York and suggests he would make a good president.

Strober, Deborah Hart, and Gerald S. Strober. *Giuliani, Flawed or Flawless? The Oral Biography.* Hoboken, N.J.: John Wiley & Sons, 2007. Presents a generally favorable portrait of Giuliani, based on more than forty superficial interviews with the former mayor's friends and critics.

SEE ALSO: Jan. 26, 1979: Former Vice President Nelson Rockefeller Dies Mysteriously; July 20, 1982: Conservative Politician John G. Schmitz Is Found to Have Children Out of Wedlock; Apr. 9, 1987: Bess Myerson Resigns as New York Commissioner of Cultural Affairs; Jan. 17, 1998: President Bill Clinton Denies Sexual Affair with a White House Intern; Oct. 2, 2003: Newspaper Claims That Arnold Schwarzenegger Groped Women; Dec. 6, 2005: Spokane, Washington, Mayor Recalled in Gay-Sex Scandal; Mar. 12, 2008: New York Governor Eliot Spitzer Resigns in Prostitution Scandal.

May 9, 2000

FORMER LOUISIANA GOVERNOR EDWIN EDWARDS IS CONVICTED ON CORRUPTION CHARGES

The administration of Edwin Edwards, the three-term governor of Louisiana, was marred by allegations of corruption for decades. In 2001, Edwards was sentenced to ten years in federal prison for corrupt practices, including extortion and money laundering, related to the issuance of contracts and licenses for riverboat casino gambling.

LOCALE: Baton Rouge, Louisiana
CATEGORIES: Corruption; law and the courts; politics; government

KEY FIGURES

Edwin Edwards (b. 1927), former governor of Louisiana, 1972-1980, 1984-1988, 1992-1996
Edward J. DeBartolo, Jr. (b. 1946), owner of the San Francisco 49ers football team and bidder for a Louisiana riverboat casino development project
Frank Polozola (b. 1942), U.S. District Court judge

SUMMARY OF EVENT

On May 9, 2000, former Louisiana governor Edwin Edwards was found guilty of racketeering, extortion, conspiracy to commit extortion, wire and mail fraud, and money laundering, among other crimes. On January 8, 2001, U.S. District Court judge Frank Polozola sentenced him to 120 months in prison, fined him $250,000, and ordered him to forfeit $1.8 million.

Five others were charged as coconspirators: Edwards's son and law partner, Stephen; Andrew Martin, Edwards's executive assistant during his fourth term as governor; Cecil Brown, a longtime friend and courier of information and cash for Edwards; Bobby Johnson, a Baton Rouge, Louisiana, contractor with ties to Edwards; Louisiana state senator Greg Tarver; and Ecotry Fuller, a member of the casino license board for Louisiana. While

Tarver and Fuller were found not guilty, the others received sentences of between five and seven years and fines between $50,000 and $60,000.

Edwards was first elected to the Crowley City Council, then as a state representative and a member of the U.S. Congress. He was a popular governor who first served from 1972 to 1980. He was constitutionally banned from seeking a third consecutive term, so he waited four years before handily winning an election to serve a third term beginning in 1984. In his third term as governor, the state had faced high unemployment and ran a significant operating deficit. The state fell further into debt and was seeking much-needed revenue.

From the early days of his political career, Edwards was accused of corruption and taking payoffs from those doing business with the state. He rarely took on the accusations directly, responding instead to his critics with sharp one-liners. For example, a gift of close to $20,000 in value from a South Korean lobbyist was simply dismissed by him as a gift to his wife.

Edwards proposed legalized-gambling options while in office, but those options did not develop until his successor, Charles "Buddy" Roemer, took office and worked with the state legislature for the approval of riverboat-casino gambling. In no time, Edwards was back as governor for a fourth term, surprising many. He, too, would play a major part in the development of gambling in the state. Louisiana would soon approve the licensing of fifteen riverboat casinos that would create jobs and generate revenue. As the contracts and licenses were being awarded, it became clear to many that those contracts were going to bidders who had some sort of business relationship with Edwards, whose final term as governor ended in early 1996.

Among those riverboat bidders was Edward DeBartolo, Jr., part owner of the San Francisco 49ers football team and son of the successful shopping-mall developer Edward DeBartolo, Sr. In

2000's

1996, DeBartolo Entertainment was in the process of bidding for the fifteenth, and final, riverboat casino license. Though Edwards was out of office at the end of 1996, he still had many powerful friends in government. The former governor used his connections to give DeBartolo confidential information from the meetings of the Louisiana Gaming Control Board.

In early March, 1997, the night before DeBartolo made his presentation for a riverboat casino and shopping-mall complex on the Red River in Bossier City, Edwards and DeBartolo met at the Baton Rouge Radisson Hotel bar. Edwards requested 1 percent of DeBartolo's casino profits and $400,000 for assisting in procuring the license. Edwards also implied that DeBartolo would have trouble getting the contract unless he complied with his request. DeBartolo agreed to Edwards's terms in that meeting.

Soon after that meeting at the Radisson, a Federal Bureau of Investigation (FBI) wiretap caught Edwards on the phone with Ralph Perlman, a member of the Gaming Control Board. Edwards asked Perlman if the vote regarding DeBartolo's contract would be encouraging. Perlman replied in the affirmative. In mid-March, Edwards again met with DeBartolo, this time to retrieve a briefcase containing $400,000 in $100 bills. The next day, the partnership of DeBartolo Entertainment and Hollywood Casino Corporation was awarded the final riverboat-casino license on a 6-0 vote. In the end, however, DeBartolo would never receive the license.

The FBI began wiretapping Edwards's phones and placing microphones in his law office to gather substantial evidence related to other possible payoffs. While Edwards was somewhat cryptic and careful with comments he made over the phone, microphones revealed he was more carefree when discussing business dealings in his law office.

On October 6, 1998, DeBartolo pleaded guilty to the charge of failing to report that Edwards had extorted him for the casino license. DeBartolo cooperated with authorities and received two years probation and agreed to pay $1 million in penalties. However, DeBartolo lost considerably more than

cash: He lost the casino license and controlling ownership of the San Francisco 49ers, which went to his sister.

Edwards, his son Stephen, and four associates were indicted on November 7 by a federal grand jury for a racketeering conspiracy to extort money from prospective businesses seeking to open riverboat casinos in Louisiana. The licenses were lucrative, and Edwards knew those interested would go to extremes to get one.

Robert Guidry, a former riverboat casino owner, testified at the former governor's trial that he paid $100,000 per month to Edwards, his son, Stephen, and an Edwards aide. During the trial, Edwards questioned the legality of the deal by claiming he was not in office as governor when he allegedly received those payments. The cornerstone of Edwards's defense in the case was that all payments were legal payments made for his lobbying and consultation expertise. However, Guidry testified that Edwards's work, while governor, in reassigning key members of the state police gaming division was essential to Guidry receiving his renewed gambling license. Without the gambling license, Guidry's riverboat contract was worthless. Guidry admitted to making payments to Edwards totaling $1.5 million by dropping amounts as much as $100,000 in cash in clandestine areas, including trash bins, in Baton Rouge from March, 1996, through April, 1997.

Multiple permits were needed to successfully operate a riverboat casino, adding to the temptation to subvert the law to get those lucrative permits. To set up a riverboat casino, a company would have to win one of the available permits to build and dock its boat. Additionally, a company would have to receive an operating license from the state police. In one instance, Edwards suggested to one company, Players Casino in Lake Charles, that they would need his help in getting approval from the state police. In turn, the company purchased $200,000 worth of goods from an Edwards-owned company.

Because the U.S. attorney had failed to convict Edwards on corruption charges during the mid-1980's, few people were absolutely confident of getting a conviction in this case, even though some of his coconspirators cooperated with prosecutors by testifying. All three had accepted plea bargain deals with federal authorities and were forthcoming with details when they took the witness stand at trial. Edwards and his son and associates were found guilty on May 9, 2000. Edwin Edwards unsuccessfully appealed his conviction, an appeal based largely on his claim that the testimony of key trial witnesses was questionable.

While still attempting to appeal his case, Edwards began serving his term at the Federal Medical Center in Fort Worth, Texas, on October 21, 2002. He later transferred to Oakdale Federal Prison in Oakdale, Louisiana. This low-security prison houses other high-profile inmates, including Enron's Andrew Fastow, Worldcom's Bernard Ebbers, and former Alabama governor Don Siegelman.

IMPACT

For a state with significant wealth in terms of natural resources, many critics lament the political corruption that has impeded the state's progress. Louisiana remains a poor state with an inadequate educational system and unstable revenue. Concern about corrupt politics has kept many businesses from establishing themselves in the state, businesses that would provide jobs, income to the state from sales taxes, and a hint of stability in a politically unstable state. Edwards's unethical and illegal dealings only made matters worse, and they did nothing more for the state than reinforce its reputation as a haven for corrupt politicians and government officials.

—John C. Kilburn, Jr.

FURTHER READING

Bridges, Tyler. *Bad Bet on the Bayou: The Rise of Gambling in Louisiana and the Fall of Governor Edwin Edwards*. New York: Farrar, Straus & Giroux, 2001. A comprehensive report on Edwin Edwards's role in the development of gaming and the corruption related to gaming in Louisiana.

Brotherton, John. *A Fistful of Kings*. Humble, Tex.: Shears Group, 2000. A story of casino gambling in Russia and Louisiana as told by a Players Casino vice president and witness for the prosecution in the Edwards case.

Parent, Wayne. *Inside the Carnival: Unmasking Louisiana Politics*. Baton Rouge: Louisiana State University Press, 2004. A comprehensive review of Louisiana politics, with substantial focus on political corruption in the state.

SEE ALSO: Oct. 22, 1923: U.S. Senate Begins Hearings on Teapot Dome Oil Leases; May 12, 1924: Kentucky Congressman John W. Langley Is Convicted of Violating the Volstead Act; Dec. 11, 1997: HUD Secretary Henry Cisneros Is Indicted for Lying to Federal Agents; Jan. 28, 2000: John Spano Is Sentenced for Fraudulent Purchase of Ice Hockey Team; Oct. 2, 2003: Newspaper Claims That Arnold Schwarzenegger Groped Women; Sept. 12, 2005: Westar Energy Executives Are Found Guilty of Looting Their Company; June 4, 2007: Congressman William J. Jefferson Is Indicted for Corruption; Mar. 12, 2008: New York Governor Eliot Spitzer Resigns in Prostitution Scandal.

2000's

September, 2000
AMERICAN SCIENTISTS ARE ACCUSED OF STARTING A MEASLES EPIDEMIC IN THE AMAZON

Patrick Tierney claimed that two renowned researchers, anthropologist Napoleon A. Chagnon and geneticist James V. Neel, started or exacerbated a measles epidemic among the indigenous Yanomami people of the Amazon in 1968. Conflicting accounts of what actually happened call into question some of Tierney's accusations, which were made in his book Darkness in El Dorado *(2000).*

LOCALE: Southern Venezuela
CATEGORIES: Publishing and journalism; medicine and health care; science and technology

KEY FIGURES
Napoleon A. Chagnon (b. 1938), American anthropologist and professor emeritus, University of California, Santa Barbara
James V. Neel (1915-2000), American geneticist
Patrick Tierney (fl. early twenty-first century), visiting scholar at the Center for Latin American Studies, University of Pittsburgh

SUMMARY OF EVENT
Patrick Tierney claims in his book *Darkness in El Dorado* (2000) that American scientists Napoleon A. Chagnon and James V. Neel administered a measles vaccine to the Yanomami people of South America in 1968, leading to or exacerbating a measles outbreak among the population and causing thousands of deaths. Others believe, however, that the vaccine actually prevented the spread of measles. Confusion exists about whether such an outbreak of measles even occurred. Estimates of the dead range from zero to thousands. Questions also remain about whether measles had been present among the Yanomami prior to the vaccination efforts.

The Yanomami, a remote tribe of indigenous, or Indian, peoples, inhabit areas of Brazil and Venezuela. They make up the largest indigenous group in South America, with an estimated population of twenty-two to twenty-seven thousand. They live in about three hundred villages that are spread out over a vast 70,000 square miles. The Yanomami are primarily hunters and farmers who live in relatively isolated areas and practice their traditional lifestyle. They comprise four Indian subdivisions, each with its own language: the Sanema of the northern sector, the Ninam of the southeastern sector, the Yanomam of the southeastern part of the Yanomami area, and the Yanomamo of the southwestern part of Yanomami area.

Chagnon and Neel spent many years working among the Yanomami. They filmed rituals and everyday life, collected genealogies, and took blood samples from the mid-1960's until the late 1990's. The government of Venezuela had banned (or revoked) Chagnon's visa to travel to the lands of the Yanomami but Chagnon managed to travel into the country by listing himself as part of a group that was traveling under Neel.

The measles vaccine scandal was initiated when Tierney accused Chagnon and Neel of questionable ethical practices in administering to the Yanomami a dangerous measles vaccine that contained a live virus—the Edmonston B. Neel used the vaccine without the permission of Venezuelan medical authorities. Neel was interested in discovering how the previously unexposed Yanomami would react to the measles vaccine. Even though a better vaccine was available, the older version, Edmonston B, was used. Edmonston B was more onerous to administer, as it was necessary (as advised by the World Health Organization, the WHO, in 1965) to give a gamma globulin shot prior to the vaccine to help control side effects.

Tierney maintains that hundreds if not thousands of Yanomami died as a result of the use of the Edmonston B vaccine. A group of researchers from the University of Michigan and University of California, Santa Barbara, found that Edmonston B was safe and had been approved by the U.S. Food and Drug Administration and the WHO. Furthermore, this same research contends that the measles outbreak had already been in evidence for one year prior to the vaccine being administered. The former director of the U.S. Centers for Disease Control, William H. Foege, said that Edmonston B, while strong and sometimes causing severe reactions that mimicked a light case of measles, would not cause the large number of deaths claimed by Tierney.

Furthermore, Tierney claimed that Neel and Chagnon did not have proper consent to use the vaccine. However, researchers from Michigan and Santa Barbara argue that the Venezuelan medical officials had approved the use. Keith Wardlaw, a visiting Christian missionary present at the time in question, maintains that while Neel had nothing to do with the outbreak and was attempting to provide vaccines to the Yanomami to prevent the spread of measles, he nevertheless was refused permission to administer the vaccine by the Society for the Protection of Indians, a Venezuelan government agency. Furthermore, Wardlaw, who with his family had been with the Yanomami Indians during the measles outbreak, actually believed his young daughter had unknowingly introduced measles to the Yanomami.

In addition, evidence shows that the 1968 outbreak was not the first among the Yanomami. Thomas Headland, a noted anthropologist, asserted that at least four measles outbreaks occurred among the Yanomami prior to the time that Chagnon and Neel arrived in the area in 1968.

Another of Tierney's assertions was that Neel did nothing to assist the Yanomami during the measles epidemic. Susan Lindee, a historian at the University of Pennsylvania who had access to Neel's field notes, found that Neel provided antibiotics to the inhabitants of the Yanomami villages he visited. The researchers from Michigan and Santa Barbara also found that Neel provided medical assistance to the Yanomami and may have saved lives through his efforts. Wardlaw supports these claims.

The alleged misconduct reported by Tierney was first brought to light by two professors of anthropol-

ogy in September, 2000. Terence Turner and Leslie Sponsel, after reading the manuscript of Tierney's soon-to-be-published *Darkness in El Dorado*, sent an e-mail message to the American Anthropological Association (AAA) to warn the organization about possible repercussions if the allegations in the book indeed were true. They also urged the AAA to conduct a formal investigation into the work. Their e-mail was leaked to the press within days. In a subsequent letter, Turner and Sponsel stated that they had not taken a position on whether the book's assertions about Neel or Chagnon were true or false. They claimed that the sole purpose of their original e-mail was to warn the AAA. Neither had done work on the Yanomami, nor had they ever written about Chagnon or Neel. Tierney, to his credit, had done field research with an indigenous population, the Kayapo of central Brazil, but not with the Yanomami. Furthermore, he has written about the ethics of working with indigenous populations.

In defense of Neel and Chagnon and countering the claims of Turner and Sponsel, the codeveloper of the Edmonston B vaccine, Samuel L. Katz, said that the same vaccine administered to the Yanomami was given to close to nineteen million children and infants around the world, including the United States, South America, Nigeria, and Burkina Faso, between 1963 and 1975 without major health problems. He insisted that the use of the Edmonston B vaccine could not have started or even exacerbated a measles epidemic.

IMPACT

Most of Tierney's allegations, and certainly the allegation that Chagnon and Neel were responsible for a massive measles epidemic that caused thousands of deaths among the Yanomami, were refuted by various groups that included the AAA, by witnesses who were present at the time in question, and by other researchers. On November 13, 2000, the provost's office at the University of Michigan, after spending hundreds of hours investigating the matter, issued a statement in support of Chagnon and Neel and against the claims made by Tierney in *Darkness in El Dorado*. Also, the office claimed that Turner and Sponsel had known about Tierney's work on the book years before sending their e-mail message to the AAA. In turn, Sponsel and Turner denied the claims made by the provost's office.

In February of 2001, the AAA convened a task force of professionals and academics who had direct knowledge of the activities in question. In its three-hundred-page report of May 18, 2002, the task force found that although Chagnon often was unethical in his research—including not obtaining proper consent from the government of Venezuela and the Yanomami for his studies—most of the allegations made against him and Neel by Tierney could not be corroborated. However, the report was rescinded by the AAA in June, 2005, for being unfair, flawed, and neglectful of Tierney's rights to due process.

The Yanomami people have changed in many ways as a result of contact with the modern world. One Yanomami tradition that has not changed, however, is the belief that bodily matter should not be kept after an individual dies. Now advocating for their rights, the Yanomami, through their representatives, have requested the return of the blood samples taken by Chagnon and Neel. (The donors had not been told that their blood would be kept indefinitely.) While researchers have promised to return the samples (or destroy them—an alternate request), the Yanomami still wait and wonder. In the meantime, the scandal led to further academic debate on the ethics of research with indigenous peoples.

—Judy L. Porter

FURTHER READING

Borofsky, Robert, with Bruce Albert et al. *Yanomami: The Fierce Controversy and What We Might Learn from It.* Berkeley: University of California Press, 2004. This introductory work for students provides an overview of the Yanomami vaccine scandal and discusses the ethics of the case.

Early, John D., and John F. Peters. *The Xilixana Yanomami of the Amazon: History, Social Structure, and Population Dynamics.* Gainesville: University Press of Florida, 2000. A study of the Yanomami before and after their contact with the modern world. Includes maps.

Peters, John F. *Life Among the Yanomami: The Story of Change Among the Xilixana on the Mucajai River in Brazil.* Peterborough, Ont.: Broadview Press, 1998. A study of the effects of modern world contact on the Yanomami, based on the author's experience of living with the Mucajai Yanomami of northern Brazil.

Tierney, Patrick. *Darkness in El Dorado: How Scientists and Journalists Devastated the Amazon.* New ed. New York: Norton, 2001. The 2000 book that brought widespread attention to the research methods and ethics of Chagnon and Neel. This edition includes a new afterword.

SEE ALSO: Mar. 21, 1928: Alberta Government Sterilizes Thousands Deemed Genetically and Mentally Unfit; Sept.-Oct., 1937: Prescription Elixir Causes More than One Hundred Deaths; 1956-1962: Prescription Thalidomide Causes Widespread Birth Disorders; July 25, 1972: Newspaper Breaks Story of Abuses in Tuskegee Syphilis Study; Nov. 26, 1997: Canadian Health Commissioner Releases Report on Tainted Blood.

September 19, 2000
EX-GAY LEADER JOHN PAULK IS PHOTOGRAPHED LEAVING A GAY BAR

John Paulk, chairman of the board for the conservative, Christian, "ex-gay" movement group Exodus International, was photographed leaving a Washington, D.C., gay bar in the fall of 2000. A former drag queen, Paulk married a woman after his experiences with Exodus and became its spokesperson. He also was a spokesperson for the conservative group Focus on the Family. Paulk claimed to have stopped at the bar to use the restroom, but not many believed him. He lost his position as Exodus board chairman.

LOCALE: Washington, D.C.

CATEGORIES: Publishing and journalism; public morals; sex; politics; social issues and reform

KEY FIGURES

John Paulk (b. 1963), Exodus International board chairman, 1995-2000, and author

Daryl Herrschaft (fl. early twenty-first century), bar patron who first spotted Paulk inside Mr. P's, a gay bar

Wayne Besen (b. c. 1971), journalist and gay activist

James Dobson (b. 1936), chairman of Focus on the Family

Anne Paulk (fl. early twenty-first century), Exodus member, author, and spouse of John Paulk

SUMMARY OF EVENT

In the year 2000, gay rights campaigning had reached into the legislatures of many U.S. states. For example, Vermont legalized gay civil unions that year, setting a favorable climate for gays and lesbians. Much of the controversy over gay rights had settled into debates about the morality of gay marriage. Conservative backlash against the movement remained strong, with right wing fundamentalist Christians leading the groups opposed to homosexuality.

Vermont's civil unions earned nationwide backlash, as voters in other states initiated constitutional amendments against same-gender marriage. Other groups, in particular, the Evangelical group Focus on the Family, hoped to "end" the practice of homosexuality altogether. With its claimed Christian focus on condemning the perceived sin, rather than the perceived sinner, the group hoped to convert gays and lesbians to heterosexuality. Focus on the Family's subgroup, Exodus International (Exodus), carried particular weight in what was called homosexual "conversions."

To that end, Exodus had two real stars. Board chairman and spokesperson John Paulk and his wife, Anne Paulk, claimed to be former gays who were now married with three children. John Paulk went on regular speaking tours to promote Exodus, with the hope of drawing other gays and lesbians to conversion. The couple wrote a book, *Love Won Out* (1998), and were featured on the cover of *Newsweek* magazine in 1998.

The "ex-gay" movement, as it is best known, became a source of much controversy. Opponents claimed it was a discriminatory farce. Gay rights activists argued that conversion groups produced more same-gender partnerships than traditional heterosexual ones, and that the groups caused irreversible emotional trauma. It came as no surprise then, that after Paulk went into a well-known gay bar in Washington, D.C., in 2000 and was exposed for doing so, the stage would be set for a noisy showdown between gay rights supporters and the activists of the ex-gay movement.

On September 19, Paulk was in Washington, D.C., participating in one of his many speaking tours for Exodus. While on his own time, he paid a visit to Mr. P's, a gay bar. Mr. P's, named for its location on P Street, existed in stark contrast to the other buildings on the block. Where those other buildings were brightly lit and modern looking, Mr. P's was stubbornly dark and concealing. The bar

913

Anne and John Paulk in 1998. (Hulton Archive/Getty Images)

had a policy against photographs being taken indoors, presumably to protect its clientele. While Paulk sat and chatted for forty minutes in the bar, he was recognized by another customer, Daryl Herrschaft, who also was a member of the gay rights lobbying organization Human Rights Campaign (HRC).

Cannily aware of what Paulk's presence in the bar could do to Exodus's reputation, Herrschaft contacted another HRC member, Wayne Besen, a journalist and gay activist. Besen rushed to the bar, camera in hand. In the dramatic showdown that followed, Besen was ejected from the bar for violating its policy against photography, but not before he had captured a fleeing Paulk on film outside the bar. From other customers, Besen learned Paulk had been flirting and using an alias.

Besen later published an exposé on Paulk that focused on his hypocrisy and the dangers of the ex-gay movement. Initially, Paulk claimed he had only stepped into the bar to use the restroom, but began chatting and stayed inside. To his credit, Paulk never pretended to have been on a conversion mission. However, given the length of his stay, the restroom excuse was quickly dismissed in both the popular press and among Paulk's colleagues who knew better.

James Dobson, chairman of Focus on the Family, confronted Paulk after the published exposé and demanded a full explanation for his apparently aberrant behavior. Paulk initially denied any homosexual inclinations, insisting he had both the support of Focus on the Family and his own wife. However, his explanation still did not hold up to scrutiny. Too many witnesses in the bar had seen him buy drinks for other men, heard him claim to be gay, and heard him use an alias from his own drag queen days. Finally, Paulk confessed that the pressures of the limelight made him want to escape, so he had been toying with the idea of again having sex with men. He quickly added that he was grateful to have been caught, feeling that God was protecting him from his own aberrant desires.

Focus on the Family removed him as Exodus's chairman of the board and sent a chaperone with him to speaking engagements. Although it was committed to supporting him, the group expressed its disappointment in what it considered a lapse in judgment, particularly as he lied about his motives until the truth was extracted from him. The group tried to downplay the incident, claiming that thousands had "escaped" homosexuality and that these successes should be considered more important than Paulk's aberrant behavior.

IMPACT

Paulk's lapse, however, effectively derailed the antigay and ex-gay movements at the height of their popularity. Although gay conversion groups, ex-gay ministries, and Exodus continued to exist, they no longer flourished. The scandal was used by gay rights supporters as an example that the ex-gay movement was harmful, and ultimately ineffective.

Exodus's choice in leadership came under heavy criticism from both sides, and the media gleefully picked apart Paulk and his hypocrisy.

For his part, Paulk continued in a lower leadership role with Focus on the Family, acting as the manager of homosexuality and gender issues until his resignation in 2003. He went on to become a chef and moved, with Anne, to Oregon, far from Washington, D.C.

Besen, in contrast, made a career out of Paulk's downfall. Always concerned with gay rights and already a vocal opponent of ex-gay ministries, Besen escalated the case against the ex-gay movement even after the hubbub over Paulk's lapse died down. Besen became executive director of the group Truth Wins OUT, which exposes hypocrisy within the ex-gay and antigay movements, started a weekly column on his own Web site, and published a book, *Anything but Straight*, in 2003. Furthermore, Besen educates parents thinking of sending their gay and lesbian children into conversion programs by demonstrating the psychological harm done by such programs.

—*Jessie Bishop Powell*

FURTHER READING

Besen, Wayne R. *Anything but Straight: Unmasking the Scandals and Lies Behind the Ex-Gay Myth.* New York: Harrington Park Press, 2003. Focuses on the hypocrisy of the gay conversion movement. Discusses "converts" who have suffered psychological harm and those who eventually affirmed a positive homosexual orientation after their participation in conversion programs.

Kirby, David. "After the Fall: Man Allegedly Cured of His Homosexuality Visits Gay Bar." *Advocate*, November 21, 2000. Examines the consequences of Paulk's being photographed at Mr. P's bar, including the loss of his position as board chairman of Exodus International.

Leland, John, et al. "Can Gays Convert?" *Newsweek*, August 17, 1998. Interviews with John and Anne Paulk discuss their support for the ex-gay movement. Also includes the words of those who oppose the movement, including gay rights activists and the American Psychological Association.

Muzzy, Frank. *Gay and Lesbian Washington, D.C.* Charleston, S.C.: Arcadia Press, 2005. Double focus on the presence of gays and lesbians in the U.S. capital and their impact on politics.

Paulk, John, and Anne Paulk. *Love Won Out: How God's Love Helped Two People Leave Homosexuality and Find Each Other*. Wheaton, Ill.: Tyndale House, 1999. Summarizes the couple's journey to heterosexuality with the help of ex-gay ministries and Christianity in general, as well as their own meeting and marriage. Generally argues that heterosexual love is stronger than homosexual love.

SEE ALSO: July 19, 1921: U.S. Senate Rebukes Navy in Homosexuality Investigation; Oct. 7, 1964: President Lyndon B. Johnson's Aide Is Arrested in Gay-Sex Sting; 1970: Study of Anonymous Gay Sex Leads to Ethics Scandal; Oct. 25, 1974: Evangelist Billy James Hargis Resigns College Presidency During Gay-Sex Scandal; Jan., 1977: Singer Anita Bryant Campaigns Against Lesbian and Gay Rights; Sept. 3, 1980: Congressman Bauman Is Arrested for Liaison with Teenage Boy; Dec., 1982: Julie Andrews and Blake Edwards Deny Being Gay; July 20, 1983: Congress Members Censured in House-Page Sex Scandal; Aug. 19, 2004: Blog "Outs" Antigay Congressman Edward Schrock; Nov. 2, 2006: Male Escort Reveals Sexual Liaisons with Evangelist Ted Haggard.

2000's

September 26, 2000
GYMNAST ANDREEA RĂDUCAN LOSES HER OLYMPIC GOLD MEDAL BECAUSE OF DRUGS

Sixteen-year-old Romanian gymnast Andreea Răducan was stripped of her gold medal in the women's individual all-around competition at the 2000 Summer Olympics in Sydney, Australia, after testing positive for the banned stimulant pseudoephedrine. The substance is a common ingredient in cold medicines, which she had been given by a team physician the night before her competition.

LOCALE: Sydney, New South Wales, Australia
CATEGORIES: Drugs; medicine and health care; sports

KEY FIGURES
Andreea Răducan (b. 1983), Romanian gymnast
Ioachim Oană (fl. early twenty-first century), Romanian Olympic team physician
Ion Tiriac (b. 1939), president of the Romanian Olympic Committee

SUMMARY OF EVENT
Andreea Răducan was born in Barlad, Romania, in 1983. She showed promise in gymnastics from an early age and was a top gymnast on the Romanian national team by the late 1990's. She lived and trained at the national training center in Deva. She became known for her high energy, skills, dance ability, and artistry, receiving comparisons to legendary Romanian gymnast Nadia Comaneci.

Răducan's specialties were the floor exercise, vault, and balance beam. She won the gold medal for the floor exercise finals and placed fifth in the individual all-around finals at the 1999 World Championships, and she was one of the top gymnasts in the world leading up to the 2000 Summer Olympic Games in Sydney, Australia.

At the 2000 Games, Răducan helped the Romanian women's gymnastics team earn the gold medal in the team competition, the first gold medal for Romania since the 1984 Summer Olympics in Los Angeles. Her scores in the team competition also qualified her for the individual all-around, floor exercise, and vault finals. She finished the preliminary round of the all-around finals with the second highest total score, just behind gold-medal favorite Svetlana Khorkina of Russia. Răducan went on to win the individual all-around gold medal in the controversial final round of the competition.

Halfway through the event, the vaulting apparatus was found to have been set to an incorrect height, a mistake that led a number of competitors to "crash"; however, there were few injuries. Khorkina had been among those who vaulted at the incorrect height and crashed. Răducan also vaulted at the incorrect height, but she completed the vault without serious error. Those who had competed at the incorrect height had the option of vaulting again, but Răducan chose not to do so. She became the first Romanian gymnast to win the Olympic individual all-around title since Comaneci at the 1976 Olympics. Romanian teammates Simona Amanar and Maria Olaru took the silver and bronze medals, respectively.

On September 26, a few days after the all-around competition, the Romanian team was notified that Răducan had tested positive for the stimulant pseudoephedrine, which was on the International Olympic Committee's (IOC) list of banned substances. She was stripped of her gold medal in the individual all-around event but was allowed to compete in the event finals, where she won the silver medal on the vault but faltered on her usually solid floor exercise to finish seventh of eight competitors. Răducan, her coaches, and Romanian Olympic Committee president Ion Tiriac protested the IOC's withdrawal of her gold medal, claiming that the pseudoephedrine had been in two tablets of Nurofen, a commonly available, over-the-counter cold medicine given to her by Romanian team physician Ioachim Oană to treat her fever and cough. The IOC rejected the protests, stating that although they believed Răducan did not knowingly ingest the substance and did not receive a performance benefit, they must enforce rules violations regardless of the circumstances.

As a result of the IOC decision, the individual all-around gold medal was awarded to second-place finisher Simona Amanar, who accepted it on behalf of Romania but qualified her acceptance by stating that Răducan was the rightful winner. Third-place finisher Olaru received the silver medal and fourth-place finisher Liu Xuan of China received the bronze medal. Răducan was allowed to keep her gold medal from the team competition and her sil-

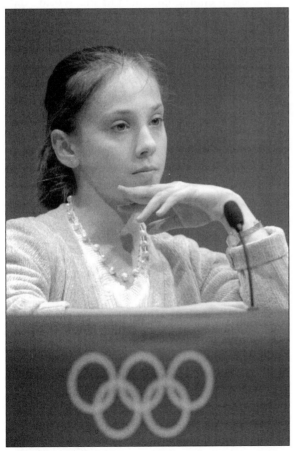

Andreea Răducan at a 2000 Summer Olympics news conference in Sydney, two days after losing her gold medal in the women's all-around gymnastics competition. (AP/Wide World Photos)

ver medal from the vault competition because she had not been tested for drugs after the team event and had passed a drug test after the event finals.

The decision to strip Răducan's medal created a wave of public sympathy for the young, petite Răducan, who did not meet the profile of an intentional doping violator. The same day her medal was stripped, Răducan and the Romanian Gymnastics Federation appealed the IOC's decision to the Court of Arbitration for Sport (CAS), the sporting world's highest court of appeal, based in Lausanne, Switzerland. An ad hoc CAS group, meeting in Sydney, ruled on September 28 that Răducan was innocent of any wrongdoing and that she had not gained a competitive advantage from the pseudoephedrine. However, it rejected her appeal to reinstate her gold medal for the individual all-around event. The court agreed with the IOC's rationale that regardless of the emotions or circumstances of the case, the Olympic antidoping code must be upheld in fairness to all athletes. Romanian team physician Oană was expelled from his job for the remainder of the Sydney Games and also was banned from the 2002 Winter Games in Salt Lake City and the 2004 Summer Games in Athens.

Răducan remained a popular figure to many both inside and outside gymnastics. The International Gymnastics Federation (IGF) also exonerated her of any wrongdoing and imposed no further sanctions, stating that the loss of her medal was punishment enough. She continued to train with and compete for the Romanian team and won five medals at the 2001 World Championships before retiring from the sport in 2002. After her retirement, she became a sports announcer, television-show host, and model and studied for a master's degree in journalism at the University of Bucharest. Oană kept his medical license but, in addition to his Olympic sanctions, received a four-year ban from the European championships and all IGF-sponsored events.

IMPACT

The withdrawal of Răducan's gold medal attracted worldwide media attention and highlighted the tougher IOC position on violations of its antidoping code. Despite the public's sympathy for Răducan,

2000's

917

many people believed nonetheless that preserving the fairness and integrity of the Games is more important for the integrity of the Olympics than any individual case.

At the time Rǎducan lost her medal, the IOC had been facing increasing public pressure to crack down on doping violators and uphold the Olympic movement's commitment to drug-free sport, a commitment that led to the more stringent antidoping policies. The uniqueness of Rǎducan's case, her proclaimed innocence, and her sympathetic nature would test the IOC's determination to enforce those policies. Its decision to follow its own rule and automatically disqualify an athlete regardless of the circumstances of the charges sent a message that accidental violations would not be tolerated, or defensible.

Oanǎ's suspension also sent the message that team physicians and other medical personnel working with athletes must know the ingredients of any and all medications they prescribe or otherwise supply, and that all persons affiliated with a team, not just athletes, could face sanctions for their carelessness.

—*Marcella Bush Trevino*

FURTHER READING

Begley, Sharon, and Devin Gordon. "Under the Shadow of Drugs: Doping—Tainted by Scandals, the IOC Starts to Crack Down." *Newsweek*, October 9, 2000. Places the Rǎducan scandal in the perspective of other doping violations at the 2000 Sydney Olympics and the public pressures that led to a stricter IOC antidoping policy.

Birchard, Karen. "Olympic Committee Bans Doctor After Doping Case." *The Lancet*, September 30, 2000. This article, in a respected medical journal, examines the case against the team physician who gave Rǎducan the medication containing the banned stimulant. Addresses the issue of physician responsibility.

Mihailovici, Sorin. "Recovery for Rǎducan: Losing the Olympic All-around Gold Has Made Andreea Rǎducan More Popular than Ever." *International Gymnast* 43, no. 1 (2001). Examines the impact of the scandal on Rǎducan's athletic career and discusses her future in gymnastics.

Pound, Richard W. *Inside the Olympics: A Behind-the-Scenes Look at the Politics, the Scandals, and the Glory of the Games.* Etobicoke, Ont.: John Wiley & Sons Canada, 2004. An inside view of the history of Olympic doping violations and scandals by a longtime member of the IOC and the founding chairman of the World Anti-Doping Agency.

Wilson, Wayne, and Ed Derse. *Doping in Elite Sport: The Politics of Drugs in the Olympic Movement.* Champaign, Ill.: Human Kinetics, 2001. Examines the movement for controlling drug use by Olympic athletes from the perspectives of science, history, social science, and politics.

SEE ALSO: June 30, 1994: Tonya Harding Is Banned from Skating After Attack on Rival; July 1, 1994: Soccer Star Diego Maradona Is Expelled from World Cup; Feb. 11, 2002: French Judge Admits Favoring Russian Figure Skaters in Winter Olympics; Mar. 17, 2005: Former Baseball Star Mark McGwire Evades Congressional Questions on Steroid Use; July 26, 2006: Tour de France Is Hit with a Doping Scandal; Oct. 5, 2007: Olympic Champion Marion Jones Admits Steroid Use.

November 5, 2000
JAPANESE AMATEUR ARCHAEOLOGIST'S "DISCOVERIES" ARE PROVEN FAKES

Amateur archaeologist Shinichi Fujimura, who had been credited with numerous major finds, was exposed as a fraud when the Japanese newspaper Mainichi Shimbun *published photographs of him burying finds he claimed to have discovered. This incident called into question the validity of his earlier work and caused a major scandal in Japan. Fujimura later admitted to fabricating all of his findings.*

ALSO KNOWN AS: Japanese paleolithic hoax

LOCALE: Tokyo, Japan

CATEGORIES: Forgery; hoaxes, frauds, and charlatanism; publishing and journalism; education; public morals; cultural and intellectual history

KEY FIGURES

Shinichi Fujimura (b. 1950), amateur archaeologist

Toshiki Takeoka (fl. early twenty-first century), archaeologist at Kyoritsu Women's University, Tokyo

Charles Keally (fl. early twenty-first century), American archaeologist at Sophia University, Tokyo

Toshiaki Kamata (fl. early twenty-first century), chairman of the Tohoku Paleolithic Institute

SUMMARY OF EVENT

On November 5, 2000, the Japanese were stunned by accusations of fraud involving one of Japan's most trusted and admired amateur archaeologists, Shinichi Fujimura. By the age of fifty, Fujimura was a leading amateur archaeologist, even though he had only a high school diploma and no formal training. He was nicknamed the Hand of God and God's Hand for his uncanny ability to find ancient artifacts.

The shy, humble father of two was working at an electronic-gadget manufacturing company in 1972 when he became interested in Japan's prehistory. Fujimura taught himself archaeology and, in 1981, had a major discovery when he found stoneware dating back 40 millennia. This discovery pushed Japan's ancient history back by 10 millennia. Fujimura's career and reputation took off, and he consistently found older artifacts as he worked on more than 180 other sites nationwide over a period of twenty years. He studied objects from the oldest of Japan's Paleolithic, or Stone Age, which dates back 600 to 1,200 millennia. The stone implements, or tools, Fujimura discovered date back 500, 600, and 700 millennia. Each discovery broke archaeological records and seemed to prove that the earliest habitation of Japan occurred 600 millennia ago and not 30 to 35 millennia ago as previously determined by the archaeological evidence.

In 1992, Fujimura made a major discovery in the Zazaragi ruins in the Miyagi Prefecture, which was the first unanimously confirmed early-middle Paleolithic site in Japan. Fujimura's finds at this site led to new avenues of research and were considered spectacular. Also in 1992, Fujimura and two trained archaeologists established the Tohoku Paleolithic Institute, a nonprofit organization in Tagajo, near Sendai, northeast of Tokyo. The institute supported the excavations of Paleolithic sites in Japan. Fujimura served as deputy director, or vice chairman. Toshiaki Kamata, an established archaeologist, served as the director.

Fujimura's findings were supported by many well-respected scientists, including anthropologists and archaeologists. Privately, some professionals expressed doubt about the age of the discoveries, but only a few expressed their doubts publicly. As early as 1985, two prominent archaeologists, the American Charles Keally from Sophia University in Tokyo and Toshiki Takeoka, a lecturer at Kyoritsu Women's University, also in Tokyo, claimed that the artifacts from one site were incorrectly

2000's

dated. Their criticisms were ignored and Keally was essentially told by other archaeologists to remain quiet about his doubts. Takeoka was forced to tone down a paper in 1997 by the editors of *Paleolithic Archaeology* when he questioned Fujimura's professionalism. Takeoka's paper was edited so that the most critical sections were removed. The editors believed these sections alluded to rumors of planted artifacts.

Because of his concerns, Takeoka encouraged journalists to watch Fujimura. Reporters had been tracking Fujimura for six months when they caught him planting artifacts, first in September, 2000, at the Soshinfudozaka ruins in Shintotsukawa, Hokkaido. The photographs, however, were not clear enough to present as evidence.

At the Kamitakamori ruins in Tsukidate, Miyagi Prefecture—about 186 miles northeast of Tokyo—Fujimura and his team announced the discovery of holes that may have held pillars or columns supporting dwellings, as well as stones believed to be more than 600 millennia old—one of the oldest indications of human habitation in Japan. On October 22, local journalists with hidden video cameras filmed Fujimura at one of the sites at dawn burying something that he had removed from his pocket. Hours later he "discovered" an artifact at the same place.

On November 5, the newspaper *Mainichi Shimbun* published three still images from the video that showed Fujimura burying the artifacts he later dug up and claimed as authentic and newly discovered. The paper published the images only after confirming the facts with Fujimura himself. In a press conference that same day, Fujimura admitted to planting many Stone Age artifacts but insisted that he had only done so at the Soshinfudozaka and Kamitakamori ruins and that all of his other finds were legitimate. He claimed that he had been tempted by the devil and by the need for the continued admiration of the archaeological community.

News of the scandal spread quickly and shocked the archaeologists who worked with Fujimura. Many defended the validity of his earlier finds, especially those who had excavated with him.

Kamata admitted that Fujimura's actions were foolish, but he also insisted that the deception involved only the two most recent sites. Fujimura resigned from Tohoku Paleolithic Institute and Kamata, as his boss, accepted full blame on behalf of the institute. Fujimura, who had been admitted to the Japanese Archaeology Association (JAA) in 1984, was expelled in 2000 after the scandal was revealed.

Shortly after the November 5 revelation, Fujimura was hospitalized after suffering an emotional breakdown. He spent the next several years in a psychiatric hospital, and all of his communication with the outside world was mediated by his doctor and lawyer. Because of his initial unavailability, it was not until May, 2001, that JAA representatives could begin five sessions of interrogation with Fujimura. Meanwhile, local governments were reexcavating the sites of his major finds. By October, with proof by others that he had faked the excavations at more than thirty sites, Fujimura admitted that all of his work was fabricated. The forgeries included sites that accounted for most of the archaeological record in Japan for the earliest period of the Paleolithic era. Fujimura wanted fame and felt pressured to continue making spectacular finds. The archaeological community was stunned and dismayed, as many of the sites were thought to be among the world's oldest human habitations.

In its report issued in May, 2002, the JAA's special investigative committee announced that none of the stone tools Fujimura identified as belonging to the Paleolithic period had academic value. Former chairman Kamata resigned from the Tohoku Paleolithic Institute, indicating that the reputation of the institute was irreparably damaged. The institute was dissolved in 2004. Fujimura eventually left the psychiatric institute, changed his name, and remarried. In 2007, he was reportedly living in a small town on the Pacific coast of Japan.

For more than twenty years, Fujimura's work was taught to children and featured in textbooks. He was a hero because his discoveries helped prove Japan's cultural uniqueness. Because archaeology is extremely popular in Japan and has been a source of great pride, the people not only felt betrayed by his fraud but also embarrassed.

IMPACT

Fujimura's method of deception was very effective, and it was difficult to detect a planted artifact unless someone was specifically looking for that item. No obvious signs of forgery existed because the planted tools were ancient, locations were favorable, and because the stone implements were dated by the stratum (layer of rock or soil) in which they were found, it was extremely difficult to differentiate between planted and real finds. Also, unusual archaeological discoveries were common, so archaeologists accepted Fujimura's sensational findings.

Fujimura also was very good at planting forgeries, often during the early morning hours but even with other people, including professionals and the press, watching him excavate. Because he was trusted and respected, any inconsistencies were explained away, ignored, or simply not noticed.

After the scandal, Fujimura critic Keally highlighted flaws in Japanese archaeology. He argued that findings were revealed at press conferences and circulated among the public and profession quickly but with little critical review or scholarly debate. Critic Takeoka said that the study of archaeology in Japan was not scholarly but rather based on the desire for incredible discoveries. Senior scholars, he said, are not challenged in Japan; to directly criticize another's work is considered a personal and professional insult.

The Fujimura scandal led the Japanese scientific community to call for major changes in how findings are announced to colleagues and the general public. Scientists also called for more time on analysis before claims were made, and for greater collaboration with foreign scientists, which would encourage more debate and raise the standards of scientific scholarship in Japan.

Japanese archaeologists and other prominent scientists, many of whom had based years of research on Fujimura's findings, found all of their work questioned, and the field itself was forced to reconsider how discoveries were verified. Trust eroded between the public and academia, as well as between colleagues, and the international reputation of Japanese archaeology suffered because of the scandal.

—*Virginia L. Salmon*

FURTHER READING

Keally, Charles T. "Dirt and Japan's Early Paleolithic Hoax." *Sophia International Review* no. 24 (2002). A look at the practice of archaeology in light of the Fujimura scandal. Written by one of Fujimura's major critics.

Normile, Dennis. "Japanese Fraud Highlights Media-Driven Research Ethic." *Science*, January 5, 2001. Discusses the impact of the revelation of Fujimura's fraud. Notes the major changes to the field of archaeology in Japan.

Romey, Kristin M. "'God's Hands' Did the Devil's Work." *Archaeology* 54, no. 1 (January-February, 2001). A brief journal article about the aftermath of Fujimura's hoax.

Wehrfritz, George, and Hideko Takayama. "With a Wave of God's Hand." *Newsweek International*, October 22, 2001. Examines the effects of Fujimura's hoax, and asks how the structure of the scientific community allowed it to happen.

Yamada, Shoh. "Politics and Personality: Japan's Worst Archaeology Scandal." *Asia Quarterly* 6, no. 3 (Summer, 2002). Detailed, well-balanced overview of the scandal and its far-reaching affect on Japanese archaeology and national pride. Includes discussion of the importance of archaeology in Japanese society.

SEE ALSO: Nov. 21, 1953: Piltdown Man Is Revealed to Be a Hoax; Mar. 23, 1989: Scientists' "Cold Fusion" Claims Cannot Be Verified; Spring, 1996: Physicist Publishes a Deliberately Fraudulent Article; Aug., 2002: Immunologist Resigns After Being Accused of Falsifying Research; Sept. 25, 2002: Inquiry Reveals That Physicist Jan Hendrik Schön Faked His Research; May 12, 2006: Scientist Is Indicted for Faking His Research on Creating Stem Cells.

2000's

December, 2000
SEXUAL ABUSE OF CHILDREN IN FRANCE LEADS TO THE OUTREAU AFFAIR

The Outreau affair was a child sex-abuse scandal that became a legal scandal. After social services alerted French prosecutors to suspected child sexual abuse, Thierry and Myriam Delay were tried for abusing their four children. The Delays admitted guilt and also implicated neighbors, creating fears of a pedophile network. Years later, cases against most of the accused, who had been incarcerated for up to thirty months while awaiting trial, were dismissed on appeal. The scandal led to major legal reform in France.

LOCALE: Outreau, France

CATEGORIES: Law and the courts; families and children; social issues and reform; sex crimes; public morals

KEY FIGURES

Myriam Delay (Myriam Badaoui; b. 1967), defendant
Thierry Delay (b. 1964), defendant
David Delplanque (b. 1973), defendant
Aurelie Grenon (b. 1980), defendant
Fabrice Burgaud (b. 1971), magistrate

SUMMARY OF EVENT

The discovery and investigation of a suspected pedophile and sex-abuse ring by authorities in Outreau, France, in December, 2000, filled the French public with horror and rage over allegations of the sexual abuse of children. Public condemnation soon shifted from the accused to the French justice system itself, in which many of the defendants were imprisoned for long stretches of time and tried based on little evidence and admittedly false accusations. The child sex-abuse scandal and the reported injustices that occurred during the investigation and trial came to be known as the Outreau affair and brought France's long-standing judicial system under scrutiny.

The Outreau child sex-abuse case began when social-service workers and teachers became concerned over the sexualized behaviors of Thierry and Myriam Delay's four children. Suspecting sexual abuse, social services staff contacted law enforcement about their observations. The Delay children were taken from their parents, placed in foster care, and questioned. The children told investigators that they were forced to perform sexual acts and watch pornographic films, and that they were molested and raped by their parents as well as some of their neighbors. Between 2001 and 2003, the children's testimonies as well as Myriam Delay's own allegations against others in the Outreau community led to an increase in the number of accused.

As the investigations came to a close, eighteen people had been charged with rape, torture, and the perpetration of barbaric acts against eighteen children, ages three to twelve, in a period of five years. Although pornographic material and sex toys had been confiscated from the Delay residence, the presence of physical evidence of child sex-abuse remained scarce. The majority of evidence gathered for the trial included, primarily, the psychological evaluations and testimonies of the children allegedly involved. The children were once again removed from the custody of their parents during the investigation and trial, and the accused were ordered to pretrial detention. One of the accused committed suicide by drug overdose after enduring over one year of pretrial incarceration. A total of seventeen adults were scheduled to go to trial over the sex-abuse allegations.

Under a firestorm of media coverage, the Outreau trial began in May, 2004, under the direction of a young magistrate, Fabrice Burgaud. In addition to the shocking stories of abuse detailed by the children, more evidence against the seventeen accused surfaced during Myriam Delay's testimony. She confessed that she and her husband,

Thierry Delay, sexually abused their children from 1995 to 2000. She also implicated her neighbors as participants in the abuse, and she explained that her own sexual victimization as a child influenced her decision to abuse her own children. The Delay's neighbors, David Delplanque and Aurelie Grenon, also confessed that they had sexually abused the Delay children.

Three critical developments changed the mood of the trial in November, 2004. First, Myriam Delay and Grenon retracted their statements about the criminal involvement of the other defendants. Second, Myriam Delay and Grenon were found to have fabricated parts of their testimonies. Third, the children's stories began to conflict with their own prior statements. Furthermore, the Delay children's stories were viewed with even more uncertainty because they also showed signs of psychological and emotional distress. Skepticism over the entire trial followed these revelations.

Nevertheless, Thierry and Myriam Delay were convicted of child abuse and rape and were sentenced to twenty and fifteen years, respectively, in prison. Delplanque and Grenon also were convicted of child abuse and rape and were sentenced to six and four years, respectively. Of the remaining thirteen defendants, seven were acquitted and released from pretrial detention while the remaining six were found guilty of child abuse. Great uncertainty over their guilt circulated until the accused appealed their convictions.

The Outreau appeals trial began on December 1, 2005, and lasted one day only. All six defendants were cleared of the charges against them. One leading reason the charges were dismissed was Myriam Delay's confession of falsely implicating her neighbors. Another reason was the weak physical and psychological evidence of sexual abuse coupled with the contradictory accounts of the children.

IMPACT

In the short term, the closure of the Outreau appeals trial marked the end of the five-year-long Outreau affair. However, in addition to affecting the children emotionally and physically, the scandal left a lasting scar on the acquitted, the public, and the French judicial system, which lost the public's confidence. Demands for legal reform followed the appeals trial.

Through detailed news coverage, the public soon learned about the pretrial mistreatment of the defen-

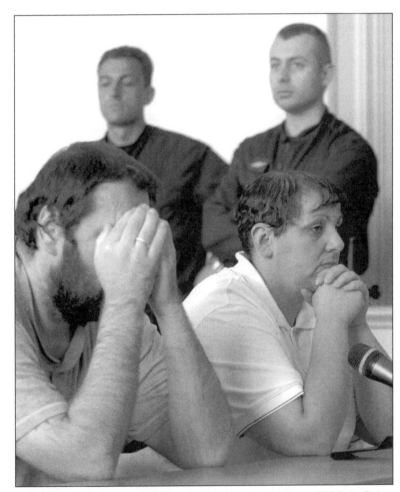

Defendants Thierry and Myriam Delay in court in June, 2004, in Saint-Omer, France. (Hulton Archive/Getty Images)

2000's

923

dants, including coerced confessions and personal losses. The media also revealed that the accused had been detained for long periods of time, some up to thirty months, before trial, were denied access to their children, and lost their jobs, marriages, and reputations. One of the defendants committed suicide prior to the trial. Outrage flared over France's pretrial detention procedures, which mandated that accused persons can remain in pretrial incarceration for up to five years. Magistrate Burgaud's inexperience as a trial judge was cited as a factor in why the case was poorly handled. Other factors were the contradictory roles and limitations placed on magistrates by the French justice system.

After the appeals ruling, French president Jacques Chirac, Prime Minister Dominique de Villepin, and Justice Minister Pascal Clément made an unprecedented apology to the wrongfully accused and promised judicial reform. In January, 2006, the French parliament ordered an investigation into the ineffective, embarrassing, and damaging legal proceedings of the case, considered a "judicial disaster" by Chirac and a "judiciary shipwreck" by others.

—Sheena Garitta

FURTHER READING

Bremner, Charles. "Outrage over Innocent Thirteen Jailed in Sex Abuse Scandal." *The Times* (London), January 20, 2006. Examines how the controversial events of the Outreau affair and the treatment of the accused during the investigations and trial prompted a government inquiry into law enforcement practices and the operations of the French judicial system.

"Exit Napoleon: The French Judicial System (The Outreau Affair)." *The Economist*, February 11, 2006. Offers a detailed account of the Outreau affair, pretrial events, the results of the trial and appeals, and the public's demand for change in France's justice system.

Hodgson, Jacqueline. "The Detention and Interrogation of Suspects in Police Custody in France: A Comparative Account." *European Journal of Criminology* 1, no. 2 (April, 2004): 163-199. An empirical study of the treatment of criminal suspects by French police before trial. A good source for any study of the French criminal justice system in the context of legal and judicial reform, especially reform demanded following the Outreau scandal.

_____. *French Criminal Justice: A Comparative Account of the Investigation and Prosecution of Crime in France*. Portland, Oreg.: Hart, 2005. A study of the French criminal justice system that includes discussion of the scandalous Outreau affair in the context of French law. Like Hodgson's 2004 study, this work is based on empirical research.

SEE ALSO: Mar. 2, 1906: Psychoanalyst Ernest Jones Is Accused of Molesting Mentally Disabled Children; Aug. 12, 1983-July 27, 1990: McMartin Preschool Is Embroiled in Child-Abuse Case; Mar., 1990: Menendez Brothers Are Arrested for Murdering Their Parents; Aug. 16, 1996: Belgian Media Reveal How Police Bungled Serial Murder Case; Mar. 4, 1999: Quebec Offers Support for Abused Duplessis Orphans; Jan. 30, 2001: Liverpool Children's Hospital Collects Body Parts Without Authorization; Dec. 18, 2003: Pop Star Michael Jackson Is Charged with Child Molestation.

2001

CLEARSTREAM FINANCIAL CLEARINGHOUSE IS ACCUSED OF FRAUD AND MONEY LAUNDERING

The Luxembourg-based financial clearinghouse Clearstream International faced public scrutiny for suspicious financial practices after the publication of the muckraking book Révélation$ *by Denis Robert and Ernest Backes. The authors accused the company of money laundering, tax evasion, managing unpublished bank accounts, and dealings with organized crime. The scandal revealed the lack of regulation and policing of financial institutions and their practices.*

LOCALE: Luxembourg

CATEGORIES: Corruption; banking and finance; business; publishing and journalism; hoaxes, frauds, and charlatanism

KEY FIGURES

Denis Robert (b. 1958), French investigative reporter

Ernest Backes (b. 1946), German author and former computer engineer and executive at Cedel

Régis Hempel (fl. early twenty-first century), former computer programmer at Clearstream

SUMMARY OF EVENT

Clearstream International was established in Luxembourg in January, 2000, through a merger of Cedel International and Deutsche Börse Clearing (DBC). Cedel was founded in 1971 to arrange transfers of U.S. dollars, or Eurodollars, deposited in banks outside the United States. DBC also performed money transfers but was not limited to Eurodollars. The founding of Clearstream combined the two companies into a single financial clearinghouse owned by the Deutsche Börse Group, based in Frankfurt, Germany.

Financial clearing is a banking industry service that facilitates the transfer of funds from one bank to another. This procedure is a matter of recording credits and debits. When bank A transfers a sum of money to bank B, the following occurs: Bank A instructs a clearinghouse, such as Clearstream, to debit its account for the sum of money agreed upon by the two banks and to credit bank B's account with the agreed-upon sum of money. This system is considered secure and quick and is used throughout the world. It is an essential element of financial transactions involving large sums of money and especially for transactions between banks operating in different currencies.

In addition to recording transfers of money, Clearstream and other financial clearinghouses maintain information on the financial position of banks in relation to other banks. This information is calculated each time a clearinghouse credits and debits accounts in the transfer of monies from one bank to another.

As early as March, 2000, the French government had issued a parliamentary report that addressed the difficulties of regulating financial activities and of preventing money laundering and other criminal activity in the realm of money transfers within Europe. The third section of the report dealt exclusively with Clearstream. On February 21, 2001, the tribunal of Luxembourg opened an investigation into possible financial manipulation by Clearstream. The tribunal found no evidence of systematic manipulation, although it did find evidence of accounting manipulation and tax evasion. No action was taken and the case was dropped on November 30, 2004, because a statute of limitations prevented prosecution.

In 2001, Denis Robert, an investigative reporter, and Ernest Backes, a former Cedel executive until he was fired in May, 1983, published *Révélation$*. The book reveals Clearstream's alleged role in the underground economy and claims the company's practices were unethical, even illegal. According to Robert and Backes, Clearstream was one of the major institutions that laundered money for banks and shell companies and for organized-crime groups.

Robert and Backes also claim that Clearstream played an important role in tax-evasion practices.

Furthermore, the book presents a detailed account of Clearstream's development of an automated system to provide unpublished accounts to banks and other clients. These claims were corroborated by Régis Hempel, a Clearstream computer programmer at the time the accounts were created. This system permitted the transfer of money without any public record or knowledge. The secret transfer of money facilitated both money laundering and tax evasion. Cedel had opened hundreds of unpublished accounts during the 1980's and 1990's.

Backes had been fired from Cedel allegedly because of an argument he had with an English banker who was a friend of the chief executive officer of Cedel. However, once the Banco Ambrosiano scandal broke during the early 1980's, Backes was convinced that he had been fired because of his knowledge of transactions between Cedel and Banco Ambrosiano. (Banco Ambrosiano, one of the major Italian banks, was implicated for money laundering funds obtained from drug and arms trafficking for organized crime and in channeling Vatican funds to revolutionary groups. The bank collapsed in 1982.)

Backes had worked with Gérard Soisson, who was the manager of Cedel and had the authority to open unpublished or secret accounts or decline them. Soisson was found dead on the island of Corsica while on vacation in July of 1983, just a few months after Backes's dismissal from Cedel.

After being fired from Cedel, Backes remained in Luxembourg to work in the stock market and eventually as manager of a butcher's cooperative. During this time, he still had friends at Cedel and began collecting the information that he and Robert would include in their book. They found that Soisson had used some discretion in granting unpublished accounts, and Backes discovered that after Soisson's death, the number of unpublished accounts at Cedel increased dramatically. Backes further discovered that Cedel had opened unpublished accounts for private companies. Backes and Robert claimed that Cedel/Clearstream had violated acceptable practices by opening secret accounts not only for banks but also for commercial and industrial companies. Robert later published a second book *La Boîte Noire* (2002), which explored issue of the unpublished accounts, or "black boxes," in greater detail.

Révélation$ brought to light other corrupt activities of Cedel and Cedel/Clearstream. One case involved the sale of six frigates to Taiwan by the French company Thomson-CSF. Joël Bûcher, an employee of the bank Société Générale, who said he left the bank after twenty years because of the money laundering that was a common practice, revealed the firm used Clearstream to launder money and keep bribes secret in the transaction.

Robert and Backes's book also led to an enormous number of lawsuits and investigations. Clearstream, and other financial institutions and individuals mentioned in the book, filed ten lawsuits for libel and defamation against Backes and Robert and the book's publisher, Arènes, in Luxembourg, France, Belgium, and Switzerland. In total, more than fifty lawsuits were filed against Robert alone. In 2003, a French court refused to award Clearstream 500,000 euros for claimed damages in its defamation case against Robert.

On June 10, 2008, a tribunal found against Robert and imposed a fine of 12,500 euros for defamation. The same day, Clearstream filed a lawsuit demanding 100,000 euros from Robert in a Luxembourg court, and the Paris bourse (stock market) recommended that he be sentenced for unlawful receipt of bank documents and dishonest reporting. Robert filed an appeal but refused to speak publicly about Clearstream or speak to the media.

IMPACT

The Clearstream scandal resulted in no major reforms in the regulation of clearinghouses and their practices, but the scandal had a significant impact on the public's awareness of clearinghouses and their function in the world of international finance. The transfer of large sums of money between countries and companies using different currencies would be almost impossible if not for the recording of transactions rather than the physical transfer of funds.

The scandal also revealed the lack of regulation and policing of financial institutions and their practices and the reluctance of courts around the world to interfere with the activities of these institutions. Also, the vast number of parliamentary commissions, judicial investigations, and trials convened as part of the Clearstream scandal show the complexity of the problem, given that the financial institutions involved do not operate in a single country nor under any one jurisdiction.

—*Shawncey Webb*

FURTHER READING

Coenen, Tracy. *Essentials of Corporate Fraud.* Hoboken, N.J.: John Wiley & Sons, 2008. An introductory guide to the white-collar crime of corporate fraud, written by a forensic, or investigative, accountant.

Loader, David. *Clearing, Settlement, and Custody.* Woburn, Mass.: Butterworth-Heinemann, 2002. A good explanation of how the finance-clearing industry functions and its critical importance to the global financial market.

Norman, Peter. *Plumbers and Visionaries: Securities Settlement and Europe's Financial Market.* New York: John Wiley & Sons, 2008. Discusses the Clearstream scandal and the work of Denis Robert. A comprehensive history of European finance clearing, how it started, and how it has changed.

SEE ALSO: Nov., 1929: Banque Oustric et Cie Failure Prompts French Inquiry; Jan. 8, 1934-Jan. 17, 1936: Stavisky's Fraudulent Schemes Rock French Government; May 28, 1970: Irish Politicians Are Tried for Conspiring to Import Weapons; Aug. 6, 1982: Banco Ambrosiano Collapses Amid Criminal Accusations; May 2, 1984: E. F. Hutton Executives Plead Guilty to Fraud; May 7, 1985: Banker Jake Butcher Pleads Guilty to Fraud; June 25, 1997: Swiss Banks Admit to Holding Accounts of Holocaust Victims; Dec. 23, 1998: Prominent Belgians Are Sentenced in Agusta-Dassault Corruption Scandal; Dec. 2, 2001: Enron Bankruptcy Reveals Massive Financial Fraud; Sept. 3, 2003: Mutual Fund Companies Are Implicated in Shady Trading Practices.

January 30, 2001
LIVERPOOL CHILDREN'S HOSPITAL COLLECTS BODY PARTS WITHOUT AUTHORIZATION

In 1992, following the death of a child at Alder Hey, a children's hospital in Liverpool, England, investigators looked into child mortality at the facility. This led to revelations about the treatment of dead children's bodies at Alder Hey and other National Health Service hospitals. In early 2001, investigators submitted their report on the matter, showing that hospitals were taking and keeping the organs and other body parts of thousands of dead children, and fetuses, without parental consent.

ALSO KNOWN AS: Alder Hey inquiry
LOCALE: Liverpool, England

CATEGORIES: Medicine and health care; government; families and children; public morals; corruption

KEY FIGURES

Dick van Velzen (b. 1950), Dutch professor of pathology at Alder Hey, 1988-1995

Alan Milburn (b. 1958), British secretary of state for health, 1999-2003

Michael Redfern (b. 1949), queen's counsel and medical law expert

Liam Donaldson (b. 1949), chief medical officer, British Department of Health

2000's

927

SUMMARY OF EVENT

Alder Hey children's hospital, near Liverpool, is one of the most respected children's hospitals in England and one of the largest children's hospitals in Western Europe. With two other leading children's hospitals, Great Ormond Street Hospital for Children in London and the Birmingham Children's Hospital, Alder Hey was caught up in a scandal that developed through the 1990's and was finally exposed to the public on January 30, 2001, with the publication of *The Report of the Royal Liverpool Children's Inquiry*, best known as the Redfern Report. The hospitals had been keeping the organs and body parts of deceased children, and fetuses, without the full consent of the parents of the deceased.

The scandal came to light indirectly. In 1996, Helen Rickard, the mother of Samantha Rickard, an infant who had died while undergoing open heart surgery at Bristol Royal Infirmary (BRI) in 1991, asked for the medical records of her daughter. She had heard of the unusually high number of deaths of children at BRI while undergoing heart surgery. These figures became known through new audit procedures instituted by the British National Health Service (NHS). Upon receiving the records, Rickard discovered a letter from the pathologist who had carried out Samantha's postmortem, stating that he had retained her heart. Shocked, she asked for its return.

Concern about BRI's poor performance and the news of the retention of the infant's heart led to the formation of a parents' action group. In February, 1999, group members called a press conference to inform the public about the retained heart. With other medical concerns about BRI, the press conference led the British government to form a public inquiry into the matter. In September, one of the witnesses at the inquiry testified under oath that Alder Hey routinely kept a large number of stored hearts of children who had undergone postmortems, and that it had been doing so since about 1948.

This fairly sensational news led to a public uproar, and the Labour government, under Health Minister Alan Milburn, promptly set up another inquiry to be chaired by Michael Redfern, a leading medical barrister (attorney) and the queen's counsel in the north of England. He was to be assisted by Jean Keeling, a consultant pediatric pathologist at the Royal Hospital for Sick Children in Edinburgh, Scotland, and a noted medical author, and Elizabeth

---

THE REDFERN REPORT

The Redfern Report on the organs scandal at Alder Hey children's hospital was released on January 30, 2001. It included the following section, "Handling the News of Organ Retention from September, 1999," which condemns all involved in the scandal.

Alder Hey and the University [of Liverpool] should have retained a paediatric pathologist to head a team to catalogue the retained organs and fragments in September 1999. This exercise would have revealed the impossibility of accounting accurately for all the organs retained because of poor record keeping and unrecorded research access to the organs. Neither Alder Hey nor the University will ever be able accurately to tell parents what happened to every organ of every child who died between 1988 and 1995. The University has never accepted its responsibility in the matter and has left Alder Hey to make a sequence of mistakes. These include four or five attempts to provide parents with accurate information relating to organ retention, not learning from and compounding mistakes made in each previous attempt. The cerebellum collection and the eye collection should have been identified and revealed earlier by both Alder Hey and the University.

Alder Hey failed to make sufficient provision for face to face communication of the news of organ retention to parents. They failed to provide suitable advice, counselling and support necessary to affected families. Even though Alder Hey were [sic] faced with a unique situation in terms of the amount and condition of organs at Myrtle Street, there was a lack of proper management which resulted in the dripfeeding of information to parents and the provision of information which was frequently inaccurate. No proper attempt at cataloguing was carried out until June 2000. The result was that each piece of news given to parents had the cumulative effect of exacerbating their reaction. From the outset they should have retained a Consultant Psychologist to assist in devising the best method for approaching parents affected.

Powell, chief officer of the Liverpool Community Health Council. They were given broad terms of reference and were instructed to one, inquire into the extent of the organ retention of children who had undergone postmortem examination and to what extent this had been done legally, and two, inquire into the roles of supervisory agents and any "such other issue relating to the above matters." In particular, the panel was to look into illegalities relating to the Human Tissue Act of 1961.

The panel was asked to report back by March, 2000, but the evidence was so extensive that the due date was extended to the end of the year. The panel's Redfern Report totaled six hundred pages. The health minister was shown a copy on January 26, 2001, and it was released to the public on January 30. Government officials expected such a furor after the report's release that police surrounded Alder Hey hospital. Relatives of the deceased children gathered at the Adelphi Hotel in central Liverpool.

The report was incredibly damning, and its chief focus was a former professor of pathology at Alder Hey who had worked under a contract from the University of Liverpool. The pathologist was Dutchman Dick van Velzen, who had worked at the hospital from 1988 to 1995. The inquiry found that from his initial interview he had lied about his credentials and his activities. The report cited twenty areas of malpractice during his seven years at Alder Hey. The hospital had retained some body parts before he arrived, but the practice mushroomed after his arrival, and, in some cases, it involved retention even without parental consent (or contrary to parental refusal).

The report criticized others as well, especially the management teams of Alder Hey and the University of Liverpool. Independent assessors had told management teams at the hospitals about inadequate staffing of the pathology departments, but they were ignored. However, it was primarily the sheer lack of supervision that accounted for the growth of the malpractice cases, plus the failure of professional colleagues to raise the alarm. A particular coroner, Roy Barter, was singled out for his poor record-keeping. The report also attacked the management's paternalism: Parents found they had very little say as to what happened to their dead children. It was assumed the medical team knew best, and that there existed a general policy of "assumed consent." Even when the scandal was breaking, management responded slowly to parents' concerns, and management was late in informing families and in returning body parts to those who requested them.

The inquiry also looked at the wider practice within the National Health Service and found evidence of some 104,000 children's body parts, organs, and fetuses being stored at more than two hundred facilities. The problem was thus much more extensive than the actions of one pathologist at one hospital. Furthermore, nearly one-half million tissue samples were also being held by hospitals. At Alder Hey, storage space had run out, and a nearby hospital was being used to store the overflow. Alder Hey and the Birmingham Children's Hospital also gave thymus glands to a pharmaceutical company in return for research funds.

Concurrent with the inquiry was the investigation of Liam Donaldson, the government's chief medical officer, who was instructed to report on organ retention at the national level, to look at the consent procedures in place, and to make recommendations for their improvement. Donaldson's findings were published as *Human Bodies, Human Choices: The Law on Human Organs and Tissue in England and Wales—A Consultation Report*, on July 1, 2002. The report found that the system of "assumed consent" should be replaced by a much more fully explicit statement of consent. He also found that more than fifty thousand organs, body parts, and fetuses were held by pathology services throughout Great Britain, a figure that reinforced the numbers in the Redfern Report.

After the inquiry, four members of the hospital staff, including the chief executive, were immediately suspended. The inquiry turned over its evidence to both the General Medical Council (GMC) for England and Wales and police. The GMC eventually banned van Velzen from practicing in Great Britain, but local police and the Crown Prosecution Service could not put together a strong enough case to warrant a criminal action against the pathologist, leading to further public outrage.

2000's

IMPACT

Health secretary Milburn accepted the report in full when it was debated in an emergency session of the British parliament. He promised a special commission to oversee the return of all organs and tissues to the families involved, if so requested. He would begin a review of the coroner's system and also of the accountability and management systems where universities and National Health Trusts worked together. Finally, he promised full support for all families at the time of their bereavement.

Early in 2003, the Alder Hey families received just over five thousand pounds (about ten thousand U.S. dollars) each in an out-of-court settlement totaling five million pounds (about twenty million U.S. dollars). By 2004, about two thousand families had filed suit against the National Health Service in the British High Court. That same year, all unidentified bodies were buried, over a short time, at Allerton Cemetery in Liverpool.

The greatest impact of the scandal was the revamping of the whole system of obtaining consent for the retention of body parts. Initially, health and medical officials feared that parental refusal would drastically reduce the needed supply of parts for medical research, but this has proven not to be the case. The procedures for aborted and miscarried fetuses also have been regularized to some extent, though many critics say that insufficient regard for human dignity still exists. Institutional mentalities tend always to be paternalistic, even indifferent, in such cases.

—David Barratt

FURTHER READING

Cowley, Christopher. *Medical Ethics, Ordinary Concepts, and Ordinary Lives.* New York: Palgrave Macmillan, 2008. Argues that the best starting point for discussions of medical ethics is "the actual words and deeds of ordinary people in ordinary disagreements." Includes a chapter on the Alder Hey scandal and inquiry and another on the postmortem.

The Times (London), January 30-31, 2001. A full investigative report of the inquiry's findings and subsequent Parliamentary debate on the matter.

Weir, Robert F., Robert Olick, and Jeffrey Murray. *The Stored Tissue Issue: Biomedical Research, Ethics, and Law in the Era of Genomic Medicine.* New York: Oxford University Press, 2004. Examines the Alder Hey inquiry in the context of concurrent developments in genetic science, law, and medical ethics. Argues that the inquiry had a major role in these developments.

SEE ALSO: Mar. 2, 1906: Psychoanalyst Ernest Jones Is Accused of Molesting Mentally Disabled Children; Feb. 23, 1943: Irish Orphan School Fire Kills Thirty-five Girls; 1956-1962: Prescription Thalidomide Causes Widespread Birth Disorders; July 25, 1972: Newspaper Breaks Story of Abuses in Tuskegee Syphilis Study; Aug. 12, 1983-July 27, 1990: McMartin Preschool Is Embroiled in Child-Abuse Case; Sept. 19, 1988: Stephen Breuning Pleads Guilty to Medical Research Fraud; Aug. 16, 1996: Belgian Media Reveal How Police Bungled Serial Murder Case; Nov. 26, 1997: Canadian Health Commissioner Releases Report on Tainted Blood; Mar. 4, 1999: Quebec Offers Support for Abused Duplessis Orphans; Dec., 2000: Sexual Abuse of Children in France Leads to the Outreau Affair; Feb. 17, 2002: Rotting Human Bodies Are Found at Georgia Crematory.

February 18, 2001

CIA Agent Robert Hanssen Is Arrested for Spying for the Russians

As one of the most effective spies in U.S. history, FBI agent Robert Hanssen sold secrets to the Soviet Union and Russia for more than twenty years. His espionage led to one of the most damaging cases of the breaching of national security in the history of the United States. Hanssen was sentenced to life imprisonment, avoiding the death penalty for treason, by pleading guilty to fifteen counts of espionage and conspiracy.

Locale: Vienna, Virginia

Categories: Espionage; government; organized crime and racketeering; corruption; law and the courts

Key Figures

Robert Hanssen (b. 1944), FBI counterintelligence agent and spy for the Soviet Union and Russia
Louis Freeh (b. 1950), FBI director, 1993-2001
Victor Cherkashin (b. 1932), Soviet KGB intelligence officer, 1952-1991

Summary of Event

Robert Hanssen, a counterintelligence officer with the Federal Bureau of Investigation (FBI) stationed in Washington, D.C., had access to large amounts of secret federal government information that he willingly sold to the Soviets and Russians. Hanssen approached the Soviets with the offer to give them U.S. secrets by writing a note and dropping it into the vehicle of a member of the Soviet embassy in Washington, D.C.

Victor Cherkashin became the Soviet case officer and handled communications with Hanssen until he retired. Hanssen, whose job with the FBI was to track spies working in the United States under diplomatic cover, kept his identity a secret from the Soviets to lessen his chances of being caught. He also asked for very little money and did not

spend in an extravagant manner. He dictated all of his tradecraft to the Soviets and was extremely careful.

In November, 2000, an unknown person clandestinely smuggled a file to FBI headquarters in Washington, D.C., from Moscow. The file contained information regarding the suspected mole, or embedded double agent, within U.S. intelligence. Included in the file was a list of the six thousand pages that this mole had turned over to the Russians. FBI investigators began to collect all documents that had been passed to the Russians and then searched for clues that would lead them to a suspect. The actual name of the mole was never used in the file, though there was some discussion regarding the mole's promotions and assignments, with dates. There also was a tape recording of a telephone conversation between the mole and a KGB officer. The FBI counterintelligence agents listened to the tape and recognized the voice as that of Hanssen.

A former KGB agent who turned defector also turned over another critical piece of evidence to the FBI: a plastic bag. Hanssen had used plastic trash bags to cover up the documents he passed to Russian intelligence. The FBI was able to pull two usable fingerprints from the bag, both of which matched Hanssen's fingerprints. Agent Hanssen was then placed under surveillance.

The FBI stationed Hanssen at its headquarters to work in the new Information Resources Division. His office was bugged and his telephones were tapped. He was being followed when he drove by Foxstone Park, his dead-drop site in nearby Vienna, Virginia, looking for a signal from his Russian handlers. By the end of January, 2001, the FBI had searched through Hanssen's Ford Taurus. They discovered chalk used for signaling, tape, garbage bags, and classified documents, which were related to ongoing FBI counterintelligence operations. A few days later, agents searched Hanssen's office,

Robert Hanssen. (AP/Wide World Photos)

where they found communications between Hanssen and Soviet-Russian intelligence.

Hanssen began to suspect that his new position was useless and that he was under surveillance. He claimed his car was bugged and that he could hear burst transmissions in his vehicle. He also wrote his final letter to Russian intelligence. In the letter he stated that he was breaking off contact for now but would contact the Russians again in one year.

On Sunday, February 18, 2001, the FBI arrest team was assembled and ready. They followed Hanssen as he drove a friend to Dulles Airport and then headed for Foxstone Park. On the way, he pulled into the parking lot of a shopping plaza and added a few more documents to his package for the drop. The FBI team relayed details of its surveillance to headquarters. Hanssen then drove to Foxstone Park, parked his car, entered the woods, and slipped the package underneath a bridge. He headed back to his car and was confronted by the FBI team, which arrested him.

FBI agents informed Hanssen's wife, Bonnie, that her husband had been arrested for espionage. Upon being questioned, she revealed that Hanssen first sold secrets to the Soviets as early as 1979. The FBI believed 1985 was the year he first contacted the Soviets.

Hanssen's arrest was announced on February 20 by FBI director Louis Freeh. Reporters discovered that Hanssen was arrested while making another document drop. Freeh briefly discussed the file the FBI received from the Russians. He added that Hanssen's espionage was a severe breach of national security. However, Freeh did not reveal the extent of the case, including that Hanssen had spied for the Soviets—and later the Russians—over a period of more than twenty years.

IMPACT

Hanssen's exploits had extremely grave consequences for U.S. security, but it is unlikely that the extent of his espionage will ever be known. What is known is that he had given the Soviets and Russians close to six thousand pages of documents and more than twenty computer disks of highly sensitive, classified information from the FBI, the CIA, the Pentagon, and perhaps most damaging, the National Security Agency. He compromised numerous intelligence sources who were embedded in Russia and U.S. intelligence efforts as a whole. He revealed the names of Russians who were working as double agents for the United States (many of whom were executed upon returning home to the Soviet Union). He informed the Russians of attempts by the United States to recruit double agents and disclosed U.S. counterintelligence techniques, which may have allowed the Russians to operate more effectively in the United States and evade surveillance or capture.

Hanssen's arrest was particularly damaging to the U.S. intelligence community as well because it revealed that even a trusted FBI agent could deceive superiors and continue spying without being detected. The FBI was now faced with damage control and a public relations nightmare. The Hanssen case came just a few years after that of agent Aldrich Ames of the U.S. Central Intelligence Agency, who was arrested for selling secrets, also to the Soviet Union. FBI director Freeh resigned because of the fallout from the Hanssen case, and the FBI also faced independent investigations about the breach of security.

—*Michael W. Cheek*

FURTHER READING

Cherkashin, Victor, with Gregory Feifer. *Spy Handler: Memoir of a KGB Officer.* New York: Basic Books, 2005. An account of Hanssen's espionage by the Soviet agent who was a main contact for Hanssen.

Havill, Adrian. *The Spy Who Stayed Out in the Cold: The Secret Life of FBI Double Agent Robert Hanssen.* New York: St. Martin's Press, 2001. A psychological study of Hanssen that also provides some background on his life before the FBI. Includes a bibliography.

Vise, David A. *The Bureau and the Mole: The Unmasking of Robert Philip Hanssen, the Most Dangerous Double Agent in FBI History.* New York: Atlantic Monthly Press, 2002. An account by a reporter for *The Washington Post.* Includes copies of e-mails and notes written by Hanssen and an appendix that summarizes the secrets he sold.

West, Nigel. *Historical Dictionary of Cold War Counterintelligence.* Lanham, Md.: Scarecrow Press, 2007. Provides a detailed history of not only the Hanssen espionage case but also Cold War-era spy cases in general. Focuses on the compromised security of the CIA.

Wise, David. *Spy: The Inside Story of How the FBI's Robert Hanssen Betrayed America.* New York: Random House, 2002. Study by a noted expert on intelligence services, written with the help of a psychiatrist who interviewed Hanssen following his arrest.

SEE ALSO: Jan. 21, 1950: Alger Hiss Is Convicted of Perjury; Sept. 12, 1962: British Civil Servant Is Arrested for Spying; Mar. 4, 1966: Munsinger Sex and Spy Scandal Rocks Canada; Aug. 19, 1985: West German Counterintelligence Chief Defects to East Germany; Mar. 2, 2003: U.S. National Security Agency Is Found to Have Spied on U.N. Officials.

April 30, 2001
WASHINGTON INTERN CHANDRA LEVY DISAPPEARS

Chandra Levy, an intern with the Federal Bureau of Prisons, disappeared just days before she was to return home to California. U.S. Congress member Gary Condit later admitted to having had a sexual relationship with Levy while she was in Washington, D.C., but he was never officially named a suspect in her disappearance. Levy's body was found in a park close to her D.C. apartment, one year after she disappeared. Condit's political career was ruined by the scandal.

LOCALE: Washington, D.C.

CATEGORIES: Murder and suicide; politics; law and the courts; public morals; sex

KEY FIGURES

Chandra Levy (1977-2001), Federal Bureau of Prisons intern and graduate student

Gary Condit (b. 1948), U.S. representative from California, 1989-2003

Susan Levy (fl. early twenty-first century), Chandra Levy's mother

Linda Zamsky (fl. early twenty-first century), Chandra Levy's aunt

SUMMARY OF EVENT

Chandra Levy had been nearing the end of her time as an intern with the Federal Bureau of Prisons in Washington, D.C. Levy, a University of Southern California graduate student in public administration, was last seen alive on April 30, 2001, doing errands, and her last e-mail correspondence with her family was made the next day. She was scheduled to return home to her family in Modesto, California, but she never made it there.

Levy's family soon reported her missing, and investigators began a search of her Washington, D.C., apartment. In addition to finding her identification there, they found that she had been packed to permanently leave the apartment. They also discovered that she, or someone in her apartment, had used her computer to search the Web for Rock Creek Park, located four miles from her apartment. (This park would play a part in the scandal as the case evolved.) Investigators immediately searched the park but found no body.

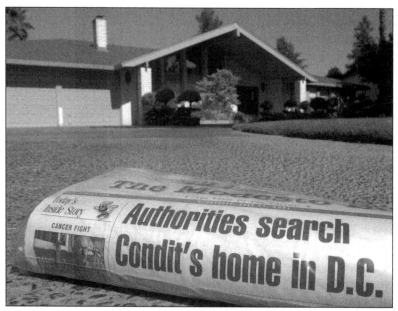

The Modesto Bee *outside the home of the parents of Chandra Levy on July 11, 2001. The local newspaper had extensive coverage of Levy's disappearance and the ensuing scandal involving Modesto-area Congress member Gary Condit.* (AP/Wide World Photos)

Investigators continued to search for Levy through the next several weeks. Levy's aunt, Linda Zamsky, told investigators in July that her niece had confided in her and told her that she had been having an affair with U.S. representative Gary Condit, who represented Levy's hometown of Modesto. Within a day and more than two months after the former intern's disappearance, Condit finally admitted to having an affair with Levy. Condit, who was married and had two children, was twenty-nine years older than Levy. Although Condit never was officially considered a suspect in Levy's disappearance and murder, the media focused on him nonetheless. Levy's parents, Susan and Robert Levy, also remained suspicious of Condit throughout the investigation. They also hired a public relations company to handle press inquiries, and they made several appearances on television to appeal for help in finding their daughter.

One person of interest to authorities had been Ingmar Guandique, a young Salvadoran immigrant who was convicted of assaulting two women at

Rock Creek Park in Washington, D.C. He was questioned by police but never charged in the disappearance of Levy. However, Guandique's victims, who survived their attacks, noted that he had approached them from behind while they were jogging and listening to their portable miniature radios, a method of attack that would later resonate in the Levy case.

Just over one year later, on May 22, 2002, parts of Levy's decomposed body were found in Rock Creek Park. A man walking his dog came upon a human skull that was later determined to be Levy's through matching dental records. Her remains were scattered, and investigators concluded she had been murdered at the park on May 1, 2001. Even though the area had been searched one year earlier, experts argued that they missed the body the first time because it was located in a desolate spot. The park, at more than 1,700 acres, is large. Unfortunately, her remains were so decomposed that medical examiners found it difficult to determine exactly how she died. They named her death a homicide in the weeks following the discovery of her remains.

Condit lost credibility during the scandal and

was not reelected. He left Congress in January, 2003, and with his family bought several Baskin-Robbins ice-cream franchise stores after relocating to Arizona. Even that venture ended in controversy, as the Condits were sued over management issues and their franchise license was revoked. Condit was interviewed in January, 2008, and expressed sadness about Levy's death, but he also appeared to have moved on from the scandal.

IMPACT

The Levy-Condit scandal resonated for several reasons, including the following: Levy was having an affair with a U.S. politician, and that politician represented her hometown. She disappeared without a trace of foul play. Her body was found in a park not far from her apartment—and Condit's apartment. Condit was secretive about the affair until finally admitting the relationship two months after Levy's disappearance, but he did so only after being pressured to come forward. The affair reminded the public of the affair between President Bill Clinton and another former intern, Monica Lewinsky, from a few years earlier.

The Levy-Condit scandal resonated for another reason: its sensationalism and the intense media attention it received. The story riveted the nation for months and subsided only after another story became the number-one news item: the terrorist attacks of September 11, 2001. After this date, media coverage of Levy's disappearance rapidly declined, but it resurfaced somewhat when her body was found a few months later.

Levy's murder remains unsolved. Her family established a Web site in her memory, hoping as well that someone might come forward with information on how Levy was killed, and by whom. In addition, Susan Levy continued her work as an advocate for victim's rights, assisting other parents who have lost their children, and has received awards for her efforts. In particular, she has lobbied for the rights of victims in cases that remain cold, or unsolved. She remained steadfast in her criticism of Condit, claiming the congressman had something to do with her daughter's disappearance and murder.

—*Gina Robertiello*

FURTHER READING

Daugherty, Ralph. *Murder on a Horse Trail: The Disappearance of Chandra Levy.* New York: iUniverse, 2004. A computer programmer drawn to the case of Chandra Levy's disappearance and murder examines the facts and attempts to explain what happened. Written in an easy-to-read style. Recommended for general readers.

Murphy, Dean E. "Hope, and a Frenzy, Fade in a Missing-Person Case." *The New York Times*, March 4, 2003. Article discusses the link between the Chandra Levy case and Laci Peterson case. Both young women were from Modesto, California.

Seelye, Katherine Q. "Police Say Intern was Slain, but They Do Not Know How." *The New York Times*, May 29, 2002. Article explains the circumstances surrounding the discovery of Chandra Levy's skeletal remains at Rock Creek Park. Because of the condition of the remains, experts were not able to confirm how she was killed, or how she died.

Sowell, Thomas. *Controversial Essays.* Stanford, Calif.: Hoover Institution Press, 2002. In a brief chapter, the author examines clues that he believes may have been overlooked in the investigation of Chandra Levy's disappearance.

Wecht, Cyril H., Mark Curriden, and Angela Powell. *Tales from the Morgue: Forensic Answers to Nine Famous Cases.* Amherst, N.Y.: Prometheus Books, 2005. Several high-profile cases, including that of Chandra Levy, are examined by a forensic pathologist. Demonstrates the methods, evidence, and the pathology techniques used to analyze a case. Hypothesizes that Levy was strangled.

Weiss, Mike. "Still No Answers." *San Francisco Chronicle*, May 22, 2007. Updated review of the Levy case, determining that there are still no answers regarding who committed the crime. Susan Levy was interviewed for the article, which notes that she meets every year with the Washington, D.C., police chief.

SEE ALSO: Oct. 7, 1974: Congressman Wilbur D. Mills's Stripper Affair Leads to His Downfall;

2000's

July 20, 1982: Conservative Politician John G. Schmitz Is Found to Have Children Out of Wedlock; July 20, 1983: Congress Members Censured in House-Page Sex Scandal; Mar., 1990: Menendez Brothers Are Arrested for Murdering Their Parents; Jan. 17, 1998: President Bill Clinton Denies Sexual Affair with a White House Intern; Dec. 5, 2002: Senator Trent Lott Praises Strom Thurmond's 1948 Presidential Campaign; Sept. 29, 2006: Congressman Mark Foley Resigns in Sex Scandal Involving a Teenage Page.

June 18, 2001
AWARD-WINNING HISTORIAN JOSEPH J. ELLIS IS ACCUSED OF LYING

The Boston Globe *reported that American historian Joseph J. Ellis had frequently lied to his students and others about serving in the Vietnam War. Ellis also lied about, or greatly exaggerated, his participation in other major events of the 1960's, including the peace and Civil Rights movements. The Ellis scandal sparked a heated debate about ethical issues of personal and professional integrity for academics.*

LOCALE: South Hadley, Massachusetts
CATEGORIES: Hoaxes, frauds, and charlatanism; publishing and journalism; cultural and intellectual history; education; ethics

KEY FIGURES
Joseph J. Ellis (b. 1943), American historian
Walter V. Robinson (b. 1949), *Boston Globe* reporter
Joanne V. Creighton (b. 1942), president of Mount Holyoke College

SUMMARY OF EVENT
By mid-2001, Joseph J. Ellis must have felt a quiet satisfaction after twenty-nine years as a respected historian, teaching at Mount Holyoke College. A fifty-seven-year-old Yale University-educated professor of history at a prestigious women's college in central Massachusetts, Ellis was among the best-known and most respected faculty members on campus. He had risen rapidly at Mount Holyoke. By 1978, within six years of his arrival, he was chairman of the history department, and by 1980 he was dean of the college faculty. For eight months in 1984, he was the interim college president.

Ellis's scholarship and teaching credentials also were outstanding. His biography of Thomas Jefferson, the latest of his eight books on early American history, had just won the Pulitzer Prize. His teaching, as measured by course evaluations, ranked consistently among the finest in the college. However, his claim to have seen combat in the Vietnam War apparently aroused suspicion. Alerted by an anonymous tip, *Boston Globe* investigative reporter Walter V. Robinson began to check the authenticity of some of Ellis's stories, recounted not only in class but also in interviews with reporters. The award of a Pulitzer Prize to Ellis convinced Robinson to complete and publish the results of his investigation on the celebrated scholar.

Robinson's article, "Professor's Past in Doubt: Discrepancies Surface in Claim of Vietnam Duty," broke on page one of the *Boston Globe* on June 18, 2001. The article stated that over a period of close to twenty years, Ellis had persistently lied about his wartime experiences to his classes at Mount Holyoke. The charges stunned Ellis's students and colleagues. Most agreed that he was a gifted storyteller. His lecture style was dynamic and was enriched by humor and personal anecdotes. He seemed to empathize with the people and topics he was discussing. Course evaluations described him as displaying a close personal relationship with his subject, leaving a kind of "you-are-there" impression with his audience. However, at some point Ellis crossed the line. In his Vietnam in American Society course, he began to claim by the early 1980's that he had taken part in combat operations and top-level planning in Vietnam.

As detailed in the *Boston Globe* article, Ellis claimed that he had parachuted into Vietnam in 1965 as a young platoon leader with the fabled 101st Airborne Division. He claimed also to have led a mop-up operation in the vicinity of My Lai in March, 1968, shortly before the massacre in that Vietnamese village. Finally, he claimed that he had served in Saigon (later Ho Chi Minh City) on the headquarters staff of General William Westmoreland, commander of U.S. forces in Vietnam. The *Boston Globe* reporter found no evidence to support these assertions but much to contradict them. Records show that in 1965, the year Ellis said he was a paratrooper in Vietnam, he was a graduate student at Yale University, where he remained until 1969.

Ellis had graduated from the College of William and Mary in 1965 with a Reserve Officers' Training Corps (ROTC) commission but had deferred active military duty until the completion of a doctorate in history from Yale. He did serve in the military from August, 1969, until June, 1972, but within the United States, teaching military history at the U.S. Military Academy at West Point, New York, his entire tour of duty. Following his honorable discharge in 1972, Ellis began his teaching career at Mount Holyoke College.

Ellis told other tall tales over the years. He claimed, for example, that in 1964, prior to his military service and while still an undergraduate at William and Mary, he had trained activists in the Civil Rights movement. Once again, the *Boston Globe* could find nothing to corroborate Ellis's claim. In addition, Ellis said that he had returned deeply disillusioned from Vietnam, and after his honorable discharge he had led antiwar protests. No one who knew him at the time could remember any active interest by him in the peace movement.

The revelations of the *Boston Globe* stunned Ellis's students and colleagues, as well as many others elsewhere who knew Ellis as a brilliant scholar. He admitted his guilt and asked for forgiveness. He later called his actions "stupid and wrong" but referred only to "personal shortcomings" as an explanation of his conduct.

Initially, the president of Mount Holyoke College, Joanne V. Creighton, defended Ellis as honorable and questioned whether the *Boston Globe's* exposé had served the public interest. However, as criticism intensified from media editorials and national professional groups, Creighton appointed a faculty committee to examine the issue. The verdict did not favor Ellis. In announcing the decision, Creighton cited Ellis's repeated serious breaches of faculty responsibility to the truth. She then suspended him without pay for one academic year, ordered that he no longer teach the Vietnam course, and stripped him of his endowed chair, which was a special badge of distinction for a professor. Ellis accepted the punishment.

IMPACT

Reaction to the Ellis scandal was mixed. While many students and faculty at Mount Holyoke objected to the severity of the penalties, others, mainly off campus, believed that he had been treated too leniently. A few regarded Ellis's offenses as so severe as to bar him from teaching. An official of the American Historical Association (AHA) argued that Ellis's behavior was a flagrant violation of the AHA code of ethics. He stated that the intellectual integrity of the classroom must never be compromised, just as historical scholarship must never be distorted or falsified. An exhaustive search of Ellis's voluminous publications found no evidence that his scholarship had been tainted by his delinquencies in the classroom. There the matter rested.

In looking at why Ellis lied to his students, it is possible to infer that he intended to make the sad lessons of Vietnam more urgent and memorable. There was general agreement that his "first-person" descriptions gave a vivid immediacy to his lectures. Perhaps Ellis was guilt-ridden because he had remained safely at home while others were serving and dying in Vietnam.

A more complex explanation was that Ellis had

2000'S

come to half-believe the lies he had so often re-peated. According to this view he had sought to re-invent himself by fashioning an alternate identity in a fantasy world. Ellis may have developed the illusion that he had personally participated in what were arguably the three central events of American society during the 1960's: the Vietnam War, the peace movement, and the Civil Rights movement.

Finally, Ellis himself weighed in as to why he had lied so blatantly. He confided to an interviewer in 2004 that he had grown up in a dysfunctional home with an alcoholic father. He said that this was probably why he had been plagued all his life by a sense of insecurity and self-doubt. He attributed much of his compulsion to overachieve to a lack of self-confidence combined with a constant craving for approval. Ellis's self-assessment is intriguing although it did not fully explain why he so casually risked self-destruction over fabrications so easily disproved.

While the Ellis scandal did, for a time, engender serious discussion about intellectual honesty and dishonesty in college classrooms, it soon became clear that many academics made a practical distinction between dishonesty or deception in the classroom and the much more stringent standards that applied to academic publications. Ellis's defenders argued that despite his classroom tales, he did not break any law.

In 2002, Ellis resumed teaching at Mount Holyoke, and in 2005 he regained the endowed chair he had lost in 2001. His biography of George Washington, written during his year under suspension, secured his reputation as among the most talented biographers and historians of his generation.

—*Donald Sullivan*

FURTHER READING

Burkett, B. G., and Glenna Whitley. *Stolen Valor: How the Vietnam Generation Was Robbed of Its Honor and Its History*. Dallas, Tex.: Veritas Press, 1998. Published prior to the Ellis scandal, this work exposes dozens of bogus claims to combat action in Vietnam. Also examines various motives of those who falsified their Vietnam service.

Hoffer, Peter C. *Past Imperfect: Facts, Fictions, Fraud—American History from Bancroft and Parkman to Ambrose, Bellesiles, Ellis, and Goodwin*. New York: PublicAffairs, 2004. In the wake of the Ellis scandal, Hoffer checked Ellis's publications for evidence of plagiarism or serious distortions but found no evidence that Ellis went beyond his sources.

Maslin, Mark. "Biographical Fraud and Traumatic Nationalism: Joseph Ellis' Vietnam Testimony." *Biography* 29 (2006): 605-614. Discusses various explanations for Ellis's serious ethical lapses and examines his publications to detect whether his classroom fabrications were echoed in his scholarship.

Robinson, Walter V. "Professor's Past in Doubt: Discrepancies Surface in Claim of Vietnam Duty." *Boston Globe*, June 18, 2001. The article that broke the story of Ellis's years of lies and fabrications.

Wiener, Jon. *Historians in Trouble: Plagiarism, Fraud, and Politics in the Ivory Tower*. New York: New Press, 2005. A detailed analysis of court documents and other evidence in the fraud scandals of historians. Includes the chapter, "Lying to Students About Vietnam: The Mythic Past of Joseph Ellis."

SEE ALSO: June 5, 1944: Australian Poets Claim Responsibility for a Literary Hoax; Nov. 13, 1969: American Massacre of Vietnamese Civilians at My Lai Is Revealed; Jan. 28, 1972: Clifford Irving Admits Faking Howard Hughes Memoirs; 1978: *Roots* Author Alex Haley Is Sued for Plagiarism; Dec. 3, 1989: Martin Luther King, Jr.'s, Doctoral-Thesis Plagiarism Is Revealed; Apr., 1998: Scottish Historian Is Charged with Plagiarism; May 11, 1998: Journalist Stephen Glass Is Exposed as a Fraud; Jan. 4, 2002: Historian Stephen E. Ambrose Is Accused of Plagiarism; Jan. 18, 2002: Historian Doris Kearns Goodwin Is Accused of Plagiarism; Oct. 25, 2002: Historian Michael A. Bellesiles Resigns After Academic Fraud Accusations; July 24, 2007: University of Colorado Fires Professor for Plagiarism and Research Falsification.

June 30, 2001
KOREAN RELIGIOUS TEACHER JUNG MYUNG SEOK IS CHARGED WITH RAPE

Jung Myung Seok, a Korean religious teacher whose doctrines reportedly present him as a savior completing the work of Jesus Christ, was sought by Korean police for rape in 2001 after several of his women followers alleged that they were sexually assaulted. Jung was sought by Interpol as well, and in 2007, he was captured by Chinese police and extradited to South Korea.

LOCALES: South Korea; Japan; Taiwan; China
CATEGORIES: Sex crimes; law and the courts; religion; hoaxes, frauds, and charlatanism

KEY FIGURE
Jung Myung Seok (b. 1945), South Korean religious leader

SUMMARY OF EVENT
South Korean religious teacher and self-proclaimed Messiah Jung Myung Seok became the center of controversy in 2001 after being charged with sexually assaulting and raping an unknown number of female followers. Allegations of the spiritual leader's use of religious authority and teachings to abuse the trust and loyalty of his female followers to rape them captured the Eastern world's attention and stirred demands for justice.

Jung's church involvement began when he was a child and intensified during the 1970's, when he became a member of the Unification Church, a Christian sect headed by Messiah figure the Reverend Sun Myung Moon. During the 1980's, Jung left Moon's congregation with several of his own followers and created his own religious sect based on the Unification Church's teachings. Jung's church was named Jesus Morning Star, or JMS (also an acronym for Jung's name), in reference to a New Testament passage from Revelation (2:24-29), which details Jesus' rule over his followers and the rewards given to those who followed him. The JMS

religious following also has been known as Setsuri (providence), the International Christian Association (ICA), and the Christian Gospel Mission (CGM). Jung claimed to be the Messiah and referred to his religious movement as the Second Coming of Christ. He asserted to his followers that he was a messenger of God and that their salvation could be obtained only through him.

Jung's following quickly spread throughout South Korea, Japan, and Taiwan. Members of the growing JMS congregation came to include people employed in state and federal organizations, law enforcement agencies, and the military, but the majority of JMS members were young university students. During the early 1990's, JMS members began recruiting intensely from universities in South Korea, Taiwan, and Japan. The group's recruitment strategy consisted of holding membership drives on college campuses to solicit students' participation in their extracurricular activities, such as sports and social clubs. Students were encouraged by JMS members to sign up for these activities without being informed about the religious nature of the clubs. Through these activities, JMS members were able to gain the trust of prospective members and draw them into Jung's following. JMS members also used university students' background and personality profiles in their recruiting processes to more effectively attract them to the church. Many of the students targeted were highly intelligent and expected to become very successful in their careers. New JMS members were encouraged and required to induct other students into the following and to give sizeable monetary donations to the church to further the JMS mission and to increase their status within the cult.

In June, 1999, the Seoul Broadcasting Service in South Korea aired the first public accusations of sexual assault and rape against Jung. Hundreds of female followers came forward to describe how

Jung used his self-proclaimed identity as the Messiah to seduce and assault women in the cult. The women explained how prospective female members were often sought out by senior members and handpicked from photographs by Jung. Women within the cult were expected to tend to Jung's needs as servants, to keep him company, and to wear makeup and dress nicely. The women explained that most of the assaults would begin in the form of a health check or bath. Jung would order them to undress and take a bath with him to undergo a spiritual cleansing or healing process that entailed Jung washing their genitals to relieve them of sin and pain. These baths were performed privately with one female member or with several female members at once, and frequently resulted in sexual intercourse with Jung. Many of the women regarded their inclusion in these activities as a blessing and privilege and as a means of achieving a higher rank in the cult. To gain control over his female followers, Jung emphasized that the only way they could atone for their sins was through sexual intercourse with him, the Messiah, and were threatened with damnation if they spoke about having sex with him.

The women also explained how Jung maintained strict control over the marriages of JMS members. Members were allowed to marry other members only and marriages between members were reviewed by Jung for approval. Many prospective brides were required to see Jung for an interview and were frequently forced to have sex with him before they were allowed to marry. Marriages could be performed only by Jung in a mass wedding ceremony, and JMS newlyweds were urged to have children to increase the church's following. The shocking accounts given by JMS victims on the broadcasting network shocked South Korea and led to demands that Jung be held accountable. As the broadcast aired, however, many JMS followers held protests outside the television station in support of Jung.

Jung fled South Korea following the allegations. Dismissing fears of retaliation and spiritual damnation, JMS victims pressed charges against Jung. On June 30, 2001, Korean police officially charged Jung with fraud, rape, and embezzlement (regarding JMS donations and funds) and initiated an international manhunt with Interpol (the International Criminal Police Organization). In 2003, he was detained for visa violations in Hong Kong but fled to China to avoid being extradited to South Korea after being released on bail.

While the search for Jung continued for several years, Japanese police raided several suspected JMS offices. During 2005-2006, Japanese police investigated a forty-four-year-old South Korean woman about an im-

Jung Myung Seok, wearing mask, is extradited to South Korea in early 2008. He was arrested in China in May, 2007, after evading arrest for six years. (AP/Wide World Photos)

migrations violation and her suspected involvement with JMS and helping Jung remain a fugitive. The woman, a senior JMS member, reportedly entered Japan in March, 2000, under false pretenses by claiming that she was working as a design planner for a printing company when she was actually conducting business for the cult. The woman also collected JMS members' donations to cover Jung's accommodations and traveling expenses while he was evading capture, and she was responsible for soliciting and sending young women (prospective followers and members) overseas to Jung to have sex with him.

Jung's fugitive status came to an end in May, 2007, after being captured by Chinese police. He was extradited to Seoul in February, 2008, after Chinese police officials confirmed his identity and completed their interrogation. Jung's arrival at a Seoul airport was met by South Korean police and hundreds of JMS followers protesting his arrest. Jung maintained that he was innocent of all charges. On August 12, he was found guilty of rape and sentenced to six years in prison.

Impact

The JMS sex scandal provided insight into the inner workings of secretive religious sects and alerted the public to the underlying activities and missions of Jung's church. Despite the knowledge of the rape allegations against Jung, many JMS members remained in the cult and continued to induct new members.

The criminal investigation into the charges against Jung was met with resistance from many JMS followers. In addition to petitions and protests, certain followers infiltrated the criminal justice and legal systems in South Korea by gaining employment in government agencies, and they have been discovered filtering classified information about Jung's case to the church, destroying evidence, and compromising the chance for an untainted and fair trial. The rape charges brought against Jung spotlighted the potential danger for religious fraud, the abuse of power, and the sexual manipulation of members in religious cults.

—*Sheena Garitta*

Further Reading

Buswell, Robert E., and Timothy S. Lee. *Christianity in Korea*. Honolulu: University of Hawaii Press, 2006. A comprehensive study of the practice of Christianity in Korea. Good for background material that contextualizes Jung's cult.

"China Extradites Chief of Alleged S. Korean Rapist Cult." *China Post*, February 21, 2008. Provides a brief description of the arrest and extradition of Jung from China to South Korea and a chronology of the criminal allegations that were filed against him.

Daley, Peter. "Jung Myung Seok: How to Spot a Woolly Wolf." *Keimyung Gazette* (Keimyung University, South Korea), February 1, 2006. Gives a detailed personal account of the cult's recruitment strategies and an inside look at life within the JMS church.

Herskovitz, Jan. "South Korean Religious Sect Leader Jailed for Rape." *Reuters*, August 12, 2008. A news service wire report of Jung's conviction and sentencing for multiple counts of rape.

See also: May 20, 1974: French Cardinal Daniélou Dies in a Prostitute's House; Oct. 31, 1975: Buddhist Teacher Orders His Students to Remove Their Clothes; Aug. 12, 1983-July 27, 1990: McMartin Preschool Is Embroiled in Child-Abuse Case; Oct. 23, 1985: Guru Bhagwan Shree Rajneesh Is Indicted for Immigration Fraud; Apr. 22, 1986: Faith Healer Peter Popoff Is Exposed as a Fraud; May 6, 1992: Irish Bishop Eamonn Casey's Romantic Affair Leads to His Resignation.

2000's

August 27, 2001
LITTLE LEAGUE BASEBALL STAR DANNY ALMONTE IS FOUND TO BE OVERAGE

Danny Almonte gained fame for exceptional pitching in the 2001 Little League Baseball World Series. Sports reporters soon discovered that he was fourteen years old, two years over the age limit for players. His team was stripped of its records for the season. Both the team's founder and Almonte's father were banned from Little League for life.

LOCALE: Williamsport, Pennsylvania
CATEGORIES: Hoaxes, frauds, and charlatanism; sports; families and children; publishing and journalism

KEY FIGURES
Danny Almonte (b. 1987), Dominican-born Little League baseball player
Rolando Paulino (fl. early twenty-first century), founder of the Rolando Paulino All Stars
Felipe Almonte (fl. early twenty-first century), Almonte's father
Sonia Rojas Breton (fl. early twenty-first century), Almonte's mother
Ian Thomsen (fl. early twenty-first century), *Sports Illustrated* writer
Luis Fernando Llosa (fl. early twenty-first century), *Sports Illustrated* writer

SUMMARY OF EVENT
Pitcher Danny Almonte, a native of the Dominican Republic, and his team, the Rolando Paulino All Stars (also known as the Baby Bronx Bombers), captured the attention of fans and the media after their participation in the 2001 Little League Baseball World Series (LLWS). The team garnered this attention not because it won the LLWS but because of scandal. The Japanese team, Tokyo-Kitasuna, won the series but was kept from the spotlight after rumors began to surface about Almonte's true age.

Reporters pressed Rolando Paulino, the founder

and president of the Bronx team, to settle the rumors. He supplied a copy of Almonte's official birth certificate, which had been filed in the Dominican Republic. The certificate indicated that Almonte was born April 7, 1989, which would have made him twelve years old during the 2001 season. Two *Sports Illustrated* writers, Ian Thomsen and Luis Fernando Llosa, tried to verify the authenticity of the birth certificate but found that there were two "official" certificates in the Dominican Republic. The documents were uncovered by a Dominican reporter.

Almonte, the Bronx team's star player, was an excellent left-handed pitcher who led his team to the LLWS semifinals in South Williamsport, Pennsylvania, for the 2001 season. Almonte's fastballs were clocked at around 70 miles per hour. His team finished third in the series after a 2-0 victory over the team from State College, Pennsylvania; it was a game in which Almonte struck out sixteen. In total, Almonte struck out forty-six batters in Williamsburg.

Almonte seemed mentally sharper than his peers, and he towered above them at 5 feet 8 inches. He was such a phenomenon that coaches in the league grew suspicious of his age. Some even hired private investigators to check on their Bronx rivals. The Associated Press reported on September 4 that these investigations revealed nothing irregular. However, it was revealed that Almonte had not attended school in New York City. Even with the suspicions of rival coaches, Almonte and his teammates received several accolades, including a victory parade in the Bronx and the keys to the city.

The two birth certificates found in the Dominican Republic were identical, except for one fact: the year of birth. Both certificates were for a child named Danny Almonte. Both indicated that he was born to the same parents, had the same government identification numbers, and was born on the same month and day—April 7. One handwritten certificate filed in the town of Moca gave 1987 as the year of birth for the baby boy, weighing six pounds. The later document, which was typed, showed 1989 as the child's birth year. Both documents had been filed by Almonte's father, Felipe Almonte. The maximum age for Little League players is twelve years. To be eligible to play in the 2001 series, players could not have been born before August 1, 1988. Had Almonte been born in 1987, the question on everyone's minds, he would have been too old to play.

The *Sports Illustrated* writers presented their findings to league officials in late August, 2001. Their article, "One for the Ages," was published in the magazine's September 3 issue but posted to its Web site on August 27. The Almonte scandal officially broke.

Sonia Rojas Breton, Almonte's birth mother, who lived in the Dominican Republic, defended the 1989 date. She provided baby pictures and her copy of the birth certificate to support her story. According to *The New York Times*, Breton said that she lived in Jamao and that months after Almonte's birth she moved to Moca. She asserted that the 1987 birth certificate was for Danny's brother, Juan, born in 1987. Other records, however, indicate that Juan was born December 15, not April 7, in Jamao al Norte. Danny Almonte's 1987 birth certificate was filed in 1994 and the 1989 birth certificate was filed in early 2000, shortly before Almonte and his father entered the United States. Almonte's family in Moca claimed that the 1987 birth certificate with Danny's name was fraudulent.

Paulino protested that the scrutiny concerning Almonte's age reflected prejudice against foreigners and poor sportsmanship. Furthermore, in what later appeared to be an effort to conceal Almonte's school records, his mother claimed that he had been educated by a friend at that friend's home. However, others in the town were proud to tell reporters that Almonte had attended a local elementary school, Escuela Primaria Andres Bello. The school's vice principal said that Almonte had completed the seventh grade.

A Dominican records official, Victor Romero, also investigated. He interviewed witnesses and ex-

amined the birth certificates of both Danny and his older brother Juan and other documents in Moca and Jamao al Norte. Contradictions surfaced regarding the later document. However, Romero did find documentation at Dr. Toribio Bencosme Hospital in Moca to support the 1987 birth date. A Dominican government official in charge of public records announced that the later birth certificates (for both Danny and Juan) were fraudulent. Danny was born April 7, 1987, and Juan was born in 1985. The same official also announced that the Almonte brothers' father would be charged with falsifying a document and that Danny's birth mother also could face charges.

Moca district attorney Juan Alberto Mendez charged Almonte's father and a mayoral staffer with falsifying the birth certificates of the Almonte brothers so that both of them could play baseball.

Danny Almonte pitching in the 2001 Little League World Series. (AP/Wide World Photos)

Felipe Almonte would likely be arrested and given a five-year prison sentence if he returned to the Dominican Republic. He also faced sanctions in the United States for failing to enroll his son in school for more than one year. Furthermore, Felipe's tourist visa, used to enter the United States, had expired in late 2000. Danny Almonte's stepmother appealed to both the United States and Dominican Republic governments for mercy in the case.

In June, 2002, Almonte graduated from Bronx Middle School 52. He attended James Monroe High School, played varsity baseball, and graduated in 2006. Before graduating he married Rosy Perdomo, a thirty-year-old hair stylist and mother of a twelve-year-old son. They initially settled in the South Bronx.

IMPACT

The Little League charter committee required that Almonte's team forfeit its wins, including the team's third place in the series, for the 2001 season. Almonte's no-hitter was struck from the records as well. The Rolando Paulino All Stars were allowed to continue as a team, but became the second team in Little League history to be stripped after reaching the semifinals. The team from Zamboanga City, Philippines, had been disqualified after its 1992 tournament win for including players from another district.

The Little League president at the time of the Almonte scandal avoided blaming Almonte. He instead blamed the adults in his life, including his father. Felipe Almonte and Paulino were banned for life from Little League baseball. Paulino had seen similar trouble years before. In 1988, his Dominican Little League team had been disqualified from a regional tournament when six players were found to be overage. In the Almonte case, however, he claimed that he was not at fault but a victim of deception by the player's father.

After the scandal, Little League Baseball began to closely scrutinize the age and residency of each player or potential player. The league now requires that birth certificates must have been filed within thirty days of a player's date of birth, or that the player provide substantial alternative verification of birth date and place. Also, players must be citizens of the country they represent or be in that country on a legal visa.

—*Camille Gibson*

FURTHER READING

Hermoso, Rafael, and Lara Petusky Coger. "Almonte Faces Arrest—His Wife Seeks Mercy." *The New York Times*, September 6, 2001. News story that discusses what happened to Almonte's family after the boy's age was determined.

Llosa, Luis Fernando. "Awkward Age." *Sports Illustrated*, May 29, 2006. Magazine article that details Almonte's life several years after the scandal. Also reports on his marriage to a thirty-year-old hair stylist, which placed him in the media's spotlight once again.

McFadden, Robert D. "Star Is 14, So Bronx Team Is Disqualified." *The New York Times*, September 1, 2001. An excellent summary of how events unfolded immediately after the Little League Baseball World Series.

Thomsen, Ian, and Luis Fernando Llosa. "One for the Ages." *Sports Illustrated*, September 3, 2001, The magazine article that broke the scandal. This article was posted to the *Sports Illustrated* Web site on August 27.

Wong, Edward, and Jean-Michel Caroit. "Parents of Bronx Ace Insist Their Son Is 12." *The New York Times*, August 30, 2001. Discusses how Almonte's family lied about the ages of Danny and Juan.

SEE ALSO: Spring, 1947: Baseball Manager Leo Durocher Is Suspended for Gambling Ties; Aug. 19, 1973: Cheating Scandal Shocks Soap Box Derby; Feb. 28, 1986: Baseball Commissioner Peter Ueberroth Suspends Players for Cocaine Use; Aug. 24, 1989: Pete Rose Is Banned from Baseball for Betting on Games; Dec. 14, 2001: Notre Dame Football Coach Resigns for Falsifying His Résumé; May 3, 2003: University of Alabama Fires New Football Coach in Sex Scandal.

December 2, 2001
ENRON BANKRUPTCY REVEALS MASSIVE FINANCIAL FRAUD

When the Texas energy corporation Enron suddenly went bankrupt, it took with it the life savings and pensions of many of its employees and revealed systematic financial corruption and mismanagement that went beyond the company's walls to a respectable accounting firm and the halls of government.

LOCALES: New York, New York; Houston, Texas
CATEGORIES: Banking and finance; corruption; business; law and the courts; ethics

KEY FIGURES
Kenneth Lay (1942-2006), Enron's chief executive officer and chairman of the board
Jeffrey Skilling (b. 1953), Enron's president and chief operating officer
Sherron Watkins (b. 1959), Enron's vice president of corporate development, who urged Lay to investigate Enron's accounting practices

SUMMARY OF EVENT
Enron Corporation began its corporate existence in 1985, when Houston Natural Gas merged with InterNorth, another natural gas company that was based in Omaha, Nebraska. The combined companies controlled a system of natural gas pipelines that stretched the length and breadth of the United States, which in theory should have given it a significant competitive advantage. However, the deregulation of natural gas transmission, part of U.S. president Ronald Reagan's policies of reducing government regulation of corporations, significantly blunted that advantage by eliminating Enron's ability to claim an exclusive right to use its pipelines.

As a result, the new company's chief executive officer (CEO), Kenneth Lay, decided to move out of the traditional areas in which the precursor companies had operated, particularly gas pipelines and power-generating plants, to such areas as telecommunications, pulp and paper, and computers. To chart Enron's new course, Lay retained the consulting firm of McKinsey & Company, which sent consultant Jeffrey Skilling to Houston. Skilling advised Enron executives to leverage the company's vast size to effectively create its own market through buying contracts that locked in both costs and prices, assuring a steady flow of business. Doing this involved creating a number of special purpose entities, or SPEs, that would carry out the transactions, often in joint ventures with other companies. By 1999, Enron even created its own stock-trading company, EnronOnline, which was used by almost all energy companies.

At first the plan worked well enough, and Enron's growth was so spectacular that Skilling was offered a senior executive position, that of chief operating officer, with Enron. However, this growth was almost entirely dependent upon the presence of a strong bull market in the larger economy as well as the rapid growth of the high-tech sector that later came to be known as the dot-com bubble because it lacked fundamentals. Because so much of Enron's growth, and the resulting rapid growth of the value of its stock, had no fundamentals, the use of SPEs became increasingly a sort of shell game, moving money from one part of the company to another to create the illusion of vibrant growth and hide unprofitable ventures. Arthur Andersen, one of the most prestigious accounting firms in the United States, was involved in this systematic deception as well, which was further enabled by lax regulatory oversight.

As the U.S. economy began to slow at the beginning of the twenty-first century, the continued rapid growth of Enron became unsustainable. More desperate financial measures had to be taken to maintain the illusion that enabled Enron's stock to continue climbing. Skilling began to crack under the strain. In one well-publicized event, he used a vulgarism in a sarcastic expression of gratitude to Wall Street analyst Richard Grubman. Although within the corporate culture of Enron the expression was frequently repeated in a way that clearly regarded

945

Former Enron chief executive officer Kenneth Lay reads a prepared statement before the U.S. Senate subcommittee investigating the Enron scandal in February, 2002. (AP/Wide World Photos)

the wrong to be that of Grubman rather than Skilling, it was a warning sign of upheavals to come.

During the middle of 2001, Skilling's mental situation had become sufficiently fragile that he resigned, giving the position of CEO back to Lay on August 14. The next day, Sherron Watkins, Enron's vice president of corporate development, wrote an e-mail to Lay that many consider to be the start of Enron's downfall. In her memo, Watkins expressed reservations about how Skilling's abrupt departure would play in the securities market and identified several key weaknesses in Enron's corporate structure, particularly the Raptor and Condor deals. Raptor and Condor were SPEs that had functioned to hedge risk in particularly tricky areas of the economy. In effect, Watkins was urging Lay to investigate Enron's accounting practices.

Lay then called a meeting with Enron's general counsel, but the wake-up call came too late. Although Enron hired the legal firm Vinson & Elkins

to conduct an internal investigation, the damage was already too extensive to be corrected. One day before Enron was scheduled to announce its third-quarter results, Vinson & Elkins returned its report, claiming that while the Raptor and Condor deals were creative, they did not represent a formal conflict of interest.

Even this positive report could not cushion the blow of October 16, when Enron revealed that it had sustained more than $100 million in losses, particularly in its new power company deal and its investment in broadband telecommunications. The news sent Enron's stock prices tumbling, and on October 22 the U.S. Securities and Exchange Commission (SEC) requested information on several key transactions. Further bad news followed when Enron announced it would have to redo a number of key filings as a result of the consolidation of several previously separate entities through which it had accomplished some of its more risky deals.

These filings revealed that many of the SPEs through which Enron had done business were in fact not independent under SEC regulations, but had been treated as though they qualified to avoid consolidating them and their financial losses into Enron's financial statements. The resulting loss of confidence led to further collapse in the value of Enron's stock, until major credit-rating agencies that had previously ranked Enron as a blue-chip stock company reevaluated it as a junk stock and nearly worthless.

In a desperate attempt to salvage a disintegrating situation, the smaller energy company Dynegy, Inc., attempted a takeover of the collapsing company. However, this deal fell through when Enron revealed that its declining credit rating would result in an additional $690 million of obligations. As a result, Enron filed for Chapter 11 bankruptcy protection in a New York bankruptcy court on December 2. Enron's subsequent corporate activities were directed to the company's dissolution and the satisfaction of its creditors.

IMPACT

Because the complicated financial wheeling and dealing that caused Enron's paper wealth to implode was difficult for people without an extensive background in high finance to understand, most of the public outcry was focused upon the scandal's effect on ordinary people: Millions of American investors, including longtime Enron employees, suddenly lost billions of dollars in savings, investments, and retirement plans. People who had thought their retirements were secure were now looking at the very real possibility of having to work until they could work no more. As a result of this betrayal of trust, employees and investors demanded accountability from the executives who had been involved in the questionable accounting practices.

Both Lay and Skilling were found criminally liable and given long prison sentences, although Lay died of a heart attack shortly before he was supposed to report for incarceration. There were even some questions about whether Lay deliberately indulged in pleasures that were apt to increase his risk

of a heart attack, either in an effort to grab a few last bits of pleasure before a sentence that might well be for life or in a cynical effort to cheat prison. The accounting firm Arthur Andersen also was implicated in the financial scandal, and it ultimately went out of business.

In addition, the scandal raised serious questions about the value of the limited-liability corporation, or LLC, and whether it enabled executives to evade the consequences of their decisions. Calls were made to make it easier to pierce the shield of incorporation and hold executives as individuals financially liable for bad decisions that materially harmed investors and involved a breach of trust. However, many analysts argued that reducing the liability protection afforded by corporate entities could actually do more harm than good by exposing ordinary investors to greater risk and by making executives more wary of taking aggressive action in pursuing business opportunities.

—Leigh Husband Kimmel

FURTHER READING

Coenen, Tracy. *Essentials of Corporate Fraud.* Hoboken, N.J.: John Wiley & Sons, 2008. An introductory guide to the white-collar crime of corporate fraud, written by a forensic, or investigative, accountant.

Fox, Loren. *Enron: The Rise and Fall.* Hoboken, N.J.: John Wiley & Sons, 2003. A corporate history of Enron, exploring how the scandal developed and spiraled out of control toward bankruptcy and the company's collapse.

Fusaro, Peter C., and Ross M. Miller. *What Went Wrong at Enron: Everyone's Guide to the Largest Bankruptcy in U.S. History.* Hoboken, N.J.: John Wiley & Sons, 2002. A detailed account of the corporate greed that led to Enron's collapse.

Jenkins, Gregory J. *The Enron Collapse.* Upper Saddle River, N.J.: Pearson Education, 2003. An executive summary of the mechanisms that led to Enron's bankruptcy and collapse. Discusses lessons learned in the scandal.

Smith, Rebecca, and John R. Meshwiller. *Twenty-four Days: How Two "Wall Street Journal" Reporters Uncovered the Lies that Destroyed Faith in Corporate America.* New York: Harper-Business, 2003. Focuses upon the investigative reporting that revealed the fatal weaknesses in the management of Enron as a corporation.

Stewart, Bennet. "The Real Reasons Enron Failed." *Journal of Applied Corporate Finance* 18, no. 2 (2006): 116-119. Argues that Enron failed as a company not because of criminal intent alone but also organizational design: that is, "bonus plans that paid managers to increase reported earnings"; "the use of market-to-market accounting"; and turning the finance department into a "profit center."

Swartz, Mimi, with Sherron Watkins. *Power Failure: The Inside Story of the Collapse of Enron.* New York: Doubleday, 2003. Offers a firsthand account from the whistle-blower, Sherron Watkins, who courageously stepped forward to unmask Enron's illegal manipulations.

SEE ALSO: 1932: Insull Utilities Trusts Collapse Prompts New Federal Regulation; Mar. 29, 1962: Billie Sol Estes Is Arrested for Corporate Fraud; Aug. 6, 1982: Banco Ambrosiano Collapses Amid Criminal Accusations; May 2, 1984: E. F. Hutton Executives Plead Guilty to Fraud; May 7, 1985: Banker Jake Butcher Pleads Guilty to Fraud; Jan. 15, 1988: ZZZZ Best Founder Is Indicted on Federal Fraud Charges; Mar. 29, 1989: Financier Michael Milken Is Indicted for Racketeering and Fraud; Apr. 5, 1991: George W. Bush Is Investigated for Insider Trading; 2001: Clearstream Financial Clearinghouse Is Accused of Fraud and Money Laundering; June 25, 2002: Internal Corruption Forces Adelphia Communications to Declare Bankruptcy; Sept. 3, 2003: Mutual Fund Companies Are Implicated in Shady Trading Practices; Mar. 5, 2004: Martha Stewart Is Convicted in Insider-Trading Scandal; Oct. 14, 2004: Insurance Brokerage Marsh & McLennan Is Charged with Fraud; Sept. 12, 2005: Westar Energy Executives Are Found Guilty of Looting Their Company; Early 2007: Subprime Mortgage Industry Begins to Collapse; Sept. 20, 2008: American Financial Markets Begin to Collapse.

December 14, 2001
NOTRE DAME FOOTBALL COACH RESIGNS FOR FALSIFYING HIS RÉSUMÉ

George O'Leary, former head football coach for the Georgia Institute of Technology, resigned as head football coach of the University of Notre Dame after only five days on the job. A reporter covering his appointment as Notre Dame's head coach found inaccuracies and falsehoods on his résumé. Upon resigning, O'Leary admitted to including fabricated athletic and academic credentials on his résumé. His resignation, however, did not negatively affect his coaching career, which prospered nonetheless.

LOCALE: Notre Dame, Indiana

CATEGORIES: Hoaxes, frauds, and charlatanism; sports; public morals; ethics

KEY FIGURES

George O'Leary (b. 1946), head football coach at the University of Notre Dame

John Hussey (1943-2008), sportswriter for the Manchester, New Hampshire, *Union Leader*

Jim Fennell (fl. early twenty-first century), reporter for the Manchester, New Hampshire, *Union Leader*

Kevin White (b. 1950), athletic director, University of Notre Dame

Louis M. Nanni (b. 1962), vice president of university relations, University of Notre Dame

Edward A. Malloy (b. 1941), president of the University of Notre Dame

Summary of Event

In late 2001, after a turbulent five-season tenure, University of Notre Dame head football coach Bob Davie was asked to resign. On December 9, shortly after Davie's departure, George O'Leary, then head football coach of the Georgia Institute of Technology (Georgia Tech), was hired to replace Davie. Shortly after he accepted the prestigious position, questions began to surface about discrepancies on O'Leary's résumé.

O'Leary stated on his résumé that he earned a master's degree in education from the State University of New York, Stony Brook. He also claimed to have earned three athletic letters playing football at the University of New Hampshire (UNH). Notre Dame officials requested that O'Leary resign as head coach after learning of his faked credentials— athletic and academic.

O'Leary began his football coaching career at Central Islip High School in New York in 1975. He continued as a high school football coach in New York until 1980, when he began coaching college football at Syracuse University. While at Syracuse, he served as the defensive-line coach and assistant head coach for six years. After he left Syracuse, he became the defensive-line coach for the San Diego Chargers of the National Football League (NFL).

In 1994, O'Leary accepted the head coaching position at Georgia Tech. During his eight seasons there, he led the Yellow Jackets to a 52-33 record, which included a five-year run in bowl appearances beginning in 1997. In 1998 and 2000, he was recognized as Coach of the Year by the Atlantic Coast Conference. In 2000, he was honored with the Bobby Dodd Award as national coach of the year. Before leaving for Notre Dame, O'Leary was considered one of Georgia Tech's most prominent and successful coaches. However, he also had a few problems while coaching at Georgia. In 1999, the National Collegiate Athletic Association (NCAA) sanctioned him for improperly lending money to a former Georgia running back. It was also later revealed that Georgia used eleven ineligible football players between the 1998-1999 and 2004-2005 seasons.

Hearing of Notre Dame's decision to hire O'Leary, John Hussey, a sportswriter for the Man-chester, New Hampshire, *Union Leader*, began his research for a report on O'Leary's accomplishment for the local newspaper. Hussey read O'Leary's résumé, in which the coach claimed to have played football at UNH, and interviewed O'Leary's former coach and teammates from UNH, neither of whom could recall O'Leary playing in a single game for the Wildcats. Upon further investigation, Hussey found that the coach did not play sports at UNH, and he certainly did not earn three letters in football.

Hussey reported his findings to Jim Fennell, another reporter for the *Union Leader*, who broke the story nationwide. On December 12, administrative officials from Notre Dame approached O'Leary regarding his claim to have received three letters in football at UNH. When questioned, O'Leary admitted to including false information about his early athletic career. Feeling shamed and embarrassed, he offered to immediately resign as the head football coach. Notre Dame officials, however, refused to accept his resignation. The vice president of university relations, Louis M. Nanni, and athletic director Kevin White agreed to overlook the misleading credentials and work with O'Leary to prepare a public apology.

The next day, however, more questions surfaced about O'Leary's résumé, this time concerning his academic background at Stony Brook. Notre Dame officials discovered that O'Leary had completed only two classes during his two semesters at Stony Brook. O'Leary later admitted that he had never earned his master's degree there. Nanni and White met with Notre Dame president Edward A. Malloy and decided that they could no longer allow O'Leary to continue as their head football coach. Without having coached a single game, O'Leary was asked to resign. He presented his formal resignation on December 14, only five days into the job, saying in a statement released by the university, "Due to a selfish and thoughtless act many years ago, I have personally embarrassed Notre Dame, its alumni and fans."

Impact

The résumé scandal at Notre Dame did not negatively affect O'Leary's coaching career. Indeed, his career prospered. In 2002, he was hired as the defensive coordinator for the Minnesota Vikings of the NFL. After spending two years coaching Minnesota, O'Leary left the Vikings and accepted the head coaching position at the University of Central Florida (UCF). During his career as the Knights' head coach, O'Leary raised the expectations for the football team and was credited with increasing his players' athletic and academic performances. In 2005, O'Leary was recognized as the Conference USA Coach of the Year and he also signed a new multiple-year contract with UCF.

Notre Dame's termination of O'Leary was one in a series of high-profile firings of college coaches for actual or perceived misconduct. In September, 2000, Bobby Knight, the head coach of the men's basketball team at Indiana University, was fired for a sequence of unacceptable actions that included allegations of choking a player. In March, 2003, Jim Harrick, head men's basketball coach at the University of Georgia, resigned under pressure after accusations surfaced that athletes received credit for classes they did not attend. Also, in May, 2003, Larry Eustachy, head men's basketball coach at Iowa State University, was forced to resign after he was seen in photographs drinking alcohol with students, as well as kissing female students.

—*Ryan Patten and Laurel Mae Chang*

FURTHER READING

Callahan, David. *The Cheating Culture: Why More Americans are Doing Wrong to Get Ahead.* Orlando, Fla.: Harcourt, 2004. This book discusses why people choose to cheat to gain an advantage over their competitors. It also devotes a chapter about résumé padding, and discusses the Notre Dame résumé scandal involving George O'Leary.

Keyes, Ralph. *The Post-Truth Era: Dishonesty and Deception in Contemporary Life.* New York: St. Martin's Press, 2004. Examines why individuals falsify information, and discusses the George O'Leary scandal in the chapter "Great Pretenders."

Kidwell, Roland E., Jr. "'Small' Lies, Big Trouble: The Unfortunate Consequences of Résumé Padding, from Janet Cooke to George O'Leary." *Journal of Business Ethics* 51, no. 2 (2004): 175-184. A historical study of the effects of including inaccurate information on résumés. Also addresses the George O'Leary scandal.

Mandel, Stewart. *Bowls, Polls, and Tattered Souls: Tackling the Chaos and Controversy that Reign over College Football.* Hoboken, N.J.: John Wiley & Sons, 2007. This book provides a detailed, behind-the-scenes look at notorious university scandals involving athletics, including the O'Leary scandal at Notre Dame.

Staurowsky, Ellen J. "Piercing the Veil of Amateurism: Commercialization, Corruption, and U.S. College Sports." In *The Commercialization of Sport*, edited by Trevor Slack. New York: Routledge, 2004. Staurowsky discusses how amateur athletics in the United States has become a commercialized and corrupt spectacle.

SEE ALSO: Feb. 25, 1987: NCAA Imposes "Death Penalty" on Southern Methodist University Football; Aug. 27, 2001: Little League Baseball Star Danny Almonte Is Found to Be Overage; Mar. 27, 2002: Georgia Basketball Coach Jim Harrick, Sr., Resigns over Fraud Allegations; May 3, 2003: University of Alabama Fires New Football Coach in Sex Scandal; July 14, 2006: *New York Times* Exposes Grading Scandal at Auburn University; Aug. 20, 2007: Football Star Michael Vick Pleads Guilty to Financing a Dogfighting Ring; Sept. 13, 2007: New England Patriots Football Team Is Fined for Spying on Other Teams.

January 4, 2002
HISTORIAN STEPHEN E. AMBROSE IS ACCUSED OF PLAGIARISM

The Weekly Standard reported that Stephen E. Ambrose, one of the most widely read scholars of American history, had plagiarized material from a closely related historical work for one of his own best-selling military histories, The Wild Blue *(2001). Subsequent investigations revealing that Ambrose had plagiarized other works damaged his reputation as an academic historian but had little negative impact on his popularity with general readers.*

LOCALE: United States
CATEGORIES: Cultural and intellectual history; education; hoaxes, frauds, and charlatanism; plagiarism; publishing and journalism

KEY FIGURES
Stephen E. Ambrose (1936-2002), American historian and best-selling author
Thomas Childers (b. 1946), American history professor
Fred Barnes (b. 1934), executive editor of *The Weekly Standard*

SUMMARY OF EVENT
One of the greatest writers of popular American history, Stephen E. Ambrose became the center of a plagiarism scandal that broke in an article first posted on the Web site of *The Weekly Standard* on January 4, 2002. The scandal, which sent shock waves through the history profession, also encompassed his colleague Doris Kearns Goodwin the same month. Before the scandal broke, Ambrose, who began his career teaching at the University of New Orleans, had earned fame and fortune writing numerous books on popular topics in military and political history, most of which sold millions of copies. His major works include *Undaunted Courage* (1996), *Band of Brothers* (1992), *D-Day* (1994), and *Citizen Soldiers* (1997).

As his fame grew, Ambrose retired from his academic position and went into business for himself as Ambrose & Ambrose, Inc., which included his son, Hugh, as his agent and all of his children as research assistants. Ambrose, who saw and promoted himself as a storyteller, increasingly became a cottage industry in the field of popular history, and his publications correspondingly increased during the 1990's. He also served as a tour guide and film consultant and wrote books that included textbooks and personal memoirs. His most famous effort in the area of entertainment was as a consultant for the film *Saving Private Ryan* (1998) and the television miniseries *Band of Brothers* (2001).

Fred Barnes, executive editor of *The Weekly Standard*, revealed in "Stephen Ambrose, Copycat" that the popular writer had closely copied passages from Thomas Childers's *Wings of the Morning: The Story of the Last American Bomber Shot Down over Germany in World War II* (1995) for *The Wild Blue: The Men and Boys Who Flew the B-24s over Germany* (2001), a popular book essentially about the same subject. Barnes's story in *The Weekly Standard*, actually a review of these two books, not only cast a shadow on academic history but also further separated Ambrose from the profession.

The scandal centered on both Ambrose's overuse of quotations from Childers's book—the story of the World War II bomber crew of Childers's uncle—and from Ambrose's failure to properly identify them as quotations. What indicated that Ambrose's work was more than a matter of simple oversight or sloppiness was the frequency with which he appropriated Childers's material without acknowledging the source and his substitution of close paraphrasing for actual quoting of the secondary material.

Because Ambrose had relied heavily on Childers to access the primary sources he indirectly quoted,

951

Ambrose was seen as a popular historian profiting from the hard work and original research of a historian who was less well known. Beyond the immediate issue of plagiarism, the scandal included Ambrose's attempt to defend himself and deflect the issue. He tried to deny that what he did was plagiarism, noting that he gave generous credit to earlier works in his book's acknowledgments, and he insisted that the lifted materials represented a small percentage of all he had written. He also argued that he was not "writing a Ph.D. dissertation" and accused his accusers, particularly academics, of having an agenda against him. At the same time, Ambrose's publishers tried to play down his wrongdoings, suggesting that the issues in question were mere oversights. Furthermore, Ambrose made no offer to search out other errors, even after he conceded those already exposed.

Childers, though outraged, initially chose not to speak publicly against the widely acclaimed Ambrose. A professor of German history at the University of Pennsylvania who had decided to put aside his usual scholarship to write a more personal history based on his uncle's letters, he understood he was in many ways following Ambrose's path. As publicity over the scandal increased, however, Childers spoke out, and Ambrose's scholarly reputation was increasingly called into question.

Eventually, Ambrose would deny that he was an academic writer, although the public would continue to see him as just that. Academic historians, too, considered him an academic writer, although Ambrose initially had the support of prominent academic historians such as Eric Foner, a past president of the American Historical Association. Although Ambrose had not been on the faculty of any university for years, his academic pedigree was widely recognized enough that people began to ask whether he got away with plagiarism because he had no position to lose. However, Ambrose's reputation continued to suffer, as revelations emerged that he had copied sources beyond the Childers book.

Ambrose was soon accused of plagiarism in writing other books, most notably *Upton and the Army* (1964), which had been based heavily on Pe-

ter Michie's *The Life and Letters of Emory Upton*, published in 1885. These discoveries led to further criticisms of Ambrose's scholarly methods. In *Upton and the Army*, Ambrose had followed his by-then familiar pattern of giving effusive credit to a source that he then failed to properly cite. Further investigation of *Upton and the Army* revealed the more egregious lifting of sources that went well beyond Michie.

Ambrose never fully recovered from the scandal. In February, 2002, one month after the story of his plagiarism broke, he announced that he was abandoning his works in progress to focus on his memoirs; six months later he died of lung cancer. Although his books continued to be widely read, his reputation as America's topmost authority on military history was permanently damaged. Remaining is the nagging question of why he did what he did. One possible explanation was the pressure he felt to produce. Also, many have argued that because he was no longer an academic historian—that he was not affiliated with an educational institution—he likely believed that he did not have to abide by the ethics and rules of academia.

IMPACT

The Ambrose scandal had a significant impact on the public's perception of history and on the self-perception of historians as a whole, especially in regard to the line between academic and popular history. In particular, the scandal has raised the question of whether celebrity historians such as Ambrose should be treated differently than their less-famous colleagues.

Aside from the fact that Ambrose was accountable to no academic institution, the success of his plagiarism also raises the issue of the complicity of editors and publishers when dealing with a writer of Ambrose's stature and popularity. Additionally, some commentators have suggested that had the history profession not chosen to make an issue of the plagiarism, Ambrose might have suffered far less consequences.

Finally, beyond the question of plagiarism, the scandal raised the issue of whether history writing, even popular history writing, is about more than simply collecting, arranging, and rehashing established facts. In the end, while academic historians have distanced themselves from Ambrose and his work, his books remain popular with general readers, most likely because they have not heard of the scandal.

—*Susan Roth Breitzer*

FURTHER READING

Ambrose, Stephen. *The Wild Blue: The Men and Boys Who Flew the B-24s over Germany.* New York: Simon & Schuster, 2001. Ambrose's popular account of World War II bomber pilots that became the source of the plagiarism scandal.

Barnes, Fred. "Stephen Ambrose, Copycat." *The Weekly Standard*, January 14, 2002. The article, written as a review of Ambrose's *The Wild Blue* and Childers's *Wings of the Morning*, which broke the scandal.

Childers, Thomas. *Wings of the Morning: The Story of the Last American Bomber Shot Down over Germany in World War II.* New York: Perseus, 1995. The original account of a World War II bomber squadron from which Ambrose copied material for *The Wild Blue.*

Hoffer, Peter Charles. *Past Imperfect: Facts, Fictions, Fraud—American History from Bancroft and Parkman to Ambrose, Belleslies, Ellis, and Goodwin.* New York: PublicAffairs, 2003. A close examination of the state of the American history profession, with a focus on problems of fraud and fabrication and their resultant scandals, including that of Ambrose.

Skinner, David. "Cheating History: Ambrose, Bellesiles, Ellis, and Goodwin—The Historians Who Let Us Down." *The Weekly Standard*, November 29, 2004. Focuses on a dozen key controversies ranging across the political spectrum and representative of a wide variety of charges of falsifying work or other academic fraud.

Weiner, John. *Historians in Trouble: Plagiarism, Fraud, and Politics in the Ivory Tower.* New York: New Press, 1995. A study of academic scandals in the fields of history and the humanities. Includes the chapter "The Plagiarists: Doris Kearns Goodwin and Stephen Ambrose."

SEE ALSO: June 5, 1944: Australian Poets Claim Responsibility for a Literary Hoax; Jan. 28, 1972: Clifford Irving Admits Faking Howard Hughes Memoirs; 1978: *Roots* Author Alex Haley Is Sued for Plagiarism; Dec. 3, 1989: Martin Luther King, Jr.'s, Doctoral-Thesis Plagiarism Is Revealed; Apr., 1998: Scottish Historian Is Charged with Plagiarism; May 11, 1998: Journalist Stephen Glass Is Exposed as a Fraud; June 18, 2001: Historian Joseph J. Ellis Is Accused of Lying; Jan. 18, 2002: Historian Doris Kearns Goodwin Is Accused of Plagiarism; Oct. 25, 2002: Historian Michael A. Bellesiles Resigns After Academic Fraud Accusations; July 24, 2007: University of Colorado Fires Professor for Plagiarism and Research Falsification.

2000's

January 6, 2002
BOSTON GLOBE REPORTS ON CHILD SEXUAL ABUSE BY ROMAN CATHOLIC PRIESTS

A series of articles in the Boston Globe *revealed the systematic efforts of the Roman Catholic archdiocese to cover up incidents of sexual abuse by priests and to silence victims wishing to bring these crimes to the attention of authorities and the public. The revelations touched off a nationwide flurry of accusations by others claiming of similar abuse, some of whom were molested decades earlier, as children.*

LOCALE: Boston, Massachusetts

CATEGORIES: Publishing and journalism; sex crimes; religion; public morals; families and children; law and the courts

KEY FIGURES

Bernard Law (b. 1931), Catholic cardinal and archbishop of Boston, 1984-2002

John Geoghan (1935-2003), Catholic priest

Mitchell Garabedian (b. 1952), Boston attorney

Constance M. Sweeney (b. 1950), Superior Court judge in Massachusetts

Joseph Birmingham (1934-1989), Catholic priest

Paul Shanley (b. 1931), Catholic priest

Wilton D. Gregory (b. 1947), president, U.S. Conference of Catholic Bishops, 2001-2004

Frank Keating (b. 1944), governor of Oklahoma, 1995-2003

John Paul II (Karol Józef Wojtyła; 1920-2005), Catholic pope, 1978-2005

Benedict XVI (Joseph Alois Ratzinger; b. 1927), Catholic pope, 2005-

SUMMARY OF EVENT

On January 6, 2002, the *Boston Globe* ran the first of what would be hundreds of news stories detailing sexual abuse by Roman Catholic clergy. The initial story, "Church Allowed Abuse by Priest for Years," focused on John Geoghan, a Catholic priest defrocked in 1998, whose eighty-six known victims accused him of molesting them. Some of his acts dated back more than three decades.

The exposure of an individual member of the clergy as a sex offender was not new to the Church. Cases had been reported in Boston and elsewhere for at least half a century. What made the 2002 story unusual, and what would eventually have a catastrophic impact on the Catholic Church in Boston and indeed throughout the country and the world, was the revelation that Geoghan and other priests had been protected from exposure and prosecution by Church authorities who had frequently reassigned priests from parish to parish, provided clandestine settlements to their accusers in return for keeping incidents secret, and in some cases intimidated victims by threatening retribution if they made their accusations public.

The Boston sexual abuse scandal began during the mid-1990's when attorney Mitchell Garabedian began filing suits on behalf of plaintiffs claiming to have been sexually assaulted by Geoghan. To determine whether other victims or other abusers existed, Garabedian petitioned for access to Church records. Because courts throughout the United States historically considered these records private, Garabedian's request was denied. However, in the course of legal proceedings in July, 2001, Boston's archbishop, Cardinal Bernard Law, admitted he had known of accusations against Geoghan since 1984 and was aware the priest had been transferred among parishes rather than removed from ministry.

Learning of Law's admission and sensing there might be a larger story, the new editor of the *Boston Globe* set out to have the court grant the newspaper access to Church files. After months of argument, Superior Court judge Constance M. Sweeney ruled that the Church would be required to turn over all relevant documents to the *Boston Globe*. Although archdiocesan attorneys appealed, Sweeney stood firm by her order that documents be released by January, 2002. Meanwhile, a special investigative unit at the paper began compiling stories based on interviews with alleged victims of Geoghan and others and documenting what it believed was a long-standing systematic attempt by Church authorities to protect pedophiles—alleged and proven—from exposure and prosecution.

When it broke the initial story about Geoghan, the paper invited other victims to contact reporters with additional information. The paper received a flood of correspondence outlining abuses by dozens of priests, some cases dating back into the 1940's. Initially, the activities of two other priests generated significant interest.

The Reverend Paul Shanley, formerly in the Boston archdiocese but at this time working in California, was accused of having sexually molested boys as early as 1966. For years, Shanley was vocal in challenging the Church's position on homosexuality and was associated with the North American Man/Boy Love Association, which advocates for consensual sex between men and boys. Shanley denied all charges, but a chorus of accusers outlined for news media and attorneys the many instances during which he had taken advantage of their trust. An even more egregious case was that involving the Reverend Joseph Birmingham, who had died in 1989. More than one hundred people came forward to relate stories of how, for more than thirty years, Birmingham had molested children.

Investigators poring over Church records discovered that Law and his predecessors had been aware of the criminal acts of Geoghan, Shanley, Birmingham, and others. Instead of removing them from ministry, however, they allowed priests accused of sex offenses to continue serving in parishes. In some cases, these men were given increasingly more important and sensitive assignments while victims were discouraged from pursuing claims against the accused. Technically, Church officials could claim they broke no laws, because priests were exempt from civil

statutes requiring officials involved in counseling or health care to report cases of suspected abuse. The Massachusetts legislature moved quickly to close that loophole in February, 2002.

Although Geoghan was tried and convicted of one count of sexual abuse in February, 2002, the *Boston Globe* continued its series on the scandal, having identified nearly one hundred priests who had at one time been accused of sexually abusing minors. As weeks passed, what started out as a local scandal quickly became a national catastrophe for the Catholic Church. Emboldened by what they saw happening in Boston, victims of clergy abuse in dioceses across the United States began telling their stories publicly. Some had already received compensation and counseling, but the media was able to

John Geoghan, left, a defrocked Roman Catholic priest, listens in court in January, 2002, after he is convicted of sexually assaulting a boy in 1991. (AP/Wide World Photos)

2000's

955

make a strong case that the problem was endemic throughout the Catholic Church in the United States. The media focused on the behavior of bishops and other Church officials in attempting to keep these incidents secret while allowing known sex offenders to continue in ministries often involving children. These official Church actions bordered on criminal misconduct. One attorney even suggested that Church officials be prosecuted under the federal law designed to root out organized crime in America.

In Boston, Cardinal Law initially attempted to stonewall attempts by the *Boston Globe* to pursue its investigation and dealt peremptorily with media and Catholic laypersons who peppered him for additional information. He refused to meet with victims, questioned the veracity of some accusations, repeatedly suggested he had not been aware of many of the incidents, and sought in other ways to deflect blame from the Church hierarchy. His actions seemed only to spur additional media attention and eventually turned many laypersons against the Church. Particularly outraged were victims-rights groups such as the Survivors' Network of those Abused by Priests (SNAP), an organization founded in 1989. While Law was insisting that confidentiality was required to protect both the victim and the accused, a number of influential lay leaders began calling the scandal the American Catholic Church's Watergate. Catholics held protests outside churches in Boston, and calls for Law's resignation began almost immediately.

At the national level, the president of the U.S. Conference of Catholic Bishops, Wilton D. Gregory, began working on measures for dealing with the spiraling problem facing his fellow prelates. By the June, 2002, meeting of the American bishops in Dallas, Gregory had managed to draft a document outlining ways bishops should deal with sex offenders under their jurisdiction. Gregory's proposal included participation by the laity in reviewing cases of clergy sexual abuse. After significant debate, the document was approved. Because each bishop in the Catholic Church can act with relative autonomy within his diocese, however, Gregory had no way of enforcing these policies. Similar guidelines had

been suggested during the mid-1990's after a scandal in Chicago, but a number of bishops—including Cardinal Law—had argued against them because they infringed on a bishop's discretionary authority. Additionally, before these procedures could be formally adopted, officials in Rome were required to approve them as well.

Despite these barriers, Gregory took the extraordinary step of appointing a thirteen-member lay commission, a national review board, to assist bishops in addressing issues concerning clergy accused of abuse. Frank Keating, the governor of Oklahoma and a strong Catholic, agreed to lead this board. The national review board was not well received by many bishops, though, as some considered it an undue intrusion of the laity into matters that had traditionally been handled by the clergy under the terms of canon law, the documents governing the organization and operation of the Church worldwide.

Prior to the June meeting, Gregory went to Rome to seek assistance from Pope John Paul II. Unfortunately, the Vatican tried to distance itself from the scandal in the United States. Already aware that sexual abuse by clergy was a worldwide problem, in 2001 the pope appointed a commission headed by Cardinal Joseph Ratzinger (the future Pope Benedict XVI), the conservative theologian then serving as prefect of the congregation for the doctrine of the faith, to propose a method for handling the problem. Their solution was a mandate: Rather than permitting reassignment, every accused was to be brought before a secret clerical tribunal.

Although the pope met with Gregory and other American prelates to discuss the growing scandal, he suggested the bishops would have to handle matters themselves. Meanwhile, Vatican officials identified two main causes for the widespread sexual abuse: a lax moral climate in which some priests were seduced to forget their calling, and the presence of gays among the clergy. Some lay Catholics and people outside the Church blamed the problem on the requirement that priests remain celibate, but the Vatican refused to consider this possibility. Neither in the United States or Rome was there any acknowledgment that clerical culture, in which priests tended to protect each other while maintaining the facade of perfection for their actions, might lie at the root of the problem.

Church officials in Rome found guidelines approved in Dallas unacceptable. A new commission consisting of American bishops and representatives of the Vatican drafted a compromise document that curtailed involvement by the laity and instead dictated that accused priests have cases heard by clerical tribunals. The revised policies were approved by the American bishops at a meeting in November.

By the fall of 2002, Law began to see the hopelessness of his position as Boston's Catholic leader. He finally met with victims to learn firsthand of their pain, but his gestures at reconciliation were too late. As the year drew to a close, suits against the Boston archdiocese were mounting. Garabedian was representing eighty-six clients, a Boston law firm was litigating against 135 priests, and other firms were involved in representing dozens of other victims. Many of the plaintiffs were suing not only the offenders but also Church officials. Law worked out a secret deal with Garabedian to settle with Geoghan's victims for somewhere between $35 and $50 million, but the deal was vetoed by his finance council, a group of lay leaders who did not want Church donations paying for priests' crimes. In early December, rumors began spreading that the archdiocese would file for bankruptcy to shield itself from further lawsuits.

Law flew to Rome and offered his resignation to the pope, who accepted it on December 13. By this time nearly every diocese in the United States had been touched by the scandal, and more than twelve hundred priests had been identified as abusers by nearly five thousand alleged victims. The *Boston Globe* ran its investigative series for more than a year, after publishing nearly nine hundred articles. The paper, which won a Pulitzer Prize in 2003 for the series, also added extensive coverage of the scandal to its Web site (boston.com/globe/spotlight/abuse/).

IMPACT

The effect of the sex abuse scandal on the Church in the United States was devastating, and it extended far beyond a single diocese. Already suffering from a shortage of priests, bishops were forced to remove more than four hundred from active ministry as a result of charges brought against them. Five bishops also were forced to resign. A handful of accused priests were tried for their crimes. Geoghan, who had gone to jail in 2002, was murdered in prison by another inmate the year after he was incarcerated. Shanley was convicted and sentenced to jail in 2005. Across the United States a number of accused priests committed suicide, and one was shot by one of his victims.

Lawsuits from individuals who had been abused in the past were settled for sums running into the hundreds of millions of dollars. For example, the Boston archdiocese eventually paid $85 million to settle claims; the archdiocese of Los Angeles paid more than $600 million, Orange (California) $100 million, Dallas $31 million, and Louisville paid nearly $26 million. Because the Church traditionally considered each diocese an independent financial entity, individual bishops had to meet these financial obligations. As a result, many dioceses filed for bankruptcy protection between 2002 and 2007.

The effect on the Catholic laity was equally devastating. Taught to trust clergy as guides of morality and character, millions were shocked and repulsed by the growing litany of accusations. Church attendance sagged and financial contributions plummeted. Many lay people who wished to help reform the Church organized groups such as Voice of the Faithful, but their efforts were frequently rebuffed by Church officials fearful of giving the laity too strong a role in oversight of Church matters. This rejection led to even further distrust and alienation, and many influential Catholics were vocal in their resentment toward the American bishops and the Vatican.

Outside the Church, many Americans who already possessed anti-Catholic or antireligious sentiments took the opportunity to revel in the predicament Catholics were experiencing. Many people, however, including clergy from other Christian denominations and those from other faiths, expressed regret and sympathy for Catholics.

The stigma attached to the priesthood in the United States prompted John Paul II's successor,

Pope Benedict XVI, to speak frequently of the matter and offer numerous apologies during his April, 2008, visit to the United States. Benedict even met with some of the victims to offer the Church's regrets for what had happened to them at the hands of men they trusted.

—*Laurence W. Mazzeno*

FURTHER READING

Berry, Jason, and Gerald Renner. *Vows of Silence: The Abuse of Power in the Papacy of John Paul II*. New York: Free Press, 2004. Explores what the authors consider to be a decades-long systematic attempt by the Vatican to cover up or ignore charges of sexual abuse by priests in the United States and elsewhere.

Cozzens, Donald B. *The Changing Face of the Priesthood*. Collegeville, Minn.: Liturgical Press, 2000. Examines reasons for the difficulties experienced by the Church in the United States in attracting a healthy cross-section of potential priests. Includes a chapter on the priesthood's long-standing problems of pedophilia and molestation.

France, David. *Our Fathers: The Secret Life of the Catholic Church in an Age of Scandal*. New York: Broadway Books, 2004. Account of the scandal's background and a detailed chronology and analysis of the crisis. Discusses the systematic attempts of Church officials to keep the scandal out of the public eye. Includes a list of principal figures and an extensive bibliography.

Greeley, Andrew M. *Priests: A Calling in Crisis*. Chicago: University of Chicago Press, 2004. Systematic examination of the priesthood in the aftermath of the 2002 scandal. Designed to explain the nature of the priesthood, dispel myths about the causes for the unusually large number of pedophiles identified subsequent to initial reports of incidents in Boston, and outline root causes for the problems plaguing the Church in the United States.

Investigative Staff of the Boston Globe. *Betrayal: The Crisis in the Catholic Church*. Boston: Little, Brown, 2002. Detailed coverage of the unearthing of the sex abuse scandal. Includes victims' graphic stories as well as discussion of the alleged official cover-up and reactions to the scandal.

Jenkins, Philip. *Pedophiles and Priests: Anatomy of a Contemporary Crisis*. 1996. New ed. Bridgewater, N.J.: Replica Books, 2000. Describes the climate in the Church that fostered reticence among those in authority to deal with matters of sexual abuse. Offers a historical perspective on the issue, which has plagued the Church for decades, if not longer.

SEE ALSO: Feb. 23, 1963: Play Accuses Pope Pius XII of Complicity in the Holocaust; May 20, 1974: French Cardinal Daniélou Dies in a Prostitute's House; Sept. 10, 1981: *Chicago Sun-Times* Reports That Cardinal Cody Diverted Church Funds; Aug. 6, 1982: Banco Ambrosiano Collapses Amid Criminal Accusations; Aug. 12, 1983-July 27, 1990: McMartin Preschool Is Embroiled in Child-Abuse Case; May 6, 1992: Irish Bishop Eamonn Casey's Romantic Affair Leads to His Resignation; Mar. 4, 1999: Quebec Offers Support for Abused Duplessis Orphans; June 30, 2001: Korean Religious Teacher Jung Myung Seok Is Charged with Rape.

January 18, 2002
HISTORIAN DORIS KEARNS GOODWIN IS ACCUSED OF PLAGIARISM

Doris Kearns Goodwin, a Harvard University professor and author of several award-winning books, was accused of plagiarizing another author's work for her best-selling and award-winning history The Fitzgeralds and the Kennedys *(1987). Goodwin created further scandal when it was revealed that in 1987, she had paid off the author whose work she plagiarized.*

LOCALE: United States

CATEGORIES: Cultural and intellectual history; education; hoaxes, frauds, and charlatanism; plagiarism; publishing and journalism

KEY FIGURES

Doris Kearns Goodwin (b. 1943), professor of American history and author

Lynne McTaggart (b. 1951), journalist and author

Bo Crader (fl. early twenty-first century), *Weekly Standard* editorial staff member

SUMMARY OF EVENT

Doris Kearns Goodwin, a Harvard University professor, political commentator, and well-regarded historian, is also the author of award-winning books. *No Ordinary Time: Franklin and Eleanor Roosevelt—The Home Front in World War II* (1994), a history of the Roosevelt White House during the years of World War II, won a Pulitzer Prize in 1995, and *The Fitzgeralds and the Kennedys: An American Saga* (1987), became the basis for the popular television series *The Kennedys of Massachusetts.*

Goodwin, whose career began as a White House Fellow and later special assistant to President Lyndon B. Johnson, also served as a Public Broadcasting Service commentator, covering the Democratic and Republican National Conventions and the presidential debates. Considering her professional credentials, it came as a shock when Bo Crader of *The Weekly Standard* reported on January 18, 2002, that Goodwin had plagiarized some of her most highly regarded books. The article, "A Historian and Her Sources," came just two weeks after the same periodical revealed the plagiarism of American historian Stephen E. Ambrose. The Goodwin scandal also involved earlier efforts by Goodwin to head off potential negative publicity in a hush-money arrangement with the author whom she had plagiarized.

The Fitzgeralds and the Kennedys, Goodwin's book that raised questions of plagiarism, had been on the best-seller list of *The New York Times* for five months and had won numerous awards after it was published in 1987. It was widely known before the scandal broke that Goodwin relied on an earlier history of the Kennedy family by Lynne McTaggart called *Kathleen Kennedy: Her Life and Times* (1983) in writing her own book. What remained unnoticed, however, was Goodwin's use of numerous quotations from McTaggart's book without attribution. Furthermore, McTaggart, a journalist by profession, had written her book in a style and format that used few footnotes, which made tracing the book's primary sources difficult and encouraged reliance on the finished work for direct quotations. Nonetheless, Goodwin's plagiarism raised a question that also came up in the Ambrose case: Did Goodwin, a popular historian, profit from the original research of a predecessor? Goodwin's case also brought up the issue of failing to fully acknowledge secondary sources.

Making matters worse was Goodwin's effort to settle her plagiarism without publicity. In 1987, soon after *The Fitzgeralds and the Kennedys* was published, McTaggart noticed the misappropriation of her work. She contacted Goodwin through an attorney, who threatened a lawsuit for copyright infringement. Goodwin responded by negotiating a deal in which her publisher would pay McTaggart a significant sum in exchange for her silence; Goodwin also promised to add the necessary quotation

2000's

Doris Kearns Goodwin speaks at a history forum in St. Paul, Minnesota, in March, 2002. It was her first public appearance since she was accused of plagiarism. (AP/Wide World Photos)

marks, attributions, or both in future editions of the book. Even as she sought to settle with McTaggart, however, Goodwin insisted that the omissions had been unintentional and few in number. She blamed many of the errors on her poor note-taking skills. McTaggart agreed to the arrangement because she did not want to harm Goodwin's reputation. However, when the 2001 edition of *The Fitzgeralds and the Kennedys* failed to include many of the agreed-upon changes—Goodwin later claimed that to have done so would have broken the flow of the narrative—McTaggart decided to go public with the story. In an interview with *The Weekly Standard*, published on January 23, she said, "There is a moral issue in general that needs to be examined. The only reason I'm talking now is just to set the record straight. At least let's have the full story."

The scandal-breaking *Weekly Standard* article of January 18 led to great controversy both within the history profession and among American readers. Goodwin's most highly regarded work, *No Ordinary Time*, also became the center of scandal when it, too, was found to include plagiarized passages. A number of historians rushed to Goodwin's defense,

most publicly in a letter to the editor in *The New York Times* (October 25, 2003) that was signed by prominent historians, including Sean Wilentz, David Halberstam, and Arthur Schlesinger, Jr., a close colleague. The letter denied that she committed plagiarism, a claim that provoked even more scandal. Critics of the letter said it was nothing more than an effort to deny the truth and rewrite the very definition of plagiarism, all for the sake of protecting a famous historian.

The American Historical Association issued a statement rejecting one defense, which claimed that Goodwin's apparent lack of intent meant that she did not plagiarize. The controversy soon took on a political dimension, as Goodwin's supporters accused her accusers of a political conspiracy against her, a charge that was fairly plausible given her prominence in liberal political circles. After the story became fully public, however, Goodwin worked to have errors and omissions corrected as they were identified.

IMPACT

The Goodwin scandal had its greatest impact in its exposure of the problem of plagiarism and cheating at the highest levels of historical scholarship, calling into question the integrity of a prominent historian and the validity of her work. Her defenders raised the issue of intention, arguing that intention matters in the definition of plagiarism.

For a time, the damage was done. Goodwin was dropped as a PBS commentator for the 2004 election season, and she also resigned her position with the Pulitzer Prize selection committee. However, the media-savvy Goodwin worked effectively to rehabilitate her image. She hired a media consultant and even made an appearance on *The Late Show with David Letterman* to poke fun at herself and explain the scandal. She eventually left her faculty position at Harvard University, although she remained on its board of overseers.

Commentators have reminded readers about the seriousness of both Goodwin's plagiarism and her attempts to cover it up; still, she made a comeback with *Team of Rivals: The Political Genius of Abraham Lincoln* (2005). She also became a popular public speaker and a remains a widely admired historian. Her Web site carefully avoids mention of the scandal, making only the briefest reference to *The Fitzgeralds and the Kennedys.*

—*Susan Roth Breitzer*

FURTHER READING

Crader, Bo. "A Historian and Her Sources." *The Weekly Standard*, January 28, 2002. The article that broke the Goodwin scandal to the public. First published on the periodical's Web site on January 18.

Goodwin, Doris Kearns. *The Fitzgeralds and the Kennedys: An American Saga.* New York: Simon & Schuster, 1987. The nine-hundred-page Kennedy family history that became the center of the plagiarism scandal.

Hoffer, Peter Charles. *Past Imperfect: Facts, Fictions, Fraud—American History from Bancroft and Parkman to Ambrose, Belleslies, Ellis, and Goodwin.* New York: PublicAffairs, 2003. A history of the American history profession, with a focus on modern problems and scandals.

McTaggart, Lynne. "Fame Can't Excuse a Plagiarist." *The New York Times*, March 16, 2002. An opinion article, written shortly after the scandal broke, in which McTaggart claims that Goodwin appropriated thousands of her words from *Kathleen Kennedy.*

_____. *Kathleen Kennedy: Her Life and Times.* New York: Dial Press, 1983. The biography of U.S. president John F. Kennedy's sister, from which Doris Kearns Goodwin was accused of stealing material.

Weiner, John. *Historians in Trouble: Plagiarism, Fraud, and Politics in the Ivory Tower.* New York: New Press, 1995. A study of academic scandals in the fields of history and the humanities. Includes the chapter "The Plagiarists: Doris Kearns Goodwin and Stephen Ambrose."

SEE ALSO: June 5, 1944: Australian Poets Claim Responsibility for a Literary Hoax; Jan. 28, 1972: Clifford Irving Admits Faking Howard Hughes Memoirs; 1978: *Roots* Author Alex Haley Is Sued for Plagiarism; Dec. 3, 1989: Martin Luther King, Jr.'s, Doctoral-Thesis Plagiarism Is Revealed; Apr., 1998: Scottish Historian Is Charged with Plagiarism; May 11, 1998: Journalist Stephen Glass Is Exposed as a Fraud; June 18, 2001: Historian Joseph J. Ellis Is Accused of Lying; Jan. 4, 2002: Historian Stephen E. Ambrose Is Accused of Plagiarism; Oct. 25, 2002: Historian Michael A. Belleslies Resigns After Academic Fraud Accusations; July 24, 2007: University of Colorado Fires Professor for Plagiarism and Research Falsification.

2000's

February 11, 2002
FRENCH JUDGE ADMITS FAVORING RUSSIAN FIGURE SKATERS IN WINTER OLYMPICS

During the 2002 Winter Olympic Games in Utah, judges awarded the Russian figure skating pair the gold medal in a decision that led to major controversy, as many thought the Canadian silver medalists deserved to win gold instead. The French judge soon admitted that her federation had pressured her to vote for the Russians in a deal designed to help the French ice dancing couple. The scandal resulted in the awarding of a second gold medal and the creation of a new judging system for figure skating at the international level of competition.

ALSO KNOWN AS: Skategate
LOCALE: Salt Lake City, Utah
CATEGORIES: Corruption; sports; international relations

KEY FIGURES
Marie Reine Le Gougne (b. 1961), French pairs-skating judge
Jamie Salé (b. 1977), Canadian pairs skater
David Pelletier (b. 1974), Canadian pairs skater
Elena Berezhnaya (b. 1977), Russian pairs skater
Anton Sikharulidze (b. 1976), Russian pairs skater
Ottavio Cinquanta (b. 1938), president of the International Skating Union
Jacques Rogge (b. 1942), president of the International Olympic Committee

SUMMARY OF EVENT
Figure skating is one of the most popular, visible, and highly anticipated events of the Winter Olympic Games. Scandal erupted at the 2002 Olympics in Salt Lake City, Utah, after judges were accused of fixing the scores of the finals in pairs figure skating. The pairs-skating event featured a rivalry between two teams, the Russians and the Canadians, both of whom had won world championships. Audiences eagerly awaited a great competition for the gold medal. Both teams skated well in the short pro-

gram, and both had a chance for the gold medal in the decisive long program held several days later. Only one team would win the gold, or so everyone thought.

On February 11, 2002, the final night of the pairs-skating event, Elena Berezhnaya and Anton Sikharulidze of Russia performed a technically difficult program, but not without errors. The Canadian pair of Jamie Salé and David Pelletier followed with a flawless but less technically difficult program set to the music from the film *Love Story*. The audience cheered the Canadians with great approval. Television commentators Scott Hamilton and Sandra Bezic, both former Olympic medalists in skating, were sure that the Canadians had delivered the gold-medal-winning performance. The judges' marks came up on the scoreboard. The Russian team received first place ordinals from five of the nine judges on the panel, giving them the gold medal in a controversial 5-4 split. The final decision was met by shock and bewilderment from spectators, commentators, and Salé and Pelletier and their coach.

Questions about judging were not new to the sport of figure skating. Judges often have been accused of voting with a bias toward either the Eastern bloc or the Western bloc, Cold War terms that divided nations along geographical and political boundaries. In the 2002 Olympics pairs-skating competition, the judges representing countries in the Eastern bloc—Russia, China, Poland, and Ukraine—placed the Russians first. The judges from the Western bloc—the United States, Canada, Germany, and Japan—placed the Canadians first. The judge from France, a Western bloc nation, placed the Russians first. That judge, Marie Reine Le Gougne, admitted shortly after the event that she had been pressured to vote for the Russian pair. She claimed at the time that the head of the French skating federation, Didier Gailhaguet, made a deal to aid French ice dancers Marina Anissina and Gwendal Peizerat, scheduled to compete later in the Games. Le Gougne recanted her story after speaking to International Skating Union (ISU) president Ottavio Cinquanta. In a press conference, Cinquanta stated that there was no evidence to prove Le Gougne's original allegations but promised an internal ISU review.

The growing scandal, not the first for these Games, received worldwide media attention. In the face of the scandal, the Canadian pair made multiple television appearances in both the United States and Canada, and the Russian pair made appearances as well. The Games in Salt Lake City already had been tainted with scandal before it had begun. The Salt Lake City Organizing Committee (SLOC) had been accused of bribing International Olympic Committee (IOC) members with cash and gifts to ensure acceptance of the city's bid to host the Olympics. Four IOC officials and two top SLOC executives had resigned during the course of the affair.

The Canadian press dubbed the pairs-skating scandal Skategate. Past instances of cheating and controversial judging decisions resurfaced during the media controversy. The IOC and the ISU were forced to take action amid accusations that figure skating results were determined in backroom deals before events. IOC president Jacques Rogge pressured the ISU to quickly resolve the situation and strongly urged it to award a second pair of gold medals to the Canadian team.

The ISU had no official guidelines on how to resolve cases of cheating in judging. Ultimately, Rogge and Cinquanta announced that the Canadians would receive their gold medals in a new medals ceremony, but the unprecedented solution did not satisfy everyone. The Canadians were happy to receive their gold medals, but they felt cheated of the moment of victory they felt they earned. The French judge was suspended while the investigation continued, but many believed she should have been permanently banned from judging. Meanwhile, the ISU introduced an interim judging system just months after the 2002 Olympics ended, and it developed an entirely new judging system—the Code of Points—for all international competitions beginning in 2006.

IMPACT

The controversial judging and the well-publicized scandal ensured embarrassment for both the sport of figure skating and the Olympics. Because of the subjective nature of its judging, many thought it best to drop figure skating, or certain events in skating, from the Olympic Games. Dropping or curtailing figure skating, however, was unlikely because of the sport's popularity with viewers; skating also is a major source of revenue for the Games. Still, the scandal had to be addressed to restore the sport's credibility, and the credibility of the Olympics.

The ISU developed its new judging system, the Code of Points, to replace the traditional judging system that had been in place for decades. The new system closely resembles those used in the sports of diving and gymnastics. In figure skating's old system, in which judges would mark skaters on a subjective scale of 0.0 to 6.0 and assign ranking ordinals, judges now give skaters set numbers of points for performed jumps, spins, and other elements. Judges also assign points for skating skills, choreography, and other elements that used to fall under the second—artistic—mark in the 6.0 system. These scores are anonymously entered into a computer, which randomly selects the scores of nine judges and eliminates the highest and lowest scores. The judges' anonymity and the assignment of points versus ranks is meant to add more objectivity to the system. The Code of Points was used for the 2006 Winter Olympic Games in Torino, Italy.

The pairs scandal was a turning point, both good and bad, in the sport of figure skating. The new judging system changed how skaters trained and developed their programs, and provided for more objective judging. However, many believe that the damage to the sport's credibility brought on by the scandal contributed to a subsequent decline in public interest in the sport, as measured by television ratings and ticket sales.

—*Marcella Bush Trevino*

FURTHER READING

Garbato, Sonia Bianchetti. *Cracked Ice: Figure Skating's Inner World*. Milan, Italy: Libreria dello Sport, 2004. Memoir of a former ISU

2000's

judge, technical committee member, and council member. Places the 2002 pairs scandal within the context of a sport riddled with scandals and corruption for years before.

Goodwin, Joy. *The Second Mark: Courage, Corruption, and the Battle for Olympic Gold*. New York: Simon & Schuster, 2004. Stories of the lives and careers of the three pairs medalists from the 2002 Olympics as well as a backstage view of the judging scandal. Emphasis on the subjectivity of the second (artistic) judging mark, formerly used in skating competitions.

Pound, Richard W. *Inside the Olympics: A Behind the Scenes Look at the Politics, the Scandals, and the Glory of the Games*. New York: John Wiley & Sons, 2004. Insider recounting of the modern history of the International Olympic

Committee from a longtime committee member.

Smith, Beverley. *Gold on Ice: The Salé and Pelletier Story*. Toronto, Ont.: Key Porter Books, 2002. A brief work that discusses the early lives and careers of the Canadian pairs team at the heart of the scandal as well as the investigations and politics of the scandal itself.

SEE ALSO: Aug. 19, 1973: Cheating Scandal Shocks Soap Box Derby; June 30, 1994: Tonya Harding Is Banned from Skating After Attack on Rival; Sept. 26, 2000: Gymnast Andreea Răducan Loses Her Olympic Gold Medal Because of Drugs; July 26, 2006: Tour de France Is Hit with a Doping Scandal; Oct. 5, 2007: Olympic Champion Marion Jones Admits Steroid Use.

February 17, 2002
ROTTING HUMAN BODIES ARE FOUND AT GEORGIA CREMATORY

More than three hundred rotting human bodies that should have been cremated were found unceremoniously dumped on the grounds of Tri-State Crematory in Noble, Georgia. Most of the corpses had to be identified using either forensic methods or the shipping records of the funeral homes that worked with Tri-State. Some of the bodies never were identified. At the time of the discovery, Georgia state funeral laws were lax on cremation requirements, licensing, and inspections, thus the dumping went unnoticed.

LOCALE: Noble, Georgia

CATEGORIES: Corruption; business; hoaxes, frauds, and charlatanism; environmental issues; government; public morals

KEY FIGURES

Ray Marsh (1928-2003), co-owner of Tri-State Crematory

Clara Marsh (b. 1931), co-owner of Tri-State Crematory

Tommy Ray-Brent Marsh (b. 1974), crematory manager, son of Ray and Clara Marsh

SUMMARY OF EVENT

In November, 2001, officials in Walker County, Georgia, were alerted by the U.S. Environmental Protection Agency that a neighbor had complained that something was not quite right at the Tri-State Crematory, which was located in a rural area of the county. The caller had reported seeing human body parts in the woods adjacent to the crematory. Sheriff's deputies visited the property but did not find anything amiss.

On February 17, 2002, following additional complaints, Walker County officials again visited the crematory and the homes of owners Ray and Clara Marsh and their son, Tommy Ray-Brent Marsh. Their homes were located on the grounds of

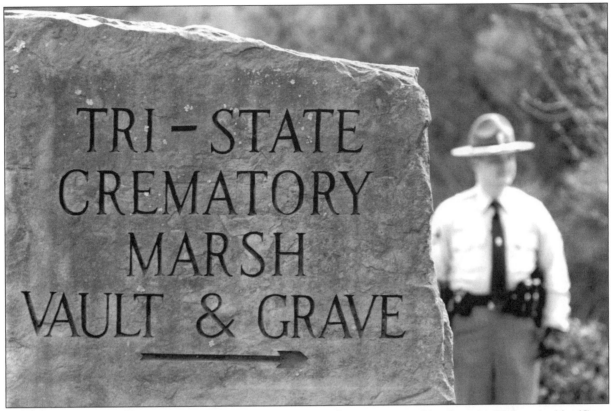

A Georgia law enforcement officer at the entrance to Tri-State Crematory in Noble, Georgia. (Hulton Archive/Getty Images)

the crematory. This time, officials made gruesome discoveries. Within a few days, hundreds of dead bodies were uncovered on the twenty-five-acre property. Some of them had been there only a few days, and others had been there for a number of years. Authorities could not tell why the corpses were dumped and not properly disposed of.

Crematory owners Ray and Clara Marsh were respected members of the Noble community. Ray, whose family was originally from the area, worked for the U.S. Postal Service. He dug ditches and graves with a backhoe in his spare time, a practice he continued for approximately ten years. In 1982, he spent about twenty thousand dollars for cremation equipment, which he housed in a shed on his property, and opened Tri-State Crematory. One of the first minority-owned crematories in the United States, it opened at a time when cremations were relatively rare in the South. Clara was originally

from Mullins, South Carolina. She taught English for the local school district for approximately forty years. Also very active in the community, she was the first African American chairman of the local Democratic committee and also was involved in the local chamber of commerce. After Ray had a debilitating stroke in 1996 and was unable to continue operation of the business, the Marsh's son Tommy kept the place running. As a high school football star, coach of the local youth group, and prospective deacon of his church, Tommy also was a respected member of the community.

As the cremation business grew in the South, Tri-State was accepting bodies not only from Georgia but also Tennessee and Alabama. Hearses were a customary sight at the Marsh property a couple of times each week. No questions were asked when Tommy began picking up the bodies himself at the funeral homes; there was no reason to believe that

965

AMENDING THE LAW ON CREMATION

In May, 2002, Georgia lawmakers amended state law on how funeral homes and crematories treat human corpses before, during, and after cremation. The revised law, excerpted here, was developed in response to the then-recent scandal at Tri-State Crematory.

- This section provides that a person who "throws away or abandons any dead human body or portion of such dead body" commits the crime of abandonment of a dead body. Further, the section makes abandonment of a dead body a felony and imposes a punishment of imprisonment for at least a year, but no more than three. The section excludes medical and other lawful uses from punishment.

- The Act amends Code section 43-18-1 by defining "crematory" as "any place where cremation is performed" excluding hospitals, clinics, laboratories, and other such facilities.

- The Act amends Code section 43-18-8 by requiring funeral directors to place identification tags that include serial numbers identifying prosthesis removed from the body prior to cremation and also requires them to provide a written statement to the person receiving the remains which verifies that the container contains "substantially the remains of the deceased."

- The Act also amends Code section 43-18-72 by requiring that those who operate crematories maintain a license, have a specific address, provide a room that seats at least thirty people, have a display room with a supply of urns, maintain a hearse, have a processing station for the grinding of cremated remains (retort) and have at least one truck. The Act further amends Code section 43-18-72 by requiring crematories to submit reports that list the names of the people it cremates and the types of containers it uses.

anything unusual was happening. The ashes of the deceased were customarily returned to the funeral homes on the next day. Tri-State charged a very reasonable fee of $200 to $250 for the service, while other crematoriums were charging $600 as a starting rate.

Neighbors began to notice that there was no black smoke coming from the crematory, but no one complained. The furnace in the shed had stopped working and needed a new part, leading to a change in the crematory's operations. The Marshes pur-

chased the needed part for less than $200. The vendor offered to install the part, but the family indicated that they did not require any assistance. This did not seem unusual to the vendor because the Marsh's had never requested service from them in all the years they had been in business. Investigators later found that the furnace was operable.

Before the search of the crematory ended, officials discovered more than 330 bodies in various stages of decomposition, strewn all over the property. Bodies were stacked on top of each other. Some were dressed formally, some were dressed in hospital gowns, and some were still in body bags. Most of the corpses did not have identification tags. About fifteen bodies were stored in a burial vault that was intended for only one body. Bodies were stuffed into abandoned vehicles, and more had been thrown into the two-acre lake on the grounds. Neighbors did not complain of the odor of deteriorating bodies because odor from the property was not unusual. However, because human remains were deteriorating at different rates, the stench was likely deplorable.

Officials were forced to deal with a macabre situation. They declared the property a disaster area so that they could receive state funds for its cleanup. After cremation, human remains are returned to family members in temporary containers, if the family did not purchase an urn. The Marshes returned these containers in a timely manner to the funeral homes. However, the urns did not contain the remains of the deceased; they contained sand, ground-up cement, or burned wood-chips mixed with dirt. The families who later discovered that they had been duped by the Marshes felt extreme betrayal, sadness, and anger, and close to seventeen hundred relatives eventually sued.

The case of the rotting bodies was horrifying in itself, but it became even more so when people realized it never should have occurred. Georgia state funeral law at the time was extremely lax in dealing with crematories. Tri-State Crematory apparently had never been inspected, but inspection was limited in the state to begin with. Furthermore, a loophole in Georgia law allowed the business to run without a license for such work. The law did not address a crematory's failure to cremate a human body, mainly because failing to do so was unthinkable. An official with the Georgia Bureau of Investigation said "We have laws against desecrating graves, but we can't find one against desecration of bodies," adding, "I guess nobody in the Legislature ever thought something like this could happen."

State forensic teams had to use a combination of methods to identify the bodies. These methods included matching dental records, DNA testing, and tracking records from the funeral homes where individual bodies originated. The remains that could be identified were cremated and returned to next of kin. About 130 bodies could not be identified and were buried in a mass grave in the fall of 2002. These bodies were not cremated; officials wanted to preserve the DNA of the corpses in case it was needed in future litigation or attempts at identification.

IMPACT

Georgia law could only treat this scandal as a misdemeanor. Tommy Ray-Brent Marsh was eventually convicted of 787 counts of theft, abuse of a corpse, and burial-service fraud. He was sentenced to two twelve-year terms for his crimes—one sentence for the state of Tennessee and one for the state of Georgia. Ray and Clara Marsh were not charged.

Relatives of the deceased filed a class action suit against Tri-State and the funeral homes involved. The award amounted to $36 million from the funeral homes and $18 million from the Marsh's homeowner's insurance policy. In addition, a portion of the Marshes land was set aside in its natural state as a tribute to those who were found there. The Marsh family retains the rights to all the land and the deed remains in their name. The crematorium was destroyed.

Georgia lawmakers rewrote the state's funeral industry laws in the years after the Tri-State scandal broke. The new laws now contain felony provisions for those who abuse them, as well as provisions for the abandonment of a human body.

—*Elizabeth Gaydou Miller*

FURTHER READING

Firestone, David, with Robert D. McFadden. "Scores of Bodies Strewn at Site of Crematory." *The New York Times*, February 17, 2002. National newspaper report of the discovery of human remains at Tri-State Crematory.

Iverson, Kenneth V. *Death to Dust: What Happens to Dead Bodies*. Tucson, Ariz.: Galen Press, 1994. A graphic discussion of the decomposition of the human body after death. Examines embalming, cremation, religious rites, and cultural biases relating to death, funerals, and human remains.

Kitch, Carolyn, and Janice Hume. *Journalism in a Culture of Grief*. New York: Routledge, 2008. Explores "the cultural meanings of death in American journalism and the role of journalism in interpretations and enactments of public grief." Includes a chapter on media coverage of the Tri-State Crematory scandal.

Prothero, Stephen. *Purified by Fire: A History of Cremation in America*. Berkeley: University of California Press, 2001. History of cremation in the United States. Includes a historical time line.

Rosen, Fred. *Cremation in America*. Amherst, N.Y.: Prometheus Books, 2004. A social and cultural history of the cremation industry in the United States. Includes a chapter on the Tri-State scandal. A good introduction, especially for younger readers.

SEE ALSO: Sept. 26, 1979: Love Canal Residents Sue Chemical Company; Jan. 30, 2001: Liverpool Children's Hospital Collects Body Parts Without Authorization.

2000's

March 27, 2002
GEORGIA BASKETBALL COACH JIM HARRICK, SR., RESIGNS OVER FRAUD ALLEGATIONS

University of Georgia basketball coach Jim Harrick, Sr., resigned following accusations of fraud and misconduct against himself and his assistant coach Jim Harrick, Jr., his son. Many people were left wondering who to blame for the scandal after the Harricks had been hired to coach at Georgia even though they had a record of misconduct while coaching at two other universities—UCLA and Rhode Island.

ALSO KNOWN AS: Harrick scandal
LOCALE: Athens, Georgia
CATEGORIES: Corruption; sports; law and the courts

KEY FIGURES
Jim Harrick, Sr. (b. 1938), University of Georgia head basketball coach
Jim Harrick, Jr. (b. 1965), University of Georgia assistant basketball coach
Michael F. Adams (b. 1948), president of the University of Georgia

SUMMARY OF EVENT
Following successful careers coaching at three other universities, Jim Harrick, Sr., was hired as head coach of the University of Georgia Bulldogs of the South Eastern Conference (SEC) at the start of the 1999 basketball season. He led Georgia to two NCAA tournament births in four years. However, the misconduct of his son, Georgia assistant coach Jim Harrick, Jr., caused the elder Harrick the most trouble and led to his resignation on March 27, 2002.

Allegations of corruption against Harrick, Jr., began to surface midway through the 2002 season. Harrick, Jr., allegedly paid a phone bill for Georgia player Tony Cole and provided additional income for high-profile players; this last claim was never proven true. The most serious accusation was that

Harrick, Jr., developed an examination specifically for Georgia basketball players enrolled in one of his classes. He also was accused of awarding A grades to three student-players—Cole, Chris Daniels, and Rashad Wright—who never attended his class.

Before accepting the job at Georgia, Harrick, Sr., had coached at Pepperdine University between 1979 and 1988 and led the Waves to regular-season championships in 1981, 1982, 1983, 1985, and 1986. He also was named West Coast Athletic Conference (WCAC) coach of the year four times and led Pepperdine to four NCAA national basketball tournaments. Harrick was hired to coach the Bruins of the University of California, Los Angeles (UCLA) in 1988. He had been an assistant coach at UCLA prior to accepting the Pepperdine job.

Harrick, Sr., coached at UCLA from 1988 to 1996. He led the Bruins to Pacific 10 Conference (Pac-10) championships in 1992, 1995, and 1996 and was Pac-10 Coach of the Year in each of these seasons as well. The 1994-1995 season ended with the Bruins winning their eleventh NCAA basketball championship. Harrick was revered as a savior after leading UCLA to its first national championship in more than twenty years. Two seasons later, he was removed as head coach of the Bruins following a National Collegiate Athletic Association (NCAA) investigation into allegations that he falsified expense records and receipts for a recruiting dinner. Although Harrick was exonerated by the NCAA, officials at UCLA held firm in their decision to fire Harrick because he lied to investigators.

Harrick, Sr., took a one-year break and returned to the game to coach the University of Rhode Island Rams of the Atlantic-10 Conference. He led the Rams to two NCAA tournament bids, an Atlantic-10 Conference Championship, and a major upset of the perennial powerhouse, the University of Kansas, in the 1998 NCAA tournament. Two years were enough for Harrick in Rhode Island. He left for

Georgia and, soon, Rhode Island supporters learned why.

Critics claimed that while he was at Rhode Island, Harrick, Sr., changed the grades of players, had others complete course assignments for players, and arranged for travel, cars, small gifts, money, and extravagant parties for players, friends, families, and potential recruits. Harrick, Jr., too, had been accused of similar improprieties while working with his father at Rhode Island. Most notably, Harrick, Jr., was accused of having falsified expense reports, just as his father had been accused of doing while coaching at UCLA. With charges of misconduct remaining charges only, father and son left Rhode Island and settled in Georgia to take the coaching jobs there.

On March 5, 2002, University of Georgia president Michael F. Adams announced that he was firing Jim Harrick, Jr., and suspending Harrick Sr. Adams's announcement followed the television broadcast of an interview with former Georgia player Cole, who alleged coaching and program misconduct. Twenty-two days after his son was fired, Harrick, Sr., resigned. He also announced his retirement from coaching.

Fearing harsh NCAA sanctions such as postseason bans, loss of scholarships, and fines, Adams imposed his own sanctions on the Georgia basketball program. The team was banned from the 2002-2003 NCAA tournament, even though the Bulldogs were ranked twenty-fifth in the nation with a record of 19-8 and were ensured of a place in postseason play. Also, Adams stripped the eligibility of two players involved in the scandal.

IMPACT

In the long run, the self-imposed sanctions likely saved the football program at Georgia, but Adams still had to contend with questions about why he hired the Harricks in the first place, knowing of their corruption-filled backgrounds. Adams said that he trusted Harrick, Sr. The two had worked together at Pepperdine dur-

ing the 1980's. Adams had entrusted Harrick, Sr., with running the school's football program and maintaining its integrity, which, Adams insisted, Harrick did with success.

The Harrick scandal followed the 2000 firing of another Georgia athletic coach, the highly respected football coach Jim Donnan. After the Donnan scandal, Adams became the fall guy at Georgia. He was booed off the field during a 2003 homecoming football game and was the subject of a petition drive in which sixty thousand students and alumni demanded he be fired as president of the university.

The firing of Harrick, Jr., and Harrick, Sr.'s, retirement did not mark the end of the Harrick scandal. Georgia's athletics program suffered further sanctions after their departure, including additional scholarship reductions and four years of probation. Adams, although unpopular with many students and alumni, remained Georgia president, but several well-known alumni withheld financial contributions to the school as a result. In a poll of faculty, nearly 70 percent had little faith in Adams as president. The poll results reflected little confidence in the school, both in athletics and academics.

The Harrick scandal had little affect on continuing corruption and misconduct at colleges and universities around the United States. Sanctions were imposed on other high-profile programs and coaches. For example, Dave Bliss was forced to resign as head coach of the Baylor Bears basketball team after player Patrick Dennehy was murdered by a

---

THE HARRICK EXAM

The so-called Harrick exam included a question that asked students to whom they attributed their playing success. The correct answer? Jim Harrick, Jr. Included here is a sampling of other multiple-choice questions from the test.

1. How many goals are on a basketball court? *Choices:* 1, 2, 3, or 4

2. In what league do the Georgia Bulldogs compete? *Choices:* ACC, Big Ten, SEC, or Pac10

3. How many points does a 3-point field goal account for in a basketball game? *Choices:* 1, 2, 3, or 4

former Baylor player. Bliss was heard on audiotape portraying Dennehy as a drug dealer. Ohio State University fired coach Jim O'Brien after he admitted to athletic director Andy Geiger that he paid more than six thousand dollars to a potential player in 1999. In 2008, Indiana University, recognized by many as a top-tier basketball program, fired coach Kelvin Sampson for having improper phone conversations with potential recruits.

High-profile coaches who are successful on the court but losers at playing by the rules still get hired by top programs to help deliver wins. With winning teams comes money—for athletic and academic scholarships, infrastructure, campus development—so questionable pasts are overlooked for the sake of victory and reputation—and cash.

—Keith J. Bell

FURTHER READING

Eitzen, D. Stanley. *Fair and Foul: Beyond the Myths and Paradoxes of Sport*. Lanham, Md.: Rowman & Littlefield, 1999. Argues that college athletics, and athletics in general, is inherently corrupt and that it breeds hypocrisy.

Harrick, Jim. *Basketball's Balanced Offense*. Indianapolis, Ind.: Masters Press, 1995. Jim Harrick, Sr., shares his coaching tips and discusses the best methods for coaching college-level basketball.

Kluger, Jeffrey. "The Coach Fouls Out." *Time*, May 12, 2003. Discusses the scandals that rocked collegiate sports in five high-profile programs in the first years of the twenty-first century. Includes the Harrick scandal.

Staurowsky, Ellen J. "Piercing the Veil of Amateurism: Commercialization, Corruption, and U.S. College Sports." In *The Commercialization of Sport*, edited by Trevor Slack. New York: Routledge, 2004. Staurowsky discusses how amateur athletics in the United States is a commercialized and corrupt spectacle.

SEE ALSO: Jan. 17, 1951: College Basketball Players Begin Shaving Points for Money; Apr. 27, 1980: Mobster's Arrest Reveals Point Shaving by Boston College Basketball Players; Feb. 25, 1987: NCAA Imposes "Death Penalty" on Southern Methodist University Football; Jan. 28, 2000: John Spano Is Sentenced for Fraudulent Purchase of Ice Hockey Team; Aug. 27, 2001: Little League Baseball Star Danny Almonte Is Found to Be Overage; Dec. 14, 2001: Notre Dame Football Coach Resigns for Falsifying His Résumé; May 3, 2003: University of Alabama Fires New Football Coach in Sex Scandal; July 14, 2006: *New York Times* Exposes Grading Scandal at Auburn University; Sept. 13, 2007: New England Patriots Football Team Is Fined for Spying on Other Teams; July 29, 2008: NBA Referee Tim Donaghy Is Sentenced to Prison for Betting on Games.

June 25, 2002
INTERNAL CORRUPTION FORCES ADELPHIA COMMUNICATIONS TO DECLARE BANKRUPTCY

At the time of its collapse, Adelphia Communications Corporation was one of the largest cable providers in the United States. In June of 2002, the company declared bankruptcy as a result of the multibillion-dollar defrauding of its own executives. John Rigas, Adelphia founder, and his son, Timothy Rigas, were convicted on charges of conspiracy, bank fraud, and securities violations and were sentenced to prison terms of fifteen and twenty years respectively. The bankruptcy was one of the largest in the history of the United States.

LOCALE: New York, New York

CATEGORIES: Law and the courts; corruption; banking and finance; communications and media

KEY FIGURES

John Rigas (b. 1924), founder and chief executive officer of Adelphia

Timothy Rigas (b. 1956), chief financial officer, board member, and executive vice president of Adelphia

Michael Rigas (b. 1953), Adelphia's vice president in charge of operations

James Rigas (b. 1958), Adelphia executive

Michael Mulcahey (b. 1957), head of internal reporting at Adelphia

SUMMARY OF EVENT

One of the largest cable providers in the United States at the time of its collapse, Adelphia Communications Corporations filed for Chapter 11 bankruptcy protection on June 25, 2002, in the United States bankruptcy court in New York. The declaration of bankruptcy was a result of the mismanagement of the company by its owner and executives, primarily John Rigas and his sons Timothy, Michael, and James. It was alleged that they had hid-

den more than $2 billion from creditors and Adelphia stockholders for their own use.

Adelphia came from modest origins. Its founder, John Rigas, and his brother Gus, were sons of Greek immigrants. The brothers began buying cable systems during the 1950's in the small Pennsylvania town of Coudersport. They named their company Adelphia, a word derived from the Greek for "brothers." During the 1980's, John Rigas bought his brother's interest in the company. By 2002, Adelphia operated cable systems in more than thirty states, notably in Pennsylvania, Ohio, Florida, and California, and had more than five million cable subscribers. Adelphia was a family-owned and family-operated company, with Rigas and his three sons holding executive positions. John Rigas, an inductee of the Cable Television Hall of Fame, was actively involved in the community and appeared to value family, charity, morals, and a solid work ethic, as evidenced by the exclusion of pornography channels on Adelphia's cable systems. The Rigas family also owned a professional hockey team: the Buffalo Sabres.

Over a three-year period from January, 1999, through May, 2002, members of the Rigas family used $2.3 billion in Adelphia funds for their own personal expenditures. For example, it was reported that company money was used to pay family debt, to buy cable systems for the family's privately owned cable company, to finance the construction of a golf course, to buy Adelphia stock, and to purchase luxuries such as an airplane, automobiles, and real estate. The Rigases used $150 million from Adelphia to buy their hockey team. To conceal the money "borrowed" from Adelphia, family members falsified financial statements and inflated profits and the number of Adelphia cable subscribers. The Rigas family made it appear that Adelphia was in better financial health than it was in truth. The fraud was not discovered until March 27, 2002,

2000's

971

After declaring bankruptcy, Adelphia lost its sponsorship of the Coliseum in Nashville, Tennessee. The corporate name was stripped from the stadium in August, 2003. (AP/Wide World Photos)

when a financial analyst from Merrill Lynch, Oren Cohen, noticed a footnote on the final page of a press release that reported the company's quarterly earnings. The footnote indicated that Adelphia was responsible for the loan of $2.3 billion to the Rigas family.

In May, after the corruption came to light, John Rigas, followed soon thereafter by his sons, resigned from the company. The Rigases were arrested in July, along with two other Adelphia executives, arrested for the same offenses: James Brown, former vice president of finance, and Michael Mulcahey, who was in charge of internal reporting. In a plea bargaining arrangement, Brown pleaded guilty and later testified against the Rigases at their trial in federal court.

While awaiting their trial, the Rigas defendants were each freed on $10 million bail. All four defendants were tried together in a single trial. John Rigas disavowed any wrongdoing. On July 8, 2004, after almost five months in court, John and Timothy Rigas (James was not charged in the criminal case) were convicted on charges of conspiracy, securities fraud, and bank fraud. They were acquitted by the jury on charges of wire fraud. Mulcahey was acquitted on all charges. The jury was unable to reach a verdict on the culpability of Michael Rigas. After pleading guilty for his role in concealing debt by falsifying an entry in the company's record, Michael Rigas later received a sentence of home confinement for ten months and probation for two years.

In July, 2005, John Rigas was sentenced to fifteen years in prison and Timothy Rigas was sentenced to twenty years in prison. The judge gave the elder Rigas a lighter sentence because of his ailing health. The octogenarian was suffering from bladder cancer and had cardiac problems. John and Michael Rigas, who appealed their convictions, were free on bail during the years their appeals were reviewed. All but one count of their convictions was upheld on appeal. After exhausting their appeals, John and Michael Rigas reported to federal prison in August, 2007. The two requested a resentencing hearing in May, 2008.

In addition to criminal penalties, the family forfeited more than $1 billion in assets to their former company. A substantial portion of the funds, more than $700 million, was used to reimburse investors who lost money when the company declared bankruptcy. Most creditors and investors were able to recoup their losses. In addition to criminal charges, the Rigas family also faced a racketeering lawsuit filed by Adelphia, a civil suit brought by the U.S. Securities and Exchange Commission, and further criminal allegations of tax evasion.

Adelphia's headquarters was relocated from Coudersport to Denver, Colorado. In 2007, the company was sold to Time Warner and Comcast for almost $18 billion and a percentage of Time Warner shares.

IMPACT

The Adelphia corruption scandal was one in a long line of similar scandals of corporate greed and unscrupulous business practices. Other white-collar scandals of the early twenty-first century include those involving Enron, WorldCom, Tyco International, subprime mortgage lenders, and to a lesser extent, Martha Stewart.

Adelphia's bankruptcy proved to be one of the largest in American history. Investors lost more than $60 billion when the company imploded. John and Michael Rigas received comparatively severe punishments for their offenses, likely because of the immense scale of their corruption and because of their adamant denials of any wrongdoing. Also a likely factor was the growing public awareness of and intolerance for white-collar crime, a view best reflected in the sanctions that have been handed down by judges and juries.

The Adelphia case underscores the complexity and depth of white-collar crime. It is possible that the Rigases' crimes remained undetected for so long because family members held several key executive roles, which limited outside scrutiny of their business practices. It was only through the close reading of an Adelphia press release that the criminality of the Rigases was discovered. In addition, this case was multifaceted, involving criminal law, civil law, and violations of business regulations and ethics.

—Margaret E. Leigey and Stephen J. Pelzer

FURTHER READING

Brancato, Carolyn Kay, and Christian A. Plath. *Corporate Governance Best Practices: A Blueprint for the Post-Enron Era.* New York: Conference Board, 2003. A study that examines corporate leadership, ethics, and responsibility at a time of increased public awareness of corporate fraud and mismanagement.

Cauley, Leslie. "Rigas Tells His Side of the Adelphia Story." *USA Today*, August 6, 2006. Serving time in a federal prison, John Rigas offers his version of the events that led to his conviction and subsequent incarceration.

Coenen, Tracy. *Essentials of Corporate Fraud.* Hoboken, N.J.: John Wiley & Sons, 2008. An introductory guide to the white-collar crime of corporate fraud, written by a forensic, or investigative, accountant.

"Judge Approves Plan by Adelphia to Pay Creditors." *Los Angeles Times*, January 4, 2007. Provides details regarding the sale of Adelphia and the plan to reimburse investors and creditors.

Leonard, Devin, Ann Harrington, and Doris Burke. "The Adelphia Story: The Sixth-Largest Cable Company Might as Well Have Been Called John Rigas & Sons." *Fortune*, August 12, 2002. Magazine article that provides a detailed history of the Rigas family and discussion of their criminal mismanagement of Adelphia.

MacDonald, Scott B., and Jane E. Hughes. *Separating Fools from Their Money: A History of American Financial Scandals.* New Brunswick, N.J.: Rutgers University Press, 2007. This book provides readers with a detailed history of American financial scandals. Limited discussion of the Adelphia scandal, but still useful for its analysis of corporate fraud in general.

SEE ALSO: 1932: Insull Utilities Trusts Collapse Prompts New Federal Regulation; Mar. 29, 1962: Billie Sol Estes Is Arrested for Corporate Fraud; May 2, 1984: E. F. Hutton Executives Plead Guilty to Fraud; Jan. 15, 1988: ZZZZ Best Founder Is Indicted on Federal Fraud Charges; Mar. 29, 1989: Financier Michael Milken Is Indicted for Racketeering and Fraud; Aug. 27, 1990: Guinness Four Are Found Guilty of Share-Trading Fraud; Dec. 2, 2001: Enron Bankruptcy Reveals Massive Financial Fraud; Sept. 3, 2003: Mutual Fund Companies Are Implicated in Shady Trading Practices; Mar. 5, 2004: Martha Stewart Is Convicted in Insider-Trading Scandal; Oct. 14, 2004: Insurance Brokerage Marsh & McLennan Is Charged with Fraud; Sept. 12, 2005: Westar Energy Executives Are Found Guilty of Looting Their Company.

2000's

July, 2002
JOURNALIST ALLEGES RELEASE OF GENETICALLY MODIFIED CORN SEEDS IN NEW ZEALAND

In his 2002 book Seeds of Distrust, *the New Zealand reporter Nicky Hager alleged that genetically modified corn had been illegally released in New Zealand. He further alleged that Prime Minister Helen Clark and her Labour government knew about the release and covered it up. These revelations and the inability of the government to deal forthrightly with the issue diminished the popularity of the Labour government and tarnished its image.*

ALSO KNOWN AS: Corngate
LOCALE: Wellington, New Zealand
CATEGORIES: Environmental issues; corruption; government; international relations; publishing and journalism; science and technology; trade and commerce

KEY FIGURES

Nicky Hager (b. 1958), New Zealand writer and investigative reporter
Helen Clark (b. 1950), prime minister of New Zealand, 1999-
John Campbell (b. 1964), New Zealand television broadcaster
Jeanette Fitzsimmons (b. 1945), member of the New Zealand parliament and Green Party leader
Marian Hobbs (b. 1947), member of the New Zealand parliament and minister of the environment, 1999-2005

SUMMARY OF EVENT

Agricultural products are sources of great national pride in New Zealand and are essential to the island nation's economy. The "naturalness" of New Zealand produce is a primary aspect of the products' appeal on world markets. To maintain that appeal, the country has extremely stringent regulations that prevent the introduction of genetically modified (GM) organisms for commercial purposes. Even the accidental introduction of GM plants would devastate the country's carefully crafted image and potentially hurt the economy.

In early July, 2002, New Zealand investigative reporter Nicky Hager's book *Seeds of Distrust: The Story of a GE Cover-up* was released, only a few weeks before parliamentary elections. Hager alleges in the book that in September and October, 2000, 5.6 tons of sweet-corn seed was shipped to three New Zealand companies. These seeds were imported from the U.S.-based company Novartis, the second-largest seed producer in the world, and were certified to be free of all genetically engineered modifications. In total, 164 hectares (405 acres) of these corn seeds were planted in the regions of Hawke's Bay, Gisborne, and Marlborough, New Zealand.

Hager further alleged that in November, the New Zealand government was alerted that a 1.7-ton lot from this shipment, designated NC9114, went to Cedenco Foods, which retested the sweet-corn seed for GM contamination. Of the eight seed lines tested, one batch tested positive for the Nos terminator, a sequence not found in healthy plants but in the soil bacterium *Agrobacterium tumefaciens. Agrobacterium* is a plant pathogen that transfers some of its genes into plants and causes the plant tissue to form a crown gall that overproduces unusual amino acids called opines, which only *Agrobacterium* can metabolize. Plant geneticists have exploited this ability to make engineered strains of *Agrobacterium* that can introduce exotic genes into plant genomes. The presence of the Nos terminator in a plant seed genome is an indication that the plant is a GM plant. Novartis informed the ministry of agriculture and forestry (MAF). The MAF and the environmental risk management authority (ERMA) ordered that no more seeds from this consignment be planted.

Further tests were ordered from three different labs, but the results were contradictory, ranging from light contamination to none. In December, 2000, ERMA stated that the contradictory results did not provide definitive evidence that the sweet-corn seed consignment was contaminated with GM seeds, and if there was contamination, it was less than 0.04 percent. Unfortunately, the New Zealand Hazardous Substances and New Organisms Act specified that no GM organisms could enter the country for commercial use. Prime Minister Helen Clark initially wanted the GM-contaminated plants pulled out and burned. However, after meetings with representatives from Novartis, Clark and her ministers changed their minds. The Novartis representatives convinced them that GM plants are ubiquitous and therefore completely GM-free seed shipments were neither practical nor possible. Thus, the Clark government considered a contamination level below 0.5 percent to be virtually GM-free. The seeds from the GM-contaminated consignment were allowed to be grown, harvested, and processed into food products. This also violated the government's own moratorium on the release of GM crops, which was not set to expire until October, 2003. More important, all of this was done with little or no public disclosure.

With the publication of Hager's book, Clark and her government ministers came under increased public pressure to answer Hager's allegations. In a July 10, 2002, television interview with broadcaster John Campbell, Clark responded angrily when asked about the claims made in Hager's book. She called Campbell "a little creep," accused the television station of ambushing her, and appealed to the broadcasting standards authority to discipline Campbell for unethical journalism.

Upon hearing about an apparent government cover-up that allowed GM plants into the country, the Green Party, which up to this point was a close political ally of the Labour Party, criticized the Clark government for violating its own policies on GM plants. Again, Clark responded by attacking the Green Party coleader, Jeanette Fitzsimmons, saying that the "Green Party and its supporters have descended to the gutter."

Even more troubling were the constant denials by government ministers that GM plants had entered the country. For example, in a July 11 interview with Campbell, the minister of the environment, Marian Hobbs, stated that there were no definitive tests that showed that the corn-seed shipment had been contaminated. Two days before, Clark also stated there was no evidence that the corn shipment was contaminated. The press named this scandal Corngate.

The 2002 election was not a disaster for the Labour Party, but it failed to gain a clear majority. The government released seven hundred pages of memos, e-mails, and other documentation, and in November, a select committee was formed to investigate the matter. After examining stacks of official documents and interviewing government officials, the committee could not reconcile the discrepancies between the oral reports given by Labour government officials and the written records provided to the committee. Furthermore, Novartis, now known as Syngenta, refused to share data from the tests it and others had run on the contaminated seed shipment.

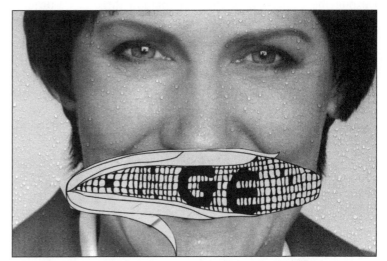

A Labour Party billboard featuring Prime Minister Helen Clark was defaced during the early days of the "Corngate" scandal. (Hulton Archive/ Getty Images)

The inquiry, however, did reveal that Clark did not leave the issue to her ministers, as she had strongly intimated, but was involved in the entire affair. Suppressed memos that were damaging to the Labour government's version of events also came to light, as did several conflicts of interest. Even though the country was largely tired of Corngate by this time, the findings of the select committee did tend to show that the Labour government altered the truth.

On July 5, 2003, the *Dominion Post*, a Wellington-based newspaper, reported that a Japanese pizza company discovered genetically engineered material in one of its toppings that used New Zealand sweet corn. This indicated that GM corn was established in New Zealand farms, despite the government bans on GM plants.

In October, 2004, the select committee completed its investigation but was still unable to ascertain what had actually happened. The presence of GM-contaminated corn or a cover-up could be neither ruled out nor confirmed. Since then, GM plants have been detected in New Zealand fields and imports and food products.

IMPACT

The Corngate scandal opened a seemingly permanent chasm between the Labour and Green parties. Despite the center-left political orientation these two parties hold in common, Corngate revealed the irreconcilable differences between the two parties on the issue of GM plants.

Corngate also marred the otherwise excellent political record of Prime Minister Clark. Normally level-headed and reasonable, Clark often lost her composure when questioned about Corngate. In many ways, Corngate struck at the very substance of Clark's government, since it looked like a murky compromise of principles in the face of pressure from industry, causing citizens who had once trusted her to become suspicious. Overall, Clark's Labour government handled the scandal quite poorly but did not suffer greatly in the end.

More important, this scandal exposed the complicated and multifaceted issues that surround the planting and harvesting of GM plants. Because of the widespread use of GM plants, it is no longer possible to keep agriculture completely GM free. Establishing a total absence of GM seeds would require testing every available seed, which would leave none to plant or eat. Accepting a low level of GM contamination is probably the most realistic policy, even if it is not the most desirable. Communicating this to a public with a poor knowledge of such matters is difficult, but it is the only way to cultivate a reasoned discussion of this issue and eventually to construct a rational and workable GM policy.

—*Michael A. Buratovich*

FURTHER READING

Espiner, Colin. "Corngate: Lend Me Your Ears." *The Press* (Christchurch), July 20, 2002. A prominent New Zealand newspaper journalist gives a summary of the political fallout shortly after the release of Hager's book and the attempts by Labour politicians to spin the story.

Hager, Nicky. *Seeds of Distrust: The Story of a GE Cover-up*. Nelson, New Zealand: Craig Potton, 2002. The book that started Corngate. A well-written exposé of the seed-contamination episode and government attempts to cover it up. Some of Hager's assertions are conspiratorial and not supported by the evidence.

Lurquin, Paul. *High Tech Harvest: Understanding Genetically Modified Food Plants*. New York: Basic Books, 2004. A user-friendly introduction to the science behind GM crops. Lurquin effectively argues that construction of a sound and reasonable GM policy requires legislators to properly understand the science behind the plant itself.

Steward, Neal C. *Genetically Modified Planet: Environmental Impacts of Genetically Engineered Plants*. New York: Oxford University Press, 2004. A nicely balanced, somewhat technical, but scientifically erudite examination of the potential benefits, concerns, and risks that surround the cultivation of GM crops. The author is quite fair to both sides.

SEE ALSO: Mar. 29, 1962: Billie Sol Estes Is Arrested for Corporate Fraud; Sept. 26, 1979: Love

Canal Residents Sue Chemical Company; Dec. 16, 1982: Congress Cites Environmental Protection Agency Chief for Contempt; July 10, 1985: French Secret Service Sinks the Greenpeace Ship *Rainbow Warrior*; Feb. 4, 1996: Whistle-Blower Reveals Tobacco Industry Corruption; Sept. 17, 2006: New Zealand Prime Minister's Husband Is "Outed" as Gay.

August, 2002

Immunologist Resigns After Being Accused of Falsifying Research

Ranjit Kumar Chandra, a well-respected Canadian immunologist and nutritionist, shocked the scientific world with the revelation that he had falsified data and fabricated research results in several published papers, particularly in papers detailing studies on infant formula and on vitamin therapy in the elderly.

Locale: St. Johns, Newfoundland, Canada
Categories: Hoaxes, frauds, and charlatanism; education; publishing and journalism; medicine and health care; science and technology

Key Figures
Ranjit Kumar Chandra (b. 1938?), Canadian immunologist and nutritionist
Marilyn Harvey (fl. early twenty-first century), Canadian nurse and research assistant
Mark Masor (fl. early twenty-first century), Canadian clinical researcher

Summary of Event

Ranjit Kumar Chandra, a Canadian immunologist and nutrition expert who published more than one hundred scholarly articles, abruptly retired from his research position at Memorial University in St. Johns, Newfoundland, in August, 2002, and moved to Switzerland. Reports soon emerged that Chandra had falsified data for countless studies, including work involving infant formula and vitamin therapy as an aid to memory in the elderly.

At the time of his resignation from the university, Chandra was a major figure in the fields of immu-

nology and human nutrition. Twice nominated for a Nobel Prize, Chandra had been the recipient of numerous research grants from both private industry and the Canadian government. Doubts about the accuracy of Chandra's research first arose following publication of research done during the 1980's into the use of infant formulas. One study, funded by the Nestlé Corporation, supported the industry's claims that artificial formula was an acceptable substitute for breast milk. Nestlé had been under fire for many years for promoting artificial formula in developing nations. As the company's markets overseas dwindled, Nestlé began promoting its Good Start infant formula in the United States. The company's advertising claimed Good Start reduced the risk of allergies. The U.S. Food and Drug Administration was skeptical, and it pressured the corporation to back up the advertising with legitimate scientific data. During the late 1980's, Nestlé hired Chandra to conduct a study to prove their claims were valid, and the study would involve comparing Nestlé's product with that of its competitor, Ross Pharmaceuticals.

Around the same time, Chandra had been hired by Ross to study its infant formula as well. Several persons close to this research project raised questions about Chandra's methods and the reliability of his findings. Mark Masor, a clinical researcher for Ross, said he became curious because Chandra never contacted him to arrange for the large amounts of Ross formula that would have been needed for the Nestlé study. Furthermore, Chandra's published conclusions stated that the number of infants involved in the study had been in the hun-

977

dreds. Masor later told journalists at the Canadian Broadcasting Company (CBC) that such a study would have required the use of twenty thousand cans of formula. In addition, the time frame for the study seemed unusually short. Masor also noted that Chandra's conclusions contradicted the findings of earlier work done by Ross researchers. Although the infant formulas marketed by Nestlé, Ross, and another competitor, Mead Johnson, had almost identical ingredients, Chandra had concluded the Nestlé and Mead Johnson formulas were effective in reducing the risk of allergies in infants, while the Ross formula was not. Along with Nestlé, Mead Johnson helped to fund Chandra's work; Ross did not.

Marilyn Harvey, a research nurse who worked directly with Chandra, also had doubts about the infant-formula studies. Her job was to enroll infants from the area for both studies. In 1989, while she was still in the process of finding infants, she was shocked to learn Chandra had published results from his Nestlé study, supporting the claims made in Nestlé's advertising.

Even more startling to Harvey was her discovery that Chandra claimed to have finished a similar study for another company, Mead Johnson, which involved two hundred infants. By the early 1990's, Chandra had published results from three separate studies claiming more than seven hundred infants as test subjects, yet Harvey knew she had not recruited more than 25 percent of that number. Sufficiently disturbed by the inconsistencies between what she knew had occurred and what Chandra had reported, she approached administrators at Memorial University. She told university officials that she suspected data fabrication.

A university committee investigated Harvey's allegations and concluded that Chandra's studies included falsified data. However, Chandra was not fired. He later filed suit against Harvey, claiming she had stolen data. Harvey was able to prove her innocence, but she remained convinced that Chandra sued simply to punish her. The suit was, in any case, an action that could have served as a deterrent for other potential whistle-blowers at Memorial University.

Chandra continued his association with Memorial until 2002. After putting the infant-formula studies behind him, he began publishing papers on the effects of multivitamins in preventing dementia in the elderly. Chandra claimed that older people who had been put on a course of vitamin supplements improved their cognitive functions from that of one suffering from dementia to that of one considered to have normal cognitive functions. The multivitamin had been developed and patented by Chandra, and he continued to market it into 2006. It was Chandra's claims about vitamin therapy, and not the controversy concerning falsified data in the infant-formula study, which led to his downfall and retirement.

Chandra had initially submitted a paper, in October, 2000, summarizing his vitamins research to the *British Medical Journal* (commonly referred to as *BMJ*). Journal editors found significant flaws in the paper, a follow-up of a study Chandra published in *The Lancet* in 1992, and were so disturbed by its contents that they asked several experts, including a statistician, to review the work. They concluded the paper presented strong evidence of having been falsified. The journal contacted officials at Memorial University and asked them to investigate.

Although rejected by *BMJ*, Chandra's paper was published by a less prestigious journal, *Nutrition*, in September, 2001. Chandra's claims in the article, "Effect of Vitamin and Trace-element Supplementation on Cognitive Function in Elderly Subjects," which focused on the almost miraculous results from using the vitamin supplements, drew the attention of science reporters at *The New York Times*, who summarized Chandra's conclusions. Skeptics of Chandra's research included Saul Sternberg, a psychology professor at the University of Pennsylvania, who read the newspaper report and then read the article as published in *Nutrition*. He then contacted a colleague, Seth Roberts of the University of California, Berkeley. They agreed Chandra's article contained glaring errors.

By the summer of 2002, Chandra knew he was under severe scrutiny. In early August, he abruptly resigned and moved to Switzerland. He announced his association with l'Universite Internationale des

Sciences de la Sante, an institution that investigative journalists from the CBC discovered (in 2006) existed, it seems, but only on paper.

IMPACT

Chandra's fraud forced serious questioning by colleagues and others in academia about what could motivate such unethical acts in a respected and successful physician-scientist. The CBC's investigation suggests the answer was simply greed. When Chandra began his research career at Memorial University, payments were often made directly to the principal investigator on a research project rather than through a university's accounting system. It was the researcher's responsibility to purchase necessary supplies and pay for support, including research assistants and clerks, from the checks they received. This was true for funds received from private companies and from the Canadian national research institutes.

Red flags had been raised during the 1990's when Chandra had been seeking a divorce from his wife. During the proceedings, it was revealed that Chandra had millions of dollars in multiple bank accounts, including several located in offshore tax havens such as the Cayman Islands. In retrospect, questions should have been asked about how a researcher on a university salary could have amassed so much wealth.

The CBC investigation also uncovered evidence that Chandra's falsification of data extended far back into his research career. Although his early work seemed free of fraud, it appears that much if not most of his later work was fraudulent. He was able to publish many papers based on studies that had never occurred. He had no patients to study and he collected no data. Some critics have suggested that Chandra used a fake name to respond to critiques of his original fraudulent articles.

The Chandra research scandal was unusual in the annals of scientific fraud both in its scope and duration. Chandra spent almost two decades building an elaborate structure of lies, the full extent of which

may never be known. It seems that he escaped detection through a combination of luck, audacity, and professional status. He was a well-respected senior researcher, which made it difficult for critics to successfully unmask him.

—*Nancy Farm Mannikko*

FURTHER READING

Roberts, Seth. "Dealing with Scientific Fraud: A Proposal." *Public Health Nutrition* 9, no. 5 (2006): 664-665. Discusses the events leading up to the discovery of Chandra's fraudulent research. Asks why it took so many years for his deceptions to come to light.

Sterken, Elizabeth. "The Impact of Scientific Misconduct on Child Health." *Public Health Nutrition* 9, no. 2 (2006): 273-274. The author deftly summarizes the adverse consequences of Chandra's falsified data being used to justify feeding infants artificial formula.

SEE ALSO: Sept.-Oct., 1937: Prescription Elixir Causes More than One Hundred Deaths; Nov. 21, 1953: Piltdown Man Is Revealed to Be a Hoax; 1956-1962: Prescription Thalidomide Causes Widespread Birth Disorders; July 25, 1972: Newspaper Breaks Story of Abuses in Tuskegee Syphilis Study; Sept. 19, 1988: Stephen Breuning Pleads Guilty to Medical Research Fraud; Mar. 23, 1989: Scientists' "Cold Fusion" Claims Cannot Be Verified; Feb. 4, 1996: Whistle-Blower Reveals Tobacco Industry Corruption; Spring, 1996: Physicist Publishes a Deliberately Fraudulent Article; Nov. 26, 1997: Canadian Health Commissioner Releases Report on Tainted Blood; Mar. 4, 1999: Quebec Offers Support for Abused Duplessis Orphans; Sept. 25, 2002: Inquiry Reveals That Physicist Jan Hendrik Schön Faked His Research; May 12, 2006: Scientist Is Indicted for Faking His Research on Creating Stem Cells; July 24, 2007: University of Colorado Fires Professor for Plagiarism and Research Falsification.

2000's

September 25, 2002
INQUIRY REVEALS THAT PHYSICIST JAN HENDRIK SCHÖN FAKED HIS RESEARCH

In one of the biggest scandals in physics in many decades, Jan Hendrik Schön published journal articles—some with coauthors—at an astonishing rate of one every eight days, on average. However, the fact that his research findings could not be replicated by others raised red flags and prompted an investigation by a committee of his peers that found he had faked his data. The ensuing scandal raised a number of controversial questions about the limits of scientists' responsibilities in dealing with intellectual fraud.

ALSO KNOWN AS: Schön affair
LOCALE: Murray Hill, New Jersey
CATEGORIES: Ethics; hoaxes, frauds, and charlatanism; publishing and journalism; science and technology

KEY FIGURES

Jan Hendrik Schön (b. 1970), German physicist employed at Bell Laboratories
Bertram J. R. Batlogg (b. 1950), Schön's mentor at Bell Laboratories and one of his main coauthors
Malcolm R. Beasley (b. 1940), professor of applied physics at Stanford University and chairman of the committee that investigated charges against Schön
Paul M. Solomon (b. 1944), superconductivity expert at IBM
Charles M. Lieber (b. 1959), Harvard University chemist
Paul L. McEuen (b. 1963), physicist at Cornell University
Lydia L. Sohn (b. 1966), Princeton University physicist

SUMMARY OF EVENT

In 1998, German physicist Jan Hendrik Schön went to work for Bell Laboratories in Murray Hill, New Jersey, and began scientific collaborations with his mentor, Bertram J. R. Batlogg, and others. By 2002,

their collaboration resulted in more than ninety articles—most of them with Schön as lead author and many of them in leading journals such as *Nature* and *Science*. His productivity became legendary: During 2001, an investigative committee determined he had written a new paper—on average—every eight days. Schön came to be viewed in the profession as a star, on the fast track to a Nobel Prize.

Such prolific research and writing would have been remarkable accomplishments for so young a scientist, even if the experiments had been less revolutionary in their implications. Schön's work seemed to show the way forward in the development of an electronics that would use organic (carbon-based) materials rather than the familiar silicon. Though other scientists also explored this area of research, Schön reported breakthrough after breakthrough in molecular electronics and superconductivity, which seemed to promise a short path to a world of nanoscale electronics.

Though many of Schön's fellow scientists were in awe of his achievements, viewing him (in Paul McEuen's phrase) as "the golden boy of condensed matter physics," there also existed an undercurrent of suspicion as his startling results could not be replicated. His work probably would have been less eagerly received had he not worked at such a prestigious laboratory as Bell and with such a distinguished colleague as Batlogg.

As early as November, 2001, IBM scientist Paul M. Solomon had written a letter of profound criticism of Schön's work with molecular field-effect transistors. *Nature* declined publication of the letter. Then, in April and May of 2002, things began to unravel rapidly for Schön, as his scientific colleagues—including Harvard's Charles M. Lieber, IBM's McEuen, and Princeton's Lydia Sohn—began to notice reused data and graphs among different articles (some even in the same article) written by Schön.

In late May, at the instigation of the management of Bell Labs, a five-member investigative committee was formed; its chairman was Stanford University scientist Malcolm R. Beasley. The committee collected comments, accusations, and concerns about twenty-five papers (involving twenty coauthors) and identified twenty-four "final allegations" to examine in detail. In late July, the committee interviewed individuals at Bell, including Schön. The final report, made public on September 25, announced that a preponderance of evidence had demonstrated scientific misconduct in two-thirds (sixteen) of the cases examined, though Schön's behavior in most of the remaining cases remained "troubling."

The committee determined, first, that Schön had repeatedly substituted data; that is, he had reused data, sometimes in distorted form, in purportedly different situations. Second, the committee found Schön's data often displayed unrealistic precision; that is, not real experimental data. Third, Schön's results often contradicted known physics; seemingly impossible results demanded an extraordinary level of scientific caution that was absent from Schön's papers. The revelations of the Beasley Report were shocking.

Responding to the devastating report, Schön acknowledged "various mistakes" and apologized "for these mistakes to the coauthors and the scientific community." He insisted that he had "observed experimentally the various physical effects reported in these publications," even though, after two years and considerable expense, others had not been able to duplicate his findings and he, too, had been unable for some months to duplicate them.

Schön's motives remain unclear. Commentators cite pressure to publish as a direct motive for fabrication (and, by encouraging so many papers, an indirect negative influence on referees). Cordelia Sealy, editor of *Materials Today*, offered the oddest suggestion—that, for male scientists such as Schön, "publishing papers is a way to attract a mate."

Impact

As a result of the committee's findings, Schön was immediately fired from Bell Laboratories. His activities since the scandal remain largely unknown. In June, 2004, his doctorate was revoked by the University of Konstanz, Germany, triggering debate over whether a doctorate is a scholarly achievement to which subsequent misconduct is irrelevant or a license to be taken seriously as a scholar worthy of tenure only if one's behavior is acceptable.

In the wake of the Beasley Report, various retractions followed. Bell Labs withdrew half-a-dozen patent applications. A number of journals retracted papers written by Schön: eight papers in *Science* in October, 2002; six papers in the *Physical Review* journals in December; four papers (with seven more flagged for caution) in *Applied Physics Letters* in February, 2003; and seven papers in *Nature* in March, 2003.

The issue of coauthor responsibility was intensely debated. The Beasley Report left this issue unresolved, exonerating Schön's coauthors of scientific misconduct but leaving the question (especially in the case of Batlogg) whether there had been inadequate oversight. Some professional organizations, such as the American Physical Society, revised their codes of ethics to place greater emphasis on collaborator responsibilities—but many issues

---

THE BEASLEY REPORT

The revelations of the Beasley Report (September 25, 2002), compiled by an investigative committee looking into accusations of research fraud by physicist Jan Hendrik Schön, shocked many in academia. The report included the following comments on Schön's research:

None of the most significant physical results was witnessed by any coauthor or other colleague.

Proper laboratory records were not systematically maintained.... virtually all primary (raw) electronic data files were deleted.... No working devices with which one might confirm claimed results are presently available, having been damaged in measurement, damaged in transit or simply discarded. Finally, key processing equipment no longer produces the unparalleled results that enabled many of the key experiments.

remained unresolved. What is the role of trust in collaboration, and who is responsible for what exactly? If coauthors bask in the glory of publication, should they be held responsible when something goes wrong? The debate expanded from coauthors to journal editors, and to referees. Were journals too quick to support trendy research? Was the system of peer review itself flawed?

In 2004, two years after the scandal, questions remained. One big question was, as intellectual property attorney Lawrence B. Ebert reported, the "potential liability of Bell Labs, the coauthors, and the journals which published the fraudulent work to all those who . . . invested resources based on a belief in the work." He questioned whether scientific journals are liable if they are "aware of problems with their published material, and yet do nothing to correct it."

After the scandal, several journals publicized the tainted character of the papers they had published. Broader issues of quality control remain. In 2006, Jennifer Couzin and Katherine Unger noted that a paper of Schön, published in 2000 and retracted in 2003, still had been "noted in research papers seventeen times since" the retraction; they pointed out that "scientists often don't know that the work they are citing has been retracted." What the chairman of the Physics Department at Schön's alma mater had characterized, in revoking his degree, as the biggest falsification scandal in physics in half a century was still not enough to prevent citation of bogus science.

—Edward Johnson

FURTHER READING

Baura, Gail D. *Engineering Ethics: An Industrial Perspective*. New York: Elsevier/Academic Press, 2006. Discusses the Schön affair in the context of other case studies in engineering ethics.

_____. "When Money Wasn't King." *IEEE Engineering in Medicine and Biology* 24, no. 2 (March-April, 2005): 15-16. A former employee reflects on corporate changes at Bell Labs that made the Schön affair possible.

Beasley, M. R., S. Datta, H. Kogelnik, H. Kroemer, and D. Monroe. *Report of the Investigation Committee on the Possibility of Scientific Misconduct in the Work of Hendrik Schön and Coauthors.* Lucent Technologies and the American Physical Society, September, 2002. This primary document, also known as the Beasley Report, explains the findings of the committee that investigated Schön's work.

Choy, Tuck, and Marshall Stoneham. "Was Schön Ever Right?" *Materials Today* 7, no. 4 (April, 2004): 64. Two physicists from London's University College suggest that some of Schön's ideas might be right-headed, even if his experiments were misleading.

Couzin, Jennifer, and Katherine Unger. "Cleaning Up the Paper Trail." *Science* 312 (April 7, 2006): 38-43. Emphasizes the difficulty, in cases such as the Schön scandal, of keeping the historical record accurate.

Ebert, Lawrence B. "There You Go Again." *Intellectual Property Today*, July, 2004. Mentions unresolved issues about liability in the Schön case and reasserts the importance of Solomon's unpublished letter to *Nature* (quoted in full in Ebert's article in the June, 2003, edition of *Intellectual Property Today*).

Service, Robert F. "Pioneering Physics Papers Under Suspicion for Data Manipulation." *Science*, May 24, 2002 "Winning Streak Brought Awe, and Then Doubt," *Science*, July 5, 2002; "Bell Lab Fires Star Physicist Found Guilty of Forging Data," *Science*, October 4, 2002. A series of reports in one of the leading science journals that provides a good overview of not only the events but also the physics involved.

SEE ALSO: Nov. 21, 1953: Piltdown Man Is Revealed to Be a Hoax; Sept. 19, 1988: Stephen Breuning Pleads Guilty to Medical Research Fraud; Mar. 23, 1989: Scientists' "Cold Fusion" Claims Cannot Be Verified; Spring, 1996: Physicist Publishes a Deliberately Fraudulent Article; Nov. 5, 2000: Japanese Amateur Archaeologist's "Discoveries" Are Proven Fakes; Aug., 2002: Immunologist Resigns After Being Accused of Falsifying Research; May 12, 2006: Scientist Is Indicted for Faking His Research on Creating Stem Cells.

September 28, 2002
BRITISH POLITICIAN REVEALS HER AFFAIR WITH PRIME MINISTER JOHN MAJOR

A conservative member of the British parliament, Edwina Currie published her memoirs in 2002, revealing that she had had a romantic affair with former prime minister John Major before working in his government. She served as junior health minister under Margaret Thatcher until she was forced to resign after claiming that British egg producers allowed salmonella to become widespread in Great Britain.

LOCALE: London, England
CATEGORIES: Publishing and journalism; sex; government; politics

KEY FIGURES
Edwina Currie (b. 1946), member of the British parliament, 1983-1997, and junior health minister, 1986-1988
John Major (b. 1943), British prime minister, 1990-1997

SUMMARY OF EVENT

The revelation of an affair between two members (MPs) of the British parliament, fourteen years after it ended, would hardly be considered scandalous in any country, except that one of the MPs, John Major, later became prime minister and was responsible for accepting the resignation of a number of his ministers whose romantic affairs were revealed while he was in office. Major's affair with Edwina Currie also revealed the political danger faced by the prime minister, having to keep the affair secret. The affair is also significant, in retrospect, because it explains why Major was so reluctant at times to fire those ministers.

Currie first published her revealing diaries about her affair with Major in serialized form in *The Times of London*, a newspaper not usually inclined to publish reports of lurid romantic affairs. She made a great deal of money from the serialization, which ran between September 28 and October 6,

2002, and the well-publicized book, *Diaries, 1987-1992*, which followed later that year. The diaries suggest a keen interest in making money, and a number of reviews took up this theme, questioning her motives. Some of these reviews were very hostile, although Currie herself was of the opinion that all publicity is good publicity.

Currie was a junior minister for health in Prime Minister Margaret Thatcher's government from 1986 to 1988. Currie was raised in an orthodox Jewish family, though later she distanced herself from any belief or practice of Judaism. A very gifted student, she won a scholarship to St. Anne's College, Oxford University, to study chemistry, but she changed her major to philosophy, politics, and economics. She then earned a master of arts degree from the London School of Economics. As a student, she became politically active in the Conservative Party and later held a seat on the Birmingham City Council. She stood for the South Derbyshire parliamentary constituency in 1983 and was elected. She was soon offered a promotion by Thatcher.

While in office, Currie actively promoted improved screening services for cancer in women, particularly breast and cervical cancer. She was an outspoken proponent in this area and caught the public's attention with her wit and assertiveness. It seemed that she had a good political career ahead of her. However, in 1988, she was forced to resign after she commented on the prevalence of salmonella in eggs produced in Great Britain. Her statement led to a loss of confidence in the British egg industry. Thatcher did not offer Currie a second chance at the job, but Major did when he became prime minister. He offered her a middle-ranking ministerial role, but she declined the offer.

The year 1988 also marked the time Currie and Major ended their four-year romantic affair. When the affair started, she was a back-bench MP and he was a government whip. During the period of the affair, she had several government jobs and he rose to

983

Edwina Currie, c. 1986. (Hulton Archive/Getty Images)

become chief secretary to the treasury, which was a cabinet post. As such, it meant that Major had a security detail with him at all times. Currie claimed that the effort needed to carry out the affair with such a security presence was what finally led her to break off the affair. She claimed to have still loved him for some time after, and it appears they remained friends.

In her diaries, Currie identifies Major with the initial B, as he was the second man in her life. It was fairly obvious to readers who B really was, and she readily admitted his identity. Her diary is more a series of personal jottings than a considered piece of writing, and it is especially notable because of its character assassinations of fellow politicians. Even Currie's lover receives a certain amount of criticism, and her husband, who had known nothing of the affair, is quickly dismissed in the diaries as well.

Later, Major claimed that he had told his wife, Norma, about the affair and that she had forgiven

him. At the time of the disclosure, he commented that it was the one event in his life of which he was most ashamed and in most fear of being made public. When it was finally disclosed, he had long since ended his term as prime minister and was no longer active in politics, so it did little actual harm to his career. However, it did bring his family the shame of public ridicule. In office, he had the image of being decent and moral, but also one with a personality somewhat grey and lackluster.

Currie's career as a politician stalled after the affair ended, though she managed to keep herself in the public eye by making speeches and helping raise funds on behalf of cancer research, especially for the charitable organization Marie Curie Cancer Care. In 1997, Currie lost her seat in Derbyshire to her Labour opponent but was promptly offered a job by the British Broadcasting Corporation as a late-night radio host for a new current-affairs program called *Late Night Currie*. This led to a television job with a commercial television company, HTV, from which she became a regular television personality. Her first marriage ended in 1997 and she remarried in 1999. She also became a prolific author of sex novels, including *A Parliamentary Affair* (1994), which are set in the world of politics.

IMPACT

The motives and timing of Currie's revelations about her affair with Major were intensely scrutinized by the press. She said she published the diaries because she believed the truth had to come out. She also believed the diaries would not harm Major, and she hoped the diaries would provoke the Conservative Party to be more realistic in its moral stance. The party at the time had been struggling to modernize itself to match Prime Minister Tony Blair's Labour Party government.

The press, however, latched on to statements in the diaries that suggested revenge at being completely left out of Major's autobiography (2000) and for his failure to offer her a higher government post. The latter seems an unrealistic criticism of her work, however, because she had been offered a job that would have been a stepping stone to higher office. (She had criticized him heavily in the past for the poor representation of women in his cabinet.)

For Major, the revelations led him to reassess his life, but his autobiography does not give the slightest hint of the affair with Currie, or any relationship with her. Currie had the power to harm him at any moment during his tenure as prime minister, but she did not do so, choosing instead to wait until after his tenure ended to reveal their affair.

—*David Barratt*

FURTHER READING

Clark, Alan. *Diaries: In Power*. London: Weidenfeld & Nicholson, 2003. Clark's diaries recount the John Major and Margaret Thatcher years of government and give intimate details into the affairs and indiscretions of a number of ministers.

Currie, Edwina. *Diaries, 1987-1992*. London: Little, Brown, 2002. Currie's memoirs, in which she exposes her affair with John Major and discusses her sense of betrayal for his failure to give her a government post or to mention her in his 2000 autobiography.

Major, John. *The Autobiography*. New York: HarperCollins, 2000. Major's autobiography, which

fails to mention his relationship, sexual or otherwise, with Currie. Instructive for bringing readers to the period in question.

SEE ALSO: 1927: President Warren G. Harding's Lover Publishes Tell-All Memoir; July 10, 1934: Sex Scandal Forces Resignation of Alberta Premier Brownlee; Dec. 10, 1936: King Edward VIII Abdicates to Marry an American Divorcée; Mar. 2-Sept. 25, 1963: John Profumo Affair Rocks British Government; Oct. 14, 1983: British Cabinet Secretary Parkinson Resigns After His Secretary Becomes Pregnant; July 25, 1987: Novelist-Politician Jeffrey Archer Wins Libel Trial Against the *Daily Star*; Aug. 10, 1989: Japanese Prime Minister Sosuke Resigns After Affair with a Geisha; Sept. 24, 1992: British Cabinet Member David Mellor Resigns over Romantic Affair; Jan. 5, 1994: British Cabinet Member Resigns After Fathering a Child Out of Wedlock; Jan. 21, 2006: British Politician Resigns After Gay-Sex Orgy; Apr. 26, 2006: Britain's Deputy Prime Minister Admits Affair with Secretary.

October 25, 2002
HISTORIAN MICHAEL A. BELLESILES RESIGNS AFTER ACADEMIC FRAUD ACCUSATIONS

Scandal followed the publication of Michael A. Bellesiles's 2000 book Arming America, *a study claiming that guns were relatively rare in the American colonies and the United States before the U.S. Civil War. Although he was accused of research falsification and distortion, Bellesiles still received the coveted Bancroft Prize for American history. However, in October, 2002, he was forced to resign his professorship after a panel of historians found him guilty of scholarly misconduct.*

LOCALE: Atlanta, Georgia
CATEGORIES: Education; cultural and intellectual history; publishing and journalism

KEY FIGURES

Michael A. Bellesiles (b. 1954), professor of history at Emory University
James Lindgren (b. 1952), professor of law at Northwestern University
Clayton E. Cramer (b. 1956), author

SUMMARY OF EVENT

Michael A. Bellesiles was a respected professor of American colonial history at prestigious Emory University in Atlanta. He was also the director of the Center for the Study of Violence and an expert in gun and frontier culture in early America. He had received fellowships to the Stanford Humanities In-

985

stitute and the Newberry Library in Chicago. In 1993, he published *Revolutionary Outlaws: Ethan Allan and the Struggle for Independence in the Early American Frontier*, a book that was well received by historians.

In late 1995, while working on a project on the early American frontier, Bellesiles claimed to have discovered that, contrary to tradition, gun ownership was rare in America during the antebellum period—the period before the American Civil War—even on the frontier, and that arms became widespread only with the mass production of firearms. As part of his research, he examined legal, probate, military, and business records, as well as travel accounts and personal letters. His discovery would soon add even more controversy to the ongoing debate between advocates of gun control and proponents of the right to bear arms, a debate that includes the belief by gun proponents that gun possession is an integral part of America's identity as a nation.

Bellesiles first published his revolutionary thesis in his article "The Origins of Gun Culture in the United States, 1760-1865" in the *Journal of American History* in 1996. His finding garnered enthusiastic reviews by many influential scholars, including Edmund Sears Morgan, an eminent authority in early American history. Also, the article won the best article of the year prize from the Organization of American Historians. However, other scholars, such as James Lindgren, professor of law at Northwestern University, were skeptical of Bellesiles's thesis, which claimed that for the years 1765 to 1770, very few probate inventories listed guns. During the late summer of 2000, Lindgren requested to see the data used for this groundbreaking theory, but Bellesiles claimed that all his notes were lost in a flood that affected Emory University that same year.

The culmination of Bellesiles's research, *Arming America: The Origins of a National Gun Culture*, was published in September of 2000. Criticism of the book followed immediately. Clayton Cramer, at the time a master's degree student at Sonoma State University in California, became Bellesiles's most persistent critic. Cramer was the first to claim that

Bellesiles had misquoted sources, taken them out of context, and even modified texts so they would fit his thesis. Similarly, in two articles published in 2002, Lindgren claimed that Bellesiles had altered statutes, dates, citations, and counts. In one case, Lindgren claims, Bellesiles provides a count of guns for seventeenth and eighteenth century Providence, Rhode Island, based on wills that did not exist. Bellesiles also claimed to have counted probate inventories that were, in fact, destroyed in the great San Francisco earthquake of 1906. Lindgren argues that Bellesiles, in effect, disregarded accounts and records that did not fit his thesis.

Despite increasing skepticism about the validity of Bellesiles's research, *Arming America* was granted Columbia University's Bancroft Prize, generally considered the most prestigious award in the field of American history. However, this honor did not stem the criticism. During the months that followed, the book became a favorite theme of academic debate, and of media scrutiny. One point that attracted significant critique was Bellesiles's analysis of the gun culture of Europe, especially in England, as part of his introduction to his investigation into gun use in America. The historian claimed that the English government outlawed the use of guns by commoners, and that all guns owned by the militia were carefully kept in governmental magazines. However, in contrast, Lindgren pointed out that there were laws exhorting commoners to practice with their muskets, and records show that guns were kept in owners' homes for personal defense and hunting.

Bellesiles further claims in the book that in the United States, guns were uncommon, either because they were expensive, inefficient, highly regulated, or simply undesired by civilians. According to Bellesiles, guns were not widely used for hunting either, a claim based on his study of less than one hundred travel accounts. Moreover, he dismisses the militias' status as professionals, remarking that their guns were mostly unusable. He also claims that just over 14 percent of men owned guns between 1765 and 1859, and that this percentage began to increase just before the Civil War, mostly due to the successful mass production of the Colt revolver.

The intense criticism and media attention forced Emory University to initiate an internal inquiry into Bellesiles's scholarship. An external investigative committee examined the matter as well. Both committees found grave errors, some due to the misuse of evidence and some due to the lack of evidence. The external committee issued its report on July 10, 2002. Emory announced Bellesiles's resignation from the university on October 25 (effective December 31).

For the first time since the award was established, Columbia rescinded Bellesiles's Bancroft Prize and asked that he return the $4,000 he was awarded. Also, his book contract with Alfred A. Knopf was dropped. In 2003, Soft Skull Press published a revised edition of *Arming America*, which was preceded by the seventy-four-page "pamphlet" *Weighed in an Even Balance*, in which Bellesiles steadfastly defends the validity of his research, pointing out that only one-fourth of his research had been contested.

IMPACT

With the publication of *Arming America*, Bellesiles found himself at the center of the ongoing debate over gun possession. Hailed as a hero by those opposed to the easy availability of weapons in the United States, Bellesiles was later vilified by proponents of the right to bear arms. He was blacklisted in academia, stripped of his Bancroft Prize, and forced to resign from his position at Emory University.

The Bellesiles scandal came at a time when other similar scandals rocked academia, especially the field of history. Concurrent with this scandal were those of historians Joseph Ellis and Doris Kearns Goodwin, who were accused of academic misconduct as well. The scandal that arose because of the inaccuracies in *Arming America* was attributed by many to the pressures of writing popular history and by others to postmodern scholarship's tendency to relativize the truth. Bellesiles argues that the scandal arose because of a higher level of scrutiny by the media.

—Concepcion Saenz-Cambra

BELLESILES RESPONDS TO THE OFFICIAL INQUIRY

In an undated letter, excerpted here, historian Michael Bellesiles responded to the final report (July 10, 2002) of an investigative committee of scholars from outside Emory University, convened to inquire into allegations that he committed academic fraud.

I remain convinced that the standard workings of academic discourse remain the best way of correcting errors and increasing our knowledge. . . . It is not evident that launching a sharply focused investigation of one small part of a scholar's work brings us closer to the truth on the subject of that research. Rather, it is my opinion that this debate has actually obscured a much more important consideration of the main issues raised by *Arming America*. Scholarship must be open to new directions, allowing scholars to build on their own earlier research, to qualify previous generalizations they have made, to correct errors in their work, and even to change their minds in the face of more compelling evidence.

FURTHER READING

Cramer, Clayton E. *Armed America: The Remarkable Story of How and Why Guns Became as American as Apple Pie.* Nashville, Tenn.: Nelson Current, 2007. Detailed critique of Bellesiles's claims, including diaries, travel accounts, and statistical evidence. Written by a leading critic of the historian's work.

Hoffer, Peter Charles. *Past Imperfect: Facts, Fictions, and Fraud—American History from Bancroft and Parkman to Ambrose, Bellesiles, Ellis, and Goodwin.* New York: PublicAffairs, 2007. Examination of the key controversies in the historical profession, including the Bellesiles case, as the culmination of the tensions between the New Left scholars and traditional historians.

Lindgren, James. "Fall from Grace: *Arming America* and the Bellesiles Scandal." *Yale Law Journal* 111, no. 8 (2002): 2195-2249. A detailed scholarly study of Bellesiles's book, the data he used, and the book's alleged errors. Written by one of his main critics.

Lindgren, James, and Justin L. Heather. "Counting Guns in Early America." *William and Mary Law*

2000's

987

Review 43, no. 5 (2002): 1777-1842. Another detailed study of Bellesiles's controversial book.

Skinner, David. "Cheating History: Ambrose, Bellesiles, Ellis, and Goodwin—The Historians Who Let Us Down." *The Weekly Standard*, November 29, 2004. Focuses on a dozen key controversies ranging across the political spectrum and representative of a wide variety of charges.

Wiener, Jon. *Historians in Trouble: Plagiarism, Fraud, and Politics in the Ivory Tower*. New York: New Press, 2005. Offers a detailed analysis of court documents and other evidence. Less partial when judging the gravity of some historians' work, lessening Bellesiles's acts, and harshly critical of historians Stephen Ambrose and Doris Kearns Goodwin.

SEE ALSO: 1928-1929: Actor Is Suspected of Falsely Claiming to Be an American Indian; Jan. 28, 1972: Clifford Irving Admits Faking Howard Hughes Memoirs; 1978: *Roots* Author Alex Haley Is Sued for Plagiarism; Spring, 1996: Physicist Publishes a Deliberately Fraudulent Article; Apr., 1998: Scottish Historian Is Charged with Plagiarism; May 11, 1998: Journalist Stephen Glass Is Exposed as a Fraud; June 18, 2001: Historian Joseph J. Ellis Is Accused of Lying; Jan. 4, 2002: Historian Stephen E. Ambrose Is Accused of Plagiarism; Jan. 18, 2002: Historian Doris Kearns Goodwin Is Accused of Plagiarism; July 24, 2007: University of Colorado Fires Professor for Plagiarism and Research Falsification.

December 5, 2002

SENATOR TRENT LOTT PRAISES STROM THURMOND'S 1948 PRESIDENTIAL CAMPAIGN

A speech delivered by Mississippi senator and Senate majority leader Trent Lott on the occasion of the one hundredth birthday of South Carolina senator Strom Thurmond praised Thurmond's 1948 so-called Dixiecrat segregationist campaign for the presidency. The resulting political fallout led to Lott's resignation as majority leader.

LOCALE: Washington, D.C.
CATEGORIES: Politics; social issues and reform; racism; government

KEY FIGURES
Trent Lott (b. 1941), U.S. senator from Mississippi, 1989-2007
Strom Thurmond (1902-2003), U.S. senator from South Carolina, 1956-2003
George W. Bush (b. 1946), president of the United States, 2001-2009
Bill Frist (b. 1952), U.S. senator from Tennessee, 1995-2007

Al Gore (b. 1948), vice president of the United States, 1993-2001

SUMMARY OF EVENT
Trent Lott's political rise as one of the "new breed" of southern conservative Republicans was, by all standards, exceptional. Obtaining his law degree in 1967 from the University of Mississippi, Lott won election to the U.S. House of Representatives at the age of thirty-one and served in the House from 1973 to 1989. Lott was then elected to the U.S. Senate and enjoyed a meteoric rise through the ranks, becoming Senate majority whip in 1995 and then majority leader in 1996 while in his first electoral term of office. He consistently held the post of either majority or minority leader into the year 2002.

Lott strongly identified with the more conservative elements in Congress. He opposed the renewal of significant civil rights bills that had been passed during the 1960's, and he assumed an active role in the impeachment trial of President Bill Clinton,

Senator Strom Thurmond, seated, celebrates his one-hundredth birthday with, from left, Vice President Dick Cheney, President George W. Bush, Senator Trent Lott, and Thurmond's daughter, Julie Thurmond Whitmer. (AP/ Wide World Photos)

working hand-in-hand with the Senate "managers" and casting his vote in favor of conviction. During the early months of the administration of George W. Bush, Lott served as a staunch, and often decisive, ally of the president—though one who sometimes showed an independent streak. In a great many instances, Lott's influence and political acumen proved to be crucial, as in the case of Bush's tax-cut scheme in 2001 and the U.S. military operations against Iraq that began in 2003. However, during the debate over the latter initiative, Lott's initial misgivings over the theory that Iraqi dictator Saddam Hussein was stockpiling weapons of mass destruction indicated that he considered himself to be a power in his own right who could not invariably be expected to accept every White House pronouncement uncritically.

It had been Senator Strom Thurmond of South Carolina who had pioneered the "switch over" of white, southern conservative politicians from the solid South Democratic Party tradition to the Republican Party, and had thus functioned as a role model for people such as Trent Lott, Newt Gingrich of Georgia, George Allen of Virginia, and Bill Frist of Tennessee. Thurmond, then South Carolina's governor, left the 1948 Democratic Party convention out of frustration with President Harry S. Truman's liberal stance on the issue of racial desegregation and had launched a prosegregationist, states' rights campaign for the presidency under the banner of the States' Rights Party, or Dixiecrat, movement. Thurmond garnered close to 1.2 million popular votes and carried the states of South Carolina, Mississippi, Alabama, and Louisiana to capture thirty-nine electoral votes.

Thurmond had subsequently been elected to the U.S. Senate, where he became a highly visible opponent of integrationist and civil rights legislation: In 1957, he set the record for a congressional filibuster, debating for twenty-four hours and eighteen minutes against the passage of the 1957 Civil Rights Act. During the acrimonious struggle over the Civil Rights Act of 1964, Thurmond was involved in a physical scuffle with liberal Democratic senator Ralph Yarborough of Texas, wherein both men ended rolling on the floor. Shortly thereafter, Thurmond announced his move into the ranks of the Republican Party, where he became instrumental in facilitating the party's rightward political tilt. By December 5, 2002, when he celebrated his one hundredth birthday, Thurmond had become the oldest serving U.S. senator in history.

At a special birthday celebration held that evening in Thurmond's honor, Lott delivered a speech praising the centenarian senator, during which he uttered words referring to Thurmond's 1948 campaign. Lott's words that were to ignite the greatest controversy included the following:

2000's

989

I want to say this about my state: When Strom Thurmond ran for president, we voted for him. We're proud of it. And if the rest of the country had followed our lead, we wouldn't have had all these problems over all these years, either.

IMPACT

Initially, little media reaction followed Lott's December 5 speech, except on Web sites and blogs. However, what the media did bring to light was Lott's voting record and past speeches supporting segregationist causes, and his association with the Sons of Confederate Veterans and the Council of Conservative Citizens (formerly the White Citizens' Councils). The repercussions then came on with a vengeance.

Lott's remarks elicited attacks from all sides. Former Civil Rights movement leaders such as John Lewis and Jesse Jackson, incensed by past memories of Thurmond's speeches and other activities against civil rights and mindful of Lott's voting record, denounced the Mississippi senator's words as a retrograde attack on the progress of civil liberties and racial integration over more than a half century.

Democratic Party legislators, considering Lott's speech a possible electoral issue, weighed in with increasingly emphatic rebuttals. Among the Democrats, Lott's most vocal critic was former vice president Al Gore—a frequent past opponent of Lott in the Senate—who called the senator's speech racist and divisive and who advocated for Lott's censure by the Senate if he failed to deliver an adequate apology.

On December 9, Lott issued an official apology for using what he called a "poor choice of words" and denied that he had indicated support for Thurmond's past segregationist ideas. However, Lott was losing support even among his conservative Republican colleagues, and his remarks were proving to be an embarrassment to the White House, which had previously initiated overtures to African American leaders in an effort to bolster support of the Republican Party among people of color. What was probably the coup de grace was delivered by President Bush in a speech in Philadelphia on December 12, in which he roundly criticized Lott's words as offensive. Throughout the following week, Lott vowed that he would fight to retain the leadership, but as more Republican senators indicated that they favored a change, Senator Frist of Tennessee, who in the wake of the December 5 incident had expressed full support for Lott, made a turnaround and announced on December 19 that he would seek the majority leader's post.

Lott resigned as Senate majority leader on December 20, and Frist, who had obtained tacit support from the Bush administration as a much more diplomatic and pliant conservative, was elected to succeed him on January 6, 2003.

—Raymond Pierre Hylton

FURTHER READING

Baker, Peter. *The Breach: Inside the Impeachment and Trial of William Jefferson Clinton.* New York: Berkley Books, 2001. Though this book was written long before Lott's speech, it is nonetheless useful in that it adroitly describes Lott's political style, modus operandi, and the extent of his political influence prior to December, 2002.

Gregg, Gary L., II, and Mark J. Rozell. *Considering the Bush Presidency.* New York: Oxford University Press, 2004. Suggests that the Lott-Thurmond incident provided the Bush administration with a pretext for replacing Lott with Bill Frist.

Kraus, Jon, Kevin J. McMahon, and David M. Rankin. *Transformed by Crisis: The Presidency of George W. Bush and American Politics.* New York: Palgrave Macmillan, 2004. Focuses on Lott's controversial speech as a crisis, with the Democrats attempting to capitalize and the Bush administration countering with damage control.

Lott, Trent. *Herding Cats: A Political Life.* New York: Regan Books, 2005. Lott's career autobiography and apologia, in which he argues that he has been misinterpreted and misunderstood. Castigates the Bush administration for backstabbing.

Schier, Steven E., ed. *High Risk and Big Ambition: The Presidency of George W. Bush.* Pittsburgh, Pa.: University of Pittsburgh Press, 2004. Implies that Lott's Thurmond birthday speech frustrated the Bush administration's outreach to African Americans.

Tiefer, Charles. *Veering Right: How the Bush Administration Subverts the Law for Conservative Causes.* Berkeley: University of California Press, 2004. A slanted account, but one that does give insight on possible preexisting motives behind Bush's quick rejection of Lott.

SEE ALSO: Mar. 1, 1967: Adam Clayton Powell, Jr., Is Excluded from Congress; June 23, 1967: Senator Thomas J. Dodd Is Censured for Misappropriating Funds; Oct. 11, 1979: Senate Denounces

Herman E. Talmadge for Money Laundering; Jan. 25, 1984: Jesse Jackson Calls New York City "Hymietown"; Sept. 23, 1987: Plagiarism Charges End Joe Biden's Presidential Campaign; May 31, 1989: Speaker of the House Jim Wright Resigns in Ethics Scandal; June 1, 1994: Congressman Dan Rostenkowski Is Indicted in House Post Office Scandal; Jan. 17, 1998: President Bill Clinton Denies Sexual Affair with a White House Intern; Dec. 17, 2003: Senator Strom Thurmond's Biracial Daughter Is Revealed; July 9, 2007: Senator David Vitter's Name Is Found in D.C. Madam's Address Book.

January 2, 2003
E-MAIL MESSAGE PROMPTS INQUIRY INTO AIR FORCE ACADEMY SEXUAL ASSAULTS

An e-mail message alleging a pattern of sexual assaults at the U.S. Air Force Academy and official cover-ups of the assaults prompted a series of investigations and changes in academy policy. The response to the scandal, while substantive, was the subject of controversy and drew criticism both from those who found it excessive and those who considered it insufficient.

LOCALE: Colorado Springs, Colorado
CATEGORIES: Sex crimes; military; government; communications and media; education; ethics

KEY FIGURES
Wayne Allard (b. 1943), U.S. senator from Colorado, 1997-
Tillie Fowler (1942-2005), U.S. representative from Florida, 1993-2001
James G. Roche (b. 1940), undersecretary of the U.S. Air Force, 2001-2005
Donald Rumsfeld (b. 1932), U.S. secretary of defense, 2001-2006
Peter B. Teets (b. 1942), acting undersecretary of the U.S. Air Force, January-March, 2005

SUMMARY OF EVENT
On January 2, 2003, the undersecretary of the U.S. Air Force, James Roche, received an e-mail from a person using the name Renee Trindle, alleging a pervasive pattern of sexual assaults at the Air Force Academy. The e-mail, which also claimed the sexual assaults were covered up and ignored by academy leadership, was copied to several prominent government officials and journalists, including the chief of staff of the Air Force and U.S. senator Wayne Allard of Colorado. The media began reporting the assaults. Subsequent investigations by the Air Force and the U.S. Congress revealed that numerous sexual assaults indeed had occurred at the academy and that administrators tried to conceal the offenses by intimidating victims and witnesses and by shielding academy staff.

The allegations, which surfaced nearly twenty-seven years after women were first admitted to the Air Force Academy, closely resembled similar allegations involving other branches of the U.S. military. Female naval officers were sexually assaulted and harassed at the 1991 convention of the Tailhook Association—an organization comprising active

2000's

991

and former U.S. Navy pilots—in Las Vegas. At the Aberdeen Proving Ground in Maryland in 1996, twelve male U.S. Army officers were arrested for sexual assault. The Tailhook and Aberdeen scandals had focused upon the conduct of small groups of people over a relatively short duration, whereas the allegations emerging from the Air Force Academy suggested a longstanding and pervasive pattern of institutional corruption that began with the commission of criminal acts and progressed to a conspiracy to conceal those acts.

Following the receipt of the e-mail, Roche directed the Air Force general counsel to form a working group to investigate the matter. The group submitted an interim report to Roche in March, 2003, leading the Air Force to implement its "Agenda for Change" on March 26. The agenda made changes to life at the academy that would make it "consistent with the Air Force concepts of no tolerance for sexual assault." The working group submitted its final report on June 17.

Roche also directed the Air Force inspector general's office (IGO) to investigate the allegations. Inquiries formed outside the Air Force as well. The secretary of defense, Donald Rumsfeld, at congressional urging, formed a seven-member panel under the leadership of Allard and former U.S. representative Tillie Fowler of Florida. In February, the Office of the Inspector General (OIG) of the Department of Defense, at the request of the Senate Armed Services Committee, began its inquiry. The complaints reviewed by the Fowler panel, as it came to be called, had been submitted by female cadets who attended the academy between 1993 and 2003. According to these complaints, the assaults took place primarily in student dormitories and typically involved upperclass male cadets and freshman and sophomore female cadets. Male cadets reportedly often provided female cadets with alcohol in violation of academy policy and, following the assaults, would blackmail their victims into remaining silent by threatening to reveal their violations of alcohol policy to administrators. Cadets who reported the attacks allegedly were ignored and then often disciplined for offenses that included alcohol violations and fraternization (with the cadets who also were

their assailants). Many who filed complaints had withdrawn from the academy. The Fowler panel issued its report on September 22 and also held that the general counsel's working group might have shielded top academy staff from accountability in the assaults.

Investigations revealed that approximately 12 percent of the female graduates of the 2003 academy class had reported that they had been sexually assaulted or faced an attempted sexual assault while attending the academy. An estimated 20 percent of all female cadets who attended the academy within the ten-year period in question had been sexually assaulted during their time at the academy. Many of the alleged assailants, like their alleged victims, failed to graduate. In a survey conducted in 2004, more than three hundred respondents reported that they had been sexually assaulted, and nearly two-thirds indicated that they had not reported the assaults.

The investigations produced a wave of negative publicity for the academy, the Air Force, and the military as a whole. Public opinion of the scandal was divided; many believed that the allegations were overblown or that the academy was being unfairly targeted for behavior equally prevalent in civilian colleges and universities; yet others viewed the scandal as a continuation of a pattern of abuse in the U.S. military. Many public officials reacted to the scandal with anger; Allard and other lawmakers harshly criticized Roche when he appeared before the U.S. Senate Armed Services Committee to testify about the allegations. Groups such as the Miles Foundation, which advocates for victims of sexual trauma in the military, were equally adamant in demanding widespread changes in academy and military policy to deter further sexual assaults and hold administrators and supervisors accountable for investigating complaints and disciplining offenders.

Although the investigations confirmed allegations of a longstanding pattern of sexual assaults, the reports issued by the respective investigatory committees stopped short of recommending harsh consequences for academy leadership. The Air Force IGO report, issued on September 14, 2004, and the Defense Department's OIG report, issued

DEFENSE DEPARTMENT RECOMMENDATIONS

In its December, 2004, report on sexual harassment at the Air Force Academy, the Office of the Inspector General, Department of Defense, recommended that the superintendent of the academy take the following actions:

1. Work with other Service Academy Superintendents and the Office of the Under Secretary of Defense (Personnel and Readiness) to formulate a single survey instrument and testing protocol that can be administered to cadets and midshipmen periodically to measure cultural changes and adherence to core values; upon completing each such survey, brief the Service Secretaries and the Inspector General of the Department of Defense on the results.

2. Increase command attention to eliminating alcohol consumption, prohibited consensual sex, and use of government equipment for pornography at the United States Air Force Academy, thereby furthering good order and discipline among cadets.

3. Ensure that orientation training for cadets includes effective training on clear standards for sexual interaction so all cadets understand clearly the boundaries, penalties for crossing them, individual leadership responsibilities, and reporting options.

4. Maintain a heightened level of command attention aimed at eliminating sexual harassment and negative attitudes toward women at the United States Air Force Academy.

5. Review current admissions criteria and consider adopting changes that emphasize core values as a part of the whole person concept, along with current measures, such as aptitude scores, grades, athletics, and extracurricular activities.

6. Implement Title 10 U.S.C. § 8583 requirements for exemplary leadership behavior into the cadet curriculum and disciplinary system to ensure that graduates possess and enforce the leadership traits essential for future leaders of the United States Air Force.

on December 3, made several recommendations for the prevention of future assaults, including a procedure for confidential reporting, improved access to counseling and medical care, and a strict protocol for investigating sexual assault allegations. Although the committees' findings appeared to confirm allegations that the victim reports had been mishandled, the findings also showed agreement that academy administrators had acted reasonably and legally in their responses to the victim reports. The committees suggested that the mishandling of the victim complaints was due primarily to failures in policy and procedure rather than the negligence or willful misconduct of administrators.

The conclusions of investigators and the response of the Air Force to the scandal met with criticism from within and outside the U.S. military and government. Critics alleged that many of the officials who were disciplined had little or no actual role in the scandal; one officer who was forced into retirement had joined the administration of the academy following the time period under investigation and had been employed at the institution for only two months. Many of the administrators involved retired voluntarily before disciplinary measures could be taken against them. Roche retired in January, 2005, in the light of unrelated allegations of misconduct and was replaced by Peter B. Teets, who in a memorandum to Secretary of Defense Rumsfeld in early 2005 advised against pursuing criminal charges against Air Force officers implicated in the scandal. Teets suggested that the officers had acted in "good faith" and were not derelict in their duties. Although Allard, other members of Congress, and victims' advocacy groups expressed dissatisfaction with the memorandum, neither Rumsfeld nor any other official authorized or initiated additional action against the accused officers.

IMPACT

The scandal and the resulting investigation led to the implementation of new policies on reporting and investigating sexual assaults at the Air Force Academy. Even with these policy changes, lingering questions remain regarding the willingness and ability of the U.S. armed services to adapt to social change and to balance a culture emphasizing loyalty and obedience with the need to address internal problems involving corruption and misconduct.

Although subsequent reports and other evidence

indicate that the service academies have made progress in deterring and prosecuting sexual assaults, other evidence, including numerous reports of sexual assaults upon active-duty female troops serving in Iraq and Afghanistan, indicate that sexual assaults still occur in the U.S. military.

—*Michael H. Burchett*

FURTHER READING

"Air Force Ignored Academy Abuse." *The New York Times*, September 23, 2003. Contains a synopsis of the Fowler panel's report and reactions to the report immediately following its release.

Higgins, M. "The Air Force Academy Scandal: Will the 'Agenda for Change' Counteract the Academy's Legal and Social Deterrents to Reporting Sexual Harassment and Assault?" *Women's Rights Law Reporter* 26, nos. 2-3 (2005): 121-138. Examines the effect of the academy's "Agenda for Change," implemented by the Air Force at the height of the sexual assault scandal.

Hunter, Mic. *Honor Betrayed: Sexual Abuse in America's Military*. Fort Lee, N.J.: Barricade Books, 2007. A social history of the masculinist culture of the U.S. military and that culture's tolerance for sexual abuse. Begins with "Why It Happens" and includes chapters on "the code of hypermasculinity," hazing, domestic violence, and women in the military. Ends with first-person accounts.

"Pentagon Sets New Policy on Reporting Sexual Assaults at Academies." *The New York Times*, March 19, 2005. Briefly describes changes in the sexual assault policies of U.S. military academies.

Smallwood, William L., and Sue Ross. *The Air Force Academy Candidate Book: How to Get In, How to Prepare, How to Survive*. Monument, Colo.: Silver Horn Books, 2007. A guide for prospective Air Force cadets that details the academy's policies and procedures on sexual assault and related issues.

Thomas, Cathy Booth. "The Air Force Academy's Rape Scandal." *Time*, March 6, 2003. Journalistic account of the scandal that provides a synopsis of key events and the perspectives of victims.

SEE ALSO: July 19, 1921: U.S. Senate Rebukes Navy in Homosexuality Investigation; June 26, 1992: U.S. Navy Secretary Resigns in the Wake of Tailhook Sexual Assault Scandal; Apr. 28, 1994: U.S. Naval Academy Expels Midshipmen for Cheating; May 20, 1997: Air Force Prosecution of Female Officer for Adultery Reveals Double Standard; June 2, 2004: U.N. Report Reveals That Secretary-General Kofi Annan Dismissed Sexual Harassment Charges; June 22, 2005: U.S. Air Force Investigates Religious Intolerance at Its Academy.

March 2, 2003

U.S. National Security Agency Is Found to Have Spied on U.N. Officials

According to an investigative report by the British newspaper The Observer, *the U.S. National Security Agency had been engaging in wiretapping and other forms of spying on United Nations personnel, including Secretary-General Kofi Annan, in preparation for seeking U.N. Security Council support for the U.S.-British invasion of Iraq in 2003.*

Locales: London, England; New York, New
   York
Categories: Espionage; government;
   international relations; military; ethics

Key Figures

Frank Koza (fl. early twenty-first century), U.S.
   National Security Agency, chief of staff of
   regional targets section
Katharine Gun (b. 1974), translator for
   Government Communications Headquarters, a
   British intelligence agency
Clare Short (b. 1946), former British cabinet
   member and international development
   secretary
Hans Blix (b. 1928), chief U.N. weapons inspector
Kofi Annan (b. 1938), secretary-general of the
   United Nations

Summary of Event

On March 2, 2003, the British newspaper *The Observer* reported that the United States had been using its National Security Agency (NSA) to tap the phones and read the e-mails of select diplomats at U.N. headquarters in New York City. According to a "top secret" internal memorandum, allegedly written by NSA official Frank Koza and sent on January 31, the agency was to conduct electronic surveillance "particularly directed at the U.N. Security Council Members," excepting those from the United States and Great Britain. The goal of the surveillance was to provide the George W. Bush adminis-

tration with information to help U.S. policymakers gain international support—particularly from the United Nations—for its planned invasion of Iraq with Britain. The text of Koza's e-mail accompanied the report by *The Observer*.

The context of the surveillance was the run-up to the impending U.N. Security Council vote on whether to authorize the use of military force against Iraq. Beginning in April, 1991, under the cease-fire that ended the U.S.-led armed attack against Iraq in response to its invasion of Kuwait, Iraq had been required by Security Council resolution no. 687 to disarm itself of chemical, biological, and nuclear weapons and to allow U.N. weapons inspectors to verify compliance with that requirement. Through the next several years, Iraq failed to comply fully with that resolution, consistently obstructing the weapons inspectors before expelling them in 1998.

After the September 11, 2001, terrorist attacks in New York and Washington, D.C., and the subsequent U.S. and British-led invasion of Afghanistan, the Bush administration turned its attention to Iraq. After weeks of negotiating exact language, the Security Council voted 15-0 on September 12, 2002, to adopt resolution no. 1441, which condemned Iraq's support of terrorist organizations, its grave violations of international human-rights laws, and its failure to comply with past Security Council resolutions, including 687.

In response to resolution 1441, Iraqi president Saddam Hussein agreed to let weapons inspectors return to his country. However, in early 2003, the chief U.N. weapons inspector, Hans Blix, told the United Nations that Iraq was unable to provide evidence and documentation of its destruction of stockpiles of chemical weapons. The United States and Britain argued that Iraq's breach of resolution 1441 called for further Security Council actions, including authorization of the use of military force against Iraq.

THE E-MAIL MEMO

U.S. National Security Agency official Frank Koza sent the following e-mail to colleagues, urging them to monitor the e-mail and phone communications of U.N. Security Council members for information that could help the United States and Great Britain in their efforts to win international approval for their planned invasion of Iraq in 2003.

To: [Recipients withheld]
From: FRANK KOZA, Def Chief of Staff (Regional Targets) CIV/NSA
Sent on Jan 31 2003 0:16
Subject: Reflections of Iraq Debate/Votes at UN-RT Actions +
  Potential for Related Contributions
Importance: HIGH
Top Secret//COMINT//X1

All,
    As you've likely heard by now, the Agency is mounting a surge particularly directed at the UN Security Council (UNSC) members (minus US and GBR of course) for insights as to how membership is reacting to the on-going debate RE: Iraq, plans to vote on any related resolutions, what related policies/ negotiating positions they may be considering, alliances/ dependencies, etc.—the whole gamut of information that could give US policymakers an edge in obtaining results favorable to US goals or to head off surprises. In RT, that means a QRC surge effort to revive/create efforts against UNSC members Angola, Cameroon, Chile, Bulgaria and Guinea, as well as extra focus on Pakistan UN matters.
    We've also asked ALL RT topi's to emphasize and make sure they pay attention to existing non-UNSC member UN-related and domestic comms [home phone and e-mail] for anything useful related to the UNSC deliberations/ debates/ votes. We have a lot of special UN-related diplomatic coverage (various UN delegations) from countries not sitting on the UNSC right now that could contribute related perspectives/ insights/ whatever. We recognize that we can't afford to ignore this possible source.
    We'd appreciate your support in getting the word to your analysts who might have similar, more in-direct access to valuable information from accesses in your product lines. I suspect that you'll be hearing more along these lines in formal channels—especially as this effort will probably peak (at least for this specific focus) in the middle of next week, following the SecState's presentation to the UNSC.

Thanks for your help.

those three countries would abstain or vote against the resolution without exercising their vetoes if enough of the nonpermanent members of the Security Council supported military action, the United States and Britain lobbied Cameroon, Guinea, Angola, Pakistan, Bulgaria, and Chile for support. (The remaining members of the Security Council that year were Mexico, Germany, and Syria.) Had those six nations been willing to support a new Security Council resolution authorizing the use of military force, the result would have been no worse than a 9-6 vote.

The perceived need for support from those six nations explains why the NSA was allegedly spying on their delegations to discern their voting intentions, as well as gathering information that could help obtain their support for military action. In the end, when it became clear that the United States and Britain could not secure the support of a majority of the Security Council, those countries did not seek a further resolution authorizing the use of military force. Instead, the United States and Britain initiated armed conflict against Iraq purportedly on the strength of resolution 1441.

In November, 2003, several months after *The Observer* published its story about the NSA's spying, British officials arrested Katharine Gun, a translator for Government Communications Headquarters, a British intelligence agency, and charged her with violating the Official Secrets Act. According to prosecutors, Gun received a copy of the NSA memorandum through

The United States and Britain (along with Spain, which also supported aggressive action against Iraq) encountered resistance from other Security Council members, including the other permanent members, France, China, and Russia. Hoping that e-mail from its author, Koza, and proceeded to leak the memo to *The Observer*. Gun pleaded not guilty and stated that she leaked the memo because she wanted to prevent an invasion of Iraq. Her trial began on February 25, 2004, but she was acquitted by the court when the prosecution declined to present evidence against her. Gun became known as the whistle-blower in the scandal and received worldwide attention and support for her efforts.

The next day, Clare Short, a former British cabinet minister who had resigned her position as international development secretary a couple of months after the March, 2003, invasion of Iraq, disclosed that the British government had helped the NSA spy on U.N. diplomats, including Secretary-General Kofi Annan. Short claimed that she had seen transcripts of Annan's conversations about Iraq, drawing criticism from British prime minister Tony Blair and others, who said that Short had endangered British national security. Soon after, Short recanted slightly, saying that the transcripts she had seen may have involved Africa, rather than Iraq.

It should be noted that the NSA surveillance of U.N. diplomats, despite its secretive nature and its implementation without warrants, does not appear to have violated domestic law. The U.S. Foreign Intelligence Surveillance Act of 1978 (FISA), which regulates domestic surveillance for foreign intelligence gathering (as opposed to criminal prosecution), requires special FISA warrants only where the surveillance is likely to target communications involving a U.S. citizen; where the communications are between nonresident aliens, however, neither FISA nor the U.S. Constitution requires a warrant for surveillance.

IMPACT

The revelation of the NSA's apparent spying on U.N. officials proved embarrassing to the Bush administration, but it did not appear to have affected the outcome of diplomacy after the passage of resolution 1441 in September, 2002. In part, this may be the case because the United States and Britain were far from alone in spying on the United Nations. In late 2004, U.N. officials discovered a hidden listening device in one of its European headquarters' offices; analysis of the device suggested that it was of Russian or East European—and hence, not U.S. or British—design.

In the United States, it is almost an exaggeration to call the spying incident scandalous. Surprisingly, *The New York Times* and many other major American newspapers did not even report on the spying, an omission that drew scathing criticism from foreign media outlets. Far more controversy ensued with the revelation nearly two years later that the NSA had also been conducting electronic surveillance, without warrants, of U.S. citizens.

—*Tung Yin*

FURTHER READING

Abrams, Norman. *Anti-Terrorism and Criminal Enforcement*. 2d ed. St. Paul, Minn.: West Group, 2008. Provides a good introduction to understanding the mechanics of the Foreign Intelligence Surveillance Act and other antiterrorist legislation.

Bright, Martin. "U.S. Stars Hail Iraq War Whistle-Blower." *The Observer*, January 18, 2004. The reporter who broke the NSA spy scandal with two colleagues reports on the widespread support for Katharine Gun, the intelligence agency staffer who leaked the Koza memo to the press.

Bright, Martin, Ed Vulliamy, and Peter Beaumont. "Revealed: U.S. Dirty Tricks to Win Vote on Iraq War." *The Observer*, March 2, 2003. Article that broke the story about the NSA spying on U.N. officials. Criticizes the Bush administration for ordering the surveillance.

Conyers, John C., et al. *Constitution in Crisis: The High Crimes of the Bush Administration and a Blueprint for Impeachment*. New York: Skyhorse, 2007. Although decidedly biased against the Bush administration, this rich work explores thousands of sources to document a pattern of corruption leading up to the invasion of Iraq. Includes discussion of the NSA spy scandal.

SEE ALSO: Jan. 21, 1950: Alger Hiss Is Convicted of Perjury; Sept. 12, 1962: British Civil Servant Is Arrested for Spying; Mar. 2-Sept. 25, 1963: John Profumo Affair Rocks British Government;

2000's

Mar. 4, 1966: Munsinger Sex and Spy Scandal Rocks Canada; Feb. 18, 2001: CIA Agent Robert Hanssen Is Arrested for Spying for the Russians; June 2, 2004: U.N. Report Reveals That

Secretary-General Kofi Annan Dismissed Sexual Harassment Charges; Jan. 15, 2005: Iqbal Riza Resigns from the United Nations in Oil-for-Food Scandal.

April 29, 2003
NEW YORK TIMES REPORTER JAYSON BLAIR IS EXPOSED AS A FRAUD

The New York Times *discovered that reporter Jayson Blair had plagiarized a story about an anguished mother of a missing U.S. soldier in Iraq, setting off an investigation that uncovered four years of Blair's fabrications and deceit. Although Blair was fired, and the newspaper took responsibility, the credibility of not only the newspaper but all news sources was questioned.*

LOCALE: New York, New York

CATEGORIES: Communications and media; hoaxes, frauds, and charlatanism; plagiarism; publishing and journalism

KEY FIGURES

Jayson Blair (b. 1976), reporter for *The New York Times*

Macarena Hernandez (b. 1974), reporter for the *San Antonio Express-News*

Howell Raines (b. 1943), executive editor of *The New York Times*

Gerald Boyd (1950-2006), managing editor of *The New York Times*

SUMMARY OF EVENT

Newspapers are generally regarded as accurate, unbiased sources of information. *The New York Times*, an American institution since 1851, had achieved an immaculate reputation for printing "all the news that's fit to print." However, the stories submitted by reporter Jayson Blair were found to be fabrications in some instances and outright plagiarism in others. The failure of the *Times* to oversee verifica-

tion of Blair's facts and perhaps a too lenient approach to a young reporter led to an examination and restructuring of newsroom procedures. Not only was Blair's career destroyed but also the careers of two high-ranking *Times* editors. The damage extended beyond the *Times* to journalism as a whole.

Blair was born on March 23, 1976, in Columbia, Maryland, the son of Thomas Blair, a career civil servant, and Frances Blair, an educator. He grew up in Centreville, Virginia, wrote for his high school paper, and interned for the *Centreville Times*, a local weekly. In 1994, he enrolled in the journalism school at the University of Maryland. Initially, fellow students and faculty alike were impressed with his charismatic manner and his enthusiasm for finding stories. However, problems began to surface about Blair missing deadlines and concerns that the work submitted might not have been his. At Maryland he rose to the rank of editor of *The Diamondback*, the student newspaper, but after an alleged plagiarism incident, he resigned.

During summer breaks, Blair interned at the *Boston Globe* and *The Washington Post*. In the summer of 1998, he won an internship at *The New York Times*. Although he was asked to stay on at the end of the summer, he left the paper, stating he had to finish some courses for his December graduation. In June, 1999, Blair returned to the *Times* and was offered an entry-level reporting job. His extraordinary promise as a reporter-writer and his being African American made his hire a natural for an organization committed to diversity. Had the human resources department checked, it would have discovered that Blair never graduated from the University of Maryland.

Blair was on the fast-track at the *Times*, scrambling for stories and working long hours. He wrote 137 stories within five months, and only one factual correction was required by editors. Due to his success, he was promoted to a higher level reporter position in November but his work began to slip, and the rate of corrections on his work exceeded that of a typical cub, or rookie, reporter. Blair was warned to be more careful.

Despite problems in his personal life, including substance abuse, and the reservations of many people at the paper, Blair was promoted to staff reporter in January, 2001. The recruiting committee, headed by Gerald M. Boyd, then a deputy managing editor, approved the promotion despite the opposition of Jonathan Landman, metropolitan editor for the paper. Blair's performance at work continued to decline. In early 2002, Landman sent warnings about Blair's work behavior to Boyd, stating, "We have to stop Jayson from writing for the *Times*. Right now." His advice was not heeded, and between January and April, Blair, who was trying to get his life under control, took two leaves of absence from the paper. When he returned, he was reassigned from the metro desk to the sports section; Landman hoped the "tighter leash" in the sports section would help the young reporter.

The Beltway sniper case in the Washington, D.C., area in October, 2002, gave Blair the opportunity to prove he was a good reporter. Executive editor Howell Raines, wishing to flood the area with reporters, transferred Blair to the national desk in Washington, D.C., especially because Blair knew the area well. He was assigned to an exclusive story, based on information gleaned from five unnamed law enforcement officers, which would be published on the front page. This and other stories on the sniper attacks led to an angry response by law enforcement officials and claims that Blair had not told the truth. Fairfax County, Virginia,

prosecutor Robert Horan claimed that 60 percent of a story Blair wrote included misquotes and incorrect information. In meetings with his editors, Blair defended his stories and was allowed to remain on the national desk.

In March, 2003, Blair began filing stories about the families of service personnel in Iraq. Although the reports were often eloquent, they were filled with inaccuracies. Later, it was discovered that Blair, in many cases, had never visited the places in his reports nor interviewed the people mentioned in his articles. He claimed to have visited the home of Army specialist Jessica Lynch, who had been captured and rescued in Iraq, but his so-called firsthand description of Lynch's home was inaccurate. Some who read Blair's stories saw the incorrect details, the fabricated scenes, and the made-up quotations, and then tried to contact the *Times* about the errors; many gave up after their concerns were not addressed. Others did not bother contacting the paper

Jayson Blair. (Hulton Archive/Getty Images)

BLAIR UNCOVERED

New York Times *national editor Jim Roberts met with reporter Jayson Blair over a two-day period beginning on April 29, 2003. Blair was accused of plagiarizing a* San Antonio Express-News *story about a missing U.S. soldier in Iraq and his mother's fears.* The New York Times *published an article, excerpted here, telling its readers of Blair's deception.*

In a series of tense meetings over two days, Mr. Roberts repeatedly pressed Mr. Blair for evidence that he had indeed interviewed the mother. . . .

''You've got to come clean with us,'' he [Roberts] said—and zeroed in on the mother's house in Texas. He asked Mr. Blair to describe what he had seen.

Mr. Blair did not hesitate. He told Mr. Roberts of the reddish roof on the white stucco house, of the red Jeep in the driveway, of the roses blooming in the yard. Mr. Roberts later inspected unpublished photographs of the mother's house, which matched Mr. Blair's descriptions in every detail.

It was not until Mr. Blair's deceptions were uncovered that Mr. Roberts learned how the reporter could have deceived him yet again: by consulting the newspaper's computerized photo archives.

What haunts Mr. Roberts now, he says, is one particular moment when editor and reporter were facing each other in a showdown over the core aim of their profession: truth.

"Look me in the eye and tell me you did what you say you did," Mr. Roberts demanded. Mr. Blair returned his gaze and said he had.

Source: Dan Barry et al., "Correcting the Record: Times Reporter Who Resigned Leaves Long Trail of Deception." *The New York Times*, May 11, 2003.

"Valley Mom Awaits News of MIA Son," about a missing U.S. soldier in Iraq and his mother's anguish. The soldier, Sergeant Edward Anguiano, had been part of Specialist Lynch's convoy when it was ambushed in March, 2003. Blair's too-similar story, "Family Waits, Now Alone, for a Missing Soldier," appeared in the *Times* on April 26. Hernandez read Blair's story, noticed the similarities, and alerted her editor, who in turn contacted editors at the *Times*. Blair met with his editors on April 29 but had no evidence to substantiate his claim that the story was his. Anguiano's mother in Texas stated that Hernandez had visited her home, but no reporter from the *Times* had visited.

Unable to prove his story was original, Blair resigned from the *Times* on May 1. On May 11 the *Times* published a lengthy front-page account of Blair's acts of fabrication and plagiarism. A staff meeting on May 14 led to extensive criticism of the failure of Raines and Boyd to detect Blair's deceptions, and both editors were forced to resign in June.

IMPACT

The results of Blair's dishonesty were both immediate and far-reaching. He not only lost his job but also destroyed the careers of Raines and Boyd. Both editors were accused of leaning too far to advance affirmative action. Boyd, also African American, denied any favoritism, but Raines admitted that he did give a second chance to Blair because of his race. Although a lengthy article detailing Blair's actions and including corrections was published on May 11, the blow to the credibility of the *Times* was severe. The scandal quickly became a source of comedy on a number of television shows and, worse still, the work of other *Times* reporters was questioned. The paper accepted responsibility for Blair's actions, apologized to the public, and sought to repair its reputation.

Corrective measures, to prevent any future viola-

---

at all, assuming nothing would be done. They also believed that once a story was published, no retraction could make a difference. Blair was filing stories with bylines from places he had never been, was not in contact with his editors, and was not submitting expense reports. The latter should have been a red flag to his supervisors, showing he was not traveling as much as his stories appeared to attest.

A reporter for another newspaper, the *San Antonio Express-News*, exposed Blair's ongoing deceptions. On April 18, 2003, the *Express-News* published a story by reporter Macarena Hernandez, tion of basic standards of reporting, included form-ing a committee to address "what went wrong." The committee, chaired by assistant managing editor Allan Siegal, recommended in its report of July 28, 2003, that two management-level positions—public editor and standards editor—be created at the pa-per. The public editor would be an ombudsperson, investigating public complaints concerning accu-racy and fairness in news reporting. The standards editor would be an "internal guardian" who ensures quality control.

While Blair's deceptions led to restructuring at the *Times*, they also produced a ripple effect, en-compassing changes in journalism as a whole. Other newspapers revisited their policies and be-came more stringent in scrutinizing the work of their reporters. In a survey conducted by the Ameri-can Society of Newspaper Editors, 350 editors stated they had taken some "specific action" be-cause of the Blair scandal.

Blair published a book in 2004, *Burning Down My Masters' House*, which is an attempt to justify his actions. The book, however, was not favorably received. Stephen Pomper, a reviewer for the *Wash-ington Monthly*, described the book as a "300-page pity party." Critics were skeptical of the book's de-tails, given Blair's history of deception.

—*Marcia B. Dinneen*

FURTHER READING

Barry, Dan, et al. "*Times* Reporter Who Resigned Leaves Long Trail of Deception." *The New York Times*, May 11, 2003. A lengthy, front-page exposé of Blair's "frequent acts of journalistic fraud," published in response to the revelations of his deception.

Blair, Jayson. *Burning Down My Masters' House: My Life at "The New York Times."* Beverly Hills, Calif.: New Millennium Press, 2004. This mem-oir chronicles Blair's four years as a reporter and how his manic-depressive illness led to his be-havior as a cheat and plagiarist.

Hassan, Adeel. "Blair's Victims: That Helpless Feeling." *Columbia Journalism Review*, July-August, 2003. Details specific examples of Blair's deceptions and examines the reactions of those directly affected by his fraud.

Mnookin, Seth. *Hard News: The Scandals at "The New York Times" and Their Meaning for Ameri-can Media*. New York: Random House, 2004. A former reporter for *Newsweek* magazine tells the story behind the scandal of Jayson Blair and the effect of the fraud and deception on the staff and readers of *The New York Times*.

Patterson, Maggie, and Steve Urbanski. "What Jayson Blair and Janet Cooke Say About the Press and the Erosion of Public Trust." *Journal-ism Studies* 7, no. 6 (2006): 828-850. A journal article that details how Blair's actions subverted the mission of journalism.

SEE ALSO: Apr. 15, 1981: Janet Cooke Admits Fab-ricating Her Pulitzer Prize-Winning Feature; June 24, 1994: *Time* Magazine Cover Uses Al-tered O. J. Simpson Photo; May 11, 1998: Jour-nalist Stephen Glass Is Exposed as a Fraud; Sept. 8, 2004: *60 Minutes II* Reports on George W. Bush's Evasion of Wartime Duty.

2000's

May 3, 2003

UNIVERSITY OF ALABAMA FIRES NEW FOOTBALL COACH IN SEX SCANDAL

Four months after agreeing to a seven-year, $10 million contract to become the new head football coach at the University of Alabama, Mike Price was fired for inappropriate behavior. An article in Sports Illustrated *magazine one week later revealed that Price—who was in Florida for a golf tournament—had spent lavishly on alcohol and private dances at a strip club and had consensual sex with two of the dancers in his hotel room. In turn, Price sued the university, Time, Inc., and the reporter for libel and defamation, and he won his case.*

LOCALE: Tuscaloosa, Alabama
CATEGORIES: Gambling; law and the courts; public morals; publishing and journalism; sex

KEY FIGURES

Mike Price (b. 1946), head football coach at the University of Alabama
Don Yaeger (b. 1962), *Sports Illustrated* reporter
Lori Boudreaux (b. 1967), dancer at Arety's Angels in Pensacola, Florida
Robert Witt (b. 1941), president of the University of Alabama

SUMMARY OF EVENT

On December 18, 2002, after fourteen years of successful leadership of the football program at Washington State University (WSU), Mike Price accepted the position of head football coach at the University of Alabama, which is arguably one of the most prestigious college football programs in the United States. He was issued, yet never signed, a seven-year, $10 million contract. The contract had a morals clause.

On May 3, 2003, only four months into his new job, Price was fired by University of Alabama president Robert Witt. According to media accounts, Price was in Pensacola, Florida, for an appearance at the Emerald Coast Classic Golf Tournament. After arriving in Pensacola on April 16, Price headed for Arety's Angels, a local strip club. The alleged sequence of events, as well as additional information that surfaced later, was accepted as true by Alabama officials, even though there was a dearth of corroborating evidence. Price was summarily terminated and earned the dubious distinction of losing his job at Alabama without ever coaching a single game.

News of the firing first surfaced on an Auburn University booster club Web site on April 23. The site posted rumors that Price had visited the strip club. Shortly after the Web site posting, radio talk shows, television sports shows, and newspapers across the United States turned the alleged rumors into headlines. They reported that exactly one week earlier, on April 16, Price spent hundreds of dollars on alcoholic beverages and private dances. Most damaging, however, were the accusations that Price also had sex with two dancers from the club that night, one of whom later spent $1,000 for hotel room service on Price's credit card. The accusations came most significantly from a May 12 article by reporter Don Yaeger in *Sports Illustrated* ("How He Met His Destiny at a Strip Club").

According to the article, Price introduced himself solely as "Mike" at the club, attempting to limit his public exposure. However, in no time, the football fans at the club recognized Price as the newly hired coach at Alabama. Club patrons even began to refer to him as "coach." Witnesses said that Price bought not only many drinks but also private dances from Lori "Destiny" Boudreaux, who had worked at the strip club for fifteen years. Price allegedly broke many of the club's rules during at least one of the dances. Boudreaux would later testify that she was propositioned by Price, who asked her to accompany him to his room at the Crowne Plaza Hotel later in the evening.

Price then left Arety's Angels to attend the sponsors' dinner for the Emerald Coast Classic Golf Tournament. He was professional at the dinner but soon returned to Arety's Angels, after the meal. According to witnesses, Price kissed and fondled a waitress at the bar, which prompted club staff to warn Price that his actions were not permissible. After moving to another table, Price bought more drinks for several dancers, prompting later allegations that he had spent hundreds of dollars at the club. Just before midnight, he headed back to his hotel room, but he was not alone.

As detailed in the *Sports Illustrated* article, two dancers accompanied Price to his hotel room. The women claimed that they engaged in consensual sex with Price. The next morning, after Price left for the golf tournament, one of the dancers ordered $1,000 worth of room service on Price's credit card, prompting a concerned hotel manager to call Price, who was by this time on the golf course.

Alabama officials were soon informed of the events in Pensacola, but the allegations did not come as a surprise to Alabama athletic director Mal Moore. A few weeks after Price had been hired, several female students at the university claimed that he bought them drinks and propositioned them while dining at Buffalo's American Grille in Tuscaloosa. Moore had spoken to Price about the accusations, stressing that this type of behavior was unacceptable. In turn, Price denied the allegations.

Price was fired on May 3, based solely on unproven allegations. In July, he filed a $20 million libel suit against the University of Alabama, Time, Inc. (which owns *Sports Illustrated*), and Yaeger, contending that the events described by Yaeger in the *Sports Illustrated* article were false. On October 10, Price settled the defamation portion of the lawsuit against Time and received an undisclosed amount. He had sued for $10 million in compensatory damages and another $10 million in punitive damages.

Boudreaux confirmed in a sworn affidavit at trial that she was Yeager's source, but she apparently did not tell the truth. Her account of what happened in Price's hotel room was deemed hearsay by the court, so her story was not admissible at trial. The court ruling left nothing but doubt in the case of Price's alleged sexual encounter with the strip-club dancers in Florida.

IMPACT

Alabama's firing of Price sent a clear message that inappropriate behavior, even if only alleged and even if off campus, can end one's career. Furthermore, the university's decision to fire Price based only on uncorroborated allegations harmed the institution's credibility. Also, following Price's dismissal, officials were forced to find their fourth head football coach in as many years but to do so in a negative climate for the university.

Price was one of several high-profile college and university coaches within a period of a few years who were accused of inappropriate behavior and had been terminated as a result. In 2003, Rick Neuheisel, then head football coach at the University of Washington, was fired after a string of transgressions dating back to 1999. Neuheisel had lied to Washington officials about a job interview with the San Francisco 49ers of the National Football League. He also broke the National Collegiate Athletic Association (NCAA) rules on gambling by betting on college basketball games. In 2005, he settled his wrongful termination lawsuit against the NCAA and Washington for $4.5 million. In 2006, Mike Pressler, then head men's lacrosse coach at Duke University, was forced to resign amid allegations that three of his players had raped a woman at a party. Ultimately, the accusations were found to be untrue and, in 2007, Duke and Pressler reached an undisclosed financial settlement over his forced resignation. In early 2008, Pressler also filed a defamation lawsuit against Duke, claiming that university representatives said he had not adequately supervised his athletes.

In Pullman, Washington, the home of Price's former employer, WSU, the legacy of the famed coach descended from that of a well-respected icon to a person tainted by the fame associated with being fired from Alabama. Price moved on from his infamous night at Arety's Angels to serve as head football coach at the University of Texas—El Paso.

—*Ryan Patten and Joseph Hurley*

FURTHER READING

Fatsis, Stefan. "Football Coach and Time Inc. Settle Libel Suit." *The Wall Street Journal*, October 11, 2005. An overview of the lawsuit settlement in *Price v. Time Inc.* in October, 2005.

Murphy, Kirsten. "The Price of Privilege." *News Media and the Law* 28, no. 2 (2004): 17-20. A journal article that provides an excellent analysis of the firing of Mike Price.

Yaeger, Don. "How He Met His Destiny at a Strip Club." *Sports Illustrated*, May 12, 2003. Examines the events that allegedly took place at Arety's Angels and in Mike Price's hotel room.

SEE ALSO: Feb. 25, 1987: NCAA Imposes "Death Penalty" on Southern Methodist University Football; Aug. 27, 2001: Little League Baseball Star Danny Almonte Is Found to Be Overage; Dec. 14, 2001: Notre Dame Football Coach Resigns for Falsifying His Resume; Mar. 27, 2002: Georgia Basketball Coach Jim Harrick, Sr., Resigns over Fraud Allegations; July 14, 2006: *New York Times* Exposes Grading Scandal at Auburn University; Aug. 20, 2007: Football Star Michael Vick Pleads Guilty to Financing a Dogfighting Ring; Sept. 13, 2007: New England Patriots Football Team Is Fined for Spying on Other Teams.

May 21, 2003
SEXUALLY PROVOCATIVE FILM *THE BROWN BUNNY* PREMIERES AT CANNES FILM FESTIVAL

The Brown Bunny, a disturbing film by iconoclastic auteur Vincent Gallo that includes a provocative sequence showing fellatio, received a mixed reception from the international film community at the prestigious Cannes Film Festival. Nominated for the Palme d'Or, the film touched off a heated debate over the relationship between filmmakers and critics and ultimately between filmmakers and their audiences.

LOCALE: Cannes, France

CATEGORIES: Film; sex; art movements; publishing and journalism; public morals; popular culture

KEY FIGURES

Vincent Gallo (b. 1961), American actor and experimental film director

Chloë Sevigny (b. 1974), Oscar-nominated American film actor

Roger Ebert (b. 1942), Pulitzer Prize-winning American film critic

SUMMARY OF EVENT

Drawing on the experimental neorealism pioneered by pop artist Andy Warhol nearly a generation earlier, Vincent Gallo's *The Brown Bunny* tells the bleak story of a motorcycle racer named Bud Clay (played by Gallo) who, desperate to escape a past that includes a passionate relationship with a woman identified only as Daisy (played by Chloë Sevigny), sets out to drive a van loaded with his motorcycle from New Hampshire to California. For most of the nearly hour and a half film, that trip is recorded in unrelieved tedium—restaurant stops, gas fill-ups, and changes of clothes, and miles of highway filmed through bug-splattered windows.

The most significant action in the film is psychological, happening behind Clay's opaque sunglasses. There are chance encounters with three different women, but in each case Clay cannot bring himself to risk the vulnerability of authentic connection, and his character is left decidedly alone. The encounters are distinguished by disjointed conversations, long stares, and cryptic silences. Along

Chloë Sevigny and Vincent Gallo at the premiere of their film The Brown Bunny *at Cannes, France, in May, 2003.* (Hulton Archive/Getty Images)

the way, Clay visits Daisy's parents, and while there he secures one of Daisy's favorite childhood stuffed animals, a brown bunny. When he finally arrives in Los Angeles, he goes to Daisy's house—but it is empty. At a hotel, however, he is joined by Daisy who coolly performs oral sex on him after smoking crack cocaine. They engage in a steadily heated conversation about her relationships with other men. What is revealed, however, is that Daisy had been gang raped during a party some months earlier; that Clay had failed to help her and had, in fact, left the party; and that she had subsequently choked to death on her own vomit. Clay is haunted (literally) not merely by her memory but by his own shame and is trying to find in his cross-country flight an escape from his sense of responsibility

(represented by the grotesque stuffed bunny he now lugs about).

Gallo hesitated when he was approached in early 2003 to premiere his film project (he was the film's producer, director, writer, and star) for consideration for the Palme d'Or at Cannes in France. Although his earlier film, 1998's *Buffalo '66*, a quirky psychological study of a released convict who kidnaps a beautiful woman to pretend to be his girlfriend when he must visit his parents, had become an award-winning independent film, his experiences at Cannes had always been strained. He knew that to meet the festival's spring deadline, given production difficulties he was facing, he would have to submit an unfinished rough cut. He decided to submit the film.

Even with the edgy experimental nature of the film—its deliberate evocation of tedium; its layers of dense, associational imagery; its dreamlike nonlinearity; its minimal action; and its unsympathetic central character—Gallo was not prepared for the reaction his film ignited. The controversy surrounding its debut on May 21 quickly became the headline of what was an otherwise routine festival. Although the film received appreciative applause, the majority of the Cannes audience was decidedly hostile to the film, booing and jeering and, for most, walking out long before the controversial sex scene. The ten-minute oral-sex sequence, which Sevigny actually performed on Gallo, was seen as entirely gratuitous. Gallo tirelessly argued long after the premiere that the scene reenforced the emptiness in the character's soul and, given that the woman was actually dead, was a powerful image for the deep narcissism of his grief.

In the wake of the disastrous showing, the most vocal critic of the film was Roger Ebert, the Pulitzer Prize-winning film critic for the *Chicago Sun-Times* and cohost of a long-running, nationally syndicated, film-review show. He has been a respected and powerful voice in the industry. He pilloried Gallo's film, not merely because of the sex scene but also the film's poor pace and lack of focus. He famously described it as the worst film Cannes had ever shown. The day after the premiere, a teary and obviously shaken Gallo admitted the film was a rough cut and apologized for wasting the judges' time with an unfinished film. There also was suspicion that the virtually unqualified support of the French press for the film may have reflected less its sensitivity to Gallo's film and more its political motivations: In the heated atmosphere leading up to the U.S. invasion of Iraq when French and U.S. relations were particularly chilly, the French ironically (and gleefully) celebrated what was widely seen as a truly awful American film.

Ebert's words, widely disseminated on the Web, ignited a lengthy and very public war of words between Gallo and Ebert—an exchange that was less a discussion of the merits (or lack thereof) of Gallo's avant-garde film and more an exchange of insults that climaxed with Gallo supposedly put-

ting a hex on Ebert's prostate. Ebert quipped that he had experienced a colonoscopy and watching that was more enjoyable than watching Gallo's film.

Within months of Cannes, Gallo returned to the film. After reediting the work (cutting about 25 minutes, although leaving the sex scene intact), he reissued the film, initially at the 2003 Toronto Film Festival, then in summer, 2004, as a Wellspring Media then Sony Pictures theatrical release, and ultimately on DVD. Not surprisingly, given the enormous attention it had received at Cannes, the film found an immediate audience in its theatrical release, most likely expecting to see one of those celebrated "so-bad-it's-kitschy" films. However, Gallo's sensitive editing had significantly altered the impact, and audiences and critics (most notably Ebert himself) found the reedited film provocative and powerful as an understated, even stark, anatomy of grief that juxtaposed images of escape and fantasy with the hard reality of guilt, doubt, sorrow, and responsibility.

IMPACT

The Brown Bunny created a scandal in itself, but the disturbing fellatio scene—although accounting for barely ten minutes of the entire film—raised difficult (and incendiary) questions about the line between art and pornography. Given that Gallo and Sevigny had maintained a high-profile off-screen relationship, the sequence blurred the line between art and voyeurism, its unflinching (and unedited) recording of the act resembling not cinema but salacious hardcore porn footage or a sleazy underground celebrity sex tape for the Web. It did not immediately register with viewers that within the larger argument of the film such a perception of the scene's coldness helped sustain a significant thematic argument about the nature of love. Indeed, the scene was sufficient to have Sevigny, an accomplished independent-film actor who had been nominated for an Oscar in 1999 for her work in *Boys Don't Cry*, summarily dropped by the prestigious William Morris talent agency. Only in its rerelease did the scene's larger argument—the de-glamorization of sex in the face of death and the pain involved in any grieving process that involves a sexual relationship—become clear.

Apart from the response to the sexual content, however, the public dust-up between Gallo and Ebert revealed the fragile nature of egos in that particular dynamic—both with the actors and those who cover their work in the press. Clearly, Gallo, like Warhol before him, crafted a film that was not intended for the general public, a film whose portrayal of the banality and absurdity of life would be inaccessible to those who see films for entertainment and spectacle. That discussion, however, never took place. Rather, the barbs between artist and critic quickly denigrated into personal attacks that could be seen cynically as part of the promotional machinery of Hollywood—indeed, given the controversy surrounding Gallo's film and the Ebert critique, an otherwise marginal film destined for limited release in art-house theaters eventually played to a much wider audience and, in the end, made far more money for its parent company, Sony Pictures.

—*Joseph Dewey*

Further Reading

Ebert, Roger. *Roger Ebert's Movie Yearbook, 2004.* Riverside, N.J.: Andrews McMeel, 2004. Includes relevant commentary by Ebert on the Gallo-*Brown Bunny* controversy as well as Ebert's original scathing review of *The Brown Bunny.*

_____. "The Whole Truth from Vincent Gallo." *Chicago Sun-Times*, August 29, 2004. A candid interview with the filmmaker Ebert had so condemned more than one year earlier after seeing the premiere of *The Brown Bunny* at Cannes.

Krzywinska, Tanya. *Sex and the Cinema.* New York: Wallflower/Columbia University Press, 2006. Thorough investigation into the differences between art and pornography that uses numerous contemporary examples (including Gallo's film) to define the new dimensions of artistic license in the age of the Web.

Sklar, Richard. "Beyond Hoopla: The Cannes Film Festival and Cultural Significance." *Cineaste* 22, no. 3 (June, 1996): 18-28. Helpful summary of the importance of Cannes as a promotional tool for maverick filmmakers and independent films.

Winter, Jessica. *The Rough Guide to American Independent Film.* New York: Rough Guides, 2006. Contextualizes Gallo's filmmaking by assessing the late twentieth century emergence of low-budget auteur films (and filmmakers) whose limited success was supported by numerous regional film festivals and by the critical press sensitive to the provocative and experimental work.

See also: Feb. 17-Mar. 15, 1913: Armory Modern Art Show Scandalizes the Public; Mar. 26, 1922: Hindemith's Opera *Sancta Susanna* Depicts a Nun's Sexual Desires; 1927: Mae West's Play About Gays Is Banned on Broadway; Dec. 3, 1930: Surrealist Film *L'Âge d'or* Provokes French Rioting; Jan. 20, 1933: Hedy Lamarr Appears Nude in the Czech Film *Exstase*; Early Nov., 2003: Paris Hilton Sex-Tape Appears on the Web.

2000's

July 1, 2003
BASKETBALL STAR KOBE BRYANT IS ACCUSED OF RAPE

Professional basketball player Kobe Bryant was accused of sexually assaulting a nineteen-year-old concierge at a hotel resort. He denied the accusation and claimed that the sexual encounter was consensual. The prosecution dropped the criminal charges after the accuser, Katelyn Faber, refused to testify on grounds that her sexual history would fuel further media attention. Faber filed a civil suit against Bryant and settled out of court for an undisclosed amount of money.

LOCALE: Edwards, Colorado
CATEGORIES: Law and the courts; public morals; publishing and journalism

KEY FIGURES
Kobe Bryant (b. 1978), professional basketball player
Katelyn Faber (b. 1985), hotel concierge and college student
Vanessa Bryant (b. 1982), Bryant's wife

SUMMARY OF EVENT
Professional basketball player Kobe Bryant, an All-Star guard with the Los Angeles Lakers, was accused on July 1, 2003, of sexually assaulting Katelyn Faber, a nineteen-year-old concierge at a hotel resort in Edwards, Colorado. Bryant had been in Colorado for scheduled knee surgery at the Steadman-Hawkins Clinic in Vail. He checked into the Lodge and Spa at Cordillera, a hotel in Edwards, on June 28.

According to Faber, who remained anonymous throughout the criminal investigation and most of the legal proceedings, Bryant invited her to his room after she gave him a tour of the hotel on the night of July 1, the day before his surgery. She told investigators that she and Bryant flirted with each other and that the flirting led to consensual kissing. She said the kissing led to unwanted groping and that Bryant blocked her exit when she tried to leave the room. She then said that Bryant physically restrained her over a chair and placed his hands

around her neck, suggesting strangulation if she resisted. She stated that Bryant then began to penetrate her sexually and that she requested several times that he stop. Faber said that Bryant continued with the sexual assault and tightened his grasp around her neck each time she asked him to stop.

Faber then told investigators that she left the room immediately after the assault and remained at the hotel until the end of her work shift. Her coworkers offered conflicting reports of her demeanor following the incident. One coworker stated that Faber did not appear to be distraught; another coworker told authorities that Faber told him that she had been sexually assaulted. That coworker said that he advised Faber to tell her parents.

The twenty-four-year-old Bryant already was a National Basketball Association veteran and would win the league's Most Valuable Player award for the 2007-2008 season. At the time of the allegations, he was married to Vanessa Bryant and had one daughter. (The couple had a second daughter in 2006.) On July 2, Bryant had his knee surgery as scheduled. On that same day, Faber told authorities at the Eagle County Sheriff's Department that she had been sexually assaulted by Bryant. Faber's allegations were videotaped by investigators. During the interview at the sheriff's station, Faber stated that Bryant used physical force to restrain her during nonconsensual sexual intercourse and that Bryant told her not to tell anyone about the sexual encounter. After her interview with police officials, Faber went to Vail Valley Medical Center for rape-kit testing.

The sheriff's office interviewed Bryant, also on July 2. Bryant told investigators that the sexual encounter with Faber was consensual and added that his wife would be upset upon learning of the allegations. Bryant's legal defense team tried, without success, to have the interview removed as evidence because it was obtained without Bryant's knowledge. On July 4, the Eagle County sheriff issued an arrest warrant for Bryant for felony assault. Already home in Los Angeles, Bryant returned to Colorado. Upon his arrest, he posted a bond of twenty-five thousand dollars and was released the same day. On July 18, Bryant was charged with felony sexual assault. He consistently denied the rape accusation, claimed the sex with Faber was consensual, and added that he was guilty of adultery only. He made several public appearances with Vanessa, including a tearful press conference in Los Angeles on the day he was formally charged.

Faber's sexual history was brought to light after medical tests concluded that her underwear was stained with the DNA of two men other than Bryant. The Colorado rape shield statute, which disallows the presentation of the sexual history of an alleged rape victim during legal proceedings, did not protect Faber in this instance. Her sexual contact with other men around the time of the alleged assault by Bryant was admitted as evidence for the defense. The defense argued that Faber's physical injuries were consistent with having intercourse on more than one occasion in a short period of time.

Prosecutors claimed in the months before trial that Bryant's attorneys were attempting to damage Faber's credibility. In addition, she was subjected to physical threats and faced unrelenting media scrutiny. The media eventually identified her by name. Furthermore, the transcripts of a closed-session hearing were mistakenly released to the media by a court reporter. The court issued an order to try to prevent the transcripts from being released to the public. Several media organizations claimed that because the transcripts were released accidentally and, thus, were obtained through no fault of their own, they were protected by the First Amendment to the U.S. Constitution and could release the information to the public. The Colorado Supreme Court ruled in favor of the court on July 19, 2004, but on August 2, the judge in the Bryant case decided to allow the media to publish the transcripts.

After months of preparation by prosecutors and defense attorneys, Faber told her attorneys that she would not testify in court, leading the prosecution to drop the criminal charges against Bryant on September 1. The following day, Bryant issued a statement, apologizing to Faber and her family for the pain they have endured through the months of the case.

Before the criminal charges were dropped, Faber had filed a civil suit against Bryant, on August 10, and the two settled out of court in March, 2005. The conditions of the settlement were not disclosed.

IMPACT

Early in his career, Bryant was an intelligent and well-spoken role model to millions of sports fans. The sexual-assault scandal is now a part of his image and it follows him everywhere. Basketball fans around the United States continue to verbally taunt him in the venues of opposing teams. His MVP award in 2008 matters little to his detractors. However, his supportive fans seemed to have forgiven him for the scandal.

The accusations of rape, nevertheless, stunned American sports fans and others as well, and the ac-

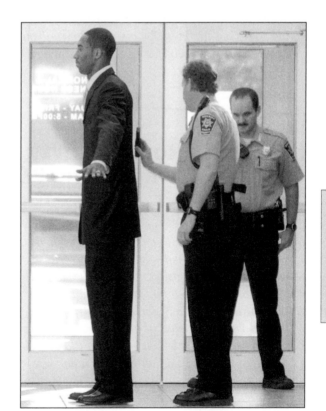

Kobe Bryant being searched upon entering the Eagle County, Colorado, courthouse in May, 2004. (AP/Wide World Photos)

companying media affair led many to call for a re-examination of sports "heroes." The infatuation with celebrity resulted in intense media presence at each phase of the case, a case filled with reports of infidelity and marked by public disgrace and disappointment. It featured a battle of words between victim's rights groups and a powerful sports world that supports its stars at all costs. Through it all, Bryant remains a "most valuable" star, and Faber remains all but forgotten.

—*Traqina Q. Emeka*

FURTHER READING

Corliss, R. "Say It Ain't So Kobe." *Time*, July 28, 2003. A popular national magazine article that explores the circumstances that led to Bryant's arrest and the criminal charge against him.

Gibeaut, J. "Celebrity Justice." *ABA Journal* 91, no. 1 (2005): 42-49. This American Bar Association journal article discusses the fascination with celebrity and how it influences the justice system.

Kirtley, J. "Gag the Press." *American Journalism Review* 26, no. 5 (2004). This journal article ad-dresses the issue of First Amendment rights and media access.

Sarche, J. "Bryant Case Moving Forward, sans Headlines, Hearing Looms." *Vail Daily*, January 25, 2005. This local-newspaper article provides a chronology of the events, from the time of the alleged assault to civil court proceedings.

SEE ALSO: May 13, 1913: Boxer Jack Johnson Is Imprisoned for Abetting Prostitution; Mar. 30, 1931: "Scottsboro Boys" Are Railroaded Through Rape Trials; July 2, 1963: Muslim Leader Elijah Muhammad Is Sued for Paternity; July 28, 1980: Magazine Reveals Baseball Star Steve Garvey's Marital Problems; Nov. 28, 1987: Black Teenager Claims to Have Been Gang-Raped by Police Officers; Mar. 30, 1991: William Kennedy Smith Is Accused of Rape; Sept. 22, 1997: Sportscaster Marv Albert Is Tried for Sexual Assault; Mar. 14, 2006: Duke Lacrosse Players Are Accused of Gang Rape; July 29, 2008: NBA Referee Tim Donaghy Is Sentenced to Prison for Betting on Games.

July 14, 2003
COLUMNIST ROBERT NOVAK LEAKS THE NAME OF CIA OPERATIVE VALERIE PLAME

CIA operative Valerie Plame's husband, Joseph Wilson, was a former U.S. ambassador who had investigated claims of sales of uranium to Iraq before the U.S.-led invasion of Iraq in 2003. Wilson publicly claimed that Iraq had not obtained uranium from Niger and that Iraq did not have weapons of mass destruction. Newspaper columnist Robert Novak then identified Plame as a CIA agent. Critics said that Plame's name was revealed to Novak by a White House official as revenge against Wilson.

ALSO KNOWN AS: Plame affair; Plamegate; CIA leak scandal

LOCALE: Washington, D.C.

CATEGORIES: Espionage; publishing and journalism; ethics; government; international relations; politics

KEY FIGURES

Robert Novak (b. 1931), newspaper columnist and political commentator

Valerie Plame (b. 1963), Central Intelligence Agency operations officer

Joseph Wilson (b. 1949), former U.S. Foreign Service diplomat

Richard Armitage (b. 1945), deputy secretary of state

Lewis "Scooter" Libby (b. 1950), Vice President
Dick Cheney's chief of staff

Karl Rove (b. 1950), deputy chief of staff to
President George W. Bush

SUMMARY OF EVENT

Joseph C. Wilson, the former acting ambassador to
Iraq who had diplomatic experience in North Africa, was sent to Niger on February 26, 2002, by the
U.S. Central Intelligence Agency (CIA) to investigate rumors (based upon forged documents) that
Iraq had purchased unrefined uranium ore in Niger.
Wilson found no evidence to confirm the rumors
and reported that such a transaction was highly unlikely. Furthermore, through his knowledge of and
contacts in Iraq, Wilson knew of no credible evidence to support contentions that Iraq had a considerable stockpile of WMDs and an ongoing program
to develop more WMDs.

On July 6, 2003, *The New York Times* published
an opinion article by Wilson, "What I Didn't Find in
Africa," that was highly critical of George W.
Bush's administration and the invasion of Iraq in
March. Wilson argued that the invasion was approved using extremely shaky evidence. As many
later claimed, White House officials leaked the
name of Wilson's wife, Valerie Plame, as a CIA operative as revenge against Wilson and to further justify the invasion.

As early as August of 2002, the administration of
U.S. president George W. Bush began zealously to
seek justification for invading Iraq and unseating
the government of dictator Saddam Hussein. Bush,
his closest advisers, and top-level federal officials
put forth three arguments to justify their proposed
attack on Iraq.

First, according to the Bush administration,
Hussein's close ties to al-Qaeda likely meant that he
was involved in planning—or, at a minimum, supporting—the September 11, 2001, terrorist attacks
on the United States. Second, Iraq had a large stockpile of weapons of mass destruction (WMDs) and a
vigorous program of WMD development. With this
stockpile, it had or soon would have first-strike ca-
pabilities against the United States. Third, Iraq had
purchased raw uranium from Niger to create its own

nuclear weapons program and was continuing to
search worldwide for additional nuclear bomb-
making materials. Iraq's WMD development program would be an imminent threat to U.S. security.
The administration concluded that, in an act of self-
defense, the United States must invade Iraq and
remove Hussein from office. Furthermore, Hussein
must be returned to the United States and tried for
his crimes.

Regardless of the evidence, Bush reported the
Niger uranium sale to Iraq as fact to the American
public in his state of the union address on January
28, 2003. The CIA even had attempted to remove
Bush's claim from his speech. On October 11,
2002, the U.S. Congress had passed a joint resolution authorizing the president to go to war if he determined that it was necessary to defend the national security of the United States. In Bush's report
to Congress on March 19, 2003, the day before the
attack began, he spoke only of Iraq's weapons of
mass destruction and U.S. national security as sufficient motive for the U.S.-led invasion of Iraq.

Within days of Wilson's *New York Times* article,
columnist Robert Novak learned from Richard Armitage, the deputy assistant secretary of state, that
Plame was a CIA operations officer with a classified, covert identity. Novak claims Armitage mentioned her name in passing. Novak then turned to
Karl Rove, Bush's deputy chief of staff, to confirm
that she was Wilson's spouse. Armitage, in October, confirmed with investigators that he was the
source of the leak.

On July 11, Novak's column, "Mission to Niger," was released by Creators Syndicate and distributed through the Associated Press. The column
was not published, however, until July 14. In the
column, Novak outed Plame, harming CIA operations and ruining her career. Most significantly,
however, the leak gambled with national security.
Novak remained adamant that his intent was not to
reveal Plame's covert identity but to investigate
why Wilson, a critic of the Bush administration,
was selected to investigate possible uranium sales
to Iraq by Niger.

On October 31, a federal grand jury was called to
investigate the leak. Patrick Fitzgerald, a U.S. attor-

2000's

NOVAK'S INFAMOUS ONE-SENTENCE LEAK

An excerpt from columnist Robert Novak's syndicated column of July 14, 2003, in which he revealed Valerie Plame's identity as a CIA operative.

Wilson never worked for the CIA, but his wife, Valerie Plame, is an Agency operative on weapons of mass destruction.

Source: Creators Syndicate.

ney for the northern district of Illinois, was appointed special counsel to pursue the federal inquiry for a possible violation of the Intelligence Identities Protection Act of 1982 and other federal crimes. Fitzgerald attempted to find out if White House officials had already leaked Plame's name to reporters before Novak's column appeared or if they later had simply repeated information already made public by Novak. Later testimony revealed that reporter Bob Woodward was the first person in the media to learn of Plame's identity and that the source of that leak was Armitage.

IMPACT

According to the House Committee on Government Reform, which investigated the leak, there had been a minimum of eleven Plame-related breaches of security by various White House staff. The committee's report, issued on July 22, 2005, also states that the White House did not comply with its obligations to either investigate the security breaches nor did the White House apply administrative sanctions to those who were involved. A number of White House officials broke several federal laws and acts that prohibit sharing classified government information, yet not one person in the Bush administration or in federal office was indicted. The White House itself was guilty of inertia for not carrying out its legal responsibilities. It made no attempt to investigate who had been leaking classified information.

The committee's report adds that the White House also downplayed the importance of Wilson's trip to Niger and that his subsequent report that Iraq did not buy uranium from Niger was dismissed.

Finally, the report said the White House disregarded Wilson's allegations that there was no evidence that Iraq had weapons of mass destruction.

In the end, no person was tried for violations of federal acts or statutes relating to the unauthorized disclosure of classified information. The only trial resulting from the grand jury investigation was that of Vice President Dick Cheney's former chief of staff, Lewis "Scooter" Libby, for perjury and for obstructing justice during the grand jury investigation. According to testimony, Libby had been told by Cheney in June, 2003, that Wilson's wife (her name apparently was not yet known) was a CIA employee.

Libby was convicted on March 6, 2007, of two counts of perjury, one count of obstruction of justice, and one count of making a false statement. On July 2, President Bush commuted his thirty-month prison sentence but did not pardon him, leaving much of Libby's sentence, including fines, intact.

The leak scandal also impacted U.S. intelligence. Blowing an agent's cover compromises intelligence-gathering methods and operations, affects the safety of intelligence agents and foreign and domestic informants, and harms recruitment efforts for agents as well as potential informants. Novak's exposure of Plame's identity likely had some significant effect on national security and foreign intelligence gathering, although the exact nature of that harm will likely remain unknown, given that it is counterproductive for the CIA, or any of the other federal intelligence-gathering agency, to admit to any harm. It should be noted, however, that Plame was working in operations related to Iran's development of nuclear weapons.

—Edward J. Schauer

FURTHER READING

Bamford, James. *A Pretext for War: 9/11, Iraq, and the Abuse of America's Intelligence Agencies.* New York: Doubleday, 2004. An excellent book that examines the prelude to the invasion of Iraq and the CIA leak scandal.

Isikoff, Michael, and David Corn. *Hubris: The Inside Story of Spin, Scandal, and the Selling of the Iraq War*. New York: Crown, 2006. More than one-third of this book is dedicated to the CIA leak scandal.

Risen, James. *State of War: The Secret History of the CIA and the Bush Administration*. New York: Free Press, 2006. Draws together the many pieces of information about the CIA and the Bush administration before and during the invasion of Iraq and before and after the CIA leak scandal.

Wilson, Joseph C. *The Politics of Truth: Inside the Lies That Led to War and Betrayed My Wife's CIA Identity—A Diplomat's Memoir*. New York:

Carroll & Graf, 2004. Wilson discusses his diplomatic career, his family and personal life, and his experiences and recollections of the Valerie Plame scandal.

Wilson, Valerie Plame. *Fair Game: My Life as a Spy, My Betrayal by the White House*. New York: Simon & Schuster, 2007. Insightful look into the life of a CIA agent, who was exposed as a covert operative by columnist Robert Novak.

SEE ALSO: Feb. 18, 2001: CIA Agent Robert Hanssen Is Arrested for Spying for the Russians; Apr. 28, 2004: CBS Broadcasts Photos of Abused and Tortured Prisoners at Abu Ghraib; Jan. 15, 2005: Iqbal Riza Resigns from the United Nations in Oil-for-Food Scandal.

September 3, 2003
MUTUAL FUND COMPANIES ARE IMPLICATED IN SHADY TRADING PRACTICES

New York State attorney general Eliot L. Spitzer filed a legal complaint against Canary Capital Partners, a hedge fund, for fraudulent late trading and time-zone arbitrage, practices that favored select clients over ordinary customers. Investigators looked at twenty-five fund companies, which led to settlements with regulators totaling over $3.1 billion, private civil lawsuits, congressional hearings and legislative proposals, and U.S. Securities and Exchange Commission oversight reforms.

LOCALE: New York, New York
CATEGORIES: Corruption; banking and finance; law and the courts; business; government

KEY FIGURE
Eliot L. Spitzer (b. 1959), New York State attorney general, 1999-2006, and governor of New York, 2006-2008

SUMMARY OF EVENT
According to the Investment Company Institute, a mutual-fund trade group, nearly 48 percent of U.S. households were mutual-fund shareholders at the end of 2003. The total assets of mutual funds came to $7.4 trillion. Mutual-fund growth paralleled the movement in American retirement plans away from employer-managed and -defined benefits plans and toward employee-managed and -defined contribution plans.

New York State attorney general Eliot L. Spitzer announced in a complaint filed with the New York Supreme Court on September 3, 2003, that his office had obtained evidence of illegal trading practices of New Jersey-based Canary Capital Partners, a hedge fund. According to Spitzer, the company was found to have engaged in fraudulent late trading and time-zone arbitrage with four large mutual fund companies at the expense of its ordinary, long-term mutual-fund investors. Even before this announcement, the mutual-fund industry was being

1013

viewed with dissatisfaction. After the technology-stock bubble burst in 2000, the stock market entered a three-year bear market, and funds performed poorly. The following background discussion of the structure and operations of mutual funds will help clarify both the dissatisfaction by 2003 and the scandals that were uncovered.

Mutual funds, also known as open-end investment companies, are not run by fund employees; rather, they are overseen by a board of directors. This board contracts with service providers: the investment adviser (a management company that makes the portfolio decisions), the transfer agent (who administers purchases and redemptions of shares and keeps customer records), and the principal underwriter (who handles distribution of shares). The U.S. Securities and Exchange Commission (SEC) regulates mutual funds, primarily through rules and through its Office of Compliance Inspections and Examinations. The SEC also regulates the securities markets.

Mutual funds are designed to help their owners (the shareholders) pool their money, diversify their portfolios, and have access to expert management at a lower cost than they could as individuals. The preamble of the Investment Company Act of 1940, which created mutual funds, states that they must be organized, operated, and managed in the interests of shareholders. Thus, mutual funds have a fiduciary duty, or legal duty of care and good faith, to shareholders.

Many analyses of the scandals point to the conflict of interest and objectives inherent in the governing structure of mutual funds. Investors (shareholders) want to maximize their returns on the money held in the funds. The investment adviser (management company) wants to maximize its profits. The investment adviser is paid a percentage of assets under management as its management fee. Prior to the scandals, funds had grown larger and larger. Fees charged to shareholders had increased, even though economies of scale should have reduced fund-management costs. The expense ratio of the average equity (stock) fund rose from 0.77 to 1.56 percent between 1959 and 2004.

Analyses of the scandals also pointed to SEC regulations requiring only that a majority of the fund directors be independent (that is, not connected to the fund adviser in the preceding five years). In addition, the board chair was not required to be independent. Critics pointed out that if a fund wanted to change advisers or negotiate lower fees, having a board chair who is affiliated with the adviser would be an inherent conflict.

Some of these issues were beginning to be investigated just before Spitzer's announcement. In February, 2003, the SEC proposed new rules that would require every mutual fund and adviser to instate compliance policies that would prevent securities law violations and to appoint a chief compliance officer. In March, the U.S. House Subcommittee on Capital Markets held a hearing, the first of ten congressional hearings (none resulting in laws passed) between 2003 and 2005. This one focused on fees, sales practices, disclosure, and fund performance and governance.

The investigations that followed the September 3 complaint were brought (in various combinations) by Spitzer, the SEC, the National Association of Securities Dealers (NASD), and the attorneys general of California, Colorado, and Massachusetts. New York's Martin Act gave Spitzer exceedingly broad powers to investigate and prosecute financial fraud. Some of the most prominent actions, with settlements ranging from $9 million to $515 million, involved the fund advisers Alliance Capital, Invesco, Bank of America/FleetBoston, Janus Capital, MFS, Morgan Stanley, Edward Jones, and Strong Capital Management.

Although several other practices were discussed in the hearings, reports, and media coverage surrounding the scandals, most of the charges brought involved two forms of arbitrage: late trading and stale pricing. Generally, arbitrage involves exploiting short-term price differences in a security to make a profit without risk. Late trading was performed by a small number of high-dollar, sophisticated investors who had a special relationship with intermediaries and the funds themselves. Stale-price, or time-zone, arbitrage, which exploits the prices of international stocks at the time foreign markets close, was well known and widely practiced by both large and small investors.

Coverage of the scandals often used the term "market timing"; this term can also mean rapid trading. By 2003, even many ordinary mutual fund shareholders were beginning to trade frequently. Although it did not reach the level of illegality, it certainly diluted returns for long-term shareholders, adding to the damage done by arbitrage. From 1950 to 1975, the average length of time investors held shares was twelve years; by 2002, it was two and a half years.

Morningstar, a mutual-fund rating and analysis company, identified hedge funds (which use risky investment methods to achieve large gains) as the source of most mutual fund arbitrage money and predicted that the scandals would lead to more regulation of them. Some hedge funds publicly listed "mutual fund timing" as their investment strategy. The SEC's November, 2003, survey found that 50 percent of the eighty largest fund companies were secretly allowing timing by certain shareholders (undoubtedly including hedge funds) that was forbidden by their own prospectus disclosures.

Because many people were surprised that Spitzer, rather than the SEC or the NASD (which regulates broker-dealers), first uncovered the scandals, the U.S. Government Accountability Office (GAO) conducted an analysis of the SEC's fund oversight program. Its April, 2005, report found that although the SEC made a good faith effort through its regulations to combat the known risks for arbitrage, it did not conduct examinations that might have uncovered this practice. Examinations are one of the SEC's two primary oversight methods.

IMPACT

One measure of the impact of the scandals is the gain they afforded violators versus the loss to long-term shareholders. A research study by Eric Zitzewitz on stale-price arbitrage documented that this activity cost long-term shareholders $4.9 billion in 2001 and that the cost had doubled since 1998-1999.

Another measure is the cost to the funds themselves, as investors lost trust and withdrew their

money. A research study calculated the losses suffered by the fifteen publicly traded mutual fund families investigated between September 3, 2003, and November 31, 2004. In the three days following the announcement of an investigation, funds lost, on average, $1.35 billion.

Numerous reforms were proposed or enacted as a result of the scandals. The SEC's new rules required fund boards of directors to designate a chief compliance officer and to conduct annual self-assessments and mandate that funds have written policies and procedures reasonably designed to prevent violations of federal securities law. Other rules relate to the disclosure of expenses as a dollar amount, the prohibition of various forms of directed brokerage using 12b-1 fees, and enhanced disclosure to shareholders of arbitrage policies. The SEC expanded its surveillance program to focus more attention on preventing wrongdoing. It instituted risk-targeted minisweeps to gather information on specific mutual fund practices, which have included soft dollars, 12b-1 fees, and revenue sharing.

The Investment Company Institute's *Mutual Fund Fact Book* shows that in 2007, $12.02 trillion was invested in eight thousand mutual funds owned by nearly 300,000 shareholders. Clearly, increasingly large amounts of the retirement and college savings of ordinary Americans are placed in mutual funds. Consumers represent two-thirds of the American economy. Thus, both the risks and the unfairness continue to grow when mutual funds are allowed to place corporate profits above their fiduciary responsibility to shareholders.

—*Glenn Ellen Starr Stilling*

FURTHER READING

Bogle, John C. "What Went Wrong in Mutual Fund America? The Triumph of Salesmanship over Stewardship." In *The Battle for the Soul of Capitalism*. New Haven, Conn.: Yale University Press, 2005. Clear, readable, passionate discussion of the scandals and the mechanisms used to perpetrate them.

MacDonald, Scott B., and Jane E. Hughes. *Separating Fools from Their Money: A History of American Financial Scandals*. New Brunswick,

N.J.: Rutgers University Press, 2007. Explains the often complex business world in an easy-to-read format. Detailed history of American financial scandals and their main players, including Eliot Spitzer, whose work is the focus of an entire chapter.

Smith, Thomas R., Jr. "Mutual Funds Under Fire: A Chronology of Developments Since January 1, 2003." *Journal of Investment Compliance* 7, no. 1 (2006): 4-33. This comprehensive account describes events initiated by Spitzer, the SEC, the U.S. Congress, mutual fund industry groups, and others.

Swensen, David F. "Hidden Causes of Poor Mutual-Fund Performance." In *Unconventional Success: A Fundamental Approach to Personal Investment.* New York: Free Press, 2005. Carefully documented explanation of the practices underlying the scandals. Unflinching in its exposure and condemnation of regulators, lobbyists, and the funds themselves.

Zitzewitz, Eric. "Who Cares About Shareholders? Arbitrage-Proofing Mutual Funds." *Journal of Law, Economics, and Organization* 19, no. 2 (2003): 245-280. Explains the mechanics of stale-price arbitrage and the extent to which it was known before the scandals.

SEE ALSO: Nov., 1929: Banque Oustric et Cie Failure Prompts French Inquiry; 1932: Insull Utilities Trusts Collapse Prompts New Federal Regulation; Nov. 28, 1967: Investor Louis Wolfson Is Convicted of Selling Stock Illegally; May 2, 1984: E. F. Hutton Executives Plead Guilty to Fraud; Jan. 15, 1988: ZZZZ Best Founder Is Indicted on Federal Fraud Charges; Mar. 29, 1989: Financier Michael Milken Is Indicted for Racketeering and Fraud; Aug. 27, 1990: Guinness Four Are Found Guilty of Share-Trading Fraud; 2001: Clearstream Financial Clearinghouse Is Accused of Fraud and Money Laundering; Dec. 2, 2001: Enron Bankruptcy Reveals Massive Financial Fraud; Mar. 5, 2004: Martha Stewart Is Convicted in Insider-Trading Scandal; Oct. 14, 2004: Insurance Brokerage Marsh & McLennan Is Charged with Fraud; Mar. 12, 2008: New York Governor Eliot Spitzer Resigns in Prostitution Scandal; Sept. 20, 2008: American Financial Markets Begin to Collapse.

October 2, 2003
NEWSPAPER CLAIMS THAT ARNOLD SCHWARZENEGGER GROPED WOMEN

As former bodybuilder and popular film actor Arnold Schwarzenegger was running for governor of California, a number of women told reporters that he had harassed or abused them years before. The Los Angeles Times *published a series about the accusations, but Schwarzenegger won the election nevertheless. He promised to have the charges investigated but did not follow through on his plan.*

ALSO KNOWN AS: Gropegate
LOCALE: Los Angeles, California

CATEGORIES: Publishing and journalism; politics; sex crimes; sex; public morals; women's issues; Hollywood

KEY FIGURES
Arnold Schwarzenegger (b. 1947), former bodybuilder, film actor, and governor of California, 2003-
John Carroll (b. 1941), editor of the *Los Angeles Times*
Maria Shriver (b. 1955), broadcast journalist and Schwarzenegger's wife

Susan Estrich (b. 1952), Democratic political commentator who chastised the *Los Angeles Times* for publishing the claims against Schwarzenegger

SUMMARY OF EVENT

According to biographer Laurence Leamer, the Austrian-born bodybuilder and film actor Arnold Schwarzenegger had a habit of sexual directness with women and, while usually charming, sometimes bullied his companions. Moving to the United States in 1968, Schwarzenegger soon became an American success. He arrived poor and could barely speak English. Through talent, good looks, hard work, business acumen, and skillful promotion, he became a multimillionaire. After breakups with two live-in girlfriends, he married the broadcast journalist Maria Shriver, a Democrat and a niece of former U.S. president John F. Kennedy.

Schwarzenegger, a Republican, held positions on social issues to the left of most members of the party but championed business and befriended the party's elite. During George H. W. Bush's administration, he chaired the President's Council on Physical Fitness and Sports. Then, as age worked against his ability to continue in action films, Schwarzenegger considered running in 2002 against Gray Davis, the incumbent governor of Schwarzenegger's adopted state of California. Schwarzenegger changed his mind, however, after an article in the March, 2001, issue of *Premiere* magazine reported that Schwarzenegger sexually harassed women and after the *National Enquirer* published an exposé of a sexual relationship it claimed he had with a former actress.

Nevertheless, Schwarzenegger played such a big role in the 2002 election in campaigning successfully to provide state money for after-school programs that when, in the summer of 2003, the recently re-elected Davis found himself subject to a recall vote scheduled for October 7 of that year, Schwarzenegger had become a prominent figure in California politics. Having received his wife's consent to run for governor, he announced his candidacy on *The Tonight Show with Jay Leno* on August 6.

Schwarzenegger knew that his fame as an actor would help him in the campaign but that his reputation as a womanizer would hurt, as would his inexperience with the intricacies of California government and the attitude of many voters that a celebrity candidate should not be taken seriously. He tried to keep from verbally stumbling by avoiding questions from the press, which he considered hostile.

Meanwhile, with the announcement of Schwarzenegger's candidacy, John Carroll, editor of the *Los Angeles Times*, began his newspaper's investigation of Schwarzenegger's alleged misdeeds with women, assigning reporters to determine whether the rumors were true. Carroll said that he believed the newspaper had a responsibility to report accurately the character of a candidate for the state's highest office and that it was better to publish the truth before voters cast their ballots rather than afterward. The newspaper, however, had opposed the recall in a staff editorial, and Carroll knew that supporters of Schwarzenegger would claim reportorial bias if the *Los Angeles Times* published articles accusing Schwarzenegger of inappropriate conduct against women.

After much effort to discover and substantiate accusations from various women, the *Los Angeles Times* published the first article of its series on what came to be called Gropegate. That article, "Women Say Schwarzenegger Groped, Humiliated Them," ran on Thursday, October 2, only five days before the election. It referred to incidents alleged to have occurred when Schwarzenegger was single and also when he was married. Several of the women who spoke to reporters did so only after the newspaper agreed to conceal their names; in each of those cases, the reporters received the assurance of a family member or a friend that the alleged victim had revealed the incident long before the campaign for governor began.

One woman claimed that Schwarzenegger stuck his arm under her skirt and grabbed her buttocks without her consent. Other women claimed he made unwelcome, crude sexual suggestions to them. Among the women who claimed that Schwarzenegger had grabbed their breasts were two who allowed their names to be used: E. Laine Stockton, recounting a 1975 incident in California, and Anna Richardson, recounting, as she had for *Premiere*, an incident she said occurred in England in 2000. Another woman at the scene in England remembered the incident differently, saying that Richardson, and not Schwarzenegger, was the person who was being sexually forward. The article also quoted a spokesperson for Schwarzenegger, who denied any sexual impropriety by the candidate and accused Democrats of trying to wreck his campaign.

The *Los Angeles Times* article of October 2 was followed by more claims of sexual harassment by Schwarzenegger, and the paper continued its series through the election and in the weeks following. By the time of the election, the newspaper had presented the cases of more than one dozen women who claimed Schwarzenegger harassed or abused them.

IMPACT

Schwarzenegger denied the allegations against him. However, on the morning in which the first *Los Angeles Times* article appeared, he did acknowledge his poor behavior toward women in the social atmospheres of bodybuilding culture and Hollywood and agreed that he likely hurt the feelings of others. Eager to put his misbehavior as a bodybuilder and actor behind him, he offered a blanket apology to those he offended.

The new governor, however, also called the *Los Angeles Times* series an act of dirty politics, and many people agreed. One commentator who sided with him was a feminist and a Democrat, Susan Estrich, whose op-ed attacking the paper for its series' original allegations appeared on October 3, 2003, in the same newspaper. A professor of law, Estrich noted that none of the women mentioned as victims had filed charges, and that the alleged incidents from years past did not constitute sexual harassment.

Most conservatives questioned the motivation of the *Los Angeles Times* in publishing lewd stories about the leading Republican candidate only a few days before the election, even though critics acknowledged that Schwarzenegger deserved his boorish reputation. With the exception of Estrich,

liberals, and certainly feminists, rejoiced at what they considered the exposure of sexist villainy. As for the electorate as a whole, however, the scandal seemed irrelevant. According to Leamer, it was Shriver who reassured voters about her husband's character. The vote on October 7 went against Davis, and Californians chose Schwarzenegger as his replacement.

On November 6, eleven days before his inauguration, Schwarzenegger announced that he was hiring a private investigative firm to look into his alleged misconduct. Many observers doubted whether any firm he hired could be impartial. As matters turned out, however, no investigation took place. On December 8, Schwarzenegger announced that he had called it off, asserting that it would solve nothing and would merely provide fodder for his political foes.

In 2006, Schwarzenegger and two of his aides settled a libel suit filed against them by alleged victim Richardson, thus removing from media attention what little remained of the scandal that began in 2003. On November 7, he was reelected governor of California.

In earlier generations, most American political careers would have been ruined by accusations such as those leveled against Schwarzenegger. The situation was reminiscent of the scandal involving Bill Clinton and former White House intern Monica Lewinsky when Clinton had been president during the late 1990's. Schwarzenegger's recovery from the allegations made against him confirmed that public attitudes of voters toward the sexual behavior of political leaders were changing, and sexual misconduct was no longer necessarily a disqualification to holding public office.

—*Victor Lindsey*

FURTHER READING

Estrich, Susan. "A Deplorable October Surprise." *Los Angeles Times*, October 3, 2003. Condemns the *Los Angeles Times* for publishing its scandalous story against Schwarzenegger of the previous day. Estrich's article is especially telling because she is a feminist and a Democrat; Schwarzenegger is a Republican.

Leamer, Laurence. *Fantastic: The Life of Arnold*

Schwarzenegger. New York: St. Martin's Press, 2005. A well-researched, balanced account of Schwarzenegger's youth and his careers as a bodybuilder, actor, and politician—with much discussion of his behavior with women.

Mathews, Joe. *The People's Machine: Arnold Schwarzenegger and the Rise of Blockbuster Democracy*. New York: PublicAffairs, 2006. A *Los Angeles Times* reporter's detailed story, in its historical context, of Schwarzenegger as a political aspirant, gubernatorial candidate, and governor.

Smolkin, Rachel. "The Women." *American Journalism Review*, December-January, 2004. A sympathetic discussion of how the *Los Angeles Times* investigated the claims of groping, the standards used by the newspaper, and the decisions of reporters and editors.

Welkos, Robert W., Gary Cohn, and Carla Hall. "Women Say Schwarzenegger Groped, Humili-ated Them." *Los Angeles Times*, October 2, 2003. The article that broke the story of allegations against Schwarzenegger's physical and verbal mistreatment and harassment of women.

SEE ALSO: July 20, 1982: Conservative Politician John G. Schmitz Is Found to Have Children Out of Wedlock; Oct. 11-13, 1991: Justice Clarence Thomas's Confirmation Hearings Create a Scandal; Jan. 17, 1998: President Bill Clinton Denies Sexual Affair with a White House Intern; May 2, 2000: New York Mayor Rudy Giuliani's Extramarital Affair Is Revealed; May 9, 2000: Former Louisiana Governor Edwin Edwards Is Convicted on Corruption Charges; Oct. 13, 2004: Television Producer Files Sex Harassment Suit Against Bill O'Reilly; Dec. 6, 2005: Spokane, Washington, Mayor Recalled in Gay-Sex Scandal; Mar. 12, 2008: New York Governor Eliot Spitzer Resigns in Prostitution Scandal.

Early November, 2003
PARIS HILTON SEX-TAPE APPEARS ON THE WEB

Paris Hilton, an heir to the Hilton Hotels fortune and actor and businessperson in her own right, became a celebrity for her famous name, beauty, and relentless partying in trendy clubs. Rick Salomon, the son of a film studio vice president, was most famous for a brief, tempestuous marriage to actor Shannon Doherty. When clips from an amateur sex tape of Salomon and Hilton appeared on the Web, it generated the first in a long line of scandals for Hilton.

LOCALE: Hollywood, California

CATEGORIES: Sex; communications and media; film; popular culture; Hollywood

KEY FIGURES

Paris Hilton (b. 1981), businesswoman, actor, and former model

Rick Salomon (b. 1968), son of a film executive

SUMMARY OF EVENT

Paris Hilton began her career as a successful model for reputable agencies in New York, Los Angeles, and London, but the very features that led to this success—her famous name and good looks—inevitably made her a favorite of paparazzi and society columnists. Soon the pop-culture cliché "famous for being famous" began to recur in media references to her, as photos and film clips of her smiling coyly at nightclubs and parties became a staple of the tabloids and celebrity television shows from the late 1990's onward.

In early November, 2003, Hilton's image was redefined when clips from a crudely filmed sex tape featuring Hilton and love interest Rick Salomon appeared on a Web site owned by the adult-film company Marvad Corp., which is based in Seattle, Washington. No longer would Hilton be merely annoyingly ubiquitous; for the rest of the decade, she

2000's

would be infamous, with the sex-tape controversy only the first of numerous scandals that helped to define the new Hilton.

A mutual friend of the former couple, Donald Thrasher, who had once been Salomon's roommate, was thought to have stolen the video from Salomon before selling it to Marvad without either Hilton's or Salomon's knowledge. The tape, filmed in Salomon's Hollywood Hills home in 2001, begins with Hilton demurely primping in a bathroom mirror and beseeching Salomon not to use profanity while he entreats her to reveal herself and have sex with him. Key scenes include Hilton performing oral sex on Salomon and, near the tape's conclusion, close-ups of Hilton's breasts taken by Hilton herself with a camcorder. News of the tape generated headlines and numerous jokes by television comedians.

Hilton was distraught over her public humiliation. One news story showed her upbraiding a clerk at a newsstand for prominently displaying periodicals featuring the scandal and expressing concern about the effect the publicity would have on her young fans. Cynics, though, pointed out that the tape had been made public scarcely a week before the debut of *The Simple Life*, a reality-television show in which Hilton and best friend Nicole Richie, daughter of R&B singer Lionel Richie, traded their indulgent West coast lifestyles for work on a farm in rural Arkansas. The series became a huge hit for Fox Television and ran for several seasons. Salomon also benefitted from the publicity stirred up by the video. He arranged for adult-film company Red Light District to market copies of the video in DVD format on the Web. Dubbed *1 Night in Paris*, the tape became a best seller and won a top award from the adult-film industry.

Despite the intense media blitz surrounding *1 Night in Paris*, it is likely that the scandal would have been short-lived; neither Hilton nor Salomon had the sort of sober, conservative reputation that would render their filming of private sex acts surprising or shocking—and by the early twenty-first century, it was not uncommon for American couples to tape themselves having sex. However, just as the initial publicity began to abate, the tape pro-

voked a heated public fight between Salomon and Hilton's parents, Kathy and Richard, who had made a number of angry public statements insinuating that Salomon was exploiting their daughter for his own fame and fortune. These comments prompted Salomon to file a $10 million lawsuit accusing the Hiltons and their daughter's personal assistant of defaming him. Paris Hilton countersued, seeking a share of the profits her former boyfriend was making from video sales.

The legal wrangling kept the controversy alive well into 2004. The pertinent legal matters were settled when Hilton was awarded a cash settlement of $400,000 and a share of the future earnings from sales of the DVD. As soon as these lawsuits were settled, Hilton garnered fresh attention after rumors began to circulate about the existence of a second tape, one alleged to feature Hilton and another model experimenting with sex toys.

Salomon continued to sell and promote *1 Night in Paris*, but just as his relationships with Hilton and actor and former girlfriend Shannon Doherty had been his original source of fame, it was his next relationship that kept him in the public eye. In 2007, he embarked on a tumultuous off-and-on-again affair with television actor Pamela Anderson. After much publicity on talk shows and in gossip columns, Anderson and Salomon married in Las Vegas in October of that year. Anderson left Salomon, however, after less than three months of married life, and their union was annulled in March of 2008.

For Hilton, the tape scandal was only the beginning of years of public humiliation and embarrassment. Although she continued to work as a celebrity "spokesmodel" for numerous companies and launched her own successful lines of clothing, jewelry, perfume, and handbags, a series of further misadventures maintained her public image as an indulgent, irresponsible scofflaw. Her license to drive was suspended after a drunk-driving conviction in 2006, and she was sentenced to forty-five days in jail after police stopped her in early 2007 for driving without a proper license and speeding. Television cameras recorded every minute of the resulting debacle: Hilton reporting for her jail term, leaving jail after only a few days for medical reasons, and returning to jail after being ordered there by an angry judge upset about not having been consulted about her early release. The media also captured her crying and screaming in court, returning to jail, leaving jail, claiming to have found religion during incarceration, and claiming interest in helping starving people in the developing world.

Hilton's later attempt to launch a singing career fizzled when her debut album *Paris* was released in 2006 to poor reviews and sales. Her acting career consisted of cameos in major films and larger roles in B movies and straight-to-video releases. Her only sizeable role in a major film remained that of the character Paige in the 2005 remake of the horror classic *House of Wax*.

IMPACT

The Hilton-Salomon sex-tape scandal illustrates how celebrities are still defined—scornfully—by a pop-culture audience thought to be open-minded and nonjudgmental. Whatever one thinks about Hilton's and Salomon's lifestyles and choices, they both—especially Hilton—have demonstrated remarkable savvy as business people. Nevertheless, the public images of both Hilton and Salomon continued to be those shaped by this scandal: Hilton as a pampered beauty and "dumb blond" sex object and Salomon as a Lothario and pornographer.

Furthermore, the sex-tape scandal revealed the power of the media, especially the speed and power of the Web. Film celebrities have been subjected to the rumor mill at least since the invention of motion pictures, but these early stories were circulated only by word of mouth, by print, and occasionally by radio and television. However, the Hilton-Salomon scandal was immediate. Because of the Web, millions were able to view clips of the sex-tape on demand. Soon thereafter, anyone could buy the video on the Web as well.

—*Thomas Du Bose*

FURTHER READING

Angelo, Marty. *One Life Matters.* Cottesloe, Wash.: Impact, 2006. Inspirational book by the prison minister who counseled Hilton during her brief time in jail. Speculates on what Hilton might have been thinking as she waited for her release.

Fahy, Thomas. "One Night in Paris (Hilton): Wealth, Celebrity, and the Politics of Humiliation." In *Pop-porn: Pornography in American Culture*, edited by Ann C. Hall and Mardia J. Bishop. Westport, Conn.: Praeger, 2007. Fahy explores the intersection of celebrity status and wealth and how its plays out in a culture of soft porn. The book itself starts with the premise that "Americans are addicted to porn, but are forced to disguise it as fashion, hygiene, class commentary, or other forms of entertainment." Hilton's life is defined, in part, by these disguises.

Hilton, Paris, with Merle Ginsberg. *Confessions of an Heiress: A Tongue-in-Chic Peek Behind the Pose.* New York: Fireside, 2004. A combination autobiography and self-help book offering much insight into Hilton's perception of herself. Made *The New York Times* best-seller list.

Newkey-Burden, Chas. *Paris Hilton: Life on the Edge—The Biography.* London: John Blake, 2007. A biographical portrait of the infamous former model and tabloid celebrity. Explores the 2003 sex-tape scandal and her time in jail in 2007.

SEE ALSO: July 18, 1988: Actor Rob Lowe Videotapes Sexual Tryst with a Minor; June 27, 1995: Film Star Hugh Grant Is Arrested for Lewd Conduct; Sept. 22, 1997: Sportscaster Marv Albert Is Tried for Sexual Assault; Apr. 7, 1998: Pop Singer George Michael Is Arrested for Lewd Conduct; May 21, 2003: Sexually Provocative Film *The Brown Bunny* Premieres at Cannes Film Festival; July 28, 2006: Actor Mel Gibson Is Caught Making Anti-Semitic Remarks; June 13, 2008: Singer R. Kelly Is Acquitted on Child Pornography Charges.

2000's

December 17, 2003
SENATOR STROM THURMOND'S BIRACIAL DAUGHTER IS REVEALED

U.S. senator Strom Thurmond, a long-time proponent of racial segregation, had a daughter named Essie Mae Washington-Williams with an African American woman in 1925, a revelation made public on the CBS television news show 60 Minutes *in late 2003. Correspondent Dan Rather interviewed Washington-Williams, closing the book on decades-long rumors that Thurmond had a biracial child out of wedlock.*

LOCALE: New York, New York

CATEGORIES: Radio and television; social issues and reform; families and children; racism

KEY FIGURES

Essie Mae Washington-Williams (b. 1925), retired school teacher and daughter of Strom Thurmond

Strom Thurmond (1902-2003), U.S. senator from South Carolina, 1948-2003

Carrie Butler (1909-1947), Washington-Williams's mother

Dan Rather (b. 1931), *CBS Evening News* anchor and *60 Minutes* correspondent

SUMMARY OF EVENT

After seventy-eight years of silence, a biracial former school teacher named Essie Mae Washington-Williams announced in a television interview with *CBS News* correspondent Dan Rather that she was the daughter of conservative Republican segregationist Strom Thurmond, a longtime U.S. senator from South Carolina. Her mother was Carrie Butler, an African American woman. Thurmond's reputation as a segregationist made the news both startling and fascinating, although rumors about his paternity of a biracial daughter had existed for decades.

Washington-Williams agreed to be interviewed by Rather because she wished to put the decades of speculation to rest and to clarify for her own children their family legacy. According to Washington-Williams, her mother was a sixteen-year-old maid

in the Thurmond household during the 1920's. The future Senator Thurmond was twenty-two years old and soon to be a lawyer. She was conceived in Edgefield, South Carolina, where the Thurmonds lived and where her mother worked. She also revealed that she was born in 1925 in Aiken, South Carolina. At age six months, she was taken to Pennsylvania to be raised by an aunt, Mary Washington, and her husband.

Washington-Williams knew that she had "a dad somewhere," although she did not know his identity. Her mother was the only person who knew the real story about her father. In 1941, when Washington-Williams was sixteen years old, her mother, by then living in Pennsylvania, arranged for her to finally meet her father, who by this time was an attorney about to go into the armed forces. Washington-Williams, who said her mother never told her that her father was white, described her meeting with Thurmond in his law office as "very nice" and that he seemed "glad" to meet her. They talked about a variety of subjects, including what she hoped to do with her life.

After their initial meeting, Thurmond and Washington-Williams stayed in contact. His political career blossomed. He was governor of South Carolina while she was a student at South Carolina State College (later University), an all-black college in Orangeburg that Thurmond recommended she attend. As governor, he regularly visited colleges around the state. In 1947, he visited South Carolina State and met with his daughter but kept secret that she was his child. According to Washington-Williams, it was common knowledge among the black people in Edgefield that she was Thurmond's child. Inasmuch as the climate of the American South before the 1950's accepted that white men and black women had relationships—some consensual, some not—there was no outcry, no backlash, no repercussions for either Thurmond or Washington-Williams.

Thurmond contributed to his daughter's financial needs while she was in college and until she married. He did not automatically send or give her money personally, but funds were always available for tuition and room and board. Many have speculated that Thurmond's financial support amounted to nothing but "hush money," a means to keep her silent about being his daughter and thus to shield the up-and-coming conservative politician from scandal. Washington-Williams insisted she saw no advantage in revealing her relationship to Thurmond, and that she did not want to hurt his political career. She said that in spite of his bigoted, segregationist policies, she believed he had done many good things for her and for all black people in South Carolina. She said that *Ebony* magazine once sent a reporter for a story about her when she was attending South Carolina State. She refused to be interviewed for what she called a family friendship.

As a strict segregationist, Thurmond fought against racial and social progress, including school desegregation. In what was the longest filibuster in Senate history—24 hours and 18 minutes—he worked to defeat civil rights legislation. He tried to derail the nomination of Thurgood Marshall to be the first African American justice of the United States. To thwart President Harry S. Truman's plan to integrate the armed forces, he ran for president in 1948 as a Dixiecrat. His own hometown newspaper (in Edgefield) ran a front-page story in 1972 that called him "unprincipled" for naming himself a "devout segregationist" while fathering "colored offspring."

Washington-Williams insists that her father did many good things: He served meritoriously in World War II, his election to the Senate in 1954 was by an unheard-of write-in vote, he recommended a black man for a federal judgeship, and he was the first senator to hire a black administrative aide. Washington-Williams said that despite the controversial views about him, he was "very good" to her and was "a great friend."

As for Thurmond, he neither confirmed nor denied that he had a child with a black woman. He usually brushed the questions aside. When he visited Washington-Williams while she was in college, the two would meet in the college president's office. Some witnesses claimed to have seen them sitting together outside in the center court of the college.

After college, Washington-Williams kept in contact with her father, by this time a U.S. senator, mostly through annual trips either to his Columbia, South Carolina, home or to his Senate office in Washington, D.C. At those times, he would give her money to help her financially, always warning her to be careful. His Senate office secretary arranged their appointments and must have known that there was some familial relationship between the two, although she never discussed that knowledge.

After his daughter married, Thurmond discontinued his financial support, except in cases of

Essie Mae Washington-Williams. (Hulton Archive/Getty Images)

emergency. She taught in the Los Angeles Unified School District for thirty years, beginning in the late 1960's. In 1964, when Washington-Williams's husband died at the age of forty-five, Thurmond once again began helping her and her four children. He met the first of his grandchildren when the baby was only six months old. Washington-Williams, who was then living in Pennsylvania, had taken the baby to Washington, D.C., for a visit with Thurmond. Thurmond did not see the other three children, however, until they were in their teens.

Washington-Williams said she believed that Thurmond "cared something" about her, which made her feel better about their unorthodox relationship. Though never publicly acknowledging her as his daughter, he said at their first meeting, "Well, you look like one of my sisters" and added that she had cheekbones like those of "our family."

By the time Thurmond died, he had slowed down considerably; he was one hundred years old. Washington-Williams, living in Los Angeles since the 1960's, had stopped making annual trips to Washington, D.C., because of her own health issues. Even as his health deteriorated and death seemed imminent, Thurmond kept his biracial daughter a secret. Upon his death in June, 2003, Washington-Williams decided to tell her story, first in an interview with Rather that was broadcast on *60 Minutes* on December 17, 2003. She also wrote *Dear Senator: A Memoir by the Daughter of Strom Thurmond* (2005), a book for her children, so that they would know the truth about their grandfather.

IMPACT

At the time of Washington-Williams's birth and for decades after, the races were segregated in the American South. The Confederate way of life was still very much a reality. Consequently, the revelation that Thurmond, one of the most outspoken defenders of that way of life, had fathered a child with a black woman was scandalous, even as late as 2003, the year of his death. Thurmond built his political career on deception and secrecy. As the public learned of his hypocrisy, reactions ranged from no surprise to criticism of Washington-Williams for having kept quiet for so long, allowing a racist bigot to have a powerful political career while supporting his biracial daughter.

—*Jane L. Ball*

FURTHER READING

Bass, Jack, and Marilyn W. Thompson. *Ol' Strom: An Unauthorized Biography of Strom Thurmond.* Atlanta: Longstreet, 1998. An anecdotal, unauthorized biography of Thurmond, the oldest and longest-serving senator of his time.

_____. *Strom: The Complicated Personal and Political Life of Strom Thurmond.* New York: PublicAffairs, 2005. Discusses his affair with Carrie Butler and his secret relationship with his biracial daughter. Explores the contradictions of his life as a segregationist.

Washington-Williams, Essie Mae, with William Stadiem. *Dear Senator: A Memoir by the Daughter of Strom Thurmond.* New York: Regan Books, 2005. Describes Washington-Williams's relationship with a generous, even affectionate father who was also a staunch segregationist. Details his support and encouragement even as he kept the relationship secret.

SEE ALSO: May 16, 1934: General Douglas MacArthur Sues Newspaper Columnist for Libel; Jan. 25, 1984: Jesse Jackson Calls New York City "Hymietown"; May, 1999: Civil Rights Leader Jesse Jackson Fathers a Child Out of Wedlock; Dec. 5, 2002: Senator Trent Lott Praises Strom Thurmond's 1948 Presidential Campaign.

December 18, 2003

Pop Star Michael Jackson Is Charged with Child Molestation

In 2003, pop-music star Michael Jackson was charged with child molestation and administering an intoxicating agent to commit that felony. Jackson was later acquitted, but his career was negatively affected.

LOCALE: Santa Maria, California

CATEGORIES: Law and the courts; families and children; communications and media; music and performing arts

KEY FIGURES

Michael Jackson (b. 1958), American musician and entertainer

Gavin Arvizo (b. 1989), boy who accused Jackson of molestation

SUMMARY OF EVENT

On December 18, 2003, global pop-music star Michael Jackson was charged with seven counts of child molestation and two counts of administering an intoxicating agent to commit that felony. The crime allegedly took place in February and March, 2003, against a thirteen-year old boy, Gavin Arvizo.

In 2000, Arvizo had been diagnosed with cancer and had his spleen and a kidney removed. Jackson paid for Arvizo's medical expenses and made accommodations for Arvizo to be transported to and from chemotherapy sessions. The boy later began to visit Jackson at his home in Santa Maria, California, and he and Jackson had many telephone conversations.

The police investigation into accusations of alleged child molestation by Jackson began after a television documentary featured an interview with the singer. The documentary *Living with Michael Jackson*, with British journalist Martin Bashir, aired in the United States on February 6, 2003. The film, which included Arvizo, showed the boy holding Jackson's hand and resting his head on Jack-

son's shoulders. Arvizo told the journalist that he and Jackson often slept in the same room but not in the same bed. Jackson said in the interview that many children, including some actors, have slept in his bed, but he adamantly maintained that nothing inappropriate occurred.

Jackson is one of the most prolific entertainers in modern history. His 1992 album *Thriller* sold more than 65 million copies and put Jackson in the *Guinness Book of World Records* for producing the world's best-selling album. Although he has had monumental success in the music and entertainment industries, he has also been one of the most ridiculed entertainers, facing accusations of odd behavior and, most critically, sexual inappropriateness with boys. Some speculate that Jackson fueled the public's perception of him as a bizarre eccentric who is obsessed with recapturing his childhood after he purchased a mansion and large property in Central California and built an amusement park there. The nearly 3,000-acre property is called Neverland Ranch.

Jackson has often stated that he prefers the company of children, adding that children are more honest than adults. Jackson befriended many children and invited many of them to his home to enjoy the amusement-park rides. Some children also slept at his home as part of their visits. Jackson has always denied any sexual contact with any of children. At the time Jackson was charged with child molestation in 2003, many individuals thought he would finally be found guilty and imprisoned. However, this would not happen.

Responding to public concerns after the airing of the documentary, the Santa Barbara County district attorney stated that, under California law, even if Arvizo had slept in the bed with Jackson, such an act would not have been deemed criminal without "affirmative and offensive conduct." On February 19, in response to the Bashir documentary, Jackson produced his own documentary to disprove accusa-

Michael Jackson arriving at the courthouse in Santa Maria, California, in early 2005. (AP/Wide World Photos)

tions of child molestation against him. In the video, Arvizo and his mother, Janet Arvizo, insisted that he had not been molested by Jackson, and Arvizo's mother claimed that Jackson was like a father to her son. She also stated that she was thinking about taking legal action against Bashir.

After the rebuttal documentary, Arvizo's mother contacted Larry Feldman, the attorney who in 1993 represented Jordan Chandler, another child who had accused Jackson of child molestation. Feldman sent Arvizo and his family to psychologist Stanley J. Katz, the same psychologist who assisted Chandler's family in determining if their son was molested by Jackson. Arvizo's brother told Katz that he witnessed Jackson touching his brother, and Katz, in return, reported what he heard to authori-

ties, citing that this was protocol for someone of his profession. He stated that he is mandated to report child abuse, although he later testified in court that he did not think Jackson was a pedophile but a regressed ten year old.

In June, 2003, the Santa Barbara County Sheriff's Department started an investigation into the allegations of child abuse. The media began to descend on Santa Maria, a town of about 90,000 residents in Central California, 170 miles north of Los Angeles. In July, the sheriff's department first interviewed Arvizo and his family. On November 18, more than seventy investigators from the district attorney's office and the sheriff's department went to Jackson's home with a search warrant. Along with the warrant to search the property, they also had a warrant for Jackson's arrest. Again, the media were there, recording the entire police action on film. On November 20, Jackson surrendered to authorities.

The felony complaint stated that Jackson had committed a lewd act with Arvizo and, on two occasions, administered an intoxicating agent with the intent to enable Arvizo in the commission of the lewd acts. Jackson was arraigned January 16, 2004, in Santa Maria and pleaded not guilty.

Jackson was indicted on all seven charges following grand jury proceedings in March. Jury selection for the trial began almost one year later, on January 31, 2005. Media from around the globe camped out at the courthouse for the entire trial. Fans and critics of Jackson camped out as well, especially as the trial neared completion. The proceedings included ninety-one prosecution witnesses and fifty defense witnesses, including comedian and late-night talk-show host Jay Leno. The judge in the case allowed Leno to joke about Jackson and the case out of court, but only if the jokes were unrelated to the incident about which Leno would act as a witness during the trial.

Arvizo's claims and those of his family members were contradictory when compared during the trial. Arvizo also stated during testimony that he lied to a school administrator that Jackson had not molested him. He stated that he feared being teased at school and that he was already being teased after the airing of the Bashir documentary.

At the trial, prosecutors introduced several pornographic books and magazines (some of which were taken from Jackson during the 1993 child molestation allegations) that had been seized at Jackson's home. The prosecution argued the periodicals and books amounted to child erotica and thus proved his sexual attraction to boys. The defense, however, argued that the books were legal to possess and that a substantial number of the books and magazines had been taken from Jackson's home long before 2003. While the books featured nudity, none reportedly displayed sexual acts.

Many of the witnesses who were called to testify at trial had problems with credibility. Arvizo's mother had been accused by several celebrities of attempting to extort money from them. One prosecution witness who stated that he had seen Jackson molest children had been accused of robbing several restaurants, a toy store, and an electronics store. Another witness, who was a former maid at Jackson's home, had been convicted of stealing a sketch of Elvis Presley made by Jackson.

IMPACT

On June 13, the jury found Jackson not guilty on all charges. Fans cheered and cried outside the courthouse as the verdicts were read. After trial, the conduct of jurors during deliberations became an issue. One juror admitted to bringing in a medical textbook and stating that Jackson fit the profile of a pedophile. The juror also claimed that she winked at Jackson's mother, Katherine Jackson, even though jurors are instructed to avoid such communication. Several jurors apparently admitted they were fans of Jackson and that they would never convict him.

Even when plagued by rumor and scandal, as Jackson has been for much of his career, the pop singer has managed to translate adversity into greater fame. Some would argue that the continuous media reports on Jackson and his erratic behavior have made him more infamous. While many argue that his work as a musical artist has been uneven, his contribution to modern music and entertainment has been enormous. The sex-abuse scandals have tarnished his reputation only to the point of making him fodder for ridicule. The scandals, however, have not diminished his overall status as one of the greatest entertainers of modern times.

—Ashley M. Miller and Jeffery T. Walker

FURTHER READING

Guest, Lynton. *The Trials of Michael Jackson*. Vale of Glamorgan, Wales: Aureus, 2006. A look at the unreported or underreported aspects of Michael Jackson's 2005 criminal trial.

Taibbi, Matt. "The Nation in the Mirror." *Rolling Stone*, June 16, 2005. A scathing critique of the circus atmosphere both outside and inside the Santa Maria courtroom during Michael Jackson's molestation trial.

Taraborrelli, J. Randy. *Michael Jackson: The Magic and the Madness*. New York: Turtle Point Press, 2004. A book chronicling the life of Michael Jackson. First published in 1991 and updated for this edition.

Wilkinson, Peter. "The Case Against Jackson." *Rolling Stone*, January 25, 2005. Details the inner workings of Jackson's trial and arguments made by the prosecution and defense.

Williams, Troy M. "The Trial of a Career." *Los Angeles Times*, June 14, 2005. Gives a detailed analysis of the 2005 trial for child molestation, with a focus on the trial's long-term effect on Jackson's singing career.

SEE ALSO: Feb. 6, 1942: Film Star Errol Flynn Is Acquitted of Rape; Nov. 23, 1946: Tennis Star Bill Tilden Is Arrested for Lewd Behavior with a Minor; Dec. 12, 1957: Rock Star Jerry Lee Lewis Marries Thirteen-Year-Old Cousin; Feb. 1, 1978: Roman Polanski Flees the United States to Avoid Rape Trial; Aug. 12, 1983-July 27, 1990: McMartin Preschool Is Embroiled in Child-Abuse Case; July 18, 1988: Actor Rob Lowe Videotapes Sexual Tryst with a Minor; Jan. 13, 1992: Woody Allen Has Affair with Lover Mia Farrow's Adopted Daughter; Apr. 7, 1998: Pop Singer George Michael Is Arrested for Lewd Conduct; Dec., 2000: Sexual Abuse of Children in France Leads to the Outreau Affair; June 13, 2008: Singer R. Kelly Is Acquitted on Child Pornography Charges.

2000's

March 4, 2004
FORMER UNITED WAY CHARITY CHIEF PLEADS GUILTY TO EMBEZZLEMENT

Oral Suer, the former chief executive officer and head of United Way in Washington, D.C., pleaded guilty to having embezzled from the organization for nearly three decades. For many years, Suer stole from the charity, taking about half a million dollars. He was sentenced to federal prison and ordered by a judge to make full restitution to United Way. The scandal led the charity to make policy changes and institute a new code of ethics.

LOCALE: Washington, D.C.
CATEGORIES: Corruption; law and the courts

KEY FIGURES

Oral Suer (b. 1935), former chief executive officer of United Way, Washington, D.C., 1974-2001

Norman Taylor (fl. early twenty-first century), Suer's successor as chief executive officer of United Way

Rodney E. Slater (b. 1955), independent head of United Way's ethics and policy task force

SUMMARY OF EVENT

United Way of the National Capital Area (UWNCA), located in Washington, D.C., was created in 1974. The D.C. agency was conceived when the United Givers Fund, the United Black Fund, and the Health and Welfare Council were merged, creating the twenty-third-largest United Way office in the United States. In roughly five years, UWNCA became the first United Way branch to include national nonprofits in its annual fund-raising campaign. Some of the most noteworthy nonprofits that participated include the American Cancer Society and the American Heart Association. By the early 1990's, UWNCA was managing one of the largest United Way campaigns in the United States.

The chief executive officer (CEO) and co-founder of the UWNCA was Oral Suer. Suer took over as the CEO of the Washington, D.C., office in 1974 and continued in that role until his retirement in 2001. During his twenty-seven year tenure as CEO, Suer helped raise more than $1 billion for local charities in the greater Washington, D.C., area. By the early 1990's, Suer helped to establish UWNCA as the second largest local United Way office in the country. At its peak, the D.C. branch was raising tens of millions of dollars annually from both private sector and federal workers.

Despite nearly three decades of leadership, Suer did not always act in the best interest of the agency and the thousands of people it served. Members of UWNCA's board, along with previous auditors, had learned early on that Suer had taken monies from the agency and that he failed to repay those funds. However, these board members chose not to fully reveal their information on Suer's possible illegal activities, which dated back to 1986. A later audit revealed that at least one United Way director was actually alerted that Suer had not reimbursed the charity an amount over half a million dollars for various items, including sick-leave and vacation cash payments and advances on his base salary. Federal investigators, along with an independent audit of the company, later revealed that Suer's illegal activities might have dated back to 1976, just two years after his start as CEO of the organization.

A federal grand jury began to investigate UWNCA's financial operations in August, 2002, not long after a series of *Washington Post* articles revealed evidence of illegalities by the recently retired Suer and his successor, Norman Taylor. The news articles claimed that Suer took an early pension payout in which he collected thousands of dollars more than he was entitled to. Additionally, the articles also claimed that Suer charged personal expenses on United Way credit cards, expenses that included vacations and trips to see his children in college. The newspaper also found that during his tenure as CEO, UWNCA purposely withheld from local D.C. charities more than $1 million it had collected for them. UWNCA top officials and board members initially denied the allegations of Suer misconduct and then fired numerous employees and board members who had demanded an internal investigation.

By the end of 2002, UWNCA administrators forced the resignation of CEO Taylor, replaced its governing board of directors, brought in a new CEO, Charles Anderson, and commissioned an outside forensic audit of both Suer and Taylor. The financial investigation was carried out by the accounting firm PricewaterhouseCoopers. Although UWNCA leadership had refused to commission such an audit, the organization's board at the time overruled that decision. In addition, the new board, which was selected in January, 2003, actually expanded the scope and nature of the forensic audit to include a comprehensive look at Suer's entire career with UWNCA.

The investigation determined that Suer had received an estimated $2.4 million from UWNCA in excess of his salary and that he repaid the agency $961,000. More specifically, the audit revealed that Suer had reimbursed himself about $20,000 more than he had actually pledged at various United Way annual fund-raisers. The report also indicated that under the authority of Taylor, Suer took some $230,000 in additional retirement benefits that were not authorized by the pension regulations of the organization.

Suer received close to $694,000 for twenty-seven years' worth of unused sick leave and vacation time, even though evidence shows that he frequently took vacations. It also was discovered that he stole more than $400,000 in cash advances and $180,000 in extra deferred compensation, none of which he was authorized to receive. From 1997 through 2001, estimates show that he charged more than $80,000 in purchases without providing receipts. In fact, it was found that many of those charges were indeed personal in nature, including charges for lavish meals and weekend getaways. For example, in 1991, Suer claimed more than $500 in expenses for a United Way conference in Tampa,

Florida; coincidentally—or not—the Super Bowl was in town that same weekend. The audit later discovered that no United Way conference had been held in Tampa for that particular weekend. The investigation concluded that Suer, along with some of his top managers, had absconded with more than $1 million during his period in office.

The results of the forensic audit were passed along to the federal investigators, who had already commenced their own inquiry into Suer's alleged illicit activities. Finally, on March 4, 2004, Suer pleaded guilty to transporting stolen money across state lines, making false statements, and concealing facts relating to an employee retirement plan. Based on his plea, he admitted to stealing close to $500,000 from the charity. In particular, he confessed to charging the organization for personal expenses and vacations, paying himself close to $333,000 for annual leave he had already used, and stealing nearly $94,000 from the charity's pension plan. On May 19, he was given the maximum sentence of twenty-seven months in federal prison and was ordered to pay $497,000 in restitution to United Way.

Suer was not the first executive officer from United Way to be indicted by a federal grand jury. In 1995, former United Way chief executive and president of twenty-two years, William Aramony, was convicted for twenty-five counts of embezzlement and imprisoned. Aramony had taken an estimated $500,000 during his tenure as CEO of the national agency. In total, some thirty United Way top executives over the last twenty years have been involved and subsequently punished for their illegal activities.

IMPACT

Suer's illegal activities had a grave impact on United Way donations. After his corruption became known to the general public in January, 2001, major longtime donors refused to give to the agency. By 2003, annual contributions declined by two-thirds, from $95 million to $34 million. A local workplace fund-raising drive among both private and government employers of the greater D.C. area in 2002 collected contributions totaling only $19 million, a small sum compared to the more than $90 million raised in 2001. Additionally, UWNCA was forced to lay off more than half of its staff. The D.C. office, which formerly employed about ninety people, was reduced to a staff of thirty-five. Furthermore, several regional offices were forced to close, causing a further reduction in charitable offerings.

By the summer of 2002, United Way's national headquarters accepted that its governance structure was partly responsible for the decaying reputation of the organization. In response, United Way appointed Rodney E. Slater, former U.S. secretary of transportation, to lead a task force focused on ethics and policy restructuring of the agency. The task force was asked to create both a new code of ethics along with a set of business and financial procedures that emphasized the essential mission of United Way. By September, 2005, the task force produced its final report, recommending a reduction of board and staff members, stronger financial controls, and the creation of an ethics committee to deal with agency misconduct, all of which were eventually instituted.

—*Paul M. Klenowski*

FURTHER READING

Coenen, Tracy. *Essentials of Corporate Fraud.* Hoboken, N.J.: John Wiley & Sons, 2008. An introductory guide to the white-collar crime of corporate fraud, written by a forensic, or investigative, accountant. Although geared to the corporate world, this work is relevant to all types of organizations that rely on sales—and donations—to succeed.

Glaser, John S. *The United Way Scandal: An Insider's Account of What Went Wrong and Why.* New York: John Wiley & Sons, 1994. An inside-account of the corrupt leadership of United Way, with a particular focus on William Aramony, United Way president who led the organization for more than two decades. Predates the Suer scandal.

Jackson, Peggy M., and Toni E. Fogarty. *Sarbanes-Oxley for Nonprofits: A Guide to Building Competitive Advantage.* New York: John Wiley & Sons, 2005. Explores the relevant themes and requirements of the Sarbanes-Oxley Act, formed to ensure the accountability of nonprofits. Addresses potential unethical actions by employees at all levels.

Zack, Gerard M. *Fraud and Abuse in Nonprofit Organizations: A Guide to Prevention and Detection.* Hoboken, N.J.: John Wiley & Sons, 2003. A guidebook for those who work in nonprofits. Useful tips on detection and deterrence of fraud.

SEE ALSO: Apr. 9, 1987: Bess Myerson Resigns as New York Commissioner of Cultural Affairs.

March 5, 2004
MARTHA STEWART IS CONVICTED IN INSIDER-TRADING SCANDAL

In a stunning, but temporary, fall from grace, home-design guru Martha Stewart was convicted of multiple federal felonies for selling stocks immediately before those stocks were expected to decrease in value. Stewart was convicted not of insider trading but rather of lying to government agents about a trade that was not illegal.

LOCALE: New York, New York

CATEGORIES: Business; corruption; drugs; law and the courts

KEY FIGURES

Martha Stewart (b. 1941), corporate executive, editor, writer, and television-show host

Peter Bacanovic (b. 1962), financial consultant

Samuel D. Waksal (b. 1947), founder and former chief executive officer of ImClone Systems

Douglas Faneuil (b. 1975), Bacanovic's assistant

Miriam Goldman Cedarbaum (b. 1929), U.S. district judge who presided over Stewart's trial

SUMMARY OF EVENT

On March 5, 2004, after deliberating for three days, a jury of four men and eight women convicted Martha Stewart, chief executive officer of Martha Stewart Omnimedia, of making false statements to the federal government, obstruction of justice, and conspiracy to make false statements and obstruct justice. Prosecutors argued that Stewart hindered a government investigation of suspected insider trading in a biotechnology firm called ImClone Systems, which was founded and being run by Samuel Waksal.

ImClone's business prospects depended almost entirely on its cancer treatment drug, Erbitux. On December 26, 2001, Waksal learned that the U.S. Food and Drug Administration was not going to approve Erbitux. Waksal tried to sell all of his personal shares of ImClone stock, even attempting to have his stake transferred to a family member to be sold. Stewart, who also had shares in ImClone, sold her entire stake on that same day. The jury found that she lied to government agents about her reasons for selling her shares.

As it turned out, Waksal and Stewart shared the same financial consultant at Merrill Lynch: Peter Bacanovic. Bacanovic was on vacation at the time, but his assistant, Douglas Faneuil, called him on December 27 to inform him of Waksal's attempted sale. According to telephone records, Bacanovic immediately called Stewart's office and left a message at 10:04 A.M., which was recorded in the company's computer system by Stewart's personal assistant, Ann Armstrong, as "Peter Bacanovic thinks ImClone is going to start trading downward." Later that day, Stewart called Bacanovic's office and reached Faneuil, who informed her—as directed by Bacanovic—that Waksal had tried to sell his entire stake of ImClone. Stewart ordered Faneuil to sell all 3,928 of her shares of ImClone, which he did the same day. ImClone stock collapsed in response to the company's announcement on December 28 of the FDA decision not to approve Erbitux. Had Stewart waited until after December 28 to sell her stock, she would have lost close to fifty thousand dollars.

By early 2002, the House Energy and Commerce Committee, the U.S. Securities and Exchange Commission (SEC), the Federal Bureau of Investigation (FBI), and the U.S. Attorney's Office had all commenced investigations into Waksal's attempted stock sale and, in the process, noticed the timing of Stewart's sale as well. SEC lawyers interviewed Bacanovic on January 7, 2002, at which point Bacanovic explained that in mid-December, 2001, he and Stewart had agreed that they would sell her ImClone stock if were to drop below sixty dollars per share.

A few weeks later, SEC lawyers, FBI agents, and federal prosecutors asked to meet Stewart. However, before that meeting took place, Stewart sat at her assistant's desk, found the record of the December 27 phone message from Bacanovic, and—in her assistant's presence—altered the message to read, "Peter Bacanovic re: ImClone." Stewart quickly asked her assistant to restore the message to its original state. On February 4, 2002, Stewart, accompanied by legal counsel, met with government lawyers and agents. At this meeting, Stewart said that she and Bacanovic had agreed sometime before early December to sell her ImClone stock if it dropped below sixty dollars per share. She also described her December 27 phone conversation as between herself and Bacanovic, not Faneuil.

Bacanovic testified formally before the SEC on February 13 and essentially repeated his statements from his January interview. SEC lawyers, FBI agents, and federal prosecutors also interviewed Stewart again, by telephone, on April 10; she repeated that she and Bacanovic had agreed on when to sell her ImClone stock, and she said that she did not remember hearing on December 27 that Waksal was trying to dump his ImClone stock.

On June 4, 2003, federal prosecutors indicted Stewart and Bacanovic on nine separate counts. In addition, the SEC charged Stewart with securities fraud. The securities fraud charge was unusual because it was based not on Stewart's sale of ImClone stock but rather on her public statements of innocence. According to the SEC, Stewart made these statements with the intention of deceiving purchasers of her company's stock.

The criminal trial began on January 20, 2004, and lasted for six and a half weeks. Stewart was represented by Robert Morvillo, an experienced criminal defense attorney. The lead prosecutor was Assistant U.S. Attorney Karen Patton Seymour, then head of the criminal division. The key witnesses against Stewart and Bacanovic were Faneuil, Armstrong, and Mariana Pasternak, a friend of Stewart. Pasternak testified that, while vacationing together in Mexico, Stewart mentioned that Waksal's stock was plunging and that she had sold her shares, observing, "Isn't it nice to have brokers who tell you those things?" The jury evidently credited the testimony of these witnesses (although it did acquit Bacanovic of a separate count alleging that he had forged a worksheet to bolster the claim that a prior agreement to sell existed).

On July 17, the trial judge, Miriam Goldman Cedarbaum, sentenced Stewart to five months in prison and five months of home detention, fined her thirty thousand dollars, and ordered nineteen months of supervised release following confinement. Although Stewart was freed on bail pending appeal, she opted to serve her prison sentence nevertheless. On October 8, she reported to Alderson Federal Prison Camp in West Virginia and served her sentence. Following the story outside the minimum-security facility for women was the media, which broadcast from outside the complex for several weeks. The U.S. Court of Appeals for the second circuit rejected her appeal. Upon her release from prison, the media followed her to her home in New York and watched her every move. Stewart embraced the publicity.

THE ORIGINAL INDICTMENT

The grand jury investigating Martha Stewart and Peter Bacanovic for various federal offenses issued its indictment against the two on June 4, 2003, in federal court in New York. The three charges were outlined in a section of the indictment called "The Conspiracy," excerpted here.

From in or about January 2002 until in or about April 2002, in the Southern District of New York and elsewhere, Peter Bacanovic and Martha Stewart, and others known and unknown, unlawfully, willfully, and knowingly did combine, conspire, confederate and agree together and with each other to commit offenses against the United States, to wit: to obstruct justice . . . ; to make false statements . . . ; and to commit perjury . . . .

IMPACT

Stewart's conviction had a mixed impact on her iconic image. Many credited her for accepting responsibility for her actions and requesting she enter prison before her appeals were processed. Her talk show *Martha Stewart Living* went off the air three days after the guilty verdict, but Stewart resurfaced on daytime television with a new program called *The Martha Stewart Show*, which made its debut on September 12, 2005.

After Stewart completed her prison term, Mark Burnett, producer of the popular reality television shows *Survivor* and *The Apprentice*, approached her to star in a spinoff of the latter to be called *The Apprentice: Martha Stewart*. That show aired on NBC in the fall of 2005, but its ratings were considered sub-par and it was not renewed.

Because the trial judge dismissed the securities fraud charge, some critics of the prosecution argued that Stewart had been convicted of lying about something that was not itself a crime. Other critics perceived gender bias among prosecutors. Stewart, a powerful businesswoman, was convicted for what many considered a trivial matter, while the federally indicted male executives of scandal-ridden corporations such as Enron, Worldcom, and Tyco remained free. (Within a couple of years, however, state and federal prosecutors obtained convictions in virtually all high-profile cases involving the executive officers of these companies, who would receive prison sentences in excess of twenty years each, but for crimes much more serious and far-reaching than those of Stewart.)

On August 7, 2006, Stewart and Bacanovic agreed to settle insider trading civil charges brought against them by the SEC on June 4, 2003, for the December, 2001, ImClone stock sales. In its press release announcing the agreement, the SEC said,

Under the settlement, Stewart and Bacanovic agree to pay disgorgement and penalties. Stewart also agrees to a five year bar from serving as a director of a public company and a five year limitation on the scope of her service as an officer or employee of a public company. In August 2004, the

Martha Stewart leaves a federal courthouse in New York City after being sentenced on July 16, 2004, in an insider-trading scandal. (AP/Wide World Photos)

commission barred Bacanovic from associating with a broker, dealer or investment adviser.

Finally, in an ironic twist, the FDA reversed itself and approved Erbitux in February, 2004, for use as a cancer treatment drug. Had Waksal not panicked in December, 2001, and acted hastily to sell his company shares, neither he nor Stewart would be convicted felons.

—Tung Yin

FURTHER READING

Byron, Christopher M. *Martha Inc.: The Incredible Story of Martha Stewart Living Omnimedia.* New York: J. Wiley, 2002. Unauthorized biography of Stewart and her company by a reporter with *The Wall Street Journal.*

Dershowitz, Alan M. "With Lawyers Like These . . ." *The Wall Street Journal*, March 8, 2004. An editorial that castigates Stewart's legal team, written by a well-known Harvard law professor and legal commentator.

2000's

Glater, Jonathan D. "Martha Stewart's Sentence: The Corporate Role—Stewart Likely to Influence Her Company, Even from Jail." *The New York Times*, July 17, 2004. Examines the legal impact of Stewart's conviction on her ability to run her business from outside the corporate office.

Hays, Constance L., and David Carr. "Before Facing Judge, Stewart Is Out and About." *The New York Times*, July 15, 2004. Describes Stewart's actions and mental-emotional state before she was sentenced.

Hays, Constance L., and Leslie Eaton. "The Martha Stewart Verdict: The Overview—Stewart Found Guilty of Lying in Sale of Stock." *The New York Times*, March 6, 2004. A recap of Stewart's trial the day after the jury in the case rendered its verdict of guilty on multiple charges.

Turow, Scott. "Cry No Tears for Martha Stewart." *The New York Times*, May 27, 2004. An article that supports Stewart's conviction for conspiracy, obstruction of justice, and making false statements to federal authorities.

SEE ALSO: Jan., 1913: British Prime Minister's Staff Is Investigated for Insider Trading; 1932: Insull Utilities Trusts Collapse Prompts New Federal Regulation; Nov. 28, 1967: Investor Louis Wolfson Is Convicted of Selling Stock Illegally; Oct. 9, 1980: Bendix Executive Resigns Amid Rumors of an Affair; May 2, 1984: E. F. Hutton Executives Plead Guilty to Fraud; Jan. 15, 1988: ZZZZ Best Founder Is Indicted on Federal Fraud Charges; Aug. 27, 1990: Guinness Four Are Found Guilty of Share-Trading Fraud; Apr. 5, 1991: George W. Bush Is Investigated for Insider Trading; Apr. 15, 1992: Hotel Tycoon Leona Helmsley Enters Prison for Tax Evasion; Dec. 2, 2001: Enron Bankruptcy Reveals Massive Financial Fraud; Sept. 18, 2006: *Newsweek* Reveals That Hewlett-Packard Spied on Its Own Board.

April 28, 2004
CBS BROADCASTS PHOTOS OF ABUSED AND TORTURED PRISONERS AT ABU GHRAIB

The CBS news program 60 Minutes II *broadcast photographs of U.S. soldiers abusing and humiliating Iraqi prisoners at Abu Ghraib prison. U.S. officials characterized the abuse as the isolated acts of renegade soldiers. Later evidence showed that "enhanced interrogation techniques" had been approved at the highest levels of the U.S. government, leading many to believe that prisoner abuse was common U.S. military practice. Also, critics claim that U.S. officials knew about and tried to cover up the abuse months before the photos were made public.*

LOCALE: Near Baghdad, Iraq
CATEGORIES: Communications and media; atrocities and war crimes; human rights; military; violence; government; publishing and journalism

KEY FIGURES
Ricardo Sanchez (b. 1951), U.S. Army lieutenant general and commander of coalition forces in Iraq, 2003-2004
Antonio Taguba (b. 1950), U.S. Army major general, who led the Army's investigation into prisoner abuse
Janis Karpinski (b. 1953), U.S. Army brigadier general, who was commander at Abu Ghraib, 2003-2004
James Schlesinger (b. 1929), former defense secretary and head of investigatory panel
Donald Rumsfeld (b. 1932), secretary of the U.S. Department of Defense, 2001-2006

SUMMARY OF EVENT
Abu Ghraib is an infamous prison near Baghdad, Iraq. It was first used as a torture chamber and exe-

cution site during Saddam Hussein's rule of Iraq. After Hussein's regime was toppled by the invasion of Iraq in 2003, the prison was transformed into a U.S. military detention facility. Soldiers from the U.S. Army's Military Police (MP) Corps abused Iraqi prisoners there, photographed their acts of torture and humiliation, and created an international scandal. The abuse came to light on April 28, 2004, when the CBS television news program *60 Minutes II* aired a story about the prison's cellblock 1A.

The *60 Minutes II* broadcast featured photographs of prisoners who were hooded and stacked in human pyramids; in positions of simulated sexual acts; chained into distorted positions; wearing women's underwear on their heads; leashed; hooded and forced to balance on a box while attached to "electrodes"; and cowering under near-attack by a dog. The photos often include U.S. soldiers smiling and flashing gestures of approval as they posed alongside the prisoners being abused. MPs Charles Graner and Sabrina Harmon, both at the rank of specialist, were shown in photos smiling and flashing an approving "thumbs up" gesture near the bruised face of a dead man on ice in a body bag. The man, Manadel al-Jamadi, died during interrogation by the U.S. Central Intelligence Agency (CIA) on November 4, 2003. Although a U.S. military autopsy established his death as a homicide, no one was charged with that death.

The compelling and troubling images, however, distinguished Abu Ghraib from other allegations of mistreatment of prisoners by U.S. troops and the CIA in Afghanistan and Guantanamo Bay, Cuba. The Abu Ghraib photos made more real the earlier claims of U.S. military abuse by military watchdog groups and human rights organizations. The photos began their journey to the public eye when a horrified MP stumbled upon them and notified the Army's Criminal Investigation Division of their existence on January 13, 2004.

The military had already been warned of inhu-

Abu Ghraib prison inmates gather outside their cells for traditional Friday prayers in May, 2004. U.S. military tents and guard towers dominate the prison landscape at the facility near Baghdad, Iraq. (AP/Wide World Photos)

mane treatment at Abu Ghraib, before the CBS broadcast in April, 2004. Internal documents show several MPs were being investigated for prisoner abuse already in late 2003. The Associated Press reported on the abuse and investigations in October, 2003. The mistreatment also came to the attention of the International Committee of the Red Cross (ICRC), which sent a team of investigators to cellblock 1A in mid-October, 2003. The team reported its findings to American officials through a confidential report, issued in February, 2004. The ICRC alleged violations of international humanitarian law that included beatings with hard objects

2000's

1035

THE TAGUBA REPORT

The commander of coalition forces in Iraq ordered U.S. Army major general Antonio Taguba to conduct a covert internal investigation into alleged abuses at Abu Ghraib. An excerpt from Taguba's March 9 report follows.

Regarding part one of the investigation, I make the following specific findings of fact:

1. That between October and December, 2003, at the Abu Ghraib Confinement Facility (BCCF), numerous incidents of sadistic, blatant, and wanton criminal abuses were inflicted on several detainees. This systemic and illegal abuse of detainees was intentionally perpetrated by several members of the military police guard force . . . in Tier (section) 1-A of the Abu Ghraib Prison (BCCF).

The allegations of abuse were substantiated by detailed witness statements and the discovery of extremely graphic photographic evidence. Due to the extremely sensitive nature of these photographs and videos, the ongoing CID [Army Criminal Investigation Division] investigation, and the potential for the criminal prosecution of several suspects, the photographic evidence is not included in the body of my investigation. . . .

I find that the intentional abuse of detainees by military police personnel included the following acts:

- Punching, slapping, and kicking detainees; jumping on their naked feet
- Videotaping and photographing naked male and female detainees
- Forcibly arranging detainees in various sexually explicit positions for photographing
- Forcing detainees to remove their clothing and keeping them naked for several days at a time
- Forcing naked male detainees to wear women's underwear
- Arranging naked male detainees in a pile and then jumping on them
- Positioning a naked detainee on an MRE [Meal, Ready-to-Eat] Box, with a sandbag on his head, and attaching wires to his fingers, toes, and penis to simulate electric torture
- Writing "I am a Rapest" (sic) on the leg of a detainee alleged to have forcibly raped a 15-year old fellow detainee, and then photographing him naked
- Placing a dog chain or strap around a naked detainee's neck and having a female Soldier pose for a picture
- A male MP guard having sex with a female detainee
- Using military working dogs (without muzzles) to intimidate and frighten detainees, and in at least one case biting and severely injuring a detainee
- Taking photographs of dead Iraqi detainees

such as firearms, placing prisoners in stress positions for hours at a time, prolonged exposure to extreme heat or cold, and sleep and sensory deprivation.

After receiving the photos from CID, Lieutenant General Ricardo Sanchez, the commander of coalition forces in Iraq, ordered Major General Antonio Taguba on January 19 to conduct a secret internal investigation. Taguba's March 9 report concluded that between October and December, 2003, "numerous incidents of sadistic, blatant, and wanton criminal abuses" were inflicted on prisoners and that the abuse was "systematic and illegal" and "intentionally perpetrated" by MPs.

The photos of abused and tortured prisoners at Abu Ghraib dominated the world media. Furthermore, both the ICRC Report and the Taguba Report had been leaked to the media in May. In the United States, the Senate opened hearings into the matter. Investigations also were implemented by the Pentagon and the Department of Defense (DOD). James Schlesinger, former defense secretary, chaired the DOD panel; its report was issued on August 24. Testifying before the Senate Armed Services Committee, Schlesinger announced that although there had been evidence of "failures of leadership" at Abu Ghraib and beyond, through the chain of command, the responsibility for the serious mistreatment rested primarily with the MPs on duty at the prison. In a press conference the day the report was released, Schlesinger elaborated the DOD panel's findings: "There was sadism on the night shift at Abu Ghraib, sadism that was certainly not authorized. It was kind of [like the popular teen film] *Animal House* on the night shift." He added that no top military or government officials bore any direct responsibility, and that "the injunction from the top was to ensure 'humane treatment' of detainees." Furthermore, the DOD panel found "no policy that encouraged or justified abuse."

The soldiers directly involved in the abuse were charged, tried, convicted, and sentenced by military courts-martial for acts that included assault, battery, conspiracy, and maltreatment of detainees. Graner was sentenced to ten years in prison, Staff Sergeant Ivan Frederick received eight years, and Private Lynndie England received three years. Eight other soldiers received lesser punishments, including imprisonment and administrative penalties such as demotion, discharge, or both. Two officers were reprimanded as well. Brigadier General Janis Karpinski, the commander of Abu Ghraib prison and other detention facilities in Iraq, was removed from that post and demoted to colonel. The commander of the military intelligence brigade, Colonel Thomas Pappas, was fined and removed from his command.

IMPACT

The Abu Ghraib scandal, which became the centerpiece in the debate about fighting the global war against terrorism, provoked inquiries into how prisoners are treated during wartime. Confidential memos were leaked to the press as questions began to mount. One memo, a telling U.S. Department of Justice (DOJ) memo from August, 2002, and addressed to White House counsel, surfaced in June, 2004. John Yoo of the Office of Legal Counsel (OLC) at the DOJ, who wrote the memo, interpreted the 1994 federal statute that ratified the United Nations Convention Against Torture and applied it in the "context of the conduct of interrogations outside the United States." Yoo's legal analysis held that for an act to be torture, the one inflicting the torture must have intended it to cause severe pain and it must cause pain that is equivalent in

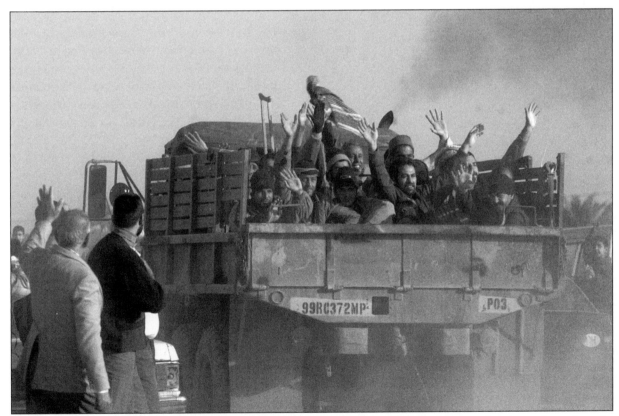

Former Iraqi prisoners of Abu Ghraib were transported from the prison by the U.S. military after their release from detention in January, 2004. Many had been abused and tortured by U.S. military personnel in a scandal that would come to light less than four months after this photograph was taken. (AP/Wide World Photos)

2000's

intensity to the pain that would accompany "serious physical injury, such as organ failure."

The Bybee memo, as it came to be called, gave Donald Rumsfeld, the secretary of the DOD, legal latitude to develop "enhanced interrogation techniques." The new chief of the OLC, Jack Goldsmith, was shocked to see this secret torture memo in October, 2003, and later stated that it was without legal foundation. The DOJ rescinded the Bybee memo on December 30, 2004.

While the DOD's enhanced interrogation techniques were not created for Abu Ghraib, it appears that at least some of the practices migrated from Guantanamo Bay to Iraq. Major General Geoffrey Miller, commander of facilities at Guantanamo Bay, visited Abu Ghraib in August and September, 2003. Miller reportedly had been assigned to "Gitmo-ize" (Guantanamo Bay is referred to by the military as Gitmo) Abu Ghraib, specifically referring to the harsh interrogation practices at Gitmo that had been approved by Rumsfeld. Some of Miller's recommendations were adopted by Sanchez for use at Abu Ghraib. Indeed, the Taguba Report concluded that the mistreatment of prisoners by MPs was a consequence of direct orders from military intelligence and other governmental agencies who "actively requested that MP guards set physical and mental conditions for favorable interrogation of witnesses," a technique Miller used at Guantanamo.

—Kimberlee Candela

FURTHER READING

Danner, Mark. *Torture and Truth: America, Abu Ghraib, and the War on Terror.* New York: New York Review of Books, 2004. Follows the paper trail, including policy statements and government reports on the mistreatment. Many original government documents are included, as well as the infamous photographs.

Hersh, Seymour. *Chain of Command: The Road from 9/11 to Abu Ghraib.* New York: Harper-Collins, 2005. Hersh, a Pulitzer Prize-winning investigative journalist, helped break the Abu Ghraib story with a May 9, 2004, article in *The New Yorker.*

Jaffer, Jameel, and Amrit Singh. *Administration of Torture: A Documentary Record from Washington to Abu Ghraib and Beyond.* New York: Columbia University Press, 2007. Jaffer and Singh, both attorneys with the American Civil Liberties Union, discuss the thousands of relevant documents, including government e-mails and autopsy reports, which they obtained for this study of the prisoner-abuse scandal.

McKelvey, Tara. *Monstering: Inside America's Policy of Secret Interrogations and Torture in the Terror War.* New York: Carroll & Graf, 2007. A study of the crimes at Abu Ghraib prison. Includes first-hand interviews with MPs who worked at Abu Ghraib and with former Iraqi prisoners.

Mayer, Jane. *The Dark Side: The Inside Story of How a War on Terror Turned into a War on American Ideals.* New York: Doubleday, 2008. A staff writer for *The New Yorker* examines the Bush administration's response to the September 11, 2001, terrorist attacks and beyond in this meticulously researched, readable account of the American war on terror.

Zimbardo, P. G. *The Lucifer Effect: Understanding How Good People Turn Evil.* New York: Random House, 2007. Zimbardo revisits his famous 1971 experiment and applies his research to the torture and humiliation at Abu Ghraib prison, challenging society to think about the situational influences that lead to oppression and abuse.

SEE ALSO: July, 1961: Psychologist Stanley Milgram Begins Obedience-to-Authority Experiments; Mar. 13, 1964: Kitty Genovese Dies as Her Cries for Help Are Ignored; Nov. 13, 1969: American Massacre of Vietnamese Civilians at My Lai Is Revealed; Aug. 20, 1971: Abusive Role-Playing Ends Stanford Prison Experiment.

June 2, 2004
U.N. Report Reveals That Secretary-General Kofi Annan Dismissed Sexual Harassment Charges

United Nations staffer Cynthia Brzak claimed that the U.N. high commissioner for refugees, Ruud Lubbers, had sexually harassed her. Despite the finding of an investigative panel in support of her claim, the U.N. secretary-general, Kofi Annan, overruled the panel's disciplinary recommendations and dismissed the charges against Lubbers, head of one of the United Nations' principal humanitarian divisions.

LOCALE: New York, New York

CATEGORIES: Politics; international relations; law and the courts; sex crimes; women's issues

KEY FIGURES

Kofi Annan (b. 1938), Ghanaian secretary-general of the United Nations, 1997-2007

Ruud Lubbers (b. 1939), former prime minister of the Netherlands, 1982-1994, and U.N. high commissioner for refugees

Cynthia Brzak (b. 1952), American U.N. staff member

Stephen M. Schwebel (b. 1929), American jurist and former president of the International Court of Justice, 1997-2000

Robert W. Sweet (b. 1922), U.S. District Court judge

SUMMARY OF EVENT

The early years of the twenty-first century have in many ways been unkind to established institutions, taking their toll on the reputations of private and public bodies alike. International governmental organizations have not been spared such public tarring. In the world of public institutions at the global level, no image has been tarnished more than that of the United Nations. Indeed, the notoriety surrounding Secretary-General Kofi Annan's response in the Ruud Lubbers sexual harassment case would almost certainly have been much less had it not been for the myriad scandals surrounding the United Nations at the time.

These U.N.-involved scandals ranged from disclosures of massive mismanagement and corruption in the institution's food-for-oil program in Iraq (including charges that the senior officer in charge of that program had taken bribes from Saddam Hussein's government), to charges that U.N. peacekeepers and relief workers have used their positions to coerce sex from local citizens in Africa, East Timor, and elsewhere, to allegations that Annan's son had been handsomely rewarded by the Swiss company for which he helped acquire a lucrative U.N. contract. Sandwiched amid these other scandals is Annan's decision to dismiss the sexual harassment charges against Lubbers, the head of the U.N. refugee relief department, a move that instantly acquired scandal status of its own.

The story behind the scandal began when Cynthia Brzak, a high-ranking aide to Lubbers and a U.N. employee for a quarter of a century, accused Lubbers of having grabbed her and rubbed up against her from behind when leaving a 2003 business meeting in Geneva, Switzerland. The charges were referred to the U.N. Office of Internal Oversight (OIOS), which on June 2, 2004, released an in-house document that supported Brzak's charges. Moreover, although Lubbers's position was that Brzak had misinterpreted a friendly gesture, the OIOS report also noted a pattern of similar, past behavior by Lubbers and recommended his official censure. Lubbers had become the United Nations' ninth high commissioner for refugees in January of 2001 and had paid his own salary while working for the United Nations.

Annan consulted American jurist Stephen M. Schwebel, a former head justice of the International Court of Justice in The Hague, the Netherlands, who found that the evidence against Lubbers did not rise to the legal standard necessary for conviction in a court of law. On July 15, Annan, basing his decision on Schwebel's finding, dismissed the charges against Lubbers as insufficiently substantiated by the evidence. Privately, however, Annan wrote a letter to Lubbers stressing his concern over both Brzak's accusation and the pattern of behavior on Lubbers's part noted in the OIOS report.

Had the matter ended there, the scandal would have never become public knowledge and no blight would have been attached to the generally distinguished public service career of Lubbers. In October, however, evidently dissatisfied with Annan's handling of the matter, the OIOS included in the publicly released summary of the work it completed during the prior year its findings in the investigation into the charges against Lubbers and its recommendations on the matter. The media quickly seized on the story as yet another controversy engulfing the United Nations and its secretary-general. Annan's alleged tolerance of sexual harassment at the highest level in one of the premier humanitarian divisions of the United Nations quickly acquired the proportions of a scandal.

IMPACT

The OIOS report's release, and the subsequent firestorm of criticism that the United Nations received over the Lubbers matter, on the whole produced mixed results for the principal figures involved. Lubbers initially tried to retain his position, but only a few months later, on February 20, 2005, he resigned, arguing that the continuing press coverage of the sexual harassment charge against him made it impossible for him to do his job effectively. More scandalous was Annan's letter to the refugee office staff the following day that called the Lubbers affair an "unwanted distraction" and that Lubbers had "not been found guilty of any offence," a claim that was wholly incorrect. Topping off the scandal were Lubbers's own words, deemed "appalling" by the OIOS. In his "farewell" to office staff, Lubbers said he had been "harassed" and "raped and raped and raped" through the investigations.

Insofar as the refugee office was at the time investigating rumors of sexual abuses committed by U.N. peacekeeping forces, including 150 charges of rape, sexual abuse of children, and the solicitation of sexual acts in Congo alone, Lubbers's continuing status as high commissioner for refugees had by this time become not only untenable but also an institutional embarrassment to the United Nations.

Brzak filed a federal lawsuit against the United Nations on May 4, 2006, on the grounds of sexual harassment and alleged discrimination against her for having raised the issue. On the last day of April, 2008, U.S. District Court judge Robert W. Sweet dismissed her suit on the grounds that the United Nations had a long-established immunity from legal action in U.S. courts in general and in the area of employee-related issues in particular, which outweighed Brzak's claims against the organization.

For Annan, the handling of the case remains another stain on his overall, generally commendable record of overseeing the increasingly vast operations of the United Nations around the world during his years as secretary-general. For the organization itself, however, the Lubbers case, combined with the companion controversies that involved the United Nations during the first decade of the twenty-first century, forced the body to undertake much needed reforms in overseeing the conduct of its permanent and contracted personnel in New York and Geneva and throughout its global operations. Thus, a Swiss consulting firm and other outside evaluators were hired to assess the performance of the United Nations' overseas operations.

Likewise, a zero-tolerance policy was adopted on matters of sexual harassment. The policy was implemented most famously in the case of the December, 2005, dismissal of Carina Perelli, the director of the electoral assistance division of the U.N. Election Services Office, despite the praise that the division had won during her seven-year tenure for its work in such trying locations as East Timor and Afghanistan.

—*Joseph R. Rudolph, Jr.*

FURTHER READING

Fleck, Fiona, and Warren Hoge. "Annan Clears Refugee Chief of Harassment Accusations." *The New York Times*, July 16, 2004. News article announcing Annan's controversial decision to dismiss the sexual harassment charges against Lubbers.

Koestler-Grack, Rachel A. *Kofi Annan.* New York: Chelsea House, 2007. Part of the Modern Peacemakers series, this work provides a brief but useful introduction to Annan's diplomatic career.

Meisler, Stanley. *Kofi Annan: A Man of Peace in a World of War.* New York: John Wiley & Sons, 2008. As the title suggests, the focus is on Annan's accomplishments as a peacemaker, both before and as the U.N. secretary-general. As such it offers a context for evaluating the place of his role in the Lubbers scandal in the context of his broad, generally distinguished career.

Weiss, Thomas G., et al. *The United Nations and Changing World Politics.* 5th ed. Boulder, Colo.: Westview Press, 2007. A good overview of United Nations operations from which to judge Lubbers's contributions to the organization's work and against which to evaluate his alleged harassment of Brzak.

SEE ALSO: Mar. 3, 1986: Former U.N. Secretary-General Kurt Waldheim's Nazi Past Is Revealed; Oct. 11-13, 1991: Justice Clarence Thomas's Confirmation Hearings Create a Scandal; June 26, 1992: U.S. Navy Secretary Resigns in the Wake of Tailhook Sexual Assault Scandal; Aug. 21, 1994: Sex Scandal Forces Dismissal of NAACP Chief Benjamin Chavis; Jan. 17, 1998: President Bill Clinton Denies Sexual Affair with a White House Intern; Jan. 2, 2003: E-mail Message Prompts Inquiry into Air Force Academy Sexual Assaults; Mar. 2, 2003: U.S. National Security Agency Is Found to Have Spied on U.N. Officials; Oct. 13, 2004: Television Producer Files Sex Harassment Suit Against Bill O'Reilly; Jan. 15, 2005: Iqbal Riza Resigns from the United Nations in Oil-for-Food Scandal.

August 19, 2004
BLOG "OUTS" ANTIGAY CONGRESSMAN EDWARD SCHROCK

Political activist Michael Rogers claimed on his blog that U.S. representative Edward Schrock was gay or bisexual. The blog entry linked to a recording alleged to be of Schrock speaking on a phone line for men seeking other men for gay sex. The outing led Schrock to end his 2004 reelection bid.

LOCALE: Washington, D.C.
CATEGORIES: Publishing and journalism; sex; politics; public morals

KEY FIGURES

Edward Schrock (b. 1941), U.S. representative from Virginia, 2001-2004
Michael Rogers (c. 1964), political activist and blogger

SUMMARY OF EVENT

When Democrat Owen B. Pickett announced he would leave the U.S. Congress at the end of his eighth term, in 2000, voters elected conservative Republican Edward Schrock to replace him. A former U.S. Navy admiral and Vietnam War veteran, Schrock won his Virginia district largely on the military vote. Already a state senator, Schrock's election to the U.S. House of Representatives came as no surprise to political prognosticators, who noted Pickett was a conservative Democrat. Across the nation, several seats vacated by conservative Democrats were won by Republicans.

On August 19, 2004, political activist Michael Rogers claimed on blogActive.com that Schrock was a closeted homosexual or bisexual. Rogers included on his blog a link to voice data to support the

2000's

Congress members Edward Schrock, right, and Tom DeLay at the White House in January, 2004. (Hulton Archive/Getty Images)

accusation. Rogers, who has been committed to outing gay lawmakers who oppose gay and lesbian rights legislation, claimed Schrock had been placing advertisements on an interactive phone line for men seeking other men for gay sex.

It took only two weeks from the time Rogers posted the taped message for Schrock to resign. In that time, Rogers's blog was accessed by countless politicians and others, who treated the findings like news they might encounter in the popular press. The popular press, in turn, had to scramble to keep up with the story, which grew quickly as people added their own perspectives by posting comments to the blog.

Schrock had made his name in the House as a strong opponent of gay and lesbian rights. Spe-

cifically, he cosponsored bills that would have banned same-gender marriage and barred lesbians and gays from openly serving in the military. With the failure of those bills, he strongly supported the official U.S. military policy known as Don't Ask, Don't Tell, a so-called compromise on the question of gays in the military. Schrock made public comments to the effect that having gays in the military was sexually dangerous, as they were impossible to recognize.

Schrock was named president of the Republican freshman House in 2001 and won a second term in the House in 2002. The Christian Coalition gave Schrock, an active Baptist, high ratings. However, his ascent came to an abrupt halt in 2004, a year marked by landslide Republican victories in Congress.

Rogers said he wanted to stop Schrock's hypocrisy, arguing that the gay community as a whole has no obligation to protect gays and lesbians who actively oppose gay rights. When the allegations came to light, the Republican Party was supportive of Schrock, making glowing statements about his congressional record and focusing on his status in the House. Initially, it was believed that the allegations would not affect Schrock's bid for reelection.

However, Schrock, on August 30, rescinded his bid for reelection, stating only that the allegations against him would prevent him from focusing on the real issues in his constituency. Rogers's accusations were not supported by any material beyond the phone message, and he could not offer further proof that the voice on the call was, in fact, that of Schrock. However, Schrock's withdrawal from the congressional race confirmed his guilt in the minds of many.

Republicans remained supportive of Schrock, who was married and had a child, and cited their disappointment that he should have to resign because of the mere suggestion of homosexuality. They claimed that his resignation was caused by Rogers's intent to push a particular political viewpoint. However, Rogers, who said he was sorry to see Schrock resign, had a slightly different slant on the issue. Although still opposed to Schrock's conservative politics and believing he was a hypocrite,

Rogers had believed that by the year 2004, homosexuality should not have been so much of an issue that it could end any politician's career.

The Republican Party chose Thelma Drake to run for the post vacated by Schrock, and she won the district that year and was reelected to a second term in 2006. By December of 2004, Schrock was back on Capitol Hill, though in a much less celebrated post, working as staff director for the House Government Reform Committee. In this diminished capacity, he was unable to block gay rights legislation and actively promote antigay legislation.

IMPACT

This scandal illustrates several points about American popular culture. Both the Republican Party and Rogers seem to agree that Schrock resigned because of the rumor that he had sought homosexual sex. Rogers argued that the rumor was true, while Schrock focused on how the claim would prevent him from working on the real issues of his election campaign. In either case, Schrock's resignation demonstrates that homosexuality remains a political nightmare for those accused of being lesbian or gay or of seeking same-gender sex. The nightmare exists in the United States, even though there are several gay and lesbian politicians who are out. Specifically, that Schrock believed he had to resign indicates the negative implications homosexuality has within the Republican Party. Though the party remained outwardly supportive of Schrock, it did so under the flag of supporting an unfairly accused colleague, not of supporting one who was potentially gay or bisexual.

Rogers's strategy is opposed by some gay and lesbian activists as well. Groups such as the Log Cabin Republicans, whose members are gay and Republican, disagree with outing closeted government officials, whatever their politics. Opponents of outing point out that no gay rights issues have been decided after outing an official, and they suggest that it is more effective to focus on the issues rather than the politicians. In turn, Rogers argues that conservative gays who oppose gay rights are effectively double dipping, enjoying gay-rights successes in their private lives while condemning those rights publicly. Other groups, such as the Human Rights Campaign, argue that outing often deepens the already entrenched views of conservative opponents of gay and lesbian rights.

Rogers had a different point. The entire purpose of his blog has been to out closeted gay politicians who oppose gay rights legislation. He believes they are hiding behind party dogmas to avoid taking responsibility for their own actions. His purpose in outing Schrock was to expose a man whom he believes was a conservative hypocrite and to demonstrate that gays are everywhere, regardless of political viewpoint. He argues that the gay community has a responsibility to expose gay politicians who hide their sexuality and, most important, do so while actively opposing legislation that harms the community.

Scandals such as the Schrock affair show a growing rift in the type of voters sought by the Republican and Democrat parties in the twenty-first century. For many years, Republicans have targeted right wing fundamentalist Christians, who have considered the Republican Party the only conservative option. Democrats have targeted a more left-wing group, selling themselves as the more liberal political party. Gay and lesbian rights have become so public, with issues such as gay marriage and gay military service regularly coming to Congress, that the Republicans and Democrats have taken largely opposing stances on these issues. In general, the Republicans oppose and the Democrats support gay rights. Thus, a stance in favor of gay rights is perceived as politically liberal, and for a group to be politically conservative and still favor gay rights seems contradictory to many, even though there is no reason the two perspectives cannot coexist. This means groups such as the Log Cabin Republicans are relatively rare and often find themselves on the outside when it comes to politics. Some conservative Republican politicians shun Log Cabin endorsements for fear of alienating other voters.

Finally, the scandal illustrates the importance of the World Wide Web and its influence on the media and politics in modern popular culture. Media influence on popular opinion affects politics and, with

2000's

the addition of blogs, popular opinion is increasingly influencing the media. This cyclical relationship became even more clear with the Schrock scandal.

—*Jessie Bishop Powell*

FURTHER READING

Muzzy, Frank. *Gay and Lesbian Washington, D.C.* Charleston, S.C.: Arcadia Press, 2005. Double focus on the presence of gays and lesbians in the nation's capital and their impact on politics.

Rauch, Jonathan. *Gay Marriage: Why It Is Good for Gays, Good for Straights, and Good for America.* New York: Times Books/Henry Holt, 2004. Summarizes the state of gay and lesbian rights at the time of Schrock's resignation. Primarily supports gay and lesbian marriage rights.

Shear, Michael D., and Chris L. Jenkins. "Va. Legislator Ends Bid for Third Term." *The Washington Post*, August 31, 2004. Contemporary account of Schrock's decision not to seek reelection, including his denial of guilt and the political community's support of his legislative

efforts. This mainstream media report was published twelve days after Rogers's blog outing of Schrock.

SEE ALSO: Oct. 7, 1964: President Lyndon B. Johnson's Aide Is Arrested in Gay-Sex Sting; 1970: Study of Anonymous Gay Sex Leads to Ethics Scandal; Oct. 25, 1974: Evangelist Billy James Hargis Resigns College Presidency During Gay-Sex Scandal; Jan., 1977: Singer Anita Bryant Campaigns Against Lesbian and Gay Rights; Aug. 4, 1978: British Politician Jeremy Thorpe Is Charged with Attempted Murder; Sept. 3, 1980: Congressman Bauman Is Arrested for Liaison with Teenage Boy; Sept. 19, 2000: Ex-gay Leader John Paulk Is Photographed Leaving a Gay Bar; Sept. 29, 2006: Congressman Mark Foley Resigns in Sex Scandal Involving a Teenage Page; Nov. 2, 2006: Male Escort Reveals Sexual Liaisons with Evangelist Ted Haggard; July 11, 2007: Florida Politician Is Arrested for Soliciting an Undercover Male Police Officer.

September 8, 2004
60 MINUTES II REPORTS ON GEORGE W. BUSH'S EVASION OF WARTIME DUTY

CBS News correspondent Dan Rather presented documents in a 2004 report on 60 Minutes II *that questioned U.S. president George W. Bush's Air National Guard service during the 1970's. The Killian documents, as they came to be called, accused Bush of having received favors to make his military record look better than it was. The documents were widely considered fakes, permanently damaging the reputations of both Rather and CBS.*

ALSO KNOWN AS: Killian documents scandal; Memogate; Rathergate

LOCALE: New York, New York

CATEGORIES: Radio and television; communications and media; publishing and journalism; politics; military

KEY FIGURES

Dan Rather (b. 1931), broadcast journalist and *CBS Evening News* anchor

George W. Bush (b. 1946), president of the United States, 2001-2009

Mary Mapes (fl. late twentieth century), *60 Minutes II* and *CBS Evening News* producer

Bill Burkett (fl. early twenty-first century), retired U.S. Army National Guard lieutenant colonel, who was the source for the Killian documents

Summary of Event

On September 8, 2004, CBS television broadcast a controversial story that was highly critical of U.S. president George W. Bush's military record with the U.S. Army Air National Guard. Almost immediately following the broadcast, reported by longtime news anchor and journalist Dan Rather, competing media sources began to question the validity of the evidence presented in the story and to criticize CBS for broadcasting the report. The Killian documents, as they came to be called, were widely considered to have been fabricated. Following the outpouring of criticism, CBS fired Mary Mapes, the producer of the segment, as well as several others who were involved in the broadcast. Rather resigned from the CBS news desk less than one year later.

At the time of the scandal, Rather was one of the most recognizable journalists of his time. He rose to become the head anchor on *CBS Evening News* in 1981 and achieved success as a contributing reporter with *60 Minutes*. He was at the top of the journalism world already during the 1960's as a hard-hitting correspondent during the Vietnam War and for his unswerving interview with President Richard Nixon during the early 1970's. He covered some of the most significant stories in the United States throughout the 1980's and 1990's, and in 2004, he broke a story that would turn out to be his most controversial yet.

On September 4, Rather decided to report a story on Bush's military record. The report presented several documents that made Bush's time in the armed services seem less than honorable. The memos, believed to be drawn up while Bush was in the National Guard during the early 1970's, documented incidences where Bush blatantly disobeyed orders by failing to report for scheduled physical examinations—leading to the revocation of his flight status—and by asking to be excused from certain activities, such as military drills. The memos also insinuated that the Bush family's political power was used to ensure that the future president's record was devoid of this negative information. In essence, the Killian documents, if real, would have proven that Bush's military record had been made to appear much better than it actually was.

Because the story was aired so close to election time, the broadcast sparked an immediate media frenzy. Many quickly stepped forward to question the validity of the documents themselves as well as the integrity and political bias of CBS and Rather. Initially, CBS stuck by the report, stating that the documents used had been well researched, but as investigations into the origin of the documents continued, it seemed more and more that the military memos were inaccurate, if not fraudulent.

As inquiries grew more tense, *60 Minutes II* segment producer Mapes came forward to defend the origin of the story's material. Mapes, an award winning journalist and long-time CBS producer, acquired the memos in question from Bill Burkett, a retired National Guard lieutenant colonel. Burkett claimed he had retrieved the memos from the personal files of the deceased lieutenant colonel Jerry B. Killian, who was President Bush's commander during his time in the National Guard. In the weeks following the story, Mapes and CBS maintained that Burkett was an accurate source and that the information he acquired regarding the president was truly from Killian's personal files.

However, as critical analysis intensified, independent researchers began to repudiate the origin of the memos and the time in which they were created. Before Rather's broadcast on September 8, Mapes and her associates had interviewed several people, in addition to Burkett, to ensure that the documents were legitimate, but this fact ultimately did not help CBS in defending its story, because the documents they had in their possession were only copies of the supposed originals. Unfortunately, Burkett told Mapes that he had burned the original Killian documents after he sent the copies to CBS headquarters, an action that fueled the argument that the documents were fraudulent.

Two weeks after the broadcast, Rather and CBS were forced to retract the story; the evidence in support of the Killian documents was simply not present. However, evidence was also lacking that the documents were faulty. Independent investigators found that the documents had inconsistencies in letterhead, signature, and date of production. Some investigators did conclude, however, that Killian's signature seemed to match the signature on the memos. Ultimately, the investigators could not prove or disprove that the documents were fraudulent because they were copies.

What led investigators and other media sources to discredit the story were the inconsistencies in Burkett's account of how he obtained the documents. Burkett changed his story several times. Initially, he said he received the documents through a warrant officer who had access to Killian's files, but he later claimed to have collected them by other means. In the end, the documents could not be authenticated.

IMPACT

CBS, Mapes, and Rather apologized publicly for reporting the story and said that they recognize their mistakes in not researching the matter fully before its broadcast. However, the damage to CBS's journalistic reputation had already been done. In response to the accusations by outside forces that CBS was operating under a liberal bias and had been trying to sabotage the coming elections, the network fired several employees associated with the production of the story. Less than one year later, Rather resigned from his news anchor position after nearly forty years in journalism.

CBS and Rather have had a difficult time recovering from the harm that was done to their reputations. Rather filed a lawsuit against CBS in 2007, alleging that the network laid the sole blame for the story on him, which permanently damaged his career. However, the greatest damage seems to have been done to the field of journalism itself.

Further investigations have looked into the Killian documents scandal, but none have proved that the documents are real. The controversy has raised many questions about the true motivation behind news reporting in the United States. The debate continues over the scandal, and many questions remain: Was the story politically biased against Bush, and was it aired to harm his campaign? Did CBS make a genuine mistake by airing the report? In any case, investigative journalism in the United States was left with a permanent scar.

—*Jennifer L. Titanski*

FURTHER READING

Hindman, Elizabeth Blanks. "Black Eye: The Ethics of CBS News and the National Guard Documents." *Journal of Mass Media Ethics* 23, no. 2 (April, 2008): 90-109. A scholarly case study of the response of mainstream media to the *60 Minutes II* broadcast of the Rather story and the resulting Killian documents scandal, with a critical focus on the ethical principles applied by these various media organizations.

Mapes, Mary. *Truth and Duty: The Press, the President, and the Privilege of Power.* New York: St. Martin's Press, 2005. Mapes tells her side of the controversial story on the Killian documents and scandal and argues that true journalism is coming to an end.

Rieder, Rem. "Breaking All the Rules: CBS' Documents Fiasco Is a Textbook Case of How Not to Do Journalism." *American Journalism Review* 27, no. 1 (February-March, 2005). A concise look at the effects of the Killian documents scandal on all those involved in the controversy.

Weisman, Alan. *Lone Star: The Extraordinary Life and Times of Dan Rather.* Hoboken, N.J.: John Wiley & Sons, 2006. Drawing on interviews from some of Dan Rather's biggest fans and most vocal critics, Alan Weisman's book explores the controversial image that Rather developed over his forty-plus years in news broadcasting.

SEE ALSO: June 13, 1971: *New York Times* Publishes the Pentagon Papers; July 8-22, 1972: Jane Fonda's Visit to North Vietnam Outrages Many Americans; Nov. 13, 1986-May 4, 1989: Iran-Contra Weapons Scandal Taints Reagan's Administration; Apr. 5, 1991: George W. Bush Is Investigated for Insider Trading.

October 13, 2004
TELEVISION PRODUCER FILES SEX HARASSMENT SUIT AGAINST BILL O'REILLY

Bill O'Reilly, a conservative political commentator best known for his Fox News television show The O'Reilly Factor, *was sued by his show's producer, Andrea Mackris, for sexual harassment. O'Reilly was first to sue Mackris, however, claiming in his preemptive suit filed the same day that Mackris and her attorney were extorting him. The matter was settled out of court for an undisclosed amount of money. In the long term, the suits had little impact on O'Reilly's or Mackris's careers in broadcasting.*

LOCALE: New York, New York

CATEGORIES: Law and the courts; radio and television; communications and media; women's issues

KEY FIGURES

Bill O'Reilly (b. 1949), host of *The O'Reilly Factor* and conservative political commentator

Andrea Mackris (b. 1971), producer of *The O'Reilly Factor*

Benedict Morelli (b. 1950), attorney for Andrea Mackris

SUMMARY OF EVENT

On October 13, 2004, Fox News talk-show host Bill O'Reilly was sued by his show's former producer, Andrea Mackris, for sexual harassment. Mackris claimed she had audiotapes of sexually provocative phone calls made to her by O'Reilly. She also claimed that O'Reilly sexually harassed her repeatedly by talking about his own sex life and fantasies and by asking her questions about her sex life, even though she expressed no interest in continuing the conversations. O'Reilly had sued Mackris first earlier on the same day, claiming she and her attorney, Benedict Morelli, a leading employment discrimination lawyer, were trying to extort him.

O'Reilly decided to file suit against Mackris and

Morelli after he received a letter from Morelli dated September 29, indicating that his law firm was representing "a young woman employee of Fox" who had "been the victim of constant and relentless" sexual harassment "by one of Fox's most prominent on-air personalities." The letter did not name names, however.

Unfortunately for O'Reilly, the details of the suit against him became readily accessible to the public on the Web. O'Reilly never denied the accusations against him, leading Mackris to amend her lawsuit on October 19. The original lawsuit against O'Reilly, Fox News Channel, News Corporation, Twentieth Century Fox Film Corporation, and Westwood One sought $60 million.

Considered by many to be one of the top-rated cable news hosts, O'Reilly graduated college with a bachelor's degree in history and received a master's degree in broadcast journalism in 1975. He began his career as a high school teacher and then became a news anchor. By 1980, he was an anchor for his own program with WCBS. In 1986, he joined ABC News, and later that year he began working on the entertainment news show *Inside Edition*. He obtained a second master's degree that year as well and became the host of his own show, *O'Reilly Report*. In 1996, the show was renamed *The O'Reilly Factor*.

The O'Reilly Factor, like his other ventures, has been very successful with millions of viewers. On the show, O'Reilly examines highly controversial issues with a conservative bent, even though he considers himself nonpartisan and is registered as an independent. He has described himself as a "traditionalist" commentator. He has never been afraid to state his opinion, regardless of others' perceptions of him. He also has written a newspaper column and published a number of books, including *The O'Reilly Factor: The Good, the Bad, and the Completely Ridiculous in American Life* (2000), *The No Spin Zone* (2003), *The O'Reilly Factor for*

2000'S

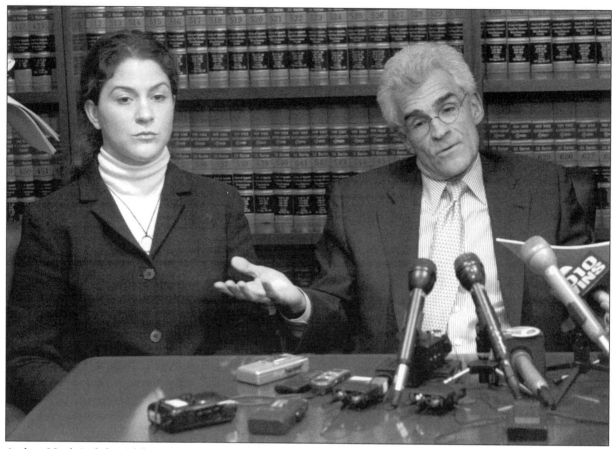

Andrea Mackris, left, with her attorney, Benedict Morelli, announce their sexual harassment lawsuit against television commentator Bill O'Reilly at a news conference in New York City on October 13, 2004. (AP/Wide World Photos)

Kids: A Survival Guide for America's Families (2004), *Culture Warrior* (2006), and *Kids Are Americans Too* (2007). He also has done some acting.

Whether the sexual harassment allegations made by Mackris are true or not, the intimate details of her complaint, including eighty-five allegations against O'Reilly, have been made public through the Web. Some of those allegations include claims that he masturbated while on the phone with Mackris, and how she was sickened by this fact. In addition, she claims he gave detailed descriptions of what he would do to her sexually if he was away with her, got her drunk, or showered with her. However, no actual tapes were ever produced in the case as evidence, and Morelli could not confirm their existence.

Initially, the parties to the lawsuits attempted to settle informally, but O'Reilly then attempted to have Mackris fired. On October 28, the case was settled out of court. Each party dropped the charges against the other, but the terms of the agreement were never made public. Mackris's attorney did state, however, that the original offer was too low to be accepted. Experts believe the settlement was probably around $10 million.

IMPACT

Ratings for *The O'Reilly Factor* jumped after Mackris's lawsuit was filed. Critics argue that the accusations may have cost O'Reilly some of his reputation as a moralist, but viewers have not wavered in their respect for his opinion. In fact, in one of the few discussions he had with his viewers regarding the accusations, he thanked them for their loyalty and support.

Even though O'Reilly claimed that there was no wrongdoing on his part—he never apologized to his viewers, to Mackris, or to his employer—he was publicly humiliated and did cancel some scheduled interviews. Before the lawsuits, O'Reilly received many accolades, including Emmy Awards, for his investigative reporting, and he continued to do so afterward.

Impacting the scandal was the ease with which the public could access the complaint against O'Reilly on the Web, leading to further embarrassment for the commentator. In one unfortunate detail from the lawsuit, Mackris claimed that O'Reilly described how he would massage her with a loofah if they were to shower together. However, O'Reilly did not use the term "loofah"; instead he referred to using a "falafel thing" to massage her. As a consequence, the scandal has been comedically referred to as the falafel scandal by his critics.

It is also difficult to ignore the irony of a sexual harassment lawsuit filed against O'Reilly, the conservative moralist who has written a children's book on sex in popular culture, among other conservative topics. Some consider him a hypocrite. Mackris, too, has been criticized for failing to complain to her employer, Fox, at the time the harassment occurred and for returning to work with O'Reilly after the alleged harassment took place.

—*Gina Robertiello*

FURTHER READING

Chowthi, Roy. *Bill O'Reilly Versus the Truth: Confronting the Propaganda of Bill O'Reilly and the Scam of the "No-Spin" Zone*. New York: iUniverse, 2007. Author argues that O'Reilly, who claims he is nonpartisan, is truly a conservative Republican who discredits and despises Democrats and liberals.

Hart, Peter. *The Oh Really? Factor: Unspinning Fox News Channel's Bill O'Reilly*. New York: Seven Stories Press, 2003. Argues that O'Reilly has misguided opinions and that he contradicts himself. Published in cooperation with the media watchdog group Fairness and Accuracy in Reporting.

Marshall, Anna-Maria. *Confronting Sexual Harassment: The Law and Politics of Everyday Life*. Burlington, Vt.: Ashgate, 2005. Examines law, social change, and the politics of workers' everyday lives, which often includes sexual harassment. Also provides a framework for studying issues of everyday life, especially in the workplace.

O'Reilly, Bill. *The No Spin Zone*. New York: Broadway Books, 2003. Discussion of current topics and getting to the truth in the context of media "spin" on those topics. Offers advice and opinion.

_____. *The O'Reilly Factor: The Good, the Bad, and the Completely Ridiculous in American Life*. New York: Broadway Books, 2000. A bestselling book, offering O'Reilly's opinion about what is right and wrong in the United States. O'Reilly gives his assumptions and views on politics, culture, and society in general.

SEE ALSO: Oct. 11-13, 1991: Justice Clarence Thomas's Confirmation Hearings Create a Scandal; June 26, 1992: U.S. Navy Secretary Resigns in the Wake of Tailhook Sexual Assault Scandal; Aug. 21, 1994: Sex Scandal Forces Dismissal of NAACP Chief Benjamin Chavis; Jan. 17, 1998: President Bill Clinton Denies Sexual Affair with a White House Intern; Oct. 2, 2003: Newspaper Claims That Arnold Schwarzenegger Groped Women; June 2, 2004: U.N. Report Reveals That Secretary-General Kofi Annan Dismissed Sexual Harassment Charges; Apr. 11, 2007: Shock Jock Don Imus Loses His Radio Show over Sexist and Racist Remarks.

2000's

October 14, 2004

INSURANCE BROKERAGE MARSH & McLENNAN IS CHARGED WITH FRAUD

Marsh & McLennan, an international insurance brokerage and professional services company, was charged with fraud in 2004 by Eliot L. Spitzer, the attorney general of New York. Confronted by pages of testimony affirming its illegal actions, the company settled out of court, paying a fine of $850 million.

LOCALE: New York

CATEGORIES: Law and the courts; business; corruption; government

KEY FIGURES

Eliot L. Spitzer (b. 1959), New York State attorney general, 1999-2006

David D. Brown IV (b. 1959), head of the New York State attorney general's Investment Protection Bureau

Jeffrey W. Greenberg (b. 1951), chief executive officer of Marsh & McLennan, 1999-2004

Michael G. Cherkasky (b. 1950), chief executive officer of Marsh & McLennan, 2004-2008

William L. Rosoff (b. 1946), general counsel of Marsh & McLennan

SUMMARY OF EVENT

As attorney general for New York State since 1999, Eliot Spitzer had acquired the nickname Caped Crusader because of his relentless pursuit of white-collar crime. In 2004, his attention turned to insurance giant Marsh & McLennan (MMC) after learning that the company had been condoning inflated bids and taking commissions for steering clients toward specific companies. In other words, it had been price-fixing. Following six months of investigation, Spitzer filed a civil complaint against the company. Media attention and a resultant drop in the price of the company's stock led MMC to fire its chief executive officer. The company also announced it would no longer accept commissions and paid $850 million into a fund to compensate policyholders.

Spitzer's action against MMC was yet another target for the attorney general, who had been waging war against corporate giants that heretofore had been protected by the concept "that's how business is done." Spitzer challenged out-of-state power plants whose emissions were polluting the skies over New York; he went after several big Wall Street investment firms, including Merrill Lynch. His actions against former New York Stock Exchange chairman Dick Grasso and other investigations into hedge funds and after-closing trading established him as a force working for consumer rights and made his name known nationally. In 2002, *Time* magazine named him its Crusader of the Year.

As the son of wealthy real-estate developer Bernard Spitzer and Anne Goldhaber Spitzer, a literature professor, Eliot was brought up in a life of privilege. He graduated from Princeton in 1981 and Harvard Law in 1984; he married Silda Wall, a fellow law-school student, in 1987. His parents instilled a strong sense of social responsibility and, following some years practicing corporate law, Spitzer ran for attorney general of New York. Following a failed attempt in 1994, he tried again in 1998 and defeated his opponent by a narrow margin.

Spitzer's crusade against MMC began with an anonymous tip. On March 30, 2004, David D. Brown, IV, in charge of the attorney general's Investment Protection Bureau, opened an envelope containing a two-page, single-spaced typed letter addressed to New York Attorney General Eliot Spitzer and signed "Concerned." The letter stated that MMC, the world's largest insurance broker, had taken two payments: first, it received commissions from its customers, those businesses it represented seeking insurance; second, it took undisclosed payments from the insurance companies that wrote the policies. Brown thought the second payment looked like a kickback and faxed the letter to

Spitzer. To ascertain the truth of the allegations, Spitzer asked Brown to subpoena the company's representatives. The subpoena was sent out three days later, and within a week William L. Rosoff, general counsel for MMC, was in the attorney general's office. Rosoff downplayed the situation and stated that although the company did take a commission, there was no harm since the customers were still getting the best deal. Spitzer was not convinced, and in April, his team began interviewing other insurance brokers and insurance companies and subpoenaed their e-mails.

Spitzer's office hired law students to go through the boxes of e-mails, and by early summer the e-mails suggested the brokers were steering business to particular insurers, not to aid the client but to earn bonuses negotiated by the insurers. On September 9, Craig Winters, a second-year law student, found an e-mail from an MMC executive with specific details concerning a faked bid for the Greenville County, South Carolina, school district: The insurer, California Association of Non-Profits, was asked to bid deliberately high to guarantee that another company, Zurich, would get the bid. The false quotes were a pretext that the bid process had been competitive.

In the course of Spitzer's investigation, two executives from American International Group (AIG), an insurance carrier, testified how the fraud worked; they testified in exchange for a lighter sentence. When a given policy was up for renewal, MMC took the following steps to assure AIG would get the business: First, MMC provided AIG with a target premium and the policy terms for the quote. If AIG agreed to the quote, it got to keep the business, regardless of whether it could have quoted a lower premium. Second, MMC let other carriers know what the winning quote was

and asked them to submit backup quotes, or B quotes, that were higher, thus eliminating them from contention for the business.

With evidence of bid-rigging by MMC, in business since 1902, Spitzer and his lawyers met with the firm's lawyers on October 12. Rosoff denied any wrongdoing and failed to understand Spitzer's investigation. Rosoff went on to state that Spitzer did not understand how things worked in the insurance business.

Two days later, on October 14, Spitzer held a press conference. He announced that he had filed a civil complaint in the New York State Supreme Court against MMC, AIG, and other brokers for security fraud and bid-rigging. In addition, Spitzer cited the commissions, called contingent commissions or market service agreements, paid to MMC for steering volume business toward a specific insurer. In 2003, the contingent commissions amounted to $800 million, the equivalent of more than one-half of the company's $1.5 billion yearly income. Spitzer's office had prepared a thirty-one-page com-

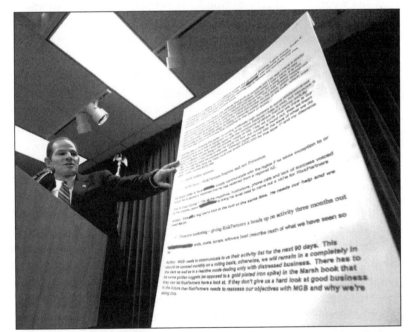

New York State attorney general Eliot Spitzer displays a copy of e-mails from the insurance brokerage firm Marsh & McLennan during a news conference in New York on October 14, 2004. Spitzer announced that he was suing the firm because of widespread corruption and fraud. (AP/Wide World Photos)

plaint and almost one hundred pages of exhibits, and he warned he would be treating the company as a criminal enterprise unless MMC's top leadership stepped down. Initially, MMC planned to fight, but, following the public reaction to Spitzer's charges, saw its stock lose 48 percent of its value in four trading days. After eleven days, MMC chief executive officer Jeffrey W. Greenberg stepped down. The next day the company announced it would stop accepting commissions from insurers.

Michael G. Cherkasky, whom Spitzer had once worked for, was installed as MMC's chief executive officer on October 25. Spitzer followed by dropping all criminal charges against the company. On January 31, 2005, MMC agreed to pay $850 million to settle the civil suit.

IMPACT

Following Spitzer's charges against MMC, the company discontinued its policy of charging commissions and fired a number of executives. Eight former MMC executives were charged with felonies for bid-rigging and price-fixing. Other companies that were also indicted by Spitzer scrambled to straighten out their business practices. Spitzer's investigation prompted similar actions by state insurance regulators and attorneys general (the insurance industry is not federally regulated). A review of business practices in the insurance industry was extended to the United Kingdom and other countries in Europe, broadening the investigation by Spitzer and his team.

In addition to inspiring a more ethical way of doing business in the insurance agency, the action against MMC confirmed the general public's view of Spitzer as their hero, fighting for the little guy against the corporate giants. His popularity led to his decision to run for governor of New York in 2006, and he won in a landslide. His first year as governor was filled with conflict and controversy, however, and in 2008, after for so long being the voice of morals and ethics in business, Spitzer was implicated in a Federal Bureau of Investigation prostitution sting. He resigned as governor on March 12.

—*Marcia B. Dinneen*

FURTHER READING

Coolidge, Carrie, and Neil Weinberg. "Pulling the Plug on Marsh." *Forbes*, November 15, 2004. Detailed coverage of Spitzer's lawsuit against Marsh & McLennan and the suit's impact on the insurance industry.

Elkind, Peter, and Joan Levinstein. "Spitzer's Crusade." *Fortune*, November 15, 2004. Focuses on Spitzer's legal work and how he carries out his campaigns against those businesses conducting unethical practices.

Fishman, Steve. "Inside Eliot's Army." *New York*, January 10, 2005. A step-by-step account of Spitzer's investigation of Marsh & McLennan.

MacDonald, Scott B., and Jane E. Hughes. *Separating Fools from Their Money: A History of American Financial Scandals*. New Brunswick, N.J.: Rutgers University Press, 2007. Detailed history of American financial scandals and their main players, including Eliot Spitzer, whose work is the focus of an entire chapter.

Masters, Brooke A. *Spoiling for a Fight: The Rise of Eliot Spitzer*. New York: Times Books, 2006. Discusses Spitzer's biggest career successes, focusing on his efforts to crack down on financial fraud.

Vickers, Marcia. "The Secret World of Marsh Mac." *BusinessWeek*, November 1, 2004. This cover story examines Spitzer's legal work against Marsh & McLennan and how the company's management and its attitude contributed to its problems.

SEE ALSO: Nov. 28, 1967: Investor Louis Wolfson Is Convicted of Selling Stock Illegally; May 2, 1984: E. F. Hutton Executives Plead Guilty to Fraud; Dec. 2, 2001: Enron Bankruptcy Reveals Massive Financial Fraud; June 25, 2002: Internal Corruption Forces Adelphia Communications to Declare Bankruptcy; Sept. 3, 2003: Mutual Fund Companies Are Implicated in Shady Trading Practices; Sept. 12, 2005: Westar Energy Executives Are Found Guilty of Looting Their Company; Early 2007: Subprime Mortgage Industry Begins to Collapse; Mar. 12, 2008: New York Governor Eliot Spitzer Resigns in Prostitution Scandal.

January 15, 2005

IQBAL RIZA RESIGNS FROM THE UNITED NATIONS IN OIL-FOR-FOOD SCANDAL

Iqbal Riza, chief of staff to U.N. secretary-general Kofi Annan, resigned his post after U.N. officials were investigated for suspected corruption, mismanagement, and conflict of interest in administering the U.N. Oil-for-Food Programme to help the people of Iraq. Riza had destroyed potentially relevant—and self-incriminating—documents during the investigation.

LOCALE: New York, New York
CATEGORIES: Corruption; international relations

KEY FIGURES

Iqbal Riza (b. 1934), Pakistani chief of staff to the U.N. secretary-general, 1997-2005
Kofi Annan (b. 1938), secretary-general of the United Nations, 1997-2007
Saddam Hussein (1937-2006), Iraqi dictator, 1979-2003
Paul Volcker (b. 1927), chairman of independent inquiry into the Oil-for-Food Programme

SUMMARY OF EVENT

The United Nations launched its Oil-for-Food Programme (OFFP) in 1995 to help the people of Iraq with food, medicine, and other basic necessities of life. As the program continued, questions began to arise about whether it was being managed properly. Allegations of corruption, mismanagement, and even bribery were made against U.N. officials administering the program. In April, 2004, the U.N. launched an independent investigation, and while the United Nations promised full cooperation, certain events led investigators to believe that the organization perhaps had a great deal to hide.

Over several months, Iqbal Riza, the chief of staff to U.N. secretary-general Kofi Annan, ordered the destruction of documents that could have contained information relevant to the investigation. Riza ultimately resigned from his position, which

only raised further suspicion about the destroyed documents and the United Nations as a whole.

The United Nations often acts as a peacekeeping force and attempts to use diplomacy and economics to solve problems in the international community. After Iraq invaded Kuwait in 1990, the United Nations placed economic sanctions on Iraq, which prevented the country from selling its oil on the global market. The sanctions were designed to ensure that the Iraqi government did not use its oil revenues for the development of weapons or to pursue military action against its neighbors. However, after the sanctions were in place for a time, U.N. investigators found that years of war, subsequent debt, and bad economic decisions made by the Iraqi government were leaving thousands of its citizens in need of basic amenities, such as food and medical supplies. In 1991, with the support of large nations such as the United States, the United Nations proposed a program that would allow the sale of oil on the global market in exchange for food and necessary supplies to the Iraqi dictator, President Saddam Hussein.

The program proposal indicated that the United Nations would monitor the oil revenues to ensure that all the profits were used either to get humanitarian goods to the Iraqi people or to pay war reparations that Iraq owed to Kuwait. Initially, the Iraqi government refused the proposal. Hussein and others believed the agreement took away too much sovereignty. Several proposals followed, which were all turned down by Hussein. Then, on April 14, 1995, the United Nations Security Council, at the urging of Secretary-General Boutros Boutros-Ghali, passed a resolution to create the OFFP, a program that increased the monetary value that was outlined in previously offered programs. Hussein agreed to the program, and Iraq began to export its oil again in late 1996.

The program ran for the next few years and funneled, according to U.N. officials but doubted by many others, billions of dollars in oil sales to the Iraqi people. It also paid Iraq's debts. Annan, U.N. secretary-general since 1997, was forced to suspend the United Nations' operation of the program on November 21, 2003, several months after the United States had invaded Iraq. The program was transferred to the Coalition Provisional Authority. Although the program ran for nearly a decade, it underwent a great deal of criticism from the United States and other countries, who suspected that the program's funds were not being used to alleviate the suffering of the Iraqi people but instead were taken by Iraqi leadership and U.N. officials. Some critics even cast suspicion on Annan, as they questioned what benefits he may have reaped from the program.

On April 21, 2004, Annan responded to these criticisms by launching an investigation into the management of the OFFP. Riza asked the former Federal Reserve chairman Paul Volcker to lead the inquiry into whether or not the program was as corrupt as some feared. Annan and Riza swore to cooperate in full with the investigation.

A Pakistani by nationality, Riza was born in India in 1934, before Pakistan was created. He began his work with the United Nations during the 1970's and had many important assignments, including work with U.N. peacekeeping efforts to stop the Rwandan genocides. He was appointed Annan's chief of staff in 1997. Riza was never directly involved in the management of the OFFP, but he had been criticized earlier for his involvement in Rwanda and in a case of nepotism involving his son, who received a job appointment with the United Nations.

Although the suspected corruption between the United Nations and Iraqi government was scandalous in itself, the alleged corruption involving Riza and the OFFP did not come to light until after the program was terminated. On April 24, soon after empaneling the investigative committee, Riza instructed other U.N. departments to hand over all relevant documentation to the panel. However, Riza would soon order the shredding of years of documentation from his own offices (specifically, the

years 1997-1999, when the OFFP was in full swing) over the course of several months.

Riza was the center of suspicion when investigators discovered that these crucial documents had been destroyed. Annan and other U.N. officials were suspect as well. The destruction of the documents led investigators to fear that Riza was hiding incriminating information, but Riza insisted that the destroyed documents were copies of materials that the commission had already seen and that his office assistant had requested that these materials be destroyed simply to make more room in the office. Investigators did not believe Riza, and he was reprimanded.

The Volcker investigation, because it was an informal body, had no legal recourse against any U.N. official, including Riza, for shredding the documents or for mismanagement of the program. On January 15, 2005, Riza stepped down as chief of staff after losing the confidence of his colleagues. However, Annan stood by Riza, even after his resignation, stating that he knew Riza had made a mistake but that he did not believe Riza deliberately interfered with the investigation. The Volcker investigation issued its final report on September 7.

IMPACT

Few doubt that the OFFP was started with the best of intentions: That is, delivering humanitarian aid to the suffering Iraqi citizens. However, Riza's order to destroy potentially critical program documents forever harmed the reputation of the program. The United Nations, too, lost some of the public's confidence. Many began to doubt that the agency could continue in its role as an effective peacekeeping and global governing body without the potential for corruption or scandal, or without independent oversight.

—*Jennifer L. Titanski*

FURTHER READING

Hsieh, Chang-Tai. *Did Iraq Cheat the United Nations? Underpricing, Bribes, and the Oil for Food Program.* Cambridge, Mass.: National Bureau of Economic Research, 2005. A statistical analysis of the OFFP that uses straight facts to explain how Iraqi leadership manipulated the United Nations' plans for the program.

Meyer, Jeffrey. *Good Intentions Corrupted: The Oil for Food Scandal and the Threat to the U.N.* New York: PublicAffairs, 2006. A detailed and critical look at the OFFP. Discusses how the program was supposed to help the Iraqi people, how it was corrupted by financial mismanagement and incompetence, and how its virtual demise harmed the United Nations itself.

Traub, James. *The Best Intentions: Kofi Annan and the U.N. in the Era of American World Power.* New York: Farrar, Straus and Giroux, 2006. Examines U.N. policies and programs, specifically the OFFP, instituted during Kofi Annan's first term as secretary-general. Details the U.S. response to these policies and programs.

Weiss, Thomas G., et al. *The United Nations and Changing World Politics.* 5th ed. Boulder, Colo.: Westview Press, 2007. A good overview of United Nations operations in the context of global politics and rapid changes in peacekeeping and humanitarian work around the world.

SEE ALSO: Mar. 3, 1986: Former U.N. Secretary-General Kurt Waldheim's Nazi Past Is Revealed; Mar. 2, 2003: U.S. National Security Agency Is Found to Have Spied on U.N. Officials; June 2, 2004: U.N. Report Reveals That Secretary-General Kofi Annan Dismissed Sexual Harassment Charges.

January 27, 2005
GERMAN SOCCER REFEREE ADMITS TO FIXING GAMES FOR MONEY

German soccer referee Robert Hoyzer admitted to fixing games by making unnecessary or questionable calls, affecting the outcome of many matches. He also admitted to fixing games during the prestigious German Cup. However, he cooperated with police, leading to the arrests of other referees as well as players. The scandal led German soccer officials to change how referees are promoted and led to heightened monitoring of gambling within the sport.

ALSO KNOWN AS: Bundesliga scandal of 2005
LOCALE: Germany
CATEGORIES: Corruption; gambling; organized crime and racketeering; sports

KEY FIGURES
Robert Hoyzer (b. 1979), German soccer referee
Ante Sapina (b. 1976), Croatian sports gambler

SUMMARY OF EVENT

Soccer is a beloved sport in Germany and a source of great national pride, passionately followed by millions of fans. It is the nation's only major professional sport and is played by almost all school children. Indeed, soccer is the world's most popular sport, so popular that the Germans were able to use their love for the sport to win the good graces of world opinion after the savagery of World War II.

Organized soccer in Germany dates back to 1900 with the creation of the German soccer federation, the Deutscher Fussball-Bund, or DFB. The German professional soccer league, called the Bundesliga and distinguished from the federation, was established under the authority of the DFB in 1962 as a sixteen-team West German professional league. It was the hope of organizers that the Bundesliga would enhance Germany's professional competitiveness, especially in forming World Cup teams. The league more than succeeded in that goal and

2000's

1055

was credited with helping form a West German team that became the runner-up in the 1966 World Cup.

The professionalization of German soccer also attracted an influx of money. In 1971, several players were caught in a bribery scandal. The affair, known as the Bundesliga scandal of 1971, was considered a national disgrace, which Germany hoped would never be repeated. Since 1974, the Bundesliga has been ranked into a first and second division comprising professional teams from different German cities. The soccer clubs compete against each other in the annual German Cup tournament.

The apex of international soccer is the World Cup tournament sponsored by the Fédération Internationale de Football Association (FIFA), a tournament of national soccer teams from around the globe. The FIFA World Cup is held in a different host country every four years. In 2004, Germans were looking forward to hosting the 2006 World Cup, but that excitement was complicated by an unexpected and scandalous turn of events.

Soccer referee Robert Hoyzer was questioned about his impartiality in refereeing a game in the first round of the 2004 German Cup. In the game between Paderborn and Hamburger SV on August 21, Hoyzer appeared to be favoring Paderborn with his calls. With Hamburg leading 2-0, he called several questionable penalties against Hamburg. Two calls resulted in goals for Paderborn and one expelled a Hamburg player for "insulting" behavior. Paderborn came back to win the game 4-2 and Hamburg was eliminated from the German Cup.

Four other German referees met with the DFB to discuss Hoyzer's calls during the August 21 game. Around the same time, a state-run betting company had detected unusual betting patterns in games Hoyzer officiated. One Berlin gambler had won big on an underdog team. The DFB president announced the finding of evidence that Hoyzer had rigged games, leading German prosecutors to launch their own investigation. They found that Hoyzer had fixed twenty-three soccer games from April to December, 2004.

Hoyzer's youth was filled with soccer. His father was a respected referee in the German soccer leagues, and the young Hoyzer had a brief career as a player. When that ended he became a referee for the DFB in 2001. Handsome, confident, and well-dressed, he also was a popular official. Over the next few years, he rose steadily in the ranks of German referees. By 2004, he had advanced to refereeing in the second division of the Bundesliga.

Hoyzer at first denied the allegations made against him by the DFB. He told the *Bild* newspaper that he had never bet on a game he refereed and that he was hurt that his refereeing colleagues could think him capable of such behavior. Faced with mounting adverse evidence, however, he confessed on January 27, 2005, that he was involved with a Croatian betting syndicate based in Berlin. He admitted to fixing seven games for $108,350. He was arrested in February and suspended from the league.

On April 29, the DFB banned Hoyzer from the sport for life. Hoyzer also began cooperating with police in establishing the guilt of other referees. He implicated referee Dominik Marks and player Steffen Karl. On March 11, Karl admitted bribing other players and was arrested. Marks was accused of earning about thirty-five thousand euros by manipulating games he was refereeing.

Hoyzer also told police about his connections to the major betting syndicate in Berlin. He said he had met Ante Sapina at Berlin's Café King sports bar, owned by Ante's brother, Milan Sapina. Ante was a shrewd gambler on German soccer, but after meeting Hoyzer, he saw an opportunity to improve his odds. He paid Hoyzer sixty-seven thousand euros and gave him a new television set to rig the games he refereed. In one game in October, Hoyzer manipulated a 1-0 victory by penalizing one team and expelling one of its players. The Sapina brothers, along with several soccer players, were arrested.

The trial of Hoyzer, the Sapina brothers, Marks, and Karl began in October. Hoyzer was charged with eleven counts of fraud. Ante Sapina was charged with forty-two counts. Given that Hoyzer had been cooperating with law enforcement in the investigation, his testimony was not surprising. He admitted to betting on soccer on a small scale until he met Ante, whom, he said, corrupted him. Ante also admitted guilt.

Investigators found that the Sapina brothers made more than two million euros by betting on rigged games. The testimonies of Hoyzer and Sapina differed at points, with the trial revealing that the Sapina brothers cleverly enticed Hoyzer into cheating with a seductive array of bribes. Prosecutors recommended that Hoyzer receive only a two-year suspended sentence, given his confession and his cooperation with their investigation. The judge in the case rejected their recommendation. In a major surprise, on November 21, the judge sentenced Hoyzer to twenty-nine months in prison. Hoyzer's crimes were well-considered, the judge explained, and Hoyzer had violated his duty of neutrality.

Ante Sapina was convicted of fraud and sentenced to thirty-five months in prison. His brothers were given suspended sentences of sixteen and twelve months, respectively. Marks was given an eighteen-month suspended sentence. The sentences of Hoyzer and the other defendants were affirmed on appeal by Germany's highest court. The chief appellate judge condemned the defendants for undermining confidence in Germany's national sport. After the trial and sentencing, German authorities announced that they would continue to investigate other players and referees. The league also ordered that most of the rigged games officiated by Hoyzer and the other implicated referees be replayed.

IMPACT

The Hoyzer scandal impacted German soccer in several ways. First, referees felt their authority and credibility had been undermined. The press began reporting that referees were making calls under a cloud of suspicion, which led to numerous refereeing mistakes. The DFB implemented new rules for referees. They are now required to serve a three-year probationary period in the lower leagues before being eligible for promotion to the higher leagues. The DFB also began using an observer to monitor all calls in games of the German Cup.

Second, the scandal impacted the betting industry in Germany. Betting is a huge business in German soccer, as it is in almost all professional sports. It is estimated that in 2004, betting on soccer amounted to 1.2 billion euros. The Hoyzer scandal

made it especially clear that corruption is a part of betting, especially when large amounts of money come into play. Although gambling is unlikely to be eliminated from professional sports, the scandal nevertheless led the FIFA and DFB to initiate stricter controls against gambling on soccer. FIFA decided to monitor betting at all World Cup tournaments, beginning with the 2006 finals in Germany.

Third, the Hoyzer scandal threatened the atmosphere of the FIFA World Cup tournament scheduled to be played in Germany in the summer of 2006. Fortunately for German soccer, its legendary former soccer star, Franz Beckenbauer, had assumed the role of president of the World Cup organizing committee. Beckenbauer was the epitome of professional integrity and success in competitive soccer. With the conclusion of the Hoyzer prosecution and Beckenbauer's adroit management, the 2006 World Cup tournament was a great success.

—*Howard Bromberg*

FURTHER READING

Brenner, Reuven, Gabrielle A. Brenner, and Aaron Brown. *A World of Chance: Betting on Religion, Games, Wall Street*. New York: Cambridge University Press, 2008. In this wide-ranging academic study of betting in human society, the authors contend that with widespread gambling in sports, the corruption of referees such as Hoyzer becomes inevitable.

Goldblatt, David. *The Ball Is Round: A Global History of Soccer*. New York: Riverhead Books, 2008. Comprehensive and readable history of soccer from its earliest days in the context of cultural and international developments. Impressive scope of research.

Hunt, Chris, ed. *The Complete Book of Soccer*. Buffalo, N.Y.: Firefly Books, 2006. A history of soccer that features biographies of great players and more than five hundred photographs. The Hoyzer scandal figures prominently in the time line of soccer scandals.

Trecker, Jamie. *Love and Blood: At the World Cup with the Footballers, Fans, and Freaks*. Orlando, Fla.: Harcourt, 2007. An account of fan passion at the 2006 World Cup in Germany. Argues that

2000's

the impassioned politics of fandom masked the significance of the Hoyzer scandal.

SEE ALSO: Apr. 2, 1915: Players Fix Liverpool-Manchester United Soccer Match; July 1, 1994:

Soccer Star Diego Maradona Is Expelled from World Cup; May 4, 2006: Media Uncover Match-Fixing in Italian Soccer; July 29, 2008: NBA Referee Tim Donaghy Is Sentenced to Prison for Betting on Games.

March 17, 2005
FORMER BASEBALL STAR MARK McGWIRE EVADES CONGRESSIONAL QUESTIONS ON STEROID USE

After being identified as a steroid user by former teammate José Canseco, Mark McGwire was asked to testify at a U.S. House of Representatives hearing on steroid use in Major League Baseball. At the hearing, McGwire refused to answer questions about his own history with performance-enhancing drugs or their use by baseball players in general.

LOCALE: Washington, D.C.
CATEGORIES: Drugs; government; medicine and health care; sports

KEY FIGURES
Mark McGwire (b. 1963), Major League Baseball player
José Canseco (b. 1964), Major League Baseball player
George J. Mitchell (b. 1933), former U.S. senator from Maine, 1980-1995, and special counsel to the commissioner of Major League Baseball
Bud Selig (b. 1934), commissioner of Major League Baseball, 1992-
Sammy Sosa (b. 1968), Major League Baseball player

SUMMARY OF EVENT
On March 17, 2005, Mark McGwire appeared before the Government Reform Committee of the U.S. House of Representatives to testify on steroid use in Major League Baseball (MLB). Also present at the hearing were MLB commissioner Bud Selig, representatives from the Major League Baseball Players Association (MLBPA), and players José

Canseco, Rafael Palmeiro, Curt Schilling, and Sammy Sosa. Player Frank Thomas appeared through video conferencing. Also testifying were medical experts and the families of young amateur baseball players who had suffered physically and emotionally from steroid use.

McGwire's testimony became the lasting symbol of the hearings, which were broadcast on national television. After choking up while reading a written statement expressing his regret that younger players had suffered from steroid abuse, McGwire refused to answer questions asked by the committee. McGwire was asked about his own use of performance-enhancing drugs, the integrity of the game of baseball, and whether steroid use constituted cheating, among other topics. McGwire's responses rarely went beyond variations of his statement "I'm not here to discuss the past." Although he did say that steroids were bad and that players should not use them, he would not answer the question of how he knew that to be true. In the end, McGwire left the hearings disgraced and ridiculed for his failure to make pertinent or revealing statements about steroid use in baseball.

McGwire was not the only casualty of the hearings. Sosa, a native of the Dominican Republic, was criticized for his use of a translator, which many journalists claimed was a ruse by the veteran player. Palmeiro testified that he had never used steroids, but within six months of the hearings, he failed a drug test and was forced to retire. Neither player could shake the taint of having used performance-enhancing drugs.

Canseco and Schilling were also disparaged for their testimony as they recanted previous statements. Canseco renounced the prosteroid rhetoric he had used in previous interviews and writings. Schilling, a vocal critic of steroid use, said that he did not know much about the steroid problem in baseball, despite having earlier estimated that a large number of players were users. Officials for both MLB and MLBPA also had a poor showing at the hearings. Members of Congress harshly condemned the weak drug-testing program that MLB and the player's union had put in place two weeks before the hearings.

McGwire had been one of the most popular Major League Baseball players of the late 1980's and 1990's. In 1987, he set the rookie record for most home runs in a season with 49 and won the American League Rookie of the Year Award. With Oakland A's teammate Canseco, McGwire was part of one of the most productive offensive tandems of the era. Playing for Oakland until 1997 and then with the St. Louis Cardinals until his retirement in 2001, McGwire was the most prolific home-run hitter in baseball from his debut in 1986 to 2001. During those sixteen seasons, only eleven of which he played more than one hundred games, he hit 583 home runs. As spectators became infatuated with home-run hitting during the 1990's, McGwire quickly became a fan favorite. His popularity only increased in 1998, when he and Chicago Cubs slugger Sosa pursued the single-season home-run record. With a total of 70 home runs in the 1998 season, McGwire eclipsed the previous record of 61, set in 1961 by Roger Maris. The excitement surrounding the home-run race between McGwire and Sosa helped baseball recover from the damage done to its popularity by the strike of 1994-1995.

Although McGwire had always been a prodigious home-run hitter, the enormous totals he and others produced during the 1990's led to public suspicion that they were using performance-enhancing drugs, particularly anabolic steroids. As early as 1988, members of the press alleged that Canseco was a steroid user, and he reportedly bragged of that use around his teammates and coaches. Although Canseco later claimed that he and McGwire used steroids together during their time in Oakland, McGwire was not generally suspected by the public of using the drug. During 1998's home-run race, a journalist revealed that McGwire's locker contained a bottle of androstenedione (andro), a legal, muscle-building supplement. When McGwire and Sosa later revealed that they also used creatine, another legal supplement, many fans and sportswriters wondered if the two players had used illegal substances as

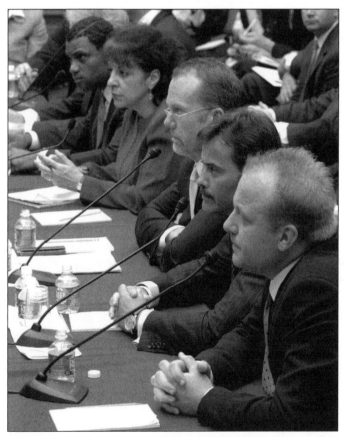

Former baseball star Mark McGwire (center, with glasses), and other players at a House committee session investigating steroid use in Major League Baseball. From left is Sammy Sosa and his translator, McGwire, Rafael Palmeiro, and Curt Schilling. (AP/ Wide World Photos)

2000's

1059

THE MITCHELL REPORT

The Mitchell Report on the use of steroids and other performance-enhancing drugs in professional baseball in the United States was issued on December 13, 2007. The report included three final recommendations on the matter to Major League Baseball.

To prevent the illegal use of performance enhancing substances in Major League Baseball, I [Special Counsel George J. Mitchell] make a series of recommendations. Some can be implemented by the Commissioner unilaterally; some are subject to collective bargaining and therefore will require the agreement of the Players Association.

- First, the Commissioner's Office should place a higher priority on the aggressive investigation of non-testing (so-called "non-analytic") evidence of possession or use, enhance its cooperation with law enforcement authorities, and make other improvements designed to keep performance enhancing substances out of major league clubhouses.

- Second, Major League Baseball needs a compelling and greatly enhanced educational program that focuses on real-life stories as well as on all the risks involved in the use of performance enhancing substances. These include health risks, career risks, and the many dangers that can result from associating with drug dealers. This program should also give significant attention to the status that major league players enjoy as role models and how their use affects the decisions of young people throughout the country. I have been warned by a number of former players that some players will use performance enhancing substances no matter what they are told. They may be right. But I also heard from other former players who wrestled long and hard with the decision to use performance enhancing substances. An education program that effectively communicates the messages described above might not deter all players from use, but it surely will deter some.

- Third, although it is clear that even the best drug testing program is, by itself, not sufficient, drug testing remains an important part of a comprehensive approach to combating the illegal use of performance enhancing substances. The Commissioner does not have the authority to act unilaterally on drug testing, however; the agreement of the Players Association is required. The current joint drug program is part of the Basic Agreement that was agreed to in 2006 and will remain in effect until 2011. Any changes to the program therefore must be negotiated with and agreed to by the Players Association. Neither party is obligated to agree to reopen the Basic Agreement to address the program, even though that is what happened in 2005. There is no way for me to know whether that will happen again.

well. Although the story was widely reported at first, it soon lost momentum as many fans accepted that andro and creatine were allowed by MLB and easily purchased over the counter.

In 2005, McGwire was in the center of the steroid maelstrom that prompted the congressional hearings. Early that year, Canseco published his tell-all memoir, *Juiced: Wild Times, Rampant 'Roids, Smash Hits, and How Baseball Got Big.* In the book, he named numerous steroid-using baseball players, including McGwire. Despite the extraordinary and damaging claims Canseco made, MLB declined to investigate the issue. The press, however, delved deeper into Canseco's allegations and found evidence to support some of his claims. In response to the press investigations, the Government Reform Committee announced it would hold hearings on steroid use in baseball.

IMPACT

McGwire's refusal to "discuss the past" at the congressional hearing destroyed his credibility with baseball fans. Only seven years earlier, he had been one of baseball's most beloved stars. In 2007, when he became eligible for election to the Hall of Fame, many voters and other sportswriters identified suspected steroid use and his testimony at the hearing as reasons they would not support his candidacy. Although McGwire had played at a level that justified his induction in the Hall of Fame, he only received support from 23.5 percent of voters, far short of the 75 percent necessary for inclusion.

McGwire became the only eligible player with more than 500 home runs to not be elected to the Hall of Fame.

The attention the hearings brought to steroid use in baseball forced MLB to become more proactive in preventing the use of performance-enhancing drugs. Although drug testing began three years prior to the hearings, the House Government Reform Committee criticized the lenient penalties that were in place, and at the end of the season, MLB toughened its steroid policy. In a plan proposed shortly before the hearings, players who failed tests would be suspended ten games for the first failure, and a fifth failed test was required before a lifetime suspension was even a possibility. Under the policy instituted in November, 2005, a first-time offender received a fifty-game suspension and a third failed test resulted in a mandatory lifetime ban from baseball. However, many continued to criticize MLB for having a drug policy that is lax when compared to that of the International Olympic Committee and other organizations.

On December 13, 2007, former U.S. senator George J. Mitchell, acting as special counsel to the commissioner of baseball, issued his report on MLB steroid use, naming McGwire and nearly ninety other players (those active in 2007 as well as former players) as suspected steroid users. In the wake of the Mitchell Report, Major League Baseball commissioner Selig announced his intention once again to strengthen MLB's testing program.

—*Jacob F. Lee*

FURTHER READING

Bryant, Howard. *Juicing the Game: Drugs, Power, and the Fight for the Soul of Major League Baseball.* New York: Viking Press, 2005. Study of the use of steroids in Major League Baseball from the 1980's through 2005. McGwire is featured prominently both for his suspected use of performance-enhancing drugs and his testimony before the House committee.

Canseco, José. *Juiced: Wild Times, Rampant 'Roids, Smash Hits, and How Baseball Got Big.* New York: Regan Books, 2005. Canseco's tell-all memoir, which instigated the 2005 hearings on steroid use in MLB.

_____. *Vindicated: Big Names, Big Liars, and the Battle to Save Baseball.* New York: Simon Spotlight Entertainment, 2008. Canseco's follow-up to the steroids scandal.

Carroll, Will, with William L. Carroll. *The Juice: The Real Story of Baseball's Drug Problems.* Chicago: Ivan R. Dee, 2005. Analyzes from a medical viewpoint a wide range of performance-enhancing drugs and their effect on players.

Fainaru-Wada, Mark, and Lance Williams. *Game of Shadows: Barry Bonds, BALCO, and the Steroids Scandal That Rocked Professional Sports.* New York: Gotham Books, 2006. Provides historical context for the problem of steroid use in professional sports, particularly baseball.

Mitchell, George. *Report to the Commissioner of Baseball of an Independent Investigation into the Illegal Use of Steroids and Other Performance Enhancing Substances by Players in Major League Baseball.* New York: Office of the Commissioner of Baseball, 2007. The official report to the MLB commissioner on the steroids era in professional baseball.

SEE ALSO: Nov. 29, 1979, and Jan. 31, 1983: Baseball Commissioner Suspends Mickey Mantle and Willie Mays for Casino Ties; Feb. 28, 1986: Baseball Commissioner Peter Ueberroth Suspends Players for Cocaine Use; Aug. 24, 1989: Pete Rose Is Banned from Baseball for Betting on Games; July 1, 1994: Soccer Star Diego Maradona Is Expelled from World Cup; Sept. 26, 2000: Gymnast Andreea Răducan Loses Her Olympic Gold Medal Because of Drugs; July 26, 2006: Tour de France Is Hit with a Doping Scandal; Oct. 5, 2007: Olympic Champion Marion Jones Admits Steroid Use.

2000's

June 22, 2005

U.S. AIR FORCE INVESTIGATES RELIGIOUS INTOLERANCE AT ITS ACADEMY

Claims that cadets and staff at the U.S. Air Force Academy were pushing cadets to accept evangelical Christianity prompted an official inquiry into the allegations. Investigators concluded that the academy faced religious insensitivity, but not discrimination. These conclusions were controversial, and debate continues over religious diversity in the military.

LOCALE: Colorado Springs, Colorado
CATEGORIES: Military; religion; education; social issues and reform; civil rights and liberties

KEY FIGURES

Michael L. Weinstein (b. 1955), U.S. Air Force Academy graduate, who notified media of religious intolerance at the academy
John A. Weida (b. 1956), U.S. Air Force brigadier general, commandant of cadets at the Air Force Academy, 2003-2005
Melinda Morton (b. 1957), U.S. Air Force captain, chaplain at the Air Force Academy
John W. Rosa (b. 1951), U.S. Air Force lieutenant general, superintendent of the Air Force Academy, 2003-2005
Roger Brady (fl. early twenty-first century), U.S. Air Force lieutenant general, who chaired an investigative panel
Kristen Leslie (fl. early twenty-first century), Yale University professor, who led an independent investigation at the academy

SUMMARY OF EVENT

A report released by a U.S. Air Force panel on June 22, 2005, concluded that even though religious insensitivity existed at the academy, discrimination based on religion did not. The Brady Report, named for Lieutenant General Roger Brady, who chaired the panel, covered the period from April, 2003, through early June, 2005, and was based on about

three hundred interviews with staff and cadets. The report, the first official recognition of religious problems at the academy, had nine findings and nine recommendations, but the recommendations were not significant and the report met with mixed reactions.

The religious atmosphere at the academy had long caused unease among some cadets, but the situation deteriorated after Brigadier General John A. Weida was appointed commandant of cadets on April 11, 2003. Weida engaged in a number of acts that upset non-Christian cadets by mixing his personal beliefs with his official duties as commandant. In one case, he told cadets that the Lord was in control, urged cadets to discuss their Christian faith with others, and introduced a "J for Jesus" hand signal to which cadets had to reply.

In December, three hundred academy staff and cadets signed a large advertisement published in the academy's newspaper, urging cadets to contact them to "discuss Jesus." The head football coach, Fisher DeBerry, referred to the football team as Team Jesus Christ. In February, 2004, after the release of Mel Gibson's controversial film *The Passion of the Christ*, zealous cadets papered the academy cafeteria with flyers that indicated the film was officially sponsored by the academy, flashed images from the film during meals, hung posters in many locations, and heavily promoted the film through e-mails.

Michael L. Weinstein, a 1977 honor graduate of the academy, heard about many discriminatory incidents, including anti-Semitic comments, at the academy and began assembling a dossier. Weinstein, who also is an attorney, a former assistant general counsel in the executive office of U.S. president Ronald Reagan, sent the dossier directly to Lieutenant General John W. Rosa, Jr., who had been appointed superintendent of the academy in July, 2003.

On Thursday, July 29, Weinstein, who is also

Jewish and the father of two cadets then at the academy, drove from his home in Albuquerque, New Mexico, to attend the academy's leadership conference, a special event to update graduates on the academy's accomplishments. At the conference he heard about more uncomfortable incidents, including proselytizing attempts, and about anti-Semitic incidents that included comments about Jews being accused of killing Jesus. He then met Rosa and received a lukewarm response to his concerns. He soon realized that Rosa likely did not receive the dossier.

In late December, an academy Protestant chaplain, Captain Melinda Morton, also alarmed over the fervent emphasis on proselytizing, invited Yale University professor Kristen Leslie to the academy to lead a team evaluating the academy's pastoral-care efforts. The team found, in part, that cadets were being told that faith in Jesus would get them through academy training and that cadets who chose not to attend church services were humiliated as heathens. The team was especially alarmed at the proselytizing of young cadets during vulnerable, severely stressful times, and criticized as divisive the academy's "overarching evangelical emphasis."

In late July, 2004, the team's report, called the Yale Report, was delivered to the academy. The academy responded by establishing the RSVP (Respecting the Spiritual Values of All People) project, with the goal of promoting religious diversity at the academy. However, RSVP was strongly opposed by evangelicals among the staff, and the project made little progress.

In September, Weinstein and Steve Aguilar released *The Religious Climate at the United States Air Force Academy*, which documented practices that were in clear violation of the First Amendment to the U.S. Constitution, which guarantees freedom of religion. Weinstein concluded that there was a major power struggle within the academy between fundamentalist evangelicals and other religious persons. He saw no internal resolution in sight, and decided to go public with his concerns.

On November 18, Pam Zubeck, chief military-affairs reporter for the *Colorado Springs Gazette*, published her first story on the controversy. Her se-

ries was picked up by national media. After months of little action, things began to move rapidly. In March, 2005, Weinstein first heard about Chaplain Morton's efforts and about the Yale Report, which had been kept secret. Zubeck found the report, wrote about it, and found herself on television, being interviewed on *60 Minutes II* and CNN. Other major national media began to cover the unfolding scandal. In the meantime, on April 28, Americans United for Separation of Church and State (AUSCS) released a report alleging systematic and pervasive religious bias and intolerance at the highest levels at the academy.

A few days after the release of the AUSCS report, the Air Force announced the formation of an investigative task force. The panel was led by Lieutenant General Brady, a born-again Christian. On June 3, Superintendent Rosa publicly acknowledged there were problems with religious diversity at the academy and said that they were so embedded that it would take years to correct. The Brady Report was released on June 22. Weida and DeBerry apologized for their actions and the Air Force chief of staff warned commanders against promoting their personal religious beliefs. *The New York Times*, in an editorial, criticized the report, arguing that its weak conclusions strained credibility.

IMPACT

The House Armed Services Committee looked into the Brady Report's findings and held a hearing on June 28, but the hearing degenerated into political debate. On July 12, the Air Force deputy chief of chaplains, Major General Cecil Richardson, said that chaplains would not proselytize but that a private chaplains'-association document gave them the right to evangelize the unchurched, ostensibly Jews and other non-Christians. On October 6, Weinstein filed a legal complaint for violations of constitutional rights against the Air Force. The Air Force withdrew the chaplains' document, but neither Weinstein nor the evangelicals were satisfied.

In early 2006, Weinstein took action and founded the Military Religious Freedom Foundation (MRFF). The foundation has received thousands of complaints of religious discrimination from military personnel, and in September, 2007, broadening its scope, Weinstein filed a lawsuit against the secretary of defense for discrimination against non-Christians in the U.S. military.

—*Abraham D. Lavender*

FURTHER READING

Loveland, Anne C. *American Evangelicals and the U.S. Military, 1942-1993*. Baton Rouge: Louisiana State University, 1996. Examines the changing demographics of the military and traces the history, strategies, and goals of American evangelicalism's tremendous success in increasing its influence on the military since World War II.

United States Congress. House of Representatives. *The Religious Climate at the U.S. Air Force Academy: Hearing Before the Military Personnel Subcommittee of the Committee on Armed Services*. Washington, D.C.: Government Printing Office, 2005. Report of the June 28, 2005, congressional hearing investigating the Air Force Academy scandal.

Weinstein, Michael L., and Davin Seay. *With God on Our Side: One Man's War Against an Evangelical Coup in America's Military*. New York: St. Martin's Griffin, 2008. The story of Weinstein's battle with evangelical fundamentalists at the Air Force Academy and his work to keep the military secular and free of religious indoctrination and intimidation. Originally published in 2006.

Welch, Bobby. *You the Warrior Leader: Applying Military Strategy for Victorious Spiritual Warfare*. Nashville, Tenn.: Broadman and Holman, 2004. The president of the Southern Baptist Convention argues in favor of the concept of evangelical militarism as the basis of U.S. military policy.

Winn, Patrick. "Religion at Issue." *Air Force Times*, August 5, 2008. A brief but telling report on the state of religion and religious practice at the Air Force Academy in the wake of the scandal and Weinstein's work in changing the academy's policies.

SEE ALSO: Apr. 4, 1976: West Point Cadets Are Caught Cheating on Exams; June 26, 1992: U.S. Navy Secretary Resigns in the Wake of Tailhook Sexual Assault Scandal; Apr. 28, 1994: U.S. Naval Academy Expels Midshipmen for Cheating; May 20, 1997: Air Force Prosecution of Female Officer for Adultery Reveals Double Standard; Jan. 2, 2003: E-mail Message Prompts Inquiry into Air Force Academy Sexual Assaults; Feb. 18, 2007: *Washington Post* Exposes Decline of Walter Reed Army Hospital.

July 1, 2005
FEDERAL AGENTS RAID CONGRESSMAN RANDALL CUNNINGHAM'S HOME

A raid by federal agents of the home of U.S. representative Randall Cunningham in an exclusive suburb north of San Diego, California, led to Cunningham's resignation from Congress and to his criminal conviction for bribery, mail and wire fraud, and income tax evasion. He pleaded guilty to accepting bribes amounting to at least $2.4 million from several defense contractors. He was sent to prison for eight years and four months, the longest prison sentence ever for a former member of Congress.

LOCALE: Rancho Santa Fe, California

CATEGORIES: Corruption; government; law and the courts; business

KEY FIGURES

Randall Cunningham (b. 1941), U.S. representative from California, 1991-2005
Brent Wilkes (b. 1954), defense contractor
Mitchell Wade (b. 1963), defense contractor
Thomas Kontogiannis (b. 1949), financier
Kyle Dustin Foggo (b. 1954), CIA official

SUMMARY OF EVENT

Political corruption in pursuit of economic gain is nothing new in U.S. politics, but few have carried it to the lengths of U.S. representative Randall Cunningham of California. Duke, as he was known to admirers and critics, received more than two million dollars in bribes from persons hoping to receive lucrative government contracts, the largest bribery amount in congressional history. The money allowed him and his wife to acquire a home in exclusive Rancho Santa Fe in northern San Diego County, California, as well as fine artworks, luxury automobiles, and a yacht in Washington, D.C., along the Potomac River for Cunningham's personal use.

Born in Los Angeles and raised in Fresno, California, and Shelbina, Missouri, Cunningham was one of the authentic aviation heroes of the Vietnam War, credited with shooting down five enemy planes. He thus achieved recognition as the only U.S. Navy ace pilot of the war. He was awarded the Navy Cross, two Silver Stars, fifteen Air Medals, and the Purple Heart. In 1972, he became an instructor with the Navy's fabled top-gun air-combat school near San Diego, and he later claimed that his experiences in Vietnam were the basis for the 1986 film *Top Gun*, which starred Tom Cruise. After retiring from the Navy in 1987, Cunningham became a Cable News Network commentator.

Narrowly elected to the U.S. Congress in 1990 from a previously Democratic district, Cunningham immediately received adulation and recognition because of his heroic exploits in Vietnam. He subsequently was reelected to Congress by increasing majorities through the 2004 election. In Congress, given his military background and heroic reputation, his initial national prominence came from his participation in the debates leading to the Gulf War. After the Republicans achieved majority status in the 1994 election, Cunningham chaired the House Intelligence Subcommittee on Human Intelligence Analysis and Counterintelligence.

As a member of the Appropriations Education Subcommittee, Cunningham was able to increase federal funds to public schools in San Diego. His voting record was predictably conservative, attacking President Bill Clinton for a lack of patriotism and for appointing judges who were supposedly soft on crime. Cunningham favored the death penalty for major drug dealers, opposed the move to allow gays and lesbians to serve openly in the military, and accused his Democratic opponents of being socialists. Interestingly, he received the designation "conservation hero" from the Audubon Society for his role in banning shark finning, or the removal of shark fins, and dumping the often still-living sharks back into the sea.

Cunningham began to use the power of his congressional position for his own benefit beginning during the mid-1990's, and initially on a fairly small scale. Brent Wilkes, head of ADCS, Inc., a San Diego defense firm, provided Cunningham with limousine service, free meals, the use of a fourteen-foot motorboat, and occasional payments of $500. In turn, the Congress member earmarked millions of dollars for Wilkes's businesses, including a $20 million document-digitization system. Other defense contractors also benefited from Cunningham's endeavors, particularly after the terrorist attacks of September 11, 2001.

Mitchell Wade was one of those defense contractors. He provided Cunningham with private jets for holidays and shopping trips, a condominium, antiques, and a Rolls Royce. Cunningham also had the use of a yacht on Washington, D.C.'s Potomac River, where he lived when Congress was in session, paying nothing and reportedly entertaining prostitutes. Because of his influence, which included the bullying of Pentagon officials, Wade's company, MZM, was awarded numerous government contracts, including a noncompetitive $250 million five-year contract in 2002. Wilkes provided Cunningham with $600 prostitutes on a trip to Hawaii.

By 2003, Cunningham's material appetites had increased significantly. Wade purchased Cunningham's residence in Del Mar Heights for $1.675 million, well over its market value, allowing the Congress member to purchase a $2.55 million, 8,000-square-foot home in Rancho Santa Fe, a luxury community twenty-five miles north of San

CUNNINGHAM'S BRIBE MENU

The U.S. government outlined its case against Representative Duke Cunningham in a March 3, 2006, sentencing memorandum to the District Court in San Diego, California. In the following excerpt, prosecutors explain how Cunningham's infamous "bribe menu" worked.

The naked avarice that animated Cunningham's corruption is starkly framed in one of Cunningham's Congressional note cards. Under the very seal of the United States Congress, Cunningham placed this nation's governance up for sale to a defense contractor—detailing the amount of bribes necessary to obtain varying levels of defense appropriations.

In this "bribe menu," the left column represented the millions in government contracts that could be "ordered" from Cunningham. The right column was the amount of the bribes that the Congressman was demanding in exchange for the contracts. For example, Cunningham's menu offered $16 million to Coconspirator No. 2 in government contracts in exchange for the contractor giving up his title to a boat ("BT") for which Coconspirator No. 2 had initially paid $140,000 ("140"). The next four rows indicate that an additional million dollars in funding was "for sale" in exchange for every additional $50,000 that Coconspirator No. 2 was willing to pay Cunningham. Once Coconspirator No. 2 had paid Cunningham $340,000 in bribes, the rates dropped; and, as the final five rows reflect, Cunningham would charge only $25,000 for each additional million dollars that was awarded in additional government contracts.

firm, MZM, received $163 million in federal contracts (not necessarily all from his dealings with Cunningham). On July 1, federal agents raided Cunningham's home in Rancho Santa Fe, MZM offices in Washington, D.C., and the forty-two-foot Potomac yacht on which Cunningham had been living for the previous year.

A few days before the raids, Cunningham stated that he had used poor judgment when he sold his Del Mar Heights home to Wade, that he had paid $13,000 for docking fees and other expenses connected to his use of Wade's yacht, and that he had never provided any illegal aid to the defense contractor. It also was reported that two weeks before the raids, officials at MZM shredded numerous documents.

IMPACT

On July 14, several days after the raid on his home, Cunningham announced that he would not run for reelection and that he and his wife would sell their Rancho Santa Fe home and donate the profits to charity. In a plea bargain agreement on November 27, Cunningham resigned his seat in Congress and pleaded guilty to accepting bribes amounting to at least $2.4 million from several defense contractors, as well as to mail and wire fraud and income tax evasion. As part of his guilty plea, Cunningham agreed to forfeit $1.8 million in antiques and other items as well as his $2.5 million home. Included as evidence was Cunningham's "bribe menu," in which he demanded $50,000 for each $1 million in value for each contract he steered to a defense contractor. In a tearful statement, Cunningham admitted that he broke the law and that he had disgraced his office, ruined his reputation, and disgraced his family and friends.

Several months later, on March 2, 2006, Cunningham was sentenced to eight years and four

Diego. Several months later, Wade sold the Del Mar Heights property for $975,000, taking a $700,000 loss on what he paid to Cunningham, in essence a bribe for the Congress member. The mortgage on the new home was paid off by defense contractors in the amount of $1.25 million. It is estimated that the various bribes to Cunningham totaled approximately $3 million, making him, according to one source, the most corrupt Congressman in U.S. history, measured in monetary terms.

In early 2005, a federal grand jury, in conjunction with the Federal Bureau of Investigation, the Defense Criminal Investigative Service, and the U.S. Internal Revenue Service, began investigating Cunningham's various financial dealings with Wade. According to the federal government's Defense Information Systems Agency, Wade's months in prison. Sixty-four years old and suffering from prostate problems, he was spared the ten-year term requested by prosecutors, in part because of his military record. Nevertheless, the sentence was one of the longest ever meted out to a former Congressman. After medical examinations, Cunningham was incarcerated in the minimum-security federal prison in Tucson, Arizona. Reporters from the *San Diego Union-Tribune* and Copley News Service shared a 2006 Pulitzer Prize for their coverage of the Cunningham scandal.

Wade, named as the principal coconspirator, pleaded guilty to numerous charges, including giving Cunningham $1 million in bribes. Wade agreed to testify against Wilkes, who was convicted of bribery in November, 2007, and sentenced to twelve years in prison. In addition to Wade and Wilkes, Long Island businessman Thomas Kontogiannis also was investigated for his role in arranging a second mortgage for Cunningham on the home in Rancho Santa Fe. Kontogiannis was sentenced to eight years in prison in 2008 for money-laundering bribes given to Cunningham. Kyle Dustin Foggo, number-three official with the U.S. Central Intelligence Agency, was indicted because of his relations with Wilkes.

Other scandals surfaced at the time as well. House Majority Leader Tom DeLay of Texas resigned as a result of his connection with the Jack Abramoff bribery affair, and California Congressman Jerry Lewis, one-time head of the House Appropriations Committee, also was investigated for his connections to Cunningham. However, Cunningham's criminal acts were more egregious and blatant.

—*Eugene Larson*

FURTHER READING

Bachrach, Judy. "Washington Babylon." *Vanity Fair*, August, 2006. Provides considerable background about Wilkes, Wade, and Foggo and their involvement in the Cunningham affair.

Cunningham, Randy, and Jeffrey L. Ethell. *Fox Two: The Story of America's First Ace in Vietnam.* 1984. New ed. New York: Warner Books, 1989. Cunningham's own dramatic account of his air-combat exploits in Vietnam, written with the assistance of a noted author who specializes in writing about military air power.

Hettena, Seth. *Feasting on the Spoils: The Life and Times of Randy "Duke" Cunningham, History's Most Corrupt Congressman.* New York: St. Martin's Press, 2007. A comprehensive journalistic exposé of Cunningham's misdeeds, including those of the other major characters in the scandal.

Stern, Marcus, Jerry Kammer, Dean Calbreath, and George E. Condon, Jr. *The Wrong Stuff: The Extraordinary Saga of Randy "Duke" Cunningham, the Most Corrupt Congressman Ever Caught.* New York: PublicAffairs, 2007. An analysis by the team of reporters who won a Pulitzer Prize in 2006 for their investigations into Cunningham's bribery and fraud.

SEE ALSO: Oct. 22, 1923: U.S. Senate Begins Hearings on Teapot Dome Oil Leases; Nov. 16, 1951: Federal Tax Official Resigns After Accepting Bribes; Oct. 10, 1973: Spiro T. Agnew Resigns Vice Presidency in Disgrace; Sept. 21, 1977: Carter Cabinet Member Resigns over Ethics Violations; Feb. 2, 1980: Media Uncover FBI Sting Implicating Dozens of Lawmakers; Jan. 22, 1987: Pennsylvania Politician Kills Himself at Televised Press Conference.

2000's

Beginning August 29, 2005

GOVERNMENT INCOMPETENCE MARS HURRICANE KATRINA RELIEF EFFORTS

As Hurricane Katrina came ashore along the Gulf coast—most specifically near the city of New Orleans, Louisiana—an ill-prepared local, state, and federal bureaucracy was deeply criticized for its failed response to the devastation. Because many of the victims were African American, critics also claimed that racism was at the heart of government ineffectiveness and inaction. The incompetence led to reform in emergency management at all levels of government and to further questions about the role of racism in how help is administered.

LOCALES: Louisiana; Mississippi; Alabama

CATEGORIES: Environmental issues; ethics; racism; government; politics; public morals; social issues and reform

KEY FIGURES

Ray Nagin (b. 1956), mayor of New Orleans, 2002-

Kathleen Babineaux Blanco (b. 1942), governor of Louisiana, 2004-2008

Michael D. Brown (b. 1954), head of the Federal Emergency Management Agency, 2003-2005

George W. Bush (b. 1946), president of the United States, 2001-2009

SUMMARY OF EVENT

On the morning of August 29, 2005, Hurricane Katrina made landfall near Buras, Louisiana, as a category 3 storm on the Saffir-Simpson scale with 135 mile-per-hour winds and a storm surge between eighteen and twenty-five feet. The storm caused catastrophic damage in Louisiana, Mississippi, and Alabama, and led to the deaths of more than eighteen hundred people; the $82 billion in damage made it the costliest hurricane in U.S. history.

Eighty percent of the city of New Orleans was inundated with water up to twenty feet deep when several levees surrounding the city failed. Local, state, and federal governments were not prepared to respond to the widespread destruction, leaving thousands of people in need of critical aid and guidance. The controversy stemmed, in part, from a lack of communication at all levels of government, both before the hurricane and after.

On September 22, the U.S. House of Representatives convened its Committee to Investigate the Preparation for and Response to Hurricane Katrina, having been given a clear mandate by Congress: "gather facts about the preparation for and response to Katrina, at all levels of government. . . . [F]ind out what went right and what went wrong." The committee issued its scathing, 520-page report to Congress on February 15, 2006. The report was deeply critical of how government agencies failed to anticipate disaster, despite clear warnings from the National Hurricane Center (NHC) and the National Weather Service (NWS), that disaster was imminent, and failed to take care of even the most basic of human needs after the hurricane made landfall along the Gulf coast. The report lauded only two government agencies—the NHC and the NWS—and commended the work of countless private citizens and groups in taking the initiative to help their neighbors.

Singled out for criticism by not only the committee but also critics across the United States were New Orleans mayor Ray Nagin, Louisiana governor Kathleen Babineaux Blanco, U.S. president George W. Bush, and numerous federal agencies, including the U.S. Department of Homeland Security and the Federal Emergency Management Agency (FEMA). Other critics of the preparation and response included politicians, scholars, entertainers, writers, social commentators, and the victims themselves.

During the five-day period between Monday, August 29, when the storm hit, and Friday, September 2, twenty to thirty thousand people were stranded at the Louisiana Superdome (a sporting and entertainment venue that was used as a shelter of last resort during the storm) and the Convention Center, both in downtown New Orleans, with little or no food or medical supplies. For nearly one week, the city of New Orleans was in chaos, and some residents took advantage of a shorthanded and ill-prepared police department and a Louisiana National Guard that was focused on keeping order at the Superdome and Convention Center, by taking food and other needed items from damaged and destroyed stores. (Critics later pointed out that blacks were described by media as looters and whites as victims looking for, finding, and taking food.)

Critics soon accused Mayor Nagin for not having a comprehensive plan to evacuate city residents, especially those with special needs, such as the elderly and disabled. Critics were especially concerned that Nagin, and other officials, failed to make evacuation plans even though NHC and NWS

scientists, five years before Katrina, had predicted what would happen if a storm such as Katrina struck in or near New Orleans. Critics also said that Nagin failed to take advantage of the city's bus system to effectively evacuate those who did not have the resources to get out of the city before the storm struck. Many also pointed out that Nagin lost precious time in failing to issue a mandatory evacuation until 9:30 A.M. on Sunday, August 28, twenty-four hours before the storm came ashore. On Thursday, September 1, a tired and frustrated Nagin went on radio and pleaded with Blanco and Bush to send more assistance, imploring them to "get off [their] asses and do something," so that they could all "fix the biggest goddamn crisis in the history of the country."

Governor Blanco was accused of failing to relinquish enough power and authority in time for the federal government to respond to the needs of thou-

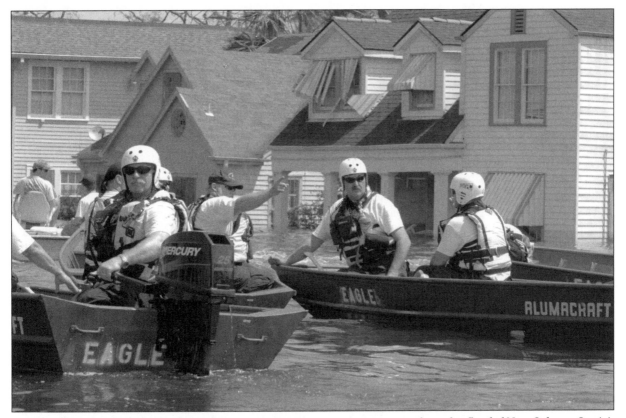

Search and rescue staff with the Federal Emergency Management Agency move through a flooded New Orleans, Louisiana, neighborhood on August 31, 2005. (Federal Emergency Management Agency)

Displaced New Orleans residents wait along the side of a closed freeway for FEMA assistance on September 2, 2005, five days after Hurricane Katrina made landfall. (Federal Emergency Management Agency)

sands of people. Blanco also was faulted for failing to redeploy hundreds of National Guard soldiers who were stationed in one of the most flood-prone areas of greater New Orleans: Jackson Barracks in Chalmette. Another charge leveled at Blanco was that she allowed personal political antipathy toward Nagin and Bush to affect her ability to work with them during the crisis.

President Bush was accused of failing to appreciate the magnitude of Katrina and its destructive aftermath, and that when he did, he did so too late. Katrina necessitated considerable federal assistance. On August 30, one day after the hurricane made landfall, Bush was posing for photographers with a country music singer at a naval base in Coronado, California.

Michael D. Brown, the Bush-appointed head of FEMA, also was singled out as the head of what turned out to be an inept federal agency. Most crit-

ics accused Brown of lacking the proper background and experience to manage FEMA and for not correcting the numerous bureaucratic impediments that prevented the agency from doing its job. Bush clearly showed that he did not understand the magnitude of the disaster, nor FEMA's incompetence, when he publicly praised Brown on Friday, September 2, for "doing a heck of a job." Many also said that Bush had cut funding for the upkeep of the levees that surrounded New Orleans, which the U.S. Army Corps of Engineers helped oversee and maintain.

The worst of the crisis ended on September 2, when Bush, with Blanco's consent, ordered the National Guard to join forces with thirty thousand regular U.S. Army soldiers. They were placed under the command of Lieutenant General Russel Honoré. Thousands of storm victims who were living in the squalid conditions at the Superdome and

Convention Center were bused to the Astrodome in Houston, Texas, leaving the two giant buildings nearly empty by Friday. Bush, Nagin, and Blanco met on Friday to discuss the lack of communication among responding agencies, including the local, state, and federal governments. In a heated but ultimately productive exchange, Nagin encouraged Blanco and Bush to "get together on the same page."

IMPACT

Criticism of the governments' response to Hurricane Katrina opened up a personal and partisan political debate, mostly involving Nagin, Blanco, and Bush. On September 12, FEMA director Brown resigned. Ten days later, the congressional investigatory committee convened, and hearings proceeded for months.

In addition to government incompetence, racism played a role in the emergency response to Katrina. The hurricane and its aftermath exposed deep socioeconomic and racial divisions in New Orleans. Critics argued that African Americans were largely forgotten in the crisis. The residents of devastated areas such as the Ninth Ward and New Orleans East were mostly black, as were most of the evacuees and those who ended up at the Superdome or Convention Center because their homes were destroyed and had nowhere else to go. Those most in need and most vulnerable, critics argued, were black, and race played a crucial role in why government officials did not move quickly enough to provide assistance. Reflecting these deep divisions, many people even accused white city officials of blowing up the levees to protect white neighborhoods. This fear was a legitimate one. During the 1927 Mississippi River flood, New Orleans city officials had dynamited several levees to save wealthier white neighborhoods at the expense of poorer African American neighborhoods. On September 2, during an NBC television fund-raiser for Katrina victims, singer-entertainer Kanye West claimed that President Bush "doesn't care" about black people.

The political fallout hurt the careers of some elected officials, including Blanco, who chose not to run for reelection in the fall of 2007. Others, including Nagin, continued their careers amid the controversy. In a January 16 speech, Nagin, who is black, made a racially insensitive remark, referring to the inevitability of New Orleans once again becoming a "chocolate city" (a black majority). Despite widespread criticism, he won a close mayoral election in the fall of 2006.

Three years of thinking about Katrina led to a different response by government officials when Hurricane Gustav, a category 2 storm, made landfall west of New Orleans on the morning of September 1, 2008. This time, evacuation plans were in order. Mayor Nagin and the governor of Louisiana, Bobby Jindal, ordered evacuations days before Gustav came ashore. The order led to the largest evacuation in the history of the state. Although this storm was predicted to be less strong than Katrina, officials would not take chances, especially given that the whole world was watching their response.

—*Christopher L. Stacey*

FURTHER READING

Brinkley, Douglas. *The Great Deluge: Hurricane Katrina, New Orleans, and the Mississippi Gulf Coast.* New York: William Morrow, 2006. Excellent detailed analysis of the immediate impact of Katrina, spanning August 27 to September 3, 2005. Brinkley marshals a wide array of sources, including interviews, newspaper articles, magazines, and secondary sources based on the history of hurricanes and the coastal South in general. Illustrated, with endnotes and index.

Dewan, Shaila. "Resources Scarce, Homelessness Persists in New Orleans." *The New York Times*, May 28, 2008. A report, nearly three years after Katrina, on the thousands of residents of New Orleans, and other places hit by the hurricane, who remain homeless.

Dyson, Michael Eric. *Come Hell or High Water: Hurricane Katrina and the Color of Disaster.* New York: Basic Civitas, 2006. Dyson's work focuses mostly on the racial dynamics of the governments' response to Katrina. Argues that an insidious racism permeated the incompetence and lack of urgency surrounding the governments' response. Illustrated, with endnotes.

2000's

Horn, Jed. *Breach of Faith: Hurricane Katrina and the Near Death of a Great American City.* New York: Random House, 2006. Horn based his study mostly on interviews and goes further in time chronologically than Brinkley. Maps, endnotes, index.

Marable, Manning, and Kristen Clarke, eds. *Seeking Higher Ground: The Hurricane Katrina Crisis, Race, and Public Policy Reader.* New York: Palgrave Macmillan, 2008. A collection exploring the intersections of public policy, government, and race in the wake of Katrina. Argues that perceptions of the disaster cannot be divorced from perceptions of New Orleans as a black city.

SEE ALSO: Sept. 26, 1979: Love Canal Residents Sue Chemical Company; Dec. 16, 1982: Congress Cites Environmental Protection Agency Chief for Contempt.

September 12, 2005
WESTAR ENERGY EXECUTIVES ARE FOUND GUILTY OF LOOTING THEIR COMPANY

David Wittig, the former chief executive officer of Westar Energy, Inc., was convicted, along with a company vice president, Douglas Lake, of stealing millions of dollars from the company for personal gain. For their crimes, in which they paid themselves millions of dollars in benefits and used company-owned property for personal matters, Wittig and Lake were heavily fined and sent to prison.

LOCALE: Topeka, Kansas
CATEGORIES: Law and the courts; banking and finance; business; corruption

KEY FIGURES
David Wittig (b. 1955), chief executive officer of Westar Energy, Inc.
Douglas Lake (fl. early twenty-first century), corporate vice president of strategy at Westar
Clinton Weidner (fl. early twenty-first century), president of Capital City Bank

SUMMARY OF EVENT
David Wittig was born in the middle-class town of Prairie Village, a suburb of Kansas City, Kansas. At a young age, he excelled in school, especially in the area of advanced mathematics. He eventually won a
scholarship to the University of Kansas and earned a bachelor of science degree in business administration and economics in 1977. Wittig then moved to New York City, where he began working as a stockbroker on Wall Street.

Wittig, who began working for the major Kansas-based utility company Westar Energy, Inc., in 1995, was rewarded for his aggressive business tactics with a promotion to chief executive officer (CEO) in 1998 and then chairman in 1999. For his next big acquisition, which ultimately led to his downfall, Wittig purchased 85 percent of the nation's second largest security company, Protection One, Inc., for $1 billion. He then made plans to sell Westar's electric assets to Public Service of New Mexico, a deal that would bring Westar an estimated $1 billion. This plan failed, along with another plan to purchase Kansas City Power & Light in 1999. However, the greatest problem for Westar became Protection One.

The U.S. Securities and Exchange Commission (SEC) began to investigate Westar's accounting practices. Additionally, Protection One customers began to complain about their services, a direct consequence of Wittig hiring managers who did not understand the businesses they were running. While Westar was losing millions of dollars, Wittig and other company executives were amassing millions of dollars in bonuses and perks. Although these bonuses were brought to light during the second federal criminal case against Wittig, the first case against him, involved an illegal deal with a prominent Topeka, Kansas, banker in 2002.

Wittig's career on Wall Street began with the Kansas-based firm H. O. Peet & Company. Then, in 1978, he took a job with Kidder Peabody & Co. He eventually was noticed by Martin Siegel, Kidder's number-one investment banker. Siegel took Wittig under his wing and began to show him the ways of Wall Street, giving him advice on acquisitions and mergers. Siegel later left Kidder to join Drexel Burnham Lambert, Inc., and was indicted in 1987 for his involvement in the federal case against Wall Street tycoon Ivan Boesky.

Wittig stayed on at Kidder and made a name for himself as an investor. He was featured on the cover of *Fortune* magazine in November, 1986. The article was about young Wall Street successes who were considered to be the next elite social class in the United States. Wittig began to master the art of medium-size deals in the deregulated utility business of the 1980's. He became close friends with many corporate executives in the Midwest, who helped him on his way to business stardom.

In 1989, Wittig joined Salomon Brothers, Inc., where he shared duties as chief of mergers and acquisitions from 1991 to 1995. In 1995, he became the executive vice president for corporate strategy for Western Resources, Inc. (later named Westar). He quickly became a major player in purchasing businesses that would be free from the regulations of the utility industry. During 1996 alone, he made a hostile takeover bid for Kansas City Power & Light and bought Westinghouse Security Systems for $368 million. Additionally, Wittig attempted a hostile $2.6 billion takeover of ADT, the nation's largest residential-security company. Although Tyco International would purchase ADT, Westar netted $864 million from the sale of the ADT shares that Wittig managed to acquire before the Tyco deal.

The first federal investigation against Wittig occurred in the fall of 2002. The case centered around an illegal business deal between Wittig and the former president of Topeka's Capital City Bank, Clinton Weidner. Weidner needed a $1.5 million loan to invest in a potentially lucrative real estate project in Scottsdale, Arizona. Wittig agreed to loan Weidner the money in return for increasing Wittig's personal credit line by $1.5 million and making another $20 million in loans available to other Westar executives.

Wittig and Weidner were tried in 2003 and found guilty on July 14, 2004, of four counts of making false bank entries and one count of money laundering. Weidner was sentenced to six years and six months in federal prison. Wittig was given a lesser sentence of four years and three months and fined $1 million.

During this same time frame, Wittig and one of his vice presidents Douglas Lake, resigned from Westar amid accusations of theft of company assets and funds. Federal investigators alleged that the two former executives had undeservedly paid themselves millions of dollars in benefits and used company-owned property for personal matters. In fact, after becoming CEO of Westar, Wittig leased two luxury jets along with a full-time aviation staff. It was discovered that Wittig had inappropriately used these aircraft to take his family on numerous shopping trips to major U.S. cities and even to Europe on occasion. Westar corporate jets also were used to fly his family and friends to popular summer vacation spots, including Wittig's luxurious rental home in Southampton, New York. Furthermore, Wittig purchased and renovated the mansion of former Kansas governor Alf Landon. The renovations alone for this project cost an estimated $2 million. Additionally, Wittig had his executive office suite redesigned for $6.6 million, a bill paid for, ultimately, by investors.

In late 2004, Wittig and Lake were indicted on thirty-nine counts for looting Westar. The counts included those for conspiracy, forfeiture, circumvention of internal controls, wire fraud, and money laundering. Wittig and Lake's first trial lasted more than two months, but jurors deadlocked on many of the charges, forcing the judge to declare a mistrial in December. In the summer of 2005, a retrial led to

2000's

guilty verdicts. On September 12, Wittig was convicted of thirty-nine counts and Lake was convicted of thirty. A fortieth count ordered them to forfeit the millions of dollars in stocks and cash they looted from the company.

On April 4, 2006, Wittig was sentenced to eighteen years in prison and ordered to pay a $5 million fine in addition to $14.5 million in restitution. He could have received a maximum sentence of 455 years in prison. Lake was given a fifteen-year sentence and ordered to pay $2.7 million in restitution and was fined $5 million. On January 5, 2007, an appeals court overturned their convictions, citing the government's lack of evidence on the charge that Wittig and Lake failed to comply with federal regulations in using corporate property. The court also ruled that they could not be retried on the most serious charges because of legal protections against double jeopardy. However, the court ordered a retrial on the conspiracy and circumvention charges and on the forfeiture order.

IMPACT

Wittig's crimes had a dramatic impact on the public perception of the company, investors and local citizens alike. Wittig's questionable business deals, coupled with his insatiable greed, put more than an entire company at grave financial risk; it also placed the people of Kansas at risk. Nearly two thousand local citizens worked for Westar, making the company one of the largest employers in Kansas.

Many Westar employees, along with thousands of customers, reported feelings of anger, betrayal, and sadness, the same emotions felt by workers and consumers who were robbed and deceived by corporate executives of other notable companies, such as Enron and Worldcom. However, Wittig and Lake were somewhat different from Kenneth Lay of Enron and Bernard Ebbers of WorldCom. Wittig and Lake were concerned mainly with their own personal gain and not the economic growth of their company.

As a result of the Wittig scandal, Westar implemented debt-reduction and restructuring plans. Furthermore, the company sold non-core-related assets, including Protection One and power plants in China and India, and remains an active utility provider in the Midwest.

—*Paul M. Klenowski*

FURTHER READING

Brickey, Kathleen. *Corporate and White Collar Crime: Cases and Materials*. 4th ed. New York: Aspen, 2006. This work offers insight into white-collar-criminal cases, including some that are similar in context to Wittig.

Coenen, Tracy. *Essentials of Corporate Fraud*. Hoboken, N.J.: John Wiley & Sons, 2008. An introductory guide to the white-collar crime of corporate fraud, written by a forensic, or investigative, accountant.

Rosoff, Stephen, Henry Pontell, and Robert Tillman. *Profit Without Honor: White Collar Crime and the Looting of America*. 4th ed. Upper Saddle River, N.J.: Prentice Hall, 2003. This text provides an excellent overview of white-collar crime in the United States, especially the numerous noteworthy cases of the early twenty-first century.

Steiner, George, and John Steiner. *Business, Government, and Society: A Managerial Perspective*. Chicago: McGraw-Hill, 2005. This book offers valuable insight into the many issues facing today's managers. Also discusses the Wittig scandal.

SEE ALSO: Mar. 29, 1962: Billie Sol Estes Is Arrested for Corporate Fraud; May 2, 1984: E. F. Hutton Executives Plead Guilty to Fraud; Jan. 15, 1988: ZZZZ Best Founder Is Indicted on Federal Fraud Charges; Mar. 29, 1989: Financier Michael Milken Is Indicted for Racketeering and Fraud; Jan. 28, 2000: John Spano Is Sentenced for Fraudulent Purchase of Ice Hockey Team; May 9, 2000: Former Louisiana Governor Edwin Edwards Is Convicted on Corruption Charges; June 25, 2002: Internal Corruption Forces Adelphia Communications to Declare Bankruptcy; Oct. 14, 2004: Insurance Brokerage Marsh & McLennan Is Charged with Fraud; Sept. 18, 2006: *Newsweek* Reveals That Hewlett-Packard Spied on Its Own Board.

September 30, 2005
DANISH NEWSPAPER'S PROPHET MUHAMMAD CARTOONS STIR VIOLENT PROTESTS

In response to self-censorship in Europe by those fearing reprisal for expressing an opinion on Islam, the Danish newspaper Jyllands-Posten *published a cartoon feature depicting artists' conceptions of the Prophet Muhammad. Critics declared that the cartoons constituted hate speech and were insulting to Muslims. While scandalized by the publication, many Westerners were scandalized by the violence of the protests as well.*

LOCALE: Copenhagen, Denmark
CATEGORIES: Publishing and journalism; religion; violence; popular culture; colonialism and imperialism; public morals

KEY FIGURES
Flemming Rose (b. 1958), editor at the *Jyllands-Posten*
Kåre Bluitgen (b. 1959), Danish writer
Vebjørn Selbekk (b. 1969), editor who first reprinted the cartoons
Anders Fogh Rasmussen (b. 1953), prime minister of Denmark, 2001-

SUMMARY OF EVENT
Political cartoons have a long history in Western culture, and by the early twenty-first century, almost any aspect of Western culture had become fair game for cartoonists' visual wit. Even Roman Catholic popes, patriarchs, and Jesus Christ were no longer considered sacrosanct. The first decade of the twenty-first century also marked an intensification of conflicts between Western secularism and radical Islamic fundamentalism, particularly after the September 11, 2001, terrorist attacks on the World Trade Center in New York and the Pentagon in Washington, D.C.

On one hand, U.S. president George W. Bush and other Western leaders were careful to avoid any statement related to the global war on terrorism that sounded like an attack on Islam rather than on the terrorists themselves. Western leaders frequently spoke positively about Islam as a religion. By contrast, Islamic fundamentalist leaders such as Osama bin Laden had openly referred to the Islamic struggle as one against not merely Western governments but Western secularism in general, which the fundamentalists condemn as decadent and immoral.

Islamic fundamentalist leaders have a history of reacting to any criticism of Islam or its prophet, Muhammad, in a manner considered to be inappropriately defensive and thin-skinned by Western standards. To leaders such as the Ayatollah Khomeini, who issued a fatwa (Islamic religious pronouncement) of death against Indian-born British novelist Salman Rushdie for his blasphemous novel *The Satanic Verses* (1988), any reference to Muhammad that was not 100 percent reverential was an insult to Islam. To dare suggest that Muhammad might be imperfect or that Islam has flaws is blasphemous, and any person who does suggest these things should be destroyed.

The potential for violence and even death deeply affected writers and artists, especially those who were Muslim or who were raised in Muslim countries. Many writers and artists felt it necessary to self-censor whenever touching on subjects related to Islam, Muslims, or the Middle East, largely as a result of fear that they too might become targets of the wrath of a radical cleric or clerics. Some people, however, took the chance to voice their opinions, knowing that criticism of Islam was problematic and controversial.

In Denmark on September 17, 2005, the newspaper *Jyllands-Posten* (Jutland post), concerned about self-censorship among intellectuals, artists, writers, and the media on the topic of Islam, published an article examining the work of writer Kåre Bluitgen and his inability to find an illustrator for his children's book *Koranen og profeten Muhammeds liv* (2006; the Qur'ān and the life of the Prophet Muhammad) because of fears of reprisal. On September 30, the *Jyllands-Posten* decided to take concrete action against that fear by publishing twelve political cartoons, commissioned by cultural editor Flemming Rose, on Muhammad and Islam. The one-page feature, "Muhammeds ansigt" (the face of Muhammad), included a cartoon that showed the prophet with a bomb in his turban and another that showed him with a crescent hanging over his turban, which could be seen either as a partial halo or a pair of devil's horns. Other cartoons even mocked the anticipated response to the cartoons.

The text that accompanied the cartoon feature, written by Rose, highlighted an unwillingness by some Muslims to accept the concept of freedom of speech and, in particular, the idea that one must be willing to accept the speech rights of others, even if that person's speech is offensive. The text also explained that the cartoon feature was a form of integration, that by publishing the cartoons, Muslims were being accepted into Danish society rather than treated as perpetual strangers.

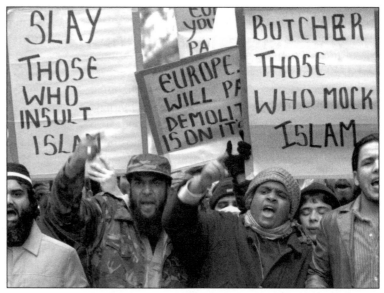

Demonstrators march to the Danish embassy in London in February, 2006, months after the Danish newspaper Jyllands-Posten *published political cartoons of the Prophet Muhammad.* (AP/Wide World Photos)

The earliest objections to the cartoon feature, which came from Danish Muslims, were reasoned and peaceful, even after Vebjørn Selbekk, editor of another Danish newspaper, reprinted them in January, 2006. Critics were concerned that the cartoons unfairly stigmatized a Danish minority and placed into danger those Muslims who deplored the terrorism committed by a few coreligionists and those Muslims who wanted only to integrate peacefully into Danish society. They also suggested that the cartoons had imperialist overtones reminiscent of the late nineteenth and early twentieth century, when European great powers carved out colonial empires in the Middle East and ruled with little sensitivity to the cultures and traditions of local peoples.

The response to the cartoons turned violent, however, as some were reprinted in newspapers around the world. First, the reactions came in the form of public protest. In Gaza, demonstrators desecrated not only the flag of Denmark but also those of Norway, the Netherlands, and Germany. As more and more demonstrations around the world—namely in the Middle East—turned violent, hundreds of protestors were killed by police. The flames of anger were further fanned by two Danish imams who assembled a dossier of other images they considered offensive to Islam, including doctored photographs of a Muslim being mounted by a dog while praying (dogs are considered unclean animals by most Muslims). Another example in the dossier referred to a contest in France in which participants put on rubber pig snouts and squealed like hogs while wearing turbans and other garments that suggested the participants were Muslim.

The responses to the cartoons then turned official, as Muslim leaders issued death threats against the cartoonists and even offered rewards for their murder. These threats were considered sufficiently serious that the artists went into hiding. In February, 2008, three people were arrested by Danish police for conspiring to murder cartoonist Kurt Westergaard, whose work depicted the Prophet Muhammad with a bomb in his turban. Boycotts against Danish goods were answered with calls to buy Danish products as a way of showing support for free speech. Denmark's prime minister, Anders Fogh Rasmussen, refused to issue a public apology, insisting that he would not compromise Denmark's commitment to freedom of speech.

In January of 2006, the controversy had become so severe that the *Jyllands-Posten* published an open letter to its readers. In the letter, the editorial staff explained that the cartoons had been presented soberly as a form of political and social commentary, and that they were not intended to insult or offend. The artist who had drawn the cartoon of Muhammad wearing a turban with a bomb explained that his intent was not to attack Islam but to protest that small segment of Muslims who, by committing terrorist attacks in the name of their religion, bring disrepute upon Islam as a whole. The open letter, which *Jyllands-Posten* put on its Web site to make it available worldwide, failed in its intent. Many considered the letter nothing more than arrogant and self-justifying.

IMPACT

The cartoon feature reinforced perceptions already held by many. Muslims consider the cartoons further evidence that Western secular culture has no respect for the sacred, specifically the sacred in Islam, while Westerners believe the ensuing riots and protests prove that Islam is antithetical to free speech. The scandal nevertheless impacted Western reporting on Islam and representations of the sacred.

In late 2006, on the first anniversary of the publication of the controversial cartoons, related controversy erupted when a videotape of members of a right-wing political youth group showed group members drawing pictures that insulted Muslims. The artists in the group had to go into hiding because they were threatened with death.

In November of 2007, a British primary school teacher in Sudan was arrested and tried for having insulted Islam by allowing her students to name a teddy bear Muhammad as part of a class project. Although the *Jyllands-Posten* cartoon controversy

was not specifically cited in coverage of the Sudan case, the coverage included the same themes of cultural misunderstanding, Muslim outrage, and international political pressure. The issue was further complicated because Muslims do not consider the name Muhammad too sacred for ordinary use, as long as the name is used for a person. Muhammad is believed to be a particularly lucky name (unlike many Christians who believe that the name Jesus is too sacred to be given to any child). Using the name Muhammad for a toy or animal is considered offensive.

—*Leigh Husband Kimmel*

FURTHER READING

Armour, Rollin S. *Islam, Christianity, and the West: A Troubled History*. Maryknoll, N.Y.: Orbis Books, 2002. A Catholic perspective on the volatile history between Islam and Christianity.

Clark, Lynn Schofield. *Religion, Media, and the Marketplace*. New Brunswick, N.J.: Rutgers University Press, 2007. Places the cartoon scandal within the larger context of the conflict between faith, the media, and secular market forces.

Majid, Anouar. *A Call for Heresy: Why Dissent Is Vital to Islam and America*. Minneapolis: University of Minnesota Press, 2007. A moderate Muslim's critique of the position within Islam that any criticism is blasphemy.

Muhammad, Tariq Ghazi. *The Cartoons Cry*. New York: AuthorHouse, 2007. Balances the public's offense at the cartoons with a consideration of how the cartoons might have revealed the fragility of Islamic civilization.

Rose, Flemming. "Why I Published Those Cartoons." *The Washington Post*, February 19, 2006. The cultural editor for *Jyllands-Posten* discusses in this telling opinion article the reasons why he commissioned the cartoons and why the paper published them.

SEE ALSO: Mar. 26, 1922: Hindemith's Opera *Sancta Susanna* Depicts a Nun's Sexual Desires; Feb. 23, 1963: Play Accuses Pope Pius XII of Complicity in the Holocaust.

2000's

November 17, 2005

LIBERIAN WORKERS SUE BRIDGESTONE FIRESTONE OVER SLAVE LABOR

Workers at the world's largest rubber plantation, in Liberia, brought a federal lawsuit against their employer, Bridgestone Firestone, in a U.S. court. Organized by the International Labor Rights Fund on behalf of some six thousand people who lived and worked on the plantation, the suit alleged a litany of abuses including low wages and poor working conditions, forced labor, and the use of children as workers.

LOCALES: Harbel, Liberia; Indianapolis, Indiana
CATEGORIES: Law and the courts; colonialism and imperialism; human rights; environmental issues; business; labor; social issues and reform

KEY FIGURES

Terry Collingsworth (b. 1956), executive director of the International Labor Rights Fund
Daniel J. Adomitis (b. 1955), president of Firestone Natural Rubber Company
David F. Hamilton (b. 1957), U.S. District Court judge

SUMMARY OF EVENT

Bridgestone Firestone, the largest tire manufacturer in the world, is an American-Japanese conglomerate with head offices in Nashville, Tennessee. In addition to its tire manufacturing concerns, the company produces a host of latex products for use in industry and construction. The company was founded in Akron, Ohio, as the Firestone Tire and Rubber Company in 1900. In 1988, Firestone was bought by the Japanese tire manufacturer Bridgestone, and the company was named Bridgestone Firestone (BF) in 1990 after the two entities merged.

At the beginning of the twentieth century, the British government held a global monopoly on rubber. In an effort to supply the growing domestic automobile market with cheaper rubber, Firestone, with the encouragement and full support of the U.S. government, explored opportunities to break Great Britain's hold on Africa. In 1926, Firestone invested in the West African nation of Liberia. It embarked on a ninety-nine-year lease with the Liberian government for a natural rubber plantation and founded the city of Harbel in Margibi County, near Monrovia. By the early twenty-first century, BF was Liberia's largest employer and held a concession on more than 1 million acres of land throughout the country. The plantation in Harbel alone measured more than 240 square miles and officially employed six thousand people.

The character of natural latex harvesting is highly labor-intensive, requiring the hand tapping of rubber trees with relatively simple tools and the collection of raw latex in portable buckets. Coupled with an impoverished local population and BF's high demand for the natural latex, perhaps it is not surprising that serious charges of abusive labor practices surfaced again in 2005. Each worker, referred to as a "tapper," had to meet a daily quota of 450 pounds of latex.

Acting on information provided by Liberian environmental law activists, Terry Collingsworth, a lawyer and executive director of the International Labor Rights Fund (ILRF; now the International Labor Rights Forum), traveled to Liberia in early October, 2005. The ILRF is a United States-based advocacy organization that focuses on working conditions and workers' rights worldwide, particularly in the developing and least developed world. Collingsworth visited the BF plantation and interviewed more than one hundred laborers about not only working conditions but also housing, sanitation, utilities, and environmental practices. Upon his return to the ILRF's offices in Washington, D.C., Collingsworth filed an Alien Tort Statute (1789) class-action lawsuit against BF on behalf of twelve adult and twenty-three child plaintiffs in the U.S. District Court in Los Angeles on November 17. The Alien Tort Statute allows non-U.S. citizens to file suit in U.S. courts for international law violations, including slavery and forced labor, that are unrecognized as law violations in the country of the plaintiff or plaintiffs.

The twelve-count claim in *John Roe I et al. v. Bridgestone* alleged that plantation conditions constituted forced labor because tappers labor up to fourteen hours per day and must enlist others (often children as young as six years old) as unpaid help, swelling the workforce to an estimated sixteen thousand people. For their work, the tappers earned the equivalent of $3.19 per day, before deductions. These wages were docked 50 percent if tappers failed to meet their quotas. In addition, because many of the tappers lived on the plantation, they relied upon BF for housing, food, access to water and electricity, education, and health care. If provided at all, these necessities were well below standard. In short, the lawsuit alleged that BF was engaged in modern-day slavery, forcing the Liberians to work in deplorable conditions by the coercion of poverty.

The suit against BF was filed in the United States, not Liberia, for several reasons. Principally, Collingsworth was able to bring suit in the United States not only because of the Alien Tort Statute but also because of the Trafficking Victims Protection Reauthorization Act of 2003, which, in part, created a civil right of action for human trafficking victims in U.S. courts, irrespective of geographic location of the offense or the nationality of victims or perpetrators. Furthermore, by filing in the United States, Collingsworth hoped to protect the plaintiffs (identified only as John, James, and Jane Roe) and the other plantation workers from retribution and a corrupt legal system in Liberia.

Predictably, BF responded immediately and aggressively to the allegations, employing its substantial legal and public relations resources. In addition to standard-

ized sound bites from a host of BF media liaisons, Firestone Natural Rubber Company president Daniel J. Adomitis was frequently cited in the media not only disputing the veracity of the charges and expostulating on the company's corporate benefice but also alleging that the ILRF was more interested in generating media attention than in serving the interests of Liberian rubber workers.

On the legal front, BF's team of attorneys simultaneously filed motions to transfer the venue from California to the Southern District of Indiana and to dismiss the case. The court granted the motion to transfer venue based on the case's lack of connection to California and the fact that the company's headquarters are located within the jurisdiction of the Southern District of Indiana. However, the court did not address BF's motion to dismiss.

The case was heard by Judge David F. Hamilton. Again, BF filed a motion to dismiss, for lack of subject-matter jurisdiction. The court denied the motion. On June 26, 2007, the court decided the matter, largely in favor of BF, and dismissed eleven of the twelve counts. In his ruling, Judge Hamilton deemed that the adult workers' principal claim of

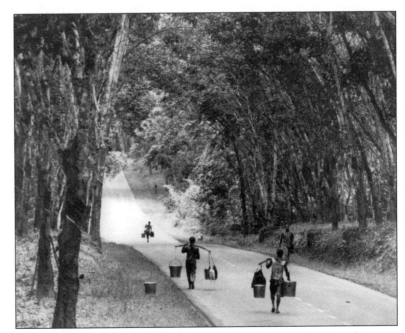

Workers in Liberia carry buckets of newly tapped rubber over long distances at Firestone's vast estate in 1978. (Hulton Archive/Getty Images)

forced labor in violation of international law was undermined by their allegations that they are afraid of losing the same jobs they claim they are being forced to perform. Furthermore, his decision specified that forced labor cannot be equated only with low wages and difficult working conditions. In short, it was the opinion of the court that the adults' working conditions on the plantation, while harsh, did not violate the specific, universal, and obligatory norms of forced labor under international law.

In a victory for the ILRF and its plaintiffs, however, the count pertaining to the child workers survived the legal challenge. Hamilton determined that BF actively encouraged parents to require children to work full-time at dangerous jobs on the plantation. The case continued as one of forced child labor.

IMPACT

The allegations that prompted the lawsuit had an immediate impact. Though the treatment of workers on Liberian rubber plantations has been suspect from the early 1930's, when it was first investigated by the League of Nations, the dire conditions have remained largely unknown in North America to all but a small cohort of labor and human rights attorneys, environmentalists, and developing-world solidarity activists.

The ILRF's case has garnered the renewed attention of the United Nations and alerted people in the developed world to the human and social costs of postcolonialism and to cases of corruption and abuse by multinational corporations. More directly, the scrutiny of BF has driven the company to address a host of labor and related issues in Liberia, including better enforcement of the company's own labor regulations, improved basic services on the plantation, and a greater investment in the commitment to provide education and training for the populace. On August 6, 2008, BF signed an agreement with the Firestone Agricultural Workers Union of Liberia to provide incremental wage increases and other benefits. The agreement marked the first such accord between the company and its plantation workers in Liberia.

—*Stephen L. Muzzatti*

FURTHER READING

Hecht, Susanna B., and Alexander Cockburn. *The Fate of the Forest Developers, Destroyers, and Defenders of the Amazon.* London: Verso, 1989. Employing an environmental humanism paradigm, the authors address the problems of natural-resource harvesting. Though the focus is on South America, the book does draw upon examples from elsewhere in the developing world.

Mullins, Christopher W., and Dawn L. Rothe. *Power, Bedlam, and Bloodshed: State Crime in Post-colonial Africa.* New York: Peter Lang, 2008. An overview of violations of international criminal law in postcolonial African states. Focuses on how crimes arise from a postcolonial environment and the potential remedies offered by international social control.

United Nations Mission in Liberia. *Human Rights in Liberia's Rubber Plantations: Tapping into the Future.* Monrovia, Liberia: United Nations, 2006. The final report of a study conducted by the U.N. human rights and protection section that highlights poverty and human-rights violations in Liberia's agricultural sector.

SEE ALSO: Nov. 15, 1908: Belgium Confiscates Congo Free State from King Leopold II; 1930: Liberia Is Accused of Selling Its Own Citizens into Slavery; Late 1955: British Atrocities in Kenya's Mau Mau Rebellion Are Revealed; Oct. 20, 1978: Firestone Recalls Millions of Defective Car Tires; June 4, 1979: South African President B. J. Vorster Resigns in Muldergate Scandal.

December 6, 2005

SPOKANE, WASHINGTON, MAYOR RECALLED IN GAY-SEX SCANDAL

Spokane mayor James E. West was a conservative Republican Washington State senator and a staunch leader against gay and lesbian rights while in the legislature. In May, 2005, local media reported that West had chatted online with a seventeen-year-old boy about having sex with him. The media also said that West had sexually molested boys years earlier and that he had been having sex with young men whom he met on the Web. West was recalled from office in 2005.

LOCALE: Spokane, Washington

CATEGORIES: Sex crimes; sex; corruption; politics; law and the courts; families and children; public morals; publishing and journalism

KEY FIGURES

James E. West (1951-2006), mayor of Spokane, Washington, 2003-2005

Shannon Sullivan (b. c. 1968), leader of the recall campaign against West

Ryan Oelrich (b. 1980 or 1981), a beneficiary of West's political favors

SUMMARY OF EVENT

In May, 2005, the *Spokane Spokesman-Review* broke a story that it had been investigating for a considerable time. Mayor James E. West, a conservative Republican, was accused of attempting to elicit sexual favors on the Web from a young man in return for an internship at Spokane City Hall. What made this accusation even more startling was that in his twenty-plus years in the Washington State legislature, West had been a staunch voice against gay and lesbian rights. Among the causes he had championed were barring gays and lesbians from working in schools, day-care centers, and some state agencies, and defining marriage as a union only between a man and a woman.

In his powerful post as Washington senate majority leader, West had effectively killed a bill that would have banned discrimination against gays. He also introduced legislation outlawing sexual intercourse between consenting teenagers. Additionally, as mayor of Spokane, he indicated that he would veto a measure to offer benefits to domestic partners of city employees. Although some of his family-values causes never became law, they were indicative of West's political leanings and presumptive evidence of his hypocrisy.

One of the most shocking aspects of the breaking story was that it involved a boy whom West believed to be only seventeen years old. In reality, the event was a sting; the presumed teenager with whom he had been in contact was someone hired by the *Spokesman-Review*. During one of their online chats, for which he called himself Right Bi-Guy, the mayor admonished the youth to remember that he was "very closeted" and that no one knew he liked men sexually.

The *Spokesman-Review* published the Web exchanges in copious detail. Even more seriously, the article accused the mayor of having molested at least two young Cub Scouts (both of whom later became convicted felons) almost twenty-five years earlier when he was a sheriff's deputy. To minimize the damage, West immediately issued a statement apologizing for the "shame" he brought to the city but vigorously denied any molestation. He did resign from a Boy Scouts council and admitted to frequenting gay Web sites and having sexual relations with adult men. Although denying he was gay, he did allow that he might be bisexual. (He had married at a relatively late age, was in that relationship for about five years, and then was divorced.)

Despite the accusations against him, West vowed to complete the mayoral term to which he had been elected in 2003, the same year he was diagnosed with colon cancer. Among the accusations was that he had promised city jobs to those with whom he hoped to have sex. One person who received a city job in exchange for sex was twenty-four-year-old Ryan Oelrich, whom the mayor did appoint to Spokane's Human Rights Commission. Oelrich resigned after six months because he claimed West would not stop pressuring him for sex. Eventually, the Federal Bureau of Investigation (FBI) stepped in to investigate the charges of public corruption.

Although West believed that he was safely closeted, rumors about his sexuality had existed for many years. In general, outrage against the mayor greeted the article, but there were people who questioned its timing. Some thought it had political overtones, and there were those who thought it was unfair entrapment. West threatened to sue the paper for invasion of privacy, but he did not do so. After admitting to the sexual indiscretions, he defended his prior antigay opinions as representing the will of the constituents who had elected him and said they were not necessarily his own beliefs. He also expressed regret about the way he had voted on some of these issues. At a news conference, he averred that the events had "helped me straighten out my personal life" but also complained he had been "brutally outed."

Shortly after the allegations surfaced, Mayor West said he would take a short leave of absence to fight the molestation charges. During an appearance on NBC television's *The Today Show*, he again claimed that he was just following the will of the voters in his antigay proposals. The city of Spokane began looking into West's use of city computers and e-mail accounts. It hired an independent investigator, who determined that West had violated city policy when he downloaded images from a gay Web site onto his office computer. The police did not immediately comment on any possible criminal charges resulting from his actions. For one thing, the statute of limitations for molestation had expired.

Although fellow Republicans and Spokane city leaders distanced themselves from the mayor, they did not push for his resignation. It was left to a single citizen, Shannon Sullivan, to instigate a recall petition. She gathered more than the required 12,600 valid signatures. The thirty-seven-year-old mother maintained it was not an antigay move but

that she just wanted a mayor whom her young son could be proud of. A Superior Court judge ruled against two counts of the petition but left a third intact. West then appealed to the Washington State Supreme Court, which ruled against him. Although not a lawyer, Sullivan herself had made the oral arguments before the court. A special mail-in recall election was then ordered and held on December 6, 2005.

During the recall campaign against him, West had few public defenders, but when a gay rights group offered him a forum to tell his side of the story, he declined. West was recalled from office by a 65 to 35 percent margin (approximately 40,000 votes for the recall and 21,500 against it). Sometime before his death from colon cancer at the age of fifty-five in July, 2006, West told a Seattle newspaper that he no longer visited gay Web sites and had been refraining from gay sex. This revelation could well be related to his hopes to run for office again.

IMPACT

Toward the end of his life, West still hoped to be rehabilitated, but his political career was finished. Although he had characterized being the mayor of Spokane as his "dream job," he apparently harbored ambitions to run for governor. (He did run for lieutenant governor in 1996 but was defeated in his party's primary.) The Republican leadership of Washington State avowed that the scandal would not reflect on their party, but it is possible that some political fallout resulted. Another right-leaning antigay conservative within the party was revealed to be a hypocrite on the issue.

The local lesbian and gay community used the West scandal to demonstrate the damage that being closeted caused to those who felt they had to conceal their sexuality. They also wanted to highlight the hypocrisy of those politicians who espoused family-values rhetoric in public but who lived very different—indeed, deeply opposed—lives in private. This case engendered much discussion in Spokane about the problems that gays and lesbians faced. A gay spokesperson said that the city had learned that "lives lived in dishonesty are lives not well-lived."

Overall, the gay and lesbian communities in Spokane and elsewhere were generally less than sympathetic to West. *The Advocate*, a leading gay news periodical, decried as "pathetic" those people, including West, who denied their sexuality.

—*Roy Liebman*

FURTHER READING

Breslau, Karen. "Spokane: A Mom vs. a Mayor." *Newsweek*, August 29, 2005. A fuller account of Sullivan's recall petition drive and her appearance delivering oral arguments before the state supreme court.

Egan, Timothy. "Spokane Mayor, Caught in Sex Sting, Is Ousted in Vote That May Advance Gay Rights." *The New York Times*, December 8, 2005. The recall election of December 6 spelled the end of West's career. Another recap of the scandal.

Kaushik, Umesh Kher. "Exposed in Spokane." *Time*, May 23, 2005. A report on the exposé by the *Spokane Spokesman-Review*, which brought to the public's attention the sexual hypocrisy of Mayor West and accused him of molesting boys many years earlier.

Saskal, Rich. "Spokane Recall Ruling." *The Bond Buyer*, August 26, 2005. News story on the Washington State Supreme Court clearing the way for Shannon Sullivan to begin collecting signatures for a recall election against West.

_____. "West Taking Leave." *The Bond Buyer*, May 15, 2005. After a local Spokane newspaper broke a sex scandal implicating Mayor James West, he announced that he would take a leave of absence to prepare his defense.

Savage, Dan. "No Excuses for West." *The Advocate*, January 31, 2006. A gay columnist's opinion piece about the West scandal and a look back at how gays of his generation coped with being forced to remain in the closet.

Williams, Juliet A., and Paul Apostolidis, eds. *Public Affairs: Politics in the Age of Sex Scandals*. Durham, N.C.: Duke University Press, 2004. Provides a context for the West case by examining other sex scandals involving political figures.

SEE ALSO: Oct. 7, 1964: President Lyndon B. Johnson's Aide Is Arrested in Gay-Sex Sting; Oct. 25, 1974: Evangelist Billy James Hargis Resigns College Presidency During Gay-Sex Scandal; Sept. 3, 1980: Congressman Bauman Is Arrested for Liaison with Teenage Boy; July 20, 1982: Conservative Politician John G. Schmitz Is Found to Have Children Out of Wedlock; July 20, 1983: Congress Members Censured in House-Page Sex Scandal; Jan. 18, 1990: Washington, D.C., Mayor Marion Barry Is Arrested for Drug Use; May 2, 2000: New York Mayor Rudy Giuliani's Extramarital Affair Is Revealed; Oct. 2, 2003: Newspaper Claims That Arnold Schwarzenegger Groped Women; Sept. 29, 2006: Congressman Mark Foley Resigns in Sex Scandal Involving a Teenage Page; Nov. 2, 2006: Male Escort Reveals Sexual Liaisons with Evangelist Ted Haggard; July 11, 2007: Florida Politician Is Arrested for Soliciting an Undercover Male Police Officer; Mar. 12, 2008: New York Governor Eliot Spitzer Resigns in Prostitution Scandal.

2000's

January 21, 2006
BRITISH POLITICIAN RESIGNS AFTER GAY-SEX ORGY

Politician Mark Oaten, an up-and-coming Liberal Democrat, was forced to relinquish his seat in the British parliament when it was revealed that he had been linked with male prostitutes and participated in gay orgies. He attributed his behavior to a midlife crisis instigated by the aging process, including the rapid loss of his hair.

LOCALE: London, England
CATEGORIES: Prostitution; government; politics; sex; public morals

KEY FIGURES

Mark Oaten (b. 1964), member of the British parliament
Tomasz (b. c. 1980), prostitute and former ballet dancer from Poland
Belinda Oaten (b. 1968), Mark Oaten's wife

SUMMARY OF EVENT

In January of 2006, the British tabloid *News of the World* published a story about the sexual peccadilloes of forty-one-year-old Mark Oaten, a Liberal Democrat member of Parliament (MP) from the constituency of Winchester, England. The titillating account described his six-month liaison with a "rent boy," the English term for a male prostitute. Identified only as Tomasz, the latter was allegedly a former ballet dancer from Poland.

It was reported that Tomasz also occasionally participated in orgies with the MP along with at least two other rent boys. The article cited "a bizarre sex act too revolting to describe" as one of Oaten's predilections. This bizarre act was later determined to involve coprophilia, a rather extreme form of sexual gratification or humiliation, or both. He also had a predilection for having the rent boys dress in soccer uniforms.

Oaten was an ambitious up-and-coming politician when the scandal broke. Born in the small town of Watford, England, he worked in public relations and as a lobbyist before entering politics when he

was elected to the Watford District Council. At the age of twenty-two, he was one of the youngest town council members in England. His eight-year service apparently gave him a taste for higher office. In 1992, he ran unsuccessfully for Parliament, but it was only a temporary setback. Five years later he won a seat for the Liberal Democrats by the very narrowest of margins—two votes—by unseating the Conservative incumbent in his new constituency of Winchester, the home of the famous cathedral.

Not unexpectedly, such a narrow voting margin was challenged, and the election was rerun. This time Oaten triumphed by the convincing margin of more than twenty-one thousand votes. His political career seemed assured. He was reelected in 2001 and 2005, albeit by decreasing margins of victory, and was considered one of the future leading lights of his party's right wing. Among his posts were those as party spokesperson for disabilities and membership on the foreign affairs and defense team.

Ultimately, Oaten became the chairman of the Parliamentary Liberal Democrats. He served in other capacities as well before becoming the party's shadow home secretary, a sign of the esteem in which the party held him. In late 2005, the alcoholism of the Liberal Democrats' leader, Charles Kennedy, was revealed and the party fell into crisis. Oaten, although publicly supporting Kennedy, was seen as maneuvering to succeed him behind the scenes.

In January, 2006, Oaten declared himself in the running for the position of party leader. If successful he would be in line to be prime minister should his perennially also-ran party ever form a government. Just a week later, Oaten withdrew from his leadership quest amid increasing rumors about his private life, although he claimed he withdrew because he did not have adequate support from his party. On January 21 the gathering storm broke with the publication of the *News of the World* story about Oaten's gay sex life.

The married father of two daughters, Oaten had used his seemingly staid "family man" image to his political advantage. He was now reviled as a hypocrite. Additionally, he had previously criticized a judge who had been fired for cavorting with rent boys. Although he would confess only to "errors in judgment," Oaten later blamed his misfortune on a midlife crisis, examples of which were the rapid loss of his hair and turning forty years of age. He did not admit to being gay even though he apparently had been a habitué of male prostitutes for at least one and one-half years before being discovered. One of the prostitutes was quoted as saying that the MP was "a very troubled man leading a very dangerous double life."

For a while after the scandal began developing, Oaten had to weather being the object of scatological jokes. One joke asked how he and Charles Kennedy were alike. The punch line (referring to one's assumed sexual practice and the other's alcoholism) was "They both like to get s—t-faced in the evening." Oaten also was derided a few months after the scandal for apparently trading in on his notoriety by appearing on a daytime-television fitness program.

Oaten apparently rose above his problems and, even though no longer in government, he staged a modest comeback. He became active in prison reform circles and became a member of the Council of Europe and the Western European Union. He also lectured on politics at Oxford University and at universities in the United States. Oaten's well-received book, *Coalition: The Politics and Personalities of Coalition Government from 1850*, was published in 2007.

IMPACT

Oaten's own political career lay in ruins. He resigned his party posts and said he would not run again for his Parliament seat in the next election; he stood very little chance of winning, according to polling data. His disgrace affected his party as well; the so-called "Oaten effect" was blamed for his party's loss of the majority on the Winchester Council.

This scandal, coming just two weeks after party leader Kennedy's resignation, greatly harmed the Liberal Democrats. Their ratings in the polls dropped to the lowest level in eight years, and it was reported that the second-place Conservative Party was hoping to gain some defectors from its ranks.

On a personal level, Oaten's marriage of thirteen years was severely affected, and his wife vented her anguish in public. Unlike many political wives in the United States whose husbands have been involved in scandal—such as the spouse of former New York governor Eliot L. Spitzer—Oaten's wife, Belinda, at first declined to play the role of the supportive spouse. According to Oaten himself, his statuesque wife threw her wedding rings at him and struck him several times. To journalists she declared that his betrayal had plunged her into "unimaginable horror." They did reconcile later, but not until after Belinda Oaten had taken the children and left home for a period of time.

The gay community in Great Britain was somewhat energized by this case. Even though Oaten did not actually come out as gay, or even as bisexual, at least one politically active gay organization in England challenged his party. The group stated that other members of the gay-friendly Liberal Democrats should now take the opportunity to go public with their own homosexuality.

—Roy Liebman

FURTHER READING

"Mark Oaten to Withdraw from Lib Dem Leader Race." *Daily Telegraph*, January 19, 2006. Just before the story broke about Mark Oaten's sexual peccadilloes, he announced he was withdrawing from the race to succeed Charles Kennedy as the Liberal Democrat Party leader.

Oaten, Mark. *Coalition: The Politics and Personalities of Coalition Government from 1850*. Petersfield, England: Harriman House, 2007. Political lessons to be learned from the activities of Great Britain's coalition governments beginning with the prime ministry of Benjamin Disraeli to the first years of the twenty-first century.

Parris, Matthew. "Oaten May Have Taken a Stupid Risk, but That Doesn't Mean He's Stupid." *The Spectator*, January 28, 2006. Analysis of why

2000's

politicians take foolhardy risks. The author concludes that their personalities lend themselves to acts of daring and risk-taking and the belief that they will never be caught.

Thurlbeck, Neville. "Lib-Dem Oaten's Three-in-Bed-Rent-Boy Shame." *News of the World*, January 21, 2006. The account of Mark Oaten's months-long relationship with a male prostitute and, on occasion, other rent boys, and a veiled but censorious account of the "degrading" sexual practices in which they engaged.

SEE ALSO: Mar. 2-Sept. 25, 1963: John Profumo Affair Rocks British Government; Aug. 4, 1978: British Politician Jeremy Thorpe Is Charged with Attempted Murder; Oct. 14, 1983: British Cabinet Secretary Parkinson Resigns After His Secretary Becomes Pregnant; July 25, 1987: Novelist-Politician Jeffrey Archer Wins Libel Trial Against the *Daily Star*; Dec. 18, 1989: Prince Charles's Intimate Phone Conversation with Camilla Parker Bowles Is Taped; Aug. 23, 1992: Princess Diana's Phone Conversation with Her Lover Is Made Public; Sept. 24, 1992: British Cabinet Member David Mellor Resigns over Romantic Affair; Jan. 5, 1994: British Cabinet Member Resigns After Fathering a Child Out of Wedlock; Aug. 31, 1997: Princess Diana Dies in a Car Crash; Sept. 28, 2002: British Politician Reveals Her Affair with Prime Minister John Major; Apr. 26, 2006: Britain's Deputy Prime Minister Admits Affair with Secretary.

March 14, 2006
DUKE LACROSSE PLAYERS ARE ACCUSED OF GANG RAPE

The Duke University men's lacrosse team received scandalous national attention when an exotic dancer accused three of the team's players of raping her during a party. The case led to heated public debate about rape, racism, and press coverage. It also led to the firing of the team's head coach, to the cancellation of the lacrosse team's season, to the disbarring and public disgrace of the prosecutor, to the exoneration of the three indicted players, and to civil lawsuits.

LOCALE: Durham, North Carolina

CATEGORIES: Law and the courts; sex crimes; publishing and journalism; women's issues; racism; social issues and reform; education

KEY FIGURES

Crystal Gail Mangum (b. 1979), exotic dancer and North Carolina Central University student

Mike Nifong (b. 1950), Durham, North Carolina, district attorney

Reade Seligmann (b. 1985), Duke lacrosse player

Collin Finnerty (b. 1986), Duke lacrosse player

David Evans (b. 1984), Duke lacrosse player

Mike Pressler (b. 1960), Duke lacrosse team head coach

Richard H. Brodhead (b. 1947), president of Duke

SUMMARY OF EVENT

On the evening of March 13, 2006, the student body of Duke University had been enjoying spring break. Remaining on the Durham, North Carolina, campus were members of the university's lacrosse team, which had games scheduled during the break. Players gathered at the rented house of a teammate at 610 West Buchanan Boulevard, opposite Duke's east campus. The house was owned by the university.

Earlier in the day, team member Dan Flannery hired two exotic dancers to provide entertainment for a party scheduled for that evening. Kim Roberts, who was African American-Asian, and Crystal Gail

Mangum, who was African American, were set to arrive at the party at 11 P.M. They were scheduled to dance for two hours and were paid eight hundred dollars in advance for their services. Kim (the two dancers used their first names only when working) arrived shortly after the scheduled time and Crystal arrived shortly before midnight. By that time the party was well under way, and many members of the team had been drinking for some time.

Shortly after midnight, Crystal and Kim locked themselves in the house's only bathroom before leaving the house around 12:20 on the morning of March 14. Kim left the property entirely but Crystal, a student at North Carolina Central University, also in Durham, remained in the yard. Perhaps intoxicated, she was photographed lying on her side at 12:37, having fallen down. At 12:41, she was photographed as she entered a car belonging to Kim, who had returned to the property. At 12:53, Kim called 911 complaining that men outside the house were shouting racial epithets at them. Two police cars arrived within five minutes, but because all was quiet, they left the residence.

At 1:22, Kim again called the police because Crystal was drunk and unconscious in her black Honda. The police arrived, removed Crystal from Kim's car, and took her to Duke University Medical Center, where, during initial screening, Crystal answered "yes" when asked whether she had been raped. One hour later, she told a police officer that she had not been raped. He called headquarters to inform the watch commander that Crystal withdrew her rape allegation. However, Crystal then told a sexual-abuse nurse that she had been raped, so her accusation of rape was not withdrawn by police.

Although Crystal's account was inconsistent, the rape charge was investigated nonetheless. On March 16, the accuser was asked to identify the alleged rapists from photographs of all forty-six members of the lacrosse team. She singled out three white men. One of the men, Reade Seligmann, had a persuasive alibi and could prove that he was not in the house at the time the rape allegedly took place. He had left the house and was taped by a surveillance camera using an automatic teller machine (ATM) some distance from Buchanan Boulevard,

Duke University lacrosse player Reade Seligmann, right, speaks with his attorney in court in Durham, North Carolina, on May 18, 2006. Seligmann and two teammates were indicted for rape but were later exonerated. (AP/ Wide World Photos)

the site of the party. His ATM transaction was made at 12:24 A.M. on March 14.

As the case developed, all forty-six lacrosse players voluntarily provided DNA samples to investigators. These samples were compared to the DNA collected from semen that was in Crystal's vagina and on her underclothing the night of the alleged rape. The samples from the lacrosse players did not match the DNA of the semen, suggesting that Crystal had sexual intercourse—consensual or by means of rape—with someone on the evening in question, but not with any of the accused.

Duke University president Richard H. Brodhead first heard of the accusations on March 20. On March 24, Coach Mike Pressler met with Duke administrators and supported the accused players. The following day, Brodhead met with advisers to discuss how best to handle the case. On March 28, Brodhead suspended the lacrosse team pending the outcome of the investigation.

Mike Nifong, acting Durham County district attorney at the time of the incident, was running for election as district attorney. He was courting the black vote, so he had a personal interest in impressing the black community with his ability to serve their interests. As he became more fully involved in the case, he won increasing support among black voters. He capitalized on the strained relations between Duke, often portrayed as a rich person's school, and the surrounding, somewhat impoverished, black community.

By March 29, the Duke scandal had received national attention when it was reported in a front-page article in *The New York Times*. On that day, Brodhead met with members of the Duke faculty senate, who urged him to suspend the lacrosse team, dissolve the lacrosse program, and fire coach Pressler. On April 5, Brodhead canceled the team's season and demanded that Pressler resign. The following day, eighty-eight members of the Duke faculty signed a statement condemning the alleged gang rape and published their statement in the *Duke Chronicle*.

On April 17, players Collin Finnerty and Seligmann were indicted on charges of first-degree forcible rape, first-degree sexual offense, and kidnapping. If found guilty, the two would have received life sentences. Senior player David Evans received his bachelor's degree on May 14 and was indicted the following day on similar charges.

As the case proceeded, Nifong's prosecution turned scandalous. He withheld from defense counsel such items as the surveillance videotape showing Seligmann using the ATM at the time the alleged rape occurred. He minimized the importance of inconsistencies in Crystal's account of the alleged rape. Most critically, he withheld the results of the DNA tests that would have instantly exonerated all three defendants.

Four days before the election, the judge in the case ordered Nifong to turn over the DNA results to the defense, but Nifong ignored this order. On November 7, he won the election. Glaring irregularities in the prosecution's case increasingly became apparent, and the rape charges against the three defendants were dropped on December 22.

On December 28, the North Carolina State Bar filed ethics charges against Nifong, claiming in its report that his conduct in the case was "prejudicial to the administration of justice." The bar's report also said that Nifong had engaged in "conduct involving dishonesty, fraud, deceit, or misrepresentation."

Nifong was sworn in as district attorney on January 2, 2007. Ten days later, he asked North Carolina attorney general Roy Cooper to take over the case. On June 16, Nifong was disbarred. In April, all remaining charges against the players were dropped by Cooper. In August, Nifong was sentenced to one day in jail and fined $500 for criminal contempt of court.

IMPACT

The initial scandal in this case was the gang rape allegations against three Duke lacrosse players. As the case moved forward, the scandal grew to include the university's rush to judgment in canceling the lacrosse season, suspending players, firing the team's head coach, and issuing a statement by its faculty senate that condemned the alleged gang rape. President Brodhead acted precipitously in suspending Finnerty and Seligmann without convincing evidence that they were guilty. The forced resignation of Coach Pressler, who helped raise the team to national prominence during his sixteen years at Duke, was brought about by external pressures and the fear of bad publicity such a case would bring to the university. Even had the three players been found guilty, Pressler's forced resignation would have been unjustified.

Even more scandalous was the self-serving prosecution of the case by a civil servant—acting district attorney Nifong—who was desperately attempting to establish his worth as a politician. His unethical actions came close to destroying the lives of three innocent university students. In the end, Duke University was forced to pay damages to those harmed by the case. Durham County and Nifong were sued for damages as well.

—*R. Baird Shuman*

FURTHER READING
Bernstein, Viv, and Joe Drape. "Rape Allegation Against Athletes Is Roiling Duke." *The New York Times*, March 29, 2006. The first national story about the scandal.
Nelson, Michael. "Bad Call." *Chronicle of Higher Education*, October 6, 2007. An insightful consideration of the role that stereotypes played in the scandal.
Smolkin, Rachel. "Justice Delayed." *American Journalism Review*, August-September, 2007. An analysis of the news media's response to the gang rape allegations. Critical of the press's rush to condemn and its assumptions of guilt in the case.
Taylor, Stuart, Jr., and K. C. Johnson. *Until Proven Innocent: Political Correctness and the Shameful Injustices of the Duke Lacrosse Rape Case.* New York: St. Martin's Press, 2007. An examination of the accusations of rape and of the refusal of the prosecutor to accept incontrovertible evidence of their innocence.
Yaeger, Don, with Mike Pressler. *It's Not About the Truth: The Untold Story of the Duke Lacrosse Case and the Lives It Shattered.* New York: Threshold Editions, 2007. An intimate look into the scandal as told by coach Mike Pressler to writer Don Yaeger.

SEE ALSO: Mar. 30, 1931: "Scottsboro Boys" Are Railroaded Through Rape Trials; Mar. 13, 1964: Kitty Genovese Dies as Her Cries for Help Are Ignored; Nov. 28, 1987: Black Teenager Claims to Have Been Gang-Raped by Police Officers; Mar. 30, 1991: William Kennedy Smith Is Accused of Rape; Sept. 22, 1997: Sportscaster Marv Albert Is Tried for Sexual Assault; July 1, 2003: Basketball Star Kobe Bryant Is Accused of Rape; June 13, 2008: Singer R. Kelly Is Acquitted on Child Pornography Charges.

April 26, 2006
BRITAIN'S DEPUTY PRIME MINISTER ADMITS AFFAIR WITH SECRETARY

After Deputy Prime Minister John Prescott admitted that he had a two-year affair with his secretary, Tracey Temple, she went public with her story and maintained that he used his power to get her into a sexual relationship, and that the two often had sex in his office. This abuse of power constituted sexual harassment, but the media focused on the relationship.

LOCALE: London, England
CATEGORIES: Sex; sex crimes; government; politics; public morals; women's issues

KEY FIGURES
John Prescott (b. 1938), British deputy prime minister, 1997-2007
Tracey Temple (b. 1962), Prescott's diary secretary
Tony Blair (b. 1953), British prime minister, 1997-2007

SUMMARY OF EVENT
John Prescott had been a key figure in Tony Blair's Labour Party government since the election of 1997. Before this time, Prescott was a combative figure in union affairs and in public debates with Conservatives. He had moved from old-style Labour to join Blair's New Labour, and for this he was valued by the new prime minister. He had been a senior cabinet minister, first as combined transport and environment minister, then picking up the employment portfolio. In 1997, he succeeded

Michael Heseltine as deputy prime minister.

In late 2002, Prescott began an affair with his newly appointed diary secretary, Tracey Temple, an affair that lasted about two years. Temple was thirty-seven years old and Prescott was sixty-one. However, it was not until 2006, some two years after the affair had ended, that Temple decided to go to Max Clifford, a leading British publicist, with her story. Clifford negotiated a $500,000 deal with the *Daily Mail* to buy her story. It was published on Sunday, April 30. The popular and competitive Sunday papers in Britain have traditionally given themselves over to scandal of all kinds, and they are always prepared to pay large sums for any story about the disgrace of a public figure. The Prescott story filled nine pages.

Prescott discovered the immanent deal between Temple and the newspaper, a deal not completed until Saturday, April 29. He decided to go public first, and on April 26 admitted to his two-year affair. Prescott's admission was followed on the Saturday of the deal with a television interview of Temple, in which she stated that she had to let people know the truth, but added, "But I never, ever thought I would actually have to do anything like this." She claimed that news of the affair was going to break anyway, that she had had minimal support from Prescott, and therefore she had decided to make her move. She claimed to have been manipulated and said that falsehoods about her were circulating.

Prescott himself denounced the publication of her story and the press's raking through details of politicians' private lives, and he also accused Temple of making up much of it. He threatened to sue. Much of this could be seen as typical bluster. More significant, the government immediately announced its continuing support for Prescott, claiming he still had a vital role to play and that the affair was a private matter that had no effect on the course of government.

The material Temple supplied to the *Daily Mail* was based on a diary she had kept, which was frequently quoted by the newspaper. The most sensational part of the diary was the rendezvous the lovers kept, which were often in government buildings or buildings occupied by Prescott on a "grace and favor" lease as part of his job. Thus, they met in his apartment in Admiralty Arch, just down the road from Whitehall, where Prescott had his office. Some of the affair was conducted in his own office, while his staff were working outside, sometimes even with the door open. More damaging, she claimed they had sex immediately after a significant public event: a memorial service for the war in Iraq, held in St. Paul's Cathedral, London, in October, 2003. They also had sex in a hotel room while Prescott's wife, Pauline, was waiting downstairs.

Prescott had made little attempt to be discreet about the relationship. He invited Temple to escort his wife to the state opening of Parliament in 2002, soon after the affair had begun at a Christmas party. This was an inappropriate invitation, given that Temple was only his diary secretary, a somewhat junior position. He had also engaged in sexual banter with her in front of other colleagues and had caressed her in public elevators in his office building.

Temple stated that she enjoyed the attention. Her boyfriend at the time, Barrie Williams, had more to tell another popular newspaper, the *Daily Mirror*. He stated that Temple's sexual appetite was large, and after a few drinks she became very adventurous and flirtatious. He had been quite unaware of the affair, even though Temple asked him to marry her just after embarking on the affair with Prescott. He thought Temple had reveled in her power, though she explicitly denied this.

IMPACT

The immediate impact of the scandal for Temple was that she was shifted to a minor position as a gardener for two months. She was then given a low-key post at the University of Westminster. Finally, in January, 2007, she was given back her old job in the deputy prime minister's office, but with no immediate contact with Prescott. In fact, very soon after, Prescott resigned and was not involved with the cabinet of the new prime minister, Gordon Brown.

For Prescott, the scandal could have cost him his job. He held a delicate position in the government, as a sort of point of contact between Blair and his chancellor, Brown. While not in Blair's innermost circle of advisers, Prescott was in a very senior position. Although there was no breach of security, and none suggested, he did become something of a figure of fun as a result of the affair, and he lost a good deal of credibility. Previous displays of inappropriate behavior made Prescott something of a liability for a while, but Blair was typically loyal to old colleagues and was prepared to protect him.

Prescott's forty-four-year marriage remained intact, though there were stories of Pauline Prescott's fury over the affair. Prescott himself asked for privacy for his family, though a television comedy about the affair, *Confessions of a Diary Secretary* (February, 2007), was hardly the answer he wanted. Rumors of an earlier affair threatened but never came to light. Prescott was thus able to remain in office.

For the government, the affair came on the heels of other embarrassing faux pas, especially the Home Office minister's admission that criminals recommended for deportation at the end of their prison sentence were not being sent back to their country of origin, and earlier sexual scandals involving Robin Cook, a former foreign secretary, and others. Many believed that Blair was losing his grip on his government ministers. However, Blair kept his equilibrium and resigned in 2007, a time of his choosing, after ten years in power.

—*David Barratt*

FURTHER READING

Brown, Colin. *Fighting Talk: Biography of John Prescott*. New York: Simon & Schuster, 1997. An account of Prescott's early rise to power, from a ship's steward to union organizer and from Old Labour to New Labour. However, the account predates his rise to deputy prime minister and the Temple affair.

Mackenzie, Kelvin. *The John Prescott Kama Sutra*. London: John Blake, 2006. An example of Prescott becoming a figure of fun after the affair. In this spoof, the author revisits the sites where Prescott and Temple had sex.

Seldon, Anthony. *Blair's Britain, 1997-2007*. New York: Cambridge University Press, 2007. This magisterial work gives the fullest account of the Blair years and Prescott's place within them.

"We Made Love in John's Office." *The Mail on Sunday* (London), April 29, 2006. The news article that continued the story of Prescott's affair with Temple.

SEE ALSO: Mar. 2-Sept. 25, 1963: John Profumo Affair Rocks British Government; Oct. 14, 1983: British Cabinet Secretary Parkinson Resigns After His Secretary Becomes Pregnant; July 25, 1987: Novelist-Politician Jeffrey Archer Wins Libel Trial Against the *Daily Star*; Dec. 18, 1989: Prince Charles's Intimate Phone Conversation with Camilla Parker Bowles Is Taped; Aug. 23, 1992: Princess Diana's Phone Conversation with Her Lover Is Made Public; Sept. 24, 1992: British Cabinet Member David Mellor Resigns over Romantic Affair; Jan. 5, 1994: British Cabinet Member Resigns After Fathering a Child Out of Wedlock; Sept. 28, 2002: British Politician Reveals Her Affair with Prime Minister John Major; Jan. 21, 2006: British Politician Resigns After Gay-Sex Orgy.

2000's

May 4, 2006
MEDIA UNCOVER MATCH-FIXING IN ITALIAN SOCCER

The Italian media revealed wire-tapped conversations between the former team manager of the popular Juventus soccer club, Luciano Moggi, and Italian Football Association officials about appointing particular referees to particular games. Four of the premier clubs in Italian soccer were implicated in the scandal, and several sports executives were convicted and imprisoned. Most shocking was the demotion of Juventus to a lower division of play.

LOCALE: Italy
CATEGORIES: Corruption; sports; organized crime and racketeering

KEY FIGURES
Luciano Moggi (b. 1937), general manager of the Juventus soccer team
Antonio Giraudo (b. 1946), chief executive of the Juventus soccer team
Silvio Berlusconi (b. 1936), owner of AC Milan and prime minister of Italy, 1994-1995, 2001-2006, 2008-

SUMMARY OF EVENT
The corruption scandal that struck Italian soccer in 2006 enveloped four of the most famous and successful teams in the history of the sport. In soccer-crazed Italy, Juventus stands as the most storied team in the country and is the third most successful soccer team in all of Europe. Formed in 1897, the Turin-based club has won more than fifty trophies. Prior to the 2006 scandal, the team spent its entire history in Serie A, the upper division of Italian soccer. Accordingly, it has the largest fan base in all of Italy with about 11 million fans, as well as 28 million registered fans throughout Europe and an estimated 170 million fans worldwide. It is the most popular soccer team in the world.

The soccer club Associazione Calcio Milan, commonly known as AC Milan or Milan, formed in 1899 and also spent most of its history in the top ranks of soccer. It has won eighteen international titles, more than any other soccer team in existence. In 1986, entrepreneur Silvio Berlusconi acquired the team and retained ownership while he served three terms as prime minister of Italy. Berlusconi owned the club during the scandal.

Società Sportiva Lazio, known as SS Lazio or Lazio, formed in Rome in 1900. Although not as successful as Juventus or AC Milan, Lazio has spent most of its history in Serie A and is not a stranger to scandal. A 1980 incident involving illegal betting resulted in the club being temporarily demoted, along with AC Milan, to Serie B. Lazio suffered a loss of season points in 1986 for illegal betting by a player. In 2002, the club's owner, Sergio Cragnotti, was involved in a financial scandal with his food-services company, which forced him to reduce spending and ultimately sell the club. By 2006, Lazio had rebounded and was enjoying a successful season with a roster of inexpensive players.

ACF Fiorentina, generally known as Fiorentina, formed in 1926 in Florence. The club has also spent most of its existence at the Serie A level. The club went bankrupt in 2002 and essentially ceased to exist for two months until being revived by a new owner. Beginning at the Serie C level, Fiorentina worked its way back to Serie A by the end of the 2003-2004 season. By 2006, the club was struggling to avoid being relegated back to Serie B and desperately needed every victory that it could obtain.

On May 4, details of match-fixing between Luciano Moggi, general manager of Juventus, and an official responsible for refereeing assignments were printed on the front page of Italy's largest newspaper. Moggi and Antonio Giraudo, a Juventus chief executive, were accused of creating a network of soccer federation officials, team owners, referees, and journalists to influence refereeing assignments and thus the outcome of league games. Moggi pressured the vice chairman of the Union of

European Football Associations (UEFA) referees committee to favor Juventus. He also spoke to Italy's interior minister to persuade him to allow Juventus to play a game with Fiorentina after that game had been postponed following the death of Pope John Paul II.

Moggi and Giraudo also were accused of detaining and berating a referee for not favoring Juventus during a November, 2004, game. Television pundits were implicated for having suppressed discussion of controversial decisions that favored Juventus. Moggi and Giraudo resigned later in the month, along with Juventus's entire board.

The Italian Football Federation (FIGC) began investigating forty-one people. In July, 2006, a FIGC prosecutor charged four teams with sports fraud. Juventus, AC Milan, Lazio, and Fiorentina were ordered before the largest sports tribunal ever held in Italy in an improvised courtroom in Rome's Olympic Stadium. The tribunal, which included a panel of six judges and twenty-six officials, including referees, was not, however, a criminal proceeding.

The prosecutor asked Italian judges to punish the clubs in a way that would deter others from thinking about corrupting soccer. He demanded that Juventus be dropped two divisions and that the other clubs also be demoted. However, justice minister Mario Clemente Mastella declared himself and many other fans to be in favor of amnesty for the clubs as a way of holding on to those star Italian players who would possibly flee abroad. After Mastella's pronouncement, other politicians aligned on the question of amnesty according to their allegiance to the various clubs. Berlusconi lobbied against a demotion for any of the teams.

A team's relegation to a lower division would result in a significant financial setback. Juventus, with stock sold on the Milan stock exchange, faced the risk of bankruptcy, as major sponsors would flee a club that no longer played Serie A. The other teams, less prominent, also would lose sponsorships and the ability to pay the salaries of top players. The four implicated teams included thirteen players from Italy's World Cup team. A number of top European soccer clubs, including England's Chelsea, Arsenal, and Manchester United, and Spain's Real Madrid, eagerly hoped for the opportunity to snag these star players.

IMPACT

On July 14, a sports tribunal announced a verdict that was not as severe as expected, perhaps because Italy defeated France in the World Cup final earlier in the week, thereby sending the entire nation of Italy into euphoria. The sentences fell short of what the prosecutor had sought, yet the fall of Juventus still struck Italy as the collapse of a monarchy.

The tribunal demoted Juventus from Serie A to Serie B for its role in the game-fixing scandal. The club also was docked 30 points, the equivalent of ten losses, which made it very difficult for the team to advance to the championship and move back to Serie A. Juventus also lost the championships it had won in 2004-2005 and 2005-2006. Fiorentina and Lazio also were demoted to Serie B and penalized 12 and 7 points, respectively. AC Milan remained in Serie A but lost 15 points. Moggi and Giraudo received five-year suspensions and fines. The vice president of AC Milan received a one-year ban from the game, and the president and honorary president of Fiorentina were suspended for several years. Lazio's president was banned for three and one-half years. Several referees were suspended.

The teams had three days to appeal the court's decision. With the verdict upheld, Juventus, AC Milan, and Fiorentina would be barred from the Champions League and Lazio would be banned from the UEFA Cup. Milan appealed and had its penalty reduced to 8 points, while keeping its Champions League participation. Milan won the competition in 2006-2007. The other teams also had their punishments reduced. On appeal, Fiorentina won reinstatement to Serie A, with a 15-point penalty. Lazio also remained in Serie A, with a 3-point reduction and a retroactive 30-point deduction that cost them qualification for the UEFA Cup. Juventus played in Serie B in the 2007-2008 season for the first time in the club's history. The team sold many of its players.

—Caryn E. Neumann

2000's

FURTHER READING

Agnew, Paddy. *Forza Italia: A Journey in Search of Italy and Its Football.* London: Ebury Press, 2006. An introduction to Italian soccer that makes the case that corruption is endemic to the sport. Includes coverage of several scandals that occurred prior to the Serie A scandal in 2006.

Foot, John. *Winning at All Costs: The Untold Story of Triumph, Tragedy, and Corruption in Italian Soccer.* New York: Nation Books, 2007. A general history of Italian soccer dating back to its northern Italian roots during the 1890's. Examines the effects of corruption on the sport.

Goldblatt, David. *The Ball Is Round: A Global History of Soccer.* New York: Riverhead Books, 2008. Extensive history of soccer that places the sport in its international context. Includes discussion of the 2006 Italian scandal.

Vialli, Gianluca, and Gabriele Marcotti. *The Italian Job: A Journey to the Heart of Two Great Footballing Cultures.* London: Bantam, 2006. Examines the differences between Italian and English soccer fans, arguably the most passionate soccer fans in the world.

SEE ALSO: Apr. 2, 1915: Players Fix Liverpool-Manchester United Soccer Match; July 1, 1994: Soccer Star Diego Maradona Is Expelled from World Cup; Jan. 27, 2005: German Soccer Referee Admits to Fixing Games for Money; July 29, 2008: NBA Referee Tim Donaghy Is Sentenced to Prison for Betting on Games.

May 12, 2006
SCIENTIST IS INDICTED FOR FAKING HIS RESEARCH ON CREATING STEM CELLS

South Korean biomedical researcher Hwang Woo-suk was charged with faking data in two landmark papers that described the production of the first cloned human embryos, the first embryonic stem cells derived from cloned embryos, and the first patient-specific embryonic stem-cell lines. Furthermore, the unfertilized human eggs used for these experiments were procured through unethical means, and Hwang misused the research funds secured for this work.

LOCALE: Seoul, South Korea

CATEGORIES: Hoaxes, frauds, and charlatanism; publishing and journalism; science and technology

KEY FIGURES

Hwang Woo-suk (b. 1952), stem-cell researcher and a former professor at Seoul National University

Gerald Schatten (b. 1949), stem-cell researcher, University of Pittsburgh School of Medicine

Chung Un-chan (b. 1946), president of Seoul National University

Roh Sung-il (b. 1952), fertility specialist, MizMedi Hospital, Seoul

Roe Jung-hye (b. 1957), dean of research, Seoul National University

Kim Sun-jong (b. 1969), biologist and former Hwang collaborator

Han Hak-soo (b. 1969), producer with the investigative news television show *PD Sucheop*

SUMMARY OF EVENT

On February 12, 2004, Seoul National University (SNU) biologist Hwang Woo-suk and his colleagues announced that they had successfully used somatic cell nuclear transfer (SCNT) to generate thirty cloned human embryos and derive an embryonic stem cell line from one of these cloned embryos. Hwang's report represented the first time SCNT was successfully used to make cloned human embryos and derive human embryonic stem cells. The results were published as "Evidence of a Pluripotent Human Embryonic Stem Cell Line Derived from a Cloned Blastocyst" in the March 12, 2004, issue of the renowned journal *Science*.

SCNT involves the removal of the nucleus (the cellular compartment that houses the chromosomes) from an unfertilized egg, followed by transplantation of a nucleus from another cell into this egg and artificial activation to initiate embryonic development. After growing in an artificial culture medium for approximately six days, surviving cloned embryos grow into semihollow

Hwang Woo-suk, center, is escorted by members of his research team after a press conference in Seoul in January, 2006. (Hulton Archive/Getty Images)

spheres called blastocysts. Blastocyst-stage embryos consist of external trophectoderm cells and internal inner-cell mass cells; the inner-cell mass cells are isolated and cultured to derive embryonic stem cell lines. The supplementary material to Hwang and colleagues' *Science* article stated that the 242 unfertilized human eggs used for these experiments were collected from sixteen female volunteers, who provided them without financial compensation.

In May, 2004, the British scientific journal *Nature* discovered that some of the eggs used by Hwang's group were donated by junior members of his own research team. Korean activists for citizens' rights and bioethicists protested, because it appeared that an overbearing boss coerced his female graduate students to undergo a potentially painful and risky procedure. Nevertheless, Hwang denied any wrongdoing.

Hwang's group announced yet another landmark advance in May, 2005. They claimed to have established eleven genetically matched patient-specific embryonic stem-cell lines. For SCNT they used nuclei from cultured fibroblasts (a cell from skin biopsies that grows well in culture) taken from nine patients who suffered from spinal cord injury, diabetes, or a disorder of the immune system. The fibroblast nuclei were transferred into nucleus-

deprived eggs from female volunteers and grown to the blastocyst stage. These blastocyst-stage embryos were cultured to make patient-specific embryonic stem-cell cultures that were genetically identical to the patients from whom the fibroblasts had been isolated. These patient-specific embryonic stem cells could potentially be used to treat catastrophic diseases that require regeneration of hopelessly damaged tissues, without rejection by the patient's immune systems. These results, published in the paper "Patient-Specific Embryonic Stem Cells Derived from Human SCNT Blastocysts" on June 17, 2005, in *Science*, were hailed throughout the international scientific community as a major breakthrough.

Although Hwang was a national hero by the time the article appeared, troubling questions and accusations arose nonetheless. On June 1, an investigative news program from the Seoul-based Munhwa Broadcasting Company (MBC) called *PD Su-cheop* had received a tip from a former Hwang research associate that there were enormous ethical problems with Hwang's egg procurements and technical problems that made the production of patient-specific stem cells impossible. Four months later, on October 15, *PD Su-cheop* producer Han Hak-soo interviewed former Hwang collaborator

Kim Sun-jong, who admitted that he had falsified two of the photographs in the 2005 *Science* paper under instructions from Hwang.

The following month, on November 12, Hwang's American coauthor, Gerald Schatten of the University of Pittsburgh, announced that he was cutting all ties with Hwang and SNU, citing significant bioethical violations in egg donor recruitment for the 2004 *Science* paper. On November 21, Roh Sung-il from MizMedi Hospital in Seoul, who supplied eggs for Hwang's research, announced that in 2002 he had paid at least twenty women approximately $1,430 each for eggs that were used in the 2004 study. These egg collections occurred before the South Koreans had passed their bioethics laws that made it a crime to pay for eggs. Roh insisted that Hwang did not know about these payments, but on November 24, Hwang admitted that he had used these eggs with full knowledge of this impropriety. He resigned his directorship of the World Stem Cell Hub but remained at SNU and vowed to continue his research.

On November 22, *PD Su-cheop* had reported the results of its preliminary analysis of Hwang's 2005 *Science* paper. MBC had acquired five samples from the patient-specific cell lines allegedly made by Hwang in his 2005 *Science* paper and sent the samples, along with tissue samples from the patients whose nuclei supposedly were used to construct the patient-specific embryonic cell lines, to an independent lab for corroboration. DNA analyses from this independent lab showed that the DNA from one of the patient-specific cell lines did not match the tissue sample as it should, which raised the distinct possibility that the embryonic stem-cell lines were not made from cloned embryos. For its efforts at exposing Hwang's fraud, the news program was taken off the air for more than one month after the public condemned its report as too harsh against the researcher.

On December 7, thirty SNU faculty members delivered a petition to SNU president Chung Un-chan, requesting that the university launch its own investigation into the results of Hwang's 2005 *Science* paper. The university began its investigation on December 12 and carefully examined all the materials allegedly generated by Hwang and his colleagues. This inquiry ended on December 29, when Roe Jung-hye, SNU dean of research, announced that "there are neither patient-specific stem-cell lines in Hwang's laboratory nor any scientific evidences to support the claim that such cell lines ever existed."

Further investigations showed that the untruths in Hwang's landmark 2004 and 2005 papers could only be the result of deliberate fabrication. Additionally, it was clear that Hwang had pressured female lab workers to donate their eggs. *Science* officially published the retraction of Hwang's 2004 and 2005 papers on January 20, 2006.

On March 6, Hwang admitted that he ordered his fellow researchers to falsify data for the 2005 *Science* paper. On March 20, SNU fired him, and he was indicted on charges of fraud, embezzlement, and violations of bioethics laws on May 12; several of his collaborators were indicted on similar charges. He reportedly opened animal-cloning laboratories near Seoul and in Thailand.

IMPACT

Hwang's faked research stifled international embryonic stem-cell research. Many labs ceased trying to clone human embryos after Hwang announced his success. After news of Hwang's fraud came to light, stem-cell labs were forced to restart the complicated task. Furthermore, the scandal led scientific journals to reevaluate the peer-review system to more effectively detect fraud before it gets published.

Hwang's ethical improprieties with egg donor recruitment also generated extensive discussions about standards for regulating egg procurement for embryonic stem-cell research. Some argue that egg donations, as is the case with organ donations, should be free of financial considerations. Others counter that because the hormonal induction used to hyperstimulate the ovaries during egg donation carries significant short- and long-term health risks, it is inappropriate to ask women to endure such risks without remuneration.

Another effect of Hwang's prevarication was its impact on the public, including investors. For example, the fraud revelation led to the temporary cancellation of *PD Su-cheop* for airing its exposé and led to the abrupt fall in stock prices of several South Korean biotechnology companies. Also, Hwang's blatant dishonesty—and the dishonesty of his colleagues—will be added to the arsenal of those opposed to embryonic stem-cell research.

—*Michael A. Buratovich*

FURTHER READING

Chong, Sei, and Dennis Normile. "Stem Cells: How Young Korean Researchers Helped Unearth a Scandal." *Science* 311 (2006). Discussion of how a South Korean investigative news show and young South Korean scientists launched the inquiry that brought Hwang's fraudulent publications to light.

Cyranoski, David. "Korean Stem-Cell Stars Dogged by Suspicion of Ethical Breach." *Nature* 429 (2004). The report that initially drew attention to the ethical breaches surrounding Hwang's recruitment of egg donors, by the science reporter who covered the Hwang scandal for this British journal.

Herold, Eve. *Stem Cell Wars*. New York: Palgrave, 2006. A supportive polemic for discussion of hu-man embryonic stem cells that focuses largely on politics, by a science reporter who interviewed Hwang on several occasions.

Hyun, Insoo. "Fair Payment or Undue Inducement?" *Nature* 442 (2006). Commentary by a Case Western Reserve University bioethicist on the dangers of egg donation and the case for financially remunerating egg donors.

Wohn, Yvette D., and Dennis Normile. "Prosecutors Allege Elaborate Deception and Missing Funds." *Science* 312 (2006). A detailed report of the charges brought against Hwang and his associates.

SEE ALSO: July 25, 1972: Newspaper Breaks Story of Abuses in Tuskegee Syphilis Study; Sept. 19, 1988: Stephen Breuning Pleads Guilty to Medical Research Fraud; Mar. 23, 1989: Scientists' "Cold Fusion" Claims Cannot Be Verified; Nov. 5, 2000: Japanese Amateur Archaeologist's "Discoveries" Are Proven Fakes; Aug., 2002: Immunologist Resigns After Being Accused of Falsifying Research; Sept. 25, 2002: Inquiry Reveals That Physicist Jan Hendrik Schön Faked His Research.

Summer, 2006-March 16, 2007

MANUFACTURER RECALLS PET FOOD THAT KILLED THOUSANDS OF AMERICAN PETS

In response to reports of the deaths of thousands of pets in the United States who consumed tainted pet food, the Chinese government and the U.S. Food and Drug Administration identified two Chinese companies that manufactured adulterated food additives with harmful chemicals to maximize their profits.

ALSO KNOWN AS: Menu Foods scandal

LOCALES: China; Canada; United States

CATEGORIES: Trade and commerce; business; law and the courts; government; medicine and health care; international relations

KEY FIGURES

Rosa L. DeLauro (b. 1943), U.S. representative from Connecticut

Richard J. Durbin (b. 1944), U.S. senator from Illinois

Paul Henderson (fl. early twenty-first century), Menu Foods president and chief executive officer

Andrew C. von Eschenbach (b. 1941), commissioner of the U.S. Food and Drug Administration

Zheng Xiaoyu (1944-2007), head of China's food and drug administration

2000's

SUMMARY OF EVENT

On March 16, 2007, Menu Foods, a producer of private-label pet foods based in Ontario, Canada, announced that it was recalling sixty million cans and packets of nearly one hundred brands of its products because of the deaths of a reported seventeen animals who were fed the products. Initially, the contaminant was unknown, and the actual number of affected pets remains unknown as well.

For weeks, as the recall continued to grow, both Menu Foods and the U.S. Food and Drug Administration (FDA) could not identify the problem and insisted that there had been no more than a handful of deaths. Veterinarians, however, reported thousands of pet deaths—cats and dogs—from causes such as kidney failure, while bloggers steadily tracked death tolls and developments. Later, two manufacturing plants in China were found to have added the nitrogen-rich chemical melamine, which is used in the production of fertilizer, plastics, and other inedible products, to wheat gluten and rice-protein concentrate to inflate their protein content. Wheat gluten and rice-protein concentrate are used as thickeners for wet pet food. Menu Foods was the leading manufacturer of wet pet-food products in North America at the time the scandal broke.

Lawsuits and mainstream media coverage of the scandal were followed—too late, many thought—by an FDA prohibition against the importation of Chinese wheat gluten and by congressional hearings into the FDA's response to the crisis and its oversight of the food supply. For a time U.S.-Chinese relations seemed threatened, but after the Chinese government identified at least one of the individuals responsible for the melamine contamination, the largest pet food recall in American history subsided.

The scandal began in the summer of 2006, when tainted wheat gluten first reached the United States, according to the FDA. Menu Foods began incorporating some of this contaminated food additive into its products on November 8. Reportedly, within six weeks, the company began receiving reports of pets being sickened by pet food produced at its plants in Streetsville, Ontario, Canada, and Emporia, Kansas, although Menu Foods said it had not received such reports until February 20, 2007. Seven days later, the company began routine feeding trials with forty to fifty cats and dogs; the same day, Menu Foods' chief executive officer, Paul Henderson, sold 12,700 of his shares in the company.

On March 7, the first of nine animals in the feeding trial died from acute renal failure. Further deaths prompted the company to switch wheat gluten suppliers four days later. However, roughly two weeks passed before Menu Foods sent samples of its products to Cornell University for testing. Unable to locate the source of the animal poisoning, Cornell in turn forwarded samples to the New York State Food Laboratory, which soon identified the chemotherapy agent aminopterin as a contaminant.

After sending food samples to Cornell, Menu Foods, on March 16, announced its first giant recall but failed to report the deaths of its test subjects. As Wall Street reacted and pet owners panicked, Menu Foods' stock declined 45 percent and its Web site was shut down. Consumers, unable to reach the company via the Web or by telephone, also were stonewalled by the FDA, which would only officially recognize the deaths of the nine animals in Menu Foods' feeding trials. The official death toll was revised to include a few pets, but it remained at fourteen even as blogs were posting reports of hundreds of deaths and veterinarians were estimating that deaths actually numbered in the thousands. By the end of March, retailers were pulling all Menu Foods products off their shelves, the company's New Jersey plant was under suspicion, and the FDA had announced that melamine was the major contaminant of the pet food.

Within hours of the FDA's announcement, other pet-food makers began announcing recalls. Still, the death toll mounted, and the announcements continued. On March 30, the FDA imposed an import restriction on wheat gluten produced by the Xuzhou Anying Biologic Technology Development Company in Jiangsu province, China. However, the public was not notified of this development until it was discovered days later by bloggers. U.S. senator Richard Durbin and U.S. representative Rosa DeLauro issued a press release on April 1 that criticized the FDA's laxity, but the release

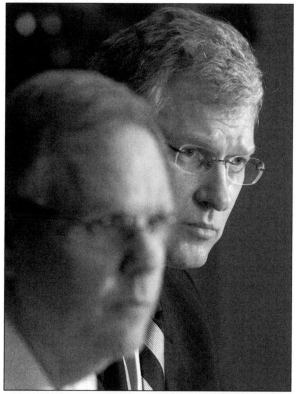

Menu Foods president and chief executive officer Paul Henderson, right, and executive vice president Richard Shields listen as a woman questions them at a news conference in March, 2007, about the death of her dog from eating Menu Foods dog food. (AP/Wide World Photos)

stated the obvious. The animal rights group People for the Ethical Treatment of Animals, or PETA, followed the next day with a public demand for the resignation of FDA commissioner Andrew C. von Eschenbach.

On April 3, tensions increased when the mainstream press speculated that tainted wheat gluten had been sold to suppliers of human food. Two days later, Durbin announced congressional hearings into the scandal. China followed with its own investigation into melamine-contaminated wheat gluten. Around April 10, investigators found that rice protein concentrate, another thickener used in food production, had been contaminated with melamine, prompting a new round of pet-food recalls and the identification of a second suspected Chinese manufacturer, in Shandong province. By the end of the

month, it was feared that contamination had reached the human food supply through surplus-tainted pet food given to chickens, hogs, and farmed fish.

On April 20, the FDA announced that it had opened a criminal investigation into the crisis. Chinese officials gave FDA inspectors permission to enter China, but they were not allowed to interview anyone involved with exporting the contaminated food products. Also, the suspect production facilities had been shut down before U.S. inspectors arrived. Around the same time, recalls of pet foods were announced in South Africa, after the deaths of animals who had consumed food laced with melamine-contaminated corn gluten. Within two months, melamine contamination was found in European products containing Chinese-produced corn gluten and rice-protein concentrate. On May 29, facing a worldwide problem, the Chinese government announced that the former head of China's food and drug administration, Zheng Xiaoyu, had been sentenced to death for accepting bribes in connection with the approval of faulty products. On June 27, Chinese officials announced a shutdown of 180 food factories accused of having improperly used industrial chemicals and expired food products. Zheng was executed on July 10.

IMPACT

Menu Foods estimated that the 2007 pet-food recall cost the company between forty-five and fifty-five million dollars. The costs to affected pet owners— in the thousands—are far higher, in both financial and emotional terms, leading to changes in U.S. law. Pet owners, both individually and collectively through class-action lawsuits, have filed countless suits against pet-food makers. Traditionally, pets have been accorded little monetary value by the courts, and as a consequence few suits concerning pets have been filed. The courts' valuation of pets— and the courts' realization of the emotional and financial ties of owners—has increased, however, and there appears to be a shift in perspective.

Pet-food manufacturers, too, suffered a major setback: eroded customer confidence. Companies have been building their own manufacturing plants and engaging in greater oversight of imported in-

2000's

gredients. The FDA, which was slow to react to the crisis, now takes seriously the issue of tainted animal food because of possible contamination of the human food supply.

Subsequent revelations of contaminated Chinese-produced medicines and health and beauty aids not only sparked a minor trade war between China and the United States over American products but also led to the realization that inadequate U.S. oversight of imports such as pet-food ingredients signals a possible threat to homeland security.

—Lisa Paddock

FURTHER READING

"Fallout from Recent Pet Food Recall." *Neutraceuticals World* 10 (June, 2007). This overview of the pet-food recall discusses how the crisis affected the human food supply and increased the demand for organic food—for people and their pets.

Kearns, Nancy. "Moving on, Moving Up: Pet Food Executives Tell Us How the Industry Has Changed, Post-Recall." *Whole Dog Journal* 10 (September, 2007). Although none of the executives interviewed for this piece were affiliated with companies implicated in the 2007 recall, the article describes how the scandal affected pet-food manufacturers, who beefed up not only production facilities but also customer relations.

Martin, Jonathan. "When a Pet Dies of Suspected Food Poisoning—What Is Its Value?" *Seattle Times*, March 22, 2006. The first class-action lawsuit filed against Menu Foods was filed in Seattle. This feature explains how the case affects pet-related laws.

Nestle, Marion. *Pet Food Politics: The Chihuahua in the Coal Mine.* Berkeley: University of California Press, 2008. A noted expert on the politics of food and food consumption investigates the pet-food scandal of 2006-2007.

Swaminathan, Nikhil. "The Poisoning of Our Pets: Scientists and Government Agencies Home in on the Cause of More than One Hundred Pet Deaths from Tainted Food." *Scientific American*, March 28, 2007. A good article outlining the course of the tainted-food case and how the scientific community and the federal government have handled the issue.

SEE ALSO: Sept.-Oct., 1937: Prescription Elixir Causes More than One Hundred Deaths; 1956-1962: Prescription Thalidomide Causes Widespread Birth Disorders; Oct. 20, 1978: Firestone Recalls Millions of Defective Car Tires; Sept. 17, 1985: Media Allege Canadian Officials Allowed Sale of Rancid Tuna; Feb. 4, 1996: Whistle-Blower Reveals Tobacco Industry Corruption; Nov. 26, 1997: Canadian Health Commissioner Releases Report on Tainted Blood; Aug. 20, 2007: Football Star Michael Vick Pleads Guilty to Financing a Dogfighting Ring.

July 14, 2006
NEW YORK TIMES EXPOSES GRADING SCANDAL AT AUBURN UNIVERSITY

A sociology professor at Auburn University contacted The New York Times *to report that his colleague was granting directed-study classes to athletes so that they could raise their grade point averages and remain eligible to play. The student athletes were given inflated grades in courses with virtually no academic work—a practice that also led to a misleading academic ranking of the university by the NCAA.*

LOCALE: Auburn, Alabama

CATEGORIES: Publishing and journalism; education; corruption; hoaxes, frauds, and charlatanism; sports

KEY FIGURES

James Gundlach (fl. early twenty-first century), chairman of the Department of Sociology, Auburn University

Thomas A. Petee (fl. early twenty-first century), professor of sociology at Auburn University

Tommy Tuberville (b. 1954), Auburn University football coach

Pete Thamel (fl. early twenty-first century), reporter for *The New York Times*

SUMMARY OF EVENT

On July 14, 2006, *New York Times* reporter Pete Thamel broke the story of a possible grading scandal involving athletes at Auburn University in Alabama. The scandal was brought to Thamel's attention by Professor James Gundlach, chairman of the Sociology Department at the university. Gundlach was reportedly watching a televised football game and heard that one of the players was a scholar-athlete with a sociology major. Because neither he nor two other full-time professors in the department had ever had the player in their respective classes, Gundlach began researching the department's academic records. He discovered that another profes-

sor, Thomas A. Petee, was offering an exorbitant number of directed-study classes that required very little course work and no class time. Though Gundlach had attempted to deal with the problem through appropriate institutional channels, reporting the issue to the provost's office months earlier, lack of attention to the problem led him to bring the issue to the media.

Concerns regarding the Auburn athletic department involved primarily the football team, which had eighteen players taking almost one hundred credit hours of Petee's directed-study courses. Though both athletes and nonathletes were enrolled in the courses, approximately 25 percent of Petee's students were athletes. One player even took as many as seven directed-study courses from Petee. Another problem for the athletic department that resulted from the study of these courses was the discovery that these eighteen players were receiving higher grades in Petee's directed-study courses, grades that raised the players' overall grade point averages to acceptable academic standards set by the National Collegiate Athletic Association (NCAA). Another issue that came to the university's attention was Petee allowing one athlete to join a course two-thirds of the way through the semester and rewarding a high grade to that student for little effort.

Whether the courses were linked specifically to the athletic department was questionable. Despite one athlete's report that the director of Auburn's Student Athlete Support Services had arranged the courses, this was not confirmed. Regardless of the large number of football players who were advanced because of these courses, Coach Tommy Tuberville repeatedly stressed his confidence that the issue was academic rather than one of athletics. He denied the involvement of the athletic department in manufacturing the courses, in advising students to take the courses, or in pressuring professors to inflate the grades of student athletes.

2000'S

Auburn's academic standing in the NCAA was top for its division for public universities, and it ranked behind only Stanford University, the U.S. Naval Academy, and Boston College in the entire division. The academic standing of Auburn athletes prompted other institutions to question how the NCAA evaluated academic standards and ranked colleges and universities based on those evaluations.

The Auburn directed-study courses were investigated by university officials after the story broke in *The New York Times*. Despite challenging areas such as statistics and theory that would better be taught in a classroom because of required intensive content, the university discovered that Petee was offering a wide variety of courses in this format. Gundlach reported that Petee had offered directed-reading courses to over 250 students the previous year (2004-2005). This load included fifteen different directed-reading courses, which put Petee's teaching load at three times the normal full-time load. Other professors and department chairs at the university confirmed that the workload Petee carried was ridiculously high, even impossible.

At the orders of university president Edward R. Richardson, Auburn conducted an internal audit. The audit discovered a number of additional problems in the Sociology Department, including alleged grade changes that brought several students' grade point averages to an acceptable level for graduation. In one instance, Professor Paul Starr was contacted about a change of grade he allegedly gave to a scholarship athlete (not a football player) never enrolled in any of his classes. The student's grade was changed from an incomplete to an A, one of four A's given to the student (the other A's were awarded by Petee, Starr's department chairman). The A grades raised this student athlete's grade point average to the university's standard for graduation. The internal audit confirmed that Petee changed approximately thirty-three grades above the average departmental grade changes in a particular semester. He was reprimanded for lack of appropriate record keeping. Auburn did share some findings with the NCAA, but the university did not expect to share the complete results of the audit.

The NCAA agreed that the problems were academic and not with the athletic program.

The internal audit and press coverage of the bogus classes and the grade inflations led to the implementation of several new requirements at Auburn. First, the directed-readings program was overhauled. The curriculum was made more challenging, and fewer courses were allowed in this format. The maximum number of courses and students per professor was limited, with a student requiring multiple signatures before he or she could sign up for more than nine hours of directed-readings and before an individual professor could supervise more than three students per semester in such courses.

Second, Petee and James Witte, the director of adult education who also awarded athletes higher-than-normal grades, lost their departmental leadership positions but not their status as classroom teachers. Petee, however, was later suspended with pay, and he refused to discuss the matter with the media. His only defense for directing so many of the reading courses was that they were necessary because the university lacked departmental resources—teachers—to cover the heavy load of courses that needed to be taught.

Auburn tried to dismiss Petee, who then countersued. He settled with the university, retained his salary, and retained his position as interim chairman of the sociology department. Gundlach had retired shortly after he brought the corruption to the media's attention, citing departmental division as his reason for leaving the university.

IMPACT

The bogus-course and grade-inflation scandal at Auburn, deemed more of an issue of academics rather than of athletics, reinforced concerns over the NCAA's ranking of academics at a given institution. Even with the scandal in the news, the NCAA ranked Auburn fifth in the United States among Division I-A public universities, leading to questions about how the NCAA ranking system worked. After the Auburn affair, the NCAA was encouraged to change its ranking system to account for academic differences among schools, that is, among those that are academically challenging and those that only pretend to be or those whose ranking was based on inflated grades and nonexistent classes.

—*Theresa L. Stowell*

FURTHER READING

Lipka, Sara. "Auburn Alters Policy on Independent Study." *Chronicle of Higher Education*, September 1, 2006. Simple overview of Auburn University's revised policies regarding directed-study classes. Especially relevant because the scandal led to academic reform at the university.

Mandel, Stewart. *Bowls, Polls, and Tattered Souls: Tackling the Chaos and Controversy That Reign over College Football*. Hoboken, N.J.: John Wiley & Sons, 2007. This book provides a detailed, behind-the-scenes look at notorious university scandals involving student athletes and college athletics.

Staurowsky, Ellen J. "Piercing the Veil of Amateurism: Commercialization, Corruption, and U.S. College Sports." In *The Commercialization of Sport*, edited by Trevor Slack. New York: Routledge, 2004. Staurowsky discusses how amateur athletics in the United States has become a commercialized and corrupt spectacle.

Thamel, Pete. "Top Grades and No Class Time for Auburn Players." *The New York Times*, July 14, 2006. Original article that broke the story. Reports on James Gundlach's concerns over Thomas Petee's directed-study courses offered to athletes at Auburn. Highlights the number of courses offered and specific students involved, and discusses Petee's response to the accusations against him.

Wasley, Paula. "Auburn U. Settles with Professor Who Handed Out Easy Grades to Athletes." *Chronicle of Higher Education*, August 10, 2007. Brief article detailing the results of Petee's lawsuit against Auburn University and the university's dismissal proceedings against him. Good for studies of the impact of the scandal on student athletics and student-athlete scholarship.

SEE ALSO: Jan. 17, 1951: College Basketball Players Begin Shaving Points for Money; Apr. 27, 1980: Mobster's Arrest Reveals Point Shaving by Boston College Basketball Players; Feb. 25, 1987: NCAA Imposes "Death Penalty" on Southern Methodist University Football; Mar. 27, 2002: Georgia Basketball Coach Jim Harrick, Sr., Resigns over Fraud Allegations; May 3, 2003: University of Alabama Fires New Football Coach in Sex Scandal; Sept. 13, 2007: New England Patriots Football Team Is Fined for Spying on Other Teams.

July 26, 2006
TOUR DE FRANCE IS HIT WITH A DOPING SCANDAL

The Tour de France, a grueling three-week bicycle race that is one of Europe's most popular sporting events, was hit with a major drug scandal in 2006. American cyclist Floyd Landis, who won the race, was stripped of his championship and banned from riding for two years after testing positive for a performance-enhancing drug. Landis maintained his innocence and appealed the rulings, but to no avail.

LOCALE: France

CATEGORIES: Sports; drugs; corruption; medicine and health care ethics

KEY FIGURES

Floyd Landis (b. 1975), American professional cyclist

Oscar Pereiro (b. 1977), Spanish professional cyclist

Tom Simpson (1937-1967), British cyclist whose death led to the implementation of drug testing in professional cycling

SUMMARY OF EVENT

Throughout its more than one-hundred-year history, the Tour de France, competitive cycling's most prestigious event, has been plagued by scandals and doping incidents. Early tour riders were believed to have consumed alcohol and used other substances to dull the pain of competing in endurance cycling. Riders also began using drugs and other substances to increase their performance rather than dull their senses. Organizing bodies, such as the Tour and the International Cycling Union, followed with policies designed to combat the illegal practices. The death of the British champion Tom Simpson on Mount Ventoux during the 1967 tour led to the implementation of drug testing policies.

American professional cyclist Floyd Landis, who joined the Phonak Cycling team after riding for several years with seven-time Tour de France champion Lance Armstrong, another American,

Floyd Landis at a press conference in Madrid, Spain, on July 28, 2006. (Hulton Archive/Getty Images)

started the 2006 season impressively with overall wins in the Amgen Tour in California and the prestigious Paris-Nice race. Landis won for a third time at the Ford Tour de Georgia just prior to start of the Tour de France. Despite these early successes, Landis was not a favorite to win cycling's most prestigious race.

On the eve of the tour's start, July 1, nine riders, including pre-race favorites Jan Ulrich from Germany and Italy's Ivan Basso, were disqualified. Their names turned up on a list of fifty-six cyclists who allegedly had contact with a Spanish doctor at the center of a doping probe in Spain. During the early stages of the tour, Landis was able to keep up with the pace set by the riders of the Rabobank team. Landis positioned himself in the overall lead until stage 13, when he and his team started a breakaway led by his former teammate, Oscar Pereiro of Spain, who took the overall lead by 89 seconds. In stage 15, on the slopes of Alpe d'Huez, Landis outrode Pereiro by almost two minutes and regained the fabled yellow jersey (worn by the tour leader) and a 10-second overall lead in the standings. Landis performed poorly during stage 16, as he fell from first to eleventh place. Pereiro took the overall lead and was eight minutes ahead of Landis with only three stages remaining.

In the following day's stage 17, Landis amazed the cycling world with a breakaway attack considered "one of the most epic days of cycling ever seen." At one point he led Pereiro by 9 minutes 4 seconds and ultimately won the stage. His win in this stage took more than 7 minutes from Pereiro's overall lead. The next stage was a 57-kilometer individual time trial. Landis's strength in time trials worked for him in this stage as he came well within striking distance of regaining the tour lead. He finished third in the time trial of stage 19, which put him 89 seconds ahead of Pereiro and 3 minutes 31 seconds ahead of Spanish rider Carlos Sastre, reclaiming the yellow jersey with a lead of 59 seconds. On July 23, Landis retained the lead through stage 20, the famous procession into Paris to end the tour, by 57 seconds.

Only days after winning the tour, Landis's team announced that its top rider had tested positive, after stage 17, for an unusually high ratio of the hormone testosterone to the hormone epitestosterone (T/E ratio). Under World Anti-Doping Agency (WDA) regulations, a ratio of testosterone to epitestosterone greater than 4:1 is considered a positive result. Any rider found to have these hormones in their system, at this ratio or greater, is to be disqualified from a race and suspended from racing for two years. Landis denied that he was doping and placed faith in a second test using his backup, or B, sample. Testing had been performed by the French government's antidoping clinical laboratory, the National Laboratory for Doping Detection (LNDD). Following the reported positive result on his A sample on July 26, Landis suggested that the results had been improperly released under the rules of the International Cycling Union (UCI). Phonak Cycling announced that Landis would be dismissed if the backup sample also tested positive. The backup sample did test positive as well, and Landis was fired from his team on August 5.

Under UCI regulations, the determination of whether or not a cyclist violated any rules must be made by the cyclist's national federation, in this case USA Cycling, which ultimately transferred the case to the United States Anti-Doping Agency (USADA). Landis claimed that he was not guilty of using banned performance-enhancing drugs. He argued that the processing of the A and B urine samples did not meet the established WDA criteria for a positive doping offense. Landis maintained the positive results on the B sample came from a sample number not assigned to him. He also claimed that the same two technicians analyzed both the original and the second validating samples. International laboratory standards forbid the same individuals from participating in both tests to prevent them from validating their own findings.

IMPACT

On May 14, 2007, the USADA and Landis began arbitration. In a bitterly contested nine-day hearing, Landis and his lawyers insisted that the French lab did not follow WDA rules in testing his urine samples. A three-person panel agreed with them, in part. The panel's eighty-four-page decision concluded the presence of problems with the way the French lab conducted some of its tests, filled out its paperwork, and handled the urine samples. Nevertheless, two of the three panelists concluded that the lab errors in question were not significant enough to dismiss the positive test. On September 20, Landis was stripped of his Tour de France title and suspended from cycling competition for two years. Second-place rider Pereiro became the official winner of the 2006 tour.

Landis appealed the decision to the Court of Arbitration for Sport, based in Lausanne, Switzerland, for his last chance at appeal. The hearings opened in New York in March, 2008. On June 30, the CAS announced from Switzerland that it was upholding the September decision to ban Landis for two years.

The Landis doping scandal affected the overall popularity of bicycle racing in the United States, placing the world's premier cycling event under a dark cloud. Fans and the media have become more cynical, and businesses are reconsidering whether it is worthwhile to invest in the sport as sponsors of team or events. The governing bodies of cycling around the world have promised more assertiveness in cleaning up the corruption.

—Mary McElroy

FURTHER READING

Hood, Andrew, and John Wilcockson. *The Tour de France 2006: Triumph and Turmoil for Floyd Landis.* Boulder, Colo.: Velo Press, 2006. An analysis of the race that covers every aspect of the grueling three-week event with maps, stage reports, and profiles of the riders. Photographs enhance the visual experience of the road race.

Landis, Floyd, and Loren Mooney. *Positively False: The Real Story of How I Won the Tour de France.* New York: Simon Spotlight, 2007. Told in Landis's own words, this memoir is a powerful indictment of the unchecked governing bodies of cycling, who he believes have compromised the integrity of the sport as a whole.

Thompson, Christopher S. *The Tour de France: A Cultural History.* 2006. New ed. Berkeley: University of California Press, 2008. This new edi-

2000's

tion, with an updated preface, explores the cultural history of the Tour de France. Includes discussion of the doping scandals that have plagued the tour from its early days into the twenty-first century.

Walsh, David. *From Lance to Landis: Inside the American Doping Controversy at the Tour De France.* New York: Ballantine Books, 2007. Explores the many facets of the cycling doping scandals in the United States and abroad. Examines how performance-enhancing drugs can infiltrate a premier sports event and why athletes succumb to the pressures to use them. Walsh conducted hundreds of hours of interviews with key figures in international cycling.

SEE ALSO: Feb. 28, 1986: Baseball Commissioner Peter Ueberroth Suspends Players for Cocaine Use; June 30, 1994: Tonya Harding Is Banned from Skating After Attack on Rival; July 1, 1994: Soccer Star Diego Maradona Is Expelled from World Cup; Sept. 26, 2000: Gymnast Andreea Răducan Loses Her Olympic Gold Medal Because of Drugs; Feb. 11, 2002: French Judge Admits Favoring Russian Figure Skaters in Winter Olympics; July 1, 2003: Basketball Star Kobe Bryant Is Accused of Rape; Mar. 17, 2005: Former Baseball Star Mark McGwire Evades Congressional Questions on Steroid Use; Oct. 5, 2007: Olympic Champion Marion Jones Admits Steroid Use.

July 28, 2006
ACTOR MEL GIBSON IS CAUGHT MAKING ANTI-SEMITIC REMARKS

Star film actor Mel Gibson was stopped for erratic driving and speeding and then arrested for drunk driving on Pacific Coast Highway in Malibu. During the traffic stop, he made anti-Semitic remarks to the sheriff's deputy who detained him. Gibson's arrest and vulgar rants were detailed by the media within hours of his arrest. The actor made several public apologies, but the scandal did not affect his career.

LOCALE: Malibu, California

CATEGORIES: Racism; law and the courts; social issues and reform; public morals; Hollywood

KEY FIGURES
Mel Gibson (b. 1956), American film actor and director

James Mee (fl. early twenty-first century), Los Angeles County Sheriff's Department deputy

SUMMARY OF EVENT
Actor and director Mel Gibson's profanity-filled, racially charged rant at Los Angeles County sher-

iff's deputy James Mee, who had stopped Gibson on Pacific Coast Highway in Malibu, California, for driving erratically and speeding, made headlines around the world in a matter of hours. Although Gibson's career seemed to hang in the balance for the next few days, he ultimately walked away from the incident relatively unscathed. His professional survival stemmed not only from his public expressions of regret but also, ironically, from his reputation as an already rough-edged and somewhat tarnished star long before Mee pulled him over in the predawn hours of July 28, 2006, and arrested him for drunk driving.

Born in New York State to an American father and an Irish-Australian mother, Gibson moved with his family to Australia just as he was about to enter his teenage years, when his father decided to relocate to his wife's homeland. Although he first drew worldwide attention among the so-called Australian New Wave filmmakers and actors of the 1970's and early 1980's, Gibson's success in a science-fiction film series in which he played an antihero named Mad Max, struggling to survive in a post-apocalyptic wasteland, made him a superstar in action films far removed from the art-film dramas favored by his early colleagues.

In addition to the Mad Max films, Gibson also starred with Danny Glover in the wildly popular *Lethal Weapon* series of seriocomic police movies. In 1990, Gibson surprised his fans with a switch to the most serious sort of drama imaginable—an adaptation of William Shakespeare's *Hamlet* directed by Franco Zeffirelli. The film was successful with both critics and viewers, encouraging Gibson to embark on a series of ambitious, serious-minded pictures, sometimes as actor, sometimes as director, and sometimes as both. Each of these films—which constituted an unofficial trilogy of historical epics—created controversy and drew attention to Gibson's beliefs about and attitudes toward various minority groups.

The hugely popular *Braveheart* (1995), which Gibson both directed and starred in, was the story of Scottish national hero William Wallace, and it drew accusations of hatred of the English as well as homophobia because of its unsympathetic and stereotyped depiction of the homosexual English king Edward II. Gibson then starred in *The Patriot* (2000), a revolutionary war drama that again drew accusations of Anglo bashing because of its one-sided portrayal of the English as vicious and wholly despicable. His pet project, *The Passion of the Christ* (2004), a film detailing the final week in the life of Jesus, incited much debate in the media, as some felt that Gibson, in an age-old slander, was placing the blame for the crucifixion of Jesus on the Jews. The film was also criticized for depicting Jesus receiving far more brutalization at the hands of his captors than is supported by New Testament texts.

All these prior controversies, centered on Gibson's perceived prejudices, haunted—but perhaps also helped—him in the wake of his drunken encounter with Mee. The deputy wrote in his arrest report that Gibson belligerently demanded to know if Mee was Jewish and subsequently went into a paranoid tirade in which he blamed Jews for every war that had ever occurred in the history of humankind. Also, Gibson allegedly insinuated that he would use

Los Angeles County Sheriff's Department booking photograph of Mel Gibson on the morning of his arrest. (Hulton Archive/Getty Images)

his power and influence in California to carry out reprisals against Mee. Gibson refused to cooperate with deputies and, at the Malibu-Lost Hills sheriff's station, he came close to relieving himself publically on the station floor. During all this brouhaha, according to Mee, Gibson made frequent use of "the F-word." Later, rumors circulated that, according to some unnamed source other than Mee, Gibson also made a crude, sexist remark to a female deputy at the sheriff's station. Despite all this drama, within five hours, Gibson was released on bail. Within twelve hours the story of his arrest and reprehensible behavior had hit the news services, and what seemed to be written copies of Deputy Mee's original arrest report were posted on the celebrity-news Web site tmz.com.

For the next month, debates raged in the media. Was the sheriff's department report posted on the Web authentic? If so, how was it obtained? Had

2000's

1107

someone at the sheriff's station leaked the report? Had Gibson been given preferential treatment because he was a celebrity? Had Mee's superiors tried to coerce him into downplaying or denying Gibson's alleged bigoted statements? Is Gibson truly an anti-Semite? Many people in the entertainment industry and prominent Jewish Americans made public statements either attacking or defending Gibson. The actor also found himself being widely spoofed in editorial cartoons, in comic routines, and on television.

Gibson's initial response was to issue a public apology the next day, July 29. However, this statement of shame never specifically addressed the charge of anti-Semitism and seemed to blame the incident on drinking and his long-term problems with alcohol. When public opinion deemed this mea culpa unsatisfactory, Gibson offered another on August 1. In this second attempt at redress, he directly denied his alleged religious bigotry and denounced not only anti-Semitism specifically but all forms of hate and prejudice. He also offered to get together with Jewish people offended by his outburst and discuss the matter openly, a ploy he had used earlier when crude, homophobic remarks he made in an interview with a Spanish reporter outraged gays and lesbians in 1991. Gibson did not contest the charge of driving while intoxicated, and on August 18 he was given three years of probation, fined thirteen hundred dollars, and ordered to take part in various alcohol rehabilitation programs.

IMPACT

In spite of the attention it received and the heated debate it sparked, the inebriated blather that Gibson spewed at Deputy Mee in July of 2006 ultimately did little damage to the star's career. He continued to make and release films and to be a powerful entertainment figure. In part, this outcome derived from the somewhat soiled and tattered reputation that Gibson brought with him to the scandal. He had already been accused of being intolerant. After media scrutiny dissipated, most people retreated to opinions that they had reached long ago about his attitudes and behavior, leaving his fans to decide to accept his excuses and apologies and his detractors

to ask themselves if they could expect anything less from him.

No doubt the scandal would have seriously jeopardized the career of a celebrity with a tamer, more level-headed public persona, as the shock would have been far keener and the additional charge of hypocrisy would have been incredibly damaging. In fact, the only concrete outcome of the incident was that it inspired the state of California to pass a law in 2007 making it a crime for law enforcement or court officials to sell or solicit for sale any information, including photographs, about the arrest of a celebrity or other high-profile detainee.

—*Thomas Du Bose*

FURTHER READING

Carr, Steven. *Hollywood and Anti-Semitism.* New York: Cambridge University Press, 2001. Although covering only the time period up to World War II, this book remains the definitive work on its subject and provides cogent background for the incident involving Mel Gibson.

Clarkson, Wensley. *Mel Gibson: Living Dangerously.* New York: Thunder's Mouth Press, 1999. Predates the 2006 scandal but provides insight into Gibson's troubled history with ethnic, racial, and sexual minorities.

Newton, Michael, and John L. French. *Celebrities and Crime.* New York: Chelsea House, 2008. Written especially for younger readers, this book examines the intersection of celebrity and crime. Discusses how law enforcement handles celebrities accused of criminal acts, as well as celebrities victimized by crime.

Parish, James Robert. *Hollywood Bad Boys: Loud, Fast, and Out of Control.* Chicago: Contemporary Books, 2002. A revealing collection of biographies of Hollywood male celebrities who are known for extremes of behavior. No biography of Gibson but helpful for understanding the culture that celebrates rough-edged actors.

SEE ALSO: Jan. 18, 1923: Actor Wallace Reid's Death in Drug Rehab Shakes Film Industry; Feb. 6, 1942: Film Star Errol Flynn Is Acquitted of Rape; Jan. 14, 1943: Film Star Frances Farmer Is

Jailed and Institutionalized; Aug. 31, 1948: Film Star Robert Mitchum Is Arrested for Drug Possession; May, 1955: Scandal Magazine Reveals Actor Rory Calhoun's Criminal Past; Feb. 25, 1977: Film Producer David Begelman Is Found to Have Forged Checks; 1980: Biographer Claims Actor Errol Flynn Was a Nazi Spy; Jan. 25, 1984: Jesse Jackson Calls New York City "Hymietown"; Dec. 1, 1987: Yale Scholar's Wartime Anti-Semitic Writings Are Revealed; July 18, 1988: Actor Rob Lowe Videotapes Sexual Tryst with a Minor; July 26, 1991: Comedian Pee-wee Herman Is Arrested for Public Indecency; June 27, 1995: Film Star Hugh Grant Is Arrested for Lewd Conduct; June 22, 2005: U.S. Air Force Investigates Religious Intolerance at Its Academy.

August 12, 2006
NOVELIST GÜNTER GRASS ADMITS TO YOUTHFUL NAZI TIES

One of Germany's leading writers, Günter Grass was long an outspoken critic of his nation's reluctance to come to terms with its criminal Nazi past. He thus created a scandal when he admitted that when he was a teenager he himself had been a member of a Waffen-SS paramilitary unit, after more than sixty years of silence about this episode in his life.

LOCALE: Germany

CATEGORIES: Publishing and journalism; literature; social issues and reform; military; ethics

KEY FIGURE

Günter Grass (b. 1927), German novelist and writer

SUMMARY OF EVENT

In an interview with the *Frankfurter Allgemeine Zeitung* (*FAZ*) about his memoir *Beim häuten der Zwiebel* (2006; *Peeling the Onion*, 2007), Günter Grass discussed his revelation in the book that he had been a member of the Waffen-SS, the combat division of the elite Nazi paramilitary force, for a brief period in 1944-1945. The SS was responsible for the majority of the atrocities perpetrated by the Nazi regime, including the Holocaust, and was condemned as a criminal organization at the Nuremberg Trials (1945-1949); the Waffen-SS, however, which included conscripted soldiers, was exempted from prosecution.

Although Grass had never concealed his enthusiasm for the Nazi movement as a teenager, he had always maintained publicly that his involvement in World War II was limited to service with FLAK, Germany's antiaircraft service, in 1944. One biography, Michael Jürgs's *Bürger Grass: Biografie eines deutschen Dichters* (2002; citizen Grass: biography of a German poet), is based on countless hours of interviews with Grass about his youth, and it perpetuates the story of his wartime service. Jürgs revised the biography and addresses Grass's Waffen-SS service and the attendant scandal in *Günter Grass: Eine deutsche Biografie* (2007; Günter Grass: a German biography). Within his private circle, Grass had confided the truth only to his wife, though not to his children, and to a small group of colleagues, including Austrian writer Robert Schindel. Schindel affirmed in a statement to the Viennese daily *Die Presse* that Grass had told him about his Waffen-SS service more than twenty years earlier and talked about it on numerous occasions.

In the *FAZ* interview, Grass addressed his treatment in *Beim häuten der Zwiebel* of his childhood in Danzig (now Gdańsk) at the beginning of the war, his involvement in the Hitler Youth, his application to join a submarine mission as a fifteen-year-old boy eager to leave home, and his unexpected summons to active, though fairly uneventful, service two years later in the Frundsberg division of the Waffen-SS. Grass's activity in the Waffen-SS was limited; he never fired a single shot in combat and spent the majority of his time either sick with jaundice or training on outmoded weaponry. Grass has affirmed that he was unaware that his assignment was to be with the Waffen-SS until he arrived in Dresden, yet even then he was willfully blind to the real nature of the organization and felt no sense of guilt or shame for his affiliation until after the war. Since then, however, he had reproached himself heavily for his susceptibility to Nazi propaganda and his failure to ask the necessary questions.

Interestingly, *Beim häuten der Zwiebel* had been distributed to reviewers several weeks prior to the publication of Grass's interview in *FAZ* on August 12, 2006. Evidently, none had been eager enough in his or her reading to come across the sparse passages devoted to Grass's recollection of his service in the Waffen-SS. The record of Grass's internment in a U.S. POW camp in Bavaria, undiscovered for over sixty years, was quickly retrieved after his admission had been made public. Similarly, several months after the scandal broke, German biographer Klaus Wagenbach came across his notes from an unfinished Grass biography from 1963 that con-

tained references to the dates, locations, and nature of Grass's military service. It would seem, therefore, that Grass had not elected to conceal his past with the Waffen-SS until after the year 1963. As it was, however, the public was completely unprepared for the "global shock" that was unleashed by the publication of the *FAZ* interview.

The prevailing immediate reaction was one of anger and disillusionment, particularly in Germany and Poland, Grass's birthplace, where the term "SS-man" is held synonymous in the Polish language with the devil and the incarnation of pure evil. Numerous literary figures and intellectuals felt compelled to speak out in defense or condemnation of their colleague. While some lauded Grass's courage in his voluntary public disclosure of his past, others joined in the general outcry against Grass's protracted silence, attacking his past indictments of Germany's repression of its criminal past—for instance, his vehement denunciation of the visit by Ronald Reagan and German chancellor Helmut Kohl in 1985 to the Bitburg military cemetery, which contained the graves of SS soldiers—as evidence of gross hypocrisy and moral duplicity.

The timing of Grass's revelation likewise gave rise to mistrust and speculation as to his motives. In the *FAZ* interview, Grass had explained simply that the truth had weighed heavily on him and had to come out, adding that the need to break his silence had, in part, motivated the writing of *Beim häuten der Zwiebel*. However, the theory that Grass deferred his announcement until after securing the Nobel Prize in Literature quickly gained widespread currency, as did the notion that his interview with *FAZ* was a publicity stunt to promote his new book. Certainly, whatever damage Grass's revelation may have done to his reputation and standing as a moral authority, it was a boon for the sales of *Beim häuten der Zwiebel*.

Press photographers swarm Günter Grass during a reading of his revealing book Peeling the Onion *in December, 2007, in Prague.* (Hulton Archive/ Getty Images)

IMPACT

In the light of the tremendous interest aroused by the *FAZ* interview, the release date of the memoir was moved from September 1 to August 15. By August 31, all 150,000 copies of the first edition had been sold, and the second printing, consisting of 100,000 copies, was already on its way to bookstores. The memoir immediately soared to the top of the bestseller lists in *Der Spiegel* and *Focus* magazines. By the same time, translations for England, the United States, France, and Denmark were already under way, with plans being made for a translation conference in December with the author and the representatives of approximately twenty European and non-European languages.

In view of Grass's admission of his involvement in the Waffen-SS, many critics called for him to be stripped of some of the many honors he had acquired over the course of his long career; most notably, of the Nobel Prize in Literature and of his honorary citizenship in the city of Gdańsk. Both of these campaigns were short-lived, however. The Nobel Foundation in Sweden issued an announcement on August 15 that the conferment of a Nobel Prize was irrevocable. Lech Wałęsa, former president of Poland, a recipient of the Nobel Peace Prize, and one of the first and most outspoken advocates for rescinding Grass's honorary citizenship, changed his position after reading Grass's explanatory and conciliatory letter of August 23 to the mayor of Gdańsk.

Other proposals for Grass's punishment or atonement quickly followed but met with little response. These proposals include those by literary critic Hellmuth Karasek, who suggested to the German broadcaster ZDF that Grass should donate his Nobel Prize money to a charitable organization for the victims of the Waffen-SS regime. Conservative German politician Erika Stein called for Grass to turn over his honorarium for *Beim häuten der Zwiebel* to Polish victims of Nazism. The Polish vice minister of national education called for Grass to use the book's proceeds to finance the printing of

history books for Polish children. Grass did, however, voluntarily refuse the prestigious Brückenpreis (Bridge Prize) from the Polish city of Görlitz that was offered to him at the end of August, out of the fear that the conferment would ultimately be revoked under the pressure of public protest.

—*Jennifer Driscoll Colosimo*

A SENSE OF SHAME

In his 2006 memoir Beim Häuten der Zwiebel, *or* Peeling the Onion *(2007), Günter Grass introduces readers to his days as a member of the Waffen-SS military unit during the final year of World War II. In this excerpt, he admits to feeling shame but also to the burden of carrying that shame for close to sixty years.*

My new marching orders made it clear where the recruit with my name was to undergo basic training: on a drill ground of the Waffen SS, as a Panzer gunner, somewhere far off in the Bohemian Woods. . . .

[F]or decades I refused to admit to the word [Waffen], and to the double letters [SS]. What I had accepted with the stupid pride of youth I wanted to conceal after the war out of a recurrent sense of shame. But the burden remained, and no one could alleviate it.

True, during the tank gunner training . . . there was no mention of the war crimes that later came to light, but the ignorance I claim could not blind me to the fact that I had been incorporated into a system that had planned, organized, and carried out the extermination of millions of people. Even if I could not be accused of active complicity, there remains to this day a residue that is all too commonly called joint responsibility. I will have to live with it for the rest of my life.

Source: Peeling the Onion, *translated by Michael Henry Heim (Orlando, Fla.: Harcourt, 2007), pp. 110-111.*

FURTHER READING

Fuchs, Anne. "'Ehrlich, du lügst wie gedruckt': Günter Grass's Autobiographical Confession and the Changing Territory of Germany's Memory Culture." *German Life and Letters* 60, no. 2 (April, 2007): 261-275. Offers a psychological-literary analysis of *Peeling the Onion* and addresses the broader issue of collective memory in Germany.

Grass, Günter. "How I Spent the War." *The New*

Yorker, June 4, 2007. A harrowing account of Grass's wartime experiences in the Waffen-SS, in which he makes no attempts to excuse himself from membership but rather ponders the difficulties in recalling events of his youth.

_____. *Peeling the Onion.* Translated by Michael Henry Heim. Orlando, Fla.: Harcourt, 2007. English translation of Grass's memoir of his youth, *Beim häuten der Zwiebel*, which included the revelation of his service in the Waffen-SS in 1944-1945.

Schade, Richard E. "Layers of Meaning, War, Art: Grass's *Beim Häuten der Zwiebel.*" *German Quarterly* 80, no. 3 (Summer, 2007): 279-301. Provides a valuable critical analysis of Grass's narrative style in the memoir and elucidates its connection to Grass's suppression of painful wartime memories and feelings of personal moral failure.

SEE ALSO: May 26, 1945: Norwegian Writer Knut Hamsun Is Arrested for Treason; Oct. 26, 1962: West German Police Raid *Der Spiegel* Magazine Offices; Feb. 23, 1963: Play Accuses Pope Pius XII of Complicity in the Holocaust; Nov. 9, 1976: German Generals Must Retire for Supporting a Neo-Nazi Pilot; 1980: Biographer Claims Actor Errol Flynn Was a Nazi Spy; Mar. 3, 1986: Former U.N. Secretary-General Kurt Waldheim's Nazi Past Is Revealed; Dec. 1, 1987: Yale Scholar's Wartime Anti-Semitic Writings Are Revealed.

September 17, 2006
NEW ZEALAND PRIME MINISTER'S HUSBAND IS "OUTED" AS GAY

In 2006, Peter Davis, the husband of New Zealand's prime minister, Helen Clark, was outed as gay when the Star-Times *newspaper and the magazine* Investigate *published pictures of him kissing a gay man. The magazine implied Davis, too, was gay, but Davis and the prime minister both denied the allegations. The slander was likely launched by a right-wing fundamentalist Christian group seeking to smear Clark's political career.*

LOCALE: Auckland, New Zealand
CATEGORIES: Publishing and journalism; sex; politics; government; public morals

KEY FIGURES
Peter Davis (b. 1947), professor of sociology at the University of Auckland and husband of Prime Minister Helen Clark
Helen Clark (b. 1950), prime minister of New Zealand, 1999-
Ian Scott (fl. early twenty-first century), medical doctor and longtime friend of Clark and Davis

SUMMARY OF EVENT
On September 17, 2006, not long after her reelection as New Zealand's prime minister, Helen Clark and her husband, Peter Davis, were the foci of a vicious smear campaign that alleged Davis was gay. The controversy was touched off when New Zealand's *Star-Times* newspaper and an alternative magazine, *Investigate,* ran photographs of Davis kissing Ian Scott, a medical doctor and longtime friend of Davis and Clark. Scott was out as gay.

Immediately, the couple's entire marriage came under scrutiny, even though they had been typically low key about their private relationships. Over the next several days, their entire marital history was played out in the newspapers, though none of the revelations amounted to anything particularly scandalous. Instead, the press was rehashing old debates about the couple, both of whom are generally regarded as quite unconventional. Davis and Clark met in 1977 and, after four years of dating, married in 1981, not long after Clark's first election to Parliament, largely because they already shared a home and believed they would be inviting moral criticism if they remained unmarried.

Over the years, Clark and Davis spent a good deal of time apart, with one or the other commuting home on weekends. The press, of course, implied that these separations indicated emotional rifts, but Davis and Clark insist they were entirely job related. Socially, they are also opposites, with Clark displaying a composed outer shell in nearly every situation and Davis remaining introverted and awkward. Davis, whose academic work is unquestionably high in quality, is nonetheless stereotyped as a househusband because he tends to more of the domestic matters. Clark also employs several women in her office who are lesbian, leading the press to speculate about her sexuality. Davis and Clark shared an embarrassing public kiss in 1994 that became front-page fodder and was used to imply a bad relationship.

In 2005, the race for the prime minister's seat was extremely tight. The National Party garnered quite a bit of support against Clark's Labour Party by focusing its campaign on tax cuts. However, Labour won a narrow victory at the polls, and Clark celebrated her reelection. However, she remained a controversial figure and retained enemies who wanted to see her ouster. Thus, when the kiss her husband received from Scott reached the press, the media immediately began hinting that Davis was gay. Clark, Davis, and Scott all denied these rumors, explaining that Scott, a family friend attending Clark's postelection victory party in 2005, was drunk and the kiss was celebratory in nature. However, the media storm outlasted the initial articles, and both Clark and Davis had to repeatedly defend their marriage in the press.

Throughout the scandal, the media granted the unspoken acceptance of homosexuality as aberrant. Even though Scott is openly gay, he, Davis, and Clark all found themselves protesting Davis's heterosexuality. In other words, if Scott had been a woman, the scandal would have been less dramatic. A simple extramarital affair would not have garnered so much attention. None of the three devoted any energy to arguing that Davis was not having an affair with Scott. Instead, they were all forced to defend Davis's heterosexuality, just as Clark had been forced to defend her own heterosexuality in the past. By implying that Davis was gay, the press effectively implied that not only was the Clark-Davis home devoid of love, but the entire marriage also was a front to conceal both parties' closet homosexuality.

The slander was probably launched by a right-wing fundamentalist Christian group called the Raven-Taylor-Hales Brethren, seeking to smear Clark's political image. An offshoot of another Christian group called the Exclusive Brethren, the Raven-Taylor-Hales Brethren oppose the Labour Party's liberal politics. Although Brethren members, who support a separatist position, do not vote, they are politically active. For instance, in 2005, they spent between $500,000 and $1 million on anti-Labour Party campaigning that hinted at support for the National Party. They also regularly campaign for conservative candidates.

After the allegations became public, Davis and Clark learned the group probably had hired a private investigator. Clark initially believed the National Party had impelled the Brethren's actions, as the attack came soon after a minor scandal in which a conservative member of Parliament was accused of having an extramarital affair. However, the Nationals adamantly denied any such participation and sympathized with the unfair situation the prime minister and her husband faced. Scott expressed his outrage, as did Davis's colleagues and friends, who maintained that the prime minister and her husband have been a devoted couple, deeply in love.

Even after the scandal had died down, the media were still gleefully looking for evidence of the couple's nontraditional lifestyle. For instance, when Davis turned sixty years old, magazines reported that Clark did not get him a gift, as he did not want one (at least one magazine hinted that her gifts were too practical for him), and that he brought her tea in bed.

IMPACT

In all reality, the scandal was barely a blip on Clark's professional record. From her perspective, it was simply an attack upon a public figure who chooses to keep her private life out of the limelight as much as possible. No charges were filed against the Brethren, and no public hue and cry was raised against Clark. However, the event is nonetheless noteworthy for several reasons.

First, the sexuality of public figures will remain a public topic. Therefore, the speculation about Clark's or Davis's being homosexual, no matter how unfair, represents a form of sport in New Zealand and, indeed, around the world. Other famous and powerful women sometimes perceived as lesbians include former U.S. first lady Eleanor Roosevelt and U.S. senator and former First Lady Hillary Rodham Clinton, among others. Second, both Clark and Davis stand well apart from stereotypical gender roles, which are more politically palatable to some. It is much harder to find potential homosexuality in a family with a domestic wife and an outspoken husband. Therefore, in spite of Clark and Davis's protestations of heterosexuality, their lifestyle will certainly grace the front pages of New Zealand's papers again.

—*Jessie Bishop Powell*

FURTHER READING

Dorman, Michael. *Dirty Politics*. New York: Delacorte, 1979. A history of smear campaigns and other dirty political tactics in the United States. A good primer of the nasty tricks politicians regularly play on each other and have played upon them by outside parties.

Edwards, Brian. *Helen: Portrait of a Prime Minister*. Auckland, New Zealand: Exisle, 2001. Includes discussions about Clark's marriage and the controversial speculations about her sexuality already afloat well before Davis received Scott's infamous kiss.

Hallett, Greg. *New Zealand: A Blackmailer's Guide*. Auckland, New Zealand: Prince of New Spain, 2007. Covers the Davis-Scott scandal along with other smear campaigns and dirty politics that have plagued the island nation.

SEE ALSO: Dec., 1982: Julie Andrews and Blake Edwards Deny Being Gay; Jan. 12 and May 11, 1987: Media Reports Spark Investigation of Australian Police Corruption.

September 18, 2006
NEWSWEEK REVEALS THAT HEWLETT-PACKARD SPIED ON ITS OWN BOARD

Newsweek *magazine revealed that Patricia Dunn, the chairperson of technology giant Hewlett-Packard, had arranged for electronic surveillance of board members and journalists to stop corporate leaks to the press. Through the use of pretexting, company investigators lied to illegally obtain telephone records. The resulting scandal led to a criminal case in California, a congressional investigation, federal criminal charges, and several company resignations.*

LOCALE: Palo Alto, California

CATEGORIES: Espionage; publishing and journalism; business and labor; corruption; law and the courts; trade and commerce

KEY FIGURES

Patricia Dunn (b. 1953), chairperson of Hewlett-Packard, 2005-2006

George A. Keyworth II (b. 1939), physicist and HP board member

Tom Perkins (b. 1932), venture capitalist and HP board member

David A. Kaplan (fl. early twenty-first century), *Newsweek* reporter and attorney

SUMMARY OF EVENT

Founded in 1939 by Stanford University classmates Bill Hewlett and Dave Packard, Hewlett-Packard Corporation (HP) became one of the most successful and admired of American businesses. It grew

                                                     Hewlett-Packard Spied on Its Own Board

into a global company dealing in information technology infrastructure, personal computing, and information access. In 2004, HP had revenues of nearly $80 billion, and by 2006 it employed 150,000 people in 170 countries.

Patricia Dunn assumed the chair of HP's board on February 7, 2005, when Carly Fiorina, arguably the most prominent female chief executive officer in the United States at the time, left the company under pressure after accusing two board members of leaking information to the press. Dunn had joined the HP board of directors in 1998 as part of an effort to diversify the firm's board, which was dominated by family members and friends of founders Packard and Hewlett. Dunn had been cochair of Barclays Global Investors, an investment banking firm. She had also served

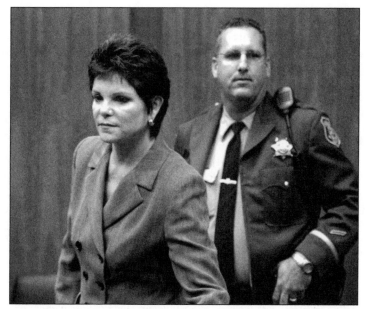

Patricia Dunn in a Santa Clara County courtroom in October, 2006. (Hulton Archive/Getty Images)

as co-chief executive officer of Wells Fargo Investment Advisers. As chair of HP's audit committee since 2002, she had earned the disdain of board members Tom Perkins and George A. Keyworth II for her detail-oriented style and enthusiastic support of the Sarbanes-Oxley Act of 2002, which established standards for corporate boards.

As a non-executive chairperson, Dunn presided over board meetings, recommended board committees and committee chairs, and made herself available for consultation with the interim chief executive officer. Dunn was told by other directors that her most important duties would be to preside over the choice of a new chief executive officer and to stop leaks of information from HP to the media. While leaks of information to the media are nearly impossible to halt, such unauthorized disclosures infuriate corporate leaders concerned about the images of their companies and the impact of such disclosures upon stock prices as well as other business dealings. A series of damaging leaks had preceded Fiorina's departure and had nearly derailed the selection of Mark Hurd, the new chief executive officer who began working in his new position on April 1, 2005. As Fiorina stated when she learned about a

leak of information from one board meeting, such disclosures are also a breach of trust—and no management team can operate without trust. Fiorina believed that Perkins and Keyworth had leaked corporate information during her tenure.

Dunn, too, was soon immersed in a leak investigation, in this case a disclosure to *The Wall Street Journal*. She turned to an HP security manager for help in proceeding, but he referred her to an outside investigator with the Boston-based company Security Outsourcing Solutions (SOS). This company, which had been under contract with HP for ten years, often hired subcontractors to carry out specific investigations, such as obtaining private telephone records. Dunn requested an investigator from SOS, which assigned Ronald R. DeLia to the job.

Dunn code-named the investigation Project Kona. She advised the board of the investigation and obtained support from a majority of the directors, though she did not provide specific details of the inquiry because board members themselves were under investigation.

In the meantime, Dunn and Perkins began to clash over company control issues. Dunn opposed

Perkins's nominees to the board while Perkins resented Dunn's focus on governance. Disagreements between the two became so frequent that Dunn coined the phrase "chairman abuse" to describe Perkins's remarks. Supporting Dunn was the chief executive officer, Hurd, who had been informed of the leaks by Dunn. In response, he warned HP managers that they would be summarily terminated for leaking information.

On June 15, private investigator DeLia informed Dunn and Ann Baskins, HP's attorney, that he had obtained the private phone records of reporters from *Businessweek* and *The New York Times*. De-Lia said that his investigators had used "pretexting"; that is, they presented themselves, in this case, as board directors to obtain "their own" phone records. Baskins expressed concern over the legality of the tactic, but DeLia informed her that he was aware of no laws banning the practice.

In January, 2006, Keyworth had lunch with reporter Dawn Kawamoto of CNET, a technology-review Web site. The two had become friends, and Keyworth thought that the lunch was purely a social occasion. However, some of Keyworth's discussion with Kawamoto subsequently appeared on CNET, in a piece by Kawamoto that presented Hurd

---

ACCEPTING RESPONSIBILITY?

Former Hewlett-Packard chair Patricia Dunn testified before a subcommittee of the House Committee on Energy and Commerce on September 28, 2006. Representative Cliff Stearns of Florida wanted to know if Dunn felt any sense of responsibility for the pretexting "fiasco" at Hewlett-Packard. His questions, and her responses, are excerpted here.

Mr. Stearns. Ms. Dunn, your written testimony is 33 pages long. You go into great detail explaining why the investigation was necessary and how you were assured that these aggressive tactics were legal. You even advocate congressional action to produce clear-cut rules on pretexting, a suggestion that this committee has endorsed. However, conspicuous by its absence in your testimony is any degree of contrition or acceptance of responsibility.

And I have listened to this testimony in my office, and you have just indicated it is wrong. You indicated you had been briefed three times, and yet, there is no suggestion that you are going to accept any responsibility and no sense that what you did was wrong. So I get the sense after reading your testimony that you still do not really believe that you did anything wrong here.

And I guess that is a question. Do you feel that you are totally innocent here and with no culpability?

Ms. Dunn. My understanding is that my opening statement is a part of my full submission.

Mr. Stearns. . . . The question I want is yes or no, do you think that your—have any culpability in this whole fiasco? Just yes or no.

Ms. Dunn. I will repeat what I said in my opening statement. I deeply regret that so many people were badly affected.

Mr. Stearns. We are not talking about other people. We are talking about you personally.

Ms. Dunn. Including me, that was said in my opening statement. And I would like to tell you what I would do differently—

Mr. Stearns. But regret is one thing, but culpability that you accept blame is another, and I am just trying to think—and I know, I mean, you could say you are not blamable. You can say that, but I am just trying to put on the record whether you think you are at fault for anything, other than regrets and you are sorry and things like that.

Is it just possible you could say yes or no, that you feel you have some culpability?

Ms. Dunn. If I knew then what I know now, I would have done things very differently and there are some specific things I would have done very differently. . . .

Mr. Stearns. I am interpreting what you say is that knowing what you know today it was wrong?

Ms. Dunn. Absolutely.

Mr. Stearns. And knowing what you do today that you have to accept responsibility, you have to accept personal responsibility for what happened. That is my interpretation of what you are telling me. Is that a correct interpretation?

Ms. Dunn. Sir, I do not accept personal responsibility for what happened.

and HP in a positive light. Keyworth liked the report but Dunn nevertheless launched another investigation to track down the leak. HP employment attorney Kevin Hunsaker headed the investigation, named Kona II, and reported weekly to Dunn and Baskins.

Kona II examined more than ten thousand articles published about HP in the preceding six years. The inquiry included pretexting to obtain telephone records and created a fictitious employee to leak news to Kawamoto. The Kona team also trailed Kawamoto and her daughter, staked out the homes of Kawamoto and Keyworth, and examined Kawamoto's phone records. They discovered several calls from Kawamoto to Keyworth. In May, Keyworth admitted to the board that he was the source of the leak to CNET. He was asked by the board to resign, but he refused. However, Perkins resigned from the board in anger and then sought legal counsel.

In July, Perkins received a letter from AT&T about an online account that he had never established. On August 14, he informed the HP board that he had direct proof of illegal hacking of phone records. He demanded that HP notify the U.S. Securities and Exchange Commission (SEC) because he was legally obliged to publicly disclose the reasons for his resignation. HP refused to notify the SEC. Perkins's legal counsel then notified the SEC, U.S. attorney offices in Manhattan and San Francisco, the California attorney general, the Federal Trade Commission, and the Federal Communications Commission. In response to these notifications, HP amended its SEC filing on September 6 to acknowledge that investigators had engaged in possibly illegal pretexting. On September 18, *Newsweek* magazine featured a cover story by reporter David A. Kaplan on Dunn and her tactics at HP, bringing the entire affair to the public. Hurd announced Dunn's resignation on September 22, effective on January 18.

IMPACT

Initially, the HP board strongly supported Dunn. The company ordered an independent investigation that concluded that she had acted properly. How-

ever, the board then asked Dunn to resign. Several resignations followed, including those of Keyworth, Baskins, and Hunsaker. Perkins charged that the entire investigation was an attempt by Dunn to eliminate the friends of Packard and Hewlett who remained on the board. The board reimbursed Perkins for $1.5 million in legal fees.

On October 4, the California attorney general charged Dunn with four felonies: fraudulent wire communication, wrongful use of computer data, identity theft, and conspiracy. She pleaded not guilty at her arraignment. Hunsaker, DeLia, and two private investigators also were charged. On January 12, 2007, one of the investigators pleaded guilty to federal charges of identity theft and conspiracy. The charges against Dunn were dropped in March, possibly in part because she was diagnosed with advanced ovarian cancer. Charges against Hunsaker, DeLia, and the second investigator were dropped after they completed community service. In December, 2006, HP had paid a $14.5 million civil settlement to the state of California, with most of the money slated to fund investigations into privacy rights and intellectual property violations.

On February 28, 2008, HP announced that it had settled for undisclosed sums the claims brought against the company by the *BusinessWeek* and *New York Times* journalists whose phone records were illegally obtained through HP pretexting. Other lawsuits were filed against HP, including one by CNET reporter Kawamoto.

—*Caryn E. Neumann*

FURTHER READING

Baer, Miriam. "Corporate Governance and Corporate Policing: What Can We Learn from the Hewlett-Packard Pretexting Scandal?" *University of Cincinnati Law Review* 77 (2009). Using the HP scandal and Dunn's role in that scandal as a starting point, this article looks at the tension between a corporate board's dual mandate to police its own and implement ethical corporate governance.

Kaplan, David A. "The Boss Who Spied on Her Board." *Newsweek*, September 18, 2006, 40-45. This cover article broke the story of the HP investigations, triggered a debate about pretexting, and led to Dunn's resignation.

Packard, David. *The HP Way: How Bill Hewlett and I Built Our Company.* New York: Collins Business, 2006. A history of Hewlett-Packard, recommended by the company as a thorough explanation of its approaches to business, people, and processes.

Stewart, James B. "The Kona Files: How an Obsession with Leaks Brought Scandal to Hewlett-Packard." *The New Yorker*, February 19, 2007, 152-170. A detailed account of the scandal and its aftermath.

SEE ALSO: Feb. 4, 1976: Lockheed Is Implicated in Bribing Foreign Officials; Oct. 9, 1980: Bendix Executive Resigns Amid Rumors of an Affair; May 2, 1984: E. F. Hutton Executives Plead Guilty to Fraud; Feb. 4, 1996: Whistle-Blower Reveals Tobacco Industry Corruption; Dec. 2, 2001: Enron Bankruptcy Reveals Massive Financial Fraud; June 25, 2002: Internal Corruption Forces Adelphia Communications to Declare Bankruptcy; Mar. 5, 2004: Martha Stewart Is Convicted in Insider-Trading Scandal; Sept. 12, 2005: Westar Energy Executives Are Found Guilty of Looting Their Company.

September 29, 2006

CONGRESSMAN MARK FOLEY RESIGNS IN SEX SCANDAL INVOLVING A TEENAGE PAGE

Congressman Mark Foley resigned from the U.S. House of Representatives when it was discovered that he sent sexually explicit e-mails and text messages to at least one teenage boy who was serving as a congressional page. The resignation triggered investigations into how House leadership addressed earlier accusations. Dennis Hastert, Speaker of the House, did not return for another term, and Republican seats in the House may have been lost because of the scandal.

LOCALE: Washington, D.C.

CATEGORIES: Government; politics; sex crimes; public morals

KEY FIGURES

Mark Foley (b. 1954), U.S. representative from Florida, 1995-2006

Jeff Trandahl (b. 1964), clerk of the House of Representatives, 1999-2005

Dennis Hastert (b. 1942), U.S. representative from Missouri, 1987-2007, and Speaker of the House, 1999-2007

SUMMARY OF EVENT

The House Page Program, a unique opportunity for students in their junior year of high school to live in Washington, D.C., allows students to experience the inner workings of the U.S. House of Representatives. Pages run errands for House members, assist with telephone calls in the cloakroom, and assist on the House floor as needed. In addition to working on Capitol Hill, pages also attend academic classes.

The program has been in place for more than two hundred years. At its inception, only males could serve as pages, but in 1973, female pages earned a permanent place in the program. Until the early 1980's, pages were responsible for finding their own lodging and were largely unsupervised after leaving work. In 1982, however, a page commission recommended creating a residence hall near Capitol Hill for all pages so they could be properly supervised. Concurrently, the commission also recommended the establishment of a page board, comprising current members of the House, to oversee the program and to provide adequate supervision and protection for the pages. Approximately seventy-two pages serve in a given year, and the program is administered by the clerk of the House. The daily activities are overseen by the residence-hall staff and school and work staff.

Pages serve on the House floor and are in contact with members on a regular basis. Many members become mentors to the pages, providing a unique glimpse into the life of a representative. As early as 2000, Mark Foley was noted for his involvement with the pages, and there was a general feeling among the staff of the Page Program that Foley was becoming too familiar with the pages. Jeff Trandahl served as clerk of the House from 1999 to 2005. According to a

Mark Foley, right, at a 2003 press conference in Washington, D.C. (AP/ Wide World Photos)

later report of the House Committee on the Standards for Official Conduct, Trandahl testified that Foley "was a distraction and was interfering with the program" and that he "failed to keep a professional distance from the pages."

Foley also reportedly visited the Page Residence Hall on more than one occasion. One evening, in June, 2000, two or more pages got into Foley's car and left the grounds of the residence hall. The pages returned not long after. Trandahl warned Foley to stay away from the pages.

In the fall of 2001, a former page (who remained anonymous) appointed by Representative Jim Kolbe contacted Kolbe's office to report that he had been communicating with Foley via e-mail since the end of his time as a page. The former page viewed the communications as a means of networking, but he had also received an e-mail from Foley that made him uncomfortable. He reported this to Kolbe's office and asked that someone handle the situation. He subsequently received an e-mail of apology from Foley but continued his communications with the Congress member. However, he was not the only page with whom Foley maintained contact.

In 2005, another former page contacted his sponsor, Representative Rodney Alexander, to report on

the nature of the e-mails he was receiving from Foley. The former page told a staff member that Foley's e-mails were "starting to freak [him] out." The House Speaker, Dennis Hastert, and clerk were both notified of the e-mails and the parents' request that the matter be handled quietly.

After talking with Alexander's office, Trandahl and Representative John Shimkus, chairman of the Page Board, approached Foley regarding the e-mails. He was told to stop communications with the former page and to cease any involvement in the page program.

On September 29, 2006, *ABC News* contacted Foley's office and informed his staff that it was in possession of instant-message exchanges between Foley and a former page that were sexually explicit. Foley's staff had a meeting regarding the messages. Foley resigned that same day, left Washington, D.C., and admitted himself into rehabilitation for alcoholism. The identity of the page involved in the exchange was not revealed, but the instant messages became widely known after being posted on various blogs and through media outlets.

The exchange of messages was the culmination of years of questionable behavior by Foley. Although he never was found to have had physical contact with current or former House pages, he had clearly crossed a line. A House ethics committee report of December, 2006, stated, "Such conduct is an abuse of power, and an abuse of trust of the pages, their parents or guardians, and the Congress itself." Because Foley resigned from the House, no official action could be taken against him by that government body.

IMPACT

Foley was not the first House member involved in a scandal involving underage pages. In 1982, Daniel Crane and Gerry Studds were both censured by the House following an investigation that revealed they had each engaged in a sexual relationship with pages. Crane apologized for the affair he had with a seventeen-year-old girl but lost his seat in Congress in the 1984 election. Studds admitted to an affair with a male page that occurred in 1973 and announced to the House that he was gay. He was re-elected in 1984 and continued to serve in the House until 1997. On the heels of the 1982 scandal, Speaker of the House Tip O'Neill formed a page commission, leading to major changes to the program in an effort to protect the pages. Positive changes included housing all pages in a dormitory located on Capitol Hill and implementing a page board to oversee activities of the page program. An official page code of conduct was developed, allowing for the immediate dismissal of any page found in violation of program rules.

Following the Foley scandal, the House Page Program was reevaluated and further changes were made to the composition of the page board. Two members from each political party (Democratic and Republican), as well as the House clerk, the sergeant at arms, a page parent, and a page alumnus, now serve on the board. House leadership hoped that making necessary changes would prevent a similar incident from occurring and would improve communication regarding the welfare of pages.

—*Tessa Li Powell*

FURTHER READING

Abrams, Jim. "House Leaders Investigate Page Program." *The Washington Post*, December 13, 2007. Amid a new page scandal and the resignation of two members of the page board, the House again called for a reevaluation of the program.

Amer, Mildred. "Pages of the United States Congress: History, Background Information, and Proposals for Change." *CRS Report for Congress*, February 6, 2007. Describes the page program and highlights changes that have been made or proposed since the Mark Foley scandal of 2006.

Babington, Charles, and Jonathan Weisman. "Rep. Foley Quits in Page Scandal." *The Washington Post*, September 30, 2006. Follows the resignation of Foley and examines the roles played in the case by congressional leadership.

Long, Kim. *The Almanac of Political Corruption, Scandals, and Dirty Politics*. New York: Delacorte Press, 2007. A wide-ranging book detailing the various scandals and corrupt practices that have plagued U.S. politics.

Turley, Jonathan. "A Page Protection Act: The Path to Saving a Historic Program." *Roll Call*, October 5, 2006. Written by a page alum and legal professor. Addresses problems with the page board and discusses possible remedies to maintain the program.

United States Congress. House of Representatives. Committee on the Standards of Official Conduct. *Investigation of Allegations Related to Improper Conduct Involving Members and Current or Former House Pages*. Washington, D.C.: Government Printing Office, 2006. Committee report written in response to the Foley scandal. Examines whether the lack of response from others in the House was a breach of ethics rules.

SEE ALSO: Oct. 7, 1974: Congressman Wilbur D. Mills's Stripper Affair Leads to His Downfall; Sept. 3, 1980: Congressman Bauman Is Arrested for Liaison with Teenage Boy; July 20, 1983: Congress Members Censured in House-Page Sex Scandal; Jan. 17, 1998: President Bill Clinton Denies Sexual Affair with a White House Intern; Apr. 30, 2001: Washington Intern Chandra Levy Disappears.

October 22, 2006
CHILEAN POLITICIANS USE COMMUNITY FUNDS FOR PERSONAL CAMPAIGNS

Officials of Chiledeportes, the Chilean government's sports agency, were accused of misusing as much as $1 million in funds designated for promoting community sports programs. An e-mail leaked to the media indicated that the Chiledeportes officials had used the money in districts represented by legislators from Concertación, or the Coalition of Parties for Democracy. Opposition legislators charged that the money had been illegally used to help political campaigns.

LOCALE: Chile
CATEGORIES: Corruption; government; politics

KEY FIGURES

Michelle Bachelet (b. 1951), president of Chile, 2006-
Ricardo Lagos (b. 1938), president of Chile, 2000-2006
Patricio Aylwin (b. 1918), president of Chile, 1990-1994

SUMMARY OF EVENT

In 2003, the Chilean government of President Ricardo Lagos responded to a series of scandals relating to corruption and influence peddling in the domestic development agency, the ministry of public works, and the central bank. In the wake of the scandals, a series of legal and administrative reforms were enacted to prevent a repeat of these scandals. The reforms clarified payments for public employees, changed campaign financing, established a permanent budget commission to oversee government spending, created a code of ethics for civil servants, and changed the way in which the ministry of public works awarded government contracts. The measures met with general approval both in Chile and abroad for increasing government transparency.

Even with this history of corruption, government corruption in Chile is relatively rare, according to the U.S. Department of State. Chile ranked about twentieth out of 163 countries in 2006 in the annual Corruption Perceptions Index released by the non-governmental group Transparency International, thereby holding a position similar to that of the United States and Belgium.

Concertación (Coalition of Parties for Democracy) had held executive power in Chile since 1990, perhaps contributing to a complacent atmosphere among lawmakers. Despite the scandals, the center-left government remained popular, with President Michelle Bachelet (who began her term on March 11, 2006) ranking as one of the most respected women in the country. Bachelet is Chile's first female president.

On October 22, 2006, a scandal emerged about the use of state funds by officials of Chiledeportes, a government agency that organizes local sporting activities. An audit of the agency revealed that about $1 million (U.S.), or about 90 percent of its budget, had been funneled into the coffers of local, leftist political campaigns. These payments to congressional candidates of the Party for Democracy (PD), which was part of the ruling Concertación, were fraudulently marked on forged invoices as electoral expenses.

The right-wing opposition immediately charged that Concertación had improperly used funds to win the last elections and was attempting a similar maneuver to win the upcoming elections. The main target of this charge appeared to be former president Lagos, who left office with a popularity rating of 70 percent and remained eligible to run again for president in the December, 2009, elections.

On October 30, Bachelet stated that she would not accept corruption in her administration. She was clearly concerned about the impact of the scandal upon Chile's newly positive international image. She assured the public that the scandal would be properly investigated and that changes would be made to avoid new corruption cases. She an-

1121

nounced that a number of actions would be taken to reform the direct allocation of public funds to state agencies to ensure that the funds directly benefit the people. Bachelet also announced a restructuring of Chiledeportes to refine the project evaluation process, strengthen internal accounting procedures and institutional oversight mechanisms, and change the sports fund guidelines to disburse money only when projects have met certain requirements as documented in the annual reports of the undersecretary for athletics.

Two former officials of Concertación, Edgardo Boeninger, a Christian Democrat and former ministry general secretariat of the presidency, and Jorge Schaulsohn, founder and former PD president, then blew the whistle in interviews. They stated that members of Concertación felt entitled to take public funds for campaign purposes since private industry generally financed right-wing political parties. Both officials alleged that a culture of corruption existed within the government. Gonzalo Martner, a former president of the Socialist Party, added to the fire by giving an interview to the newspaper *El Mercurio*, in which he supported Schaulsohn's claims. Martner stated that the governing parties had used discretionary government funds, exempt from public scrutiny, to fund campaigns. Other former government officials supported the charges. Schaulsohn was expelled from the party in December. Schaulsohn, Boeninger, and Martner all opposed Lagos, and their attacks gave further support to the notion that much of the furor over Chiledeportes was part of an effort to block Lagos from again running for president.

Senator Camilo Escalona, Socialist Party president, stated that no members of Concertación had received money from discretionary funds since the establishment of democratic government in 1990. He charged that right-wing parties had received illegal campaign funds during the administration of dictator Augusto Pinochet Ugarte. The charge prompted the right-wing opposition Alliance for Chile to sue and attempt to subpoena more than one hundred people who had held high public office since 1990. The judge in the case blocked the subpoenas.

Emerging next was the claim that candidates for the right-wing National Renewal had used the same company as the PD to inflate their election expenses. Meanwhile, prosecutor Xavier Armendtriz pursued an investigation into Chiledeportes. Bachelet publicly supported the head of Chiledeportes and undersecretary for athletics, Catalina Depassier, and denied that a culture of corruption existed. Patricio Aylwin, president of Chile from 1990 to 1994 and a member of the coalition, stated that no culture of corruption existed, even though some government officials in his cabinet had used public funds for campaign purposes. Depassier resigned after it became known that she had lied about her educational credentials.

On November 23, 2006, Bachelet announced new anticorruption measures by releasing a thirty-two-page report produced by the minister of finance. The measures focus upon combating corruption, improving transparency in the public sector, modernizing government, and reforming campaign finance. A day later, Guillermo Díaz, president of the national railway system, faced fraud charges relating to his employment with the public works ministry under the administration of Lagos. The media charged that Díaz's employment, even after he was suspected of fraud, demonstrated a lack of concern by Concertación-led governments about public corruption. Newspapers called for greater reforms as well as concrete actions to demonstrate the government's willingness to stop abuses.

IMPACT

On November 24, the government established a legislative commission to investigate the scandal. Both progovernment and rightist Alliance for Chile members formed the commission. Nicolás Monckeberg, a deputy from the rightist National Renovation Party, headed the commission. When progovernment legislators presented a vote of no confidence against Monckeberg for allegedly abusing his leadership role by questioning government employees linked to the scandal, the opposition politicians withdrew from the commission. They argued that no credible outcome could be reached if the investigation into the government was led by progovernment politicians. The official report charged one official, Luis Guastavino, with corruption. A separate report issued by the alliance implicated PD officials Rodrigo González, Marco Antonio Núñez, and Laura Soto, as well as Socialist deputy Marco Enríquez-Ominami. Only Soto ultimately faced charges of embezzlement for using state funds.

The opposition's actions stalled when it, too, became the focus of political scandal. In December, Bachelet called for an investigation into the improper use of public funds to create the two major right-wing parties, the Independent Democratic Union and National Renewal, at the end of Pinochet's dictatorship during the late 1980's. Members of Bachelet's Socialist Party argued that the use of public funds in this case should also be examined if the Right was truly interested in reform.

—*Caryn E. Neumann*

FURTHER READING

Angell, Alan. *Democracy After Pinochet: Politics, Parties, and Elections in Chile.* Washington, D.C.: Brookings Institution Press, 2007. Exam-

ines the political situation in Chile at the time of the sports scandal, which began in October, 2006.

Oppenheim, Lois Hecht. *Politics in Chile: Socialism, Authoritarianism, and Market Democracy.* Boulder, Colo.: Westview Press, 2007. A good study of Chilean politics and economic development through 2006.

Rector, John L. *The History of Chile.* New York: Palgrave Macmillan, 2005. An excellent and updated general history of Chile.

SEE ALSO: Jan., 1913: British Prime Minister's Staff Is Investigated for Insider Trading; May 23, 1981: Italian Justice Minister Resigns Because of Crime Connection; Jan. 12 and May 11, 1987: Media Reports Spark Investigation of Australian Police Corruption; Feb. 28, 1995: Former Mexican President Carlos Salinas's Brother Is Arrested for Murder; Nov. 3, 1996: Car Crash Reveals Depth of Government Corruption in Turkey; Jan., 1997: Pyramid Investment Schemes Cause Albanian Government to Fall.

November 2, 2006
EVANGELIST KENT HOVIND IS CONVICTED OF FEDERAL TAX VIOLATIONS

American evangelist Kent Hovind, who founded Creation Science Evangelism in 1989 but never paid payroll or income taxes despite his lucrative income, was found guilty of tax fraud. After an investigation by the U.S. Internal Revenue Service that included a raid of his home and business, he was convicted of fifty-eight tax-related offenses and sentenced to ten years in federal prison.

LOCALE: Pensacola, Florida
CATEGORIES: Law and the courts; corruption; hoaxes, frauds, and charlatanism; religion

KEY FIGURES
Kent Hovind (b. 1953), American evangelist and creationist

Jo Delia Hovind (b. 1956), codefendant in tax-evasion case and Kent Hovind's spouse
Eric Hovind (b. 1978), son of the Hovinds
David Charles Gibbs (b. 1968), attorney

SUMMARY OF EVENT

Kent Hovind was born in East Peoria, Illinois, in 1953. He converted to Christianity at the age of sixteen and graduated from East Peoria Community High School in 1971. After high school, he earned several degrees in Christian education from unaccredited institutions and was ordained as a Baptist minister. Despite having a doctorate from an unaccredited school, Hovind consistently referred to himself as Dr. Dino.

After serving as the pastor of several churches

2000's

and teaching science at several Christian schools, Hovind moved to Pensacola, Florida, in 1989 and started a ministry called Creation Science Evangelism (CSE). In 2001, he built Dinosaur Adventure Land, a small theme park and small fossil museum that taught creationist principles. He spoke at hundreds of churches and other venues, peddling his unique and offbeat brand of recent creationism called Young Earth creationism, which teaches that the earth and universe are less than 6,000-10,000 years old and were created by God, and that the bulk of the geologic features preserved in the crust of the earth were generated by the flood of Noah. Hovind's presentations were filled with erroneous and demonstrably false statements.

Hovind bluntly stated in his lectures and on his Web site that he did not believe in paying taxes to the government. His CSE ministry employed many people, but it never withheld taxes from their salaries. Because Hovind had never registered CSE as a tax-exempt religious organization, he was obligated to pay taxes on all his earnings and the salaries he paid to his employees. Upon learning about his antitax philosophy and attempts to evade paying taxes, administrators at nearby Pensacola Christian College (PCC) reported Hovind to the U.S. Internal Revenue Service (IRS) and forbade PCC students from working at CSE.

Because the IRS had no record that Hovind had ever filed a tax return, in 1996 it attempted to collect back taxes for 1989-1995. To escape responsibility for paying federal income taxes, Hovind filed bankruptcy on March 1, 1996. In his bankruptcy petition, he argued that because he is a minister of God, everything he owns belongs to God and is not subject to taxation. On June 5, the U.S. Bankruptcy Court rejected the petition, ruling that it had been filed in bad faith. The court found that even though Hovind had stated that he received no income, had no expenses, and owned no property, the IRS investigation revealed that he owned a house (on which he made regular payments) and had several automobiles, and that he had enough disposable income to send his children to a private Christian school (at $4,800 per year in tuition) and install central heating and air conditioning in his home (for $3,265).

As a result of the legal action against him, Hovind agreed to pay the IRS $432.33 per month for sixty months.

In May, 1998, Hovind made another concerted effort to evade paying federal income taxes. He and his wife, Jo Delia Hovind, filed a Power of Attorney and Revocation of Signature form with the Escambia County, Florida, clerk of courts. This document argued that they had been misled and were forced to sign government documents that specified their payment schedule and therefore did not owe the government any more money. They also renounced their U.S. citizenship and declared themselves, individually, as "a natural citizen of 'America' and a natural sojourner." This, in their minds, rescinded their obligation to pay federal income taxes.

In 2002, Hovind was once again delinquent in his tax payments and attempted to sue the IRS for harassment. He referred to his home state of Florida as the "state of Florida Body-Politic Corporation" and argued that he was a citizen of the state of Florida and not of the United States and, therefore, was not required to pay federal income taxes.

An April, 2004, IRS raid of Hovind's home and business showed that he lacked a business license and tax-exempt status. Bank deposits recovered from the raid showed that Hovind had deposited well over one million dollars into various bank accounts since 1997 and had neither reported nor paid taxes on any of this income. On June 3, the IRS filed a tax lien of over half a million dollars against Hovind and his son, Eric Hovind, who helped his father hide income. The lien was placed on their businesses, too.

On July 11, 2006, Hovind was charged in the U.S. District Court for the Northern District of Florida in Pensacola with twelve counts of failing to pay employee-related taxes; forty-five counts of "smurfing," a banking industry term for evading reporting requirements by making multiple cash withdrawals just under $10,000; and one count of interfering with an IRS investigation. Jo Hovind, who had handled the money for her husband's enterprises, was charged with forty-four related counts.

After his indictment, Hovind vociferously maintained his innocence and stated that he had no idea who was charging him or what his crime was. After stating that he did not recognize the government authority in tax matters, Hovind attempted to enter a plea of "subornation of false muster," a legally nonsensical phrase that, some have said, is more reminiscent of militia terminology. When U.S. magistrate Gordon Miles Davis offered to enter a plea for him, Hovind switched his plea to not guilty under duress. Davis also confiscated Hovind's passport because he was a flight risk and his guns because he had threatened IRS agents.

Hovind's trial began on October 21. At trial, he tried to argue that the approximately thirty people who worked for him were missionaries and not employees. He also maintained that his amusement park, admission, and merchandise sales belonged to God and could not be taxed. Nevertheless, some of Hovind's workers testified that they punched time cards, took vacation and sick days, and were docked pay if they spent too much time on the phone. Attorney David Charles Gibbs, who provided free legal aid to churches nationwide, testified that Hovind enthusiastically explained to him how he "beat the tax system" and had no obligation to pay taxes. After closing arguments on November 2, the jury deliberated for three hours and found Hovind guilty of all fifty-eight counts and Jo Hovind guilty of all forty-four counts. On January 19, 2007, Hovind was sentenced to ten years in prison and three years probation. He was ordered to pay the court more than one million dollars in restitution and legal fees. Jo Hovind was sentenced in June to one year in prison and three years probation, and was fined $8,000.

IMPACT

Hovind's conviction was embarrassing to the American creationist movement because Hovind was one of its most visible figures. Even more troubling was Hovind's reprehensible behavior throughout the IRS investigation and his trial. He filed false lawsuits and criminal charges against the IRS, threatened IRS investigators and those who cooperated with them, and destroyed records. Had he cooper-

ated with the government, he might have avoided prison time, but his avowed recalcitrance precipitated his incarceration.

Furthermore, the bizarre and ridiculous nature of Hovind's tax-evasion arguments and his inability to accept correction from others revealed a person desperately divorced from reality. Hovind's deplorable demeanor reflected very badly on the creationist movement as a whole and tended to reinforce the quixotic stereotype already associated with modern creationists. Hovind's controversial statements and divisive tactics also contributed to the 2005 schism of the largest international creationist organization, Answers in Genesis.

—*Michael A. Buratovich*

FURTHER READING

Fail, Angela. "Christian College Leader Says Taxes Are Part of Religion: Hovind Argues God's Workers Are Exempt." *Pensacola News Journal*, October 20, 2006. News story about the Pensacola Christian College vice president who reported Hovind's tax evasion to the IRS.

Huston, Peter. *More Scams from the Great Beyond! How to Make Even More Money Off Creationism, Evolution, Environmentalism, Fringe Politics, Weird Science, the Occult, and Other Strange Beliefs*. Boulder, Colo.: Paladin Press, 2002. An astonishing collection of scams based on strange religious and other fringe beliefs.

Levicoff, Steve. *Name It and Frame It? New Opportunities in Adult Education and How to Avoid Being Ripped Off by "Christian" Degree Mills*. 4th ed. Ambler, Pa.: Institute on Religion and Law, 1995. A disturbing survey of Christian diploma mills in the United States. Also examines Patriot University, Hovind's alma mater.

Martinez, Greg. "Stupid Dino Tricks: A Visit to Kent Hovind's Dinosaur Adventure Land." *Skeptical Inquirer* 26 (November-December, 2004): 47-51. A visitor to Dinosaur Adventure Land describes the park and associated museum and notes the many scientific inaccuracies that pockmark the displays.

Pigliucci, Massimo. *Denying Evolution: Creation,*

2000's

Scientism, and the Nature of Science. Sunderland, Mass.: Sinauer, 2002. A severe critique of creationism by a prominent evolutionary biologist who debated Hovind and marveled at his ignorance of modern evolutionary biology.

Steward, Michael. "Creationist's Fight with Uncle Sam May Evolve into Painful Defeat." *Pensacola News Journal,* July 19, 2006. A news report detailing the case against Hovind and the risk he took to fight that case.

SEE ALSO: May-June, 1926: Evangelist Aimee Semple McPherson Claims She Was Kidnapped; June 27, 1978: Evangelist Herbert W. Armstrong Excommunicates His Own Son; Oct. 23, 1985: Guru Bhagwan Shree Rajneesh Is Indicted for Immigration Fraud; Apr. 22, 1986: Faith Healer Peter Popoff Is Exposed as a Fraud; Mar. 19, 1987: Jim Bakker Resigns as Head of PTL Television Network; Feb. 21, 1988: Evangelist Jimmy Swaggart Tearfully Confesses His Adultery.

November 2, 2006
MALE ESCORT REVEALS SEXUAL LIAISONS WITH EVANGELIST TED HAGGARD

Ted Haggard, the founder and senior pastor of New Life Church in Colorado, was disgraced after a male escort revealed on television that Haggard had sex with him over a three-year period. Haggard, asked by the church to leave his ministry and the Colorado Springs area, also resigned his leadership position with the influential National Association of Evangelicals. A church overseer claimed Haggard was "completely heterosexual" following three weeks of "restorative" therapy.

LOCALE: Colorado Springs, Colorado
CATEGORIES: Drugs; prostitution; religion; sex; social issues and reform

KEY FIGURES
Ted Haggard (b. 1956), evangelical preacher
Michael Jones (b. 1957), male escort
Tim Ralph (fl. early twenty-first century), pastor and counselor

SUMMARY OF EVENT
Ted Haggard was the lead pastor of New Life Church, which boasted a membership of fourteen thousand people. He had founded the megachurch in 1984 in the basement of his home in Colorado

Michael Jones. (AP/Wide World Photos)

Springs. Haggard also was the head of the thirty-million-member National Association of Evangelicals (NAE). In 2005, *Time* magazine named him as one of the top twenty-five most influential evangelicals in the United States.

Haggard also openly condemned homosexuality and preached against same-gender marriage, but he reportedly visited gay bars and invited gays to attend his church services. On November 2, 2006, Haggard was outed by a male escort, Michael Jones, who claimed that the popular pastor had paid him for sex and that the encounters occurred during a three-year period. Jones, who made his announcement on a Denver, Colorado, television station, also claimed that Haggard often used the drug crystal methamphetamine when they were together. He also said that Haggard had revealed sexual fantasies to him, one involving a group of young college men.

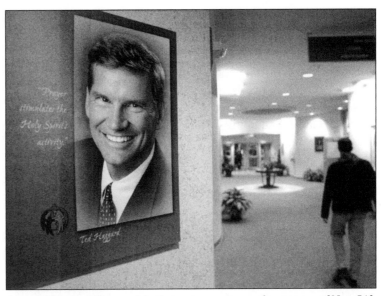

A portrait of Ted Haggard in the prayer center on the campus of New Life Church near Colorado Springs, Colorado. (AP/Wide World Photos)

Initially, Jones knew Haggard by the name Art (Haggard's middle name is Arthur). After learning that Art was the well-known pastor Haggard, who railed against homosexuality and same-gender marriage, Jones decided to come forward about his sexual encounters with Haggard. He believed he should expose Haggard's hypocrisy. Rumors had already been circulating in the gay community in Denver, Colorado, about Haggard's sexuality. When first confronted with the gay-sex allegations, Haggard claimed he did not know Jones and denied having ever used drugs. A few days later, however, he admitted that he had purchased methamphetamine but never used the drug.

On November 4, 2006, the board of the New Life Church issued a statement from its membership, which had concluded that Haggard's alleged actions constituted sexually immoral conduct. Drawing on church bylaws, the board reported that Haggard's conduct compelled them to remove him from his job with the church. Attached to a severance package from the church was the stipulation that Haggard also leave the Colorado Springs area. Haggard already had tendered his resignation from the presidency of the NAE on November 2. The NAE reported that during its more than sixty years of existence, it had never had moral failure in its leadership.

Haggard issued a statement on November 5 that was read before his church by another pastor. Haggard admitted to having had gay sex but claimed it was a "dark" part of his life. He further expressed sorrow for his behavior and said he was "a deceiver and a liar." He said the church board acted appropriately in removing him from his ministry and that the removal would be permanent.

Haggard also said in his statement that he had been "warring against" his sexual desires for his entire adult life. By all appearances he led a heterosexual life that included a marriage and children, a life choice not uncommon for those with same-gender sexual desires who also are deeply committed to their religion and who fear reprisal. Conservative churches in the United States, as elsewhere, speak harshly about same-gender sexuality and condemn it as immoral. They also severely punish sexual transgressors.

2000's

IMPACT

Haggard lost his ministry, church, and evangelical standing. In February, 2007, after three months of silence, he sent an e-mail message to friends, telling them he was moving from Colorado Springs with his wife, Gayle, and family to start a process of personal "restoration." This process, which involved examining all aspects of his life, included counseling by a team of ministers who were appointed by the New Life Church. Haggard also entered a treatment center in Arizona. Tim Ralph, one of the team counselors, said that Haggard, after three weeks of therapy, was now "completely heterosexual" and that Haggard's declaration of heterosexuality was supported by evidence. First, no other person had claimed Haggard engaged in gay sex, and second, gay sex was not a constant in Haggard's life. Haggard's accuser, Jones, responded to Ralph's report by saying that he thought Haggard indeed was gay.

In August, Haggard released a statement that asked for monetary donations to help support his family while he and his wife attended college classes. He wanted to pursue a degree in counseling, and his wife was to study psychology. He also reported that his family was moving into the Dream Center, a halfway house based in Phoenix, Arizona, that ministers to recovering convicts, drug addicts, prostitutes, and others. Within days, however, the restoration team reported that Haggard would not be working at the Dream Center or in any ministry, and it advised Haggard to seek employment outside the church. Steering Haggard away from a return to ministry was based, in part, on Haggard's high profile. The team cited biblical passages about the need to hold influential figures to a higher standard of behavior.

—Ski Hunter

FURTHER READING

Banerjee, Neela. "Accused of Gay Liaison, Head of Evangelical Group Resigns." *The New York Times*, November 3, 2006. News of Jones's out-

---

> ## HAGGARD AND JONES
>
> *The Reverend Ted Haggard apologized to the congregants of the New Life Church. His statement, read by another pastor before the church and published by the* Colorado Springs Gazette *on November 5, 2006, begins,*
>
> To my New Life Church family.
>
> I am so sorry. I am sorry for the disappointment, the betrayal, and the hurt. I am sorry for the horrible example I have set for you. . . . I alone am responsible for the confusion caused by my inconsistent statements. The fact is, I am guilty of sexual immorality, and I take responsibility for the entire problem.
>
> *Michael Jones, the male escort who outed Haggard, told* The New York Times *in a June 7, 2007, interview,*
>
> I've been with some pretty famous people, and I would never out them. This was a unique situation. Here is Ted preaching about being shameful . . . and then he sneaks around with me.

---

ing and Haggard's resignation from the newspaper of record.

Goodstein, L. "Minister's Own Rules Sealed His Fate." *The New York Times*, November 19, 2006. Discusses the dismissal of Haggard from his church, a dismissal caused, in part, by Haggard's own preaching.

"Haggard's Cure Claim Greeted by Skepticism." *Christian Century*, March 6, 2007. Editorial that questions the legitimacy of Haggard's claim that he had been "cured" and was now completely heterosexual after three weeks of therapy.

Ireland, J. "The Escort Who Spoke Out." *Advocate*, December 5, 2006. Focuses on Haggard's accuser, Jones, and how he decided to out Haggard. Jones says that he outed the pastor because of his hypocrisy.

Jones, Mike, with Sam Gallegos. *I Had to Say Something: The Art of Ted Haggard's Fall*. New York: Seven Stories Press, 2007. Jones discusses the Haggard case, focusing on how Haggard's hypocrisy urged him to out the pastor on a Denver television station.

Miller, Brett A. *Divine Apology: The Discourse of Religious Image Restoration*. Westport, Conn.:

Praeger, 2002. Analyzes religious figures accused of sexual misconduct. Includes a section on fundamentalist Christian pastors and preachers.

"Reviewing the Fundamentals." *Christianity Today*, January, 2007. Focuses on the sex scandal in the context of the biblical teachings of the New Testament. Cites the book of James, which instructs that Christian leaders should be placed under strict standards of conduct.

SEE ALSO: 1970: Study of Anonymous Gay Sex Leads to Ethics Scandal; Oct. 25, 1974: Evangelist Billy James Hargis Resigns College Presidency During Gay-Sex Scandal; Jan., 1977: Singer Anita Bryant Campaigns Against Lesbian and Gay Rights; Aug. 4, 1978: British Politician

Jeremy Thorpe Is Charged with Attempted Murder; Sept. 3, 1980: Congressman Bauman Is Arrested for Liaison with Teenage Boy; Dec., 1982: Julie Andrews and Blake Edwards Deny Being Gay; Mar. 19, 1987: Jim Bakker Resigns as Head of PTL Television Network; Feb. 21, 1988: Evangelist Jimmy Swaggart Tearfully Confesses His Adultery; Sept. 19, 2000: Ex-gay Leader John Paulk Is Photographed Leaving a Gay Bar; Aug. 19, 2004: Blog "Outs" Antigay Congressman Edward Schrock; Dec. 6, 2005: Spokane, Washington, Mayor Recalled in Gay-Sex Scandal; Sept. 29, 2006: Congressman Mark Foley Resigns in Sex Scandal Involving a Teenage Page.

November 20, 2006
NEWS CORP ABANDONS PLAN TO PUBLISH O. J. SIMPSON'S BOOK

News Corp announced plans to publish a book by the notorious former football star O. J. Simpson called If I Did It, *an allegedly speculative account of how Simpson would have murdered his former wife, Nicole Brown Simpson, and her friend, Ronald Goldman. Public reaction was so overwhelmingly negative that News Corp canceled both its planned television special and the book's release. Goldman's family received legal title to the book and published it in 2007 as Simpson's actual confession.*

LOCALES: New York, New York; Miami, Florida; Los Angeles, California
CATEGORIES: Publishing and journalism; radio and television; public morals; business

KEY FIGURES
O. J. Simpson (b. 1947), former professional football player and actor
Judith Regan (b. 1953), editor and publisher of ReganBooks

Pablo F. Fenjves (b. 1953), ghostwriter and screenwriter
Denise Brown (b. 1957), advocate for victims of domestic violence
Fred Goldman (b. 1940), father of Ronald Goldman

SUMMARY OF EVENT
On November 20, 2006, News Corporation (News Corp) announced that it would cancel publication of O. J. Simpson's book *If I Did It*. The book, planned for publication by ReganBooks, a News Corp subsidiary, allegedly was a hypothetical confession by Simpson of how he would have murdered his former wife and her friend. Also planned was a two-part television interview *O. J. Simpson: If I Did It, Here's How It Happened* on Fox Television, also a News Corp subsidiary. The interview special, earmarked to promote the book, was scheduled to be broadcast in the final week of the television ratings sweeps. The announcement was followed by overwhelming public condemnation of ReganBooks and Fox.

2000's

Two weeks earlier, on October 30, the gossip tabloid *National Enquirer* first alleged that Simpson was working secretly on a manuscript in which he would confess to the 1994 murders of Nicole Brown Simpson and Ronald Goldman. That manuscript, *If I Did It*, was acquired by ReganBooks, an imprint of HarperCollins. Simpson was to receive $3.5 million for the book contract. Pablo F. Fenjves, *If I Did It*'s ghostwriter, was recruited by ReganBooks and led to believe the book was to be the confession of a murderer. Fenjves himself believes that Simpson murdered Brown Simpson and Goldman.

The *National Enquirer* also suggested that Simpson intended to quickly spend the contract money to avoid paying on the civil judgment against him. Indeed, the $630,000 he was paid in advance, which should have gone to the Goldmans (beneficiaries of the civil judgment), was funneled through a shell corporation, Lorraine Brooke Associates, named for two of his children. He used the money to pay bills, including his mortgage and Internal Revenue Service debts.

On the evening of the announcement by News Corp, Ronald Goldman's father, Fred Goldman, appeared on *Larry King Live* on CNN and strongly urged people to not buy the book. Ronald's family launched a Web site (dontpayoj.com) the next morning, gathering signatures for a petition to stop the book's publication. The family argued that a killer (Simpson was acquitted of the murders in criminal court but found liable in civil court) should not profit from his or her crime.

On November 15, ReganBooks publisher Judith Regan had called Simpson a killer and claimed the book indeed was his confession. She said she contracted the book to bring further awareness to violence against women, which included herself. She also said that her motive for publishing the book was vengeance. By November 20, more than one dozen stations affiliated with Fox refused to air the special. Also, many bookstores refused to sell the book; those that did donated sales profits to charities.

The public's passionate response to the book and television interview was understandable, given that many considered Simpson's acquittal nothing less than a gross miscarriage of justice. The planned interview was likened to a snuff film, and even Simpson agreed that book earnings would be blood money. Finally, the public, journalists, and other media professionals questioned the ethics of News Corp, Fox, and ReganBooks.

On November 21, Denise Brown, Nicole Brown Simpson's sister, announced that News Corp attempted to buy off the Brown and Goldman families by offering millions of dollars for their silence but that News Corp would still publish the book and air the interview. When the Brown family refused News Corp's offer, the company's chairman, Rupert Murdoch, canceled the book and interview and asked booksellers to return all unsold copies. However, some copies of the book circulated after its first printing, and *Vanity Fair* magazine got hold of one. It published a detailed book review in its January 22, 2007, issue, and by June 13, the book was available on the Web.

If I Did It reached merchants once again in September, 2007, although in a somewhat different form. Earlier that summer, a federal bankruptcy judge awarded rights to the original manuscript to the Goldman family. The retitled *If I Did It: Confessions of the Killer* was published as a book of nonfiction—a true O. J. Simpson confession—by Beaufort Books and includes commentary by the ghostwriter, Fenjves, and victim-rights advocate Dominick Dunne. The Goldman family received 90 percent of the profits from sales of the book. Denise Brown responded to the 2007 publication with an online petition, requesting the publisher cancel further printings. By February 14, 2008, the petition's "close" date, more than 6,600 people had signed in support of Brown's campaign.

IMPACT

The scandal surrounding the planned publication of *If I Did It* and its accompanying television special raised anew many ethical dilemmas. First, critics asked whether a person found liable for human pain, suffering, and death should profit from those acts.

Second, critics asked if a media giant, such as

News Corp, should pay a person (Simpson), believed by many to be a murderer, to "confess" on television while hiding behind a criminal court's finding of his not being guilty, and pay the "interviewer" (Regan) to take part in such a charade. Third, critics questioned whether or not any subject is taboo in a world in which networks are attempting to boost sagging ratings. Fourth, is it ethical for journalists to exploit a miscarriage of justice for personal gain?

Finally, many believe that Simpson decided to write the book not only for the money but also to get back in the limelight: He had enjoyed his celebrity for thirty years before the murders, and he clearly basked in this status. However, if these were Simpson's intentions, they failed. He did not receive money for the book, short of the advance, and did not regain his positive celebrity status. If anything, he remains a pariah.

—*Edward J. Schauer*

FURTHER READING

Bugliosi, Vincent T. *Outrage: The Five Reasons Why O. J. Simpson Got Away with Murder*. New York: W. W. Norton, 1996. Study of the murder case by a well-known felony prosecutor. Includes an explanation of how the abundant and quality evidence pointed solely to Simpson as the murderer. Explains in detail how the murder trial went wrong.

Clark, Marcia, and Teresa Carpenter. *Without a Doubt*. New York: Viking Press, 1997. Critical appraisal of all major actors and actions in the Simpson trial by Marcia Clark, the deputy district attorney who led the prosecution.

Cochran, Johnnie L., Jr., with Tim Rutten. *Journey to Justice*. New York: Ballantine Books, 1996. Cochran led the legal team in the successful criminal defense of Simpson. A key to Cochran's perspective on the trial may be found in the title of chapter 14, "From Seeds of Doubt, Justice Flowers."

Dunne, Dominick. *Justice: Crimes, Trials, and Punishments*. New York: Three Rivers Press, 2001. The author, a much-read journalist and major advocate of justice for murder victims, devotes ten chapters to his observations and insight regarding the murder trial of Simpson. Dunne sat through the entire trial and had regular interaction with the families of Nicole Brown Simpson and Ron Goldman after the murders.

The Goldman Family, Pablo F. Fenjves, and Dominick Dunne. *If I Did It: Confessions of the Killer*. New York: Beaufort Books, 2007. Contains an exact replication of the original manuscript of *I Did It*, with commentary by the Goldman family, a prologue by ghostwriter Fenjves, and an afterword by Dunne.

SEE ALSO: Summer, 1936: Film Star Mary Astor's Diary Becomes a Public Sensation; 1978: Actor Joan Crawford's Daughter Publishes Damning Memoir, *Mommie Dearest*; June 12, 1994: Double Murder Leads to Sensational O. J. Simpson Trial; June 24, 1994: *Time* Magazine Cover Uses Altered O. J. Simpson Photo.

2000's

November 23, 2006
FORMER RUSSIAN SECURITY SERVICE OFFICER DIES FROM RADIATION POISONING

Alexander Litvinenko was an officer in the Russian federal security service, once assigned to protect billionaire Boris Berezovsky, who later fell out with the Russian government. After Litvinenko accused the Russian government of scheming to kill Berezovsky, he fled to England. There, he developed a strange illness, later found to be radiation poisoning, and died. Many believe Litvinenko was killed by the Russian government, possibly on orders from President Vladimir Putin.

LOCALE: London, England

CATEGORIES: Murder and suicide; politics; corruption; international relations; government; medicine and health care

KEY FIGURES

Alexander Litvinenko (1962-2006), former senior operational officer in the Federal Security Service of the Russian Federation

Boris Berezovsky (b. 1946), Russian businessman, dissident, and former deputy secretary of Russia's security council

Vladimir Putin (b. 1952), president of the Russian Federation, 1999-2008, and prime minister, 2008-

Andrei Lugovoi (b. 1966), Russian politician and businessman

SUMMARY OF EVENT

Alexander Litvinenko's death is largely the story of three men—Litvinenko, Boris Berezovsky, and Vladimir Putin—and the turbulence of political change in postcommunist Russia. The fall of communism created a Wild West type of environment in Russia, which was ready made for profiteers and unscrupulous businessmen willing to exploit the country's political disorganization and breakdown in law and order for their personal gain. Business disagreements were sometimes resolved by competitors being gunned down. One of the country's

major tourist cities, St. Petersburg, became its crime capital as well.

Regional governors created their own private fiefdoms across the great Eurasian expanse of Russia, and the country's privatization process allowed politically well-connected, and lucky, private entrepreneurs such as Berezovsky (who survived at least two assassination attempts during the mid-1990's) to gain control of the country's major industries and amass personal fortunes through pyramid schemes, money laundering, smuggling, and other illicit activities.

Once in office in 1999, Vladimir Putin focused his presidency on regaining control of Russia's political process. He pushed through laws that made regional governors appointees of the center and extended government control over its key, privatized industries. The latter efforts led him to target, among others, Berezovsky, who by the time of Putin's presidency had become a billionaire with holdings in Russia's oil industry and substantial investments in Russia's media, its automobile sector, and Aeroflot, the country's airline. One technique that Putin regularly employed to regain control over such sectors was the use of legal proceedings against his targets, and so it was for Berezovsky. Indicted for fraud in Russia, Berezovsky fled to Great Britain and then sought asylum in 2001.

Meanwhile, Litvinenko also became embroiled in a conflict with Russian authorities—in his case, with the Federal Security Service of the Russian Federation (FSB), in which he had been an officer for many years but whose return to the brutal practices of the Soviet Union he publicly attacked in 1998 at a Moscow press conference. In particular, he accused the FSB of conducting assassinations and other illegal acts to maintain its position in the leadership of a post-Soviet Russia, which was then theoretically democratizing under the presidency of Boris Yeltsin. Subsequently imprisoned twice for his comments, Litvinenko fled to Britain in 2000, where he merged into a large colony of Russian expatriates (duly infiltrated by undercover Russian security agents) and where he was granted political asylum in 2001. (He later acquired British citizenship.)

Upon Berezovsky's arrival in London, Litvinenko and Berezovsky resumed a friendship that had begun in 1998, when Litvinenko reputedly refused an order to assassinate Berezovsky while serving as his bodyguard. Rejoined in London, they inaugurated an escalating series of charges against the Putin regime that gained increasing credibility in Western circles. Putin's critics in the Russian media were not just harassed but also began to die either accidently or in more violent ways, usually without anyone being charged with their murder. Against this backdrop, Litvinenko's 2006 death in London under mysterious circumstances, and by a highly exotic form of poisoning, immediately acquired both a sinister and scandalous aura.

The facts relating to the poisoning itself remained somewhat disputed despite the intensity of investigative efforts. There is, for example, still a small debate over whether Litvinenko had been poisoned prior to November 1, or only once, on the day he fell ill. It is certain that he was poisoned on the first of November and almost certainly while having a drink at the Millennium Hotel in central London with two former associates in the Soviet KGB, Andrei Lugovoi and Dimitri Kovtun. An inspection of the hotel's kitchen area found a highly radioactive tea cup with traces of polonium-210, radioactive material that laboratory findings later confirmed as the poison that killed Litvinenko. After seeing Lugovoi and Kovtun, Litvinenko journeyed to a restaurant for a scheduled meeting with an Italian security specialist (Mario Scaramella), who had offered to provide him with information on the death of a Russian investigative journalist (Anna Politkovskaya) suspected of being poisoned by Russian agents in 2004 and then assassinated in October, 2006.

Subsequent rumors indicated that Litvinenko was poisoned yet again in the hospital where he was taken for treatment. His recovery there was followed by a subsequent sharp decline in his condition; he then died on November 23. Medical evidence has thoroughly discredited that theory, however, with Litvinenko's initial recovery now being credited to his generally good health and his subsequent relapse seen as a normal consequence of the nature of the radioactive poison he had consumed. Significantly, before he died, Litvinenko recovered enough to make a deathbed statement in which he blamed Putin and Russian security forces operating under Putin's command for his murder. Seven months later, in June of 2007, Berezovsky was alerted by British intelligence that he, too, was being targeted for murder. He fled England in fear for his life.

IMPACT

The British media—and not just the London tabloids—were closely reporting on the scandalous story of Litvinenko's poisoning and eventual death and on the clues that seemed to point to Moscow for having a part in his demise. When media accusations continued as the story unfolded, Britain's diplomatic relations with Russia began to suffer. Moscow retaliated for the unwanted media attention, first by disrupting the British Broadcasting Corporation's broadcasts in Russia and later by expelling several British diplomats from Moscow.

London-Moscow relations further worsened in May of 2007, when British authorities narrowed their suspect list to Lugovoi after having found traces of radioactive material in several places where Lugovoi stayed en route to London and after arriving in London prior to his November 1 meeting with Litvinenko (Litvinenko became ill that same day). On May 22—after tracing the polonium-210 radioactive material used to kill Litvinenko to a Russian nuclear plant as well—British authorities formerly charged Lugovoi with Litvinenko's murder. The British Foreign Office requested Lugovoi's extradition to face charges in Britain. In response, Russian authorities, whose own request for Berezovsky's extradition had been previously refused, rejected the British request on the grounds that it would violate Russia's constitution.

—Joseph R. Rudolph, Jr.

FURTHER READING

Goldfarb, Alex, with Marina Litvinenko. *Death of a Dissident: The Poisoning of Alexander Litvinenko and the Return of the KGB*. New York: Free Press, 2007. Written by a close friend of Litvinenko and by Litvinenko's wife, this work makes the case that Litvinenko's death was a KGB-styled execution intended to send a message to other would-be critics of Putin's Russia.

Litvinenko, Alexander, and Yuri Felshtinsky. *Blowing Up Russia: The Secret Plot to Bring Back KGB Terror*. New York: Encounter Books, 2007. Part of a three-volume set of articles, interviews, and other materials compiled by Boris Berezovsky, this book focuses on the 1998-2005 period of conflict between Litvinenko and the FSB, whom he suspected would some day kill him.

Litvinenko, Alexander, and Pavel Stroilov. *Allegations: Selected Works by Alexander Litvinenko*. Slough, England: Aquilion, 2007. Published a year after Litvinenko's death, Stroilov's work as editor and translator offers a carefully selected anthology of Litvinenko's allegations of misconduct at the highest levels in the Russian government.

SEE ALSO: Oct. 25, 1924: Forged Communist Letter Brings Down British Government; Jan. 8, 1934-Jan. 17, 1936: Stavisky's Fraudulent Schemes Rock French Government; June, 1956: George F. Kennan Proves Russian Sisson Documents Are Fakes; Sept. 12, 1962: British Civil Servant Is Arrested for Spying.

Early 2007
SUBPRIME MORTGAGE INDUSTRY BEGINS TO COLLAPSE

During the 2000-2006 housing boom, American lenders issued a staggering total of $1.5 trillion in risky subprime mortgages, relying on rapidly appreciating home values to protect their investments. As home prices began declining in 2006, record numbers of debtors defaulted, leading to soaring home foreclosure rates, lender bankruptcies, and a general weakening of the U.S. economy. Mismanagement and outright fraud at all levels created a cascading national and international financial crisis leading to industry and government reform.

LOCALE: United States
CATEGORIES: Banking and finance; business; corruption; government

KEY FIGURES

Ben Bernanke (b. 1953), chairman of the Federal Reserve, 2006-2010
Henry Paulson (b. 1946), secretary of the U.S. Treasury, 2006-2009

SUMMARY OF EVENT

Home ownership has always been considered a bulwark of the American way of life. From the end of World War II until the presidency of Ronald Reagan, most home financing required at minimum a 20 percent down payment and featured fixed interest rates, a payoff period not exceeding thirty years, and strict requirements for income and creditworthiness that ensured a low default rate but priced lower income people out of the market. One of the arguments for deregulation was the claim that the lending industry, if freed from constraints, could supplant government subsidies to those otherwise unable to afford a home. The mortgage lending industry, specifically those companies specializing in subprime mortgages, began collapsing even before New Century Financial Corporation, one of the largest such lenders in the United States, declared bankruptcy in April, 2007. Many believe the collapse began earlier in the year.

During the early 1980's, freed from federal regulations, what emerged was a new class of mortgage lending institutions, whose operations were based on originating large numbers of mortgages and selling them to Wall Street investment firms, which in turn sold bonds backed by mortgage investment portfolios. This process is called securitization. Rating agencies gave such investments their highest (AAA) rating based on high dividend rates and assumptions that the underlying mortgage loans were entirely secured by collateral and the risks of borrower default were low. Both assumptions proved to be false. There is suspicion that the ratings agencies themselves may have colluded with investment firms.

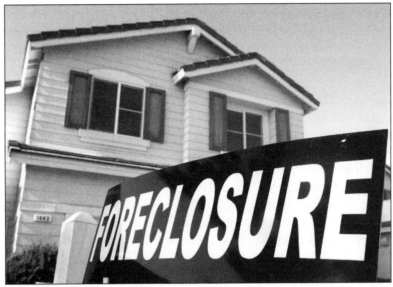

A foreclosed home for sale in Stockton, California, in April, 2008. (Hulton Archive/Getty Images)

The enormous profitability of home loans to investors led to aggressive marketing of subprime instead of prime mortgages, especially those with adjustable interest rates that rise after two or so years, to risky borrowers. A subprime loan is a loan issued to a risky borrower. According to the federal government, risky borrowers are those with a credit score usually below 650 and who have a lower income, an unstable employment history, or a history of financial problems (such as a previous foreclosure, repossession, or bankruptcy).

Between 2000 and 2006, refinance transactions tapping home equity became much more common as well. The availability of so much credit was one factor in the rapid escalation of home prices between 2000 and 2006, marking the housing bubble. Inflation-adjusted home prices, which on the average increased by 0.4 percent per year between 1980 and 2000, nearly doubled between 2000 and 2006, putting a conventional mortgage beyond the means of most first-time home buyers. This inflationary trend created phantom equity for people who bought homes during the 1990's, equity they were encouraged to tap by refinancing homes to pay off other debts, cope with a financial crisis, or simply indulge themselves.

The essentially fraudulent nature of the subprime mortgage industry is epitomized by Angelo Mozilo, cofounder and chief executive officer of Countrywide Financial Corporation, based in Calabasas, California. Mozilo's annual salary at the height of the housing bubble topped $200 million. He was investigated for deliberately propelling his company toward financial collapse as he withdrew his own investment at the last minute and left ordinary stockholders with huge losses. Bank of America announced its $4 billion purchase of Countrywide in January, 2008. The name Countrywide is now synonymous with the subprime mortgage scandal.

There are many different types of subprime mortgages, and many classes of borrowers, including some who qualified for a conventional mortgage but were steered toward a subprime lender by an unscrupulous broker who collected a hefty commission. Racial minorities and the elderly were frequently singled out for the most predatory loans. Home builders and real estate agents and brokers participated in the subprime scandal by selling properties to buyers who clearly could not afford them. Brokers, who were paid on commission and had no further stake in the loan, told borrowers who worried about repayment terms that they could always refinance at a later date, taking advantage of appreciation in the interim. This proved an empty promise when property values started to decline and lending standards tightened.

One of the commonest types of subprime loan is the adjustable rate mortgage, or ARM. A typical ARM has an artificially low interest rate (often called a teaser rate) and correspondingly low payments for the first few years after issuance, after which interest rates and payments rise rapidly and become unmanageable for many with lower or fixed incomes. In theory, in these first years, the homeowner's property appreciates and the homeowner's credit rating improves, allowing for refi-

nancing to a fixed-rate mortgage. Little known was that the refinancing homeowner would end up paying substantially in additional lender fees and a prepayment penalty.

Another common feature of a subprime loan is the balloon payment. Instead of paying down the loan in regular increments, the borrower pays interest only, or interest plus a small sum, and agrees to make a large lump sum payment at some point in the future. These optional-payment mortgages represent a minefield for the borrower, because they allow the borrower to pay less than the interest amount and add the deficiency to the principal of the loan, up to 110 percent of the original loan amount. This is known as negative amortization.

Another troublesome type of loan, the Alt-A or "liar mortgage," proliferated during the same period. Also called stated-income loans, these were issued to people with good credit but without documentation of income. Carrying high interest rates and other undesirable terms, Alt-A loans appealed to speculators, or investors, who defaulted in large numbers when property values declined. Although the typical Alt-A borrower is perceived by the public and legislators as being undeserving of rescue (in contrast to a lower income borrower whose primary residence is threatened with foreclosure), the consequences of the collapse of this market to financial institutions and communities has been more devastating than that created by classic subprime loans.

In 2006, as interest rates on the large numbers of ARMs from 2004 started to reset to higher rates, a number of problems emerged and the housing bubble began to burst. Credit started to contract, with lenders refusing the most marginal loan requests. Home prices in the most rapidly appreciating markets, which coincided with the highest levels of subprime lending, began to decline. Unable to meet payments or refinance, people put their homes

---

DEFINING "SUBPRIME"

The board of governors of the U.S. Federal Reserve and other federal financial agencies issued "Expanded Guidance for Subprime Lending Programs" on January 31, 2001. In the document, the term "subprime" is defined.

The term "subprime" refers to the credit characteristics of individual borrowers. Subprime borrowers typically have weakened credit histories that include payment delinquencies, and possibly more severe problems such as charge-offs, judgments, and bankruptcies. They may also display reduced repayment capacity as measured by credit scores, debt-to-income ratios, or other criteria that may encompass borrowers with incomplete credit histories. Subprime loans are loans to borrowers displaying one or more of these characteristics at the time of origination or purchase. Such loans have a higher risk of default than loans to prime borrowers. Generally, subprime borrowers will display a range of credit risk characteristics that may include one or more of the following:
- Two or more 30-day delinquencies in the last 12 months, or one or more 60-day delinquencies in the last 24 months;
- Judgment, foreclosure, repossession, or charge-off in the prior 24 months;
- Bankruptcy in the last 5 years;
- Relatively high default probability as evidenced by, for example, a credit bureau risk score (FICO) of 660 or below (depending on the product/collateral), or other bureau or proprietary scores with an equivalent default probability likelihood; and/or
- Debt service-to-income ratio of 50% or greater, or otherwise limited ability to cover family living expenses after deducting total monthly debt-service requirements from monthly income.

up for sale. This created a feedback loop, especially in Florida, Nevada, and California. More homes on the market, with fewer buyers able to purchase them, meant further price declines.

Lenders began the process of short sales—working with a homeowner to sell a property valued less than the remaining mortgage due—and foreclosures at record levels. In the heyday of subprime lending, foreclosure did not pose a threat to lender profits because property appreciation canceled out foreclosure costs. The lending industry counted on this. When the system started breaking down, investment firms stopped buying securitized subprime mortgages. Primary lenders, cut off from their main source of capital, shut their doors in droves.

In August of 2007, the nation's secondary mortgage market temporarily shut down, leaving private-sector lenders without a source of money for home buyers. Countrywide Financial, the largest originator of subprime loans in the United States, appeared headed for bankruptcy. The Federal Reserve, headed by Ben Bernanke, responded by lowering the prime interest rate. The conduits for funding most home mortgages shifted to institutions with Federal Housing Administration (FHA) backing and to the Government Sponsored Enterprises (GSEs) of Fannie Mae and Freddie Mac. Investors were still willing to buy mortgage-backed securities backed by FHA insurance or the GSE guarantee.

By mid-2008, it was apparent that the collapse of the subprime market had created a ripple effect extending through the home mortgage market to the economy in general. Nationwide, property values were dropping by 7.47 percent per year, and one in 171 homes was involved in foreclosure. Several regional banks heavily invested in the subprime market had failed outright, and many more were in serious trouble. In July, the U.S. government responded by enacting a sweeping housing rescue bill—the Housing and Economic Recovery Act—that included a provision for refinancing subprime mortgages with an FHA guarantee, a bailout of Fannie Mae and Freddie Mac (as recommended by Secretary of the Treasury Henry Paulson) that cost an estimated $25 billion, and grants and loans to communities to buy vacant foreclosed properties. Fannie Mae and Freddie Mac were bailed out by federal regulators in September.

IMPACT

In terms of its impact on the average American, the subprime mortgage crisis must rank near the top of the list of modern economic scandals. The effects are not confined to the United States, however, but have had serious repercussions in Europe and Asia because of heavy investment by foreign companies and sovereign wealth funds in mortgage-backed securities. Although a number of other factors, notably a sharp increase in energy costs, contributed to the overall decline in economic well-being in the United States between mid-2006 and mid-2008, the collapse of the housing market was clearly the triggering event.

Between December, 2007, and July, 2008, unemployment and bankruptcy filings rose significantly, while housing prices (in most areas), retail sales, and stock values continued to decline, leading to increasingly pessimistic predictions of the duration and depth of the recession. Any final assessment of the impact of the mortgage industry collapse must necessarily await the results of remedial legislation and future elections.

Securing a home loan now involves a process similar to that before the 1990's: paying a 20 percent down payment and meeting strict requirements for income and creditworthiness. Furthermore, consumers who qualify for these harder-to-get loans now focus on securing fixed interest rates.

—*Martha A. Sherwood*

FURTHER READING

DiMartino, Danielle, and John V. Duca. "The Rise and Fall of Subprime Mortgages." *Economic Letter: Insights from the Federal Reserve Bank of Dallas* 2, no. 11 (November, 2007). A good introduction to the subprime mortgage crisis.

Gramlich, Edward M. *Subprime Mortgages: America's Latest Boom and Bust.* Washington, D.C.: Urban Institute Press, 2006. Written by a member of the Federal Reserve Board. The bulk of the book treats subprime lending as a positive force.

2000's

The title and introduction, added just before the book went into print, show how rapidly conditions changed.

Renuart, Elizabeth, and Alys Cohen. *Stop Predatory Lending: A Guide for Legal Advocates.* Boston: National Consumer Law Center, 2007. A good source of information on lender practices contributing to the subprime mortgage crisis.

Sabry, Faten, and Thomas Schopflocher. "The Subprime Meltdown: A Primer." New York: National Economic Research Associates, June 21, 2007. A brief introductory guide to the crisis in the subprime mortgage industry.

SEE ALSO: May 7, 1985: Banker Jake Butcher Pleads Guilty to Fraud; Mar. 29, 1989: Financier Michael Milken Is Indicted for Racketeering and Fraud; Dec. 2, 2001: Enron Bankruptcy Reveals Massive Financial Fraud; Sept. 3, 2003: Mutual Fund Companies Are Implicated in Shady Trading Practices; Sept. 20, 2008: American Financial Markets Begin to Collapse.

February 18, 2007
WASHINGTON POST EXPOSES DECLINE OF WALTER REED ARMY HOSPITAL

The Washington Post *published the first in a series of exposés on the medical neglect and deplorable living conditions of wounded soldiers at Walter Reed Army Medical Center, the Army's major hospital. The exposé led to a national scandal and public condemnation, the resignations of top government and military officials, the formation of a presidential commission to investigate the matter, and new, focused programs for soldier-patients systemwide.*

LOCALE: Washington, D.C.
CATEGORIES: Publishing and journalism; military; medicine and health care; government; politics

KEY FIGURES
Dana Priest (b. 1959), staff writer for *The Washington Post*
Anne Hull (fl. early twenty-first century), staff writer for *The Washington Post*
George W. Weightman (b. 1951), commander of Walter Reed Army Medical Center, 2006-2007
Francis J. Harvey (b. 1943), secretary of the U.S. Army

Kevin C. Kiley (b. 1950), Army surgeon general and commander of Walter Reed Army Medical Center, 2002-2004
Robert Gates (b. 1943), U.S. secretary of defense

SUMMARY OF EVENT
On February 18, 2007, *The Washington Post* (*The Post*) published the first in a series of articles that chronicled inadequate medical care and neglect at Walter Reed Army Medical Center for troops returning from the wars in Iraq and Afghanistan. The articles, written by staff writers Dana Priest and Anne Hull, were the result of four months of interviews and countless visits with Walter Reed patients, staff, and family members of troops. Beginning with the first article in the series, "Soldiers Face Neglect, Frustration at Army's Top Medical Facility," Priest and Hull described rampant neglect and bureaucratic bungling at the medical center, as well as deteriorated facilities and poor management.

Walter Reed was once among the military's premier medical facilities. Located only five miles from the White House in Washington, D.C., the hospital has served more than 150,000 active duty, National Guard, reserve, and retired military personnel. With fifty-five hundred rooms and more than twenty-eight acres of floor space, it is one of the world's largest medical facilities. U.S. presidents, members of Congress, and foreign dignitaries also have received treatment at the facility.

Allegations of poor care and bureaucracy had been raised in Web-based features in 2004 and 2005 (on Salon.com). Furthermore, two members of Congress, both Republicans, were briefed about the problems as early as 2004 but failed to investigate for fear of embarrassing the Army. Also, an internal Walter Reed memorandum in September, 2006, had warned of possible "mission failure" because of the privatization and outsourcing of many of its services. However, it was the coverage by *The Post* that launched a national, public scandal.

The scandal led to the firing of several medical center and military officials. Countless investigations followed, all causing significant embarrassment to George W. Bush and his administration. Moreover, a House of Representatives panel investigating the Walter Reed allegations concluded that the hospital's problems were likely emblematic of the military's health care system in general.

Among the scandal's casualties was the medical center's commander, Major General George W. Weightman, who had claimed to be unaware of the center's shoddy conditions and overwhelming red tape. Weightman was relieved of his command on March 1. Others were forced to resign, including on March 2 Secretary of the Army Francis J. Harvey. Lieutenant General Kevin C. Kiley, the Army's surgeon general and the center's commander from 2002 to 2004, retired on March 12.

Although *The Post* hailed the inpatient area of the medical center as "a place of scrubbed-down order and daily miracles, with medical advances saving more soldiers than ever," much of the controversy was centered on outpatient treatment. Outpatients at Walter Reed traditionally have been active-duty personnel assigned to special outpatient military units at the center. At the height of the scandal, these patients were housed in base facilities and dozens of nearby hotels and apartments contracted by the military. Such facilities were described as a "holding ground" for hundreds of outpatients—

LIFE AT WALTER REED

A scathing news feature on living conditions for wounded soldiers at Walter Reed Army Medical Center opened with a startling exposé of neglect and filth.

Behind the door of Army Spec. Jeremy Duncan's room, part of the wall is torn and hangs in the air, weighted down with black mold. When the wounded combat engineer stands in his shower and looks up, he can see the bathtub on the floor above through a rotted hole. The entire building, constructed between the world wars, often smells like greasy carry-out. Signs of neglect are everywhere: mouse droppings, belly-up cockroaches, stained carpets, cheap mattresses.

Source: Dana Priest and Anne Hull, "Soldiers Face Neglect, Frustration at Army's Top Medical Facility." *The Washington Post*, February 18, 2007.

---

mostly soldiers and Marines—and Walter Reed's staff and facilities became overwhelmed by the legions of injured personnel from years of war in the Middle East.

Although the average stay following inpatient treatment was about ten months, many outpatients were assigned to Walter Reed's outpatient units for two years or more. According *The Post*, outpatients quickly outnumbered inpatients by a ratio of 17-1. Many were amputees or had suffered head and brain injuries; still others had severe psychological problems. According to an interview with General Weightman, problems at the center stemmed from the Army's intense scrutiny of medical discharges during two concurrent, long-term wars using an all-volunteer force.

Among the biggest complaints waged by those interviewed by *The Post* was the amount of paperwork and bureaucracy soldiers and their families had to surmount to receive basic services. Investigators reported that the typical soldier filled out twenty-two forms—filed with eight different commands, many of them off post—to enter or exit the military medical system. Furthermore, to process the forms, the Army relied on sixteen incompatible

2000's

1139

data systems and three incompatible personnel systems. Separate and incompatible pay and medical records systems were used as well. Because of these bureaucratic hurdles, records were frequently lost, forcing injured soldiers to bring in medals, photographs, and personal documents to prove they were injured in war. Soldiers and their families apparently received little guidance in navigating this arcane system.

While paperwork may have frustrated soldiers and their families, public outcry came after *The Post* described life at Walter Reed's inferior outpatient facilities, particularly a former hotel just outside the gates of the post identified as Building 18. This outpatient building had everything from vermin to mold and stained carpeting. Worse, injured and disfigured soldiers—many of whom also were

suffering from post-traumatic stress disorder, paranoid delusional disorders, and schizophrenia—reportedly spent their days wandering aimlessly through the facility. Most were waiting for a bureaucrat's decision on whether they would be discharged from the service or returned to active duty.

Reporters Priest and Hull noted that the alarming conditions were exacerbated because many patients housed in Building 18 subsisted on carry-out food and used hotplates for warming up food because the medical center's mess hall was located far from their barracks. Building 18 lacked adequate security and was located in an area of the city known for drug dealing and other crimes. In addition, noncommissioned officers, themselves with serious psychological disorders, frequently supervised other patients, some at risk of suicide.

Building 18 originally had been slated for renovation, but that project was put on hold because the medical center was scheduled for closure. In addition, a thirty-thousand-dollar grant for upgrades and recreational equipment for the residents was canceled in December, 2006, just before the Christmas holidays, because an official was concerned that such expenditures could trigger an audit. By January, the funds were no longer available. Army vice chief of staff Richard Cody, along with Harvey, walked through the facility and insisted that changes were in order.

Ultimately, medical center leaders were accused of having unqualified military personnel and overworked and under-trained case managers help injured soldiers and their families. In addition to assisting patients with housing and pay, these medical center personnel were tasked with helping soldiers with such apparently simple, but almost insurmountable, issues such as replacing their destroyed uniforms, ruined when the soldiers were injured. The task seemed simple enough. In one case, however, a soldier receiving a medal for his war service was disciplined for showing up for the ceremony in sweat

---

ARMY'S FIRST RESPONSE

General Richard Cody, the Army's vice chief of staff, announced to the press on February 21, 2007, that he would "personally oversee" the renovations of Building 18, the Walter Reed Army Medical Center facility that had deplorable living conditions.

Many of you have read or have heard reports this past weekend concerning the outpatient care of our Wounded Warriors at Walter Reed Army Medical Center. The Secretary of the Army Francis J. Harvey and I visited one outpatient care building mentioned in those reports yesterday, Building 18, and were absolutely disappointed in the status of the rooms and found the delays and lack of attention to building repairs inexcusable.

I am disappointed that I had to learn of the conditions of that building through media reports. Despite frequent visits to Walter Reed facilities and informal and formal discussion with patients and their families, I have never been made aware of Building 18, its condition, or any complaints our Wounded Warriors may have had.

Clearly, a breakdown in leadership and bureaucratic medical and contractual processes bogged down a speedy solution to these problems. I can assure you that appropriate vigor and leadership is being applied to this issue and we will correct any problems immediately. I will personally oversee the plan to upgrade Building 18 and other facilities and ensure our soldiers and their families, who have sacrificed so much, receive the care and housing they so deserve.

pants and shirt; he had not received replacement uniforms. The Army requires outpatient soldiers, even amputees and personnel using wheelchairs, to wear uniforms during treatment.

IMPACT

Beyond the firings and forced resignations, investigators began to examine the medical care of not only Walter Reed but also the military health care system in general. An independent review panel appointed by Defense Secretary Robert Gates confirmed in April, 2007, that many of the allegations made in *The Washington Post* and elsewhere were indeed true. The panel's report cited neglect and "virtually incomprehensible" inattention to maintenance at Walter Reed.

On March 6, shortly after the story broke in *The Washington Post*, President Bush appointed the Task Force on Returning Global War on Terror Heroes and convened the Commission on Care for America's Returning Wounded Warriors to investigate the allegations. The commission, which included former secretary of health and human services Donna Shalala and former Republican senator Bob Dole, issued its findings on April 19. Among its recommendations was that the health care systems of both the departments of Defense and Veterans Affairs be restructured and more closely aligned. In addition, the military's disability and compensation systems needed to be revamped. The commission also recommended that an aggressive incentive package be developed to attract an excellent medical staff.

Although many of the commission's recommendations were mired in bureaucratic red tape, one suggestion made news headlines: assigning so-called recovery coordinators from outside the military to each seriously wounded soldier to help shepherd him or her through the system. Also, as a result of the recommendations, several pieces of so-called wounded-warrior legislation were proposed in Congress.

The Government Accountability Office reported in September that the Pentagon's promised fixes at Walter Reed and elsewhere in the military health care system remained threatened by staff shortages and a lack of clarity on how best to care for wounded troops. Adding to concerns of staff shortages and stalled improvements in medical care was the slated closure of Walter Reed by the Defense Base Realignment and Closure Commission. The commission announced in 2005 that the facility was to be renamed the Walter Reed National Military Medical Center and relocated to the nearby National Naval Medical Center in Maryland. In the face of the scandal, Walter Reed continued to be a major source of care for soldiers returning from the wars in Iraq and Afghanistan.

—*Cheryl Pawlowski*

FURTHER READING

Priest, Dana, and Anne Hull. "Soldiers Face Neglect, Frustration at Army's Top Medical Facility." *The Washington Post*, February 18, 2007. The first article in the special investigative report on Walter Reed Army Medical Center. This is the story that broke the scandal.

United States Congress. Senate Armed Services Committee. *Care, Living Conditions, and Administration of Outpatients at Walter Reed Army Medical Center.* Washington, D.C.: Government Printing Office, 2007. The Senate report of its hearings on the Walter Reed Hospital medical neglect scandal. The hearings began on March 6, 2007.

Vogel, Steve. "Report Says Fixes Slow to Come to Walter Reed." *The Washington Post*, September 27, 2007. Reporter Vogel follows up on the initial February, 2007, exposé and investigates the progress of promised changes at Walter Reed Hospital.

SEE ALSO: May, 1915: British Government Falls Because of Munitions Shortages and Military Setbacks; July 28, 1932: U.S. Troops Drive World War I Veterans from Washington; May 16, 1934: General Douglas MacArthur Sues Newspaper Columnist for Libel; June 13, 1971: *New York Times* Publishes the Pentagon Papers; Apr. 15, 1981: Janet Cooke Admits Fabricating Her Pulitzer Prize-Winning Feature; Nov. 26, 1997: Canadian Health Commissioner Releases

Report on Tainted Blood; Jan. 30, 2001: Liverpool Children's Hospital Collects Body Parts Without Authorization; Sept. 8, 2004: *60 Minutes II* Reports on George W. Bush's Evasion of Wartime Duty; June 22, 2005: U.S. Air Force Investigates Religious Intolerance at Its Academy.

April 11, 2007
SHOCK JOCK DON IMUS LOSES HIS RADIO SHOW OVER SEXIST AND RACIST REMARKS

On his morning radio show, notorious shock jock Don Imus referred to members of the Rutgers University women's basketball team as "nappy-headed hos" after his cohost said they were "hardcore hos," creating a national furor. The scandal cost Imus his job, temporarily, and prompted a nationwide discussion of racist and sexist speech on the radio.

LOCALE: New York, New York

CATEGORIES: Racism; radio and television; sports; social issues and reform; women's issues; civil rights and liberties; popular culture

KEY FIGURES

Don Imus (b. 1940), radio talk-show host

Bernard McGuirk (fl. early twenty-first century), radio show producer and Imus's cohost

Al Sharpton (b. 1954), civil rights leader and syndicated radio talk-show host

C. Vivian Stringer (b. 1948), coach of the Rutgers University women's basketball team

Kia Vaughn (b. 1987), Rutgers University basketball player

SUMMARY OF EVENT

Don Imus, one of the most notorious radio hosts in the United States, is best known for his syndicated radio and television show *Imus in the Morning*. The show began as a local broadcast in New York, where it reached about one-half million listeners on the radio station WFAN. The show became nationally syndicated in 1993 and began simulcasting on paid television—on MSNBC—in 1996. The radio show was broadcast on more than sixty CBS Radio stations across the United States and had generated millions of dollars in revenue.

On April 4, 2007, the morning after the Rutgers University women's basketball team lost to the University of Tennessee in the finals of the National Collegiate Athletic Association's (NCAA) championship series, Imus commented on the appearance of the Rutgers basketball players, most of whom were African American, and called them "rough girls," apparently in reference to their tattoos. Imus's executive producer and sidekick, Bernard McGuirk, referred to the players as "hardcore hos." Imus continued the derogatory conversation and described the young women as "nappy-headed hos."

Leaders from women's groups and, most particularly, the African American community were outraged. The National Association of Black Journalists called for a national boycott of the show. Imus responded by dismissing the incident as nothing more than amusing. Two days later, following a barrage of calls demanding that he be fired, Imus issued an apology, but his expression of regret for his words was not enough. His many critics pointed to a pattern of insensitive remarks voiced on his network show over the years.

The Reverend Al Sharpton, a leader in the African American community, called Imus's comments abominable, racist, and sexist and demanded that Imus be fired immediately. In an attempt to remedy the situation, Imus appeared on Sharpton's syndicated radio talk show on April 9 to address the controversy and provide a more complete apology for what he said. Despite the appearance on Sharpton's radio show, a growing number of black leaders called for Imus's dismissal and continued to threaten to organize a boycott of his show's sponsors. Critics also called upon the Federal Communications Commission (FCC) to take action against him and radio stations that carry his program. As a result of intensifying public pressure, numerous sponsors of his morning show, including American Express, Sprint Nextel, Staples, Procter & Gamble, and General Motors, pulled their advertising. The FCC would not get involved in the matter.

MSNBC was the first to act. On April 11, NBC News announced that MSNBC would no longer simulcast *Imus in the Morning*. In announcing the decision, NBC News president Steve Capus said Imus's "comments were deeply hurtful to many, many people." The next day, CBS Radio canceled *Imus in the Morning* as well. Leslie Moonves, CBS Corporation president and chief executive officer, said the network made the decision to help change a media "culture that permits a certain level of objectionable expression that hurts and demeans a wide range of people."

Several days after the incident, Rutgers players held a news conference attended by players' parents, coaches, Rutgers administrators, religious leaders, and Imus himself at the New Jersey governor's mansion in Princeton. The three-hour meeting was arranged by Buster Soaries, a former New Jersey secretary of state and the pastor of Rutgers basketball coach C. Vivian Stringer. New Jersey's governor, Jon Corzine, was injured in a car accident on his way to the meeting, so he could not attend.

Players were deeply hurt by Imus's words. Team captain Essence Carson said Imus had "stolen a moment of pure grace from the team." At the New Jersey news conference, Coach Stringer said Imus's words affected not her team alone but all women and all persons of color. Several days after the news conference, Stringer said her players had accepted Imus's personal apology and that the team was in the process of forgiving.

Prior to his termination from the airways, Imus had signed a five-year, $40 million contract extension with CBS Radio. Upon notification of his firing, Imus hired a prominent attorney, Martin Garbus, to pursue a wrongful termination lawsuit against CBS, threatening to sue for $120 million. On August 14, he reached a settlement with CBS for an undisclosed amount of money, leaving him free to pursue other media opportunities.

Imus also faced a lawsuit from one of the Rutgers players. Kia Vaughn sued Imus for libel, slander, and defamation. The lawsuit alleged that his use of the slanderous terms was intentional and motivated by greed and financial gain. The lawsuit claimed that the insults were made purely to increase ratings for Imus and his show. Vaughn requested monetary damages of an unspecified amount, but she decided to drop the lawsuit because she wanted to focus on her university studies and basketball.

Don Imus. (AP/Wide World Photos)

IMPACT

The scandal caused by Imus's racist and sexist comments proved that such behavior is facing growing condemnation, yet such vulgar talk is widespread in American popular culture, including in the lyrics of rap, hip-hop, rock, and other musical genres. Imus's derogatory remarks, scandalous as they were, also reignited the debate over freedom of speech, a debate that moved the focus from racism and sexism—the primary reason for the scandal—to individual rights. Imus's supporters argued that it was within his First Amendment rights to express his opinions on the air, regardless of how controversial, and that he should not have been fired. The FCC determined that Imus had been fired by a private employer who believed his remarks were objectionable, and thus the case was not technically one of censorship or a violation of free speech rights.

In the end, Imus's career suffered little after his dismissal. Eight months after being fired, he launched a return to radio. On November 1, Citadel Broadcasting announced it had agreed to what was reportedly a multiyear syndication contract with Imus. The new *Imus in the Morning* program was distributed nationally by ABC radio networks and was based at Citadel, which owned WABC in New York City. It started broadcasting in December. Imus introduced two African American comedians, Karith Foster and Tony Powell, as cast members of his show.

—*Mary McElroy*

FURTHER READING

Goldstein, Hilary. "Tuning into Democracy: Community Radio, Free Speech, and the Democratic Promise." *Alternate Routes* 20 (2004): 59-106. Investigation into the connection between free speech and democracy using case studies of two radio networks.

Leets, Laura. "Disentangling Perceptions of Subtle Racist Speech: A Cultural Perspective." *Journal of Language and Social Psychology* 22, no. 2 (2003): 145-148. An experimental study that examines how racist slurs made by dominant groups in society cause harm to others.

Reed, James. *Everything Imus: All You Ever Wanted to Know About Don Imus.* New York: Birch Lane Press, 1999. A profile of one of radio's most controversial personalities. Covers more than thirty years of the career of the shock jock. Includes discussion of his propensity to use racial and sexist slurs and his battle with drugs and alcohol.

SEE ALSO: Mar. 14, 1960: FCC Chairman John C. Doerfer Resigns for Accepting Gifts from Networks; Oct. 4, 1976: Agriculture Secretary Earl Butz Resigns After Making Obscene Joke; Sept. 22, 1997: Sportscaster Marv Albert Is Tried for Sexual Assault; Oct. 13, 2004: Television Producer Files Sex Harassment Suit Against Bill O'Reilly.

May 28, 2007
JAPANESE POLITICIAN CHARGED WITH CORRUPTION HANGS HIMSELF

Japanese agricultural minister Toshikatsu Matsuoka received months of publicity for claiming questionable reimbursements and expenses and for connections with business executives arrested for rigging bids for public works projects. After he was found dead, hanging from a dog leash in an apparent suicide, Prime Minister Shinzo Abe's administration was subjected to even greater public scrutiny and suffered loss of support, culminating in the prime minister's resignation in September, 2007.

LOCALE: Tokyo, Japan

CATEGORIES: Murder and suicide; corruption; government; politics

KEY FIGURES

Toshikatsu Matsuoka (1945-2007), Japanese minister of agriculture, forestry, and fisheries, 2006-2007

Shinzo Abe (b. 1954), prime minister of Japan, 2006-2007

Norihiko Akagi (b. 1959), Japanese minister of agriculture, 2007

Taku Yamamoto (b. 1952), Japanese politician

SUMMARY OF EVENT

Toshikatsu Matsuoka was a six-time elected member of Japan's house of representatives for Kumamoto Prefecture's third district. He served as the minister of agriculture, forestry, and fisheries in the Shinzo Abe cabinet. The sixty-two-year-old Matsuoka committed suicide on May 28, 2007, during the middle of a financial scandal, marking the first time a Japanese cabinet minister killed himself since World War II. (Army minister Anami Korechika committed suicide on news of Japan's surrender.)

Matsuoka's duties included work on free-trade agreements with Australia and on diplomacy with the United States over beef-import concerns, but he received the most attention when he announced a plan to certify Japanese food restaurants outside Japan. He wanted certification to help distinguish pseudo-Japanese food restaurants from those that are "genuine." Many foreign media criticized the system, and Matsuoka was forced to retract his plan.

The real political damage to Matsuoka sprang from questions he faced over high utility expenses, for which he had claimed more than 28 million yen ($236,600) from government funds. Similarly high expenses ($42,000) for utilities had been claimed as far back as 2005. Matsuoka tried to quiet the scandal by saying that the money had been spent on purified water. One oft-quoted line from Matsuoka, "Nobody drinks tap water anymore," led *The New York Times* to suggest that he made statements "bordering on the absurd." Matsuoka had become the butt of national and international ridicule, prompting television crews and opposition politicians to visit his office to request tastings of the costly purified water.

In addition to the utilities expenses, public records also show that Matsuoka claimed another $1.2 million as "office costs" from 2001 to 2005, even though his office in a parliamentary building was rent-free. Opposition members of Parliament called for his resignation over these expenses, though Prime Minister Abe vigorously defended his minister, often against the advice of some within his own party, saying Matsuoka had fulfilled his legal responsibilities in making these declarations and that he had detailed knowledge of agricultural policy. In response to the growing public outcry, the governing Liberal Democratic Party proposed new rules requiring receipts for every expense exceeding 50,000 yen, or about $410. However, the proposal backfired, drawing attention to the policy that lawmakers are not required to file receipts for many of the expenses they report to the government. Op-

2000's

position parties responded by calling for receipts for all expenses, a requirement the governing party traditionally had resisted.

The utilities debacle was just one of a series of money scandals and policy missteps that plagued the Abe administration. Critics pointed to Abe's weak management skills and poor political judgment. Matsuoka was embroiled in other financially related scandals, having been forced to apologize shortly after taking office for failing to declare political donations amounting to $75,000. In a parallel investigation by Tokyo prosecutors that was coming to a head the week prior to Matsuoka's suicide, a company was linked to a bid-rigging scandal involving road construction projects administered by Matsuoka's ministry. Six construction-industry executives and consultants were arrested and accused of violating antimonopoly laws by colluding on bids.

The Japanese press reported that the vice farm minister, Taku Yamamoto, had said during a speech that Matsuoka might have used the money on geishas in the Asakusa entertainment district of Tokyo, but Yamamoto later retracted his statement, saying that he intended it as a joke. The accusation has never been proved.

Matsuoka took his own life in his apartment, hours before scheduled questioning in the national parliament by an audit committee in connection with political donations and allegations of misappropriation of government funds. He was discovered unconscious, hanging by his dog leash, in his pajamas, from the hinge of a door in his living room. He died at Keio University hospital in Tokyo shortly afterward. A police postmortem examination confirmed that he died after he had hanged himself. Police refused to comment on reports in the Japanese press that he had left a number of suicide notes in his apartment, including ones addressed to Japan's prime minister and the public apologizing for his actions. "He was certainly under pressure in Parliament," Abe said of Matsuoka after his death. "He was giving his all to the job, and I had very high expectations of him, so this is really too bad."

Suicides have a longstanding tradition in Japan, where they are seen as a face-saving move to avoid public humiliation. The suicide of someone who has disgraced him- or herself, or his or her office, is likely to be seen not as a means of escape from the situation but rather as a way of rectifying that problem. Japan's suicide rate is among the highest in the industrialized world and reached a record high in 2007. In 2004, more than thirty-two thousand Japanese nationals killed themselves.

IMPACT

"The effects on the cabinet will be great," a visibly shaken Prime Minister Abe declared as he left to attend a wake for the deceased minister. "I feel deeply conscious of my responsibility as prime minister, and as the one who appointed him."

Political analysts such as Minoru Morita, who runs an independent research institute in Tokyo, said the suicide could hurt Abe by drawing still more scrutiny to the scandals. After Matsuoka's suicide, Abe's approval rating dropped from 43 percent to remain below 30 percent for months. Abe's ruling Liberal Democratic Party consequently suffered great losses in the election to the upper house of councillors on July 29, losing its majority, while the Democratic Party of Japan managed to gain the largest margin since its formation in 1996. Matsuoka's replacement, Norihiko Akagi, who was suspected of unethical conduct similar to that of Matsuoka, resigned after the election. Abe was free from leadership contests from within the ruling party but was nevertheless obliged to resign as a result of the mounting pressures on his administration.

—Stefan Halikowski Smith

FURTHER READING

Fackler, Martin. "Facing Inquiry, Japanese Official Commits Suicide." *The New York Times*, May 28, 2007. Next-day reportage in the international press of Matsuoka's suicide and its political ramifications.

Mamoru, Iga. *The Thorn in the Chrysanthemum: Suicide and Economic Success in Modern Japan.* Berkeley: University of California Press, 1986. Examines the problem of suicide in Japan; discusses Japanese values, culture, and pressures for economic success; and describes the suicides of five prominent authors.

"Political Suicide." *The Economist*, June 6, 2007. An article suggesting that Matsuoka's suicide had deep consequences for Japanese politics, turning a rising Abe administration into one with serious problems.

Shinzo, Abe. "For a Beautiful Country: The New Prime Minister of Japan Speaks Out." *Vertical Inc.*, October 23, 2007. Offers a rare inside look at one of the most controversial and lauded prime ministers to be put in office, explaining the Japa-nese prime minister's pro-United States stand on world politics.

SEE ALSO: Feb. 3, 1975: Honduras's "Bananagate" Bribery Scandal Leads to Executive's Suicide; Jan. 22, 1987: Pennsylvania Politician Kills Himself at Televised Press Conference; June, 1988-June, 1989: Insider-Trading Scandal Rocks Japanese Government; Aug. 10, 1989: Japanese Prime Minister Sosuke Resigns After Affair with a Geisha.

June 4, 2007
CONGRESSMAN WILLIAM J. JEFFERSON IS INDICTED FOR CORRUPTION

In March, 2005, the Federal Bureau of Investigation began investigating Louisiana congressman William J. Jefferson for corrupt business dealings. Jefferson had been videotaped receiving $100,000 from an investor-informer to establish business contacts in Nigeria. The FBI searched Jefferson's home and found $90,000 of the cash in his refrigerator freezer. The agency later raided his office in Washington, D.C., which provoked intense debate about the right of law enforcement to search congressional offices.

LOCALES: Washington, D.C.; New Orleans, Louisiana

CATEGORIES: Law and the courts; corruption; civil rights and liberties; government; politics

KEY FIGURES

William J. Jefferson (b. 1947), U.S. representative from Louisiana, 1991-2009

Lori Mody (fl. early twenty-first century), business investor

SUMMARY OF EVENT

A Democratic congressman from Louisiana, William J. Jefferson became the subject of one of the largest criminal and legal scandals to strike the U.S. Congress in modern times. On June 4, 2007, a federal grand jury indicted him for a pattern of corruption. According to the ninety-four-page indictment, Jefferson solicited thousands of dollars in bribes, sometimes in the form of stock and retainer fees, in the years between 2000 and 2005. While the indictment proved shocking, the discovery of thousands of dollars in Jefferson's refrigerator freezer at his home by agents with the Federal Bureau of Investigation (FBI) grabbed the public's attention. Furthermore, a subsequent search of his congressional office infuriated members of Congress and all concerned with search-and-seizure rights.

Jefferson was elected to Congress in 1991, becoming the first African American Congress member from Louisiana since the days of Reconstruction. Jefferson, one of ten children of poor sharecroppers, grew up in Lake Providence, Louisiana. He earned a degree from Southern University A&M College before graduating from Harvard University Law School in 1972. He arrived in Washington, D.C., after serving three terms in the Louisiana senate. While serving in Congress, Jefferson earned a master's degree in taxation laws from Georgetown University. He established a rep-

2000's

1147

utation as an expert on trade and tax issues, serving on the House Committees on Ways and Means and Small Business as well as with the Congressional Black Caucus and the Africa Trade and Investment Caucus.

However, Jefferson, who was nicknamed Dollar Bill by his opponents in New Orleans, also gained a reputation for being eager to make a buck. He broke with his mentor, Ernest N. Morial, New Orleans's first black mayor, during the late 1970's over a large bill for legal work that Morial had assumed was free. Political observers suggested that Jefferson did not want to leave his family in the financial straits from which he began life. Jefferson and his wife, Andrea Jefferson, had five daughters.

In March, 2005, business investor Lori Mody of McLean, Virginia, approached the FBI to complain about dealings over the previous nine months with Jefferson and several of his associates. Mody had initially sought to use Jefferson's influence to win contracts to install telephone and Internet service in the African nations of Nigeria and Ghana. At the request of U.S. government officials, she agreed to wear a hidden microphone for subsequent meetings with Jefferson.

Meeting at a restaurant in May, Jefferson and the informant negotiated, on paper, the percentage of the company that Jefferson wanted for his children: 30 percent. On July 12, following a trip to Ghana, Jefferson informed Mody that she now co-owned a Ghanaian company, International Broad Band Services, with the Jeffersons. On July 30, Jefferson met Mody for breakfast at the Ritz-Carlton Hotel near the Pentagon. As they left the restaurant, Jefferson took from Mody's car a reddish-brown leather briefcase, which contained $100,000 in cash to bribe Nigerian officials. While the FBI videotaped him, Jefferson put the money in his vehicle and drove away. Four days later, the FBI raided his home and found $90,000 of the marked bills hidden in frozen-food containers in the freezer of his northeast Washington, D.C., home. The remaining $10,000 was recovered from his office assistant and his lawyer.

On May 20-21, 2006, the FBI spent eighteen hours searching Jefferson's office at the Rayburn House Office Building in Washington, D.C. Seized documents were submitted to an independent team of two U.S. Justice Department lawyers and an FBI agent for evaluation. This search marked the first time that the office of a member of Congress was searched in a criminal inquiry, and the incident touched off a firestorm of protest from both Republican and Democratic lawmakers, who argued that the search interfered with their legislative prerogatives. Justice Department officials countered that members of Congress were not above the law and that congressional offices should not be turned into sanctuaries or places for members to engage in illegal conduct. On May 25, U.S. president George W. Bush ordered the attorney general's office to seal the materials seized from Jefferson's office for forty-five days until the dispute between the House and prosecutors was resolved; some documents, however, were used to prepare an indictment against Jefferson. Meanwhile, Jefferson went to federal court in a futile effort to force the return of his documents.

The *Times-Picayune* of New Orleans called for Jefferson to resign before he inflicted even more pain on a district traumatized by Hurricane Katrina. House Speaker Nancy Pelosi, a fellow Democrat, recommended that Jefferson resign from the House Ways and Means Committee, which writes tax laws. She stated that the charges, if true, constituted an abuse of public trust and power. On June 8, House Democratic leaders endorsed an effort to oust Jefferson from his post on the committee. The Congressional Black Caucus opposed the decision on the grounds that Jefferson was presumed innocent and that removing him from his committee post before any criminal charges had been filed would be unprecedented. Jefferson viewed efforts to force him from the committee as discriminatory.

Meanwhile, the government prosecuted two persons who were closely associated with Jefferson. In January, 2006, Brett M. Pfeffer, once a top aide to Jefferson, pleaded guilty to federal bribery charges and said his boss (Jefferson) had demanded kickbacks for facilitating business deals in Nigeria. A Kentucky businessman, Vernon L. Jackson, pleaded guilty on May 3 to paying between $400,000 and

$1 million to Jefferson's family in exchange for Jefferson's help in obtaining Nigerian business deals for iGate, a telecommunications company that Jackson headed and that Jefferson and Mody were negotiating to purchase. The FBI alleged that Jefferson tried to conceal his involvement by funneling the payments to his daughters. Pfeffer and Jackson cooperated with the government's investigation of the congressman.

On December 9, Jefferson surprised most observers by winning reelection to Louisiana's Second Congressional District. He received 57 percent of the vote, cast by only about 16 percent of eligible voters in a hotly contested election. Political analysts suggested that the voters in the district, which spans most of New Orleans and the west bank of neighboring Jefferson Parish, were more concerned with maintaining the status quo than with change. The district was flooded after Hurricane Katrina made landfall on August 29, 2005, and many voters believed that Jefferson could better help residents than his less experienced opponent.

Jefferson's reelection did not stop the Justice Department from pursuing the Congress member. On June 4, 2007, he was indicted by a federal grand jury on sixteen corruption-related felony counts, including bribery, racketeering, conspiracy, money laundering, and obstruction of justice. In particular, investigators claimed that he targeted companies involved in oil, communications, satellite transmission, and sugar, all of which sought to do business in Africa. In exchange for money, Jefferson used his official position as a member of the House Ways and Means subcommittee on trade to promote these ventures. The indictment stated that Jefferson led official delegations to Africa, wrote letters to U.S. and foreign officials, and assigned members of his staff to promote ventures in Nigeria, Ghana, and Equatorial Guinea, ventures in which he had a financial interest. Jefferson pleaded not guilty on June 8 and faced trial in January, 2009.

IMPACT

The investigation into Jefferson's activities undercut efforts by Democrats to link the Republican-controlled Congress to a culture of corruption. In the 2006 elections, Republicans frequently invoked the Jefferson case to defend their party from charges of corruption. Louisiana voters appeared blasé about the investigation, perhaps because the state has a long history of corrupt politicians. During the 1990's and into the twenty-first century, Louisiana saw the convictions of an attorney general, Congress member, a state senate president, a federal judge, and numerous local officials. Jefferson's own brother-in-law, a judge, was imprisoned for mail fraud.

—*Caryn E. Neumann*

FURTHER READING

Long, Kim. *The Almanac of Political Corruption, Scandals, and Dirty Politics*. New York: Delacorte Press, 2007. A wide-ranging book detailing the various scandals and corrupt practices that have plagued U.S. politics. A good general study of political scandals.

Murray, Shailagh, and Allan Lengel. "Lawmakers Demand FBI Return Raid Files: Capitol Hill Search Stirs Constitution Fight." *The Washington Post*, May 25, 2006. News story reporting on the scandal provoked by the FBI's raid on Jefferson's office in Congress.

Parent, Wayne. *Inside the Carnival: Unmasking Louisiana Politics*. Baton Rouge: Louisiana State University Press, 2006. Although this book does not focus specifically on Jefferson, it describes the problematic and troublesome atmosphere of Louisiana politics.

Wolfensberger, Don. "Punishing Disorderly Behavior in Congress: The First Century—An Introductory Essay." Washington, D.C.: Woodrow Wilson International Center for Scholars, 2006. A wide-ranging discussion of corruption in Congress. Based on a paper prepared for the seminar Congressional Ethics Enforcement: Is Congress Fulfilling Its Constitutional Role?

SEE ALSO: Jan. 23, 1904: Senator Joseph R. Burton Is Convicted of Bribery; May 12, 1924: Kentucky Congressman John W. Langley Is Convicted of Violating the Volstead Act; Aug. 4, 1948: Columnist Drew Pearson Exposes Con-

2000's

gressman's Corruption; Mar. 1, 1967: Adam Clayton Powell, Jr., Is Excluded from Congress; June 23, 1967: Senator Thomas J. Dodd Is Censured for Misappropriating Funds; Dec. 11, 1997: HUD Secretary Henry Cisneros Is Indicted for Lying to Federal Agents; May 9, 2000:

Former Louisiana Governor Edwin Edwards Is Convicted on Corruption Charges; Beginning Aug. 29, 2005: Government Incompetence Mars Hurricane Katrina Relief Efforts; July 9, 2007: Senator David Vitter's Name Is Found in D.C. Madam's Address Book.

July 9, 2007
SENATOR DAVID VITTER'S NAME IS FOUND IN D.C. MADAM'S ADDRESS BOOK

Deborah Jeane Palfrey was convicted of racketeering for running a Washington, D.C., prostitution ring. One of her clients was David Vitter, a conservative Republican senator from Louisiana famed for long-time public dedication to traditional family values. His name, and the names of her other clients, was released by Palfrey, and Vitter admitted to having sinned. The scandal embarrassed Vitter but cost Palfrey her life; Palfrey committed suicide in 2008.

LOCALE: Washington, D.C.
CATEGORIES: Prostitution; sex; sex crimes; organized crime and racketeering; politics; law and the courts; murder and suicide

KEY FIGURES
David Vitter (b. 1961), U.S. senator from Louisiana, 2005-
Deborah Jeane Palfrey (1956-2008), owner of the escort agency Pamela Martin & Associates

SUMMARY OF EVENT
American history is replete with scandals involving politicians and women engaged in marginalized, sexually oriented businesses such as prostitution and escort services. The case of U.S. senator David Vitter in 2007 and 2008 was in many ways typical. He was a rising figure in the Republican Party who made a name for himself in his home state of Louisiana and in Washington, D.C., stumping for conser-

vative causes. He found his career endangered by an alleged connection to an upscale prostitution ring while party to a highly publicized court case. What distinguished this case from many others of the same ilk was the apparent ease with which Vitter managed to weather the scandal and the aspects of his character, history, and conduct that allowed him to survive politically.

Vitter was a young Republican senator from Louisiana who had devoted most of his political career to socially conservative causes such as public prayer in schools, abstinence-based sex education, and opposition to abortion and same-gender marriage. Despite his dedication to these family-values issues, rumors that he patronized prostitutes plagued him from as early as 2002, when the rumors effectively sank his hopes for becoming governor of Louisiana in 2002.

Deborah Jeane Palfrey was an enigmatic figure who came from a background not unlike that of Vitter. She grew up in Pennsylvania and Florida in a religious, working-class family. (Upon her death in the spring of 2008, a haunting image of her smiling beatifically in her communion dress was used in newspaper and magazine photos accompanying the story.) Like Vitter (and his wife, Wendy), Palfrey initially intended to become a lawyer. However, after obtaining an undergraduate degree in criminal justice and enrolling in law school, she at some point lost focus and drifted into the demimonde of high-class call girls, cultured women elegantly coiffed and garbed and who were paid enormous fees for their sexual services. Later, Palfrey tried to suggest that her entering the sex-for-hire business was in large part an attempt at social reform. She wanted to provide escorts with a healthy and safe work environment free of the violence and substance abuse that traditionally characterized the business.

Palfrey also made huge profits from her endeavors in this field, and her enterprise soon grew to such proportions that it attracted the attention of the law. In 1992, after two years of legal wrangling and trials, she was found guilty of pimping and pandering and imprisoned for one and one-half years. Her experiences behind bars so traumatized her that she vowed never to return to prison, a remark that would soon come back to haunt her. However unpleasant was her jail time, it did not discourage her from reentering the escort business after her release, and she founded her next venture, Pamela Martin & Associates (PMA), in Washington, D.C.

Using small-venue newspapers aimed at specialized readerships (such as campus newspapers), Palfrey recruited women from all walks of life, including college students and women already earning high salaries in respected professions. Soon, PMA had profits of hundreds of thousands of dollars per year—and yet again, Palfrey's successful sex business grew so large that it attracted the attention of the police and other legal authorities.

Palfrey first revealed her business in an interview that aired on ABC's *20/20* on May 4, 2007. She released her list of clients, which included Senator Vitter, on July 9. She was arrested in the fall of 2007 for prostitution, using the U.S. mail service for illegal purposes, and other crimes. American news media began to cover the story closely when it was revealed that many of the clients of the call-girl ring included prominent politicians, business executives, lobbyists, military officers, and international

David Vitter and his wife, Wendy Vitter, at a news conference in Metairie, Louisiana, on July 16, 2007. The senator was making his first public appearance since acknowledging that his name and phone number were in the address book of the D.C. Madam. (AP/Wide World Photos)

officials and that PMA had kept meticulous records of its contacts with clients, including their telephone numbers. (Palfrey estimated that the number of clients listed on the agency's records topped ten thousand.) Two on the list were Deputy Secretary of State Randall L. Tobias and military strategist-columnist Harlan K. Ullman; Tobias resigned because of the scandal.

Initially, Palfrey and her lawyers released only an abridged list of clients that titillated the public's prurient interest but elicited little shock or surprise. However, on July 9, when she at last provided on her Web site an exhaustive roster of the men who had patronized her agency, the name of the ultra-conservative senator from Louisiana surprised many who were unfamiliar with earlier rumors about Vitter's behavior. In the months that followed the release of the phone records, the names of Vitter and Palfrey—who was variously dubbed the D.C. madam, the Washington madam, and the Beltway madam by the media—were staples in the media.

2000's

1151

To complicate matters, a New Orleans brothel owner also contended in print that the senator had been a client of hers years earlier. Vitter denied these latter allegations.

Vitter and his family and staff acted quickly. On the day Palfrey released her complete list of clients, Vitter, with his wife by his side, made a public announcement that he had indeed used PMA's services five times during the late 1990's and in early 2000 when he first came to Washington, D.C., and was a member of the House of Representatives—but not during his term as senator. Wording his announcement in religious terms, he confessed that he had sinned, that God and his wife had forgiven him, and that he hoped that the rest of the country could do likewise. This modest, apparently humble reaction to Palfrey's scandalous revelation seemed to placate his party and his constituents in Louisiana. In fact, he seemed to suffer little in the wake of the revelation, even managing to avoid having to testify during Palfrey's criminal trial, during which she was convicted, on April 15, of a number of charges including racketeering and money laundering.

Determined not to return to prison, Palfrey hanged herself in a shed outside her mother's home in Tarpon Springs, Florida, on May 1. Her conviction was abated—that is, dismissed—on May 20.

IMPACT

The fallout from Vitter's association with PMA failed to scuttle his political career for a number of reasons. First, his quickly arranged press conference was a masterstroke of media spin. By couching his admission in religious terms, he turned the conference into a public act of confession and contrition, thereby strengthening his image as a devout Christian at the very moment he was most liable to accusations of patent hypocrisy. Furthermore, his open, low-keyed demeanor before the cameras was a refreshing contrast to that of other public figures in similar situations, for example, the brazen denials of Bill Clinton during the Monica Lewinsky scandal and the maudlin hysterics of evangelist Jimmy Swaggart, who wept copiously on national television when his own dalliance with a prostitute was made public.

Furthermore, to many in Louisiana, the mistakes Vitter made in his personal life, however much they might have contradicted his public persona, were outweighed by his accomplishments, as he was seen by many in his home state as a champion against foes to Louisiana far more serious than prostitution: David Duke and Hurricane Katrina. When former Ku Klux Klan member and neo-Nazi sympathizer Duke tried to make a political comeback in 1999 in the congressional race that Vitter ultimately won, Vitter emerged as a veritable representative of the New South who was cultured and well-spoken and who had attended Harvard and Oxford. More important, though, was his record as a tireless campaigner for his state in the aftermath of Hurricane Katrina in 2005, often expressing the anger and resentment that many people in the state felt about the abysmally inadequate and incompetent response of the federal government to the disaster.

—*Thomas Du Bose*

FURTHER READING

Benjamin, Mark. "Fall Girls." *Ms.*, Summer, 2008. Investigative reporter Mark Benjamin examines the circumstances of Deborah Jeane Palfrey's indictment for prostitution as her johns, "including sanctimonious U.S. senator David Vitter—walked away uncensured and unscathed."

Duggan, Paul. "Four Former Call Girls Testify at Palfrey Trial." *The Washington Post*, April 9, 2008. A brief but interesting news story about the testimony of four former escorts who worked for Palfrey at Pamela Martin & Associates.

Meadows, Bob, et al. "D.C. Madam: Suicide." *People*, May, 2008. A touching account of Palfrey's troubled life and her suicide upon being convicted.

Murray, Shailagh. "Senator's Number on 'Madam' Phone List." *The Washington Post*, July 10, 2007. A thoroughly detailed news report of the scandal as it was first breaking.

SEE ALSO: Dec. 7, 1980: Rita Jenrette's "Diary of a Mad Congresswife" Scandalizes Washington; July 20, 1982: Conservative Politician John G. Schmitz Is Found to Have Children Out of Wedlock; July 20, 1983: Congress Members Censured in House-Page Sex Scandal; Jan. 17, 1998: President Bill Clinton Denies Sexual Affair with a White House Intern; Beginning Aug. 29, 2005: Government Incompetence Mars Hurricane Katrina Relief Efforts; June 4, 2007: Congressman William J. Jefferson Is Indicted for Corruption; July 11, 2007: Florida Politician Is Arrested for Soliciting an Undercover Male Police Officer; Mar. 12, 2008: New York Governor Eliot Spitzer Resigns in Prostitution Scandal.

July 11, 2007
FLORIDA POLITICIAN IS ARRESTED FOR SOLICITING AN UNDERCOVER MALE POLICE OFFICER

Elected to the Florida House of Representatives in 2000, Bob Allen attempted to pay a male undercover police officer twenty dollars to perform oral sex on the officer in a public restroom at a Florida park. The arrest drew national attention for its tawdriness and hypocrisy, and for Allen's connections to Republican presidential candidate John McCain.

LOCALE: Titusville, Florida
CATEGORIES: Prostitution; sex crimes; law and the courts; politics; government; public morals

KEY FIGURES
Bob Allen (b. 1958), member of the Florida House of Representatives, 2000-2008
Daniel Kavanaugh (fl. early twenty-first century), Titusville police officer

SUMMARY OF EVENT
Bob Allen gained national notoriety as one of several socially conservative politicians involved in sex scandals in 2007. Allen was elected to the Florida House of Representatives in 2000. Essentially a professional politician, most of his income came from his government salary, although he also earned $15,000 from his marketing company, the Allen Florida Group. A graduate of Valencia Community College, he lived with his wife and daughter in Merritt Island.

Allen spent seven years in the legislature, focusing chiefly on the economic development of the state and gaining a reputation as a confrontational legislator devoid of finesse but with a sense of humor. He did little of lasting impact. Allen joined Enterprise Florida, a part of the legislature, in 2002 to attract businesses to Florida. His district, in a part of Florida known as the space coast, included NASA's Kennedy Space Center. Accordingly, in 2002, Allen received an appointment to serve with the Florida Space Authority (now part of Space Florida), which is responsible for expanding and diversifying the state's aerospace industry. Allen put $100,000 in the budget for improvements to the Space Walk of Fame at Riverfront Park, but this effort was vetoed by Governor Charlie Crist. In 2007, Allen became chairman of the house energy committee. He also served as a cochairman of U.S. senator John McCain's Florida campaign for U.S. president.

Notably, especially in the light of later developments, Allen sponsored legislation that toughened penalties for lewd or lascivious conduct in public, such as in or near a park, from a misdemeanor to a felony. The bill (HB 1475) did not pass. Allen also was instrumental in creating a new provision in Florida law that gave some sexual predators life imprisonment for their offenses. Allen had dubbed the bill the sexual predator elimination act. For his record of socially conservative voting, Allen received a 92 percent rating from the Christian Coalition of Florida prior to his 2006 reelection bid. In 2007, about two weeks before his arrest, the Florida Police Benevolent Association named Allen its Legislator of the Year for his support of law enforcement.

On July 11, Allen parked his car and entered the men's restroom at Titusville's Space View Park. Titusville police officer Daniel Kavanaugh, who was conducting a plainclothes stakeout of a nearby condominium in the hope of catching a burglar, observed Allen enter the park on foot, walk into the restroom, exit the restroom, and walk toward a park bench. Kavanaugh, concerned about possible countersurveillance, then entered the restroom to adjust his police radio. On his way out of the men's room, Kavanaugh almost bumped into Allen, who was reentering the room. Allen changed his course of direction and went back toward a park bench. Kavanaugh spoke with two other plainclothes officers sitting on a bench, then entered the restroom and began washing his hands. Allen entered the restroom and went into the first stall. Realizing that there were no paper towels to dry his hands, Kavanaugh walked into the stall marked for the disabled to find paper. As he stood in the stall drying his hands, the police officer observed Allen peering over the door of the stall and attempting to make eye contact. Allen then stepped away, returned to the door of the stall, and again made eye contact. The officer said "hey buddy," to which Allen replied "hi," and then stepped back.

According to the officer's report, about five seconds later, Allen pushed open the door to Kavanaugh's stall and stepped inside. Kavanaugh was standing against the far wall of the stall and said "what's up?" Allen said, "hi, this is kind of a public place isn't it?" Kavanaugh replied, "Do you have somewhere else we can go?" Allen answered, "How about across the bridge? It's quiet over there." The two men then had a conversation in which Kavanaugh said, "I'm looking to get some money. Can you hook me up with $20?" Allen agreed to pay $20 to perform oral sex on the officer. Allen stated that he wanted to travel with the officer across the river before performing the act and turning over the money. Before entering Allen's vehicle, Kavanaugh identified himself as a police officer and arrested Allen. Allen was later released after posting $500 bail.

Allen subsequently explained that he was intimidated by the presence of a "stocky black guy" in the restroom and was worried that other "stocky black guys" in the park might rob him. Although the statement was excluded from his trial, Allen's statement became fodder for late-night talk-show hosts and political cartoonists. The McCain campaign forced his resignation.

In the wake of the arrest, Allen held a press conference in which he proclaimed his innocence and warned his constituents to not jump to conclusions. He stated that the incident brought him closer to his wife and teenage daughter, and he described the event as the worst thing that had happened to his family. He also plowed ahead with his campaign for a Brevard County senate seat that was expected to be vacant in 2008. However, Republican leadership in the Florida house immediately stripped Allen of his chairship of the energy committee and began to isolate him.

On November 9, 2007, a jury convicted Allen of soliciting a sex act. He faced up to sixty days in jail and a five-hundred-dollar fine. He became the first sitting house member to be convicted of a crime since 1998, when Lake City Democrat Randy Mackey was convicted of tax fraud and resigned three months later. Allen's fellow Republicans immediately pressured him to resign to spare the legislature from political damage, but Allen proclaimed his innocence and resolved to continue to fight the charge. The house majority leader, Adam Hasner, announced plans to force Allen from office. However, house rules mandate the removal of a member only upon a felony conviction. Allen was convicted of a second-degree misdemeanor. To remove him, the house could form a select committee to review the case and make a recommendation to the entire house. Removing him would require a vote of two-thirds of the members at a time when Republicans held seventy-seven seats in the legislature while Democrats held forty-two; one seat remained vacant.

Allen was sentenced on November 15. He received six months probation and a $250 fine. The judge required him to pay $245 in restitution to the Titusville Police Department for the initial investigation, to pay court costs, to attend an awareness class on sexually transmitted diseases (STDs), and to undergo STD testing. Allen also was banned from returning to Space View Park. On November 16, he resigned from the state legislature, effective February 15, 2008.

IMPACT

The Allen scandal may have had little long-term impact. Anthony P. Sasso III, a Cocoa Beach ship inspector and former marine engineer, replaced Allen in a special election. Sasso became the first Democratic legislator to be elected from Brevard County since 1996, defeating Republican rival Sean Campbell despite being heavily outspent. The Democrats did not give Allen credit for Sasso's victory because voters and campaign workers did not appear to be especially interested in the scandal, regarding it as old news.

However, 2008 was not a good year for Republican candidates across the United States. It is not clear whether Sasso's election reflected strong support for the candidate, a backlash against the Republican Party for being the party of Allen, or part of a nationwide reaction against the Republicans.

—*Caryn E. Neumann*

FURTHER READING

Colburn, David R. *From Yellow Dog Democrats to Red State Republicans: Florida and Its Politics Since 1940.* Gainesville: University of Florida Press, 2007. A good history of state politics in Florida in the modern era.

Williams, Juliet A., and Paul Apostolidis, eds. *Public Affairs: Politics in the Age of Sex Scandals.* Durham, N.C.: Duke University Press, 2004. Although the Allen case is not examined in this book, the text does help set the scandal in the context of other sex scandals involving political figures.

SEE ALSO: 1970: Study of Anonymous Gay Sex Leads to Ethics Scandal; Oct. 25, 1974: Evangelist Billy James Hargis Resigns College Presidency During Gay-Sex Scandal; Sept. 3, 1980: Congressman Bauman Is Arrested for Liaison with Teenage Boy; July 20, 1982: Conservative Politician John G. Schmitz Is Found to Have Children Out of Wedlock; Sept. 19, 2000: Ex-gay Leader John Paulk Is Photographed Leaving a Gay Bar; Aug. 19, 2004: Blog "Outs" Anti-gay Congressman Edward Schrock; Dec. 6, 2005: Spokane, Washington, Mayor Recalled in Gay-Sex Scandal; Sept. 29, 2006: Congressman Mark Foley Resigns in Sex Scandal Involving a Teenage Page; Nov. 2, 2006: Male Escort Reveals Sexual Liaisons with Evangelist Ted Haggard.

July 24, 2007
UNIVERSITY OF COLORADO FIRES PROFESSOR FOR PLAGIARISM AND RESEARCH FALSIFICATION

Under intense public and academic scrutiny for writing an inflammatory essay about the September 11, 2001, terrorist attacks in the United States, university professor Ward Churchill was subjected to an academic misconduct investigation and subsequently fired for plagiarism and for fabricating and falsifying information. He filed a lawsuit seeking reinstatement.

LOCALE: Boulder, Colorado

CATEGORIES: Cultural and intellectual history; education; ethics; plagiarism; publishing and journalism

KEY FIGURES

Ward Churchill (b. 1947), professor and former chairman of the ethnic studies department at the University of Colorado, Boulder

Phil DiStefano (b. 1946), interim chancellor of Churchill's university

Marianne Wesson (b. 1948), a university law professor and chairman of the university's investigative committee

SUMMARY OF EVENT

Known for his incendiary criticism of the mistreatment of American Indians and political dissidents by the U.S. government, author and University of Colorado, Boulder, professor Ward Churchill drew condemnation and intense scrutiny after public attention focused on his essay about the September 11, 2001, terrorist attacks in the United States. In the essay, which circulated on the World Wide Web beginning on September 12, Churchill argued that the workers at the World Trade Center had deserved to die in the attacks.

The essay, and Churchill, began to attract widespread attention and condemnation, but not until early 2005. Old criticisms of Churchill's academic work resurfaced as well. The University of Colorado began an investigation into allegations that Churchill had engaged in academic misconduct, including fabrication, falsification, and plagiarism in his scholarly work. Subsequently, the university fired Churchill, who responded by filing a lawsuit against the university for reinstatement.

The September 11, 2001, terrorist attacks ("9/11") in the United States brought to mind for many Americans the question, "Why do they hate us enough to do something like this?" In "Some People Push Back," circulated on the Web, Churchill addressed this question by arguing that the answer lay primarily in U.S. foreign policy. Churchill was not alone in making this argument. Other notable figures who made the same point include linguist and writer Noam Chomsky and 2008 Republican presidential candidate Ron Paul (who later clarified his remarks). What made Churchill stand out, many believe, was his apparent lack of compassion—his sheer contempt—for those who died on September 11.

Although the essay was on the Web in September, 2001, it did not gain widespread attention until January, 2005. Churchill had been scheduled to participate on a panel at Hamilton College in Clinton, New York. In advance of the panel, which planned to discuss the "limits of dissent," the editor of Hamilton's student newspaper researched Churchill on the Web and found the 2001 essay. Soon, political conservatives such as Bill O'Reilly heard of the essay and quickly condemned Churchill. Goaded by O'Reilly and other conservatives, viewers complained to Hamilton College about Churchill's invitation. In the end, Hamilton canceled the event, citing death threats against the college community and against Churchill.

The interim chancellor of the University of Colorado, Phil DiStefano, publicly condemned Churchill on January 25, and by January 31, Churchill had resigned as chairman of the Ethnic Studies Department. Nevertheless, he remained on the university's faculty and continued to draw scrutiny.

On March 29 the university received a formal research-misconduct complaint against Churchill, who had been subject to academic criticism long before the Hamilton College controversy. Earlier in his career he had been accused of plagiarism, fabrication of research data, and lying about his ethnic background as an American Indian. However, as far as the university was concerned, March 29 marked the first time it had received a formal complaint about Churchill that required a response.

The university's Standing Committee on Research Misconduct appointed an investigative committee chaired by law professor Marianne Wesson. The committee included four other professors in law, American and English literature, history, and sociology; in total, three of the five committee members were CU professors, one was from Arizona State University, and another was from the University of Texas at Austin.

The complaint against Churchill listed nine different grounds of misconduct, but the investigative committee elected not to proceed with two of the charges: that Churchill "had misrepresented his ethnicity in order to gain greater credibility and scholarly 'voice,'" and that Churchill "had violated copyrights in his use of certain articles." The investigative committee considered these allegations outside the CU definition of academic misconduct.

The remaining charges included the following: that Churchill misrepresented the General Allotment Act of 1887 and the Indian Arts and Crafts Act of 1990, fabricated the allegation that the U.S. Army had spread disease among American Indians by giving them smallpox-infected blankets, fabricated his description of a smallpox epidemic at Fort Clark in 1837-1840, plagiarized a pamphlet by Dam the Dams, plagiarized work by Rebecca Robbins, and plagiarized work by Fay Cohen.

The investigative committee concluded that Churchill had falsified the evidence supporting his claims about the General Allotment Act and the Indian Arts and Crafts Act. It further concluded that he had falsified and fabricated his claims about the smallpox epidemics. It also concluded that while he had plagiarized work by Dam the Dams and by Professor Cohen, he had not plagiarized Professor Robbins, but only because he had written the work under Robbins's name—itself a violation of the university's academic standards. Finally, the committee determined that Churchill's violations were serious and deliberate.

The committee did not reach agreement, however, on how to proceed against Churchill. Three members concluded that Churchill's misconduct was serious enough to justify being fired, though only one of the three actually recommended dismissal. Two members recommended a five-year suspension without pay, and the other two members recommended a two-year suspension without pay. The Standing Committee on Research Misconduct was similarly split, with six members voting for dismissal, two voting for a five-year suspension without pay, and one voting for a two-year suspension without pay. On June 26, 2006, Chancellor DiStefano announced that he would recommend that university regents fire Churchill. A year later, on July 24, 2007, the university terminated his employment.

Churchill condemned the investigative committee's report, attacking it as flawed and biased. According to Churchill, the committee should have included a Native American or an American Indian studies expert. (One of the committee members was Arizona State University law professor Robert Clinton, an expert on American Indian law.) Churchill

---

"LITTLE EICHMANNS"

Ward Churchill wrote a deeply critical article following the September 11, 2001, terrorist attacks in New York City and at the Pentagon. His supporters claimed that outrage over the article, which circulated on the Web just days after the attacks, led to later investigations into Churchill's credibility and, ultimately, led to his dismissal from the University of Colorado.

As to those in the World Trade Center . . . Let's get a grip here, shall we? True enough, they were civilians of a sort. But innocent? Gimme a break. They formed a technocratic corps at the very heart of America's global financial empire—the "mighty engine of profit" to which the military dimension of U.S. policy has always been enslaved—and they did so both willingly and knowingly. . . . If there was a better, more effective, or in fact any other way of visiting some penalty befitting their participation upon the little Eichmanns inhabiting the sterile sanctuary of the twin towers, I'd really be interested in hearing about it.

Source: Ward Churchill, "Some People Push Back" (2001).

---

also raised procedural objections to the investigation, arguing that he was not provided with clear information about "the standards being applied" or "which allegations were at issue." With respect to the academic misconduct findings themselves, Churchill dismissed the committee's focus on his citations, arguing that his work consisted of a synthesis of other material and that it was not feasible to "delve into minute detail with respect to each piece or the 'big picture' will be lost." Finally, regarding the plagiarism charges, Churchill argued that he had either ghostwritten the allegedly plagiarized materials or that he had merely copyedited the volume.

The day after he was fired, Churchill filed a lawsuit against the university in a Colorado state court. His suit claims that his dismissal violated his First Amendment rights and that he should be reinstated.

IMPACT

The Churchill case revealed deep divisions, both in American society and in academia. Throughout the controversy, Churchill supporters have argued that

2000's

the case amounts to the censoring of an outspoken, radical critic of the U.S. government. His opponents, however, consider him an academic fraud whose hire, tenure, and promotion reflect a liberal bias in the academy. In any case, the scandal that ensued has yet to abate, and the divisions reflect a strong, unyielding politics at the heart of commentary in the United States.

—Tung Yin

FURTHER READING

Churchill, Ward. *On the Justice of Roosting Chickens: Reflections on the Consequences of U.S. Imperial Arrogance and Criminality.* Oakland, Calif.: AK Press, 2003. Expanded version of Churchill's original 2001 essay, "Some People Push Back," which argued that the United States brought the September 11, 2001, terrorist attacks on itself, in part because of its unilateral foreign policy.

_____. *Struggle for the Land: Native North American Resistance to Genocide, Ecocide, and Colonization.* New ed. San Francisco, Calif.: City Lights Books, 2002. A series of essays on American Indian resistance to the federal government. Includes "The Water Plot," which was used as an example of academic misconduct in the Churchill investigation.

Healy, Patrick D. "College Cancels Speech by Professor Who Disparaged 9/11 Attack Victims." *The New York Times*, February 2, 2005. A news report about Hamilton College canceling Churchill's speech on its campus following death threats and a barrage of e-mails to college officials.

SEE ALSO: 1928-1929: Actor Is Suspected of Falsely Claiming to Be an American Indian; 1978: *Roots* Author Alex Haley Is Sued for Plagiarism; Dec. 3, 1989: Martin Luther King, Jr.'s, Doctoral-Thesis Plagiarism Is Revealed; Spring, 1996: Physicist Publishes a Deliberately Fraudulent Article; Apr., 1998: Scottish Historian Is Charged with Plagiarism; May 11, 1998: Journalist Stephen Glass Is Exposed as a Fraud; June 18, 2001: Historian Joseph J. Ellis Is Accused of Lying; Jan. 4, 2002: Historian Stephen E. Ambrose Is Accused of Plagiarism; Jan. 18, 2002: Historian Doris Kearns Goodwin Is Accused of Plagiarism; Oct. 25, 2002: Historian Michael A. Bellesiles Resigns After Academic Fraud Accusations.

August 20, 2007
FOOTBALL STAR MICHAEL VICK PLEADS GUILTY TO FINANCING A DOGFIGHTING RING

Michael Vick, a star quarterback in the National Football League, and three other men were convicted and imprisoned for their roles in a dogfighting ring on property owned by Vick in rural Virginia. Vick was suspended from the NFL, lost lucrative commercial contracts, was sued for millions of dollars by his creditors, and was ordered to pay for the long-term care of the dogs rescued from his property.

LOCALE: Richmond, Virginia

CATEGORIES: Sports; gambling; law and the courts; organized crime and racketeering; violence; public morals; ethics

KEY FIGURES
Michael Vick (b. 1980), professional football player
Purnell A. Peace (fl. early twenty-first century), coconspirator
Tony Taylor (fl. early twenty-first century), coconspirator

Quanis Phillips (fl. early twenty-first century),
   coconspirator

Summary of Event

On August 20, 2007, National Football League
(NFL) quarterback Michael Vick pleaded guilty to
one count of criminal conspiracy to operate a
dogfighting ring across state lines. The case also involved the abuse and killing of dogs. Vick, who
played for the Atlanta Falcons, faced state felony
charges in Virginia as well for his role in the
dogfighting ring and related gambling activities.

Vick had been a standout quarterback at Virginia
Tech University and then was drafted in 2001 by
Atlanta. His early NFL career included setting
many new records, multiple playoff appearances,
and high-paying commercial endorsements. In 2004,
he became the NFL's highest-paid player with a
long-term contract for $130 million.

On April 25, 2007, law enforcement officials,
searching for evidence in a drug case involving
Vick's cousin, found dogfighting and dog-training
facilities on Vick's fifteen-acre property near Smith-
field, Virginia. The facilities were known as Bad
Newz Kennels. Officials also found more than fifty
pit bulls (and other dogs), treadmills modified for
dogs, and other dogfighting paraphernalia.

Dogfighting is generally regarded as a cruel, brutal, and inhumane practice. So gruesome is the practice that even experienced investigators have been
horrified by what they discovered at raids. Dogs
used for fighting are trained to kill using a variety of
methods. To ensure the animals' aggression, the
dogs are beaten, chained, and even fed gunpowder,
illegal drugs, and live animals; often they are not
fed at all for long periods. Dogs are also trained
through the use of bait dogs, which are non-pit-
trained animals used strictly as a target to kill. Bait
dogs are tied to a chain while the pit fighter is free to
roam, or the pit dog is duct-taped around the muzzle
or legs, or both, so its cannot run or fight back. If a
trained fighting dog fails to win in the ring, it is
beaten, shot, or electrocuted to death, or it is fed to
other dogs and killed or otherwise left to die.

On July 2, prosecutors alleged that Bad Newz
Kennels had operated on Vick's property for five

*Michael Vick leaving federal court in Richmond, Vir-
ginia, on July 26, 2007, following his arraignment on
dogfighting charges.* (AP/Wide World Photos)

years. On July 17, the U.S. district attorney's office
announced the federal grand-jury indictments of
Vick and three coconspirators—Purnell A. Peace,
Tony Taylor, and Quanis Phillips. On July 26,
Peace, Taylor, and Phillips all pleaded guilty and
were convicted for dogfighting conspiracy. Vick,
who initially pleaded not guilty, admitted in a plea
bargain that he paid for the dog fights and for the operation of the ring. He denied personally killing any
dogs deemed unfit for fighting, although he admitted to being part of the effort to kill those dogs. He
also denied placing side bets to profit from individual dog fights.

At the federal trial, U.S. District Court judge
Henry E. Hudson found that Vick had been fully involved in the dogfighting ring, stating "You were
instrumental in promoting, funding, and facilitating

this cruel and inhumane sporting activity," and he also noted Vick's lack of cooperation during the inquiry. The judge also cited him for using drugs while free on bail and awaiting sentencing. In December, Vick was sentenced to twenty-three months in prison and three years probation and was fined five thousand dollars. He also was indicted by prosecutors in Surry County, Virginia, on two felony counts—dogfighting and animal cruelty. His state trial was postponed until his release from prison on the federal conviction.

In August, 2007, Vick was suspended from the NFL indefinitely by league commissioner Roger Goodell, who stated in a letter to Vick, "Your admitted conduct was not only illegal, but also cruel and reprehensible. Your team, the NFL, and NFL fans have all been hurt by your actions." The Falcons sought to reclaim bonus money the team paid to Vick, and an arbitrator ruled the team was entitled to recoup $19.9 million. Vick also lost most of his product-endorsement contracts, leaving him virtually bankrupt.

Several companies, beginning with Nike on July 19 and including Upper Deck, Donruss, Rawlings, and Reebok, canceled their contracts with Vick. Nike announced that it suspended the release of a product bearing his name. Retail businesses removed products related to the player—even those products he endorsed—from their store shelves and Web sites, hoping to avoid any connection to Vick, Bad Newz Kennels, animal cruelty, or criminality in any form. Furthermore, Vick was forced to liquidate some of his real estate assets to pay his bills, and several banks sued him to recover about $5 million in loans on which he defaulted.

IMPACT

The dogfighting and animal cruelty scandal was met with widespread public disapproval and condemnation of Vick and his coconspirators. Especially shocking was the mistreatment and killing of the dogs. Federal authorities asked the judge to order Vick to set aside nearly $1 million of his own money to care for the dogs rescued from his property. The judge issued that order. A court-appointed veterinary specialist said that many of the dogs re-

quired long-term special care. By July, 2008, some of the more aggressive dogs were in the care of an animal sanctuary in Utah and others had been adopted or fostered. A documentary, "Saving the Michael Vick Dogs," aired on the series *DogTown* on the National Geographic Channel in September.

Like many professional athletes, Vick had been a role model, and he even started a foundation in 2006 to help at-risk youth and help fund after-school programs. After his arrest, fund-raisers and other organizers canceled his scheduled appearance at their respective events.

Also following Vick's arrest was the passage of a federal law against dogfighting. The Animal Fighting Prohibition Enforcement Act, signed into law in May, made organizing a dog fight a felony. Also prohibited under the new law is the transport of animals for fighting. The law also bans the use of the U.S. Postal Service to mail dogfighting paraphernalia, and it includes a civil-lawsuit provision.

—Karen L. Hayslett-McCall

FURTHER READING

Adut, Ari. *On Scandal: Moral Disturbances in Society, Politics, and Art*. New York: Cambridge University Press, 2008. A comprehensive analysis of scandals of all types. The author explores the contexts in which "wrong-doings generate scandals and when they do not." Focuses on how people experience scandals emotionally and cognitively.

Evans, Rhonda, Deann K. Gauthier, and Craig J. Forsyth. "Dog Fighting: Symbolic Expression and Validation of Masculinity." *Sex Roles* 39, nos. 11/12 (December, 1998). A scholarly study of dogfighting as a means to validate one's masculinity.

Ledbetter, D. Orlando. "Vick Enters Drug Program: Rehab, Move to Kansas May Cut Prison Time." *Atlanta Journal-Constitution*, January 1, 2008. An updated news report that details Vick's enrollment in a drug-rehabilitation program in prison.

Maske, Mark. "Falcons' Vick Indicted in Dog Fighting Case: Star QB Alleged to Have Been

Highly Involved." *The Washington Post*, July 18, 2007. A news report that discusses Vick's indictment in the dogfighting ring case.

Smith, Stephen A. "Falls from Grace: What Young Black Athletes Should Learn from the Michael Vick and Marion Jones Dramas." *Ebony*, January 1, 2008. Magazine feature on Michael Vick and Olympic sprinter Marion Jones and their fall from the top of their respective sports.

SEE ALSO: Feb. 28, 1986: Baseball Commissioner Peter Ueberroth Suspends Players for Cocaine Use; Feb. 25, 1987: NCAA Imposes "Death Penalty" on Southern Methodist University Football; June 30, 1994: Tonya Harding Is Banned from Skating After Attack on Rival; Dec. 14, 2001: Notre Dame Football Coach Resigns for Falsifying His Résumé; May 3, 2003: University of Alabama Fires New Football Coach in Sex Scandal; Mar. 17, 2005: Former Baseball Star Mark McGwire Evades Congressional Questions on Steroid Use; Sept. 13, 2007: New England Patriots Football Team Is Fined for Spying on Other Teams.

September 13, 2007

NEW ENGLAND PATRIOTS FOOTBALL TEAM IS FINED FOR SPYING ON OTHER TEAMS

The National Football League levied the highest fines in league history against the New England Patriots after collecting evidence that Patriots coaches had violated league rules against videotaping opponents' private signals. Coach Bill Belichick and the team were fined. The unprecedented penalties underlined the severity of the misconduct, damaged the credibility of three league championships, and helped foster public cynicism about ethics in professional sports.

ALSO KNOWN AS: Spygate
LOCALE: Foxboro, Massachusetts
CATEGORIES: Sports; corruption; espionage; communications and media; public morals

KEY FIGURES
Bill Belichick (b. 1952), head coach of the New England Patriots
Roger Goodell (b. 1959), commissioner of the National Football League
Eric Mangini (b. 1971), head coach of the New York Jets
Matt Walsh (fl. early twenty-first century), former Patriots video assistant

SUMMARY OF EVENT

On September 9, 2007, assistant coaches for the New England Patriots were caught illegally videotaping signals being sent from the New York sideline to their defensive players on the field during the first game of the 2007 season. The incident was reported to the National Football League (NFL) and its commissioner, Roger Goodell, who acted swiftly in levying the largest penalties in league history. The September 13 sanction was meant to punish the Patriots and warn other teams not to break league rules. Critics wanted stronger penalties, and conspiracy theorists were roused when it was learned that the NFL destroyed the evidence after issuing the penalty. The whole situation became a media storm that raged through the season and off-season.

The NFL allows teams to use two cameras to videotape games from the end zones and other specified areas and had sent multiple memorandums to all teams reiterating these rules. These end-zone angles are wide enough to see the entire field and to see how offensive and defensive players are deployed. The tapes are referred to as coaches film. The Patriots were taping the end-zone angles but

2000's

1161

they were also taping from their sideline across the field to the Jets defensive coaches and to the scoreboard that was recording ball placement and time. Offensive signals are verbally transmitted to a team's quarterback via timed, one-way, encrypted wireless communications monitored by the NFL. Defensive signals, though, are sent either verbally by a substituting player who can relay the information or by hand signals and signs using gestures, numbers, and colors. Officials with the Jets noticed this action, confiscated the videotape, and filed a complaint with the NFL.

The Jets knew at first hand that Patriots head coach Bill Belichick had a penchant for videotaping and intelligence gathering; Jets head coach Eric Mangini had worked for Belichick for more than ten years, mostly with the Patriots, until he took the Jets job. Mangini violated many of the unwritten rules in NFL coaching circles, which prohibited poaching other players, coaching a rival team, and snitching. Belichick and Mangini reportedly had a great friendship that was obliterated. Now they were archenemies.

The NFL penalized the Patriots just four days later. It demanded all other videotapes from the team and spoke with coach Belichick and team owner Robert Kraft. "This episode represents a calculated and deliberate attempt to avoid longstanding rules designed to encourage fair play and promote honest competition on the playing field," commissioner Goodell wrote in a letter to the Patriots.

Belichick released a statement following the punishment, stating "Part of my job as head coach is to ensure that our football operations are conducted in compliance of the league rules and all accepted interpretations of them. My interpretation of a rule in the constitution and bylaws was incorrect."

The infraction, punishment, and apology should have ended the cycle but only fueled the controversy. The NFL destroyed the videotape evidence, citing security reasons, as a leaked tape was aired on a Fox Sports NFL telecast the following Sunday. Conspiracy theorists believed the league was hiding something or even coddling the immensely popular Patriots. Critics claimed the Patriots had so much

recent success because of the taped defensive signals, which they in turn deciphered and used during the same game; that claim, however, was unfounded by the NFL investigation. Belichick stated that he was not taping a game to help the team in the same game; implementing such a task, he added, would be nearly impossible.

The scandal was a scandal because, first, it involved the Patriots, the dominant team of the decade, and second, sports, in general, had been under a cloud of suspicion for the use by athletes of performance-enhancing drugs such as steroids and human growth hormone. The scandal was even more compelling because it featured the Boston and New York sports markets, the deteriorating relationship between Belichick and Mangini, and a Patriots team that was on a ruthless winning streak.

The Patriots advanced to Super Bowl XLII against the New York Giants, and the scandal developed a new twist. Accusations were made by former Patriots video assistant Matt Walsh were printed in the *Boston Herald*, which stated the Patriots videotaped the St. Louis Rams' final practice before the Super Bowl.

Walsh met with NFL commissioner Goodell and Specter separately in May, and the NFL stated that no further discipline was coming to the Patriots. Specter, however, believed the idea of an independent investigation similar to former Senator George Mitchell's report on steroids in Major League Baseball might be effective in understanding the Patriots scandal.

The *Boston Herald* used the entire front and back pages of its May 14 edition to apologize to the Patriots and their fans, stating the columnist who reported the Patriots had videotaped the Rams' final practice before the Super Bowl did not have credible sources. The Patriots accepted the apology but noted that the damage was already done when the article was published on the eve of the Super Bowl, usually the top television draw of the year.

IMPACT

After being caught cheating, fined by the league, and vilified by most after the first game of the season, the Patriots and their beleaguered coach went on an unprecedented undefeated streak, ending their season in a loss to the New York Giants in Super Bowl XLII. The Patriots had a 16-0 record during the 2007 regular season. Players and coaches, approached and pressed by the media after every practice and game, played on the field like no other team in history, breaking a number of long-standing NFL records. Belichick was voted NFL Coach of the Year by the Associated Press, his second time winning the award. Many of the same writers who criticized Belichick in print and across electronic media had no choice but to award the coach of one of the greatest professional football teams in history.

The NFL owners voted in early 2008 to allow defensive signals to be radioed in to a team's defensive captain, in a manner similar to how quarterbacks are given plays. Quarterback communications are proven to be secure. This new method of communication will eliminate the interception of signals because radio usage is tightly controlled by the NFL.

The Patriots cheating scandal and actions taken by the league will likely never be forgotten. The legacy of the great Patriots franchise, once thought of as the model franchise in the league, was irreparably tarnished, and many believe that the team's three Super Bowl victories in the first decade of the twenty-first century should have asterisks denoting the victories came during a cheating scandal.

—*Jonathan E. Dinneen*

FURTHER READING

Callahan, David. *The Cheating Culture: Why More Americans Are Doing Wrong to Get Ahead*. Orlando, Fla.: Harcourt, 2004. This book discusses why people choose to cheat to gain an advantage over their competitors.

Crossman, Matt. "Tricks, Spies, and Videotapes." *Sporting News*, September 24, 2007. The author reports on the potential long-term fallout of the taping scandal. Discusses the various theories on why Patriot coach Bill Belichick recorded opposing-team signals and includes reactions to the scandal from National Football League representatives.

King, Peter. "The NFL's Mob Mentality." *Sports Illustrated*, September 24, 2007. Article argues that in making public the accusation against Belichick, Jets coach Eric Mangini broke a code of silence observed by NFL coaches.

Lupica, Mike. "Patriot Act Not New to Belichick." *Daily News* (New York), September 16, 2007. A senior columnist discusses how Belichick thinks he is above the law and how his actions tarnish the near-perfect image owner Robert Kraft has created for the Patriots.

Sandomir, Richard. "Goodell Defends Punishment and Warns of Other Sanctions." *The New York Times*, September 17, 2007. Includes quotations from NFL commissioner Goodell justifying fines levied against the Patriots and Coach Belichick.

Tomase, John. "How It Went Wrong." *Boston Herald*, May 16, 2008. The story behind the *Boston Herald*'s report of the scandal on the eve of the Super Bowl in 2008.

SEE ALSO: Aug. 19, 1973: Cheating Scandal Shocks Soap Box Derby; Feb. 25, 1987: NCAA Imposes "Death Penalty" on Southern Methodist University Football; Dec. 14, 2001: Notre Dame Football Coach Resigns for Falsifying His Résumé; Mar. 27, 2002: Georgia Basketball Coach Jim Harrick, Sr., Resigns over Fraud Allegations; May 3, 2003: University of Alabama Fires New Football Coach in Sex Scandal; Mar. 17, 2005: Former Baseball Star Mark McGwire Evades Congressional Questions on Steroid Use; July 14, 2006: *New York Times* Exposes Grading Scandal at Auburn University; Aug. 20, 2007: Football Star Michael Vick Pleads Guilty to Financing a Dogfighting Ring.

2000's

October 5, 2007
OLYMPIC CHAMPION MARION JONES ADMITS STEROID USE

Olympic track star Marion Jones admitted in court to having lied to federal investigators in 2003 about her use of performance-enhancing drugs and about her knowledge of the involvement of a former boyfriend and former coach in a scheme to cash millions of dollars worth of stolen and forged checks. Jones was jailed and ordered to forfeit her Olympic medals.

LOCALE: United States
CATEGORIES: Drugs; law and the courts; medicine and health care; public morals; sports

KEY FIGURES

Marion Jones (b. 1975), American Olympic track-and-field medalist
Victor Conte (b. 1954), self-taught pharmacist and founder of Bay Area Laboratory Co-operative, or Balco
C. J. Hunter (b. 1968), American Olympic shot putter who was briefly married to Jones
Tim Montgomery (b. 1975), American Olympic runner who is the father of Jones's eldest son

SUMMARY OF EVENT

Marion Jones was the premier female runner of her generation. In 1997, after a four-year absence from track-and-field competition and after only a few months of serious training, she won the U.S. championship in the 100-meter sprint. That victory earned for her instant recognition as the fastest woman in the world. During the next season, she participated in a world tour that was unprecedented for its ambition. She entered meets at a frenzied pace, returning home just long enough to become the first woman in fifty years to win three events at the U.S. championships in New Orleans, Louisiana.

In 1998, Jones participated in thirty-seven different running and long-jumping events and won thirty-six of them. By the time the year ended, she held the number one position in the world in the 100 meters, 200 meters, and long jump. She capped off the year by marrying shot put champion C. J. Hunter, a future Olympic athlete.

A charismatic and attractive woman, Jones quickly became a media favorite and one of the most famous female athletes in the world. Reporters and fans speculated that she would win five gold medals—more than any other woman ever in track and field—at the 2000 Sydney Olympics. Jones came close, winning the 100-meter race by the second-widest margin in Olympic history—among both men and women. She won the 200-meter race by the largest margin since Wilma Rudolph's victory at Rome in 1960. Jones took a third gold medal, as part of the U.S. 1,600-meter relay team. In the 400-meter relay, the U.S. team botched the baton handoff between the second and third legs. Jones made up some ground, but the Americans took the bronze for third place. The long jump, traditionally Jones's weakest event, left her with a fifth medal, a second bronze. In recognition of her achievements, Jones was named the Associated Press Female Athlete of the Year.

The track-and-field world, as with other sports, had long been dogged by allegations that athletes use performance-enhancing drugs. Jones stated repeatedly throughout her career that she wanted a drug-free sport and that she never used illegal drugs. However, there were persistent rumors that she used drugs. On September 26, 2000, her husband, Hunter, tested positive for steroid use. He was suspended for two years, and then he retired. The couple divorced in 2002. In the autumn of 2003, Jones testified before a federal grand jury in San Francisco, California, that was investigating athlete steroid use and those athletes' possible connections with a local company, Bay Area Laboratory Co-operative (Balco). The grand jury found a calendar at Balco with the initials "MJ" written on it, seeming to indicate a schedule for steroid use by Marion Jones ("MJ") in 2001. Hunter also reportedly told investigators that he had injected Jones with banned substances and witnessed her doing the same.

On May 16, 2004, Jones insisted that she was drug free and stated her intent to sue if the U.S. Anti-Doping Agency barred her from competing in that year's Athens Olympics without a positive drug test. In August at Athens, Jones finished fifth in the long jump, and her 4 × 100 relay team failed to finish after a bad baton handoff. By this time, sponsors had begun to drop Jones because of the rumors of drug use.

On December 7, the International Olympic Committee (IOC) opened an investigation into doping allegations against Jones after Balco founder Victor Conte alleged that he supplied her with an array of banned drugs before and after the Sydney Olympics. One year later, on December 13, 2005, an American Olympic sprinter and former boyfriend of Jones, Tim Montgomery, received a two-year ban from the sport based on evidence gathered in the Balco investigation. Jones was now linked to a second athlete convicted of using steroids. (Montgomery and Jones had a son together in 2003.)

Nevertheless, Jones remained adamant that she was drug free. On February 5, 2006, she settled a $25 million federal defamation lawsuit against Conte for damaging her reputation by declaring on ABC's *20/20* that he supplied her and Montgomery with performance-enhancing drugs. Five days later, the IOC announced that it would continue to investigate whether Jones took illegal substances at the 2000 Sydney Games. On June 23, Jones's "A" sample from the U.S. Track and Field Championships tested positive for the banned endurance-boosting hormone erythropoietin (EPO), a lab result that could lead to a possible two-year ban from the sport. However, on September 6, Jones's backup, or "B," sample came back from the lab negative. She was therefore cleared of any wrongdoing and allowed to return to competition. Observers later noted that it is very rare for a "B" sample to fail to confirm the "A" sample and speculated that any EPO in the "B" sample could have deteriorated beyond recognition.

While she had once planned to compete until she was in her forties, Jones soon declared that she had grown weary of defending herself. She married Barbadian sprinter Obadele Thompson in 2007 and retired to raise a family. However, the steroid scandal would not go away. On October 5, Jones tearfully admitted in federal court that she had used the performance-enhancing drug known as "the clear" from September, 2000, through July, 2001, and asked for forgiveness. She was on trial for providing false statements to federal investigators in the Balco case and in a check fraud case involving Montgomery and her former coach, Steven Riddick. Montgomery cashed stolen and forged checks, and Jones had received one of those checks, which was deposited into her checking account but never cleared. Jones pleaded guilty to lying to investigators at the October 5 trial.

In January, 2008, Jones received a six-month jail sentence and was ordered to perform four hundred hours of community service in each of the two years

Marion Jones at an October 5, 2007, news conference admitting that she had used steroids to enhance her athletic performance. (AP/Wide World Photos)

following her release. On March 7, Jones began her sentence at the Federal Medical Center Carswell, located at the Naval Air Station, Joint Reserve Base, in Fort Worth, Texas. Although the facility specializes in medical and mental health services, it also has inmates (including Jones) who do not require such care. She was released on September 5.

IMPACT

On April 10, after Jones was sentenced, the women who won Olympic medals in 2000 by running relays with Jones were ordered by Olympic officials to forfeit their victories and return their medals. The IOC stripped gold medals from Jearl-Miles Clark, Monique Hennagan, LaTasha Colander-Richardson, and Andrea Anderson. Runners Chryste Gaines, Torri Edwards, Nanceen Perry, and Passion Richardson were ordered to forfeit their bronze medals. The women were not accused of any wrongdoing, but the Jones scandal tainted their victories. However, they refused to surrender their medals, arguing it would be unfair to punish them for Jones's actions, and challenged the IOC through the Court of Arbitration for Sport.

In July, Jones asked U.S. president George W. Bush to commute her sentence. A commutation reduces or eliminates a sentence but does not remove civil liabilities stemming from a criminal conviction. Doug Logan, the chief executive officer of U.S. Track and Field, publicly opposed commutation because to do so would send a terrible message to youths. Logan added that a commutation would send the wrong message to the international community as well. By cheating and lying, Jones had violated the principles of track and field as well as international Olympic competition. Logan was especially angry that Jones had challenged anyone who doubted her purity, talent, and work ethic, and that she had successfully duped many people into giving her the benefit of the doubt.

Bush did not commute Jones's sentence, leading some observers to wonder if the harshness of the sentence Jones received, including not receiving a commutation, and the demonizing of her in the media had more to do with race than justice, given that champion black athletes have historically been targets of suspicion and doubt.

—Caryn E. Neumann

FURTHER READING

Cazeneuve, Brian. "Running on Empty: With Funds and Friends in Short Supply, Marion Jones May Face Prison." *Sports Illustrated*, January 14, 2008. Details the consequences of Jones's steroid use and continued deceptions.

Gutman, Bill. *Marion Jones*. New York: Simon Pulse, 2004. A standard athletic biography that glorifies Jones's quest to become the fastest woman in the world.

Jones, Marion, and Kate Sekules. *Marion Jones: Life in the Fast Lane*. New York: Warner Books, 2004. In this heavily illustrated autobiography, Jones discusses Hunter's steroid use but is not entirely forthcoming about her own involvement with performance-enhancing drugs.

Rapoport, Ron. *See How She Runs: Marion Jones and the Making of a Champion*. Chapel Hill, N.C.: Algonquin Books, 2000. Standard biography of a champion athlete, written to capitalize on Jones's success at the 2000 Olympics.

Smith, Stephen A. "Falls from Grace: What Young Black Athletes Should Learn from the Michael Vick and Marion Jones Dramas." *Ebony*, January 1, 2008. Magazine feature on Marion Jones and former professional football quarterback Michael Vick and their falls from the top of their respective sports.

SEE ALSO: July 1, 1994: Soccer Star Diego Maradona Is Expelled from World Cup; Sept. 26, 2000: Gymnast Andreea Răducan Loses Her Olympic Gold Medal Because of Drugs; Feb. 11, 2002: French Judge Admits Favoring Russian Figure Skaters in Winter Olympics; Mar. 17, 2005: Former Baseball Star Mark McGwire Evades Congressional Questions on Steroid Use; July 26, 2006: Tour de France Is Hit with a Doping Scandal; Aug. 20, 2007: Football Star Michael Vick Pleads Guilty to Financing a Dogfighting Ring.

March 12, 2008

New York Governor Eliot Spitzer Resigns in Prostitution Scandal

Eliot L. Spitzer a former New York attorney general who built his reputation by crusading aggressively against Wall Street corruption, resigned as the governor of New York following news reports that he had spent tens of thousands of dollars patronizing prostitutes with an escort service.

Locale: New York, New York

Categories: Prostitution; sex crimes; government; politics; publishing and journalism

Key Figures

Eliot L. Spitzer (b. 1959), governor of New York, 2006-2008, and former state attorney general, 1999-2006

Silda Wall Spitzer (b. 1957), Spitzer's wife and a former lawyer

Ashley Alexandra Dupré (b. 1985), waitress, aspiring musician, and prostitute

Summary of Event

On March 12, 2008, two days after every major media outlet reported that he had paid for a sexual encounter in Washington, D.C., with a New York prostitute, Eliot Spitzer announced his resignation as the governor of New York. As the New York attorney general, Spitzer had built a national reputation by aggressively pursuing Wall Street corporations he accused of corrupt business practices, and he had successfully catapulted himself into the governorship on the strength of that reputation.

To his supporters, Spitzer was a tenacious reformer who enforced the law against the rich and powerful. Critics, however, saw Spitzer as a bully who tried his cases in the press instead of the courtroom and who essentially coerced his targets into settling for large financial contributions to the state of New York by threat of indictment. Therefore,

Spitzer's shocking downfall was seen either as government overreaching to stifle a powerful reformer or just deserts, depending on one's initial view of Spitzer.

The impetus for the press reports was a federal indictment against four men and women accused of running a high-class prostitution ring called the Emperors Club VIP. Although the Emperors Club was based in New York, it provided prostitutes to clients in Washington, D.C., San Francisco, and Los Angeles. Federal authorities had jurisdiction over the investigation because of the interstate nature of the criminal enterprise, which involved possible violations of the Mann Act of 1910, which prohibits interstate transportation of women for prostitution.

According to an affidavit prepared by Federal Bureau of Investigation (FBI) special agent Kenneth Hosey in connection with the government's investigation of the Emperors Club VIP, a "Client-9"—later identified by *The New York Times* and other media outlets as Spitzer—spent two days arranging advance payment before setting up an encounter with a prostitute named "Kristen" in a Washington, D.C., hotel room, on February 13. The conversations arranging the encounter were recorded on a federal wiretap. Client-9 also paid for Kristen's train ride from New York to Washington, D.C. The affidavit contained salacious details such as the fact that other Emperors Club prostitutes considered Spitzer to be a "difficult" client in that he preferred "unsafe" activities—perhaps a reference to unprotected intercourse. Kristen, according to the affidavit, disagreed with that assessment and indicated in a text message to her supervisor that she liked Client-9, who identified himself to the Emperors Club as George Fox. Spitzer had registered for his hotel room under the name Fox, which, it turned out, is the name of an actual friend of Spitzer who contributed to his campaign.

1167

Eliot Spitzer, with his wife, Silda Spitzer, announces his resignation on March 12, 2008. (AP/Wide World Photos)

The New York Times subsequently revealed Kristen to be a twenty-two-year-old waitress and aspiring musician named Ashley Alexandra Dupré. Dupré later received immunity in exchange for her testimony before the grand jury. Federal investigators ultimately concluded that Spitzer may have paid the Emperors Club as much as eighty thousand dollars over the past few years, including time when he was serving as the attorney general and directing prosecution of other prostitution rings.

Spitzer's use of the escort service was not the initial focus of the federal investigation that would end up catching him. What spurred the inquiry was Spitzer's large cash transactions in 2007, which, it was later revealed, were used to pay the Emperors Club. His bank was mandated to report the transactions to the U.S. Internal Revenue Service (IRS). Under federal law, financial transactions in excess of ten thousand dollars generate currency transaction reports (CTRs) to the IRS that are designed to

help that agency keep track of the movement of U.S. funds as well as to help the federal government fight money laundering. Spitzer was no doubt aware of these regulations, as he apparently structured his transactions so as to bring them each below the reporting threshold. (Structuring done with the intent to evade the reporting requirements can itself be a federal crime, but is difficult to prove.) After federal investigators began looking into the transactions, they wondered whether Spitzer was the victim of extortion or identity theft. It was while investigating Spitzer that they discovered his patronage of the Emperors Club.

Spitzer's scandal had superficial similarities to President Bill Clinton's sexual scandal with former White House intern Monica Lewinsky in that both involved male politicians involved with women young enough to be their daughters, and Spitzer repeatedly emphasized, as Clinton had, that this was a "private" matter. In his first public statement on

March 10, accompanied by his wife, Silda Wall Spitzer, the governor said, "I have acted in a way that violates my obligation to my family and violates my sense of right or wrong," without specifying the conduct in question. Whereas Clinton remained popular, however, Spitzer's aggressive political character appeared to leave him with few political allies, even among Democrats, willing to stand by him. Moreover, Clinton had never been a prosecutor; Spitzer, as noted, had prosecuted prostitution rings, thus leaving himself vulnerable to criticism of hypocrisy and worse, such as placing himself above the law. Meanwhile, numerous Wall Street personalities positively delighted in the news that Spitzer had been brought down by a scandal, and Spitzer's Republican foes increased the pressure on him, calling for impeachment hearings if he did not resign.

On March 12, again accompanied by his wife, Spitzer stated publicly at a press conference that

> I cannot allow for my private failings to disrupt the people's work. Over the course of my public life, I have insisted—I believe correctly—that people take responsibility for their conduct. I can and will ask no less of myself. For this reason, I am resigning from the office of governor.

Following Spitzer's announcement, speculation increased that he had reached an agreement with federal prosecutors, perhaps resigning in exchange for the U.S. attorney's forbearance from prosecution. On November 6, prosecutors announced that Spitzer would not be charged in the case, citing a lack of evidence to support claims that Spitzer misued public funds.

IMPACT

Once considered a rising star in the Democratic Party and a potential future U.S. presidential candidate, Spitzer now had a political future that appeared to be fatally wounded by the prostitution scandal. He had been a prominent supporter of U.S. senator Hillary Rodham Clinton's bid for nomination as the Democratic Party's presidential candidate. Had Clinton won the White House, he would have been an obvious contender for the position of U.S. attorney general. However, after his resignation, the Clinton campaign removed all references to Spitzer from its Web site.

Taking Spitzer's place was David Paterson, who became the first African American and first blind governor of New York. Paterson immediately disclosed publicly that both he and his wife had a history of extramarital affairs. Perhaps because the press was still focusing on Spitzer, or perhaps because there were no illegal acts, Paterson's disclosure resulted in no apparent backlash.

—Tung Yin

FURTHER READING

Apostolidis, Paul, and Juliet A. Williams, eds. *Public Affairs: Politics in the Age of Sex Scandals*. Durham, N.C.: Duke University Press, 2004. A study of politics and political culture in the context of sex scandals.

Federal Bureau of Investigation. *Eliot Spitzer and the Prostitution Ring: The FBI Files*. Minneapolis, Minn.: Filibust, 2008. A compilation of government documents related to the case, including the federal indictment against the Emperors Club defendants and Eliot Spitzer.

Feuer, Alan, and Ian Urbina. "Client 9 in Room 871: Notes on a Rendezvous." *The New York Times*, March 11, 2008. Discusses the identification of Eliot Spitzer as Client 9 in an FBI agent's affidavit.

Hakim, Danny, and William K. Rashbaum. "Spitzer Is Linked to Prostitution Ring." *The New York Times*, March 10, 2008. The initial story that broke the scandal. Includes Spitzer's first public statement on the matter.

Lucchetti, Aaron. "Wall Street Cheers as Its Nemesis Falls from Grace." *The Wall Street Journal*, March 11, 2008. A roundup of Wall Street's reaction to news of the Spitzer prostitution-ring scandal.

Masters, Brooke A. *Spoiling for a Fight: The Rise of Eliot Spitzer*. New York: Henry Holt 2006. A largely favorable biography written with Spitzer's cooperation.

2000's

SEE ALSO: Dec. 7, 1980: Rita Jenrette's "Diary of a Mad Congresswife" Scandalizes Washington; July 20, 1982: Conservative Politician John G. Schmitz Is Found to Have Children Out of Wedlock; July 20, 1983: Congress Members Censured in House-Page Sex Scandal; July 19, 1985: Mayflower Madam Pleads Guilty to Promoting Prostitution; Jan. 17, 1998: President Bill Clinton Denies Sexual Affair with a White House Intern; May 2, 2000: New York Mayor Rudy Giuliani's Extramarital Affair Is Revealed; Oct. 2, 2003: Newspaper Claims That Arnold Schwarzenegger Groped Women; Oct. 14, 2004: Insurance Brokerage Marsh & McLennan Is Charged with Fraud; Beginning Aug. 29, 2005: Government Incompetence Mars Hurricane Katrina Relief Efforts; June 4, 2007: Congressman William J. Jefferson Is Indicted for Corruption; July 9, 2007: Senator David Vitter's Name Is Found in D.C. Madam's Address Book.

June 13, 2008
SINGER R. KELLY IS ACQUITTED ON CHILD PORNOGRAPHY CHARGES

American singer Robert Kelly, better known as R. Kelly, was indicted for sexual molestation and child pornography after a videotape surfaced that appeared to show him having sex with an underage girl. The tape was widely circulated. The sexual molestation charges were dropped and Kelly was ultimately found not guilty on charges of soliciting a minor for child pornography.

LOCALE: Chicago, Illinois

CATEGORIES: Law and the courts; music and performing arts; sex crimes; publishing and journalism; families and children; communications and media; popular culture

KEY FIGURE

R. Kelly (b. 1967), musician, songwriter, and music producer

SUMMARY OF EVENT

R. Kelly experienced success as a rhythm and blues (R&B) musician from the mid-1990's through the first few years of the twenty-first century. His fame was highlighted by hit songs and Grammy Awards. He sold more than 36 million albums worldwide and recorded more Top 40 hits and more number one hits than any other male R&B solo artist of the 1990's. Music critics referred to Kelly as an R&B superstar, "The king of Seductive R and B," and the hip-hop generation's greatest singer-songwriter. His career was overshadowed in 2000 by allegations of sex with underage girls and in 2002 with producing child pornography by videotaping himself having sex with a minor.

Kelly's legal troubles began in 1994, when he married a fifteen-year-old singer, Aaliyah, using a falsified marriage certificate claiming she was eighteen years old. The marriage was annulled six months later when Aaliyah's parents found out about the union. Kelly's legal troubles continued in 1996, when Tiffany Hawkins filed suit claiming she and Kelly were involved sexually in 1991, when she was fifteen years old. Hawkins's lawsuit was settled out of court in 1998 for $250,000. In 2001, Tracy Sampson filed a lawsuit against Kelly claiming that in 2000, when she was seventeen years old, she and Kelly had a sexual relationship. Sampson's lawsuit was later settled for $50,000. In 2002, a lawsuit was filed by Patrice Jones, who claimed that in 1998, when she was sixteen years old, she became pregnant by Kelly and that he later persuaded her to have an abortion.

In February, 2002, the *Chicago Sun Times* reported that police were investigating a twenty-six-minute video allegedly showing Kelly involved in sexual acts with a girl investigators believed to be fourteen or fifteen years old. The video was anonymously sent to the *Chicago Sun Times*, which had earlier published a series of investigative reports on Kelly, beginning in December, 2000. The newspaper claimed in that series that it found "a pattern of R. Kelly abusing his wealth and fame as a pop star to enter into sexual relationships with underage girls." The newspaper turned over the anonymously sent video to Chicago police. The video was believed to have been made in Kelly's home in Chicago sometime between 1997 and 2002. A former protégé of Kelly, known as Sparkle, identified the girl on the sex tape as her niece. Copies of the tape began surfacing on the Web, through Internet file sharing, and through street vendors across the United States.

Chicago police then sent the tape to the Federal Bureau of Investigation's crime lab, which identified Kelly through vein patterns in his hands. The police also conducted interviews with more than fifty people. On June 6, 2002, Kelly was charged with twenty-one counts of having sex with a minor. The charges were later reduced to soliciting a minor for child pornography. Kelly denied the charges, stating that he was not in the video. He called the tape bogus and the charges blackmail. Kelly further suggested that the video was a fabrication from a disgruntled former manager. If found guilty, Kelly could have received a fifteen-year prison sentence and a fine of up to $100,000.

The girl alleged to be in the video reported to a grand jury that she was not in the videotape, leaving prosecutors without a victim. Prosecutors then attempted to link the girl to the video through witness testimony. In early 2003, while Kelly was free on bond, he was facing additional child pornography charges in Florida after he was found in possession of a digital camera that allegedly showed him having sex with minors. The new felony charges were dismissed because the search was deemed illegal. In 2006, Kelly's brother, Kerry Kelly, claimed his brother had offered him a record deal of $50,000 and a house if he would say the man in the video was not Kelly but himself.

After several delays, Kelly's trial finally began on May 20, 2008. Shortly before the trial began, the *Chicago Sun Times* claimed that a woman would come forward who had reported to authorities that she and the girl in the video had performed a threesome with Kelly in the past. She testified to the identity of the girl in the video as well as to the girl being underage at the time of its taping. Nevertheless, a jury took less than one day to determine that Kelly was not guilty on all counts of soliciting a minor for child pornography. The verdict came on June 13, six years after he was initially indicted.

Impact

Kelly's legal troubles did not impact his career in the long term. Critics had predicted, especially after the child pornography allegations, that Kelly's career would suffer greatly, but after an initial negative phase, in which a tour with hip-hop artist Jay-Z was canceled and album sales reached only 610,000, his career rebounded. Jive Records, Kelly's record label, continued to support and endorse him through the allegations. Kelly sold 12 million albums and produced either platinum or multiplatinum albums from 2002 to 2008. His 2006 tour earned millions of dollars.

Cases such as Kelly's continue to influence public opinion about the criminal justice system and its treatment of celebrities. Cynics believe the legal system provides celebrity offenders preferential treatment, and that Kelly was acquitted only adds legitimacy to their claims.

The Kelly scandal also exposed the growing problem of child pornography on the Web. The videotape was widely distributed, bringing new concerns for lawmakers and law enforcement. Additionally, the wide circulation of the video before the trial presented difficulties in finding an impartial jury.

Other critics of the Kelly indictment argued that the case highlighted the low status of girls and women in the music industry and the unaffected careers of those who perpetuate—even celebrate—that status. Kelly's career is accompanied by a history of legal issues involving underage girls and jokes about child pornography, but he is still regarded as the king of R&B.

—J. Bradley McSherry and Jeffery T. Walker

2000's

FURTHER READING

Brown, Jake. *Your Body's Calling Me: Music, Love, Sex, and Money—The Story and the Life and Times of "Robert" R. Kelly*. Phoenix, Ariz.: Colossus Books, 2004. An unauthorized biography of R. Kelly. Explores his childhood, which included abuse and poverty. Also examines the child pornography allegations against the singer.

Gillespie, Alisdair A. "Indecent Images of Children: The Ever Changing Law." *Child Abuse Review* 14 (2005): 430-443. Discusses the nature and difficulties in enacting child pornography legislation.

Kitzinger, Jenny, and Paul Skidmore. "Playing Safe: Media Coverage of Child Sexual Abuse Prevention Strategies." *Child Abuse Review* 4 (1995): 47-56. Examines the influence of the media's coverage on criminal justice in cases of child sexual abuse and molestation.

Newton, Michael, and John L. French. *Celebrities and Crime*. New York: Chelsea House, 2008. Written especially for younger readers, this book examines the intersection of celebrity and crime. Discusses how law enforcement handles celebrities accused of criminal acts and celebrities victimized by crime.

SEE ALSO: July 18, 1988: Actor Rob Lowe Videotapes Sexual Tryst with a Minor; June 27, 1995: Film Star Hugh Grant Is Arrested for Lewd Conduct; Sept. 22, 1997: Sportscaster Marv Albert Is Tried for Sexual Assault; Apr. 7, 1998: Pop Singer George Michael Is Arrested for Lewd Conduct; Early Nov., 2003: Paris Hilton Sex-Tape Appears on the Web; Dec. 18, 2003: Pop Star Michael Jackson Is Charged with Child Molestation.

July 29, 2008
NBA REFEREE TIM DONAGHY IS SENTENCED TO PRISON FOR BETTING ON GAMES

A veteran referee, Tim Donaghy put the integrity of the National Basketball Association at risk by gambling on basketball games, including those in the postseason, and making calls that may have affected games. Professional basketball referees in the United States are not permitted to gamble, except at racetracks during the NBA off-season. Donaghy was sentenced to fifteen months in federal prison.

LOCALE: United States
CATEGORIES: Gambling; corruption; ethics; law and the courts; sports

KEY FIGURES
Tim Donaghy (b. 1967), National Basketball Association referee, 1994-2007
David Stern (b. 1942), NBA commissioner, 1984-

SUMMARY OF EVENT

Gambling is a mixed blessing for organized sports. While betting by fans increases interest in spectator sports, some gamblers may seek to influence the outcomes of games to win money. The professional leagues have strict rules that protect the integrity of their particular sport by prohibiting gambling by players and officials. Professional baseball's 1919 Chicago Black Sox scandal is perhaps the best-known episode of players throwing a game for money. A 1951 collegiate basketball scandal over point shaving almost killed the sport at the college level. Players and coaches at the professional level have been fined or suspended for betting on games, but no official had been caught in a betting scandal before referee Tim Donaghy was caught in 2007.

Donaghy, a referee with a stellar background, was respected by National Basketball Association

(NBA) administrators. He officiated in 772 regular season games and 20 playoff games in a career that spanned thirteen seasons. He played college basketball at Villanova University and is the son of a respected former college basketball referee, Jerry Donaghy, and the nephew of former NBA referee Bill Oakes. Donaghy worked his way into the NBA, serving apprenticeships as a Pennsylvania high school referee and, for seven seasons, as an official with the Continental Basketball Association, a lesser-known professional league in the United States. In 1994, he became one of only sixty NBA referees.

Donaghy had two previous brushes with scandal during his officiating career, but he could not be blamed for either incident. In 2003, he called a technical foul on Rasheed Wallace of the Portland Trail Blazers for throwing a ball at another official during a game. Wallace subsequently confronted Donaghy after the game, screamed obscenities, and issued threats. The NBA suspended Wallace for seven games. On November 19, 2004, Donaghy was one of three referees who worked the infamous Detroit Pistons-Indiana Pacers contest that ended with players from Indiana fighting Pistons fans in the stands.

By 2007, Donaghy earned $260,000 annually. He also had an addiction to gambling and gained a reputation among his peers as someone who was unusually eager to make a few more dollars. In 2003, he reportedly punched former high school classmate and fellow referee Joe Crawford in the face during an NBA referees' camp in New Jersey. It appears Donaghy did so because Crawford did not invite him to a morning television show that paid $500 for an appearance. Furthermore, although respected for his officiating, Donaghy apparently had few friends among his colleagues.

In 2003, Donaghy began placing bets on NBA games with a friend. In mid-December, 2006, James Battista, a professional gambler with the nicknames Baba and Sheep, confronted Donaghy about betting on NBA games and suggested that Donaghy be paid for his correct pick. Donaghy began calling Thomas Martino, who would then call Battista to give him inside information, including

Tim Donaghy leaves federal court in Brooklyn, New York, after his sentencing on July 29, 2008. (AP/Wide World Photos)

what crew would officiate a particular game and how officials and players interacted. Cell phone records indicate hundreds of calls among Donaghy, Battista, and Martino between October 1, 2006, and May 1, 2007.

On June 20, 2007, the FBI contacted the NBA to discuss allegations that a referee was gambling on games—charges that reportedly surfaced in a separate investigation of organized-crime activities. Donaghy resigned in July amid rumors that the FBI was investigating him for betting on games that he officiated during the prior four seasons and that he made calls affecting the point spread in those games. NBA commissioner David Stern called Donaghy a rogue who betrayed the league. He stated that the situation was the worst that he had experienced as an NBA fan, NBA lawyer, or NBA

2000's

commissioner. Stern also stated that he would have fired Donaghy but was advised not to by the FBI because of the ongoing investigation.

In subsequent court papers, the FBI did not specify games in which Donaghy officiated and also allegedly placed bets. The court documents did indicate that Donaghy provided a tip about an NBA game on December 13, 2006, during which he officiated—Boston Celtics-76ers game in Philadelphia. The point spread moved 2 points before tip-off—a sizable swing—with Boston going from a 1.5-point favorite to a 3.5-point choice. Boston ultimately won by 20 points. The next day, Donaghy met with coconspirators to receive a $5,000 cash payment for his tip. He also was rumored to have improperly influenced the outcome of game three of the Western Conference semifinal match between the Phoenix Suns and the San Antonio Spurs in 2007.

On August 15, 2007, Donaghy pleaded guilty in a Brooklyn, New York, federal court to two felony charges involving conspiracy to commit wire fraud as part of a scheme to defraud the NBA and conspiracy to transmit wagering information across state lines. The first charge carried a penalty of up to twenty years in prison while the second could bring an additional five years. Donaghy admitted taking cash payoffs from gamblers and betting on games that he officiated. He told the court that between December, 2006, and April, 2007, he had used "nonpublic information" to pick the winners of particular NBA games and to cover the point spread set by professional bookmakers. Other individuals would then use Donaghy's picks to place bets. He admitted making phone calls to communicate his picks, often using a coded language. If a pick did not win, Donaghy would not be paid, but he would not lose money either.

Donaghy also agreed to turn over the names of about twenty former colleagues who bet at golf courses, racetracks during the season, and casinos, and who also participated in football betting pools. The activities are not illegal in themselves but do violate the letter of the referees' contract with the NBA. Donaghy was released on a $250,000 bond and was sentenced on July 29, 2008, to fifteen

months in federal prison and three years of supervised release.

To the public, Donaghy offered a general apology, claiming he was the victim of pressure from the Gambino Mafia crime family. At his sentencing, he told the judge, "I've brought shame on myself, my family, and the profession." Two others also were sentenced. Battista and Thomas Martino, a friend of Battista, were sentenced to fifteen months and to twelve months, one day in prison, respectively. All three were ordered jointly to pay $217,000 in restitution to the federal government. On September 23, 2008, Donaghy reported to the federal prison in Pensacola, Florida, to begin serving his term.

IMPACT

Donaghy's actions badly damaged the reputation of NBA referees and officiating. In the wake of the case, fans upset by calls began to yell "fix" or "How much do you have on the game?" at referees. Hurt and confused by the scandal, many referees sharply condemned Donaghy for betraying his friends in the league. Some referees pointed out that a zero-tolerance approach to gambling by the NBA would result in about 75 percent of referees being fired for doing everything from playing in a $5 card game to pulling the levers on slot machines in casinos. Officials are allowed to attend shows at casinos during the off-season, but they are not permitted to enter gambling areas. NBA officials acknowledged that casual gambling existed among their ranks, but they feared that Donaghy would exaggerate the extent of the gambling to better his own situation. The NBA stated that it had received no evidence that any referee other than Donaghy bet on games.

A number of NBA fans charged that the league conspired to fix games. Such allegations infuriated NBA commissioner David Stern, who resented claims that he and the league were engaged in criminal activity. Donaghy's betting embarrassed the league and gave support to conspiracy-minded fans. Both the league and the referees sought to prevent a repeat of the Donaghy scandal for the sake of the future of the sport. The NBA opened a review into its gambling policies and how it hires, trains, and monitors officials. In August, 2007, an attorney with the National Basketball Referees Association represented the union in connection with the NBA's review of its basketball operations and officiating programs. Referee crews and supervisors afterward had to review all games on videotape. Every late call that impinges on the point spread is apt to be red-flagged for additional review, a practice that did not exist before the Donaghy scandal.

—*Caryn E. Neumann*

FURTHER READING

Brenner, Reuven, Gabrielle A. Brenner, and Aaron Brown. *A World of Chance: Betting on Religion, Games, Wall Street.* New York: Cambridge University Press, 2008. In this wide-ranging academic study of betting in human society, the authors contend that with widespread gambling in sports, the corruption of referees such as Donaghy becomes inevitable.

Kirchberg, Connie. *Hoop Lore: A History of the National Basketball Association.* Jefferson, N.C.: McFarland, 2007. This exhaustive study presents a history of the National Basketball Association.

Schwarz, Alan, and William K. Rashbaum. "N.B.A. Referee Is the Focus of a Federal Inquiry." *The New York Times*, July 21, 2007. A brief but helpful news report outlining the details of the Donaghy gambling scandal.

SEE ALSO: Jan. 17, 1951: College Basketball Players Begin Shaving Points for Money; Sept. 23, 1977: Horse-Swapping Fraud Staggers Belmont Park Raceway; Apr. 27, 1980: Mobster's Arrest Reveals Point Shaving by Boston College Basketball Players; Mar. 27, 2002: Georgia Basketball Coach Jim Harrick, Sr., Resigns over Fraud Allegations; July 1, 2003: Basketball Star Kobe Bryant Is Accused of Rape; Jan. 27, 2005: German Soccer Referee Admits to Fixing Games for Money; Aug. 20, 2007: Football Star Michael Vick Pleads Guilty to Financing a Dogfighting Ring.

September 7, 2008
FINANCIAL INSTITUTIONS AND MARKETS BEGIN TO COLLAPSE

Led by a complex web of actions that included a drive to maximize profits and an abandonment of prudence and responsibility, major financial institutions in the United States began to fail. By September, 2008, excessive risk-taking, inadequate cash reserves, excessive debt levels, and the subprime mortgage crisis led to financial collapse. The dire financial condition, coupled with an economic recession in the United States, forced U.S. government interventions that, by November 24, totaled $7.7 trillion in bailouts for these financial institutions.

LOCALE: United States
CATEGORIES: Banking and finance; economics; government

KEY FIGURES

Ben Bernanke (b. 1953), chairman of the U.S. Federal Reserve, 2006-2010
Henry Paulson (b. 1946), U.S. secretary of the Treasury, 2006-2009
Phil Gramm (b. 1942), U.S. senator from Texas, 1985-2002

SUMMARY OF EVENT

On September 7, 2008, the U.S. government took control of the institutions known as Fannie Mae (Federal National Mortgage Association) and Freddie Mac (Federal Home Loan Mortgage Corporation). These government sponsored entities, whose purpose was to guarantee and purchase mortgages for low- and moderate-income appli-

2000's

cants for home loans, had funded nearly two-thirds of all mortgages sold in the United States.

Following the takeover of Fannie Mae and Freddie Mac was the collapse of the investment bank Lehman Brothers on September 15, amounting to the largest bankruptcy filing in U.S. history. The following day, the U.S. Federal Reserve, led by Ben Bernanke, loaned AIG (American International Group), one of the world's largest insurance companies, $85 billion in exchange for nearly 80 percent of its stock. By September 22, all five Wall Street investment banks (including Lehman Brothers, Merrill Lynch, Morgan Stanley, and Goldman Sachs) had either gone bankrupt, been sold, or been restructured.

On October 3, a $700 billion government rescue plan was signed into law. On October 14, the U.S. Treasury Department, led by Henry Paulson, said it would spend $250 billion to purchase stock in banks, hoping to unfreeze credit markets. The first $125 billion would be spent on forced purchases in the nine largest depository banks, a move that amounted to partial nationalization. By October 27, fifteen smaller banks had taken funding from this federal allocation. On November 23, the U.S. government agreed to guarantee $306 billion in troubled assets held by Citigroup, one of the world's largest financial services firms.

All financial systems have a measure of risk built into them, but in healthy economies these risks are balanced by the prudent management of assets in the private sector and an effective set of public sector (governmental) regulatory practices that control risk while encouraging innovation. However, between 2000 and 2008, this ideal of balance disappeared as regulators lost power and financial managers found themselves with new freedoms to design and market risky new financial instruments.

Between 2001 and 2007, securitization (the process of pooling debt—such as mortgages—then packaging it and selling it to investors) produced sales for U.S. financial firms of $27 trillion, almost twice the 2007 U.S. gross domestic product. Part of this process of securitization was the use of so-called structured finance to create complex investments. However, there were dangers inherent in these investments. On October 21, 2008, Joseph E. Stiglitz, who had been awarded the 2001 Nobel Prize in Economics, told a congressional hearing on financial services regulation that

> Securitization was based on the premise that a "fool was born every minute." Globalization meant that there was a global landscape on which they could search for those fools—and they found them everywhere. Mortgage originators didn't have to ask, Is this a good loan? but only, Is this a mortgage I can somehow pass on to others?

These structured finance products would not have been sold in such vast quantities had they not been portrayed as safe and high quality. The financial firms that put together these products also ensured buyers that the products were triple-A rated and insured. Unfortunately, both of these protections proved to be flawed.

The excesses and failures of the credit rating companies (Moody's; Standard and Poor's, or S&P; and Fitch) played a crucial role in the financial crisis. Both Moody's and S&P testified before the U.S. Congress that they accepted raw data on the securitized mortgages underlying these products without checking that data. The two companies testified that they had revised their ratings models in 2004 in ways that eased the rigor of the ratings and kept the companies competitive in giving top ratings. Perhaps the most troubling issue, however, was that the credit rating companies were paid by the financial firms whose products they were rating. Moody's analysts admitted that on several occasions they raised their ratings on pools of mortgage-backed securities issued by Countrywide Financial Corporation after Countrywide complained about initial ratings.

Investor protection, through insurance, also was flawed. Structured finance products are insured by what are called credit default swaps (CDS). CDS are private contracts protecting parties, usually banks, against defaults on debts, and they have a global reach. The financial products unit of insurance giant AIG began in 1998 to sell CDS that were tied to mortgage-backed structured finance products put together by Citigroup, Merrill Lynch, and others. The deals earned AIG around $750,000 each. Over time, more and more of these products contained subprime mortgages. The Commodity Futures Modernization Act of 2000, sponsored by U.S. senator Phil Gramm, had ensured that CDS would remain unregulated. As a result, the CDS market grew from over $100 billion in 2000 to $62 trillion at the end of 2007. The sheer size of this global market led to concerns that financial firms issuing a large volume of CDS might set off a chain reaction if they failed. These concerns, however, went unheeded, and the financial system began to collapse.

By the time AIG stopped all of its CDS and subprime mortgage-related business in the summer of 2005, it had insured 420 structured finance deals, making $315 to $400 million but assuming a debt of $63 billion. The U.S. government bailout of AIG provided $85 billion to the failing company on September 16, 2008, but later increased the amount to $123 billion.

Another critical U.S. regulatory change in the early 2000's had allowed banks to keep mortgage-related structured finance products off their balance sheets (that is, they were not required to include them in their financial report that summarizes their total assets, liabilities, and shareholders' ownership stakes). Investors were thus left uninformed about the nature and amount of risk that banks held. Also, the U.S. Office of Thrift Supervision, which regulates thrifts (also called savings and loans), including Countrywide, IndyMac, Washington Mutual, and Downey—all heavily involved in mortgage lending—permitted these institutions to take excessive risks. These risks included allowing the com-

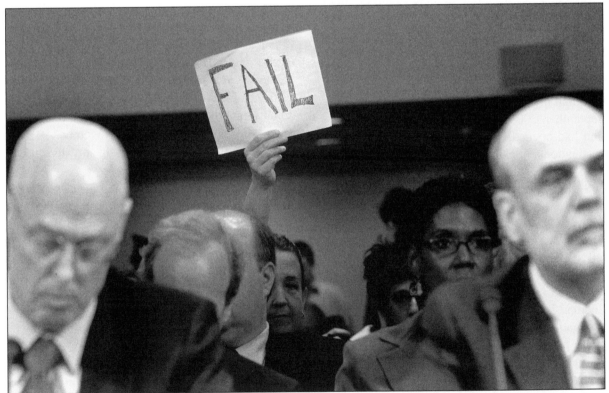

A protestor holds up a sign behind Treasury secretary Henry Paulson, left, and Federal Reserve chair Ben Bernanke at a hearing of the Senate Housing and Urban Affairs Committee on September 23, 2008, in Washington, D.C. The committee began hearing arguments from federal officials for a $700 billion government bailout of American financial institutions. (Hulton Archive/Getty Images)

panies' reserves to decline to the lowest level in two decades. The thrifts also were allowed to expand risky forms of loans, such as option adjustable-rate mortgages. By 2008, several of these companies had been seized by regulators or forced to sell themselves to avoid failure.

Excesses and risk also were at the root of Fannie Mae's and Freddie Mac's failure. During the subprime mortgage boom, mortgage lenders, including Countrywide, threatened to sell directly to Wall Street firms (including Goldman Sachs, Lehman Brothers, and Bear Stearns) unless Fannie Mae would buy some of its riskier loans. Thus, between 2005 and 2007, Fannie Mae took on more and more subprime and Alt-A loans (those for which applicants did not have conventional documentation of their income or assets). Risk officers and other officials warned of the dangers involved in these practices, but by December, 2008, the two owned or guaranteed one in three subprime mortgages and almost one in two Alt-A loans, comprising 34 percent of their single-family mortgage holdings.

IMPACT

Criminal investigations began quickly, and by late September, 2008, the Federal Bureau of Investigation had opened twenty-six preliminary fraud investigations, including investigations of Fannie Mae, Freddie Mac, Lehman Brothers, and AIG. The U.S. Securities and Exchange Commission (SEC) opened more than fifty investigations of insurers, banks, and credit rating firms. The SEC charged Fannie Mae and Freddie Mac with having committed accounting fraud in 2006 and 2007, and the two paid $450 million in penalties. On December 11, 2008, the trustee in charge of the liquidation of Lehman Brothers (already the subject of other investigations) asked the bankruptcy court for subpoena power to investigate the collapse of Lehman Brothers.

Several class action lawsuits were filed against the financial firms for violations of securities law. Securities are financial instruments that may be publicly traded, such as stocks, bonds, and mutual funds. On December 4, 2008, a class action lawsuit was filed against Citigroup on behalf of investors who had purchased Citigroup stock between January, 2004, and November 21, 2007. One successful lawsuit was filed on the principle of breach of fiduciary duty, which is a legal duty of care and good faith to act only in the interests of the beneficiary (for example, a company's shareholders). The Teachers' Retirement System of Louisiana sued four former executives of AIG for breach of fiduciary duty. On September 30, 2008, parties to the suit announced a settlement of $115 million.

By the end of September, government leaders from around the world were openly blaming the United States, particularly the federal government, for allowing the crisis to fester and thus threaten markets and economies worldwide. World leaders denounced everyone from financial speculators to managers of global financial firms who took huge risks out of greed.

The financial crisis, combined with the global recession, had a startling impact on not only the U.S. financial markets and economy but also the world economy. By late October, overall U.S. stock market losses amounted to $8 trillion for the preceding fifteen months, affecting savings and retirement accounts as well as endowments, pension funds, and international investments. By November 21, the S&P 500 stock index was down 46 percent from its peak.

On November 15, leaders of the Group of 20 (the largest developed and emerging-market world economies), which had been meeting in Washington, D.C., issued a lengthy, detailed statement on what they believed caused the financial collapse. The statement included many suggestions for reform (both immediate and medium-term) to prevent another collapse. The size of the U.S. government's intervention showed that these reforms were clearly needed. By November 24, the day after the U.S. government guarantee of Citigroup's debt, the combined amount of government funding pledged in the various parts of the financial bailout was $7.7 trillion. This equaled $24,000 for each person in the United States.

—Glenn Ellen Starr Stilling

Further Reading

Mizen, Paul. "The Credit Crunch of 2007-2008: A Discussion of the Background, Market Reactions, and Policy Responses." *Review* (Federal Reserve Bank of St. Louis), September/October, 2008. A detailed, scholarly examination of the financial crisis, with special attention to its global dimensions.

Roubini, Nouriel. "The Rising Risk of a Systemic Financial Meltdown: The Twelve Steps to Financial Disaster." *RGEmonitor*, February 5, 2008. Predicts several of the events of the financial crisis. Explains in detail the conditions that contribute to each step in such a crisis.

Roush, Chris. "Unheeded Warnings." *American Journalism Review* 30, no. 6 (December/January, 2009). Documents extensive coverage, beginning in 2000, of the conditions that led to the financial crisis. Includes discussion of coverage by *The New York Times*, *The Wall Street Journal*, the *Washington Post*, *Fortune*, and *Business Week*.

United States Congress. House of Representatives. Committee on Financial Services. *The Future of Financial Services Regulation*. Washington, D.C.: Government Printing Office, October 21, 2008. Offers clear and wide-ranging testimony by Joseph E. Stiglitz on the regulatory causes of the financial crisis. Stiglitz discusses topics such as transparency, securitization of mortgages, excessive corporate risk-taking, executive compensation, off-balance-sheet accounting, exploitive lending practices, and credit rating agencies.

Zandi, Mark. *Financial Shock: A Three-Hundred-Sixty Degree Look at the Subprime Mortgage Implosion, and How to Avoid the Next Financial Crisis.* Upper Saddle River, N.J.: Financial Times Press, 2008. Readable, thoroughly documented, comprehensive examination of the roots of the financial crisis. Discusses the Federal Reserve's policy of extremely low lending rates, the roles of various types of mortgage buyers (first-time, trade-up, investors, and flippers), overseas investors, mortgage bankers and brokers, structured finance, the credit crunch, and more.

See also: August 6, 1982: Banco Ambrosiano Collapses Amid Criminal Accusations; May 7, 1985: Banker Jake Butcher Pleads Guilty to Fraud; March 29, 1989: Financier Michael Milken Is Indicted for Racketeering and Fraud; December 2, 2001: Enron Bankruptcy Reveals Massive Financial Fraud; September 3, 2003: Mutual Fund Companies Are Implicated in Shady Trading Practices; Early 2007: Subprime Mortgage Industry Begins to Collapse.

2000's

Appendixes

BIBLIOGRAPHY

Contents

General Studies 1183
Academia 1183
Business and Economics. 1184
Celebrities 1185
Crime—General Studies. 1185
Ethics 1185
Government and Politics. 1186

Marriage, Family, and Children 1187
News Media and Journalism. 1187
Organized Crime. 1187
Religion 1187
Science and Medicine 1187
Sex and Sex Crimes 1188
Sports 1188

GENERAL STUDIES

Adut, Ari. *On Scandal: Moral Disturbances in Society, Politics, and Art.* New York: Cambridge University Press, 2008.

Caldero, M. A., and J. P. Crank. *Police Ethics: The Corruption of Noble Cause.* 2d ed. Cincinnati, Ohio: Anderson, 2004.

Callahan, David. *The Cheating Culture: Why More Americans Are Doing Wrong to Get Ahead.* Orlando, Fla.: Harcourt, 2004.

Dabney, Dean A., ed. *Crime Types: A Text/Reader.* Belmont, Calif.: Thomson/Wadsworth, 2004.

Farquhar, Michael. *A Treasury of Deception: Liars, Misleaders, Hoodwinkers, and the Extraordinary True Stories of History's Greatest Hoaxes, Fakes, and Frauds.* New York: Penguin Books, 2005.

Fernandez, Justin. *Victimless Crimes: Crime, Justice, and Punishment.* Philadelphia: Chelsea House, 2002.

Great Stories of the Century: The Major Events of the Twentieth Century as Reported in the Pages of "The New York Times." New York: Galahad Books, 1999.

Knappman, Edward W., ed. *Great American Trials: Two Hundred and One Compelling Courtroom Dramas from Salem Witchcraft to O. J. Simpson.* New York: Barnes & Noble, 2004.

Kohn, George Childs. *The New Encyclopedia of American Scandal: More than Four Hundred Fifty Famous Incidents from the 1600's to the Present.* New York: Facts On File, 2001.

Lipset, Seymour M., and Earl Raab. *The Politics of Unreason: Right-Wing Extremism in America, 1790-1970.* New York: Harper & Row, 1970.

Mallon, Thomas. *Stolen Words.* Rev. ed. New York: Harcourt, 2001.

Payne, Robert. *The Corrupt Society: From Ancient Greece to Present-Day America.* New York: Praeger, 1975.

Sherwin, Richard K. *When Law Goes Pop: The Vanishing Line Between Law and Popular Culture.* Chicago: University of Chicago Press, 2002.

Sifakis, Carl. *Frauds, Deceptions, and Swindles.* New York: Checkmark Books, 2001.

Spiegel, James S. *Hypocrisy: Moral Fraud and Other Vices.* Grand Rapids, Mich.: Baker Books, 1999.

Wilson, Colin, and Donald Seaman. *Scandal! An Encyclopedia.* London: Weidenfeld and Nicolson, 1986.

Wright, Ed. *History's Greatest Scandals: Shocking Stories of Powerful People.* New York: Barnes & Noble, 2007.

Zinn, Howard. *The Twentieth Century: A People's History.* New York: HarperPerennial, 2003.

ACADEMIA

Anderson, Judy. *Plagiarism, Copyright Violation, and Other Thefts of Intellectual Property: An Annotated Bibliography with a Lengthy Introduction.* Jefferson, N.C.: McFarland, 1998.

Ellen, David. *The Scientific Examination of Docu-*

ments: *Methods and Techniques*. 2d ed. Boca Raton, Fla.: CRC Press, 1997.

Hauptman, Robert. *Documentation: A History and Critique of Attribution, Commentary, Glosses, Marginalia, Notes, Bibliographies, Works-cited Lists, and Citation Indexing and Analysis*. Jefferson, N.C.: McFarland, 2008.

LaFollette, Marcel C. *Stealing into Print: Fraud, Plagiarism, and Misconduct in Scientific Publishing*. Berkeley: University of California Press, 2007.

McCabe, Donald L., L. K. Trevino, and K. D. Butterfield. "Academic Integrity in Honor Code and Non-Honor Code Environments." *Journal of Higher Education* 70 (1999): 211-234.

Yanikoski, Charles S. "When the Trial Is the Punishment: The Ethics of Plagiarism Accusations." *Journal of Information Ethics* 3, no. 1 (Spring, 1994): 83–88.

BUSINESS AND ECONOMICS

Berend, Ivan T. *An Economic History of Twentieth-Century Europe: Economic Regimes from Laissez Faire to Globalization*. New York: Cambridge University Press, 2006.

Blackburn, John D., Elliott I. Klayman, and Martin H. Malin. *The Legal Environment of Business*. 6th ed. Boston: Pearson, 2003.

Block, Alan A., and Constance A. Weaver. *All Is Clouded by Desire: Global Banking, Money Laundering, and International Organized Crime*. Westport, Conn.: Praeger, 2004.

Coenen, Tracy. *Essentials of Corporate Fraud*. Hoboken, N.J.: John Wiley & Sons, 2008.

Coleman, James William. *The Criminal: Understanding White-Collar Crime*. 5th ed. New York: Worth, 2002.

De George, Richard T. "Whistle-Blowing." In *Business Ethics*. 6th ed. Upper Saddle River, N.J.: Pearson/Prentice Hall, 2006.

Derber, Charles. *The Wilding of America: Money, Mayhem, and the American Dream*. 3d ed. New York: Worth, 2004.

Dunn, Donald H. *Ponzi: The Incredible True Story of the King of Financial Cons*. 1975. Reprint. New York: Broadway Books, 2004.

Ermann, M. D., and R. L. Lundman, eds. *Corporate and Governmental Deviance: Problems of Organizational Behavior in Contemporary Society*. New York: Oxford University Press, 2002.

Fraser, Steve. *Every Man a Speculator: A History of Wall Street in American Life*. San Francisco, Calif.: HarperCollins, 2005.

Geisst, Charles R. *Wall Street: A History—From Its Beginnings to the Fall of Enron*. Rev. ed. New York: Oxford University Press, 2004.

Gerber, Jurg, and Eric L. Jensen. *Encyclopedia of White-Collar Crime*. Westport, Conn.: Greenwood Press, 2007.

Gup, Benton E., ed. *Too Big to Fail: Policies and Practices in Government Bailouts*. Westport, Conn.: Praeger, 2004.

Heald, Morrell. *The Social Responsibilities of Business: Company and Community, 1900-1960*. 1970. Reprint. New Brunswick, N.J.: Transaction Books, 2005.

Ingham, Geoffrey. *Capitalism*. Malden, Mass.: Polity Press, 2008.

Jeter, Lynne. *Disconnected: Deceit and Betrayal at WorldCom*. Hoboken, N.J.: Wiley & Sons, 2003.

Katz, L. *Ill-Gotten Gains: Evasion, Blackmail, Fraud, and Kindred Puzzles of the Law*. Chicago: University of Chicago Press, 1996.

Kindleberger, Charles P., Robert Z. Aliber, and Robert Solow. *Manias, Panics, and Crashes: A History of Financial Crises*. New ed. New York: John Wiley & Sons, 2006.

Levi, Michael, and Andrew Pithouse. *Victims of White Collar Crime: The Social and Media Construction of Business Fraud*. New York: Oxford University Press, 2005.

Lu, Shen-Shin. *Insider Trading and the Twenty-four Hour Securities Market: A Case Study of Legal Regulation in the Emerging Global Economy*. Hanover, Mass.: Christopher Publishing House, 1999.

MacDonald, Scott B., and Jane E. Hughes. *Separating Fools from Their Money: A History of American Financial Scandals*. New Brunswick, N.J.: Rutgers University Press, 2007.

Podgor, Ellen S., and Jerold H. Israel. *White Collar*

Crime in a Nutshell. 3d ed. St. Paul, Minn.: West, 2004.

Rosoff, Stephen, Henry Pontell, and Robert Tillman. *Looting America: Greed, Corruption, Villains, and Victims.* Upper Saddle River, N.J.: Prentice Hall, 2003.

_____. *Profit Without Honor: White Collar Crime and the Looting of America.* 4th ed. Upper Saddle River, N.J.: Prentice Hall, 2003.

Salinger, Lawrence M. *Encyclopedia of White-Collar and Corporate Crime.* Thousand Oaks, Calif.: Sage, 2005.

Shapiro, Susan P. *Wayward Capitalists: Target of the Securities and Exchange Commission.* New Haven, Conn.: Yale University Press, 1984.

Shichor, David, Larry Gaines, and Richard Ball, eds. *Readings in White-Collar Crime.* Prospect Heights, Ill.: Waveland Press, 2002.

Von Drehle, David. *Triangle: The Fire That Changed America.* New York: Atlantic Monthly Press, 2003.

CELEBRITIES

Anger, Kenneth. *Hollywood Babylon: The Legendary Underground Classic of Hollywood's Darkest and Best Kept Secrets.* New York: Dell, 1981.

Jacobson, Laurie. *Dishing Hollywood: The Real Scoop on Tinseltown's Most Notorious Scandals.* Nashville, Tenn.: Cumberland House, 2003.

Kast, Marlise Elizabeth. *Tabloid Prodigy: Dishing the Dirt, Getting the Gossip, and Selling My Soul in the Cutthroat World of Hollywood Reporting.* Philadelphia: Running Press, 2008.

Newton, Michael, and John L. French. *Celebrities and Crime.* New York: Chelsea House, 2008.

Parish, James Robert. *Hollywood Bad Boys: Loud, Fast, and Out of Control.* Chicago: Contemporary Books, 2002.

_____. *The Hollywood Book of Death: The Bizarre, Often Sordid, Passings of More than One Hundred Twenty-Five American Movie and TV Idols.* Chicago: Contemporary Books, 2001.

Porter, Dawn, and Danforth Prince. *Hollywood Babylon—It's Back.* New York: Blood Moon, 2008.

Shiach, Don. *At the Movies: Behind the Big Screen—The History, Scandals, Directors, Studios, and Stars.* London: Southwater, 2005.

CRIME—GENERAL STUDIES

Blanche, Tony, and Brad Schreiber. *Death in Paradise: An Illustrated History of the Los Angeles County Department of Coroner.* New York: Four Walls Eight Windows, 2001.

Chermak Steven M., and Frankie Y. Bailey, eds. *Crimes and Trials of the Century.* 2 vols. Westport, Conn.: Greenwood Press, 2007.

Fox, James Alan, and Jack Levin. *The Will to Kill: Making Sense of Senseless Murder.* Boston: Allyn and Bacon, 2001.

Hornberger, Francine. *Mistresses of Mayhem: The Book of Women Criminals.* Indianapolis, Ind.: Alpha, 2002.

Law Commission of Canada, ed. *What Is a Crime? Defining Criminal Conduct in Contemporary Society.* Vancouver: University of British Columbia Press, 2004.

Parrish, Michael. *For the People: Inside the Los Angeles District Attorney's Office, 1850-2000.* Santa Monica, Calif.: Angel City Press, 2001.

Regan, Tom, and Peter Singer, eds. *Animal Rights and Human Obligations.* 2d ed. Englewood Cliffs, N.J.: Prentice-Hall, 1989.

Renzetti, C. M., D. J. Curran, and P. J. Carr, eds. *Theories of Crime: A Reader.* Boston: Allyn & Bacon, 2003.

Theoharis, Athan. *The FBI and American Democracy: A Brief Critical History.* Lawrence: University Press of Kansas, 2004.

Waddell, Terrie, ed. *Cultural Expressions of Evil and Wickedness: Wrath, Sex, Crime.* New York: Rodopi, 2003.

ETHICS

Arthur, John, ed. *Morality and Moral Controversies: Readings in Moral, Social, and Political Philosophy.* 6th ed. Upper Saddle River, N.J.: Prentice Hall, 2002.

Best, Geoffrey. *Honour Among Men and Nations: Transformations of an Idea.* Toronto, Ont.: University of Toronto Press, 1981.

Bok, Sissela. *Lying: Moral Choice in Public and Private Life*. 2d ed. New York: Vintage Books, 1999.

Caldwell, Mark. *A Short History of Rudeness: Manners, Morals, and Misbehavior in Modern America*. New York: Picador USA, 1999.

Cohen, Martin. *One Hundred One Ethical Dilemmas*. New York: Routledge, 2003.

Cook, Fred J. *The Corrupted Land: The Social Morality of Modern America*. New York: Macmillan, 1966.

Childs, James M., Jr. *Greed: Economics and Ethics in Conflict*. Minneapolis, Minn.: Fortress Press, 2000.

Goldberg, M. Hirsh. *The Book of Lies: Schemes, Scams, Fakes, and Frauds That Have Changed the Course of History and Affect Our Daily Lives*. New York: Morrow, 1990.

Gould, David B. L. *A Handbook for Developing and Sustaining Honor Codes*. Atlanta: Council for Spiritual and Ethical Education, 1999.

Hinde, Robert A. *Why Good Is Good: The Sources of Morality*. New York: Routledge, 2002.

Hospers, John. *Human Conduct*. 3d ed. Fort Worth, Tex.: Harcourt Brace College, 1996.

Kane, Robert, ed. *The Oxford Handbook of Free Will*. New York: Oxford University Press, 2002.

Owen, Nicholas, ed. *Human Rights, Human Wrongs: The Oxford Amnesty Lectures, 2001*. New York: Oxford University Press, 2003.

Ross, William D. *The Right and the Good*. New ed. New York: Oxford University Press, 2002.

Singer, Peter, ed. *A Companion to Ethics*. Cambridge, Mass.: Blackwell Reference, 1993.

Tangney, June Price, and Rhonda L. Dearing. *Shame and Guilt*. New York: Guilford Press, 2002.

GOVERNMENT AND POLITICS

Bull, Martin J., and James L. Newell, eds. *Corruption in Contemporary Politics*. New York: Palgrave Macmillan, 2003.

Carter, John J. *Covert Operations and the Emergence of the Modern American Presidency, 1920-1960*. Lewiston, N.Y.: Edwin Mellen Press, 2002.

Dudley, William. *Political Scandals: Opposing Viewpoints*. San Diego, Calif.: Greenhaven Press, 2000.

Grant, Ruth W. *Hypocrisy and Integrity: Machiavelli, Rousseau, and the Ethics of Politics*. Chicago: University of Chicago Press, 1997.

Grossman, Mark. *Political Corruption in America: An Encyclopedia of Scandals, Power, and Greed*. 2d ed. Millerton, N.Y.: Grey House, 2008.

Jeffreys-Jones, Rhodri. *Cloak and Dollar: A History of American Secret Intelligence*. New Haven, Conn.: Yale University Press, 2002.

Kessler, Ronald. *The Bureau: The Secret History of the FBI*. New York: St. Martin's Press, 2002.

Long, Kim. *The Almanac of Political Corruption, Scandals, and Dirty Politics*. New York: Delacorte Press, 2007.

Melanson, Philip H., and Peter F. Stevens. *The Secret Service: The Hidden History of an Enigmatic Agency*. New York: Carroll & Graf, 2002.

Murray, Robert K. *The Harding Era: Warren G. Harding and His Administration*. 1969. Reprint. Newtown, Conn.: American Political Biography Press, 2000.

Roberts, Robert North. *Ethics in U.S. Government: An Encyclopedia of Investigations, Scandals, Reforms, and Legislation*. Westport, Conn.: Greenwood Press, 2001.

Rose-Ackerman, Susan. *Corruption and Government: Causes, Consequences, and Reform*. New York: Cambridge University Press, 1999.

_____. *International Handbook on the Economics of Corruption*. Northampton, Mass.: Edward Elgar, 2006.

Scherer, Randy. *Political Scandals*. Detroit, Mich.: Greenhaven Press, 2008.

Schultz, Jeffrey D. *Presidential Scandals*. Washington, D.C.: CQ Press, 1999.

West, Nigel. *Historical Dictionary of Cold War Counterintelligence*. Lanham, Md.: Scarecrow Press, 2007.

Williams, Juliet A., and Paul Apostolidis, eds. *Public Affairs: Politics in the Age of Sex Scandals*. Durham, N.C.: Duke University Press, 2004.

MARRIAGE, FAMILY, AND CHILDREN

Shapiro, Michael J. *For Moral Ambiguity: National Culture and the Politics of the Family.* Minneapolis: University of Minnesota Press, 2001.

Simon, Rita J., and Howard Alstein. *Global Perspectives on Social Issues: Marriage and Divorce.* Lanham, Md.: Lexington Books, 2003.

Vieth, Victor I., Bette L. Bottoms, and Alison Perona, eds. *Ending Child Abuse: New Efforts in Prevention, Investigation, and Training.* Binghamton, N.Y.: Haworth Press, 2006.

Yalom, Marilyn. *A History of the Wife.* New York: HarperCollins, 2001.

NEWS MEDIA AND JOURNALISM

Bisbort, Alan. *Media Scandals.* Westport, Conn.: Greenwood Press, 2008.

Chiasson, Lloyd, ed. *The Press on Trial: Crimes and Trials as Media Events.* Westport, Conn.: Greenwood Press, 1997.

Fox, Richard, and Robert Van Sickel. *Tabloid Justice.* Boulder, Colo.: Lynne Rienner, 2001.

Gorman, Lyn, and David McLean. *Media and Society in the Twentieth Century.* Malden, Mass.: Blackwell, 2003.

Levy, Beth, and Denis M. Bonilla, eds. *The Power of the Press.* New York: H. W. Wilson, 1999.

Lipschultz, Jeremy H., and Michael L. Hilt. *Crime and Local TV News: Dramatic, Breaking, and Live from the Scene.* Mahwah, N.J.: Lawrence Erlbaum, 2002.

Pavlik, John V. *Journalism and New Media.* New York: Columbia University Press, 2001.

Surette, Raymond. *Media, Crime, and Criminal Justice.* 2d ed. Pacific Grove, Calif.: Brooks Cole, 1997.

Tebbel, John, and Mary Ellen Zuckerman. *The Magazine in America, 1741-1990.* New York: Oxford University Press, 1991.

ORGANIZED CRIME

Abadinsky, Howard. *Organized Crime.* 8th ed. Belmont, Calif.: Thomson/Wadsworth, 2007.

Cressey, Donald Ray. *Theft of the Nation: The Structure and Operations of Organized Crime in America.* New York: Harper & Row, 1969.

Ryan, Patrick J., and George E. Rush, eds. *Understanding Organized Crime in Global Perspective: A Reader.* Thousand Oaks, Calif.: Sage, 1997.

Witwer, David Scott. *Shadow of the Racketeer: Scandal in Organized Labor.* Urbana: University of Illinois Press, 2009.

RELIGION

France, David. *Our Fathers: The Secret Life of the Catholic Church in an Age of Scandal.* New York: Broadway Books, 2004.

Frykholm, Amy. *Rapture Culture: Left Behind in Evangelical America.* New York: Oxford University Press, 2004.

Galli, Mark. *Jesus Mean and Wild: The Unexpected Love of an Untamable God.* Grand Rapids, Mich.: Baker Books, 2006.

Hadden, Jeffrey K., and Anson Shupe. *Televangelism: Power and Politics on God's Frontier.* New York: Henry Holt, 1988.

Marsden, George. *Fundamentalism and American Culture.* 2d ed. New York: Oxford University Press, 2006.

Martin, William. *With God on Our Side: The Rise of the Religious Right in America.* New York: Broadway Books, 1996.

SCIENCE AND MEDICINE

Bell, Robert. *Impure Science: Fraud, Compromise, and Political Influence in Scientific Research.* New York: John Wiley & Sons, 1992.

Blass, Thomas, ed. *Obedience to Authority: Current Perspectives on the Milgram Paradigm.* Mahwah, N.J.: Lawrence Erlbaum, 2000.

Clouthier, Shawn G. "Institutionalized Plagiarism: Honor Among Thieves Remains an Impediment to Purging Misconduct from Scientific Inquiry." *Scientist* 18, no. 15 (2004).

Erling, Jonathon, and Joseph Spillane, eds. *Federal Drug Control: The Evolution of Policy and Practice.* Binghamton, N.Y.: Pharmaceutical Products Press, 2004.

Foster, Claire. *The Ethics of Medical Research on Humans.* New York: Cambridge University Press, 2001.

Hawthorne, Fran. *Inside the FDA: The Business and Politics Behind the Drugs We Take and the Food We Eat.* New York: John Wiley & Sons, 2005.

Hilts, Philip J. *Protecting America's Health: The FDA, Business, and One Hundred Years of Regulation.* New York: Alfred A. Knopf, 2003.

Krimsky, Sheldon. *Science in the Private Interest: Has the Lure of Profits Corrupted Biomedical Research?* Lanham, Md.: Rowman & Littlefield, 2003.

SEX AND SEX CRIMES

Amann, Joseph Minton, and Tom Breuer. *The Brotherhood of the Disappearing Pants: A Field Guide to Conservative Sex Scandals.* New York: Nation Books, 2007.

Blackburn, Simon. *Lust: The Seven Deadly Sins.* New York: Oxford University Press, 2004.

Goodwin, Robin, and Duncan Cramer, eds. *Inappropriate Relationships: The Unconventional, the Disapproved, and the Forbidden.* Mahwah, N.J.: Lawrence Erlbaum, 2002.

Holmes, Stephen T., and Ronald M. Holmes. *Sex Crimes: Patterns and Behavior.* 2d ed. Thousand Oaks, Calif.: Sage, 2002.

Plummer, Kenneth. *Intimate Citizenship: Private Decisions and Public Dialogues.* Seattle: University of Washington Press, 2003.

Schueler, G. F. *Desire: Its Role in Practical Reason and the Explanation of Action.* Cambridge, Mass.: MIT Press, 1995.

SPORTS

Brenner, Reuven, Gabrielle A. Brenner, and Aaron Brown. *A World of Chance: Betting on Religion, Games, Wall Street.* New York: Cambridge University Press, 2008.

Ginsberg, Daniel E. *The Fix Is In: A History of Baseball Gambling and Game Fixing Scandals.* New York: McFarland, 2004.

Kalb, Elliott. *The Thirty Greatest Sports Conspiracy Theories of All-Time: Ranking Sports' Most Notorious Fixes, Cover-Ups, and Scandals.* New York: Skyhorse, 2009.

Newton, David E. *Drug Testing: An Issue for School, Sports, and Work.* Springfield, N.J.: Enslow, 1999.

Pound, Richard W. *Inside the Olympics: A Behind-the-Scenes Look at the Politics, the Scandals, and the Glory of the Games.* Etobicoke, Ont.: John Wiley & Sons Canada, 2004.

—Desiree Dreeuws

CHRONOLOGICAL LIST OF ENTRIES

1901-1910

1904: Theodore Roosevelt Is Accused of Accepting Corporate Funds

January 23, 1904: Senator Joseph R. Burton Is Convicted of Bribery

December, 1904: Boston Alderman Is Reelected While in Jail for Fraud

1906-1909: Emperor William II's Homosexual "Circle" Scandalizes Germany

March 2, 1906: Psychoanalyst Ernest Jones Is Accused of Molesting Mentally Disabled Children

June 25, 1906: Millionaire Heir Murders Architect Stanford White

July 12, 1906: French Court Declares Alfred Dreyfus Innocent of Treason

December 8, 1906: Former U.S. Senator Arthur Brown Is Murdered by Lover

1907: Elinor Glyn's Novel *Three Weeks* Shocks Readers

June 13, 1907: San Francisco Mayor Schmitz Is Found Guilty of Extortion

November 15, 1908: Belgium Confiscates Congo Free State from King Leopold II

1909-1916: Dancer Isadora Duncan Begins Affair with Millionaire Heir

1910: Nobelist Marie Curie Has Affair with Physicist Paul Langevin

1911-1920

March 25, 1911: Nearly 150 Workers Die in Triangle Shirtwaist Factory Fire

January, 1913: British Prime Minister's Staff Is Investigated for Insider Trading

January 13, 1913: Federal Judge Is Impeached for Profiting from His Office

February 17-March 15, 1913: Armory Modern Art Show Scandalizes the Public

May 13, 1913: Boxer Jack Johnson Is Imprisoned for Abetting Prostitution

April 2, 1915: Players Fix Liverpool-Manchester United Soccer Match

May, 1915: British Government Falls Because of Munitions Shortages and Military Setbacks

July 27, 1917: Millionaire Socialite Dies Under Suspicious Circumstances

1919-1920: Ponzi Schemes Are Revealed as Investment Frauds

September 21, 1919: White Sox Players Conspire to Lose World Series in "Black Sox" Scandal

1921-1930

July 19, 1921: U.S. Senate Rebukes Navy in Homosexuality Investigation

February 1, 1922: Director Taylor's Murder Ruins Mabel Normand's Acting Career

March 26, 1922: Hindemith's Opera *Sancta Susanna* Depicts a Nun's Sexual Desires

April 12, 1922: Film Star Fatty Arbuckle Is Acquitted of Manslaughter

June 22, 1922: British Prime Minister David Lloyd George Is Accused of Selling Honors

January 18, 1923: Actor Wallace Reid's Death in Drug Rehab Shakes Film Industry

March 2, 1923: U.S. Senate Investigates Veterans Bureau Chief for Fraud

May 30, 1923: U.S. Attorney General Harry M. Daugherty's Aide Commits Suicide

October 22, 1923: U.S. Senate Begins Hearings on Teapot Dome Oil Leases

January 1, 1924: Film Star Mabel Normand's Chauffeur Shoots Millionaire Courtland S. Dines

May 12, 1924: Kentucky Congressman John W. Langley Is Convicted of Violating the Volstead Act

October 25, 1924: Forged Communist Letter Brings Down British Government

November 19, 1924: Film Producer Thomas H. Ince Dies After Weekend on Hearst's Yacht

July, 1925: *Nosferatu* Is Found to Have Violated *Dracula* Copyright

May-June, 1926: Evangelist Aimee Semple McPherson Claims She Was Kidnapped

December 26, 1926: Ty Cobb and Tris Speaker Are Accused of Fixing Baseball Games

1927: Mae West's Play About Gays Is Banned on Broadway

1927: President Warren G. Harding's Lover Publishes Tell-All Memoir

Early 1928: Joseph P. Kennedy Begins an Affair with Gloria Swanson

1928-1929: Actor Is Suspected of Falsely Claiming to Be an American Indian

March 21, 1928: Alberta Government Sterilizes Thousands Deemed Genetically and Mentally Unfit

June 6, 1929: Luis Buñuel's *Un Chien Andalou* Shocks Parisian Audience

November, 1929: Banque Oustric et Cie Failure Prompts French Inquiry

1930: Liberia Is Accused of Selling Its Own Citizens into Slavery

May, 1930: Postmaster's Division of Airmail Routes Creates a Scandal

December 3, 1930: Surrealist Film *L'Âge d'or* Provokes French Rioting

1931-1940

March 30, 1931: "Scottsboro Boys" Are Railroaded Through Rape Trials

1932: Insull Utilities Trusts Collapse Prompts New Federal Regulation

July 28, 1932: U.S. Troops Drive World War I Veterans from Washington

September 4, 1932: Film Star Jean Harlow's Husband Is an Apparent Suicide

January 20, 1933: Hedy Lamarr Appears Nude in the Czech Film *Exstase*

March 31, 1933: *New York Times* Reporter Denies Reports of a Soviet Famine

January 8, 1934-January 17, 1936: Stavisky's Fraudulent Schemes Rock French Government

May 16, 1934: General Douglas MacArthur Sues Newspaper Columnist for Libel

July 10, 1934: Sex Scandal Forces Resignation of Alberta Premier Brownlee

December 16, 1935: Film Star Thelma Todd's Death Cannot Be Explained

May 20, 1936: British Cabinet Member Resigns After Budget Information Leak

Summer, 1936: Film Star Mary Astor's Diary Becomes a Public Sensation

December 10, 1936: King Edward VIII Abdicates to Marry an American Divorcée

March 17, 1937: Atherton Report Exposes San Francisco Police Corruption

September-October, 1937: Prescription Elixir Causes More than One Hundred Deaths

October 11-22, 1937: Duke and Duchess of Windsor Visit Nazi Germany

May 22, 1939: Kansas City's Boss Pendergast Pleads Guilty to Income Tax Evasion

1941-1950

February 6, 1942: Film Star Errol Flynn Is Acquitted of Rape

February 19, 1942: President Roosevelt Orders Internment of Japanese Americans

April 22, 1942: French Prime Minister Pierre Laval Wants Germany to Win World War II

December 5, 1942: Industrialist Charles Bedaux Is Arrested for Nazi Collaboration

January 14, 1943: Film Star Frances Farmer Is Jailed and Institutionalized

February 23, 1943: Irish Orphan School Fire Kills Thirty-five Girls

June 4, 1943: Actor Charles Chaplin Is Sued for Paternity

June 5, 1944: Australian Poets Claim Responsibility for a Literary Hoax

May 9, 1945: Norwegian Politician Quisling Is Arrested for Nazi Collaboration

May 26, 1945: Norwegian Writer Knut Hamsun Is Arrested for Treason

August 14, 1945: French War Hero Pétain Is Convicted of Nazi Collaboration

December 14, 1945: Poet Ezra Pound Is Charged with Treason and Institutionalized

November 23, 1946: Tennis Star Bill Tilden Is Arrested for Lewd Behavior with a Minor

Spring, 1947: Baseball Manager Leo Durocher Is Suspended for Gambling Ties

July 5, 1948: Actor Carole Landis Commits Suicide During Affair with Rex Harrison

August 4, 1948: Columnist Drew Pearson Exposes Congressman's Corruption

August 31, 1948: Film Star Robert Mitchum Is Arrested for Drug Possession

May 27, 1949: Actor Rita Hayworth Marries Aly Khan After Adulterous Affair

August 26, 1949: Viet Minh Broadcasts French General's Damaging Report

January 21, 1950: Alger Hiss Is Convicted of Perjury

February 7, 1950: Swedish Film Star Ingrid Bergman Has a Child Out of Wedlock

February 9, 1950: U.S. Senator Joseph McCarthy Launches Communist Witch Hunt

May 3, 1950: U.S. Senate Committee Begins Investigating Organized Crime

1951-1960

January 17, 1951: College Basketball Players Begin Shaving Points for Money

July 16, 1951: Belgium's Disgraced King Leopold III Abdicates

November 16, 1951: Federal Tax Official Resigns After Accepting Bribes

September 19, 1952: Actor Charles Chaplin Cannot Reenter the United States

September 23, 1952: Richard Nixon Denies Taking Illegal Campaign Contributions

December 1, 1952: George Jorgensen Becomes Christine Jorgensen

November 21, 1953: Piltdown Man Is Revealed to Be a Hoax

May, 1955: Scandal Magazine Reveals Actor Rory Calhoun's Criminal Past

Late 1955: British Atrocities in Kenya's Mau Mau Rebellion Are Revealed

1956-1962: Prescription Thalidomide Causes Widespread Birth Disorders

March 9, 1956: British Conductor-Composer Is Arrested for Possessing Pornography

June, 1956: George F. Kennan Proves Russian Sisson Documents Are Fakes

June 25, 1956: President Truman's Appointments Secretary Is Convicted of Tax Conspiracy

December 12, 1957: Rock Star Jerry Lee Lewis Marries Thirteen-Year-Old Cousin

April 4, 1958: Actor Lana Turner's Daughter Kills Turner's Gangster Lover

September 22, 1958: President Eisenhower's Chief of Staff Resigns for Influence Selling

May, 1959: Teamsters Leader Dave Beck Is Convicted of Tax Fraud

November 2, 1959: Charles Van Doren Admits to Being Fed Answers on Television Quiz Show

February 7, 1960: President Kennedy's Romantic Affair Links Him to Organized Crime

February 8, 1960: U.S. Congress Investigates Payola in Pop Music Industry

March 14, 1960: FCC Chairman John C. Doerfer Resigns for Accepting Gifts from Networks

1961-1970

July, 1961: Psychologist Stanley Milgram Begins Obedience-to-Authority Experiments

March 29, 1962: Billie Sol Estes Is Arrested for Corporate Fraud

May 19, 1962: Marilyn Monroe Sings "Happy Birthday, Mr. President"

September 12, 1962: British Civil Servant Is Arrested for Spying

October 26, 1962: West German Police Raid *Der Spiegel* Magazine Offices

February 23, 1963: Play Accuses Pope Pius XII of Complicity in the Holocaust

March 2-September 25, 1963: John Profumo Affair Rocks British Government

July 2, 1963: Muslim Leader Elijah Muhammad Is Sued for Paternity

August 14, 1963: Madame Nhu Derides Self-Immolation of Vietnamese Buddhists

October 7, 1963: Vice President Lyndon B. Johnson Aide Resigns over Crime Connections

March 13, 1964: Kitty Genovese Dies as Her Cries for Help Are Ignored

October 7, 1964: President Lyndon B. Johnson's Aide Is Arrested in Gay-Sex Sting

October 29, 1965: Moroccan Politician Mehdi Ben Barka Disappears in Paris

March 4, 1966: Munsinger Sex and Spy Scandal Rocks Canada

March 1, 1967: Adam Clayton Powell, Jr., Is Excluded from Congress

June 23, 1967: Senator Thomas J. Dodd Is Censured for Misappropriating Funds

September 5, 1967: Socialite Nancy Wakeman Shoots Her Politician-Husband

November 28, 1967: Investor Louis Wolfson Is Convicted of Selling Stock Illegally

May 9, 1969: Supreme Court Justice Abe Fortas Is Accused of Bribery

July 18, 1969: Senator Edward Kennedy's Driving Accident Kills Mary Jo Kopechne

Fall, 1969-Winter, 1971: Japanese Baseball Players Are Implicated in Game Fixing

November 13, 1969: American Massacre of Vietnamese Civilians at My Lai Is Revealed

December 30, 1969: United Mine Workers Leader Joseph Yablonski Is Murdered

1970: Study of Anonymous Gay Sex Leads to Ethics Scandal

May 4, 1970: National Guardsmen Kill Protesting Kent State Students

May 28, 1970: Irish Politicians Are Tried for Conspiring to Import Weapons

1971-1980

June 13, 1971: *New York Times* Publishes the Pentagon Papers

August 20, 1971: Abusive Role-Playing Ends Stanford Prison Experiment

January 28, 1972: Clifford Irving Admits Faking Howard Hughes Memoirs

June 17, 1972-August 9, 1974: Watergate Break-in Leads to President Nixon's Resignation

June 22, 1972: Police Arrest Architect John Poulson for Bribery and Fraud

July 8-22, 1972: Jane Fonda's Visit to North Vietnam Outrages Many Americans

July 25, 1972: Newspaper Breaks Story of Abuses in Tuskegee Syphilis Study

July 31, 1972: Thomas F. Eagleton Withdraws from Vice Presidential Race

August 19, 1973: Cheating Scandal Shocks Soap Box Derby

October 10, 1973: Spiro T. Agnew Resigns Vice Presidency in Disgrace

April 15, 1974: Kidnapped Heir Patty Hearst Helps Rob a Bank

May 14, 1974: *Washington Post* Reveals That the Nixons Received Jewelry Gifts

May 20, 1974: French Cardinal Daniélou Dies in a Prostitute's House

Summer, 1974: Dalkon Shield Contraceptive Is Removed from the Market

October 7, 1974: Congressman Wilbur D. Mills's Stripper Affair Leads to His Downfall

October 25, 1974: Evangelist Billy James Hargis Resigns College Presidency During Gay-Sex Scandal

November 20, 1974: British Politician John Stonehouse Fakes His Suicide

February 3, 1975: Honduras's "Bananagate" Bribery Scandal Leads to Executive's Suicide

October 31, 1975: Buddhist Teacher Orders His Students to Remove Their Clothes

1976: Peace Corps Conceals Murder of Volunteer in Tonga

1976-1977: U.S. Congress Members Are Implicated in Koreagate Scandal

February 4, 1976: Lockheed Is Implicated in Bribing Foreign Officials

March 21, 1976: Actor Claudine Longet Kills Ski Champion Vladimir Sabich

April 4, 1976: West Point Cadets Are Caught Cheating on Exams

May 23, 1976: *Washington Post* Exposes Congressman Wayne L. Hays's Affair

September 1, 1976: Former Beatle George Harrison Loses Plagiarism Lawsuit

September, 1976: Jimmy Carter Admits Committing Adultery in His Heart

October 4, 1976: Agriculture Secretary Earl Butz Resigns After Making Obscene Joke

November 9, 1976: German Generals Must Retire for Supporting a Neo-Nazi Pilot

January, 1977: Singer Anita Bryant Campaigns Against Lesbian and Gay Rights

February 25, 1977: Film Producer David Begelman Is Found to Have Forged Checks

September 21, 1977: Carter Cabinet Member Resigns over Ethics Violations

September 23, 1977: Horse-Swapping Fraud Upsets Belmont Park Raceway

1978: Actor Joan Crawford's Daughter Publishes Damning Memoir, *Mommie Dearest*

1978: *Roots* Author Alex Haley Is Sued for Plagiarism

February 1, 1978: Roman Polanski Flees the United States to Avoid Rape Trial

June 27, 1978: Evangelist Herbert W. Armstrong Excommunicates His Own Son

July 23, 1978: Utah Millionaire Is Murdered by His Grandson

August 4, 1978: British Politician Jeremy Thorpe Is Charged with Attempted Murder

October 20, 1978: Firestone Recalls Millions of Defective Car Tires

January 26, 1979: Former Vice President Nelson Rockefeller Dies Mysteriously

April 18, 1979: Actor Lee Marvin Is Ordered to Pay Palimony to Former Lover

June 4, 1979: South African President B. J. Vorster Resigns in Muldergate Scandal

September 26, 1979: Love Canal Residents Sue Chemical Company

October 10, 1979: French President Giscard d'Estaing Is Accused of Taking a Bribe

October 11, 1979: Senate Denounces Herman E. Talmadge for Money Laundering

November 29, 1979, and January 31, 1983: Baseball Commissioner Suspends Mickey Mantle and Willie Mays for Casino Ties

1980: Biographer Claims Actor Errol Flynn Was a Nazi Spy

February 2, 1980: Media Uncover FBI Sting Implicating Dozens of Lawmakers

March 10, 1980: Scarsdale Diet Doctor Is Killed by His Lover

April 27, 1980: Mobster's Arrest Reveals Point Shaving by Boston College Basketball Players

Late July, 1980: President's Brother, Billy Carter, Registers as a Paid Agent for Libya

July 28, 1980: Magazine Reveals Baseball Star Steve Garvey's Marital Problems

September 3, 1980: Congressman Bauman Is Arrested for Liaison with Teenage Boy

October 9, 1980: Bendix Executive Resigns Amid Rumors of an Affair

December 7, 1980: Rita Jenrette's "Diary of a Mad Congresswife" Scandalizes Washington

1981-1990

April 15, 1981: Janet Cooke Admits Fabricating Her Pulitzer Prize-Winning Feature

April 28, 1981: Tennis Star Billie Jean King Is Sued for Palimony

May 23, 1981: Italian Justice Minister Resigns Because of Crime Connection

May 29, 1981: Court Finds That Ford Ignored Pinto's Safety Problems

September 10, 1981: *Chicago Sun-Times* Reports That Cardinal Cody Diverted Church Funds

May 11, 1982: Philippine President Marcos Forces the Entire Supreme Court to Resign

July 20, 1982: Conservative Politician John G. Schmitz Is Found to Have Children Out of Wedlock

August 6, 1982: Banco Ambrosiano Collapses Amid Criminal Accusations

October 19, 1982: Car Manufacturer John De Lorean Is Arrested in a Drug Sting

December, 1982: Julie Andrews and Blake Edwards Deny Being Gay

December 16, 1982: Congress Cites Environmental Protection Agency Chief for Contempt

April 25, 1983: German Magazine Publishes Faked Hitler Diaries

July 20, 1983: Congress Members Censured in House-Page Sex Scandal

August 12, 1983-July 27, 1990: McMartin Preschool Is Embroiled in Child-Abuse Case

August 21, 1983: Filipino Opposition Leader Aquino Is Assassinated on Return Home

October 14, 1983: British Cabinet Secretary Parkinson Resigns After His Secretary Becomes Pregnant

January 25, 1984: Jesse Jackson Calls New York City "Hymietown"

May 2, 1984: E. F. Hutton Executives Plead Guilty to Fraud

July 23, 1984: Vanessa Williams Is the First Miss America to Resign

December 22, 1984: Subway Vigilante Bernhard Goetz Shoots Four Black Youths

1985-1986: Westland Affair Shakes Prime Minister Thatcher's Government

May 7, 1985: Banker Jake Butcher Pleads Guilty to Fraud

July 10, 1985: French Secret Service Sinks the Greenpeace Ship *Rainbow Warrior*

July 19, 1985: Mayflower Madam Pleads Guilty to Promoting Prostitution

August 19, 1985: West German Counterintelligence Chief Defects to East Germany

September 17, 1985: Media Allege Canadian Officials Allowed Sale of Rancid Tuna

October 23, 1985: Guru Bhagwan Shree Rajneesh Is Indicted for Immigration Fraud

February 28, 1986: Baseball Commissioner Peter Ueberroth Suspends Players for Cocaine Use

March 3, 1986: Former U.N. Secretary-General Kurt Waldheim's Nazi Past Is Revealed

April 22, 1986: Faith Healer Peter Popoff Is Exposed as a Fraud

November 13, 1986-May 4, 1989: Iran-Contra Weapons Scandal Taints Reagan's Administration

January 12 and May 11, 1987: Media Reports Spark Investigation of Australian Police Corruption

January 22, 1987: Pennsylvania Politician Kills Himself at Televised Press Conference

February 25, 1987: NCAA Imposes "Death Penalty" on Southern Methodist University Football

March 19, 1987: Jim Bakker Resigns as Head of PTL Television Network

April 9, 1987: Bess Myerson Resigns as New York Commissioner of Cultural Affairs

July 25, 1987: Novelist-Politician Jeffrey Archer Wins Libel Trial Against the *Daily Star*

September 23, 1987: Plagiarism Charges End Joe Biden's Presidential Campaign

November 28, 1987: Black Teenager Claims to Have Been Gang-Raped by Police Officers

December 1, 1987: Yale Scholar's Wartime Anti-Semitic Writings Are Revealed

January 15, 1988: ZZZZ Best Founder Is Indicted on Federal Fraud Charges

February 21, 1988: Evangelist Jimmy Swaggart Tearfully Confesses His Adultery

June, 1988-June, 1989: Insider-Trading Scandal Rocks Japanese Government

July 18, 1988: Actor Rob Lowe Videotapes His Sexual Encounter with a Minor

September 19, 1988: Stephen Breuning Pleads Guilty to Medical Research Fraud

March 23, 1989: Scientists' "Cold Fusion" Claims Cannot Be Verified

March 29, 1989: Financier Michael Milken Is Indicted for Racketeering and Fraud

May 31, 1989: Speaker of the House Jim Wright Resigns in Ethics Scandal

August 10, 1989: Japanese Prime Minister Sosuke Resigns After Affair with a Geisha

August 24, 1989: Pete Rose Is Banned from Baseball for Betting on Games

December 3, 1989: Martin Luther King, Jr.'s, Doctoral-Thesis Plagiarism Is Revealed

December 15-25, 1989: Harassment of a Christian Minister Sparks the Romanian Revolution

December 18, 1989: Prince Charles's Intimate Phone Conversation with Camilla Parker Bowles Is Taped

January 18, 1990: Washington, D.C., Mayor Marion Barry Is Arrested for Drug Use

March, 1990: Menendez Brothers Are Arrested for Murdering Their Parents

August 27, 1990: Guinness Four Are Found Guilty of Share-Trading Fraud

November 19, 1990: Lip-Synching Duo Milli Vanilli Lose Grammy Award

1991-2000

March 30, 1991: William Kennedy Smith Is Accused of Rape

April 5, 1991: George W. Bush Is Investigated for Insider Trading

July 26, 1991: Comedian Pee-wee Herman Is Arrested for Public Indecency

October 11-13, 1991: Justice Clarence Thomas's Confirmation Hearings Create a Scandal

January 13, 1992: Woody Allen Has Affair with Lover Mia Farrow's Adopted Daughter

April 15, 1992: Hotel Tycoon Leona Helmsley Enters Prison for Tax Evasion

May 6, 1992: Irish Bishop Eamonn Casey's Romantic Affair Leads to His Resignation

May 19, 1992: Amy Fisher Shoots Mary Jo Buttafuoco

June 26, 1992: U.S. Navy Secretary Resigns in the Wake of Tailhook Sexual Assault Scandal

August 23, 1992: Princess Diana's Phone Conversation with Her Lover Is Made Public

September 24, 1992: British Cabinet Member David Mellor Resigns over Romantic Affair

June 23, 1993: Lorena Bobbitt Severs Her Husband's Penis

January 5, 1994: British Cabinet Member Resigns After Fathering a Child Out of Wedlock

April 28, 1994: U.S. Naval Academy Expels Midshipmen for Cheating

June 1, 1994: Congressman Dan Rostenkowski Is Indicted in House Post Office Scandal

June 12, 1994: Double Murder Leads to Sensational O. J. Simpson Trial

June 24, 1994: *Time* Magazine Cover Uses Altered O. J. Simpson Photo

June 30, 1994: Tonya Harding Is Banned from Skating After Attack on Rival

July 1, 1994: Soccer Star Diego Maradona Is Expelled from World Cup

August 5, 1994: Kenneth Starr Is Appointed to the Whitewater Investigation

August 21, 1994: Sex Scandal Forces Dismissal of NAACP Chief Benjamin Chavis

February 28, 1995: Former Mexican President Carlos Salinas's Brother Is Arrested for Murder

June 27, 1995: Film Star Hugh Grant Is Arrested for Lewd Conduct

November 18, 1995: Former Canadian Premier Brian Mulroney Is Exposed in Airbus Scandal

February 4, 1996: Whistle-Blower Reveals Tobacco Industry Corruption

Spring, 1996: Physicist Publishes a Deliberately Fraudulent Article

August 16, 1996: Belgian Media Reveal How Police Bungled Serial Murder Case

November 3, 1996: Car Crash Reveals Depth of Government Corruption in Turkey

January, 1997: Pyramid Investment Schemes Cause Albanian Government to Fall

February 26, 1997: Teacher Mary Kay Letourneau Is Arrested for Statutory Rape

March 12, 1997: Prize-Winning Aborigine Novelist Revealed as a Fraud

May 20, 1997: Air Force Prosecution of Female Officer for Adultery Reveals Double Standard

June 25, 1997: Swiss Banks Admit to Holding Accounts of Holocaust Victims

August 31, 1997: Princess Diana Dies in Car Crash

September 22, 1997: Sportscaster Marv Albert Is Tried for Sexual Assault

November 26, 1997: Canadian Health Commissioner Releases Report on Tainted Blood

December 11, 1997: HUD Secretary Henry Cisneros Is Indicted for Lying to Federal Agents

January 17, 1998: President Bill Clinton Denies Sexual Affair with a White House Intern

April, 1998: Scottish Historian Is Charged with Plagiarism

April 7, 1998: Pop Singer George Michael Is Arrested for Lewd Conduct

May, 1998: Police Corruption Is Revealed in Los Angeles's Rampart Division

May 11, 1998: Journalist Stephen Glass Is Exposed as a Fraud

December 23, 1998: Prominent Belgians Are Sentenced in Agusta-Dassault Corruption Scandal

March 4, 1999: Quebec Offers Support for Abused Duplessis Orphans

May, 1999: Civil Rights Leader Jesse Jackson Fathers a Child Out of Wedlock

May 7, 1999-March 2, 2001: Ethics Counselor Exonerates Canadian Prime Minister Jean Chrétien

January 28, 2000: John Spano Is Sentenced for Fraudulent Purchase of Ice Hockey Team

May 2, 2000: New York Mayor Rudy Giuliani's Extramarital Affair Is Revealed

May 9, 2000: Former Louisiana Governor Edwin Edwards Is Convicted on Corruption Charges

September, 2000: American Scientists Are Accused of Starting a Measles Epidemic in the Amazon

September 19, 2000: Ex-gay Leader John Paulk Is Photographed Leaving a Gay Bar

September 26, 2000: Gymnast Andreea Răducan Loses Her Olympic Gold Medal Because of Drugs

November 5, 2000: Japanese Amateur Archaeologist's "Discoveries" Are Proven Fakes

December, 2000: Sexual Abuse of Children in France Leads to the Outreau Affair

2001-2010

2001: Clearstream Financial Clearinghouse Is Accused of Fraud and Money Laundering

January 30, 2001: Liverpool Children's Hospital Collects Body Parts Without Authorization

February 18, 2001: CIA Agent Robert Hanssen Is Arrested for Spying for the Russians

April 30, 2001: Washington Intern Chandra Levy Disappears

June 18, 2001: Award-Winning Historian Joseph J. Ellis Is Accused of Lying

June 30, 2001: Korean Religious Teacher Jung Myung Seok Is Charged with Rape

August 27, 2001: Little League Baseball Star Danny Almonte Is Found to Be Overage

December 2, 2001: Enron Bankruptcy Reveals Massive Financial Fraud

December 14, 2001: Notre Dame Football Coach Resigns for Falsifying His Résumé

January 4, 2002: Historian Stephen E. Ambrose Is Accused of Plagiarism

January 6, 2002: *Boston Globe* Reports on Child Sexual Abuse by Roman Catholic Priests

January 18, 2002: Historian Doris Kearns Goodwin Is Accused of Plagiarism

February 11, 2002: French Judge Admits Favoring Russian Figure Skaters in Winter Olympics

February 17, 2002: Rotting Human Bodies Are Found at Georgia Crematory

March 27, 2002: Georgia Basketball Coach Jim Harrick, Sr., Resigns over Fraud Allegations

June 25, 2002: Internal Corruption Forces Adelphia Communications to Declare Bankruptcy

July, 2002: Journalist Alleges Release of Genetically Modified Corn Seeds in New Zealand

August, 2002: Immunologist Resigns After Being Accused of Falsifying Research

September 25, 2002: Inquiry Reveals That Physicist Jan Hendrik Schön Faked His Research

September 28, 2002: British Politician Reveals Her Affair with Prime Minister John Major

October 25, 2002: Historian Michael A. Bellesiles Resigns After Academic Fraud Accusations

December 5, 2002: Senator Trent Lott Praises Strom Thurmond's 1948 Presidential Campaign

January 2, 2003: E-mail Message Prompts Inquiry into Air Force Academy Sexual Assaults

March 2, 2003: U.S. National Security Agency Is Found to Have Spied on U.N. Officials

April 29, 2003: *New York Times* Reporter Jayson Blair Is Exposed as a Fraud

May 3, 2003: University of Alabama Fires New Football Coach in Sex Scandal

May 21, 2003: Sexually Provocative Film *The Brown Bunny* Premieres at Cannes Film Festival

July 1, 2003: Basketball Star Kobe Bryant Is Accused of Rape

July 14, 2003: Columnist Robert Novak Leaks the Name of CIA Operative Valerie Plame

September 3, 2003: Mutual Fund Companies Are Implicated in Shady Trading Practices

October 2, 2003: Newspaper Claims That Arnold Schwarzenegger Groped Women

Early November, 2003: Paris Hilton Sex-Tape Appears on the Web

December 17, 2003: Senator Strom Thurmond's Biracial Daughter Is Revealed

December 18, 2003: Pop Star Michael Jackson Is Charged with Child Molestation

March 4, 2004: Former United Way Charity Chief Pleads Guilty to Embezzlement

March 5, 2004: Martha Stewart Is Convicted in Insider-Trading Scandal

April 28, 2004: CBS Broadcasts Photos of Abused and Tortured Prisoners at Abu Ghraib

June 2, 2004: U.N. Report Reveals That Secretary-General Kofi Annan Dismissed Sexual Harassment Charges

August 19, 2004: Blog "Outs" Antigay Congressman Edward Schrock

September 8, 2004: *60 Minutes II* Reports on George W. Bush's Evasion of Wartime Duty

October 13, 2004: Television Producer Files Sex Harassment Suit Against Bill O'Reilly

October 14, 2004: Insurance Brokerage Marsh & McLennan Is Charged with Fraud

January 15, 2005: Iqbal Riza Resigns from the United Nations in Oil-for-Food Scandal

January 27, 2005: German Soccer Referee Admits to Fixing Games for Money

March 17, 2005: Former Baseball Star Mark McGwire Evades Congressional Questions on Steroid Use

June 22, 2005: U.S. Air Force Investigates Religious Intolerance at Its Academy

July 1, 2005: Federal Agents Raid Congressman Randall Cunningham's Home

Beginning August 29, 2005: Government Incompetence Mars Hurricane Katrina Relief Efforts

September 12, 2005: Westar Energy Executives Are Found Guilty of Looting Their Company

September 30, 2005: Danish Newspaper's Prophet Muhammad Cartoons Stir Violent Protests

November 17, 2005: Liberian Workers Sue Bridgestone Firestone over Slave Labor

December 6, 2005: Spokane, Washington, Mayor Recalled in Gay-Sex Scandal

January 21, 2006: British Politician Resigns After Gay-Sex Orgy

March 14, 2006: Duke Lacrosse Players Are Accused of Gang Rape

April 26, 2006: Britain's Deputy Prime Minister Admits Affair with Secretary

May 4, 2006: Media Uncover Match-Fixing in Italian Soccer

May 12, 2006: Scientist Is Indicted for Faking His Research on Creating Stem Cells

Summer, 2006-March 16, 2007: Manufacturer Recalls Pet Food That Killed Thousands of American Pets

July 14, 2006: *New York Times* Exposes Grading Scandal at Auburn University

July 26, 2006: Tour de France Is Hit with a Doping Scandal

July 28, 2006: Actor Mel Gibson Is Caught Making Anti-Semitic Remarks

August 12, 2006: Novelist Günter Grass Admits to Youthful Nazi Ties

September 17, 2006: New Zealand Prime Minister's Husband Is "Outed" as Gay

September 18, 2006: *Newsweek* Reveals That Hewlett-Packard Spied on Its Own Board

September 29, 2006: Congressman Mark Foley Resigns in Sex Scandal Involving a Teenage Page

October 22, 2006: Chilean Politicians Use Community Funds for Personal Campaigns

November 2, 2006: Evangelist Kent Hovind Is Convicted of Federal Tax Violations

November 2, 2006: Male Escort Reveals Sexual Liaisons with Evangelist Ted Haggard

November 20, 2006: News Corp Abandons Plan to Publish O. J. Simpson's Book

November 23, 2006: Former Russian Security Service Officer Dies from Radiation Poisoning

Early 2007: Subprime Mortgage Industry Begins to Collapse

February 18, 2007: *Washington Post* Exposes Decline of Walter Reed Army Hospital

April 11, 2007: Shock Jock Don Imus Loses His Radio Show over Sexist and Racist Remarks

May 28, 2007: Japanese Politician Charged with Corruption Hangs Himself

June 4, 2007: Congressman William J. Jefferson Is Indicted for Corruption

July 9, 2007: Senator David Vitter's Name Is Found in D.C. Madam's Address Book

July 11, 2007: Florida Politician Is Arrested for Soliciting an Undercover Male Police Officer

July 24, 2007: University of Colorado Fires Professor for Plagiarism and Research Falsification

August 20, 2007: Football Star Michael Vick Pleads Guilty to Financing a Dogfighting Ring

September 13, 2007: New England Patriots Football Team Is Fined for Spying on Other Teams

October 5, 2007: Olympic Champion Marion Jones Admits Steroid Use

March 12, 2008: New York Governor Eliot Spitzer Resigns in Prostitution Scandal

June 13, 2008: Singer R. Kelly Is Acquitted on Child Pornography Charges

July 29, 2008: NBA Referee Tim Donaghy Is Sentenced to Prison for Betting on Games

September 7, 2008: Financial Institutions and Markets Begin to Collapse

GEOGRAPHICAL INDEX

List of Geographical Regions

Africa 1200	Kenya 1207
Albania. 1201	Liberia 1207
Algeria. 1201	Libya. 1207
Argentina 1201	Luxembourg 1207
Asia 1201	Mexico. 1207
Australasia. 1201	Middle East 1207
Australia 1201	Morocco 1207
Austria 1201	New Zealand. 1207
Belgium 1202	Nicaragua 1207
Canada. 1202	Northern Ireland 1207
Central African Republic 1202	Norway 1208
Central and South America 1202	Pakistan 1208
Chile 1202	Philippines 1208
China. 1202	Romania 1208
Congo, Democratic Republic of the 1202	Russia 1208
Czech Republic 1202	Scotland 1208
Denmark. 1202	South Africa 1208
Dominican Republic. 1202	South Korea 1208
Egypt. 1203	Soviet Union. 1208
England 1203	Spain. 1208
Europe 1203	Sweden. 1208
France 1205	Switzerland 1208
Germany 1206	Tonga 1208
Honduras. 1206	Turkey 1209
Iran. 1206	United States. 1209
Iraq. 1206	Vatican City 1215
Ireland 1206	Venezuela 1215
Italy 1207	Vietnam 1215
Japan. 1207	

AFRICA

Nov. 15, 1908: Belgium Confiscates Congo Free State from King Leopold II, 31

1930: Liberia Is Accused of Selling Its Own Citizens into Slavery, 142

Dec. 5, 1942: Industrialist Charles Bedaux Is Arrested for Nazi Collaboration, 212

Late 1955: British Atrocities in Kenya's Mau Mau Rebellion Are Revealed, 298

Oct. 29, 1965: Moroccan Politician Mehdi Ben Barka Disappears in Paris, 374

June 4, 1979: South African President B. J. Vorster Resigns in Muldergate Scandal, 543

Oct. 10, 1979: French President Giscard d'Estaing Is Accused of Taking a Bribe, 550

Nov. 17, 2005: Liberian Workers Sue Bridgestone Firestone over Slave Labor, 1078

ALBANIA

Jan., 1997: Pyramid Investment Schemes Cause Albanian Government to Fall, 846

ALGERIA

Dec. 5, 1942: Industrialist Charles Bedaux Is Arrested for Nazi Collaboration, 212

ARGENTINA

July 1, 1994: Soccer Star Diego Maradona Is Expelled from World Cup, 815

ASIA. *See also* MIDDLE EAST

Aug. 26, 1949: Viet Minh Broadcasts French General's Damaging Report, 257

Aug. 14, 1963: Madame Nhu Derides Self-Immolation of Vietnamese Buddhists, 362

Fall, 1969-Winter, 1971: Japanese Baseball Players Are Implicated in Game Fixing, 398

Nov. 13, 1969: American Massacre of Vietnamese Civilians at My Lai Is Revealed, 401

July 8-22, 1972: Jane Fonda's Visit to North Vietnam Outrages Many Americans, 434

Feb. 4, 1976: Lockheed Is Implicated in Bribing Foreign Officials, 482

May 11, 1982: Philippine President Marcos Forces the Entire Supreme Court to Resign, 600

Aug. 21, 1983: Filipino Opposition Leader Aquino Is Assassinated on Return Home, 628

June, 1988-June, 1989: Insider-Trading Scandal Rocks Japanese Government, 714

Aug. 10, 1989: Japanese Prime Minister Sosuke Resigns After Affair with a Geisha, 733

Nov. 5, 2000: Japanese Amateur Archaeologist's "Discoveries" Are Proven Fakes, 919

June 30, 2001: Korean Religious Teacher Jung Myung Seok Is Charged with Rape, 939

May 12, 2006: Scientist Is Indicted for Faking His Research on Creating Stem Cells, 1094

Summer, 2006-Mar. 16, 2007: China Recalls Pet Food That Has Killed Thousands of American Pets, 1097

May 28, 2007: Japanese Politician Charged with Corruption Hangs Himself, 1145

AUSTRALASIA

June 5, 1944: Australian Poets Claim Responsibility for a Literary Hoax, 223

Mar. 9, 1956: British Conductor-Composer Is Arrested for Possessing Pornography, 304

Nov. 20, 1974: British Politician John Stonehouse Fakes His Suicide, 468

1976: Peace Corps Conceals Murder of Volunteer in Tonga, 476

July 10, 1985: French Secret Service Sinks the Greenpeace Ship *Rainbow Warrior*, 651

Jan. 12 and May 11, 1987: Media Reports Spark Investigation of Australian Police Corruption, 681

Mar. 12, 1997: Prize-Winning Aborigine Novelist Revealed as a Fraud, 852

Sept. 26, 2000: Gymnast Andreea Răducan Loses Her Olympic Gold Medal Because of Drugs, 916

July, 2002: Journalist Alleges Release of Genetically Modified Corn Seeds in New Zealand, 974

Sept. 17, 2006: New Zealand Prime Minister's Husband Is "Outed" as Gay, 1112

AUSTRALIA

June 5, 1944: Australian Poets Claim Responsibility for a Literary Hoax, 223

Mar. 9, 1956: British Conductor-Composer Is Arrested for Possessing Pornography, 304

Nov. 20, 1974: British Politician John Stonehouse Fakes His Suicide, 468

Jan. 12 and May 11, 1987: Media Reports Spark Investigation of Australian Police Corruption, 681

Mar. 12, 1997: Prize-Winning Aborigine Novelist Revealed as a Fraud, 852

Sept. 26, 2000: Gymnast Andreea Răducan Loses Her Olympic Gold Medal Because of Drugs, 916

AUSTRIA

Mar. 3, 1986: Former U.N. Secretary-General Kurt Waldheim's Nazi Past Is Revealed, 669

BELGIUM

Nov. 15, 1908: Belgium Confiscates Congo Free State from King Leopold II, 31

July 16, 1951: Belgium's Disgraced King Leopold III Abdicates, 276

Aug. 16, 1996: Belgian Media Reveal How Police Bungled Serial Murder Case, 840

Dec. 23, 1998: Prominent Belgians Are Sentenced in Agusta-Dassault Corruption Scandal, 889

CANADA

1928-1929: Actor Is Suspected of Falsely Claiming to Be an American Indian, 130

Mar. 21, 1928: Alberta Government Sterilizes Thousands Deemed Genetically and Mentally Unfit, 133

July 10, 1934: Sex Scandal Forces Resignation of Alberta Premier Brownlee, 176

Mar. 4, 1966: Munsinger Sex and Spy Scandal Rocks Canada, 377

Sept. 17, 1985: Media Allege Canadian Officials Allowed Sale of Rancid Tuna, 660

Nov. 18, 1995: Former Canadian Premier Brian Mulroney Is Exposed in Airbus Scandal, 830

Nov. 26, 1997: Canadian Health Commissioner Releases Report on Tainted Blood, 868

Mar. 4, 1999: Quebec Offers Support for Abused Duplessis Orphans, 892

May 7, 1999-Mar. 2, 2001: Ethics Counselor Exonerates Canadian Prime Minister Jean Chrétien, 898

Aug., 2002: Immunologist Resigns After Being Accused of Falsifying Research, 977

Summer, 2006-Mar. 16, 2007: China Recalls Pet Food That Has Killed Thousands of American Pets, 1097

CARIBBEAN. *See* **CENTRAL AND SOUTH AMERICA**

CENTRAL AFRICAN REPUBLIC

Oct. 10, 1979: French President Giscard d'Estaing Is Accused of Taking a Bribe, 550

CENTRAL AND SOUTH AMERICA

Feb. 3, 1975: Honduras's "Bananagate" Bribery Scandal Leads to Executive's Suicide, 471

Nov. 13, 1986-May 4, 1989: Iran-Contra Weapons Scandal Taints Reagan's Administration, 676

July 1, 1994: Soccer Star Diego Maradona Is Expelled from World Cup, 815

Feb. 28, 1995: Former Mexican President Carlos Salinas's Brother Is Arrested for Murder, 824

Sept., 2000: American Scientists Are Accused of Starting a Measles Epidemic in the Amazon, 910

Aug. 27, 2001: Little League Baseball Star Danny Almonte Is Found to Be Overage, 942

Oct. 22, 2006: Chilean Politicians Use Community Funds for Personal Campaigns, 1121

CHILE

Oct. 22, 2006: Chilean Politicians Use Community Funds for Personal Campaigns, 1121

CHINA

Summer, 2006-Mar. 16, 2007: China Recalls Pet Food That Has Killed Thousands of American Pets, 1097

CONGO, DEMOCRATIC REPUBLIC OF THE

Nov. 15, 1908: Belgium Confiscates Congo Free State from King Leopold II, 31

CZECH REPUBLIC

Jan. 20, 1933: Hedy Lamarr Appears Nude in the Czech Film *Exstase*, 163

DENMARK

Dec. 1, 1952: George Jorgensen Becomes Christine Jorgensen, 289

Sept. 30, 2005: Danish Newspaper's Prophet Muhammad Cartoons Stir Violent Protests, 1075

DOMINICAN REPUBLIC

Aug. 27, 2001: Little League Baseball Star Danny Almonte Is Found to Be Overage, 942

EGYPT

Aug. 31, 1997: Princess Diana Dies in a Car Crash, 861

ENGLAND

Mar. 2, 1906: Psychoanalyst Ernest Jones Is Accused of Molesting Mentally Disabled Children, 12

1907: Elinor Glyn's Novel *Three Weeks* Shocks Readers, 25

Jan., 1913: British Prime Minister's Staff Is Investigated for Insider Trading, 43

Apr. 2, 1915: Players Fix Liverpool-Manchester United Soccer Match, 55

May, 1915: British Government Falls Because of Munitions Shortages and Military Setbacks, 58

June 22, 1922: British Prime Minister David Lloyd George Is Accused of Selling Honors, 83

Oct. 25, 1924: Forged Communist Letter Brings Down British Government, 105

July, 1925: *Nosferatu* Is Found to Have Violated *Dracula* Copyright, 111

May 20, 1936: British Cabinet Member Resigns After Budget Information Leak, 181

Dec. 10, 1936: King Edward VIII Abdicates to Marry an American Divorcée, 187

Oct. 11-22, 1937: Duke and Duchess of Windsor Visit Nazi Germany, 196

Nov. 21, 1953: Piltdown Man Is Revealed to Be a Hoax, 292

Dec. 12, 1957: Rock Star Jerry Lee Lewis Marries Thirteen-Year-Old Cousin, 313

Sept. 12, 1962: British Civil Servant Is Arrested for Spying, 347

Mar. 2-Sept. 25, 1963: John Profumo Affair Rocks British Government, 355

June 22, 1972: Police Arrest Architect John Poulson for Bribery and Fraud, 431

Nov. 20, 1974: British Politician John Stonehouse Fakes His Suicide, 468

Aug. 4, 1978: British Politician Jeremy Thorpe Is Charged with Attempted Murder, 531

Oct. 14, 1983: British Cabinet Secretary Parkinson Resigns After His Secretary Becomes Pregnant, 631

1985-1986: Westland Affair Shakes Prime Minister Thatcher's Government, 645

July 25, 1987: Novelist-Politician Jeffrey Archer Wins Libel Trial Against the *Daily Star*, 696

Dec. 3, 1989: Martin Luther King, Jr.'s, Doctoral-Thesis Plagiarism Is Revealed, 739

Dec. 18, 1989: Prince Charles's Intimate Phone Conversation with Camilla Parker Bowles Is Taped, 745

Aug. 27, 1990: Guinness Four Are Found Guilty of Share-Trading Fraud, 753

Aug. 23, 1992: Princess Diana's Phone Conversation with Her Lover Is Made Public, 789

Sept. 24, 1992: British Cabinet Member David Mellor Resigns over Romantic Affair, 792

Jan. 5, 1994: British Cabinet Member Resigns After Fathering a Child Out of Wedlock, 798

Aug. 31, 1997: Princess Diana Dies in a Car Crash, 861

Jan. 30, 2001: Liverpool Children's Hospital Collects Body Parts Without Authorization, 927

Sept. 28, 2002: British Politician Reveals Her Affair with Prime Minister John Major, 983

Jan. 21, 2006: British Politician Resigns After Gay-Sex Orgy, 1084

Apr. 26, 2006: Britain's Deputy Prime Minister Admits Affair with Secretary, 1089

Nov. 23, 2006: Former Russian Security Service Officer Dies from Radiation Poisoning, 1132

EUROPE

1906-1909: Emperor William II's Homosexual "Circle" Scandalizes Germany, 9

Mar. 2, 1906: Psychoanalyst Ernest Jones Is Accused of Molesting Mentally Disabled Children, 12

July 12, 1906: French Court Declares Alfred Dreyfus Innocent of Treason, 19

1907: Elinor Glyn's Novel *Three Weeks* Shocks Readers, 25

Nov. 15, 1908: Belgium Confiscates Congo Free State from King Leopold II, 31

1909-1916: Dancer Isadora Duncan Begins Affair with Millionaire Heir, 34

1910: Nobelist Marie Curie Has Affair with Physicist Paul Langevin, 37

Jan., 1913: British Prime Minister's Staff Is Investigated for Insider Trading, 43

Apr. 2, 1915: Players Fix Liverpool-Manchester United Soccer Match, 55

May, 1915: British Government Falls Because of Munitions Shortages and Military Setbacks, 58

Mar. 26, 1922: Hindemith's Opera *Sancta Susanna* Depicts a Nun's Sexual Desires, 76

June 22, 1922: British Prime Minister David Lloyd George Is Accused of Selling Honors, 83

Oct. 25, 1924: Forged Communist Letter Brings Down British Government, 105

July, 1925: *Nosferatu* Is Found to Have Violated *Dracula* Copyright, 111

June 6, 1929: Luis Buñuel's *Un Chien Andalou* Shocks Parisian Audience, 136

Nov., 1929: Banque Oustric et Cie Failure Prompts French Inquiry, 139

1930: Liberia Is Accused of Selling Its Own Citizens into Slavery, 142

Dec. 3, 1930: Surrealist Film *L'Âge d'or* Provokes French Rioting, 147

Jan. 20, 1933: Hedy Lamarr Appears Nude in the Czech Film *Exstase*, 163

Mar. 31, 1933: *New York Times* Reporter Denies Reports of a Soviet Famine, 167

Jan. 8, 1934-Jan. 17, 1936: Stavisky's Fraudulent Schemes Rock French Government, 170

May 20, 1936: British Cabinet Member Resigns After Budget Information Leak, 181

Dec. 10, 1936: King Edward VIII Abdicates to Marry an American Divorcée, 187

Oct. 11-22, 1937: Duke and Duchess of Windsor Visit Nazi Germany, 196

Apr. 22, 1942: French Prime Minister Pierre Laval Wants Germany to Win World War II, 209

Feb. 23, 1943: Irish Orphan School Fire Kills Thirty-five Girls, 217

May 9, 1945: Norwegian Politician Quisling Is Arrested for Nazi Collaboration, 226

May 26, 1945: Norwegian Writer Knut Hamsun Is Arrested for Treason, 229

Aug. 14, 1945: French War Hero Pétain Is Convicted of Nazi Collaboration, 232

Dec. 14, 1945: Poet Ezra Pound Is Charged with Treason and Institutionalized, 236

May 27, 1949: Actor Rita Hayworth Marries Aly Khan After Adulterous Affair, 254

Aug. 26, 1949: Viet Minh Broadcasts French General's Damaging Report, 257

Feb. 7, 1950: Swedish Film Star Ingrid Bergman Has a Child Out of Wedlock, 263

July 16, 1951: Belgium's Disgraced King Leopold III Abdicates, 276

Dec. 1, 1952: George Jorgensen Becomes Christine Jorgensen, 289

Nov. 21, 1953: Piltdown Man Is Revealed to Be a Hoax, 292

1956-1962: Prescription Thalidomide Causes Widespread Birth Disorders, 301

June, 1956: George F. Kennan Proves Russian Sisson Documents Are Fakes, 307

Dec. 12, 1957: Rock Star Jerry Lee Lewis Marries Thirteen-Year-Old Cousin, 313

Sept. 12, 1962: British Civil Servant Is Arrested for Spying, 347

Oct. 26, 1962: West German Police Raid *Der Spiegel* Magazine Offices, 349

Feb. 23, 1963: Play Accuses Pope Pius XII of Complicity in the Holocaust, 353

Mar. 2-Sept. 25, 1963: John Profumo Affair Rocks British Government, 355

Oct. 29, 1965: Moroccan Politician Mehdi Ben Barka Disappears in Paris, 374

Mar. 4, 1966: Munsinger Sex and Spy Scandal Rocks Canada, 377

May 28, 1970: Irish Politicians Are Tried for Conspiring to Import Weapons, 413

June 22, 1972: Police Arrest Architect John Poulson for Bribery and Fraud, 431

May 20, 1974: French Cardinal Daniélou Dies in a Prostitute's House, 456

Nov. 20, 1974: British Politician John Stonehouse Fakes His Suicide, 468

Nov. 9, 1976: German Generals Must Retire for Supporting a Neo-Nazi Pilot, 503

Feb. 1, 1978: Roman Polanski Flees the United States to Avoid Rape Trial, 522

Aug. 4, 1978: British Politician Jeremy Thorpe Is Charged with Attempted Murder, 531

Oct. 10, 1979: French President Giscard d'Estaing Is Accused of Taking a Bribe, 550

May 23, 1981: Italian Justice Minister Resigns Because of Crime Connection, 591

Aug. 6, 1982: Banco Ambrosiano Collapses Amid Criminal Accusations, 606

Oct. 19, 1982: Car Manufacturer John De Lorean Is Arrested in a Drug Sting, 609

Apr. 25, 1983: German Magazine Publishes Faked Hitler Diaries, 618

Oct. 14, 1983: British Cabinet Secretary Parkinson Resigns After His Secretary Becomes Pregnant, 631

1985-1986: Westland Affair Shakes Prime Minister Thatcher's Government, 645

Aug. 19, 1985: West German Counterintelligence Chief Defects to East Germany, 657

Mar. 3, 1986: Former U.N. Secretary-General Kurt Waldheim's Nazi Past Is Revealed, 669

July 25, 1987: Novelist-Politician Jeffrey Archer Wins Libel Trial Against the *Daily Star*, 696

Dec. 3, 1989: Martin Luther King, Jr.'s, Doctoral-Thesis Plagiarism Is Revealed, 739

Dec. 15-25, 1989: Harassment of a Christian Minister Sparks the Romanian Revolution, 742

Dec. 18, 1989: Prince Charles's Intimate Phone Conversation with Camilla Parker Bowles Is Taped, 745

Aug. 27, 1990: Guinness Four Are Found Guilty of Share-Trading Fraud, 753

May 6, 1992: Irish Bishop Eamonn Casey's Romantic Affair Leads to His Resignation, 779

Aug. 23, 1992: Princess Diana's Phone Conversation with Her Lover Is Made Public, 789

Sept. 24, 1992: British Cabinet Member David Mellor Resigns over Romantic Affair, 792

Jan. 5, 1994: British Cabinet Member Resigns After Fathering a Child Out of Wedlock, 798

Aug. 16, 1996: Belgian Media Reveal How Police Bungled Serial Murder Case, 840

Nov. 3, 1996: Car Crash Reveals Depth of Government Corruption in Turkey, 843

Jan., 1997: Pyramid Investment Schemes Cause Albanian Government to Fall, 846

June 25, 1997: Swiss Banks Admit to Holding Accounts of Holocaust Victims, 858

Aug. 31, 1997: Princess Diana Dies in a Car Crash, 861

Apr., 1998: Scottish Historian Is Charged with Plagiarism, 879

Dec. 23, 1998: Prominent Belgians Are Sentenced in Agusta-Dassault Corruption Scandal, 889

Dec., 2000: Sexual Abuse of Children in France Leads to the Outreau Affair, 922

2001: Clearstream Financial Clearinghouse Is Accused of Fraud and Money Laundering, 925

Jan. 30, 2001: Liverpool Children's Hospital Collects Body Parts Without Authorization, 927

Feb. 18, 2001: CIA Agent Robert Hanssen Is Arrested for Spying for the Russians, 931

Feb. 11, 2002: French Judge Admits Favoring Russian Figure Skaters in Winter Olympics, 962

Sept. 28, 2002: British Politician Reveals Her Affair with Prime Minister John Major, 983

May 21, 2003: Sexually Provocative Film *The Brown Bunny* Premieres at Cannes Film Festival, 1004

Jan. 27, 2005: German Soccer Referee Admits to Fixing Games for Money, 1055

Sept. 30, 2005: Danish Newspaper's Prophet Muhammad Cartoons Stir Violent Protests, 1075

Jan. 21, 2006: British Politician Resigns After Gay-Sex Orgy, 1084

Apr. 26, 2006: Britain's Deputy Prime Minister Admits Affair with Secretary, 1089

May 4, 2006: Media Uncover Match-Fixing in Italian Soccer, 1092

Aug. 12, 2006: Novelist Günter Grass Admits to Youthful Nazi Ties, 1109

Nov. 23, 2006: Former Russian Security Service Officer Dies from Radiation Poisoning, 1132

FRANCE

July 12, 1906: French Court Declares Alfred Dreyfus Innocent of Treason, 19

1909-1916: Dancer Isadora Duncan Begins Affair with Millionaire Heir, 34

1910: Nobelist Marie Curie Has Affair with Physicist Paul Langevin, 37

May, 1915: British Government Falls Because of Munitions Shortages and Military Setbacks, 58

June 6, 1929: Luis Buñuel's *Un Chien Andalou* Shocks Parisian Audience, 136

Nov., 1929: Banque Oustric et Cie Failure Prompts French Inquiry, 139

Dec. 3, 1930: Surrealist Film *L'Âge d'or* Provokes French Rioting, 147

Jan. 8, 1934-Jan. 17, 1936: Stavisky's Fraudulent Schemes Rock French Government, 170

Apr. 22, 1942: French Prime Minister Pierre Laval Wants Germany to Win World War II, 209

Aug. 14, 1945: French War Hero Pétain Is Convicted of Nazi Collaboration, 232

May 27, 1949: Actor Rita Hayworth Marries Aly Khan After Adulterous Affair, 254

Aug. 26, 1949: Viet Minh Broadcasts French General's Damaging Report, 257

Oct. 29, 1965: Moroccan Politician Mehdi Ben Barka Disappears in Paris, 374

May 20, 1974: French Cardinal Daniélou Dies in a Prostitute's House, 456

Feb. 1, 1978: Roman Polanski Flees the United States to Avoid Rape Trial, 522

Oct. 10, 1979: French President Giscard d'Estaing Is Accused of Taking a Bribe, 550

July 10, 1985: French Secret Service Sinks the Greenpeace Ship *Rainbow Warrior*, 651

Aug. 31, 1997: Princess Diana Dies in a Car Crash, 861

Dec., 2000: Sexual Abuse of Children in France Leads to the Outreau Affair, 922

Feb. 11, 2002: French Judge Admits Favoring Russian Figure Skaters in Winter Olympics, 962

May 21, 2003: Sexually Provocative Film *The Brown Bunny* Premieres at Cannes Film Festival, 1004

GERMANY

1906-1909: Emperor William II's Homosexual "Circle" Scandalizes Germany, 9

Mar. 26, 1922: Hindemith's Opera *Sancta Susanna* Depicts a Nun's Sexual Desires, 76

July, 1925: *Nosferatu* Is Found to Have Violated *Dracula* Copyright, 111

Oct. 11-22, 1937: Duke and Duchess of Windsor Visit Nazi Germany, 196

1956-1962: Prescription Thalidomide Causes Widespread Birth Disorders, 301

Oct. 26, 1962: West German Police Raid *Der Spiegel* Magazine Offices, 349

Feb. 23, 1963: Play Accuses Pope Pius XII of Complicity in the Holocaust, 353

Nov. 9, 1976: German Generals Must Retire for Supporting a Neo-Nazi Pilot, 503

Apr. 25, 1983: German Magazine Publishes Faked Hitler Diaries, 618

Aug. 19, 1985: West German Counterintelligence Chief Defects to East Germany, 657

Jan. 27, 2005: German Soccer Referee Admits to Fixing Games for Money, 1055

Aug. 12, 2006: Novelist Günter Grass Admits to Youthful Nazi Ties, 1109

GREAT BRITAIN. *See* **ENGLAND; SCOTLAND**

HONDURAS

Feb. 3, 1975: Honduras's "Bananagate" Bribery Scandal Leads to Executive's Suicide, 471

IRAN

Nov. 13, 1986-May 4, 1989: Iran-Contra Weapons Scandal Taints Reagan's Administration, 676

IRAQ

July 14, 2003: Columnist Robert Novak Leaks the Name of CIA Operative Valerie Plame, 1010

Apr. 28, 2004: CBS Broadcasts Photos of Abused and Tortured Prisoners at Abu Ghraib, 1034

IRELAND. *See also* **NORTHERN IRELAND**

Feb. 23, 1943: Irish Orphan School Fire Kills Thirty-five Girls, 217

May 6, 1992: Irish Bishop Eamonn Casey's Romantic Affair Leads to His Resignation, 779

Italy

Dec. 14, 1945: Poet Ezra Pound Is Charged with Treason and Institutionalized, 236

Feb. 7, 1950: Swedish Film Star Ingrid Bergman Has a Child Out of Wedlock, 263

May 23, 1981: Italian Justice Minister Resigns Because of Crime Connection, 591

Aug. 6, 1982: Banco Ambrosiano Collapses Amid Criminal Accusations, 606

May 4, 2006: Media Uncover Match-Fixing in Italian Soccer, 1092

Japan

Fall, 1969-Winter, 1971: Japanese Baseball Players Are Implicated in Game Fixing, 398

Feb. 4, 1976: Lockheed Is Implicated in Bribing Foreign Officials, 482

June, 1988-June, 1989: Insider-Trading Scandal Rocks Japanese Government, 714

Aug. 10, 1989: Japanese Prime Minister Sosuke Resigns After Affair with a Geisha, 733

Nov. 5, 2000: Japanese Amateur Archaeologist's "Discoveries" Are Proven Fakes, 919

May 28, 2007: Japanese Politician Charged with Corruption Hangs Himself, 1145

Kenya

Late 1955: British Atrocities in Kenya's Mau Mau Rebellion Are Revealed, 298

Liberia

1930: Liberia Is Accused of Selling Its Own Citizens into Slavery, 142

Nov. 17, 2005: Liberian Workers Sue Bridgestone Firestone over Slave Labor, 1078

Libya

Late July, 1980: President's Brother, Billy Carter, Registers as a Paid Agent for Libya, 571

Luxembourg

2001: Clearstream Financial Clearinghouse Is Accused of Fraud and Money Laundering, 925

Mexico

May-June, 1926: Evangelist Aimee Semple McPherson Claims She Was Kidnapped, 115

Feb. 28, 1995: Former Mexican President Carlos Salinas's Brother Is Arrested for Murder, 824

Middle East. *See also* Africa; Asia

Oct. 29, 1965: Moroccan Politician Mehdi Ben Barka Disappears in Paris, 374

Nov. 13, 1986-May 4, 1989: Iran-Contra Weapons Scandal Taints Reagan's Administration, 676

Nov. 3, 1996: Car Crash Reveals Depth of Government Corruption in Turkey, 843

Aug. 31, 1997: Princess Diana Dies in a Car Crash, 861

July 14, 2003: Columnist Robert Novak Leaks the Name of CIA Operative Valerie Plame, 1010

Apr. 28, 2004: CBS Broadcasts Photos of Abused and Tortured Prisoners at Abu Ghraib, 1034

Morocco

Oct. 29, 1965: Moroccan Politician Mehdi Ben Barka Disappears in Paris, 374

New Zealand

July 10, 1985: French Secret Service Sinks the Greenpeace Ship *Rainbow Warrior*, 651

July, 2002: Journalist Alleges Release of Genetically Modified Corn Seeds in New Zealand, 974

Sept. 17, 2006: New Zealand Prime Minister's Husband Is "Outed" as Gay, 1112

Nicaragua

Nov. 13, 1986-May 4, 1989: Iran-Contra Weapons Scandal Taints Reagan's Administration, 676

North America. *See* Canada; United States

Northern Ireland

May 28, 1970: Irish Politicians Are Tried for Conspiring to Import Weapons, 413

Oct. 19, 1982: Car Manufacturer John De Lorean Is Arrested in a Drug Sting, 609

NORWAY

May 9, 1945: Norwegian Politician Quisling Is Arrested for Nazi Collaboration, 226

May 26, 1945: Norwegian Writer Knut Hamsun Is Arrested for Treason, 229

PACIFIC ISLANDS. *See* **AUSTRALASIA**

PAKISTAN

May 27, 1949: Actor Rita Hayworth Marries Aly Khan After Adulterous Affair, 254

Jan. 15, 2005: Iqbal Riza Resigns from the United Nations in Oil-for-Food Scandal, 1053

PHILIPPINES

May 11, 1982: Philippine President Marcos Forces the Entire Supreme Court to Resign, 600

Aug. 21, 1983: Filipino Opposition Leader Aquino Is Assassinated on Return Home, 628

ROMANIA

Dec. 15-25, 1989: Harassment of a Christian Minister Sparks the Romanian Revolution, 742

Sept. 26, 2000: Gymnast Andreea Răducan Loses Her Olympic Gold Medal Because of Drugs, 916

RUSSIA. *See also* **SOVIET UNION**

Mar. 31, 1933: *New York Times* Reporter Denies Reports of a Soviet Famine, 167

June, 1956: George F. Kennan Proves Russian Sisson Documents Are Fakes, 307

Sept. 12, 1962: British Civil Servant Is Arrested for Spying, 347

Mar. 4, 1966: Munsinger Sex and Spy Scandal Rocks Canada, 377

Feb. 18, 2001: CIA Agent Robert Hanssen Is Arrested for Spying for the Russians, 931

Feb. 11, 2002: French Judge Admits Favoring Russian Figure Skaters in Winter Olympics, 962

Nov. 23, 2006: Former Russian Security Service Officer Dies from Radiation Poisoning, 1132

SCOTLAND

Apr., 1998: Scottish Historian Is Charged with Plagiarism, 879

SOUTH AFRICA

June 4, 1979: South African President B. J. Vorster Resigns in Muldergate Scandal, 543

SOUTH AMERICA. *See* **CENTRAL AND SOUTH AMERICA**

SOUTH KOREA

1976-1977: U.S. Congress Members Are Implicated in Koreagate Scandal, 479

June 30, 2001: Korean Religious Teacher Jung Myung Seok Is Charged with Rape, 939

May 12, 2006: Scientist Is Indicted for Faking His Research on Creating Stem Cells, 1094

SOVIET UNION. *See also* **RUSSIA**

Mar. 31, 1933: *New York Times* Reporter Denies Reports of a Soviet Famine, 167

Sept. 12, 1962: British Civil Servant Is Arrested for Spying, 347

SPAIN

1930: Liberia Is Accused of Selling Its Own Citizens into Slavery, 142

SWEDEN

Feb. 7, 1950: Swedish Film Star Ingrid Bergman Has a Child Out of Wedlock, 263

SWITZERLAND

1930: Liberia Is Accused of Selling Its Own Citizens into Slavery, 142

1956-1962: Prescription Thalidomide Causes Widespread Birth Disorders, 301

June 25, 1997: Swiss Banks Admit to Holding Accounts of Holocaust Victims, 858

TONGA

1976: Peace Corps Conceals Murder of Volunteer in Tonga, 476

TURKEY
Nov. 3, 1996: Car Crash Reveals Depth of Government Corruption in Turkey, 843

UNITED KINGDOM. *See* **ENGLAND; NORTHERN IRELAND; SCOTLAND**

UNITED STATES
1904: Theodore Roosevelt Is Accused of Accepting Corporate Funds, 1
Jan. 23, 1904: Senator Joseph R. Burton Is Convicted of Bribery, 4
Dec., 1904: Boston Alderman Is Reelected While in Jail for Fraud, 6
June 25, 1906: Millionaire Heir Murders Architect Stanford White, 16
Dec. 8, 1906: Former U.S. Senator Arthur Brown Is Murdered by Lover, 22
1907: Elinor Glyn's Novel *Three Weeks* Shocks Readers, 25
June 13, 1907: San Francisco Mayor Schmitz Is Found Guilty of Extortion, 28
Mar. 25, 1911: Nearly 150 Workers Die in Triangle Shirtwaist Factory Fire, 40
Jan. 13, 1913: Federal Judge Is Impeached for Profiting from His Office, 46
Feb. 17-Mar. 15, 1913: Armory Modern Art Show Scandalizes the Public, 49
May 13, 1913: Boxer Jack Johnson Is Imprisoned for Abetting Prostitution, 52
July 27, 1917: Millionaire Socialite Dies Under Suspicious Circumstances, 60
1919-1920: Ponzi Schemes Are Revealed as Investment Frauds, 63
Sept. 21, 1919: White Sox Players Conspire to Lose World Series in "Black Sox" Scandal, 66
July 19, 1921: U.S. Senate Rebukes Navy in Homosexuality Investigation, 70
Feb. 1, 1922: Director Taylor's Murder Ruins Mabel Normand's Acting Career, 73
Apr. 12, 1922: Film Star Fatty Arbuckle Is Acquitted of Manslaughter, 79
Jan. 18, 1923: Actor Wallace Reid's Death in Drug Rehab Shakes Film Industry, 86
Mar. 2, 1923: U.S. Senate Investigates Veterans Bureau Chief for Fraud, 89
May 30, 1923: U.S. Attorney General Harry M. Daugherty's Aide Commits Suicide, 92
Oct. 22, 1923: U.S. Senate Begins Hearings on Teapot Dome Oil Leases, 95
Jan. 1, 1924: Film Star Mabel Normand's Chauffeur Shoots Millionaire Courtland S. Dines, 100
May 12, 1924: Kentucky Congressman John W. Langley Is Convicted of Violating the Volstead Act, 103
Nov. 19, 1924: Film Producer Thomas H. Ince Dies After Weekend on Hearst's Yacht, 108
May-June, 1926: Evangelist Aimee Semple McPherson Claims She Was Kidnapped, 115
Dec. 26, 1926: Ty Cobb and Tris Speaker Are Accused of Fixing Baseball Games, 118
1927: Mae West's Play About Gays Is Banned on Broadway, 122
1927: President Warren G. Harding's Lover Publishes Tell-All Memoir, 124
Early 1928: Joseph P. Kennedy Begins an Affair with Gloria Swanson, 127
1928-1929: Actor Is Suspected of Falsely Claiming to Be an American Indian, 130
May, 1930: Postmaster's Division of Airmail Routes Creates a Scandal, 144
Mar. 30, 1931: "Scottsboro Boys" Are Railroaded Through Rape Trials, 150
1932: Insull Utilities Trusts Collapse Prompts New Federal Regulation, 154
July 28, 1932: U.S. Troops Drive World War I Veterans from Washington, 156
Sept. 4, 1932: Film Star Jean Harlow's Husband Is an Apparent Suicide, 160
May 16, 1934: General Douglas MacArthur Sues Newspaper Columnist for Libel, 173
Dec. 16, 1935: Film Star Thelma Todd's Death Cannot Be Explained, 178
Summer, 1936: Film Star Mary Astor's Diary Becomes a Public Sensation, 184
Mar. 17, 1937: Atherton Report Exposes San Francisco Police Corruption, 191
Sept.-Oct., 1937: Prescription Elixir Causes More than One Hundred Deaths, 193
May 22, 1939: Kansas City's Boss Pendergast Pleads Guilty to Income Tax Evasion, 199

Feb. 6, 1942: Film Star Errol Flynn Is Acquitted of Rape, 202

Feb. 19, 1942: President Roosevelt Orders Internment of Japanese Americans, 205

Jan. 14, 1943: Film Star Frances Farmer Is Jailed and Institutionalized, 214

June 4, 1943: Actor Charles Chaplin Is Sued for Paternity, 220

Dec. 14, 1945: Poet Ezra Pound Is Charged with Treason and Institutionalized, 236

Nov. 23, 1946: Tennis Star Bill Tilden Is Arrested for Lewd Behavior with a Minor, 239

Spring, 1947: Baseball Manager Leo Durocher Is Suspended for Gambling Ties, 242

July 5, 1948: Actor Carole Landis Commits Suicide During Affair with Rex Harrison, 245

Aug. 4, 1948: Columnist Drew Pearson Exposes Congressman's Corruption, 248

Aug. 31, 1948: Film Star Robert Mitchum Is Arrested for Drug Possession, 251

Jan. 21, 1950: Alger Hiss Is Convicted of Perjury, 259

Feb. 9, 1950: U.S. Senator Joseph McCarthy Launches Communist Witch Hunt, 266

May 3, 1950: U.S. Senate Committee Begins Investigating Organized Crime, 270

Jan. 17, 1951: College Basketball Players Begin Shaving Points for Money, 274

Nov. 16, 1951: Federal Tax Official Resigns After Accepting Bribes, 279

Sept. 19, 1952: Actor Charles Chaplin Cannot Reenter the United States, 283

Sept. 23, 1952: Richard Nixon Denies Taking Illegal Campaign Contributions, 286

Dec. 1, 1952: George Jorgensen Becomes Christine Jorgensen, 289

May, 1955: Scandal Magazine Reveals Actor Rory Calhoun's Criminal Past, 295

June, 1956: George F. Kennan Proves Russian Sisson Documents Are Fakes, 307

June 25, 1956: President Truman's Appointments Secretary Is Convicted of Tax Conspiracy, 310

Dec. 12, 1957: Rock Star Jerry Lee Lewis Marries Thirteen-Year-Old Cousin, 313

Apr. 4, 1958: Actor Lana Turner's Daughter Kills Turner's Gangster Lover, 317

Sept. 22, 1958: President Eisenhower's Chief of Staff Resigns for Influence Selling, 320

May, 1959: Teamsters Leader Dave Beck Is Convicted of Tax Fraud, 323

Nov. 2, 1959: Charles Van Doren Admits to Being Fed Answers on Television Quiz Show, 326

Feb. 7, 1960: President Kennedy's Romantic Affair Links Him to Organized Crime, 329

Feb. 8, 1960: U.S. Congress Investigates Payola in Pop Music Industry, 332

Mar. 14, 1960: FCC Chairman John C. Doerfer Resigns for Accepting Gifts from Networks, 335

July, 1961: Psychologist Stanley Milgram Begins Obedience-to-Authority Experiments, 338

Mar. 29, 1962: Billie Sol Estes Is Arrested for Corporate Fraud, 341

May 19, 1962: Marilyn Monroe Sings "Happy Birthday, Mr. President," 344

July 2, 1963: Muslim Leader Elijah Muhammad Is Sued for Paternity, 359

Oct. 7, 1963: Vice President Lyndon B. Johnson Aide Resigns over Crime Connections, 365

Mar. 13, 1964: Kitty Genovese Dies as Her Cries for Help Are Ignored, 369

Oct. 7, 1964: President Lyndon Johnson's Aide Is Arrested in Gay-Sex Sting, 371

Mar. 1, 1967: Adam Clayton Powell, Jr., Is Excluded from Congress, 380

June 23, 1967: Senator Thomas J. Dodd Is Censured for Misappropriating Funds, 384

Sept. 5, 1967: Socialite Nancy Wakeman Shoots Her Politician-Husband, 386

Nov. 28, 1967: Investor Louis Wolfson Is Convicted of Selling Stock Illegally, 389

May 9, 1969: Supreme Court Justice Abe Fortas Is Accused of Bribery, 391

July 18, 1969: Senator Edward Kennedy's Driving Accident Kills Mary Jo Kopechne, 394

Dec. 30, 1969: United Mine Workers Leader Joseph Yablonski Is Murdered, 404

1970: Study of Anonymous Gay Sex Leads to Ethics Scandal, 407

May 4, 1970: National Guardsmen Kill Protesting Kent State Students, 410

June 13, 1971: *New York Times* Publishes the Pentagon Papers, 416

Aug. 20, 1971: Abusive Role-Playing Ends Stanford Prison Experiment, 420

Jan. 28, 1972: Clifford Irving Admits Faking Howard Hughes Memoirs, 422

June 17, 1972-Aug. 9, 1974: Watergate Break-in Leads to President Nixon's Resignation, 425

July 25, 1972: Newspaper Breaks Story of Abuses in Tuskegee Syphilis Study, 437

July 31, 1972: Thomas F. Eagleton Withdraws from Vice Presidential Race, 440

Aug. 19, 1973: Cheating Scandal Shocks Soap Box Derby, 444

Oct. 10, 1973: Spiro T. Agnew Resigns Vice Presidency in Disgrace, 447

Apr. 15, 1974: Kidnapped Heir Patty Hearst Helps Rob a Bank, 450

May 14, 1974: *Washington Post* Reveals That the Nixons Received Jewelry Gifts, 453

Summer, 1974: Dalkon Shield Contraceptive Is Removed from the Market, 459

Oct. 7, 1974: Congressman Wilbur D. Mills's Stripper Affair Leads to His Downfall, 462

Oct. 25, 1974: Evangelist Billy James Hargis Resigns College Presidency During Gay-Sex Scandal, 465

Feb. 3, 1975: Honduras's "Bananagate" Bribery Scandal Leads to Executive's Suicide, 471

Oct. 31, 1975: Buddhist Teacher Orders His Students to Remove Their Clothes, 474

1976-1977: U.S. Congress Members Are Implicated in Koreagate Scandal, 479

Feb. 4, 1976: Lockheed Is Implicated in Bribing Foreign Officials, 482

Mar. 21, 1976: Actor Claudine Longet Kills Ski Champion Vladimir Sabich, 485

Apr. 4, 1976: West Point Cadets Are Caught Cheating on Exams, 488

May 23, 1976: *Washington Post* Exposes Congressman Wayne L. Hays's Affair, 491

Sept. 1, 1976: Former Beatle George Harrison Loses Plagiarism Lawsuit, 494

Sept., 1976: Jimmy Carter Admits Committing Adultery in His Heart, 497

Oct. 4, 1976: Agriculture Secretary Earl Butz Resigns After Making Obscene Joke, 500

Jan., 1977: Singer Anita Bryant Campaigns Against Lesbian and Gay Rights, 506

Feb. 25, 1977: Film Producer David Begelman Is Found to Have Forged Checks, 509

Sept. 21, 1977: Carter Cabinet Member Resigns over Ethics Violations, 511

Sept. 23, 1977: Horse-Swapping Fraud Upsets Belmont Park Raceway, 514

1978: Actor Joan Crawford's Daughter Publishes Damning Memoir, *Mommie Dearest*, 517

1978: *Roots* Author Alex Haley Is Sued for Plagiarism, 520

Feb. 1, 1978: Roman Polanski Flees the United States to Avoid Rape Trial, 522

June 27, 1978: Evangelist Herbert W. Armstrong Excommunicates His Own Son, 525

July 23, 1978: Utah Millionaire Is Murdered by His Grandson, 528

Oct. 20, 1978: Firestone Recalls Millions of Defective Car Tires, 534

Jan. 26, 1979: Former Vice President Nelson Rockefeller Dies Mysteriously, 537

Apr. 18, 1979: Actor Lee Marvin Is Ordered to Pay Palimony to Former Lover, 540

Sept. 26, 1979: Love Canal Residents Sue Chemical Company, 546

Oct. 11, 1979: Senate Denounces Herman E. Talmadge for Money Laundering, 553

Nov. 29, 1979, and Jan. 31, 1983: Baseball Commissioner Suspends Mickey Mantle and Willie Mays for Casino Ties, 556

1980: Biographer Claims Actor Errol Flynn Was a Nazi Spy, 559

Feb. 2, 1980: Media Uncover FBI Sting Implicating Dozens of Lawmakers, 561

Mar. 10, 1980: Scarsdale Diet Doctor Is Killed by His Lover, 565

Apr. 27, 1980: Mobster's Arrest Reveals Point Shaving by Boston College Basketball Players, 568

Late July, 1980: President's Brother, Billy Carter, Registers as a Paid Agent for Libya, 571

July 28, 1980: Magazine Reveals Baseball Star Steve Garvey's Marital Problems, 574

Sept. 3, 1980: Congressman Bauman Is Arrested for Liaison with Teenage Boy, 577

Oct. 9, 1980: Bendix Executive Resigns Amid Rumors of an Affair, 580

Dec. 7, 1980: Rita Jenrette's "Diary of a Mad Congresswife" Scandalizes Washington, 582

Apr. 15, 1981: Janet Cooke Admits Fabricating Her Pulitzer Prize-Winning Feature, 585

Apr. 28, 1981: Tennis Star Billie Jean King Is Sued for Palimony, 588

May 29, 1981: Court Finds That Ford Ignored Pinto's Safety Problems, 594

Sept. 10, 1981: *Chicago Sun-Times* Reports That Cardinal Cody Diverted Church Funds, 597

July 20, 1982: Conservative Politician John G. Schmitz Is Found to Have Children Out of Wedlock, 603

Oct. 19, 1982: Car Manufacturer John De Lorean Is Arrested in a Drug Sting, 609

Dec., 1982: Julie Andrews and Blake Edwards Deny Being Gay, 612

Dec. 16, 1982: Congress Cites Environmental Protection Agency Chief for Contempt, 615

July 20, 1983: Congress Members Censured in House-Page Sex Scandal, 621

Aug. 12, 1983-July 27, 1990: McMartin Preschool Is Embroiled in Child-Abuse Case, 624

Jan. 25, 1984: Jesse Jackson Calls New York City "Hymietown," 633

May 2, 1984: E. F. Hutton Executives Plead Guilty to Fraud, 636

July 23, 1984: Vanessa Williams Is the First Miss America to Resign, 638

Dec. 22, 1984: Subway Vigilante Bernhard Goetz Shoots Four Black Youths, 641

May 7, 1985: Banker Jake Butcher Pleads Guilty to Fraud, 648

July 19, 1985: Mayflower Madam Pleads Guilty to Promoting Prostitution, 654

Oct. 23, 1985: Guru Bhagwan Shree Rajneesh Is Indicted for Immigration Fraud, 662

Feb. 28, 1986: Baseball Commissioner Peter Ueberroth Suspends Players for Cocaine Use, 666

Apr. 22, 1986: Faith Healer Peter Popoff Is Exposed as a Fraud, 673

Nov. 13, 1986-May 4, 1989: Iran-Contra Weapons Scandal Taints Reagan's Administration, 676

Jan. 22, 1987: Pennsylvania Politician Kills Himself at Televised Press Conference, 684

Feb. 25, 1987: NCAA Imposes "Death Penalty" on Southern Methodist University Football, 687

Mar. 19, 1987: Jim Bakker Resigns as Head of PTL Television Network, 690

Apr. 9, 1987: Bess Myerson Resigns as New York Commissioner of Cultural Affairs, 693

Sept. 23, 1987: Plagiarism Charges End Joe Biden's Presidential Campaign, 698

Nov. 28, 1987: Black Teenager Claims to Have Been Gang-Raped by Police Officers, 702

Dec. 1, 1987: Yale Scholar's Wartime Anti-Semitic Writings Are Revealed, 705

Jan. 15, 1988: ZZZZ Best Founder Is Indicted on Federal Fraud Charges, 708

Feb. 21, 1988: Evangelist Jimmy Swaggart Tearfully Confesses His Adultery, 711

July 18, 1988: Actor Rob Lowe Videotapes His Sexual Encounter with a Minor, 717

Sept. 19, 1988: Stephen Breuning Pleads Guilty to Medical Research Fraud, 720

Mar. 23, 1989: Scientists' "Cold Fusion" Claims Cannot Be Verified, 723

Mar. 29, 1989: Financier Michael Milken Is Indicted for Racketeering and Fraud, 726

May 31, 1989: Speaker of the House Jim Wright Resigns in Ethics Scandal, 730

Aug. 24, 1989: Pete Rose Is Banned from Baseball for Betting on Games, 735

Jan. 18, 1990: Washington, D.C., Mayor Marion Barry Is Arrested for Drug Use, 748

Mar., 1990: Menendez Brothers Are Arrested for Murdering Their Parents, 750

Nov. 19, 1990: Lip-Synching Duo Milli Vanilli Lose Grammy Award, 756

Mar. 30, 1991: William Kennedy Smith Is Accused of Rape, 759

Apr. 5, 1991: George W. Bush Is Investigated for Insider Trading, 762

July 26, 1991: Comedian Pee-wee Herman Is Arrested for Public Indecency, 765

Oct. 11-13, 1991: Justice Clarence Thomas's Confirmation Hearings Create a Scandal, 768

Jan. 13, 1992: Woody Allen Has Affair with Lover Mia Farrow's Adopted Daughter, 773

Apr. 15, 1992: Hotel Tycoon Leona Helmsley Enters Prison for Tax Evasion, 776

May 19, 1992: Amy Fisher Shoots Mary Jo Buttafuoco, 781

June 26, 1992: U.S. Navy Secretary Resigns in the Wake of Tailhook Sexual Assault Scandal, 784

June 23, 1993: Lorena Bobbitt Severs Her Husband's Penis, 795

Apr. 28, 1994: U.S. Naval Academy Expels Midshipmen for Cheating, 800

June 1, 1994: Congressman Dan Rostenkowski Is Indicted in House Post Office Scandal, 803

June 12, 1994: Double Murder Leads to Sensational O. J. Simpson Trial, 806

June 24, 1994: *Time* Magazine Cover Uses Altered O. J. Simpson Photo, 810

June 30, 1994: Tonya Harding Is Banned from Skating After Attack on Rival, 812

July 1, 1994: Soccer Star Diego Maradona Is Expelled from World Cup, 815

Aug. 5, 1994: Kenneth Starr Is Appointed to the Whitewater Investigation, 818

Aug. 21, 1994: Sex Scandal Forces Dismissal of NAACP Chief Benjamin Chavis, 821

June 27, 1995: Film Star Hugh Grant Is Arrested for Lewd Conduct, 827

Feb. 4, 1996: Whistle-Blower Reveals Tobacco Industry Corruption, 833

Spring, 1996: Physicist Publishes a Deliberately Fraudulent Article, 837

Feb. 26, 1997: Teacher Mary Kay Letourneau Is Arrested for Statutory Rape, 849

May 20, 1997: Air Force Prosecution of Female Officer for Adultery Reveals Double Standard, 855

Sept. 22, 1997: Sportscaster Marv Albert Is Tried for Sexual Assault, 865

Dec. 11, 1997: HUD Secretary Henry Cisneros Is Indicted for Lying to Federal Agents, 872

Jan. 17, 1998: President Bill Clinton Denies Sexual Affair with a White House Intern, 874

Apr. 7, 1998: Pop Singer George Michael Is Arrested for Lewd Conduct, 881

May, 1998: Police Corruption Is Revealed in Los Angeles's Rampart Division, 884

May 11, 1998: Journalist Stephen Glass Is Exposed as a Fraud, 887

May, 1999: Civil Rights Leader Jesse Jackson Fathers a Child Out of Wedlock, 895

Jan. 28, 2000: John Spano Is Sentenced for Fraudulent Purchase of Ice Hockey Team, 901

May 2, 2000: New York Mayor Rudy Giuliani's Extramarital Affair Is Revealed, 904

May 9, 2000: Former Louisiana Governor Edwin Edwards Is Convicted on Corruption Charges, 907

Sept. 19, 2000: Ex-gay Leader John Paulk Is Photographed Leaving a Gay Bar, 913

Feb. 18, 2001: CIA Agent Robert Hanssen Is Arrested for Spying for the Russians, 931

Apr. 30, 2001: Washington Intern Chandra Levy Disappears, 933

June 18, 2001: Award-Winning Historian Joseph J. Ellis Is Accused of Lying, 936

Dec. 2, 2001: Enron Bankruptcy Reveals Massive Financial Fraud, 945

Dec. 14, 2001: Notre Dame Football Coach Resigns for Falsifying His Résumé, 948

Jan. 4, 2002: Historian Stephen E. Ambrose Is Accused of Plagiarism, 951

Jan. 6, 2002: *Boston Globe* Reports on Child Sexual Abuse by Roman Catholic Priests, 954

Jan. 18, 2002: Historian Doris Kearns Goodwin Is Accused of Plagiarism, 959

Feb. 11, 2002: French Judge Admits Favoring Russian Figure Skaters in Winter Olympics, 962

Feb. 17, 2002: Rotting Human Bodies Are Found at Georgia Crematory, 964

Mar. 27, 2002: Georgia Basketball Coach Jim Harrick, Sr., Resigns over Fraud Allegations, 968

June 25, 2002: Internal Corruption Forces Adelphia Communications to Declare Bankruptcy, 971

Sept. 25, 2002: Inquiry Reveals That Physicist Jan Hendrik Schön Faked His Research, 980

Oct. 25, 2002: Historian Michael A. Bellesiles Resigns After Academic Fraud Accusations, 985

Dec. 5, 2002: Senator Trent Lott Praises Strom Thurmond's 1948 Presidential Campaign, 988

Jan. 2, 2003: E-mail Message Prompts Inquiry into Air Force Academy Sexual Assaults, 991

Mar. 2, 2003: U.S. National Security Agency Is Found to Have Spied on U.N. Officials, 995

Apr. 29, 2003: *New York Times* Reporter Jayson Blair Is Exposed as a Fraud, 998

May 3, 2003: University of Alabama Fires New Football Coach in Sex Scandal, 1002

July 1, 2003: Basketball Star Kobe Bryant Is Accused of Rape, 1008

July 14, 2003: Columnist Robert Novak Leaks the Name of CIA Operative Valerie Plame, 1010

Sept. 3, 2003: Mutual Fund Companies Are Implicated in Shady Trading Practices, 1013

Oct. 2, 2003: Newspaper Claims That Arnold Schwarzenegger Groped Women, 1016

Early Nov., 2003: Paris Hilton Sex-Tape Appears on the Web, 1019

Dec. 17, 2003: Senator Strom Thurmond's Biracial Daughter Is Revealed, 1022

Dec. 18, 2003: Pop Star Michael Jackson Is Charged with Child Molestation, 1025

Mar. 4, 2004: Former United Way Charity Chief Pleads Guilty to Embezzlement, 1028

Mar. 5, 2004: Martha Stewart Is Convicted in Insider-Trading Scandal, 1031

June 2, 2004: U.N. Report Reveals That Secretary-General Kofi Annan Dismissed Sexual Harassment Charges, 1039

Aug. 19, 2004: Blog "Outs" Antigay Congressman Edward Schrock, 1041

Sept. 8, 2004: *60 Minutes II* Reports on George W. Bush's Evasion of Wartime Duty, 1044

Oct. 13, 2004: Television Producer Files Sex Harassment Suit Against Bill O'Reilly, 1047

Oct. 14, 2004: Insurance Brokerage Marsh & McLennan Is Charged with Fraud, 1050

Jan. 15, 2005: Iqbal Riza Resigns from the United Nations in Oil-for-Food Scandal, 1053

Mar. 17, 2005: Former Baseball Star Mark McGwire Evades Congressional Questions on Steroid Use, 1058

June 22, 2005: U.S. Air Force Investigates Religious Intolerance at Its Academy, 1062

July 1, 2005: Federal Agents Raid Congressman Randall Cunningham's Home, 1064

Beginning Aug. 29, 2005: Government Incompetence Mars Hurricane Katrina Relief Efforts, 1068

Sept. 12, 2005: Westar Energy Executives Are Found Guilty of Looting Their Company, 1072

Nov. 17, 2005: Liberian Workers Sue Bridgestone Firestone over Slave Labor, 1078

Dec. 6, 2005: Spokane, Washington, Mayor Recalled in Gay-Sex Scandal, 1081

Mar. 14, 2006: Duke Lacrosse Players Are Accused of Gang Rape, 1086

Summer, 2006-Mar. 16, 2007: China Recalls Pet Food That Has Killed Thousands of American Pets, 1097

July 14, 2006: *New York Times* Exposes Grading Scandal at Auburn University, 1101

July 28, 2006: Actor Mel Gibson Is Caught Making Anti-Semitic Remarks, 1106

Sept. 18, 2006: *Newsweek* Reveals That Hewlett-Packard Spied on Its Own Board, 1114

Sept. 29, 2006: Congressman Mark Foley Resigns in Sex Scandal Involving a Teenage Page, 1118

Nov. 2, 2006: Evangelist Kent Hovind Is Convicted of Federal Tax Violations, 1123

Nov. 2, 2006: Male Escort Reveals Sexual Liaisons with Evangelist Ted Haggard, 1126

Nov. 20, 2006: News Corp Abandons Plan to Publish O. J. Simpson's Book, 1129

Early 2007: Subprime Mortgage Industry Begins to Collapse, 1134

Feb. 18, 2007: *Washington Post* Exposes Decline of Walter Reed Army Hospital, 1138

Apr. 11, 2007: Shock Jock Don Imus Loses His Radio Show over Sexist and Racist Remarks, 1142

June 4, 2007: Congressman William J. Jefferson Is Indicted for Corruption, 1147

July 9, 2007: Senator David Vitter's Name Is Found in D.C. Madam's Address Book, 1150

July 11, 2007: Florida Politician Is Arrested for Soliciting an Undercover Male Police Officer, 1153

July 24, 2007: University of Colorado Fires Professor for Plagiarism and Research Falsification, 1155

Aug. 20, 2007: Football Star Michael Vick Pleads Guilty to Financing a Dogfighting Ring, 1158

Sept. 13, 2007: New England Patriots Football Team Is Fined for Spying on Other Teams, 1161

Oct. 5, 2007: Olympic Champion Marion Jones Admits Steroid Use, 1164

Mar. 12, 2008: New York Governor Eliot Spitzer Resigns in Prostitution Scandal, 1167

June 13, 2008: Singer R. Kelly Is Acquitted on Child Pornography Charges, 1170

July 29, 2008: NBA Referee Tim Donaghy Is Sentenced to Prison for Betting on Games, 1172

Sept. 7, 2008: Financial Institutions and Markets Begin to Collapse, 1175

VATICAN CITY

Feb. 23, 1963: Play Accuses Pope Pius XII of Complicity in the Holocaust, 353

Aug. 6, 1982: Banco Ambrosiano Collapses Amid Criminal Accusations, 606

VENEZUELA

Sept., 2000: American Scientists Are Accused of Starting a Measles Epidemic in the Amazon, 910

VIETNAM

Aug. 26, 1949: Viet Minh Broadcasts French General's Damaging Report, 257

Aug. 14, 1963: Madame Nhu Derides Self-Immolation of Vietnamese Buddhists, 362

Nov. 13, 1969: American Massacre of Vietnamese Civilians at My Lai Is Revealed, 401

July 8-22, 1972: Jane Fonda's Visit to North Vietnam Outrages Many Americans, 434

CATEGORY INDEX

List of Categories

Art movements 1216
Atrocities and war crimes 1216
Banking and finance 1217
Business 1217
Business and labor 1219
Civil rights and liberties 1219
Colonialism and imperialism 1219
Communications and media 1219
Corruption 1220
Cultural and intellectual history 1223
Drugs 1223
Economics 1224
Education 1224
Environmental issues 1225
Espionage 1225
Ethics 1225
Families and children 1226
Film 1227
Forgery 1227
Gambling 1228
Government 1228
Hoaxes, frauds, and charlatanism 1232
Hollywood 1233
Human rights 1233
International relations 1234
Labor 1234
Law and the courts 1234

Literature 1238
Medicine and health care 1238
Military 1239
Murder and suicide 1240
Music and performing arts 1241
Organized crime and racketeering 1241
Performing arts 1242
Plagiarism 1242
Politics 1242
Popular culture 1245
Prostitution 1246
Psychology and psychiatry 1246
Public morals 1246
Publishing and journalism 1248
Racism 1251
Radio and television 1251
Religion 1252
Royalty 1252
Science and technology 1253
Sex 1253
Sex crimes 1255
Social issues and reform 1256
Space and aviation 1257
Sports 1257
Trade and commerce 1258
Violence 1258
Women's issues 1259

ART MOVEMENTS

Feb. 17-Mar. 15, 1913: Armory Modern Art Show Scandalizes the Public, 49

June 6, 1929: Luis Buñuel's *Un Chien Andalou* Shocks Parisian Audience, 136

Dec. 3, 1930: Surrealist Film *L'Âge d'or* Provokes French Rioting, 147

Jan. 20, 1933: Hedy Lamarr Appears Nude in the Czech Film *Exstase*, 163

May 21, 2003: Sexually Provocative Film *The Brown Bunny* Premieres at Cannes Film Festival, 1004

ATROCITIES AND WAR CRIMES

Nov. 15, 1908: Belgium Confiscates Congo Free State from King Leopold II, 31

Dec. 5, 1942: Industrialist Charles Bedaux Is Arrested for Nazi Collaboration, 212

May 9, 1945: Norwegian Politician Quisling Is Arrested for Nazi Collaboration, 226

May 26, 1945: Norwegian Writer Knut Hamsun Is Arrested for Treason, 229

Late 1955: British Atrocities in Kenya's Mau Mau Rebellion Are Revealed, 298

Nov. 13, 1969: American Massacre of

Vietnamese Civilians at My Lai Is Revealed, 401

May 28, 1970: Irish Politicians Are Tried for Conspiring to Import Weapons, 413

Mar. 3, 1986: Former U.N. Secretary-General Kurt Waldheim's Nazi Past Is Revealed, 669

Dec. 15-25, 1989: Harassment of a Christian Minister Sparks the Romanian Revolution, 742

June 25, 1997: Swiss Banks Admit to Holding Accounts of Holocaust Victims, 858

Apr. 28, 2004: CBS Broadcasts Photos of Abused and Tortured Prisoners at Abu Ghraib, 1034

BANKING AND FINANCE

1904: Theodore Roosevelt Is Accused of Accepting Corporate Funds, 1

1919-1920: Ponzi Schemes Are Revealed as Investment Frauds, 63

Nov., 1929: Banque Oustric et Cie Failure Prompts French Inquiry, 139

1932: Insull Utilities Trusts Collapse Prompts New Federal Regulation, 154

Jan. 8, 1934-Jan. 17, 1936: Stavisky's Fraudulent Schemes Rock French Government, 170

May 20, 1936: British Cabinet Member Resigns After Budget Information Leak, 181

Mar. 29, 1962: Billie Sol Estes Is Arrested for Corporate Fraud, 341

Nov. 28, 1967: Investor Louis Wolfson Is Convicted of Selling Stock Illegally, 389

Feb. 3, 1975: Honduras's "Bananagate" Bribery Scandal Leads to Executive's Suicide, 471

Feb. 25, 1977: Film Producer David Begelman Is Found to Have Forged Checks, 509

Sept. 21, 1977: Carter Cabinet Member Resigns over Ethics Violations, 511

Oct. 11, 1979: Senate Denounces Herman E. Talmadge for Money Laundering, 553

Aug. 6, 1982: Banco Ambrosiano Collapses Amid Criminal Accusations, 606

May 2, 1984: E. F. Hutton Executives Plead Guilty to Fraud, 636

May 7, 1985: Banker Jake Butcher Pleads Guilty to Fraud, 648

Jan. 15, 1988: ZZZZ Best Founder Is Indicted on Federal Fraud Charges, 708

June, 1988-June, 1989: Insider-Trading Scandal Rocks Japanese Government, 714

Mar. 29, 1989: Financier Michael Milken Is Indicted for Racketeering and Fraud, 726

Aug. 27, 1990: Guinness Four Are Found Guilty of Share-Trading Fraud, 753

Apr. 5, 1991: George W. Bush Is Investigated for Insider Trading, 762

June 25, 1997: Swiss Banks Admit to Holding Accounts of Holocaust Victims, 858

May 7, 1999-Mar. 2, 2001: Ethics Counselor Exonerates Canadian Prime Minister Jean Chrétien, 898

Jan. 28, 2000: John Spano Is Sentenced for Fraudulent Purchase of Ice Hockey Team, 901

2001: Clearstream Financial Clearinghouse Is Accused of Fraud and Money Laundering, 925

Dec. 2, 2001: Enron Bankruptcy Reveals Massive Financial Fraud, 945

June 25, 2002: Internal Corruption Forces Adelphia Communications to Declare Bankruptcy, 971

Sept. 3, 2003: Mutual Fund Companies Are Implicated in Shady Trading Practices, 1013

Sept. 12, 2005: Westar Energy Executives Are Found Guilty of Looting Their Company, 1072

Early 2007: Subprime Mortgage Industry Begins to Collapse, 1134

Sept. 7, 2008: Financial Institutions and Markets Begin to Collapse, 1175

BUSINESS

Jan. 23, 1904: Senator Joseph R. Burton Is Convicted of Bribery, 4

Jan., 1913: British Prime Minister's Staff Is Investigated for Insider Trading, 43

Oct. 22, 1923: U.S. Senate Begins Hearings on Teapot Dome Oil Leases, 95

Nov., 1929: Banque Oustric et Cie Failure Prompts French Inquiry, 139

May, 1930: Postmaster's Division of Airmail Routes Creates a Scandal, 144

1932: Insull Utilities Trusts Collapse Prompts New Federal Regulation, 154

Dec. 5, 1942: Industrialist Charles Bedaux Is Arrested for Nazi Collaboration, 212

Nov. 16, 1951: Federal Tax Official Resigns After Accepting Bribes, 279

June 25, 1956: President Truman's Appointments Secretary Is Convicted of Tax Conspiracy, 310

Sept. 22, 1958: President Eisenhower's Chief of Staff Resigns for Influence Selling, 320

Nov. 2, 1959: Charles Van Doren Admits to Being Fed Answers on Television Quiz Show, 326

Feb. 8, 1960: U.S. Congress Investigates Payola in Pop Music Industry, 332

Mar. 29, 1962: Billie Sol Estes Is Arrested for Corporate Fraud, 341

Nov. 28, 1967: Investor Louis Wolfson Is Convicted of Selling Stock Illegally, 389

June 22, 1972: Police Arrest Architect John Poulson for Bribery and Fraud, 431

Summer, 1974: Dalkon Shield Contraceptive Is Removed from the Market, 459

Feb. 3, 1975: Honduras's "Bananagate" Bribery Scandal Leads to Executive's Suicide, 471

Feb. 4, 1976: Lockheed Is Implicated in Bribing Foreign Officials, 482

Feb. 25, 1977: Film Producer David Begelman Is Found to Have Forged Checks, 509

Sept. 23, 1977: Horse-Swapping Fraud Upsets Belmont Park Raceway, 514

July 23, 1978: Utah Millionaire Is Murdered by His Grandson, 528

Oct. 20, 1978: Firestone Recalls Millions of Defective Car Tires, 534

Sept. 26, 1979: Love Canal Residents Sue Chemical Company, 546

Oct. 9, 1980: Bendix Executive Resigns Amid Rumors of an Affair, 580

May 29, 1981: Court Finds That Ford Ignored Pinto's Safety Problems, 594

Aug. 6, 1982: Banco Ambrosiano Collapses Amid Criminal Accusations, 606

Oct. 19, 1982: Car Manufacturer John De Lorean Is Arrested in a Drug Sting, 609

Dec. 16, 1982: Congress Cites Environmental Protection Agency Chief for Contempt, 615

May 2, 1984: E. F. Hutton Executives Plead Guilty to Fraud, 636

1985-1986: Westland Affair Shakes Prime Minister Thatcher's Government, 645

May 7, 1985: Banker Jake Butcher Pleads Guilty to Fraud, 648

July 19, 1985: Mayflower Madam Pleads Guilty to Promoting Prostitution, 654

Sept. 17, 1985: Media Allege Canadian Officials Allowed Sale of Rancid Tuna, 660

Apr. 22, 1986: Faith Healer Peter Popoff Is Exposed as a Fraud, 673

Jan. 15, 1988: ZZZZ Best Founder Is Indicted on Federal Fraud Charges, 708

June, 1988-June, 1989: Insider-Trading Scandal Rocks Japanese Government, 714

Mar. 29, 1989: Financier Michael Milken Is Indicted for Racketeering and Fraud, 726

Aug. 27, 1990: Guinness Four Are Found Guilty of Share-Trading Fraud, 753

Apr. 5, 1991: George W. Bush Is Investigated for Insider Trading, 762

Apr. 15, 1992: Hotel Tycoon Leona Helmsley Enters Prison for Tax Evasion, 776

Nov. 18, 1995: Former Canadian Premier Brian Mulroney Is Exposed in Airbus Scandal, 830

Feb. 4, 1996: Whistle-Blower Reveals Tobacco Industry Corruption, 833

Jan., 1997: Pyramid Investment Schemes Cause Albanian Government to Fall, 846

Nov. 26, 1997: Canadian Health Commissioner Releases Report on Tainted Blood, 868

Dec. 23, 1998: Prominent Belgians Are Sentenced in Agusta-Dassault Corruption Scandal, 889

2001: Clearstream Financial Clearinghouse Is Accused of Fraud and Money Laundering, 925

Dec. 2, 2001: Enron Bankruptcy Reveals Massive Financial Fraud, 945

Feb. 17, 2002: Rotting Human Bodies Are Found at Georgia Crematory, 964

Sept. 3, 2003: Mutual Fund Companies Are Implicated in Shady Trading Practices, 1013

Mar. 5, 2004: Martha Stewart Is Convicted in Insider-Trading Scandal, 1031

Oct. 14, 2004: Insurance Brokerage Marsh & McLennan Is Charged with Fraud, 1050

July 1, 2005: Federal Agents Raid Congressman Randall Cunningham's Home, 1064

Sept. 12, 2005: Westar Energy Executives Are Found Guilty of Looting Their Company, 1072

Nov. 17, 2005: Liberian Workers Sue Bridgestone Firestone over Slave Labor, 1078

Summer, 2006-Mar. 16, 2007: China Recalls Pet Food That Has Killed Thousands of American Pets, 1097

Nov. 20, 2006: News Corp Abandons Plan to Publish O. J. Simpson's Book, 1129

Early 2007: Subprime Mortgage Industry Begins to Collapse, 1134

Business and labor
Sept. 18, 2006: *Newsweek* Reveals That Hewlett-Packard Spied on Its Own Board, 1114

Civil rights and liberties
July 12, 1906: French Court Declares Alfred Dreyfus Innocent of Treason, 19

Mar. 21, 1928: Alberta Government Sterilizes Thousands Deemed Genetically and Mentally Unfit, 133

July 28, 1932: U.S. Troops Drive World War I Veterans from Washington, 156

Feb. 19, 1942: President Roosevelt Orders Internment of Japanese Americans, 205

Feb. 9, 1950: U.S. Senator Joseph McCarthy Launches Communist Witch Hunt, 266

Sept. 19, 1952: Actor Charles Chaplin Cannot Reenter the United States, 283

Oct. 26, 1962: West German Police Raid *Der Spiegel* Magazine Offices, 349

May 4, 1970: National Guardsmen Kill Protesting Kent State Students, 410

July 25, 1972: Newspaper Breaks Story of Abuses in Tuskegee Syphilis Study, 437

Apr. 18, 1979: Actor Lee Marvin Is Ordered to Pay Palimony to Former Lover, 540

Jan. 25, 1984: Jesse Jackson Calls New York City "Hymietown," 633

Oct. 23, 1985: Guru Bhagwan Shree Rajneesh Is Indicted for Immigration Fraud, 662

June 22, 2005: U.S. Air Force Investigates Religious Intolerance at Its Academy, 1062

Apr. 11, 2007: Shock Jock Don Imus Loses His Radio Show over Sexist and Racist Remarks, 1142

June 4, 2007: Congressman William J. Jefferson Is Indicted for Corruption, 1147

Colonialism and imperialism
Nov. 15, 1908: Belgium Confiscates Congo Free State from King Leopold II, 31

May, 1915: British Government Falls Because of Munitions Shortages and Military Setbacks, 58

1930: Liberia Is Accused of Selling Its Own Citizens into Slavery, 142

Aug. 26, 1949: Viet Minh Broadcasts French General's Damaging Report, 257

Late 1955: British Atrocities in Kenya's Mau Mau Rebellion Are Revealed, 298

Feb. 3, 1975: Honduras's "Bananagate" Bribery Scandal Leads to Executive's Suicide, 471

June 4, 1979: South African President B. J. Vorster Resigns in Muldergate Scandal, 543

Sept. 30, 2005: Danish Newspaper's Prophet Muhammad Cartoons Stir Violent Protests, 1075

Nov. 17, 2005: Liberian Workers Sue Bridgestone Firestone over Slave Labor, 1078

Communications and media
June 25, 1906: Millionaire Heir Murders Architect Stanford White, 16

Sept. 23, 1952: Richard Nixon Denies Taking Illegal Campaign Contributions, 286

Mar. 14, 1960: FCC Chairman John C. Doerfer Resigns for Accepting Gifts from Networks, 335

Oct. 26, 1962: West German Police Raid *Der Spiegel* Magazine Offices, 349

June 27, 1978: Evangelist Herbert W. Armstrong Excommunicates His Own Son, 525

Apr. 15, 1981: Janet Cooke Admits Fabricating Her Pulitzer Prize-Winning Feature, 585

Apr. 22, 1986: Faith Healer Peter Popoff Is Exposed as a Fraud, 673

Jan. 22, 1987: Pennsylvania Politician Kills Himself at Televised Press Conference, 684

July 18, 1988: Actor Rob Lowe Videotapes His Sexual Encounter with a Minor, 717

Dec. 18, 1989: Prince Charles's Intimate Phone Conversation with Camilla Parker Bowles Is Taped, 745

Mar., 1990: Menendez Brothers Are Arrested for Murdering Their Parents, 750

May 19, 1992: Amy Fisher Shoots Mary Jo Buttafuoco, 781

Aug. 23, 1992: Princess Diana's Phone Conversation with Her Lover Is Made Public, 789

June 24, 1994: *Time* Magazine Cover Uses Altered O. J. Simpson Photo, 810

Aug. 31, 1997: Princess Diana Dies in a Car Crash, 861

May 11, 1998: Journalist Stephen Glass Is Exposed as a Fraud, 887

June 25, 2002: Internal Corruption Forces Adelphia Communications to Declare Bankruptcy, 971

Jan. 2, 2003: E-mail Message Prompts Inquiry into Air Force Academy Sexual Assaults, 991

Apr. 29, 2003: *New York Times* Reporter Jayson Blair Is Exposed as a Fraud, 998

Early Nov., 2003: Paris Hilton Sex-Tape Appears on the Web, 1019

Dec. 18, 2003: Pop Star Michael Jackson Is Charged with Child Molestation, 1025

Apr. 28, 2004: CBS Broadcasts Photos of Abused and Tortured Prisoners at Abu Ghraib, 1034

Sept. 8, 2004: *60 Minutes II* Reports on George W. Bush's Evasion of Wartime Duty, 1044

Oct. 13, 2004: Television Producer Files Sex Harassment Suit Against Bill O'Reilly, 1047

Sept. 13, 2007: New England Patriots Football Team Is Fined for Spying on Other Teams, 1161

June 13, 2008: Singer R. Kelly Is Acquitted on Child Pornography Charges, 1170

CORRUPTION

1904: Theodore Roosevelt Is Accused of Accepting Corporate Funds, 1

Jan. 23, 1904: Senator Joseph R. Burton Is Convicted of Bribery, 4

Dec., 1904: Boston Alderman Is Reelected While in Jail for Fraud, 6

June 13, 1907: San Francisco Mayor Schmitz Is Found Guilty of Extortion, 28

Jan., 1913: British Prime Minister's Staff Is Investigated for Insider Trading, 43

Jan. 13, 1913: Federal Judge Is Impeached for Profiting from His Office, 46

Apr. 2, 1915: Players Fix Liverpool-Manchester United Soccer Match, 55

Sept. 21, 1919: White Sox Players Conspire to Lose World Series in "Black Sox" Scandal, 66

June 22, 1922: British Prime Minister David Lloyd George Is Accused of Selling Honors, 83

Mar. 2, 1923: U.S. Senate Investigates Veterans Bureau Chief for Fraud, 89

May 30, 1923: U.S. Attorney General Harry M. Daugherty's Aide Commits Suicide, 92

Oct. 22, 1923: U.S. Senate Begins Hearings on Teapot Dome Oil Leases, 95

May 12, 1924: Kentucky Congressman John W. Langley Is Convicted of Violating the Volstead Act, 103

Dec. 26, 1926: Ty Cobb and Tris Speaker Are Accused of Fixing Baseball Games, 118

May, 1930: Postmaster's Division of Airmail Routes Creates a Scandal, 144

Mar. 31, 1933: *New York Times* Reporter Denies Reports of a Soviet Famine, 167

Jan. 8, 1934-Jan. 17, 1936: Stavisky's Fraudulent Schemes Rock French Government, 170

May 20, 1936: British Cabinet Member Resigns After Budget Information Leak, 181

Mar. 17, 1937: Atherton Report Exposes San Francisco Police Corruption, 191

Sept.-Oct., 1937: Prescription Elixir Causes More than One Hundred Deaths, 193

May 22, 1939: Kansas City's Boss Pendergast Pleads Guilty to Income Tax Evasion, 199

Spring, 1947: Baseball Manager Leo Durocher Is Suspended for Gambling Ties, 242

Aug. 4, 1948: Columnist Drew Pearson Exposes Congressman's Corruption, 248

Aug. 26, 1949: Viet Minh Broadcasts French General's Damaging Report, 257

Feb. 9, 1950: U.S. Senator Joseph McCarthy Launches Communist Witch Hunt, 266

Jan. 17, 1951: College Basketball Players Begin Shaving Points for Money, 274

Nov. 16, 1951: Federal Tax Official Resigns After Accepting Bribes, 279

June 25, 1956: President Truman's Appointments Secretary Is Convicted of Tax Conspiracy, 310

Sept. 22, 1958: President Eisenhower's Chief of Staff Resigns for Influence Selling, 320

May, 1959: Teamsters Leader Dave Beck Is Convicted of Tax Fraud, 323

Nov. 2, 1959: Charles Van Doren Admits to Being Fed Answers on Television Quiz Show, 326

Feb. 8, 1960: U.S. Congress Investigates Payola in Pop Music Industry, 332

Mar. 14, 1960: FCC Chairman John C. Doerfer Resigns for Accepting Gifts from Networks, 335

Mar. 29, 1962: Billie Sol Estes Is Arrested for Corporate Fraud, 341

Oct. 7, 1963: Vice President Lyndon B. Johnson Aide Resigns over Crime Connections, 365

June 23, 1967: Senator Thomas J. Dodd Is Censured for Misappropriating Funds, 384

Nov. 28, 1967: Investor Louis Wolfson Is Convicted of Selling Stock Illegally, 389

May 9, 1969: Supreme Court Justice Abe Fortas Is Accused of Bribery, 391

Fall, 1969-Winter, 1971: Japanese Baseball Players Are Implicated in Game Fixing, 398

May 28, 1970: Irish Politicians Are Tried for Conspiring to Import Weapons, 413

June 17, 1972-Aug. 9, 1974: Watergate Break-in Leads to President Nixon's Resignation, 425

June 22, 1972: Police Arrest Architect John Poulson for Bribery and Fraud, 431

Aug. 19, 1973: Cheating Scandal Shocks Soap Box Derby, 444

Oct. 10, 1973: Spiro T. Agnew Resigns Vice Presidency in Disgrace, 447

Feb. 3, 1975: Honduras's "Bananagate" Bribery Scandal Leads to Executive's Suicide, 471

1976: Peace Corps Conceals Murder of Volunteer in Tonga, 476

1976-1977: U.S. Congress Members Are Implicated in Koreagate Scandal, 479

Feb. 4, 1976: Lockheed Is Implicated in Bribing Foreign Officials, 482

Apr. 4, 1976: West Point Cadets Are Caught Cheating on Exams, 488

Feb. 25, 1977: Film Producer David Begelman Is Found to Have Forged Checks, 509

Sept. 21, 1977: Carter Cabinet Member Resigns over Ethics Violations, 511

Sept. 23, 1977: Horse-Swapping Fraud Upsets Belmont Park Raceway, 514

June 4, 1979: South African President B. J. Vorster Resigns in Muldergate Scandal, 543

Oct. 10, 1979: French President Giscard d'Estaing Is Accused of Taking a Bribe, 550

Oct. 11, 1979: Senate Denounces Herman E. Talmadge for Money Laundering, 553

Nov. 29, 1979, and Jan. 31, 1983: Baseball Commissioner Suspends Mickey Mantle and Willie Mays for Casino Ties, 556

Feb. 2, 1980: Media Uncover FBI Sting Implicating Dozens of Lawmakers, 561

Apr. 27, 1980: Mobster's Arrest Reveals Point Shaving by Boston College Basketball Players, 568

Late July, 1980: President's Brother, Billy Carter, Registers as a Paid Agent for Libya, 571

Dec. 7, 1980: Rita Jenrette's "Diary of a Mad Congresswife" Scandalizes Washington, 582

May 23, 1981: Italian Justice Minister Resigns Because of Crime Connection, 591

Sept. 10, 1981: *Chicago Sun-Times* Reports That Cardinal Cody Diverted Church Funds, 597

May 11, 1982: Philippine President Marcos Forces the Entire Supreme Court to Resign, 600

Aug. 6, 1982: Banco Ambrosiano Collapses Amid Criminal Accusations, 606

Dec. 16, 1982: Congress Cites Environmental Protection Agency Chief for Contempt, 615

May 2, 1984: E. F. Hutton Executives Plead Guilty to Fraud, 636

May 7, 1985: Banker Jake Butcher Pleads Guilty to Fraud, 648

Aug. 19, 1985: West German Counterintelligence Chief Defects to East Germany, 657

Sept. 17, 1985: Media Allege Canadian Officials Allowed Sale of Rancid Tuna, 660

Feb. 28, 1986: Baseball Commissioner Peter Ueberroth Suspends Players for Cocaine Use, 666

Nov. 13, 1986-May 4, 1989: Iran-Contra Weapons Scandal Taints Reagan's Administration, 676

Jan. 12 and May 11, 1987: Media Reports Spark Investigation of Australian Police Corruption, 681

Jan. 22, 1987: Pennsylvania Politician Kills Himself at Televised Press Conference, 684

Feb. 25, 1987: NCAA Imposes "Death Penalty" on Southern Methodist University Football, 687

Apr. 9, 1987: Bess Myerson Resigns as New York Commissioner of Cultural Affairs, 693

Jan. 15, 1988: ZZZZ Best Founder Is Indicted on Federal Fraud Charges, 708

June, 1988-June, 1989: Insider-Trading Scandal Rocks Japanese Government, 714

Mar. 29, 1989: Financier Michael Milken Is Indicted for Racketeering and Fraud, 726

May 31, 1989: Speaker of the House Jim Wright Resigns in Ethics Scandal, 730

Aug. 24, 1989: Pete Rose Is Banned from Baseball for Betting on Games, 735

Jan. 18, 1990: Washington, D.C., Mayor Marion Barry Is Arrested for Drug Use, 748

Aug. 27, 1990: Guinness Four Are Found Guilty of Share-Trading Fraud, 753

Apr. 5, 1991: George W. Bush Is Investigated for Insider Trading, 762

Apr. 15, 1992: Hotel Tycoon Leona Helmsley Enters Prison for Tax Evasion, 776

Apr. 28, 1994: U.S. Naval Academy Expels Midshipmen for Cheating, 800

June 1, 1994: Congressman Dan Rostenkowski Is Indicted in House Post Office Scandal, 803

June 30, 1994: Tonya Harding Is Banned from Skating After Attack on Rival, 812

Aug. 5, 1994: Kenneth Starr Is Appointed to the Whitewater Investigation, 818

Feb. 28, 1995: Former Mexican President Carlos Salinas's Brother Is Arrested for Murder, 824

Nov. 18, 1995: Former Canadian Premier Brian Mulroney Is Exposed in Airbus Scandal, 830

Feb. 4, 1996: Whistle-Blower Reveals Tobacco Industry Corruption, 833

Aug. 16, 1996: Belgian Media Reveal How Police Bungled Serial Murder Case, 840

Nov. 3, 1996: Car Crash Reveals Depth of Government Corruption in Turkey, 843

Jan., 1997: Pyramid Investment Schemes Cause Albanian Government to Fall, 846

June 25, 1997: Swiss Banks Admit to Holding Accounts of Holocaust Victims, 858

Dec. 11, 1997: HUD Secretary Henry Cisneros Is Indicted for Lying to Federal Agents, 872

May, 1998: Police Corruption Is Revealed in Los Angeles's Rampart Division, 884

May 11, 1998: Journalist Stephen Glass Is Exposed as a Fraud, 887

Dec. 23, 1998: Prominent Belgians Are Sentenced in Agusta-Dassault Corruption Scandal, 889

Mar. 4, 1999: Quebec Offers Support for Abused Duplessis Orphans, 892

May 7, 1999-Mar. 2, 2001: Ethics Counselor Exonerates Canadian Prime Minister Jean Chrétien, 898

Jan. 28, 2000: John Spano Is Sentenced for Fraudulent Purchase of Ice Hockey Team, 901

May 9, 2000: Former Louisiana Governor Edwin Edwards Is Convicted on Corruption Charges, 907

2001: Clearstream Financial Clearinghouse Is Accused of Fraud and Money Laundering, 925

Jan. 30, 2001: Liverpool Children's Hospital Collects Body Parts Without Authorization, 927

Feb. 18, 2001: CIA Agent Robert Hanssen Is Arrested for Spying for the Russians, 931

Dec. 2, 2001: Enron Bankruptcy Reveals Massive Financial Fraud, 945

Feb. 11, 2002: French Judge Admits Favoring Russian Figure Skaters in Winter Olympics, 962

Feb. 17, 2002: Rotting Human Bodies Are Found at Georgia Crematory, 964

Mar. 27, 2002: Georgia Basketball Coach Jim Harrick, Sr., Resigns over Fraud Allegations, 968

June 25, 2002: Internal Corruption Forces Adelphia Communications to Declare Bankruptcy, 971

July, 2002: Journalist Alleges Release of Genetically Modified Corn Seeds in New Zealand, 974

Sept. 3, 2003: Mutual Fund Companies Are Implicated in Shady Trading Practices, 1013

Mar. 4, 2004: Former United Way Charity Chief Pleads Guilty to Embezzlement, 1028

Mar. 5, 2004: Martha Stewart Is Convicted in Insider-Trading Scandal, 1031

Oct. 14, 2004: Insurance Brokerage Marsh & McLennan Is Charged with Fraud, 1050

Jan. 15, 2005: Iqbal Riza Resigns from the United Nations in Oil-for-Food Scandal, 1053

Jan. 27, 2005: German Soccer Referee Admits to Fixing Games for Money, 1055

July 1, 2005: Federal Agents Raid Congressman Randall Cunningham's Home, 1064

Sept. 12, 2005: Westar Energy Executives Are Found Guilty of Looting Their Company, 1072

Dec. 6, 2005: Spokane, Washington, Mayor Recalled in Gay-Sex Scandal, 1081

May 4, 2006: Media Uncover Match-Fixing in Italian Soccer, 1092

July 14, 2006: *New York Times* Exposes Grading Scandal at Auburn University, 1101

July 26, 2006: Tour de France Is Hit with a Doping Scandal, 1103

Sept. 18, 2006: *Newsweek* Reveals That Hewlett-Packard Spied on Its Own Board, 1114

Oct. 22, 2006: Chilean Politicians Use Community Funds for Personal Campaigns, 1121

Nov. 2, 2006: Evangelist Kent Hovind Is Convicted of Federal Tax Violations, 1123

Nov. 23, 2006: Former Russian Security Service Officer Dies from Radiation Poisoning, 1132

Early 2007: Subprime Mortgage Industry Begins to Collapse, 1134

May 28, 2007: Japanese Politician Charged with Corruption Hangs Himself, 1145

June 4, 2007: Congressman William J. Jefferson Is Indicted for Corruption, 1147

Sept. 13, 2007: New England Patriots Football Team Is Fined for Spying on Other Teams, 1161

July 29, 2008: NBA Referee Tim Donaghy Is Sentenced to Prison for Betting on Games, 1172

CULTURAL AND INTELLECTUAL HISTORY

Mar. 2, 1906: Psychoanalyst Ernest Jones Is Accused of Molesting Mentally Disabled Children, 12

Feb. 17-Mar. 15, 1913: Armory Modern Art Show Scandalizes the Public, 49

June 6, 1929: Luis Buñuel's *Un Chien Andalou* Shocks Parisian Audience, 136

July, 1961: Psychologist Stanley Milgram Begins Obedience-to-Authority Experiments, 338

Oct. 31, 1975: Buddhist Teacher Orders His Students to Remove Their Clothes, 474

Sept. 1, 1976: Former Beatle George Harrison Loses Plagiarism Lawsuit, 494

May 11, 1982: Philippine President Marcos Forces the Entire Supreme Court to Resign, 600

Mar. 23, 1989: Scientists' "Cold Fusion" Claims Cannot Be Verified, 723

Dec. 3, 1989: Martin Luther King, Jr.'s, Doctoral-Thesis Plagiarism Is Revealed, 739

Mar. 12, 1997: Prize-Winning Aborigine Novelist Revealed as a Fraud, 852

Apr., 1998: Scottish Historian Is Charged with Plagiarism, 879

Nov. 5, 2000: Japanese Amateur Archaeologist's "Discoveries" Are Proven Fakes, 919

June 18, 2001: Award-Winning Historian Joseph J. Ellis Is Accused of Lying, 936

Jan. 4, 2002: Historian Stephen E. Ambrose Is Accused of Plagiarism, 951

Jan. 18, 2002: Historian Doris Kearns Goodwin Is Accused of Plagiarism, 959

Oct. 25, 2002: Historian Michael A. Bellesiles Resigns After Academic Fraud Accusations, 985

July 24, 2007: University of Colorado Fires Professor for Plagiarism and Research Falsification, 1155

DRUGS

June 25, 1906: Millionaire Heir Murders Architect Stanford White, 16

Jan. 18, 1923: Actor Wallace Reid's Death in Drug Rehab Shakes Film Industry, 86

Jan. 1, 1924: Film Star Mabel Normand's

Chauffeur Shoots Millionaire Courtland S. Dines, 100

Sept.-Oct., 1937: Prescription Elixir Causes More than One Hundred Deaths, 193

Aug. 31, 1948: Film Star Robert Mitchum Is Arrested for Drug Possession, 251

1956-1962: Prescription Thalidomide Causes Widespread Birth Disorders, 301

May 19, 1962: Marilyn Monroe Sings "Happy Birthday, Mr. President," 344

Mar. 21, 1976: Actor Claudine Longet Kills Ski Champion Vladimir Sabich, 485

Feb. 1, 1978: Roman Polanski Flees the United States to Avoid Rape Trial, 522

Apr. 27, 1980: Mobster's Arrest Reveals Point Shaving by Boston College Basketball Players, 568

Apr. 15, 1981: Janet Cooke Admits Fabricating Her Pulitzer Prize-Winning Feature, 585

Oct. 19, 1982: Car Manufacturer John De Lorean Is Arrested in a Drug Sting, 609

July 20, 1983: Congress Members Censured in House-Page Sex Scandal, 621

Feb. 28, 1986: Baseball Commissioner Peter Ueberroth Suspends Players for Cocaine Use, 666

Nov. 13, 1986-May 4, 1989: Iran-Contra Weapons Scandal Taints Reagan's Administration, 676

July 18, 1988: Actor Rob Lowe Videotapes His Sexual Encounter with a Minor, 717

Sept. 19, 1988: Stephen Breuning Pleads Guilty to Medical Research Fraud, 720

Jan. 18, 1990: Washington, D.C., Mayor Marion Barry Is Arrested for Drug Use, 748

July 1, 1994: Soccer Star Diego Maradona Is Expelled from World Cup, 815

Feb. 28, 1995: Former Mexican President Carlos Salinas's Brother Is Arrested for Murder, 824

Nov. 3, 1996: Car Crash Reveals Depth of Government Corruption in Turkey, 843

Nov. 26, 1997: Canadian Health Commissioner Releases Report on Tainted Blood, 868

Apr. 7, 1998: Pop Singer George Michael Is Arrested for Lewd Conduct, 881

Sept. 26, 2000: Gymnast Andreea Răducan Loses Her Olympic Gold Medal Because of Drugs, 916

Mar. 5, 2004: Martha Stewart Is Convicted in Insider-Trading Scandal, 1031

Mar. 17, 2005: Former Baseball Star Mark McGwire Evades Congressional Questions on Steroid Use, 1058

July 26, 2006: Tour de France Is Hit with a Doping Scandal, 1103

Nov. 2, 2006: Male Escort Reveals Sexual Liaisons with Evangelist Ted Haggard, 1126

Oct. 5, 2007: Olympic Champion Marion Jones Admits Steroid Use, 1164

ECONOMICS

Sept. 7, 2008: Financial Institutions and Markets Begin to Collapse, 1175

EDUCATION

Feb. 23, 1943: Irish Orphan School Fire Kills Thirty-five Girls, 217

Nov. 21, 1953: Piltdown Man Is Revealed to Be a Hoax, 292

July, 1961: Psychologist Stanley Milgram Begins Obedience-to-Authority Experiments, 338

1970: Study of Anonymous Gay Sex Leads to Ethics Scandal, 407

May 4, 1970: National Guardsmen Kill Protesting Kent State Students, 410

Aug. 20, 1971: Abusive Role-Playing Ends Stanford Prison Experiment, 420

Oct. 25, 1974: Evangelist Billy James Hargis Resigns College Presidency During Gay-Sex Scandal, 465

Apr. 4, 1976: West Point Cadets Are Caught Cheating on Exams, 488

Aug. 12, 1983-July 27, 1990: McMartin Preschool Is Embroiled in Child-Abuse Case, 624

Feb. 25, 1987: NCAA Imposes "Death Penalty" on Southern Methodist University Football, 687

Dec. 1, 1987: Yale Scholar's Wartime Anti-Semitic Writings Are Revealed, 705

Sept. 19, 1988: Stephen Breuning Pleads Guilty to Medical Research Fraud, 720

Mar. 23, 1989: Scientists' "Cold Fusion" Claims Cannot Be Verified, 723

Dec. 3, 1989: Martin Luther King, Jr.'s, Doctoral-Thesis Plagiarism Is Revealed, 739

Apr. 28, 1994: U.S. Naval Academy Expels Midshipmen for Cheating, 800

Spring, 1996: Physicist Publishes a Deliberately Fraudulent Article, 837

Nov. 5, 2000: Japanese Amateur Archaeologist's "Discoveries" Are Proven Fakes, 919

June 18, 2001: Award-Winning Historian Joseph J. Ellis Is Accused of Lying, 936

Jan. 4, 2002: Historian Stephen E. Ambrose Is Accused of Plagiarism, 951

Jan. 18, 2002: Historian Doris Kearns Goodwin Is Accused of Plagiarism, 959

Aug., 2002: Immunologist Resigns After Being Accused of Falsifying Research, 977

Oct. 25, 2002: Historian Michael A. Bellesiles Resigns After Academic Fraud Accusations, 985

Jan. 2, 2003: E-mail Message Prompts Inquiry into Air Force Academy Sexual Assaults, 991

June 22, 2005: U.S. Air Force Investigates Religious Intolerance at Its Academy, 1062

Mar. 14, 2006: Duke Lacrosse Players Are Accused of Gang Rape, 1086

July 14, 2006: *New York Times* Exposes Grading Scandal at Auburn University, 1101

July 24, 2007: University of Colorado Fires Professor for Plagiarism and Research Falsification, 1155

Environmental issues

Sept. 26, 1979: Love Canal Residents Sue Chemical Company, 546

Dec. 16, 1982: Congress Cites Environmental Protection Agency Chief for Contempt, 615

July 10, 1985: French Secret Service Sinks the Greenpeace Ship *Rainbow Warrior*, 651

Feb. 4, 1996: Whistle-Blower Reveals Tobacco Industry Corruption, 833

Feb. 17, 2002: Rotting Human Bodies Are Found at Georgia Crematory, 964

July, 2002: Journalist Alleges Release of Genetically Modified Corn Seeds in New Zealand, 974

Beginning Aug. 29, 2005: Government Incompetence Mars Hurricane Katrina Relief Efforts, 1068

Nov. 17, 2005: Liberian Workers Sue Bridgestone Firestone over Slave Labor, 1078

Espionage

July 12, 1906: French Court Declares Alfred Dreyfus Innocent of Treason, 19

Feb. 19, 1942: President Roosevelt Orders Internment of Japanese Americans, 205

Feb. 9, 1950: U.S. Senator Joseph McCarthy Launches Communist Witch Hunt, 266

June, 1956: George F. Kennan Proves Russian Sisson Documents Are Fakes, 307

Sept. 12, 1962: British Civil Servant Is Arrested for Spying, 347

Mar. 2-Sept. 25, 1963: John Profumo Affair Rocks British Government, 355

Mar. 4, 1966: Munsinger Sex and Spy Scandal Rocks Canada, 377

June 13, 1971: *New York Times* Publishes the Pentagon Papers, 416

June 17, 1972-Aug. 9, 1974: Watergate Break-in Leads to President Nixon's Resignation, 425

Aug. 19, 1985: West German Counterintelligence Chief Defects to East Germany, 657

Feb. 18, 2001: CIA Agent Robert Hanssen Is Arrested for Spying for the Russians, 931

Mar. 2, 2003: U.S. National Security Agency Is Found to Have Spied on U.N. Officials, 995

July 14, 2003: Columnist Robert Novak Leaks the Name of CIA Operative Valerie Plame, 1010

Sept. 18, 2006: *Newsweek* Reveals That Hewlett-Packard Spied on Its Own Board, 1114

Sept. 13, 2007: New England Patriots Football Team Is Fined for Spying on Other Teams, 1161

Ethics

Jan., 1913: British Prime Minister's Staff Is Investigated for Insider Trading, 43

Sept.-Oct., 1937: Prescription Elixir Causes More than One Hundred Deaths, 193

June 13, 1971: *New York Times* Publishes the Pentagon Papers, 416

Aug. 20, 1971: Abusive Role-Playing Ends Stanford Prison Experiment, 420

May 14, 1974: *Washington Post* Reveals That the Nixons Received Jewelry Gifts, 453

Apr. 4, 1976: West Point Cadets Are Caught Cheating on Exams, 488

Oct. 20, 1978: Firestone Recalls Millions of Defective Car Tires, 534

Sept. 17, 1985: Media Allege Canadian Officials Allowed Sale of Rancid Tuna, 660

May 31, 1989: Speaker of the House Jim Wright Resigns in Ethics Scandal, 730

Apr. 28, 1994: U.S. Naval Academy Expels Midshipmen for Cheating, 800

June 24, 1994: *Time* Magazine Cover Uses Altered O. J. Simpson Photo, 810

Apr., 1998: Scottish Historian Is Charged with Plagiarism, 879

May, 1999: Civil Rights Leader Jesse Jackson Fathers a Child Out of Wedlock, 895

May 7, 1999-Mar. 2, 2001: Ethics Counselor Exonerates Canadian Prime Minister Jean Chrétien, 898

June 18, 2001: Award-Winning Historian Joseph J. Ellis Is Accused of Lying, 936

Dec. 2, 2001: Enron Bankruptcy Reveals Massive Financial Fraud, 945

Dec. 14, 2001: Notre Dame Football Coach Resigns for Falsifying His Résumé, 948

Sept. 25, 2002: Inquiry Reveals That Physicist Jan Hendrik Schön Faked His Research, 980

Jan. 2, 2003: E-mail Message Prompts Inquiry into Air Force Academy Sexual Assaults, 991

Mar. 2, 2003: U.S. National Security Agency Is Found to Have Spied on U.N. Officials, 995

July 14, 2003: Columnist Robert Novak Leaks the Name of CIA Operative Valerie Plame, 1010

Beginning Aug. 29, 2005: Government Incompetence Mars Hurricane Katrina Relief Efforts, 1068

July 26, 2006: Tour de France Is Hit with a Doping Scandal, 1103

Aug. 12, 2006: Novelist Günter Grass Admits to Youthful Nazi Ties, 1109

July 24, 2007: University of Colorado Fires Professor for Plagiarism and Research Falsification, 1155

Aug. 20, 2007: Football Star Michael Vick Pleads Guilty to Financing a Dogfighting Ring, 1158

July 29, 2008: NBA Referee Tim Donaghy Is Sentenced to Prison for Betting on Games, 1172

FAMILIES AND CHILDREN

Mar. 2, 1906: Psychoanalyst Ernest Jones Is Accused of Molesting Mentally Disabled Children, 12

Dec. 8, 1906: Former U.S. Senator Arthur Brown Is Murdered by Lover, 22

Mar. 25, 1911: Nearly 150 Workers Die in Triangle Shirtwaist Factory Fire, 40

Feb. 23, 1943: Irish Orphan School Fire Kills Thirty-five Girls, 217

June 4, 1943: Actor Charles Chaplin Is Sued for Paternity, 220

May 27, 1949: Actor Rita Hayworth Marries Aly Khan After Adulterous Affair, 254

Feb. 7, 1950: Swedish Film Star Ingrid Bergman Has a Child Out of Wedlock, 263

1956-1962: Prescription Thalidomide Causes Widespread Birth Disorders, 301

Dec. 12, 1957: Rock Star Jerry Lee Lewis Marries Thirteen-Year-Old Cousin, 313

Aug. 19, 1973: Cheating Scandal Shocks Soap Box Derby, 444

1978: Actor Joan Crawford's Daughter Publishes Damning Memoir, *Mommie Dearest*, 517

Feb. 1, 1978: Roman Polanski Flees the United States to Avoid Rape Trial, 522

June 27, 1978: Evangelist Herbert W. Armstrong Excommunicates His Own Son, 525

July 23, 1978: Utah Millionaire Is Murdered by His Grandson, 528

Sept. 26, 1979: Love Canal Residents Sue Chemical Company, 546

July 28, 1980: Magazine Reveals Baseball Star Steve Garvey's Marital Problems, 574

July 20, 1982: Conservative Politician John G. Schmitz Is Found to Have Children Out of Wedlock, 603

July 20, 1983: Congress Members Censured in House-Page Sex Scandal, 621

Aug. 12, 1983-July 27, 1990: McMartin Pre-school Is Embroiled in Child-Abuse Case, 624

Oct. 14, 1983: British Cabinet Secretary Parkinson Resigns After His Secretary Becomes Pregnant, 631

Nov. 28, 1987: Black Teenager Claims to Have Been Gang-Raped by Police Officers, 702

Jan. 13, 1992: Woody Allen Has Affair with Lover Mia Farrow's Adopted Daughter, 773

May 6, 1992: Irish Bishop Eamonn Casey's Romantic Affair Leads to His Resignation, 779

May 19, 1992: Amy Fisher Shoots Mary Jo Buttafuoco, 781

Jan. 5, 1994: British Cabinet Member Resigns After Fathering a Child Out of Wedlock, 798

Aug. 16, 1996: Belgian Media Reveal How Police Bungled Serial Murder Case, 840

Feb. 26, 1997: Teacher Mary Kay Letourneau Is Arrested for Statutory Rape, 849

Mar. 4, 1999: Quebec Offers Support for Abused Duplessis Orphans, 892

May, 1999: Civil Rights Leader Jesse Jackson Fathers a Child Out of Wedlock, 895

May 2, 2000: New York Mayor Rudy Giuliani's Extramarital Affair Is Revealed, 904

Dec., 2000: Sexual Abuse of Children in France Leads to the Outreau Affair, 922

Jan. 30, 2001: Liverpool Children's Hospital Collects Body Parts Without Authorization, 927

Aug. 27, 2001: Little League Baseball Star Danny Almonte Is Found to Be Overage, 942

Jan. 6, 2002: *Boston Globe* Reports on Child Sexual Abuse by Roman Catholic Priests, 954

Dec. 17, 2003: Senator Strom Thurmond's Biracial Daughter Is Revealed, 1022

Dec. 18, 2003: Pop Star Michael Jackson Is Charged with Child Molestation, 1025

Dec. 6, 2005: Spokane, Washington, Mayor Recalled in Gay-Sex Scandal, 1081

June 13, 2008: Singer R. Kelly Is Acquitted on Child Pornography Charges, 1170

FILM

Feb. 1, 1922: Director Taylor's Murder Ruins Mabel Normand's Acting Career, 73

Jan. 18, 1923: Actor Wallace Reid's Death in Drug Rehab Shakes Film Industry, 86

July, 1925: *Nosferatu* Is Found to Have Violated *Dracula* Copyright, 111

Early 1928: Joseph P. Kennedy Begins an Affair with Gloria Swanson, 127

June 6, 1929: Luis Buñuel's *Un Chien Andalou* Shocks Parisian Audience, 136

Dec. 3, 1930: Surrealist Film *L'Âge d'or* Provokes French Rioting, 147

Jan. 20, 1933: Hedy Lamarr Appears Nude in the Czech Film *Exstase*, 163

1978: Actor Joan Crawford's Daughter Publishes Damning Memoir, *Mommie Dearest*, 517

May 21, 2003: Sexually Provocative Film *The Brown Bunny* Premieres at Cannes Film Festival, 1004

Early Nov., 2003: Paris Hilton Sex-Tape Appears on the Web, 1019

FORGERY

Oct. 25, 1924: Forged Communist Letter Brings Down British Government, 105

Summer, 1936: Film Star Mary Astor's Diary Becomes a Public Sensation, 184

Nov. 21, 1953: Piltdown Man Is Revealed to Be a Hoax, 292

June, 1956: George F. Kennan Proves Russian Sisson Documents Are Fakes, 307

Jan. 28, 1972: Clifford Irving Admits Faking Howard Hughes Memoirs, 422

Feb. 25, 1977: Film Producer David Begelman Is Found to Have Forged Checks, 509

Oct. 10, 1979: French President Giscard d'Estaing Is Accused of Taking a Bribe, 550

Apr. 25, 1983: German Magazine Publishes Faked Hitler Diaries, 618

May 7, 1985: Banker Jake Butcher Pleads Guilty to Fraud, 648

June 24, 1994: *Time* Magazine Cover Uses Altered O. J. Simpson Photo, 810

Jan. 28, 2000: John Spano Is Sentenced for Fraudulent Purchase of Ice Hockey Team, 901

Nov. 5, 2000: Japanese Amateur Archaeologist's "Discoveries" Are Proven Fakes, 919

GAMBLING

Apr. 2, 1915: Players Fix Liverpool-Manchester United Soccer Match, 55

Sept. 21, 1919: White Sox Players Conspire to Lose World Series in "Black Sox" Scandal, 66

Dec. 26, 1926: Ty Cobb and Tris Speaker Are Accused of Fixing Baseball Games, 118

Jan. 8, 1934-Jan. 17, 1936: Stavisky's Fraudulent Schemes Rock French Government, 170

May 20, 1936: British Cabinet Member Resigns After Budget Information Leak, 181

Mar. 17, 1937: Atherton Report Exposes San Francisco Police Corruption, 191

May 22, 1939: Kansas City's Boss Pendergast Pleads Guilty to Income Tax Evasion, 199

Spring, 1947: Baseball Manager Leo Durocher Is Suspended for Gambling Ties, 242

May 3, 1950: U.S. Senate Committee Begins Investigating Organized Crime, 270

Jan. 17, 1951: College Basketball Players Begin Shaving Points for Money, 274

Fall, 1969-Winter, 1971: Japanese Baseball Players Are Implicated in Game Fixing, 398

Nov. 29, 1979, and Jan. 31, 1983: Baseball Commissioner Suspends Mickey Mantle and Willie Mays for Casino Ties, 556

Apr. 27, 1980: Mobster's Arrest Reveals Point Shaving by Boston College Basketball Players, 568

Aug. 24, 1989: Pete Rose Is Banned from Baseball for Betting on Games, 735

May 3, 2003: University of Alabama Fires New Football Coach in Sex Scandal, 1002

Jan. 27, 2005: German Soccer Referee Admits to Fixing Games for Money, 1055

Aug. 20, 2007: Football Star Michael Vick Pleads Guilty to Financing a Dogfighting Ring, 1158

July 29, 2008: NBA Referee Tim Donaghy Is Sentenced to Prison for Betting on Games, 1172

GOVERNMENT

1904: Theodore Roosevelt Is Accused of Accepting Corporate Funds, 1

Jan. 23, 1904: Senator Joseph R. Burton Is Convicted of Bribery, 4

Dec., 1904: Boston Alderman Is Reelected While in Jail for Fraud, 6

June 13, 1907: San Francisco Mayor Schmitz Is Found Guilty of Extortion, 28

Nov. 15, 1908: Belgium Confiscates Congo Free State from King Leopold II, 31

Jan., 1913: British Prime Minister's Staff Is Investigated for Insider Trading, 43

Jan. 13, 1913: Federal Judge Is Impeachd for Profiting from His Office, 46

May, 1915: British Government Falls Because of Munitions Shortages and Military Setbacks, 58

June 22, 1922: British Prime Minister David Lloyd George Is Accused of Selling Honors, 83

Mar. 2, 1923: U.S. Senate Investigates Veterans Bureau Chief for Fraud, 89

May 30, 1923: U.S. Attorney General Harry M. Daugherty's Aide Commits Suicide, 92

Oct. 22, 1923: U.S. Senate Begins Hearings on Teapot Dome Oil Leases, 95

May 12, 1924: Kentucky Congressman John W. Langley Is Convicted of Violating the Volstead Act, 103

Oct. 25, 1924: Forged Communist Letter Brings Down British Government, 105

1927: President Warren G. Harding's Lover Publishes Tell-All Memoir, 124

Nov., 1929: Banque Oustric et Cie Failure Prompts French Inquiry, 139

1930: Liberia Is Accused of Selling Its Own Citizens into Slavery, 142

May, 1930: Postmaster's Division of Airmail Routes Creates a Scandal, 144

Mar. 30, 1931: "Scottsboro Boys" Are Railroaded Through Rape Trials, 150

1932: Insull Utilities Trusts Collapse Prompts New Federal Regulation, 154

July 28, 1932: U.S. Troops Drive World War I Veterans from Washington, 156

July 10, 1934: Sex Scandal Forces Resignation of Alberta Premier Brownlee, 176

May 20, 1936: British Cabinet Member Resigns After Budget Information Leak, 181

Dec. 10, 1936: King Edward VIII Abdicates to Marry an American Divorcée, 187

Feb. 19, 1942: President Roosevelt Orders Internment of Japanese Americans, 205

Apr. 22, 1942: French Prime Minister Pierre Laval Wants Germany to Win World War II, 209

Dec. 5, 1942: Industrialist Charles Bedaux Is Arrested for Nazi Collaboration, 212

June 4, 1943: Actor Charles Chaplin Is Sued for Paternity, 220

May 9, 1945: Norwegian Politician Quisling Is Arrested for Nazi Collaboration, 226

May 26, 1945: Norwegian Writer Knut Hamsun Is Arrested for Treason, 229

Aug. 14, 1945: French War Hero Pétain Is Convicted of Nazi Collaboration, 232

Aug. 4, 1948: Columnist Drew Pearson Exposes Congressman's Corruption, 248

Aug. 26, 1949: Viet Minh Broadcasts French General's Damaging Report, 257

Jan. 21, 1950: Alger Hiss Is Convicted of Perjury, 259

Feb. 9, 1950: U.S. Senator Joseph McCarthy Launches Communist Witch Hunt, 266

May 3, 1950: U.S. Senate Committee Begins Investigating Organized Crime, 270

July 16, 1951: Belgium's Disgraced King Leopold III Abdicates, 276

Nov. 16, 1951: Federal Tax Official Resigns After Accepting Bribes, 279

Sept. 19, 1952: Actor Charles Chaplin Cannot Reenter the United States, 283

Sept. 23, 1952: Richard Nixon Denies Taking Illegal Campaign Contributions, 286

Late 1955: British Atrocities in Kenya's Mau Mau Rebellion Are Revealed, 298

June, 1956: George F. Kennan Proves Russian Sisson Documents Are Fakes, 307

June 25, 1956: President Truman's Appointments Secretary Is Convicted of Tax Conspiracy, 310

Sept. 22, 1958: President Eisenhower's Chief of Staff Resigns for Influence Selling, 320

Nov. 2, 1959: Charles Van Doren Admits to Being Fed Answers on Television Quiz Show, 326

Feb. 7, 1960: President Kennedy's Romantic Affair Links Him to Organized Crime, 329

Feb. 8, 1960: U.S. Congress Investigates Payola in Pop Music Industry, 332

Mar. 14, 1960: FCC Chairman John C. Doerfer Resigns for Accepting Gifts from Networks, 335

Mar. 29, 1962: Billie Sol Estes Is Arrested for Corporate Fraud, 341

Sept. 12, 1962: British Civil Servant Is Arrested for Spying, 347

Mar. 2-Sept. 25, 1963: John Profumo Affair Rocks British Government, 355

Aug. 14, 1963: Madame Nhu Derides Self-Immolation of Vietnamese Buddhists, 362

Oct. 7, 1963: Vice President Lyndon B. Johnson Aide Resigns over Crime Connections, 365

Oct. 7, 1964: President Lyndon Johnson's Aide Is Arrested in Gay-Sex Sting, 371

Oct. 29, 1965: Moroccan Politician Mehdi Ben Barka Disappears in Paris, 374

Mar. 4, 1966: Munsinger Sex and Spy Scandal Rocks Canada, 377

Mar. 1, 1967: Adam Clayton Powell, Jr., Is Excluded from Congress, 380

June 23, 1967: Senator Thomas J. Dodd Is Censured for Misappropriating Funds, 384

May 9, 1969: Supreme Court Justice Abe Fortas Is Accused of Bribery, 391

July 18, 1969: Senator Edward Kennedy's Driving Accident Kills Mary Jo Kopechne, 394

Nov. 13, 1969: American Massacre of Vietnamese Civilians at My Lai Is Revealed, 401

May 28, 1970: Irish Politicians Are Tried for Conspiring to Import Weapons, 413

June 13, 1971: *New York Times* Publishes the Pentagon Papers, 416

June 17, 1972-Aug. 9, 1974: Watergate Break-in Leads to President Nixon's Resignation, 425

June 22, 1972: Police Arrest Architect John Poulson for Bribery and Fraud, 431

July 25, 1972: Newspaper Breaks Story of Abuses in Tuskegee Syphilis Study, 437

July 31, 1972: Thomas F. Eagleton Withdraws from Vice Presidential Race, 440

Oct. 10, 1973: Spiro T. Agnew Resigns Vice Presidency in Disgrace, 447

May 14, 1974: *Washington Post* Reveals That the Nixons Received Jewelry Gifts, 453

Oct. 7, 1974: Congressman Wilbur D. Mills's Stripper Affair Leads to His Downfall, 462

Nov. 20, 1974: British Politician John Stonehouse Fakes His Suicide, 468

1976-1977: U.S. Congress Members Are Implicated in Koreagate Scandal, 479

Feb. 4, 1976: Lockheed Is Implicated in Bribing Foreign Officials, 482

May 23, 1976: *Washington Post* Exposes Congressman Wayne L. Hays's Affair, 491

Sept., 1976: Jimmy Carter Admits Committing Adultery in His Heart, 497

Oct. 4, 1976: Agriculture Secretary Earl Butz Resigns After Making Obscene Joke, 500

Nov. 9, 1976: German Generals Must Retire for Supporting a Neo-Nazi Pilot, 503

Sept. 21, 1977: Carter Cabinet Member Resigns over Ethics Violations, 511

Aug. 4, 1978: British Politician Jeremy Thorpe Is Charged with Attempted Murder, 531

Oct. 20, 1978: Firestone Recalls Millions of Defective Car Tires, 534

June 4, 1979: South African President B. J. Vorster Resigns in Muldergate Scandal, 543

Oct. 10, 1979: French President Giscard d'Estaing Is Accused of Taking a Bribe, 550

Oct. 11, 1979: Senate Denounces Herman E. Talmadge for Money Laundering, 553

Feb. 2, 1980: Media Uncover FBI Sting Implicating Dozens of Lawmakers, 561

Late July, 1980: President's Brother, Billy Carter, Registers as a Paid Agent for Libya, 571

Sept. 3, 1980: Congressman Bauman Is Arrested for Liaison with Teenage Boy, 577

May 23, 1981: Italian Justice Minister Resigns Because of Crime Connection, 591

May 11, 1982: Philippine President Marcos Forces the Entire Supreme Court to Resign, 600

July 20, 1982: Conservative Politician John G. Schmitz Is Found to Have Children Out of Wedlock, 603

Dec. 16, 1982: Congress Cites Environmental Protection Agency Chief for Contempt, 615

July 20, 1983: Congress Members Censured in House-Page Sex Scandal, 621

Aug. 21, 1983: Filipino Opposition Leader Aquino Is Assassinated on Return Home, 628

Oct. 14, 1983: British Cabinet Secretary Parkinson Resigns After His Secretary Becomes Pregnant, 631

1985-1986: Westland Affair Shakes Prime Minister Thatcher's Government, 645

July 10, 1985: French Secret Service Sinks the Greenpeace Ship *Rainbow Warrior*, 651

Aug. 19, 1985: West German Counterintelligence Chief Defects to East Germany, 657

Sept. 17, 1985: Media Allege Canadian Officials Allowed Sale of Rancid Tuna, 660

Oct. 23, 1985: Guru Bhagwan Shree Rajneesh Is Indicted for Immigration Fraud, 662

Mar. 3, 1986: Former U.N. Secretary-General Kurt Waldheim's Nazi Past Is Revealed, 669

Nov. 13, 1986-May 4, 1989: Iran-Contra Weapons Scandal Taints Reagan's Administration, 676

Jan. 12 and May 11, 1987: Media Reports Spark Investigation of Australian Police Corruption, 681

Jan. 22, 1987: Pennsylvania Politician Kills Himself at Televised Press Conference, 684

Apr. 9, 1987: Bess Myerson Resigns as New York Commissioner of Cultural Affairs, 693

July 25, 1987: Novelist-Politician Jeffrey Archer Wins Libel Trial Against the *Daily Star*, 696

Sept. 23, 1987: Plagiarism Charges End Joe Biden's Presidential Campaign, 698

June, 1988-June, 1989: Insider-Trading Scandal Rocks Japanese Government, 714

May 31, 1989: Speaker of the House Jim Wright Resigns in Ethics Scandal, 730

Aug. 10, 1989: Japanese Prime Minister Sosuke Resigns After Affair with a Geisha, 733

Dec. 15-25, 1989: Harassment of a Christian Minister Sparks the Romanian Revolution, 742

Jan. 18, 1990: Washington, D.C., Mayor Marion Barry Is Arrested for Drug Use, 748

Apr. 5, 1991: George W. Bush Is Investigated for Insider Trading, 762

Oct. 11-13, 1991: Justice Clarence Thomas's Confirmation Hearings Create a Scandal, 768

June 26, 1992: U.S. Navy Secretary Resigns in the Wake of Tailhook Sexual Assault Scandal, 784

Sept. 24, 1992: British Cabinet Member David Mellor Resigns over Romantic Affair, 792

Jan. 5, 1994: British Cabinet Member Resigns After Fathering a Child Out of Wedlock, 798

Apr. 28, 1994: U.S. Naval Academy Expels Midshipmen for Cheating, 800

June 1, 1994: Congressman Dan Rostenkowski Is Indicted in House Post Office Scandal, 803

Aug. 5, 1994: Kenneth Starr Is Appointed to the Whitewater Investigation, 818

Feb. 28, 1995: Former Mexican President Carlos Salinas's Brother Is Arrested for Murder, 824

Nov. 18, 1995: Former Canadian Premier Brian Mulroney Is Exposed in Airbus Scandal, 830

Jan., 1997: Pyramid Investment Schemes Cause Albanian Government to Fall, 846

June 25, 1997: Swiss Banks Admit to Holding Accounts of Holocaust Victims, 858

Nov. 26, 1997: Canadian Health Commissioner Releases Report on Tainted Blood, 868

Dec. 11, 1997: HUD Secretary Henry Cisneros Is Indicted for Lying to Federal Agents, 872

Jan. 17, 1998: President Bill Clinton Denies Sexual Affair with a White House Intern, 874

May, 1998: Police Corruption Is Revealed in Los Angeles's Rampart Division, 884

Dec. 23, 1998: Prominent Belgians Are Sentenced in Agusta-Dassault Corruption Scandal, 889

Mar. 4, 1999: Quebec Offers Support for Abused Duplessis Orphans, 892

May 7, 1999-Mar. 2, 2001: Ethics Counselor Exonerates Canadian Prime Minister Jean Chrétien, 898

May 9, 2000: Former Louisiana Governor Edwin Edwards Is Convicted on Corruption Charges, 907

Jan. 30, 2001: Liverpool Children's Hospital Collects Body Parts Without Authorization, 927

Feb. 18, 2001: CIA Agent Robert Hanssen Is Arrested for Spying for the Russians, 931

Feb. 17, 2002: Rotting Human Bodies Are Found at Georgia Crematory, 964

July, 2002: Journalist Alleges Release of Genetically Modified Corn Seeds in New Zealand, 974

Sept. 28, 2002: British Politician Reveals Her Affair with Prime Minister John Major, 983

Dec. 5, 2002: Senator Trent Lott Praises Strom Thurmond's 1948 Presidential Campaign, 988

Jan. 2, 2003: E-mail Message Prompts Inquiry into Air Force Academy Sexual Assaults, 991

Mar. 2, 2003: U.S. National Security Agency Is Found to Have Spied on U.N. Officials, 995

July 14, 2003: Columnist Robert Novak Leaks the Name of CIA Operative Valerie Plame, 1010

Sept. 3, 2003: Mutual Fund Companies Are Implicated in Shady Trading Practices, 1013

Apr. 28, 2004: CBS Broadcasts Photos of Abused and Tortured Prisoners at Abu Ghraib, 1034

Oct. 14, 2004: Insurance Brokerage Marsh & McLennan Is Charged with Fraud, 1050

Mar. 17, 2005: Former Baseball Star Mark McGwire Evades Congressional Questions on Steroid Use, 1058

July 1, 2005: Federal Agents Raid Congressman Randall Cunningham's Home, 1064

Beginning Aug. 29, 2005: Government Incompetence Mars Hurricane Katrina Relief Efforts, 1068

Jan. 21, 2006: British Politician Resigns After Gay-Sex Orgy, 1084

Apr. 26, 2006: Britain's Deputy Prime Minister Admits Affair with Secretary, 1089

Summer, 2006-Mar. 16, 2007: China Recalls Pet Food That Has Killed Thousands of American Pets, 1097

Sept. 17, 2006: New Zealand Prime Minister's Husband Is "Outed" as Gay, 1112

Sept. 29, 2006: Congressman Mark Foley Resigns in Sex Scandal Involving a Teenage Page, 1118

Oct. 22, 2006: Chilean Politicians Use Community Funds for Personal Campaigns, 1121

Nov. 23, 2006: Former Russian Security Service Officer Dies from Radiation Poisoning, 1132

Early 2007: Subprime Mortgage Industry Begins to Collapse, 1134

Feb. 18, 2007: *Washington Post* Exposes Decline of Walter Reed Army Hospital, 1138

May 28, 2007: Japanese Politician Charged with Corruption Hangs Himself, 1145

June 4, 2007: Congressman William J. Jefferson Is Indicted for Corruption, 1147

July 11, 2007: Florida Politician Is Arrested for Soliciting an Undercover Male Police Officer, 1153

Mar. 12, 2008: New York Governor Eliot Spitzer Resigns in Prostitution Scandal, 1167

Sept. 7, 2008: Financial Institutions and Markets Begin to Collapse, 1175

HOAXES, FRAUDS, AND CHARLATANISM

1919-1920: Ponzi Schemes Are Revealed as Investment Frauds, 63

Oct. 25, 1924: Forged Communist Letter Brings Down British Government, 105

May-June, 1926: Evangelist Aimee Semple McPherson Claims She Was Kidnapped, 115

Dec. 26, 1926: Ty Cobb and Tris Speaker Are Accused of Fixing Baseball Games, 118

1928-1929: Actor Is Suspected of Falsely Claiming to Be an American Indian, 130

Mar. 31, 1933: *New York Times* Reporter Denies Reports of a Soviet Famine, 167

Jan. 8, 1934-Jan. 17, 1936: Stavisky's Fraudulent Schemes Rock French Government, 170

June 5, 1944: Australian Poets Claim Responsibility for a Literary Hoax, 223

Jan. 17, 1951: College Basketball Players Begin Shaving Points for Money, 274

Nov. 21, 1953: Piltdown Man Is Revealed to Be a Hoax, 292

June, 1956: George F. Kennan Proves Russian Sisson Documents Are Fakes, 307

Nov. 2, 1959: Charles Van Doren Admits to Being Fed Answers on Television Quiz Show, 326

Mar. 14, 1960: FCC Chairman John C. Doerfer Resigns for Accepting Gifts from Networks, 335

Mar. 29, 1962: Billie Sol Estes Is Arrested for Corporate Fraud, 341

Jan. 28, 1972: Clifford Irving Admits Faking Howard Hughes Memoirs, 422

Feb. 25, 1977: Film Producer David Begelman Is Found to Have Forged Checks, 509

Sept. 23, 1977: Horse-Swapping Fraud Upsets Belmont Park Raceway, 514

Apr. 15, 1981: Janet Cooke Admits Fabricating Her Pulitzer Prize-Winning Feature, 585

May 11, 1982: Philippine President Marcos Forces the Entire Supreme Court to Resign, 600

Apr. 25, 1983: German Magazine Publishes Faked Hitler Diaries, 618

Aug. 12, 1983-July 27, 1990: McMartin Preschool Is Embroiled in Child-Abuse Case, 624

May 2, 1984: E. F. Hutton Executives Plead Guilty to Fraud, 636

Apr. 22, 1986: Faith Healer Peter Popoff Is Exposed as a Fraud, 673

Nov. 28, 1987: Black Teenager Claims to Have Been Gang-Raped by Police Officers, 702

Jan. 15, 1988: ZZZZ Best Founder Is Indicted on Federal Fraud Charges, 708

Sept. 19, 1988: Stephen Breuning Pleads Guilty to Medical Research Fraud, 720

Dec. 3, 1989: Martin Luther King, Jr.'s, Doctoral-Thesis Plagiarism Is Revealed, 739

Nov. 19, 1990: Lip-Synching Duo Milli Vanilli Lose Grammy Award, 756

June 1, 1994: Congressman Dan Rostenkowski Is Indicted in House Post Office Scandal, 803

Spring, 1996: Physicist Publishes a Deliberately Fraudulent Article, 837

Jan., 1997: Pyramid Investment Schemes Cause Albanian Government to Fall, 846

Mar. 12, 1997: Prize-Winning Aborigine Novelist Revealed as a Fraud, 852

Apr., 1998: Scottish Historian Is Charged with Plagiarism, 879

May 11, 1998: Journalist Stephen Glass Is Exposed as a Fraud, 887

Jan. 28, 2000: John Spano Is Sentenced for Fraudulent Purchase of Ice Hockey Team, 901

Nov. 5, 2000: Japanese Amateur Archaeologist's "Discoveries" Are Proven Fakes, 919

2001: Clearstream Financial Clearinghouse Is Accused of Fraud and Money Laundering, 925

June 18, 2001: Award-Winning Historian Joseph J. Ellis Is Accused of Lying, 936

June 30, 2001: Korean Religious Teacher Jung Myung Seok Is Charged with Rape, 939

Aug. 27, 2001: Little League Baseball Star Danny Almonte Is Found to Be Overage, 942

Dec. 14, 2001: Notre Dame Football Coach Resigns for Falsifying His Résumé, 948

Jan. 4, 2002: Historian Stephen E. Ambrose Is Accused of Plagiarism, 951

Jan. 18, 2002: Historian Doris Kearns Goodwin Is Accused of Plagiarism, 959

Feb. 17, 2002: Rotting Human Bodies Are Found at Georgia Crematory, 964

Aug., 2002: Immunologist Resigns After Being Accused of Falsifying Research, 977

Sept. 25, 2002: Inquiry Reveals That Physicist Jan Hendrik Schön Faked His Research, 980

Apr. 29, 2003: *New York Times* Reporter Jayson Blair Is Exposed as a Fraud, 998

May 12, 2006: Scientist Is Indicted for Faking His Research on Creating Stem Cells, 1094

July 14, 2006: *New York Times* Exposes Grading Scandal at Auburn University, 1101

Nov. 2, 2006: Evangelist Kent Hovind Is Convicted of Federal Tax Violations, 1123

HOLLYWOOD

Feb. 1, 1922: Director Taylor's Murder Ruins Mabel Normand's Acting Career, 73

Jan. 18, 1923: Actor Wallace Reid's Death in Drug Rehab Shakes Film Industry, 86

Jan. 1, 1924: Film Star Mabel Normand's Chauffeur Shoots Millionaire Courtland S. Dines, 100

Nov. 19, 1924: Film Producer Thomas H. Ince Dies After Weekend on Hearst's Yacht, 108

Early 1928: Joseph P. Kennedy Begins an Affair with Gloria Swanson, 127

Sept. 4, 1932: Film Star Jean Harlow's Husband Is an Apparent Suicide, 160

Dec. 16, 1935: Film Star Thelma Todd's Death Cannot Be Explained, 178

Summer, 1936: Film Star Mary Astor's Diary Becomes a Public Sensation, 184

Feb. 6, 1942: Film Star Errol Flynn Is Acquitted of Rape, 202

Jan. 14, 1943: Film Star Frances Farmer Is Jailed and Institutionalized, 214

June 4, 1943: Actor Charles Chaplin Is Sued for Paternity, 220

July 5, 1948: Actor Carole Landis Commits Suicide During Affair with Rex Harrison, 245

Aug. 31, 1948: Film Star Robert Mitchum Is Arrested for Drug Possession, 251

May, 1955: Scandal Magazine Reveals Actor Rory Calhoun's Criminal Past, 295

Apr. 4, 1958: Actor Lana Turner's Daughter Kills Turner's Gangster Lover, 317

May 19, 1962: Marilyn Monroe Sings "Happy Birthday, Mr. President," 344

Feb. 25, 1977: Film Producer David Begelman Is Found to Have Forged Checks, 509

1978: Actor Joan Crawford's Daughter Publishes Damning Memoir, *Mommie Dearest*, 517

Feb. 1, 1978: Roman Polanski Flees the United States to Avoid Rape Trial, 522

Apr. 18, 1979: Actor Lee Marvin Is Ordered to Pay Palimony to Former Lover, 540

July 18, 1988: Actor Rob Lowe Videotapes His Sexual Encounter with a Minor, 717

June 27, 1995: Film Star Hugh Grant Is Arrested for Lewd Conduct, 827

Oct. 2, 2003: Newspaper Claims That Arnold Schwarzenegger Groped Women, 1016

Early Nov., 2003: Paris Hilton Sex-Tape Appears on the Web, 1019

July 28, 2006: Actor Mel Gibson Is Caught Making Anti-Semitic Remarks, 1106

HUMAN RIGHTS

Nov. 15, 1908: Belgium Confiscates Congo Free State from King Leopold II, 31

Mar. 21, 1928: Alberta Government Sterilizes Thousands Deemed Genetically and Mentally Unfit, 133

1930: Liberia Is Accused of Selling Its Own Citizens into Slavery, 142

Late 1955: British Atrocities in Kenya's Mau Mau Rebellion Are Revealed, 298

July 25, 1972: Newspaper Breaks Story of Abuses in Tuskegee Syphilis Study, 437

1976-1977: U.S. Congress Members Are Implicated in Koreagate Scandal, 479

Jan., 1977: Singer Anita Bryant Campaigns Against Lesbian and Gay Rights, 506

Mar. 4, 1999: Quebec Offers Support for Abused Duplessis Orphans, 892

Apr. 28, 2004: CBS Broadcasts Photos of Abused and Tortured Prisoners at Abu Ghraib, 1034

Nov. 17, 2005: Liberian Workers Sue Bridgestone Firestone over Slave Labor, 1078

INTERNATIONAL RELATIONS

Oct. 25, 1924: Forged Communist Letter Brings Down British Government, 105

1930: Liberia Is Accused of Selling Its Own Citizens into Slavery, 142

Oct. 11-22, 1937: Duke and Duchess of Windsor Visit Nazi Germany, 196

Apr. 22, 1942: French Prime Minister Pierre Laval Wants Germany to Win World War II, 209

Sept. 19, 1952: Actor Charles Chaplin Cannot Reenter the United States, 283

Sept. 12, 1962: British Civil Servant Is Arrested for Spying, 347

Aug. 14, 1963: Madame Nhu Derides Self-Immolation of Vietnamese Buddhists, 362

Oct. 29, 1965: Moroccan Politician Mehdi Ben Barka Disappears in Paris, 374

May 14, 1974: *Washington Post* Reveals That the Nixons Received Jewelry Gifts, 453

1976-1977: U.S. Congress Members Are Implicated in Koreagate Scandal, 479

Feb. 4, 1976: Lockheed Is Implicated in Bribing Foreign Officials, 482

Oct. 10, 1979: French President Giscard d'Estaing Is Accused of Taking a Bribe, 550

Late July, 1980: President's Brother, Billy Carter, Registers as a Paid Agent for Libya, 571

Aug. 19, 1985: West German Counterintelligence Chief Defects to East Germany, 657

Mar. 3, 1986: Former U.N. Secretary-General Kurt Waldheim's Nazi Past Is Revealed, 669

Nov. 13, 1986-May 4, 1989: Iran-Contra Weapons Scandal Taints Reagan's Administration, 676

June 25, 1997: Swiss Banks Admit to Holding Accounts of Holocaust Victims, 858

Feb. 11, 2002: French Judge Admits Favoring Russian Figure Skaters in Winter Olympics, 962

July, 2002: Journalist Alleges Release of Genetically Modified Corn Seeds in New Zealand, 974

Mar. 2, 2003: U.S. National Security Agency Is Found to Have Spied on U.N. Officials, 995

July 14, 2003: Columnist Robert Novak Leaks the Name of CIA Operative Valerie Plame, 1010

June 2, 2004: U.N. Report Reveals That Secretary-General Kofi Annan Dismissed Sexual Harassment Charges, 1039

Jan. 15, 2005: Iqbal Riza Resigns from the United Nations in Oil-for-Food Scandal, 1053

Summer, 2006-Mar. 16, 2007: China Recalls Pet Food That Has Killed Thousands of American Pets, 1097

Nov. 23, 2006: Former Russian Security Service Officer Dies from Radiation Poisoning, 1132

LABOR

Mar. 25, 1911: Nearly 150 Workers Die in Triangle Shirtwaist Factory Fire, 40

1930: Liberia Is Accused of Selling Its Own Citizens into Slavery, 142

May, 1959: Teamsters Leader Dave Beck Is Convicted of Tax Fraud, 323

Dec. 30, 1969: United Mine Workers Leader Joseph Yablonski Is Murdered, 404

Nov. 17, 2005: Liberian Workers Sue Bridgestone Firestone over Slave Labor, 1078

LAW AND THE COURTS

Jan. 23, 1904: Senator Joseph R. Burton Is Convicted of Bribery, 4

Mar. 2, 1906: Psychoanalyst Ernest Jones Is Accused of Molesting Mentally Disabled Children, 12

June 25, 1906: Millionaire Heir Murders Architect Stanford White, 16

July 12, 1906: French Court Declares Alfred Dreyfus Innocent of Treason, 19

Dec. 8, 1906: Former U.S. Senator Arthur Brown Is Murdered by Lover, 22

1907: Elinor Glyn's Novel *Three Weeks* Shocks Readers, 25

Mar. 25, 1911: Nearly 150 Workers Die in Triangle Shirtwaist Factory Fire, 40

Jan., 1913: British Prime Minister's Staff Is Investigated for Insider Trading, 43

Jan. 13, 1913: Federal Judge Is Impeached for Profiting from His Office, 46

May 13, 1913: Boxer Jack Johnson Is Imprisoned for Abetting Prostitution, 52

Apr. 2, 1915: Players Fix Liverpool-Manchester United Soccer Match, 55

1919-1920: Ponzi Schemes Are Revealed as Investment Frauds, 63

July 19, 1921: U.S. Senate Rebukes Navy in Homosexuality Investigation, 70

Apr. 12, 1922: Film Star Fatty Arbuckle Is Acquitted of Manslaughter, 79

Mar. 2, 1923: U.S. Senate Investigates Veterans Bureau Chief for Fraud, 89

Jan. 1, 1924: Film Star Mabel Normand's Chauffeur Shoots Millionaire Courtland S. Dines, 100

May 12, 1924: Kentucky Congressman John W. Langley Is Convicted of Violating the Volstead Act, 103

July, 1925: *Nosferatu* Is Found to Have Violated *Dracula* Copyright, 111

May-June, 1926: Evangelist Aimee Semple McPherson Claims She Was Kidnapped, 115

Mar. 21, 1928: Alberta Government Sterilizes Thousands Deemed Genetically and Mentally Unfit, 133

Nov., 1929: Banque Oustric et Cie Failure Prompts French Inquiry, 139

Mar. 30, 1931: "Scottsboro Boys" Are Railroaded Through Rape Trials, 150

1932: Insull Utilities Trusts Collapse Prompts New Federal Regulation, 154

May 16, 1934: General Douglas MacArthur Sues Newspaper Columnist for Libel, 173

July 10, 1934: Sex Scandal Forces Resignation of Alberta Premier Brownlee, 176

Mar. 17, 1937: Atherton Report Exposes San Francisco Police Corruption, 191

Feb. 6, 1942: Film Star Errol Flynn Is Acquitted of Rape, 202

Feb. 19, 1942: President Roosevelt Orders Internment of Japanese Americans, 205

Dec. 5, 1942: Industrialist Charles Bedaux Is Arrested for Nazi Collaboration, 212

Jan. 14, 1943: Film Star Frances Farmer Is Jailed and Institutionalized, 214

June 4, 1943: Actor Charles Chaplin Is Sued for Paternity, 220

June 5, 1944: Australian Poets Claim Responsibility for a Literary Hoax, 223

May 26, 1945: Norwegian Writer Knut Hamsun Is Arrested for Treason, 229

Dec. 14, 1945: Poet Ezra Pound Is Charged with Treason and Institutionalized, 236

Nov. 23, 1946: Tennis Star Bill Tilden Is Arrested for Lewd Behavior with a Minor, 239

Aug. 31, 1948: Film Star Robert Mitchum Is Arrested for Drug Possession, 251

Jan. 21, 1950: Alger Hiss Is Convicted of Perjury, 259

Jan. 17, 1951: College Basketball Players Begin Shaving Points for Money, 274

Mar. 9, 1956: British Conductor-Composer Is Arrested for Possessing Pornography, 304

May, 1959: Teamsters Leader Dave Beck Is Convicted of Tax Fraud, 323

Sept. 12, 1962: British Civil Servant Is Arrested for Spying, 347

Oct. 26, 1962: West German Police Raid *Der Spiegel* Magazine Offices, 349

July 2, 1963: Muslim Leader Elijah Muhammad Is Sued for Paternity, 359

Oct. 7, 1964: President Lyndon Johnson's Aide Is Arrested in Gay-Sex Sting, 371

Mar. 1, 1967: Adam Clayton Powell, Jr., Is Excluded from Congress, 380

Nov. 28, 1967: Investor Louis Wolfson Is Convicted of Selling Stock Illegally, 389

May 9, 1969: Supreme Court Justice Abe Fortas Is Accused of Bribery, 391

July 18, 1969: Senator Edward Kennedy's Driving Accident Kills Mary Jo Kopechne, 394

May 28, 1970: Irish Politicians Are Tried for Conspiring to Import Weapons, 413

June 13, 1971: *New York Times* Publishes the Pentagon Papers, 416

June 22, 1972: Police Arrest Architect John Poulson for Bribery and Fraud, 431

Oct. 10, 1973: Spiro T. Agnew Resigns Vice Presidency in Disgrace, 447

Apr. 15, 1974: Kidnapped Heir Patty Hearst Helps Rob a Bank, 450

Summer, 1974: Dalkon Shield Contraceptive Is Removed from the Market, 459

1976: Peace Corps Conceals Murder of Volunteer in Tonga, 476

Feb. 4, 1976: Lockheed Is Implicated in Bribing Foreign Officials, 482

Mar. 21, 1976: Actor Claudine Longet Kills Ski Champion Vladimir Sabich, 485

Sept. 1, 1976: Former Beatle George Harrison Loses Plagiarism Lawsuit, 494

Oct. 4, 1976: Agriculture Secretary Earl Butz Resigns After Making Obscene Joke, 500

Feb. 25, 1977: Film Producer David Begelman Is Found to Have Forged Checks, 509

1978: *Roots* Author Alex Haley Is Sued for Plagiarism, 520

Feb. 1, 1978: Roman Polanski Flees the United States to Avoid Rape Trial, 522

Aug. 4, 1978: British Politician Jeremy Thorpe Is Charged with Attempted Murder, 531

Apr. 18, 1979: Actor Lee Marvin Is Ordered to Pay Palimony to Former Lover, 540

Sept. 26, 1979: Love Canal Residents Sue Chemical Company, 546

Feb. 2, 1980: Media Uncover FBI Sting Implicating Dozens of Lawmakers, 561

Mar. 10, 1980: Scarsdale Diet Doctor Is Killed by His Lover, 565

Apr. 27, 1980: Mobster's Arrest Reveals Point Shaving by Boston College Basketball Players, 568

Late July, 1980: President's Brother, Billy Carter, Registers as a Paid Agent for Libya, 571

Sept. 3, 1980: Congressman Bauman Is Arrested for Liaison with Teenage Boy, 577

Apr. 28, 1981: Tennis Star Billie Jean King Is Sued for Palimony, 588

May 29, 1981: Court Finds That Ford Ignored Pinto's Safety Problems, 594

Sept. 10, 1981: *Chicago Sun-Times* Reports That Cardinal Cody Diverted Church Funds, 597

May 11, 1982: Philippine President Marcos Forces the Entire Supreme Court to Resign, 600

Aug. 6, 1982: Banco Ambrosiano Collapses Amid Criminal Accusations, 606

Oct. 19, 1982: Car Manufacturer John De Lorean Is Arrested in a Drug Sting, 609

Aug. 12, 1983-July 27, 1990: McMartin Preschool Is Embroiled in Child-Abuse Case, 624

May 2, 1984: E. F. Hutton Executives Plead Guilty to Fraud, 636

Dec. 22, 1984: Subway Vigilante Bernhard Goetz Shoots Four Black Youths, 641

May 7, 1985: Banker Jake Butcher Pleads Guilty to Fraud, 648

July 19, 1985: Mayflower Madam Pleads Guilty to Promoting Prostitution, 654

Oct. 23, 1985: Guru Bhagwan Shree Rajneesh Is Indicted for Immigration Fraud, 662

Feb. 28, 1986: Baseball Commissioner Peter Ueberroth Suspends Players for Cocaine Use, 666

Jan. 12 and May 11, 1987: Media Reports Spark Investigation of Australian Police Corruption, 681

Mar. 19, 1987: Jim Bakker Resigns as Head of PTL Television Network, 690

Apr. 9, 1987: Bess Myerson Resigns as New York Commissioner of Cultural Affairs, 693

July 25, 1987: Novelist-Politician Jeffrey Archer Wins Libel Trial Against the *Daily Star*, 696

Nov. 28, 1987: Black Teenager Claims to Have Been Gang-Raped by Police Officers, 702

Jan. 15, 1988: ZZZZ Best Founder Is Indicted on Federal Fraud Charges, 708

Mar. 29, 1989: Financier Michael Milken Is Indicted for Racketeering and Fraud, 726

Aug. 24, 1989: Pete Rose Is Banned from Baseball for Betting on Games, 735

Jan. 18, 1990: Washington, D.C., Mayor Marion Barry Is Arrested for Drug Use, 748

Mar., 1990: Menendez Brothers Are Arrested for Murdering Their Parents, 750

Aug. 27, 1990: Guinness Four Are Found Guilty of Share-Trading Fraud, 753

Mar. 30, 1991: William Kennedy Smith Is Accused of Rape, 759

Apr. 5, 1991: George W. Bush Is Investigated for Insider Trading, 762

Oct. 11-13, 1991: Justice Clarence Thomas's Confirmation Hearings Create a Scandal, 768

Jan. 13, 1992: Woody Allen Has Affair with Lover Mia Farrow's Adopted Daughter, 773

Apr. 15, 1992: Hotel Tycoon Leona Helmsley Enters Prison for Tax Evasion, 776

May 19, 1992: Amy Fisher Shoots Mary Jo Buttafuoco, 781

June 23, 1993: Lorena Bobbitt Severs Her Husband's Penis, 795

June 1, 1994: Congressman Dan Rostenkowski Is Indicted in House Post Office Scandal, 803

June 12, 1994: Double Murder Leads to Sensational O. J. Simpson Trial, 806

June 30, 1994: Tonya Harding Is Banned from Skating After Attack on Rival, 812

Aug. 5, 1994: Kenneth Starr Is Appointed to the Whitewater Investigation, 818

Aug. 21, 1994: Sex Scandal Forces Dismissal of NAACP Chief Benjamin Chavis, 821

Feb. 28, 1995: Former Mexican President Carlos Salinas's Brother Is Arrested for Murder, 824

June 27, 1995: Film Star Hugh Grant Is Arrested for Lewd Conduct, 827

Aug. 16, 1996: Belgian Media Reveal How Police Bungled Serial Murder Case, 840

Feb. 26, 1997: Teacher Mary Kay Letourneau Is Arrested for Statutory Rape, 849

May 20, 1997: Air Force Prosecution of Female Officer for Adultery Reveals Double Standard, 855

Aug. 31, 1997: Princess Diana Dies in a Car Crash, 861

Sept. 22, 1997: Sportscaster Marv Albert Is Tried for Sexual Assault, 865

Nov. 26, 1997: Canadian Health Commissioner Releases Report on Tainted Blood, 868

Dec. 11, 1997: HUD Secretary Henry Cisneros Is Indicted for Lying to Federal Agents, 872

Apr. 7, 1998: Pop Singer George Michael Is Arrested for Lewd Conduct, 881

May, 1998: Police Corruption Is Revealed in Los Angeles's Rampart Division, 884

Dec. 23, 1998: Prominent Belgians Are Sentenced in Agusta-Dassault Corruption Scandal, 889

Jan. 28, 2000: John Spano Is Sentenced for Fraudulent Purchase of Ice Hockey Team, 901

May 9, 2000: Former Louisiana Governor Edwin Edwards Is Convicted on Corruption Charges, 907

Dec., 2000: Sexual Abuse of Children in France Leads to the Outreau Affair, 922

Feb. 18, 2001: CIA Agent Robert Hanssen Is Arrested for Spying for the Russians, 931

Apr. 30, 2001: Washington Intern Chandra Levy Disappears, 933

June 30, 2001: Korean Religious Teacher Jung Myung Seok Is Charged with Rape, 939

Dec. 2, 2001: Enron Bankruptcy Reveals Massive Financial Fraud, 945

Jan. 6, 2002: *Boston Globe* Reports on Child Sexual Abuse by Roman Catholic Priests, 954

Mar. 27, 2002: Georgia Basketball Coach Jim Harrick, Sr., Resigns over Fraud Allegations, 968

June 25, 2002: Internal Corruption Forces Adelphia Communications to Declare Bankruptcy, 971

May 3, 2003: University of Alabama Fires New Football Coach in Sex Scandal, 1002

July 1, 2003: Basketball Star Kobe Bryant Is Accused of Rape, 1008

Sept. 3, 2003: Mutual Fund Companies Are Implicated in Shady Trading Practices, 1013

Dec. 18, 2003: Pop Star Michael Jackson Is Charged with Child Molestation, 1025

Mar. 4, 2004: Former United Way Charity Chief Pleads Guilty to Embezzlement, 1028

Mar. 5, 2004: Martha Stewart Is Convicted in Insider-Trading Scandal, 1031

June 2, 2004: U.N. Report Reveals That

Secretary-General Kofi Annan Dismissed Sexual Harassment Charges, 1039

Oct. 13, 2004: Television Producer Files Sex Harassment Suit Against Bill O'Reilly, 1047

Oct. 14, 2004: Insurance Brokerage Marsh & McLennan Is Charged with Fraud, 1050

July 1, 2005: Federal Agents Raid Congressman Randall Cunningham's Home, 1064

Sept. 12, 2005: Westar Energy Executives Are Found Guilty of Looting Their Company, 1072

Nov. 17, 2005: Liberian Workers Sue Bridgestone Firestone over Slave Labor, 1078

Dec. 6, 2005: Spokane, Washington, Mayor Recalled in Gay-Sex Scandal, 1081

Mar. 14, 2006: Duke Lacrosse Players Are Accused of Gang Rape, 1086

Summer, 2006-Mar. 16, 2007: China Recalls Pet Food That Has Killed Thousands of American Pets, 1097

July 28, 2006: Actor Mel Gibson Is Caught Making Anti-Semitic Remarks, 1106

Sept. 18, 2006: *Newsweek* Reveals That Hewlett-Packard Spied on Its Own Board, 1114

Nov. 2, 2006: Evangelist Kent Hovind Is Convicted of Federal Tax Violations, 1123

June 4, 2007: Congressman William J. Jefferson Is Indicted for Corruption, 1147

July 9, 2007: Senator David Vitter's Name Is Found in D.C. Madam's Address Book, 1150

July 11, 2007: Florida Politician Is Arrested for Soliciting an Undercover Male Police Officer, 1153

Aug. 20, 2007: Football Star Michael Vick Pleads Guilty to Financing a Dogfighting Ring, 1158

Oct. 5, 2007: Olympic Champion Marion Jones Admits Steroid Use, 1164

June 13, 2008: Singer R. Kelly Is Acquitted on Child Pornography Charges, 1170

July 29, 2008: NBA Referee Tim Donaghy Is Sentenced to Prison for Betting on Games, 1172

LITERATURE

1907: Elinor Glyn's Novel *Three Weeks* Shocks Readers, 25

July, 1925: *Nosferatu* Is Found to Have Violated *Dracula* Copyright, 111

June 5, 1944: Australian Poets Claim Responsibility for a Literary Hoax, 223

May 26, 1945: Norwegian Writer Knut Hamsun Is Arrested for Treason, 229

Dec. 14, 1945: Poet Ezra Pound Is Charged with Treason and Institutionalized, 236

Nov. 21, 1953: Piltdown Man Is Revealed to Be a Hoax, 292

Jan. 28, 1972: Clifford Irving Admits Faking Howard Hughes Memoirs, 422

1978: *Roots* Author Alex Haley Is Sued for Plagiarism, 520

Mar. 12, 1997: Prize-Winning Aborigine Novelist Revealed as a Fraud, 852

Aug. 12, 2006: Novelist Günter Grass Admits to Youthful Nazi Ties, 1109

MEDICINE AND HEALTH CARE

Jan. 18, 1923: Actor Wallace Reid's Death in Drug Rehab Shakes Film Industry, 86

Mar. 21, 1928: Alberta Government Sterilizes Thousands Deemed Genetically and Mentally Unfit, 133

Sept.-Oct., 1937: Prescription Elixir Causes More than One Hundred Deaths, 193

Dec. 1, 1952: George Jorgensen Becomes Christine Jorgensen, 289

1956-1962: Prescription Thalidomide Causes Widespread Birth Disorders, 301

July 25, 1972: Newspaper Breaks Story of Abuses in Tuskegee Syphilis Study, 437

Summer, 1974: Dalkon Shield Contraceptive Is Removed from the Market, 459

Sept. 26, 1979: Love Canal Residents Sue Chemical Company, 546

Sept. 17, 1985: Media Allege Canadian Officials Allowed Sale of Rancid Tuna, 660

Feb. 28, 1986: Baseball Commissioner Peter Ueberroth Suspends Players for Cocaine Use, 666

Sept. 19, 1988: Stephen Breuning Pleads Guilty to Medical Research Fraud, 720

July 1, 1994: Soccer Star Diego Maradona Is Expelled from World Cup, 815

Feb. 4, 1996: Whistle-Blower Reveals Tobacco Industry Corruption, 833

Nov. 26, 1997: Canadian Health Commissioner Releases Report on Tainted Blood, 868

Sept., 2000: American Scientists Are Accused of Starting a Measles Epidemic in the Amazon, 910

Sept. 26, 2000: Gymnast Andreea Răducan Loses Her Olympic Gold Medal Because of Drugs, 916

Jan. 30, 2001: Liverpool Children's Hospital Collects Body Parts Without Authorization, 927

Aug., 2002: Immunologist Resigns After Being Accused of Falsifying Research, 977

Mar. 17, 2005: Former Baseball Star Mark McGwire Evades Congressional Questions on Steroid Use, 1058

Summer, 2006-Mar. 16, 2007: China Recalls Pet Food That Has Killed Thousands of American Pets, 1097

July 26, 2006: Tour de France Is Hit with a Doping Scandal, 1103

Nov. 23, 2006: Former Russian Security Service Officer Dies from Radiation Poisoning, 1132

Feb. 18, 2007: *Washington Post* Exposes Decline of Walter Reed Army Hospital, 1138

Oct. 5, 2007: Olympic Champion Marion Jones Admits Steroid Use, 1164

MILITARY

1906-1909: Emperor William II's Homosexual "Circle" Scandalizes Germany, 9

July 12, 1906: French Court Declares Alfred Dreyfus Innocent of Treason, 19

May, 1915: British Government Falls Because of Munitions Shortages and Military Setbacks, 58

July 19, 1921: U.S. Senate Rebukes Navy in Homosexuality Investigation, 70

May, 1930: Postmaster's Division of Airmail Routes Creates a Scandal, 144

July 28, 1932: U.S. Troops Drive World War I Veterans from Washington, 156

Feb. 19, 1942: President Roosevelt Orders Internment of Japanese Americans, 205

Apr. 22, 1942: French Prime Minister Pierre Laval Wants Germany to Win World War II, 209

May 9, 1945: Norwegian Politician Quisling Is Arrested for Nazi Collaboration, 226

Aug. 14, 1945: French War Hero Pétain Is Convicted of Nazi Collaboration, 232

Aug. 26, 1949: Viet Minh Broadcasts French General's Damaging Report, 257

July 16, 1951: Belgium's Disgraced King Leopold III Abdicates, 276

Late 1955: British Atrocities in Kenya's Mau Mau Rebellion Are Revealed, 298

June, 1956: George F. Kennan Proves Russian Sisson Documents Are Fakes, 307

Nov. 13, 1969: American Massacre of Vietnamese Civilians at My Lai Is Revealed, 401

May 4, 1970: National Guardsmen Kill Protesting Kent State Students, 410

June 13, 1971: *New York Times* Publishes the Pentagon Papers, 416

Apr. 4, 1976: West Point Cadets Are Caught Cheating on Exams, 488

Nov. 9, 1976: German Generals Must Retire for Supporting a Neo-Nazi Pilot, 503

Mar. 3, 1986: Former U.N. Secretary-General Kurt Waldheim's Nazi Past Is Revealed, 669

Nov. 13, 1986-May 4, 1989: Iran-Contra Weapons Scandal Taints Reagan's Administration, 676

Dec. 15-25, 1989: Harassment of a Christian Minister Sparks the Romanian Revolution, 742

June 26, 1992: U.S. Navy Secretary Resigns in the Wake of Tailhook Sexual Assault Scandal, 784

Apr. 28, 1994: U.S. Naval Academy Expels Midshipmen for Cheating, 800

May 20, 1997: Air Force Prosecution of Female Officer for Adultery Reveals Double Standard, 855

Jan. 2, 2003: E-mail Message Prompts Inquiry into Air Force Academy Sexual Assaults, 991

Mar. 2, 2003: U.S. National Security Agency Is Found to Have Spied on U.N. Officials, 995

Apr. 28, 2004: CBS Broadcasts Photos of Abused and Tortured Prisoners at Abu Ghraib, 1034

Sept. 8, 2004: *60 Minutes II* Reports on George W. Bush's Evasion of Wartime Duty, 1044

June 22, 2005: U.S. Air Force Investigates Religious Intolerance at Its Academy, 1062

Aug. 12, 2006: Novelist Günter Grass Admits to Youthful Nazi Ties, 1109

Feb. 18, 2007: *Washington Post* Exposes Decline of Walter Reed Army Hospital, 1138

MURDER AND SUICIDE

June 25, 1906: Millionaire Heir Murders Architect Stanford White, 16

Dec. 8, 1906: Former U.S. Senator Arthur Brown Is Murdered by Lover, 22

July 27, 1917: Millionaire Socialite Dies Under Suspicious Circumstances, 60

Feb. 1, 1922: Director Taylor's Murder Ruins Mabel Normand's Acting Career, 73

Apr. 12, 1922: Film Star Fatty Arbuckle Is Acquitted of Manslaughter, 79

May 30, 1923: U.S. Attorney General Harry M. Daugherty's Aide Commits Suicide, 92

Jan. 1, 1924: Film Star Mabel Normand's Chauffeur Shoots Millionaire Courtland S. Dines, 100

Nov. 19, 1924: Film Producer Thomas H. Ince Dies After Weekend on Hearst's Yacht, 108

1928-1929: Actor Is Suspected of Falsely Claiming to Be an American Indian, 130

Sept. 4, 1932: Film Star Jean Harlow's Husband Is an Apparent Suicide, 160

Jan. 8, 1934-Jan. 17, 1936: Stavisky's Fraudulent Schemes Rock French Government, 170

Dec. 16, 1935: Film Star Thelma Todd's Death Cannot Be Explained, 178

Dec. 5, 1942: Industrialist Charles Bedaux Is Arrested for Nazi Collaboration, 212

July 5, 1948: Actor Carole Landis Commits Suicide During Affair with Rex Harrison, 245

Apr. 4, 1958: Actor Lana Turner's Daughter Kills Turner's Gangster Lover, 317

July 2, 1963: Muslim Leader Elijah Muhammad Is Sued for Paternity, 359

Mar. 13, 1964: Kitty Genovese Dies as Her Cries for Help Are Ignored, 369

Oct. 29, 1965: Moroccan Politician Mehdi Ben Barka Disappears in Paris, 374

Sept. 5, 1967: Socialite Nancy Wakeman Shoots Her Politician-Husband, 386

Dec. 30, 1969: United Mine Workers Leader Joseph Yablonski Is Murdered, 404

May 4, 1970: National Guardsmen Kill Protesting Kent State Students, 410

May 20, 1974: French Cardinal Daniélou Dies in a Prostitute's House, 456

Feb. 3, 1975: Honduras's "Bananagate" Bribery Scandal Leads to Executive's Suicide, 471

1976: Peace Corps Conceals Murder of Volunteer in Tonga, 476

Mar. 21, 1976: Actor Claudine Longet Kills Ski Champion Vladimir Sabich, 485

July 23, 1978: Utah Millionaire Is Murdered by His Grandson, 528

Aug. 4, 1978: British Politician Jeremy Thorpe Is Charged with Attempted Murder, 531

Mar. 10, 1980: Scarsdale Diet Doctor Is Killed by His Lover, 565

Aug. 6, 1982: Banco Ambrosiano Collapses Amid Criminal Accusations, 606

Aug. 21, 1983: Filipino Opposition Leader Aquino Is Assassinated on Return Home, 628

July 10, 1985: French Secret Service Sinks the Greenpeace Ship *Rainbow Warrior*, 651

Jan. 22, 1987: Pennsylvania Politician Kills Himself at Televised Press Conference, 684

Mar., 1990: Menendez Brothers Are Arrested for Murdering Their Parents, 750

June 12, 1994: Double Murder Leads to Sensational O. J. Simpson Trial, 806

Feb. 28, 1995: Former Mexican President Carlos Salinas's Brother Is Arrested for Murder, 824

Aug. 16, 1996: Belgian Media Reveal How Police Bungled Serial Murder Case, 840

May, 1998: Police Corruption Is Revealed in Los Angeles's Rampart Division, 884

Dec. 23, 1998: Prominent Belgians Are Sentenced in Agusta-Dassault Corruption Scandal, 889

Apr. 30, 2001: Washington Intern Chandra Levy Disappears, 933

Nov. 23, 2006: Former Russian Security Service Officer Dies from Radiation Poisoning, 1132

May 28, 2007: Japanese Politician Charged with Corruption Hangs Himself, 1145

July 9, 2007: Senator David Vitter's Name Is Found in D.C. Madam's Address Book, 1150

MUSIC AND PERFORMING ARTS

Mar. 26, 1922: Hindemith's Opera *Sancta Susanna* Depicts a Nun's Sexual Desires, 76

Mar. 9, 1956: British Conductor-Composer Is Arrested for Possessing Pornography, 304

Dec. 12, 1957: Rock Star Jerry Lee Lewis Marries Thirteen-Year-Old Cousin, 313

Feb. 8, 1960: U.S. Congress Investigates Payola in Pop Music Industry, 332

May 19, 1962: Marilyn Monroe Sings "Happy Birthday, Mr. President," 344

Sept. 1, 1976: Former Beatle George Harrison Loses Plagiarism Lawsuit, 494

Jan., 1977: Singer Anita Bryant Campaigns Against Lesbian and Gay Rights, 506

Nov. 19, 1990: Lip-Synching Duo Milli Vanilli Lose Grammy Award, 756

Apr. 7, 1998: Pop Singer George Michael Is Arrested for Lewd Conduct, 881

Dec. 18, 2003: Pop Star Michael Jackson Is Charged with Child Molestation, 1025

June 13, 2008: Singer R. Kelly Is Acquitted on Child Pornography Charges, 1170

ORGANIZED CRIME AND RACKETEERING

June 13, 1907: San Francisco Mayor Schmitz Is Found Guilty of Extortion, 28

Apr. 2, 1915: Players Fix Liverpool-Manchester United Soccer Match, 55

Sept. 21, 1919: White Sox Players Conspire to Lose World Series in "Black Sox" Scandal, 66

Mar. 17, 1937: Atherton Report Exposes San Francisco Police Corruption, 191

May 22, 1939: Kansas City's Boss Pendergast Pleads Guilty to Income Tax Evasion, 199

Spring, 1947: Baseball Manager Leo Durocher Is Suspended for Gambling Ties, 242

May 3, 1950: U.S. Senate Committee Begins Investigating Organized Crime, 270

Apr. 4, 1958: Actor Lana Turner's Daughter Kills Turner's Gangster Lover, 317

May, 1959: Teamsters Leader Dave Beck Is Convicted of Tax Fraud, 323

Feb. 7, 1960: President Kennedy's Romantic Affair Links Him to Organized Crime, 329

Oct. 7, 1963: Vice President Lyndon B. Johnson Aide Resigns over Crime Connections, 365

Fall, 1969-Winter, 1971: Japanese Baseball Players Are Implicated in Game Fixing, 398

Dec. 30, 1969: United Mine Workers Leader Joseph Yablonski Is Murdered, 404

June 17, 1972-Aug. 9, 1974: Watergate Break-in Leads to President Nixon's Resignation, 425

Sept. 23, 1977: Horse-Swapping Fraud Upsets Belmont Park Raceway, 514

Feb. 2, 1980: Media Uncover FBI Sting Implicating Dozens of Lawmakers, 561

Apr. 27, 1980: Mobster's Arrest Reveals Point Shaving by Boston College Basketball Players, 568

May 23, 1981: Italian Justice Minister Resigns Because of Crime Connection, 591

Aug. 6, 1982: Banco Ambrosiano Collapses Amid Criminal Accusations, 606

Oct. 19, 1982: Car Manufacturer John De Lorean Is Arrested in a Drug Sting, 609

Oct. 23, 1985: Guru Bhagwan Shree Rajneesh Is Indicted for Immigration Fraud, 662

Feb. 28, 1986: Baseball Commissioner Peter Ueberroth Suspends Players for Cocaine Use, 666

Jan. 15, 1988: ZZZZ Best Founder Is Indicted on Federal Fraud Charges, 708

Mar. 29, 1989: Financier Michael Milken Is Indicted for Racketeering and Fraud, 726

Nov. 3, 1996: Car Crash Reveals Depth of Government Corruption in Turkey, 843

Dec. 23, 1998: Prominent Belgians Are Sentenced in Agusta-Dassault Corruption Scandal, 889

Feb. 18, 2001: CIA Agent Robert Hanssen Is Arrested for Spying for the Russians, 931

Jan. 27, 2005: German Soccer Referee Admits to Fixing Games for Money, 1055

May 4, 2006: Media Uncover Match-Fixing in Italian Soccer, 1092

July 9, 2007: Senator David Vitter's Name Is Found in D.C. Madam's Address Book, 1150

Aug. 20, 2007: Football Star Michael Vick Pleads Guilty to Financing a Dogfighting Ring, 1158

PERFORMING ARTS

1909-1916: Dancer Isadora Duncan Begins Affair with Millionaire Heir, 34

1927: Mae West's Play About Gays Is Banned on Broadway, 122

Feb. 23, 1963: Play Accuses Pope Pius XII of Complicity in the Holocaust, 353

PLAGIARISM

Jan. 28, 1972: Clifford Irving Admits Faking Howard Hughes Memoirs, 422

Sept. 1, 1976: Former Beatle George Harrison Loses Plagiarism Lawsuit, 494

1978: *Roots* Author Alex Haley Is Sued for Plagiarism, 520

Sept. 23, 1987: Plagiarism Charges End Joe Biden's Presidential Campaign, 698

Dec. 3, 1989: Martin Luther King, Jr.'s, Doctoral-Thesis Plagiarism Is Revealed, 739

Apr., 1998: Scottish Historian Is Charged with Plagiarism, 879

Jan. 4, 2002: Historian Stephen E. Ambrose Is Accused of Plagiarism, 951

Jan. 18, 2002: Historian Doris Kearns Goodwin Is Accused of Plagiarism, 959

Apr. 29, 2003: *New York Times* Reporter Jayson Blair Is Exposed as a Fraud, 998

July 24, 2007: University of Colorado Fires Professor for Plagiarism and Research Falsification, 1155

POLITICS

1904: Theodore Roosevelt Is Accused of Accepting Corporate Funds, 1

Jan. 23, 1904: Senator Joseph R. Burton Is Convicted of Bribery, 4

Dec., 1904: Boston Alderman Is Reelected While in Jail for Fraud, 6

1906-1909: Emperor William II's Homosexual "Circle" Scandalizes Germany, 9

June 13, 1907: San Francisco Mayor Schmitz Is Found Guilty of Extortion, 28

Jan., 1913: British Prime Minister's Staff Is Investigated for Insider Trading, 43

Jan. 13, 1913: Federal Judge Is Impeached for Profiting from His Office, 46

June 22, 1922: British Prime Minister David Lloyd George Is Accused of Selling Honors, 83

Mar. 2, 1923: U.S. Senate Investigates Veterans Bureau Chief for Fraud, 89

May 30, 1923: U.S. Attorney General Harry M. Daugherty's Aide Commits Suicide, 92

Oct. 22, 1923: U.S. Senate Begins Hearings on Teapot Dome Oil Leases, 95

May 12, 1924: Kentucky Congressman John W. Langley Is Convicted of Violating the Volstead Act, 103

Oct. 25, 1924: Forged Communist Letter Brings Down British Government, 105

1927: President Warren G. Harding's Lover Publishes Tell-All Memoir, 124

Nov., 1929: Banque Oustric et Cie Failure Prompts French Inquiry, 139

May, 1930: Postmaster's Division of Airmail Routes Creates a Scandal, 144

July 28, 1932: U.S. Troops Drive World War I Veterans from Washington, 156

Mar. 31, 1933: *New York Times* Reporter Denies Reports of a Soviet Famine, 167

July 10, 1934: Sex Scandal Forces Resignation of Alberta Premier Brownlee, 176

Dec. 10, 1936: King Edward VIII Abdicates to Marry an American Divorcée, 187

Oct. 11-22, 1937: Duke and Duchess of Windsor Visit Nazi Germany, 196

May 22, 1939: Kansas City's Boss Pendergast Pleads Guilty to Income Tax Evasion, 199

Apr. 22, 1942: French Prime Minister Pierre Laval Wants Germany to Win World War II, 209

May 26, 1945: Norwegian Writer Knut Hamsun Is Arrested for Treason, 229

Aug. 14, 1945: French War Hero Pétain Is Convicted of Nazi Collaboration, 232

Dec. 14, 1945: Poet Ezra Pound Is Charged with Treason and Institutionalized, 236

Aug. 4, 1948: Columnist Drew Pearson Exposes Congressman's Corruption, 248

Aug. 26, 1949: Viet Minh Broadcasts French General's Damaging Report, 257

Jan. 21, 1950: Alger Hiss Is Convicted of Perjury, 259

Feb. 9, 1950: U.S. Senator Joseph McCarthy Launches Communist Witch Hunt, 266

July 16, 1951: Belgium's Disgraced King Leopold III Abdicates, 276

Nov. 16, 1951: Federal Tax Official Resigns After Accepting Bribes, 279

Sept. 19, 1952: Actor Charles Chaplin Cannot Reenter the United States, 283

Sept. 23, 1952: Richard Nixon Denies Taking Illegal Campaign Contributions, 286

June, 1956: George F. Kennan Proves Russian Sisson Documents Are Fakes, 307

June 25, 1956: President Truman's Appointments Secretary Is Convicted of Tax Conspiracy, 310

Sept. 22, 1958: President Eisenhower's Chief of Staff Resigns for Influence Selling, 320

Feb. 7, 1960: President Kennedy's Romantic Affair Links Him to Organized Crime, 329

Mar. 29, 1962: Billie Sol Estes Is Arrested for Corporate Fraud, 341

May 19, 1962: Marilyn Monroe Sings "Happy Birthday, Mr. President," 344

Sept. 12, 1962: British Civil Servant Is Arrested for Spying, 347

Oct. 26, 1962: West German Police Raid *Der Spiegel* Magazine Offices, 349

Mar. 2-Sept. 25, 1963: John Profumo Affair Rocks British Government, 355

Aug. 14, 1963: Madame Nhu Derides Self-Immolation of Vietnamese Buddhists, 362

Oct. 7, 1963: Vice President Lyndon B. Johnson Aide Resigns over Crime Connections, 365

Oct. 7, 1964: President Lyndon Johnson's Aide Is Arrested in Gay-Sex Sting, 371

Oct. 29, 1965: Moroccan Politician Mehdi Ben Barka Disappears in Paris, 374

Mar. 4, 1966: Munsinger Sex and Spy Scandal Rocks Canada, 377

Mar. 1, 1967: Adam Clayton Powell, Jr., Is Excluded from Congress, 380

June 23, 1967: Senator Thomas J. Dodd Is Censured for Misappropriating Funds, 384

May 9, 1969: Supreme Court Justice Abe Fortas Is Accused of Bribery, 391

July 18, 1969: Senator Edward Kennedy's Driving Accident Kills Mary Jo Kopechne, 394

May 28, 1970: Irish Politicians Are Tried for Conspiring to Import Weapons, 413

June 13, 1971: *New York Times* Publishes the Pentagon Papers, 416

June 17, 1972-Aug. 9, 1974: Watergate Break-in Leads to President Nixon's Resignation, 425

July 8-22, 1972: Jane Fonda's Visit to North Vietnam Outrages Many Americans, 434

July 31, 1972: Thomas F. Eagleton Withdraws from Vice Presidential Race, 440

Oct. 10, 1973: Spiro T. Agnew Resigns Vice Presidency in Disgrace, 447

Apr. 15, 1974: Kidnapped Heir Patty Hearst Helps Rob a Bank, 450

May 14, 1974: *Washington Post* Reveals That the Nixons Received Jewelry Gifts, 453

Oct. 7, 1974: Congressman Wilbur D. Mills's Stripper Affair Leads to His Downfall, 462

Nov. 20, 1974: British Politician John Stonehouse Fakes His Suicide, 468

May 23, 1976: *Washington Post* Exposes Congressman Wayne L. Hays's Affair, 491

Sept., 1976: Jimmy Carter Admits Committing Adultery in His Heart, 497

Oct. 4, 1976: Agriculture Secretary Earl Butz Resigns After Making Obscene Joke, 500

Nov. 9, 1976: German Generals Must Retire for Supporting a Neo-Nazi Pilot, 503

Jan., 1977: Singer Anita Bryant Campaigns Against Lesbian and Gay Rights, 506

Sept. 21, 1977: Carter Cabinet Member Resigns over Ethics Violations, 511

Aug. 4, 1978: British Politician Jeremy Thorpe Is Charged with Attempted Murder, 531

Jan. 26, 1979: Former Vice President Nelson Rockefeller Dies Mysteriously, 537

June 4, 1979: South African President B. J. Vorster Resigns in Muldergate Scandal, 543

Oct. 11, 1979: Senate Denounces Herman E. Talmadge for Money Laundering, 553

Late July, 1980: President's Brother, Billy Carter, Registers as a Paid Agent for Libya, 571

Sept. 3, 1980: Congressman Bauman Is Arrested for Liaison with Teenage Boy, 577

Dec. 7, 1980: Rita Jenrette's "Diary of a Mad Congresswife" Scandalizes Washington, 582

May 23, 1981: Italian Justice Minister Resigns Because of Crime Connection, 591

May 11, 1982: Philippine President Marcos Forces the Entire Supreme Court to Resign, 600

July 20, 1982: Conservative Politician John G. Schmitz Is Found to Have Children Out of Wedlock, 603

Dec. 16, 1982: Congress Cites Environmental Protection Agency Chief for Contempt, 615

Aug. 21, 1983: Filipino Opposition Leader Aquino Is Assassinated on Return Home, 628

Oct. 14, 1983: British Cabinet Secretary Parkinson Resigns After His Secretary Becomes Pregnant, 631

Jan. 25, 1984: Jesse Jackson Calls New York City "Hymietown," 633

1985-1986: Westland Affair Shakes Prime Minister Thatcher's Government, 645

July 10, 1985: French Secret Service Sinks the Greenpeace Ship *Rainbow Warrior*, 651

Mar. 3, 1986: Former U.N. Secretary-General Kurt Waldheim's Nazi Past Is Revealed, 669

Nov. 13, 1986-May 4, 1989: Iran-Contra Weapons Scandal Taints Reagan's Administration, 676

Jan. 12 and May 11, 1987: Media Reports Spark Investigation of Australian Police Corruption, 681

Jan. 22, 1987: Pennsylvania Politician Kills Himself at Televised Press Conference, 684

Apr. 9, 1987: Bess Myerson Resigns as New York Commissioner of Cultural Affairs, 693

July 25, 1987: Novelist-Politician Jeffrey Archer Wins Libel Trial Against the *Daily Star*, 696

Sept. 23, 1987: Plagiarism Charges End Joe Biden's Presidential Campaign, 698

June, 1988-June, 1989: Insider-Trading Scandal Rocks Japanese Government, 714

May 31, 1989: Speaker of the House Jim Wright Resigns in Ethics Scandal, 730

Aug. 10, 1989: Japanese Prime Minister Sosuke Resigns After Affair with a Geisha, 733

Dec. 15-25, 1989: Harassment of a Christian Minister Sparks the Romanian Revolution, 742

Dec. 18, 1989: Prince Charles's Intimate Phone Conversation with Camilla Parker Bowles Is Taped, 745

Jan. 18, 1990: Washington, D.C., Mayor Marion Barry Is Arrested for Drug Use, 748

Oct. 11-13, 1991: Justice Clarence Thomas's Confirmation Hearings Create a Scandal, 768

June 26, 1992: U.S. Navy Secretary Resigns in the Wake of Tailhook Sexual Assault Scandal, 784

Sept. 24, 1992: British Cabinet Member David Mellor Resigns over Romantic Affair, 792

Jan. 5, 1994: British Cabinet Member Resigns After Fathering a Child Out of Wedlock, 798

June 1, 1994: Congressman Dan Rostenkowski Is Indicted in House Post Office Scandal, 803

Aug. 5, 1994: Kenneth Starr Is Appointed to the Whitewater Investigation, 818

Feb. 28, 1995: Former Mexican President Carlos Salinas's Brother Is Arrested for Murder, 824

Nov. 3, 1996: Car Crash Reveals Depth of Government Corruption in Turkey, 843

May 20, 1997: Air Force Prosecution of Female Officer for Adultery Reveals Double Standard, 855

Dec. 11, 1997: HUD Secretary Henry Cisneros Is Indicted for Lying to Federal Agents, 872

Jan. 17, 1998: President Bill Clinton Denies Sexual Affair with a White House Intern, 874

Dec. 23, 1998: Prominent Belgians Are Sentenced in Agusta-Dassault Corruption Scandal, 889

May, 1999: Civil Rights Leader Jesse Jackson Fathers a Child Out of Wedlock, 895

May 7, 1999-Mar. 2, 2001: Ethics Counselor Exonerates Canadian Prime Minister Jean Chrétien, 898

May 2, 2000: New York Mayor Rudy Giuliani's Extramarital Affair Is Revealed, 904

May 9, 2000: Former Louisiana Governor Edwin Edwards Is Convicted on Corruption Charges, 907

Sept. 19, 2000: Ex-gay Leader John Paulk Is Photographed Leaving a Gay Bar, 913

Apr. 30, 2001: Washington Intern Chandra Levy Disappears, 933

Sept. 28, 2002: British Politician Reveals Her Affair with Prime Minister John Major, 983

Dec. 5, 2002: Senator Trent Lott Praises Strom Thurmond's 1948 Presidential Campaign, 988

July 14, 2003: Columnist Robert Novak Leaks the Name of CIA Operative Valerie Plame, 1010

Oct. 2, 2003: Newspaper Claims That Arnold Schwarzenegger Groped Women, 1016

June 2, 2004: U.N. Report Reveals That Secretary-General Kofi Annan Dismissed Sexual Harassment Charges, 1039

Aug. 19, 2004: Blog "Outs" Antigay Congressman Edward Schrock, 1041

Sept. 8, 2004: *60 Minutes II* Reports on George W. Bush's Evasion of Wartime Duty, 1044

Beginning Aug. 29, 2005: Government Incompetence Mars Hurricane Katrina Relief Efforts, 1068

Dec. 6, 2005: Spokane, Washington, Mayor Recalled in Gay-Sex Scandal, 1081

Jan. 21, 2006: British Politician Resigns After Gay-Sex Orgy, 1084

Apr. 26, 2006: Britain's Deputy Prime Minister Admits Affair with Secretary, 1089

Sept. 17, 2006: New Zealand Prime Minister's Husband Is "Outed" as Gay, 1112

Sept. 29, 2006: Congressman Mark Foley Resigns in Sex Scandal Involving a Teenage Page, 1118

Oct. 22, 2006: Chilean Politicians Use Community Funds for Personal Campaigns, 1121

Nov. 23, 2006: Former Russian Security Service Officer Dies from Radiation Poisoning, 1132

Feb. 18, 2007: *Washington Post* Exposes Decline of Walter Reed Army Hospital, 1138

May 28, 2007: Japanese Politician Charged with Corruption Hangs Himself, 1145

June 4, 2007: Congressman William J. Jefferson Is Indicted for Corruption, 1147

July 9, 2007: Senator David Vitter's Name Is Found in D.C. Madam's Address Book, 1150

July 11, 2007: Florida Politician Is Arrested for Soliciting an Undercover Male Police Officer, 1153

Mar. 12, 2008: New York Governor Eliot Spitzer Resigns in Prostitution Scandal, 1167

POPULAR CULTURE

Feb. 17-Mar. 15, 1913: Armory Modern Art Show Scandalizes the Public, 49

Jan. 18, 1923: Actor Wallace Reid's Death in Drug Rehab Shakes Film Industry, 86

Nov. 19, 1924: Film Producer Thomas H. Ince Dies After Weekend on Hearst's Yacht, 108

Dec. 3, 1930: Surrealist Film *L'Âge d'or* Provokes French Rioting, 147

Jan. 20, 1933: Hedy Lamarr Appears Nude in the Czech Film *Exstase*, 163

June 4, 1943: Actor Charles Chaplin Is Sued for Paternity, 220

July 5, 1948: Actor Carole Landis Commits Suicide During Affair with Rex Harrison, 245

May 3, 1950: U.S. Senate Committee Begins Investigating Organized Crime, 270

Aug. 19, 1973: Cheating Scandal Shocks Soap Box Derby, 444

1978: Actor Joan Crawford's Daughter Publishes Damning Memoir, *Mommie Dearest*, 517

July 28, 1980: Magazine Reveals Baseball Star Steve Garvey's Marital Problems, 574

Feb. 28, 1986: Baseball Commissioner Peter Ueberroth Suspends Players for Cocaine Use, 666

July 18, 1988: Actor Rob Lowe Videotapes His Sexual Encounter with a Minor, 717

Nov. 19, 1990: Lip-Synching Duo Milli Vanilli Lose Grammy Award, 756

Sept. 22, 1997: Sportscaster Marv Albert Is Tried for Sexual Assault, 865

Apr. 7, 1998: Pop Singer George Michael Is Arrested for Lewd Conduct, 881

May 21, 2003: Sexually Provocative Film *The Brown Bunny* Premieres at Cannes Film Festival, 1004

Early Nov., 2003: Paris Hilton Sex-Tape Appears on the Web, 1019

Sept. 30, 2005: Danish Newspaper's Prophet Muhammad Cartoons Stir Violent Protests, 1075

Apr. 11, 2007: Shock Jock Don Imus Loses His Radio Show over Sexist and Racist Remarks, 1142

June 13, 2008: Singer R. Kelly Is Acquitted on Child Pornography Charges, 1170

PROSTITUTION

May 13, 1913: Boxer Jack Johnson Is Imprisoned for Abetting Prostitution, 52

Mar. 17, 1937: Atherton Report Exposes San Francisco Police Corruption, 191

Nov. 23, 1946: Tennis Star Bill Tilden Is Arrested for Lewd Behavior with a Minor, 239

Mar. 4, 1966: Munsinger Sex and Spy Scandal Rocks Canada, 377

May 20, 1974: French Cardinal Daniélou Dies in a Prostitute's House, 456

Sept. 3, 1980: Congressman Bauman Is Arrested for Liaison with Teenage Boy, 577

July 19, 1985: Mayflower Madam Pleads Guilty to Promoting Prostitution, 654

Feb. 21, 1988: Evangelist Jimmy Swaggart Tearfully Confesses His Adultery, 711

June 27, 1995: Film Star Hugh Grant Is Arrested for Lewd Conduct, 827

Jan. 21, 2006: British Politician Resigns After Gay-Sex Orgy, 1084

Nov. 2, 2006: Male Escort Reveals Sexual Liaisons with Evangelist Ted Haggard, 1126

July 9, 2007: Senator David Vitter's Name Is Found in D.C. Madam's Address Book, 1150

July 11, 2007: Florida Politician Is Arrested for Soliciting an Undercover Male Police Officer, 1153

Mar. 12, 2008: New York Governor Eliot Spitzer Resigns in Prostitution Scandal, 1167

PSYCHOLOGY AND PSYCHIATRY

Mar. 2, 1906: Psychoanalyst Ernest Jones Is Accused of Molesting Mentally Disabled Children, 12

Mar. 21, 1928: Alberta Government Sterilizes Thousands Deemed Genetically and Mentally Unfit, 133

Jan. 14, 1943: Film Star Frances Farmer Is Jailed and Institutionalized, 214

Dec. 14, 1945: Poet Ezra Pound Is Charged with Treason and Institutionalized, 236

July, 1961: Psychologist Stanley Milgram Begins Obedience-to-Authority Experiments, 338

Mar. 13, 1964: Kitty Genovese Dies as Her Cries for Help Are Ignored, 369

Aug. 20, 1971: Abusive Role-Playing Ends Stanford Prison Experiment, 420

July 31, 1972: Thomas F. Eagleton Withdraws from Vice Presidential Race, 440

Apr. 15, 1974: Kidnapped Heir Patty Hearst Helps Rob a Bank, 450

Sept. 19, 1988: Stephen Breuning Pleads Guilty to Medical Research Fraud, 720

May 19, 1992: Amy Fisher Shoots Mary Jo Buttafuoco, 781

June 23, 1993: Lorena Bobbitt Severs Her Husband's Penis, 795

Mar. 4, 1999: Quebec Offers Support for Abused Duplessis Orphans, 892

PUBLIC MORALS

1907: Elinor Glyn's Novel *Three Weeks* Shocks Readers, 25

1909-1916: Dancer Isadora Duncan Begins Affair with Millionaire Heir, 34

1910: Nobelist Marie Curie Has Affair with Physicist Paul Langevin, 37

Jan., 1913: British Prime Minister's Staff Is Investigated for Insider Trading, 43

May 13, 1913: Boxer Jack Johnson Is Imprisoned for Abetting Prostitution, 52

July 19, 1921: U.S. Senate Rebukes Navy in Homosexuality Investigation, 70

Mar. 26, 1922: Hindemith's Opera *Sancta Susanna* Depicts a Nun's Sexual Desires, 76

May-June, 1926: Evangelist Aimee Semple McPherson Claims She Was Kidnapped, 115

1927: Mae West's Play About Gays Is Banned on Broadway, 122

1927: President Warren G. Harding's Lover Publishes Tell-All Memoir, 124

Early 1928: Joseph P. Kennedy Begins an Affair with Gloria Swanson, 127

June 6, 1929: Luis Buñuel's *Un Chien Andalou* Shocks Parisian Audience, 136

Jan. 20, 1933: Hedy Lamarr Appears Nude in the Czech Film *Exstase*, 163

July 10, 1934: Sex Scandal Forces Resignation of Alberta Premier Brownlee, 176

Summer, 1936: Film Star Mary Astor's Diary Becomes a Public Sensation, 184

Feb. 6, 1942: Film Star Errol Flynn Is Acquitted of Rape, 202

Jan. 14, 1943: Film Star Frances Farmer Is Jailed and Institutionalized, 214

Aug. 14, 1945: French War Hero Pétain Is Convicted of Nazi Collaboration, 232

Nov. 23, 1946: Tennis Star Bill Tilden Is Arrested for Lewd Behavior with a Minor, 239

Aug. 31, 1948: Film Star Robert Mitchum Is Arrested for Drug Possession, 251

May 27, 1949: Actor Rita Hayworth Marries Aly Khan After Adulterous Affair, 254

Feb. 7, 1950: Swedish Film Star Ingrid Bergman Has a Child Out of Wedlock, 263

May, 1955: Scandal Magazine Reveals Actor Rory Calhoun's Criminal Past, 295

Mar. 9, 1956: British Conductor-Composer Is Arrested for Possessing Pornography, 304

Dec. 12, 1957: Rock Star Jerry Lee Lewis Marries Thirteen-Year-Old Cousin, 313

Feb. 7, 1960: President Kennedy's Romantic Affair Links Him to Organized Crime, 329

Mar. 2-Sept. 25, 1963: John Profumo Affair Rocks British Government, 355

Oct. 7, 1964: President Lyndon Johnson's Aide Is Arrested in Gay-Sex Sting, 371

July 18, 1969: Senator Edward Kennedy's Driving Accident Kills Mary Jo Kopechne, 394

July 8-22, 1972: Jane Fonda's Visit to North Vietnam Outrages Many Americans, 434

Oct. 7, 1974: Congressman Wilbur D. Mills's Stripper Affair Leads to His Downfall, 462

Oct. 25, 1974: Evangelist Billy James Hargis Resigns College Presidency During Gay-Sex Scandal, 465

Oct. 31, 1975: Buddhist Teacher Orders His Students to Remove Their Clothes, 474

Sept., 1976: Jimmy Carter Admits Committing Adultery in His Heart, 497

1978: *Roots* Author Alex Haley Is Sued for Plagiarism, 520

Feb. 1, 1978: Roman Polanski Flees the United States to Avoid Rape Trial, 522

Nov. 29, 1979, and Jan. 31, 1983: Baseball Commissioner Suspends Mickey Mantle and Willie Mays for Casino Ties, 559

Sept. 3, 1980: Congressman Bauman Is Arrested for Liaison with Teenage Boy, 577

July 20, 1982: Conservative Politician John G. Schmitz Is Found to Have Children Out of Wedlock, 603

July 20, 1983: Congress Members Censured in House-Page Sex Scandal, 621

Oct. 14, 1983: British Cabinet Secretary Parkinson Resigns After His Secretary Becomes Pregnant, 631

Apr. 22, 1986: Faith Healer Peter Popoff Is Exposed as a Fraud, 673

Mar. 19, 1987: Jim Bakker Resigns as Head of PTL Television Network, 690

Feb. 21, 1988: Evangelist Jimmy Swaggart Tearfully Confesses His Adultery, 711

July 18, 1988: Actor Rob Lowe Videotapes His Sexual Encounter with a Minor, 717

Dec. 18, 1989: Prince Charles's Intimate Phone Conversation with Camilla Parker Bowles Is Taped, 745

Jan. 18, 1990: Washington, D.C., Mayor Marion Barry Is Arrested for Drug Use, 748

Mar., 1990: Menendez Brothers Are Arrested for Murdering Their Parents, 750

July 26, 1991: Comedian Pee-wee Herman Is Arrested for Public Indecency, 765

Jan. 13, 1992: Woody Allen Has Affair with Lover Mia Farrow's Adopted Daughter, 773

May 6, 1992: Irish Bishop Eamonn Casey's Romantic Affair Leads to His Resignation, 779

Aug. 23, 1992: Princess Diana's Phone Conversation with Her Lover Is Made Public, 789

Jan. 5, 1994: British Cabinet Member Resigns After Fathering a Child Out of Wedlock, 798

June 27, 1995: Film Star Hugh Grant Is Arrested for Lewd Conduct, 827

Feb. 26, 1997: Teacher Mary Kay Letourneau Is Arrested for Statutory Rape, 849

June 25, 1997: Swiss Banks Admit to Holding Accounts of Holocaust Victims, 858

Apr., 1998: Scottish Historian Is Charged with Plagiarism, 879

Apr. 7, 1998: Pop Singer George Michael Is Arrested for Lewd Conduct, 881

May, 1999: Civil Rights Leader Jesse Jackson Fathers a Child Out of Wedlock, 895

May 2, 2000: New York Mayor Rudy Giuliani's Extramarital Affair Is Revealed, 904

Sept. 19, 2000: Ex-gay Leader John Paulk Is Photographed Leaving a Gay Bar, 913

Nov. 5, 2000: Japanese Amateur Archaeologist's "Discoveries" Are Proven Fakes, 919

Dec., 2000: Sexual Abuse of Children in France Leads to the Outreau Affair, 922

Jan. 30, 2001: Liverpool Children's Hospital Collects Body Parts Without Authorization, 927

Apr. 30, 2001: Washington Intern Chandra Levy Disappears, 933

Dec. 14, 2001: Notre Dame Football Coach Resigns for Falsifying His Résumé, 948

Jan. 6, 2002: *Boston Globe* Reports on Child Sexual Abuse by Roman Catholic Priests, 954

Feb. 17, 2002: Rotting Human Bodies Are Found at Georgia Crematory, 964

May 3, 2003: University of Alabama Fires New Football Coach in Sex Scandal, 1002

May 21, 2003: Sexually Provocative Film *The Brown Bunny* Premieres at Cannes Film Festival, 1004

July 1, 2003: Basketball Star Kobe Bryant Is Accused of Rape, 1008

Oct. 2, 2003: Newspaper Claims That Arnold Schwarzenegger Groped Women, 1016

Aug. 19, 2004: Blog "Outs" Antigay Congressman Edward Schrock, 1041

Beginning Aug. 29, 2005: Government Incompetence Mars Hurricane Katrina Relief Efforts, 1068

Sept. 30, 2005: Danish Newspaper's Prophet Muhammad Cartoons Stir Violent Protests, 1075

Dec. 6, 2005: Spokane, Washington, Mayor Recalled in Gay-Sex Scandal, 1081

Jan. 21, 2006: British Politician Resigns After Gay-Sex Orgy, 1084

Apr. 26, 2006: Britain's Deputy Prime Minister Admits Affair with Secretary, 1089

July 28, 2006: Actor Mel Gibson Is Caught Making Anti-Semitic Remarks, 1106

Sept. 17, 2006: New Zealand Prime Minister's Husband Is "Outed" as Gay, 1112

Sept. 29, 2006: Congressman Mark Foley Resigns in Sex Scandal Involving a Teenage Page, 1118

Nov. 20, 2006: News Corp Abandons Plan to Publish O. J. Simpson's Book, 1129

July 11, 2007: Florida Politician Is Arrested for Soliciting an Undercover Male Police Officer, 1153

Aug. 20, 2007: Football Star Michael Vick Pleads Guilty to Financing a Dogfighting Ring, 1158

Sept. 13, 2007: New England Patriots Football Team Is Fined for Spying on Other Teams, 1161

Oct. 5, 2007: Olympic Champion Marion Jones Admits Steroid Use, 1164

PUBLISHING AND JOURNALISM

1906-1909: Emperor William II's Homosexual "Circle" Scandalizes Germany, 9

Mar. 2, 1906: Psychoanalyst Ernest Jones Is Accused of Molesting Mentally Disabled Children, 12

June 25, 1906: Millionaire Heir Murders Architect Stanford White, 16

1907: Elinor Glyn's Novel *Three Weeks* Shocks Readers, 25

Jan., 1913: British Prime Minister's Staff Is Investigated for Insider Trading, 43

July 27, 1917: Millionaire Socialite Dies Under Suspicious Circumstances, 60

Feb. 1, 1922: Director Taylor's Murder Ruins Mabel Normand's Acting Career, 73

Oct. 25, 1924: Forged Communist Letter Brings Down British Government, 105

Nov. 19, 1924: Film Producer Thomas H. Ince Dies After Weekend on Hearst's Yacht, 108

May-June, 1926: Evangelist Aimee Semple McPherson Claims She Was Kidnapped, 115

1927: President Warren G. Harding's Lover Publishes Tell-All Memoir, 124

1928-1929: Actor Is Suspected of Falsely Claiming to Be an American Indian, 130

Sept. 4, 1932: Film Star Jean Harlow's Husband Is an Apparent Suicide, 160

Mar. 31, 1933: *New York Times* Reporter Denies Reports of a Soviet Famine, 167

May 16, 1934: General Douglas MacArthur Sues Newspaper Columnist for Libel, 173

Summer, 1936: Film Star Mary Astor's Diary Becomes a Public Sensation, 184

June 5, 1944: Australian Poets Claim Responsibility for a Literary Hoax, 223

May 26, 1945: Norwegian Writer Knut Hamsun Is Arrested for Treason, 229

Aug. 4, 1948: Columnist Drew Pearson Exposes Congressman's Corruption, 248

Aug. 26, 1949: Viet Minh Broadcasts French General's Damaging Report, 257

May 3, 1950: U.S. Senate Committee Begins Investigating Organized Crime, 270

Dec. 1, 1952: George Jorgensen Becomes Christine Jorgensen, 289

May, 1955: Scandal Magazine Reveals Actor Rory Calhoun's Criminal Past, 295

Mar. 9, 1956: British Conductor-Composer Is Arrested for Possessing Pornography, 304

May 19, 1962: Marilyn Monroe Sings "Happy Birthday, Mr. President," 344

Oct. 26, 1962: West German Police Raid *Der Spiegel* Magazine Offices, 349

Feb. 23, 1963: Play Accuses Pope Pius XII of Complicity in the Holocaust, 353

Aug. 14, 1963: Madame Nhu Derides Self-Immolation of Vietnamese Buddhists, 362

Mar. 4, 1966: Munsinger Sex and Spy Scandal Rocks Canada, 377

May 9, 1969: Supreme Court Justice Abe Fortas Is Accused of Bribery, 391

Nov. 13, 1969: American Massacre of Vietnamese Civilians at My Lai Is Revealed, 401

1970: Study of Anonymous Gay Sex Leads to Ethics Scandal, 407

June 13, 1971: *New York Times* Publishes the Pentagon Papers, 416

Jan. 28, 1972: Clifford Irving Admits Faking Howard Hughes Memoirs, 422

June 17, 1972-Aug. 9, 1974: Watergate Break-in Leads to President Nixon's Resignation, 425

July 25, 1972: Newspaper Breaks Story of Abuses in Tuskegee Syphilis Study, 437

May 14, 1974: *Washington Post* Reveals That the Nixons Received Jewelry Gifts, 453

May 20, 1974: French Cardinal Daniélou Dies in a Prostitute's House, 456

May 23, 1976: *Washington Post* Exposes Congressman Wayne L. Hays's Affair, 491

Sept., 1976: Jimmy Carter Admits Committing Adultery in His Heart, 497

1978: Actor Joan Crawford's Daughter Publishes Damning Memoir, *Mommie Dearest*, 517

Jan. 26, 1979: Former Vice President Nelson Rockefeller Dies Mysteriously, 537

June 4, 1979: South African President B. J. Vorster Resigns in Muldergate Scandal, 543

Oct. 10, 1979: French President Giscard d'Estaing Is Accused of Taking a Bribe, 550

Nov. 29, 1979, and Jan. 31, 1983: Baseball Commissioner Suspends Mickey Mantle and Willie Mays for Casino Ties, 559

July 28, 1980: Magazine Reveals Baseball Star Steve Garvey's Marital Problems, 574

Dec. 7, 1980: Rita Jenrette's "Diary of a Mad Congresswife" Scandalizes Washington, 582

Apr. 15, 1981: Janet Cooke Admits Fabricating Her Pulitzer Prize-Winning Feature, 585

Sept. 10, 1981: *Chicago Sun-Times* Reports That Cardinal Cody Diverted Church Funds, 597

Dec., 1982: Julie Andrews and Blake Edwards Deny Being Gay, 612

Apr. 25, 1983: German Magazine Publishes Faked Hitler Diaries, 618

Jan. 25, 1984: Jesse Jackson Calls New York City "Hymietown," 633

July 23, 1984: Vanessa Williams Is the First Miss America to Resign, 638

July 19, 1985: Mayflower Madam Pleads Guilty to Promoting Prostitution, 654

Mar. 3, 1986: Former U.N. Secretary-General Kurt Waldheim's Nazi Past Is Revealed, 669

Jan. 12 and May 11, 1987: Media Reports Spark Investigation of Australian Police Corruption, 681

Jan. 22, 1987: Pennsylvania Politician Kills Himself at Televised Press Conference, 684

July 25, 1987: Novelist-Politician Jeffrey Archer Wins Libel Trial Against the *Daily Star*, 696

Sept. 23, 1987: Plagiarism Charges End Joe Biden's Presidential Campaign, 698

Dec. 1, 1987: Yale Scholar's Wartime Anti-Semitic Writings Are Revealed, 705

Aug. 10, 1989: Japanese Prime Minister Sosuke Resigns After Affair with a Geisha, 733

Dec. 3, 1989: Martin Luther King, Jr.'s, Doctoral-Thesis Plagiarism Is Revealed, 739

Mar., 1990: Menendez Brothers Are Arrested for Murdering Their Parents, 750

Mar. 30, 1991: William Kennedy Smith Is Accused of Rape, 759

Jan. 13, 1992: Woody Allen Has Affair with Lover Mia Farrow's Adopted Daughter, 773

Aug. 23, 1992: Princess Diana's Phone Conversation with Her Lover Is Made Public, 789

Sept. 24, 1992: British Cabinet Member David Mellor Resigns over Romantic Affair, 792

June 12, 1994: Double Murder Leads to Sensational O. J. Simpson Trial, 806

June 24, 1994: *Time* Magazine Cover Uses Altered O. J. Simpson Photo, 810

June 27, 1995: Film Star Hugh Grant Is Arrested for Lewd Conduct, 827

Nov. 18, 1995: Former Canadian Premier Brian Mulroney Is Exposed in Airbus Scandal, 830

Feb. 4, 1996: Whistle-Blower Reveals Tobacco Industry Corruption, 833

Spring, 1996: Physicist Publishes a Deliberately Fraudulent Article, 837

Mar. 12, 1997: Prize-Winning Aborigine Novelist Revealed as a Fraud, 852

Aug. 31, 1997: Princess Diana Dies in a Car Crash, 861

Jan. 17, 1998: President Bill Clinton Denies Sexual Affair with a White House Intern, 874

Apr., 1998: Scottish Historian Is Charged with Plagiarism, 879

Apr. 7, 1998: Pop Singer George Michael Is Arrested for Lewd Conduct, 881

May 11, 1998: Journalist Stephen Glass Is Exposed as a Fraud, 887

Sept., 2000: American Scientists Are Accused of Starting a Measles Epidemic in the Amazon, 910

Sept. 19, 2000: Ex-gay Leader John Paulk Is Photographed Leaving a Gay Bar, 913

Nov. 5, 2000: Japanese Amateur Archaeologist's "Discoveries" Are Proven Fakes, 919

2001: Clearstream Financial Clearinghouse Is Accused of Fraud and Money Laundering, 925

June 18, 2001: Award-Winning Historian Joseph J. Ellis Is Accused of Lying, 936

Aug. 27, 2001: Little League Baseball Star Danny Almonte Is Found to Be Overage, 942

Jan. 4, 2002: Historian Stephen E. Ambrose Is Accused of Plagiarism, 951

Jan. 6, 2002: *Boston Globe* Reports on Child Sexual Abuse by Roman Catholic Priests, 954

Jan. 18, 2002: Historian Doris Kearns Goodwin Is Accused of Plagiarism, 959

July, 2002: Journalist Alleges Release of Genetically Modified Corn Seeds in New Zealand, 974

Aug., 2002: Immunologist Resigns After Being Accused of Falsifying Research, 977

Sept. 25, 2002: Inquiry Reveals That Physicist Jan Hendrik Schön Faked His Research, 980

Sept. 28, 2002: British Politician Reveals Her Affair with Prime Minister John Major, 983

Oct. 25, 2002: Historian Michael A. Bellesiles Resigns After Academic Fraud Accusations, 985

Apr. 29, 2003: *New York Times* Reporter Jayson Blair Is Exposed as a Fraud, 998

May 3, 2003: University of Alabama Fires New Football Coach in Sex Scandal, 1002

May 21, 2003: Sexually Provocative Film *The Brown Bunny* Premieres at Cannes Film Festival, 1004

July 1, 2003: Basketball Star Kobe Bryant Is Accused of Rape, 1008

July 14, 2003: Columnist Robert Novak Leaks the Name of CIA Operative Valerie Plame, 1010

Oct. 2, 2003: Newspaper Claims That Arnold Schwarzenegger Groped Women, 1016

Apr. 28, 2004: CBS Broadcasts Photos of Abused and Tortured Prisoners at Abu Ghraib, 1034

Aug. 19, 2004: Blog "Outs" Antigay Congressman Edward Schrock, 1041

Sept. 8, 2004: *60 Minutes II* Reports on George W. Bush's Evasion of Wartime Duty, 1044

Sept. 30, 2005: Danish Newspaper's Prophet Muhammad Cartoons Stir Violent Protests, 1075

Dec. 6, 2005: Spokane, Washington, Mayor Recalled in Gay-Sex Scandal, 1081

Mar. 14, 2006: Duke Lacrosse Players Are Accused of Gang Rape, 1086

May 12, 2006: Scientist Is Indicted for Faking His Research on Creating Stem Cells, 1094

July 14, 2006: *New York Times* Exposes Grading Scandal at Auburn University, 1101

Aug. 12, 2006: Novelist Günter Grass Admits to Youthful Nazi Ties, 1109

Sept. 17, 2006: New Zealand Prime Minister's Husband Is "Outed" as Gay, 1112

Sept. 18, 2006: *Newsweek* Reveals That Hewlett-Packard Spied on Its Own Board, 1114

Nov. 20, 2006: News Corp Abandons Plan to Publish O. J. Simpson's Book, 1129

Feb. 18, 2007: *Washington Post* Exposes Decline of Walter Reed Army Hospital, 1138

July 24, 2007: University of Colorado Fires Professor for Plagiarism and Research Falsification, 1155

Mar. 12, 2008: New York Governor Eliot Spitzer Resigns in Prostitution Scandal, 1167

June 13, 2008: Singer R. Kelly Is Acquitted on Child Pornography Charges, 1170

RACISM

May 13, 1913: Boxer Jack Johnson Is Imprisoned for Abetting Prostitution, 52

Mar. 30, 1931: "Scottsboro Boys" Are Railroaded Through Rape Trials, 150

Feb. 19, 1942: President Roosevelt Orders Internment of Japanese Americans, 205

Late 1955: British Atrocities in Kenya's Mau Mau Rebellion Are Revealed, 298

Mar. 1, 1967: Adam Clayton Powell, Jr., Is Excluded from Congress, 380

July 25, 1972: Newspaper Breaks Story of Abuses in Tuskegee Syphilis Study, 437

Oct. 4, 1976: Agriculture Secretary Earl Butz Resigns After Making Obscene Joke, 500

Jan. 25, 1984: Jesse Jackson Calls New York City "Hymietown," 633

July 23, 1984: Vanessa Williams Is the First Miss America to Resign, 638

Dec. 22, 1984: Subway Vigilante Bernhard Goetz Shoots Four Black Youths, 641

Nov. 28, 1987: Black Teenager Claims to Have Been Gang-Raped by Police Officers, 702

Dec. 1, 1987: Yale Scholar's Wartime Anti-Semitic Writings Are Revealed, 705

Oct. 11-13, 1991: Justice Clarence Thomas's Confirmation Hearings Create a Scandal, 768

June 12, 1994: Double Murder Leads to Sensational O. J. Simpson Trial, 806

June 24, 1994: *Time* Magazine Cover Uses Altered O. J. Simpson Photo, 810

Mar. 12, 1997: Prize-Winning Aborigine Novelist Revealed as a Fraud, 852

May, 1998: Police Corruption Is Revealed in Los Angeles's Rampart Division, 884

Dec. 5, 2002: Senator Trent Lott Praises Strom Thurmond's 1948 Presidential Campaign, 988

Dec. 17, 2003: Senator Strom Thurmond's Biracial Daughter Is Revealed, 1022

Beginning Aug. 29, 2005: Government Incompetence Mars Hurricane Katrina Relief Efforts, 1068

Mar. 14, 2006: Duke Lacrosse Players Are Accused of Gang Rape, 1086

July 28, 2006: Actor Mel Gibson Is Caught Making Anti-Semitic Remarks, 1106

Apr. 11, 2007: Shock Jock Don Imus Loses His Radio Show over Sexist and Racist Remarks, 1142

RADIO AND TELEVISION

Dec. 14, 1945: Poet Ezra Pound Is Charged with Treason and Institutionalized, 236

May 3, 1950: U.S. Senate Committee Begins Investigating Organized Crime, 270

Sept. 23, 1952: Richard Nixon Denies Taking Illegal Campaign Contributions, 286

Nov. 2, 1959: Charles Van Doren Admits to Being Fed Answers on Television Quiz Show, 326

Feb. 8, 1960: U.S. Congress Investigates Payola in Pop Music Industry, 332

Mar. 14, 1960: FCC Chairman John C. Doerfer

Resigns for Accepting Gifts from Networks, 335

June 27, 1978: Evangelist Herbert W. Armstrong Excommunicates His Own Son, 525

Apr. 22, 1986: Faith Healer Peter Popoff Is Exposed as a Fraud, 673

Jan. 12 and May 11, 1987: Media Reports Spark Investigation of Australian Police Corruption, 681

Jan. 22, 1987: Pennsylvania Politician Kills Himself at Televised Press Conference, 684

Mar. 19, 1987: Jim Bakker Resigns as Head of PTL Television Network, 690

Feb. 21, 1988: Evangelist Jimmy Swaggart Tearfully Confesses His Adultery, 711

Nov. 19, 1990: Lip-Synching Duo Milli Vanilli Lose Grammy Award, 756

July 26, 1991: Comedian Pee-wee Herman Is Arrested for Public Indecency, 765

Oct. 11-13, 1991: Justice Clarence Thomas's Confirmation Hearings Create a Scandal, 768

June 12, 1994: Double Murder Leads to Sensational O. J. Simpson Trial, 806

Feb. 4, 1996: Whistle-Blower Reveals Tobacco Industry Corruption, 833

Sept. 22, 1997: Sportscaster Marv Albert Is Tried for Sexual Assault, 865

Dec. 17, 2003: Senator Strom Thurmond's Biracial Daughter Is Revealed, 1022

Sept. 8, 2004: *60 Minutes II* Reports on George W. Bush's Evasion of Wartime Duty, 1044

Oct. 13, 2004: Television Producer Files Sex Harassment Suit Against Bill O'Reilly, 1047

Nov. 20, 2006: News Corp Abandons Plan to Publish O. J. Simpson's Book, 1129

Apr. 11, 2007: Shock Jock Don Imus Loses His Radio Show over Sexist and Racist Remarks, 1142

RELIGION

Mar. 26, 1922: Hindemith's Opera *Sancta Susanna* Depicts a Nun's Sexual Desires, 76

May-June, 1926: Evangelist Aimee Semple McPherson Claims She Was Kidnapped, 115

Dec. 3, 1930: Surrealist Film *L'Âge d'or* Provokes French Rioting, 147

May 27, 1949: Actor Rita Hayworth Marries Aly Khan After Adulterous Affair, 254

Feb. 23, 1963: Play Accuses Pope Pius XII of Complicity in the Holocaust, 353

July 2, 1963: Muslim Leader Elijah Muhammad Is Sued for Paternity, 359

Oct. 25, 1974: Evangelist Billy James Hargis Resigns College Presidency During Gay-Sex Scandal, 465

Oct. 31, 1975: Buddhist Teacher Orders His Students to Remove Their Clothes, 474

Jan., 1977: Singer Anita Bryant Campaigns Against Lesbian and Gay Rights, 506

June 27, 1978: Evangelist Herbert W. Armstrong Excommunicates His Own Son, 525

Sept. 10, 1981: *Chicago Sun-Times* Reports That Cardinal Cody Diverted Church Funds, 597

Oct. 23, 1985: Guru Bhagwan Shree Rajneesh Is Indicted for Immigration Fraud, 662

Apr. 22, 1986: Faith Healer Peter Popoff Is Exposed as a Fraud, 673

Mar. 19, 1987: Jim Bakker Resigns as Head of PTL Television Network, 690

Feb. 21, 1988: Evangelist Jimmy Swaggart Tearfully Confesses His Adultery, 711

May 6, 1992: Irish Bishop Eamonn Casey's Romantic Affair Leads to His Resignation, 779

Mar. 4, 1999: Quebec Offers Support for Abused Duplessis Orphans, 892

June 30, 2001: Korean Religious Teacher Jung Myung Seok Is Charged with Rape, 939

Jan. 6, 2002: *Boston Globe* Reports on Child Sexual Abuse by Roman Catholic Priests, 954

June 22, 2005: U.S. Air Force Investigates Religious Intolerance at Its Academy, 1062

Sept. 30, 2005: Danish Newspaper's Prophet Muhammad Cartoons Stir Violent Protests, 1075

Nov. 2, 2006: Evangelist Kent Hovind Is Convicted of Federal Tax Violations, 1123

Nov. 2, 2006: Male Escort Reveals Sexual Liaisons with Evangelist Ted Haggard, 1126

ROYALTY

1906-1909: Emperor William II's Homosexual "Circle" Scandalizes Germany, 9

1907: Elinor Glyn's Novel *Three Weeks* Shocks Readers, 25

Nov. 15, 1908: Belgium Confiscates Congo Free State from King Leopold II, 31

June 22, 1922: British Prime Minister David Lloyd George Is Accused of Selling Honors, 83

Dec. 10, 1936: King Edward VIII Abdicates to Marry an American Divorcée, 187

Oct. 11-22, 1937: Duke and Duchess of Windsor Visit Nazi Germany, 196

May 27, 1949: Actor Rita Hayworth Marries Aly Khan After Adulterous Affair, 254

July 16, 1951: Belgium's Disgraced King Leopold III Abdicates, 276

Dec. 18, 1989: Prince Charles's Intimate Phone Conversation with Camilla Parker Bowles Is Taped, 745

Aug. 23, 1992: Princess Diana's Phone Conversation with Her Lover Is Made Public, 789

Aug. 31, 1997: Princess Diana Dies in a Car Crash, 861

SCIENCE AND TECHNOLOGY

Mar. 21, 1928: Alberta Government Sterilizes Thousands Deemed Genetically and Mentally Unfit, 133

Sept.-Oct., 1937: Prescription Elixir Causes More than One Hundred Deaths, 193

Nov. 21, 1953: Piltdown Man Is Revealed to Be a Hoax, 292

1956-1962: Prescription Thalidomide Causes Widespread Birth Disorders, 301

July, 1961: Psychologist Stanley Milgram Begins Obedience-to-Authority Experiments, 338

Aug. 20, 1971: Abusive Role-Playing Ends Stanford Prison Experiment, 420

Sept. 19, 1988: Stephen Breuning Pleads Guilty to Medical Research Fraud, 720

Mar. 23, 1989: Scientists' "Cold Fusion" Claims Cannot Be Verified, 723

Sept., 2000: American Scientists Are Accused of Starting a Measles Epidemic in the Amazon, 910

July, 2002: Journalist Alleges Release of Genetically Modified Corn Seeds in New Zealand, 974

Aug., 2002: Immunologist Resigns After Being Accused of Falsifying Research, 977

Sept. 25, 2002: Inquiry Reveals That Physicist Jan Hendrik Schön Faked His Research, 980

May 12, 2006: Scientist Is Indicted for Faking His Research on Creating Stem Cells, 1094

SEX

1906-1909: Emperor William II's Homosexual "Circle" Scandalizes Germany, 9

Dec. 8, 1906: Former U.S. Senator Arthur Brown Is Murdered by Lover, 22

1907: Elinor Glyn's Novel *Three Weeks* Shocks Readers, 25

1909-1916: Dancer Isadora Duncan Begins Affair with Millionaire Heir, 34

1910: Nobelist Marie Curie Has Affair with Physicist Paul Langevin, 37

July 19, 1921: U.S. Senate Rebukes Navy in Homosexuality Investigation, 70

Mar. 26, 1922: Hindemith's Opera *Sancta Susanna* Depicts a Nun's Sexual Desires, 76

1927: Mae West's Play About Gays Is Banned on Broadway, 122

1927: President Warren G. Harding's Lover Publishes Tell-All Memoir, 124

Early 1928: Joseph P. Kennedy Begins an Affair with Gloria Swanson, 127

Jan. 20, 1933: Hedy Lamarr Appears Nude in the Czech Film *Exstase*, 163

May 16, 1934: General Douglas MacArthur Sues Newspaper Columnist for Libel, 173

July 10, 1934: Sex Scandal Forces Resignation of Alberta Premier Brownlee, 176

Summer, 1936: Film Star Mary Astor's Diary Becomes a Public Sensation, 184

July 5, 1948: Actor Carole Landis Commits Suicide During Affair with Rex Harrison, 245

May 27, 1949: Actor Rita Hayworth Marries Aly Khan After Adulterous Affair, 254

Feb. 7, 1950: Swedish Film Star Ingrid Bergman Has a Child Out of Wedlock, 263

Feb. 7, 1960: President Kennedy's Romantic Affair Links Him to Organized Crime, 329

May 19, 1962: Marilyn Monroe Sings "Happy Birthday, Mr. President," 344

Sept. 12, 1962: British Civil Servant Is Arrested for Spying, 347

Mar. 2-Sept. 25, 1963: John Profumo Affair Rocks British Government, 355

Oct. 7, 1963: Vice President Lyndon B. Johnson Aide Resigns over Crime Connections, 365

Oct. 7, 1964: President Lyndon Johnson's Aide Is Arrested in Gay-Sex Sting, 371

Mar. 4, 1966: Munsinger Sex and Spy Scandal Rocks Canada, 377

Sept. 5, 1967: Socialite Nancy Wakeman Shoots Her Politician-Husband, 386

1970: Study of Anonymous Gay Sex Leads to Ethics Scandal, 407

May 20, 1974: French Cardinal Daniélou Dies in a Prostitute's House, 456

Oct. 7, 1974: Congressman Wilbur D. Mills's Stripper Affair Leads to His Downfall, 462

Oct. 25, 1974: Evangelist Billy James Hargis Resigns College Presidency During Gay-Sex Scandal, 465

Nov. 20, 1974: British Politician John Stonehouse Fakes His Suicide, 468

May 23, 1976: *Washington Post* Exposes Congressman Wayne L. Hays's Affair, 491

Sept., 1976: Jimmy Carter Admits Committing Adultery in His Heart, 497

Jan., 1977: Singer Anita Bryant Campaigns Against Lesbian and Gay Rights, 506

Jan. 26, 1979: Former Vice President Nelson Rockefeller Dies Mysteriously, 537

Mar. 10, 1980: Scarsdale Diet Doctor Is Killed by His Lover, 565

Oct. 9, 1980: Bendix Executive Resigns Amid Rumors of an Affair, 580

Dec. 7, 1980: Rita Jenrette's "Diary of a Mad Congresswife" Scandalizes Washington, 582

Apr. 28, 1981: Tennis Star Billie Jean King Is Sued for Palimony, 588

July 20, 1982: Conservative Politician John G. Schmitz Is Found to Have Children Out of Wedlock, 603

Dec., 1982: Julie Andrews and Blake Edwards Deny Being Gay, 612

July 20, 1983: Congress Members Censured in House-Page Sex Scandal, 621

Oct. 14, 1983: British Cabinet Secretary Parkinson Resigns After His Secretary Becomes Pregnant, 631

July 23, 1984: Vanessa Williams Is the First Miss America to Resign, 638

July 19, 1985: Mayflower Madam Pleads Guilty to Promoting Prostitution, 654

Mar. 19, 1987: Jim Bakker Resigns as Head of PTL Television Network, 690

July 25, 1987: Novelist-Politician Jeffrey Archer Wins Libel Trial Against the *Daily Star*, 696

Feb. 21, 1988: Evangelist Jimmy Swaggart Tearfully Confesses His Adultery, 711

Aug. 10, 1989: Japanese Prime Minister Sosuke Resigns After Affair with a Geisha, 733

Dec. 18, 1989: Prince Charles's Intimate Phone Conversation with Camilla Parker Bowles Is Taped, 745

Oct. 11-13, 1991: Justice Clarence Thomas's Confirmation Hearings Create a Scandal, 768

Jan. 13, 1992: Woody Allen Has Affair with Lover Mia Farrow's Adopted Daughter, 773

May 6, 1992: Irish Bishop Eamonn Casey's Romantic Affair Leads to His Resignation, 779

Aug. 23, 1992: Princess Diana's Phone Conversation with Her Lover Is Made Public, 789

Sept. 24, 1992: British Cabinet Member David Mellor Resigns over Romantic Affair, 792

Jan. 5, 1994: British Cabinet Member Resigns After Fathering a Child Out of Wedlock, 798

Aug. 5, 1994: Kenneth Starr Is Appointed to the Whitewater Investigation, 818

Dec. 11, 1997: HUD Secretary Henry Cisneros Is Indicted for Lying to Federal Agents, 872

Jan. 17, 1998: President Bill Clinton Denies Sexual Affair with a White House Intern, 874

May, 1999: Civil Rights Leader Jesse Jackson Fathers a Child Out of Wedlock, 895

May 2, 2000: New York Mayor Rudy Giuliani's Extramarital Affair Is Revealed, 904

Sept. 19, 2000: Ex-gay Leader John Paulk Is Photographed Leaving a Gay Bar, 913

Apr. 30, 2001: Washington Intern Chandra Levy Disappears, 933

Sept. 28, 2002: British Politician Reveals Her Affair with Prime Minister John Major, 983

May 3, 2003: University of Alabama Fires New Football Coach in Sex Scandal, 1002

May 21, 2003: Sexually Provocative Film *The Brown Bunny* Premieres at Cannes Film Festival, 1004

Oct. 2, 2003: Newspaper Claims That Arnold Schwarzenegger Groped Women, 1016

Early Nov., 2003: Paris Hilton Sex-Tape Appears on the Web, 1019

Aug. 19, 2004: Blog "Outs" Antigay Congressman Edward Schrock, 1041

Dec. 6, 2005: Spokane, Washington, Mayor Recalled in Gay-Sex Scandal, 1081

Jan. 21, 2006: British Politician Resigns After Gay-Sex Orgy, 1084

Apr. 26, 2006: Britain's Deputy Prime Minister Admits Affair with Secretary, 1089

Sept. 17, 2006: New Zealand Prime Minister's Husband Is "Outed" as Gay, 1112

Nov. 2, 2006: Male Escort Reveals Sexual Liaisons with Evangelist Ted Haggard, 1126

July 9, 2007: Senator David Vitter's Name Is Found in D.C. Madam's Address Book, 1150

SEX CRIMES

Mar. 2, 1906: Psychoanalyst Ernest Jones Is Accused of Molesting Mentally Disabled Children, 12

June 25, 1906: Millionaire Heir Murders Architect Stanford White, 16

Apr. 12, 1922: Film Star Fatty Arbuckle Is Acquitted of Manslaughter, 79

Feb. 6, 1942: Film Star Errol Flynn Is Acquitted of Rape, 202

Nov. 23, 1946: Tennis Star Bill Tilden Is Arrested for Lewd Behavior with a Minor, 239

Mar. 9, 1956: British Conductor-Composer Is Arrested for Possessing Pornography, 304

Oct. 7, 1964: President Lyndon Johnson's Aide Is Arrested in Gay-Sex Sting, 371

Feb. 1, 1978: Roman Polanski Flees the United States to Avoid Rape Trial, 522

Sept. 3, 1980: Congressman Bauman Is Arrested for Liaison with Teenage Boy, 577

July 20, 1983: Congress Members Censured in House-Page Sex Scandal, 621

Aug. 12, 1983-July 27, 1990: McMartin Preschool Is Embroiled in Child-Abuse Case, 624

July 19, 1985: Mayflower Madam Pleads Guilty to Promoting Prostitution, 654

July 18, 1988: Actor Rob Lowe Videotapes His Sexual Encounter with a Minor, 717

Mar. 30, 1991: William Kennedy Smith Is Accused of Rape, 759

July 26, 1991: Comedian Pee-wee Herman Is Arrested for Public Indecency, 765

June 26, 1992: U.S. Navy Secretary Resigns in the Wake of Tailhook Sexual Assault Scandal, 784

Aug. 21, 1994: Sex Scandal Forces Dismissal of NAACP Chief Benjamin Chavis, 821

June 27, 1995: Film Star Hugh Grant Is Arrested for Lewd Conduct, 827

Feb. 26, 1997: Teacher Mary Kay Letourneau Is Arrested for Statutory Rape, 849

May 20, 1997: Air Force Prosecution of Female Officer for Adultery Reveals Double Standard, 855

Sept. 22, 1997: Sportscaster Marv Albert Is Tried for Sexual Assault, 865

Apr. 7, 1998: Pop Singer George Michael Is Arrested for Lewd Conduct, 881

Dec., 2000: Sexual Abuse of Children in France Leads to the Outreau Affair, 922

June 30, 2001: Korean Religious Teacher Jung Myung Seok Is Charged with Rape, 939

Jan. 6, 2002: *Boston Globe* Reports on Child Sexual Abuse by Roman Catholic Priests, 954

Jan. 2, 2003: E-mail Message Prompts Inquiry into Air Force Academy Sexual Assaults, 991

Oct. 2, 2003: Newspaper Claims That Arnold Schwarzenegger Groped Women, 1016

June 2, 2004: U.N. Report Reveals That Secretary-General Kofi Annan Dismissed Sexual Harassment Charges, 1039

Dec. 6, 2005: Spokane, Washington, Mayor Recalled in Gay-Sex Scandal, 1081

Mar. 14, 2006: Duke Lacrosse Players Are Accused of Gang Rape, 1086

Apr. 26, 2006: Britain's Deputy Prime Minister Admits Affair with Secretary, 1089

Sept. 29, 2006: Congressman Mark Foley Resigns in Sex Scandal Involving a Teenage Page, 1118

July 9, 2007: Senator David Vitter's Name Is Found in D.C. Madam's Address Book, 1150

July 11, 2007: Florida Politician Is Arrested for Soliciting an Undercover Male Police Officer, 1153

Mar. 12, 2008: New York Governor Eliot Spitzer Resigns in Prostitution Scandal, 1167

June 13, 2008: Singer R. Kelly Is Acquitted on Child Pornography Charges, 1170

SOCIAL ISSUES AND REFORM

Dec., 1904: Boston Alderman Is Reelected While in Jail for Fraud, 6

July 12, 1906: French Court Declares Alfred Dreyfus Innocent of Treason, 19

Mar. 25, 1911: Nearly 150 Workers Die in Triangle Shirtwaist Factory Fire, 40

May 13, 1913: Boxer Jack Johnson Is Imprisoned for Abetting Prostitution, 52

1928-1929: Actor Is Suspected of Falsely Claiming to Be an American Indian, 130

Mar. 30, 1931: "Scottsboro Boys" Are Railroaded Through Rape Trials, 150

July 28, 1932: U.S. Troops Drive World War I Veterans from Washington, 156

Feb. 19, 1942: President Roosevelt Orders Internment of Japanese Americans, 205

Dec. 1, 1952: George Jorgensen Becomes Christine Jorgensen, 289

Late 1955: British Atrocities in Kenya's Mau Mau Rebellion Are Revealed, 298

July 2, 1963: Muslim Leader Elijah Muhammad Is Sued for Paternity, 359

Aug. 14, 1963: Madame Nhu Derides Self-Immolation of Vietnamese Buddhists, 362

Mar. 13, 1964: Kitty Genovese Dies as Her Cries for Help Are Ignored, 369

May 4, 1970: National Guardsmen Kill Protesting Kent State Students, 410

July 8-22, 1972: Jane Fonda's Visit to North Vietnam Outrages Many Americans, 434

July 31, 1972: Thomas F. Eagleton Withdraws from Vice Presidential Race, 440

Apr. 15, 1974: Kidnapped Heir Patty Hearst Helps Rob a Bank, 450

Oct. 4, 1976: Agriculture Secretary Earl Butz Resigns After Making Obscene Joke, 500

Jan., 1977: Singer Anita Bryant Campaigns Against Lesbian and Gay Rights, 506

Apr. 18, 1979: Actor Lee Marvin Is Ordered to Pay Palimony to Former Lover, 540

June 4, 1979: South African President B. J. Vorster Resigns in Muldergate Scandal, 543

Apr. 28, 1981: Tennis Star Billie Jean King Is Sued for Palimony, 588

Jan. 25, 1984: Jesse Jackson Calls New York City "Hymietown," 633

July 23, 1984: Vanessa Williams Is the First Miss America to Resign, 638

Dec. 22, 1984: Subway Vigilante Bernhard Goetz Shoots Four Black Youths, 641

Oct. 23, 1985: Guru Bhagwan Shree Rajneesh Is Indicted for Immigration Fraud, 662

Feb. 28, 1986: Baseball Commissioner Peter Ueberroth Suspends Players for Cocaine Use, 666

Jan. 12 and May 11, 1987: Media Reports Spark Investigation of Australian Police Corruption, 681

Nov. 28, 1987: Black Teenager Claims to Have Been Gang-Raped by Police Officers, 702

Dec. 15-25, 1989: Harassment of a Christian Minister Sparks the Romanian Revolution, 742

Oct. 11-13, 1991: Justice Clarence Thomas's Confirmation Hearings Create a Scandal, 768

June 24, 1994: *Time* Magazine Cover Uses Altered O. J. Simpson Photo, 810

Mar. 12, 1997: Prize-Winning Aborigine Novelist Revealed as a Fraud, 852

June 25, 1997: Swiss Banks Admit to Holding Accounts of Holocaust Victims, 858

Sept. 19, 2000: Ex-gay Leader John Paulk Is Photographed Leaving a Gay Bar, 913

Dec., 2000: Sexual Abuse of Children in France Leads to the Outreau Affair, 922

Dec. 5, 2002: Senator Trent Lott Praises Strom Thurmond's 1948 Presidential Campaign, 988

Dec. 17, 2003: Senator Strom Thurmond's Biracial Daughter Is Revealed, 1022

June 22, 2005: U.S. Air Force Investigates Religious Intolerance at Its Academy, 1062

Beginning Aug. 29, 2005: Government Incompetence Mars Hurricane Katrina Relief Efforts, 1068

Nov. 17, 2005: Liberian Workers Sue Bridgestone Firestone over Slave Labor, 1078

Mar. 14, 2006: Duke Lacrosse Players Are Accused of Gang Rape, 1086

July 28, 2006: Actor Mel Gibson Is Caught Making Anti-Semitic Remarks, 1106

Aug. 12, 2006: Novelist Günter Grass Admits to Youthful Nazi Ties, 1109

Nov. 2, 2006: Male Escort Reveals Sexual Liaisons with Evangelist Ted Haggard, 1126

Apr. 11, 2007: Shock Jock Don Imus Loses His Radio Show over Sexist and Racist Remarks, 1142

SPACE AND AVIATION

May, 1930: Postmaster's Division of Airmail Routes Creates a Scandal, 144

Feb. 4, 1976: Lockheed Is Implicated in Bribing Foreign Officials, 482

1985-1986: Westland Affair Shakes Prime Minister Thatcher's Government, 645

June 26, 1992: U.S. Navy Secretary Resigns in the Wake of Tailhook Sexual Assault Scandal, 784

Nov. 18, 1995: Former Canadian Premier Brian Mulroney Is Exposed in Airbus Scandal, 830

May 20, 1997: Air Force Prosecution of Female Officer for Adultery Reveals Double Standard, 855

SPORTS

May 13, 1913: Boxer Jack Johnson Is Imprisoned for Abetting Prostitution, 52

Apr. 2, 1915: Players Fix Liverpool-Manchester United Soccer Match, 55

Sept. 21, 1919: White Sox Players Conspire to Lose World Series in "Black Sox" Scandal, 66

Dec. 26, 1926: Ty Cobb and Tris Speaker Are Accused of Fixing Baseball Games, 118

Nov. 23, 1946: Tennis Star Bill Tilden Is Arrested for Lewd Behavior with a Minor, 239

Spring, 1947: Baseball Manager Leo Durocher Is Suspended for Gambling Ties, 242

Jan. 17, 1951: College Basketball Players Begin Shaving Points for Money, 274

Fall, 1969-Winter, 1971: Japanese Baseball Players Are Implicated in Game Fixing, 398

Aug. 19, 1973: Cheating Scandal Shocks Soap Box Derby, 444

Sept. 23, 1977: Horse-Swapping Fraud Upsets Belmont Park Raceway, 514

Nov. 29, 1979, and Jan. 31, 1983: Baseball Commissioner Suspends Mickey Mantle and Willie Mays for Casino Ties, 556

Apr. 27, 1980: Mobster's Arrest Reveals Point Shaving by Boston College Basketball Players, 568

Feb. 28, 1986: Baseball Commissioner Peter Ueberroth Suspends Players for Cocaine Use, 666

Feb. 25, 1987: NCAA Imposes "Death Penalty" on Southern Methodist University Football, 687

Aug. 24, 1989: Pete Rose Is Banned from Baseball for Betting on Games, 735

June 30, 1994: Tonya Harding Is Banned from Skating After Attack on Rival, 812

July 1, 1994: Soccer Star Diego Maradona Is Expelled from World Cup, 815

Jan. 28, 2000: John Spano Is Sentenced for Fraudulent Purchase of Ice Hockey Team, 901

Sept. 26, 2000: Gymnast Andreea Răducan Loses Her Olympic Gold Medal Because of Drugs, 916

Aug. 27, 2001: Little League Baseball Star Danny Almonte Is Found to Be Overage, 942

Dec. 14, 2001: Notre Dame Football Coach Resigns for Falsifying His Résumé, 948

Feb. 11, 2002: French Judge Admits Favoring Russian Figure Skaters in Winter Olympics, 962

Mar. 27, 2002: Georgia Basketball Coach Jim Harrick, Sr., Resigns over Fraud Allegations, 968

Jan. 27, 2005: German Soccer Referee Admits to Fixing Games for Money, 1055

Mar. 17, 2005: Former Baseball Star Mark McGwire Evades Congressional Questions on Steroid Use, 1058

May 4, 2006: Media Uncover Match-Fixing in Italian Soccer, 1092

July 14, 2006: *New York Times* Exposes Grading Scandal at Auburn University, 1101

July 26, 2006: Tour de France Is Hit with a Doping Scandal, 1103

Apr. 11, 2007: Shock Jock Don Imus Loses His Radio Show over Sexist and Racist Remarks, 1142

Aug. 20, 2007: Football Star Michael Vick Pleads Guilty to Financing a Dogfighting Ring, 1158

Sept. 13, 2007: New England Patriots Football Team Is Fined for Spying on Other Teams, 1161

Oct. 5, 2007: Olympic Champion Marion Jones Admits Steroid Use, 1164

July 29, 2008: NBA Referee Tim Donaghy Is Sentenced to Prison for Betting on Games, 1172

TRADE AND COMMERCE

Jan., 1913: British Prime Minister's Staff Is Investigated for Insider Trading, 43

1930: Liberia Is Accused of Selling Its Own Citizens into Slavery, 142

Nov. 28, 1967: Investor Louis Wolfson Is Convicted of Selling Stock Illegally, 389

Feb. 3, 1975: Honduras's "Bananagate" Bribery Scandal Leads to Executive's Suicide, 471

Feb. 4, 1976: Lockheed Is Implicated in Bribing Foreign Officials, 482

May 29, 1981: Court Finds That Ford Ignored Pinto's Safety Problems, 594

1985-1986: Westland Affair Shakes Prime Minister Thatcher's Government, 645

Aug. 27, 1990: Guinness Four Are Found Guilty of Share-Trading Fraud, 753

Nov. 18, 1995: Former Canadian Premier Brian Mulroney Is Exposed in Airbus Scandal, 830

July, 2002: Journalist Alleges Release of Genetically Modified Corn Seeds in New Zealand, 974

Summer, 2006-Mar. 16, 2007: China Recalls Pet Food That Has Killed Thousands of American Pets, 1097

Sept. 18, 2006: *Newsweek* Reveals That Hewlett-Packard Spied on Its Own Board, 1114

VIOLENCE

July 12, 1906: French Court Declares Alfred Dreyfus Innocent of Treason, 19

Dec. 3, 1930: Surrealist Film *L'Âge d'or* Provokes French Rioting, 147

July 28, 1932: U.S. Troops Drive World War I Veterans from Washington, 156

Late 1955: British Atrocities in Kenya's Mau Mau Rebellion Are Revealed, 298

Aug. 14, 1963: Madame Nhu Derides Self-Immolation of Vietnamese Buddhists, 362

Nov. 13, 1969: American Massacre of Vietnamese Civilians at My Lai Is Revealed, 401

Aug. 20, 1971: Abusive Role-Playing Ends Stanford Prison Experiment, 420

Apr. 15, 1974: Kidnapped Heir Patty Hearst Helps Rob a Bank, 450

Aug. 21, 1983: Filipino Opposition Leader Aquino Is Assassinated on Return Home, 628

Dec. 22, 1984: Subway Vigilante Bernhard Goetz Shoots Four Black Youths, 641

July 10, 1985: French Secret Service Sinks the Greenpeace Ship *Rainbow Warrior*, 651

Dec. 15-25, 1989: Harassment of a Christian Minister Sparks the Romanian Revolution, 742

May 19, 1992: Amy Fisher Shoots Mary Jo Buttafuoco, 781

June 23, 1993: Lorena Bobbitt Severs Her Husband's Penis, 795

June 30, 1994: Tonya Harding Is Banned from Skating After Attack on Rival, 812

Aug. 16, 1996: Belgian Media Reveal How Police Bungled Serial Murder Case, 840

Nov. 3, 1996: Car Crash Reveals Depth of Government Corruption in Turkey, 843

Jan., 1997: Pyramid Investment Schemes Cause Albanian Government to Fall, 846

May, 1998: Police Corruption Is Revealed in Los Angeles's Rampart Division, 884

Apr. 28, 2004: CBS Broadcasts Photos of Abused and Tortured Prisoners at Abu Ghraib, 1034

Sept. 30, 2005: Danish Newspaper's Prophet Muhammad Cartoons Stir Violent Protests, 1075

Aug. 20, 2007: Football Star Michael Vick Pleads Guilty to Financing a Dogfighting Ring, 1158

WOMEN'S ISSUES

1907: Elinor Glyn's Novel *Three Weeks* Shocks Readers, 25

1909-1916: Dancer Isadora Duncan Begins Affair with Millionaire Heir, 34

1910: Nobelist Marie Curie Has Affair with Physicist Paul Langevin, 37

Mar. 25, 1911: Nearly 150 Workers Die in Triangle Shirtwaist Factory Fire, 40

Dec. 1, 1952: George Jorgensen Becomes Christine Jorgensen, 289

July 2, 1963: Muslim Leader Elijah Muhammad Is Sued for Paternity, 359

Mar. 13, 1964: Kitty Genovese Dies as Her Cries for Help Are Ignored, 369

Summer, 1974: Dalkon Shield Contraceptive Is Removed from the Market, 459

Apr. 18, 1979: Actor Lee Marvin Is Ordered to Pay Palimony to Former Lover, 540

July 28, 1980: Magazine Reveals Baseball Star Steve Garvey's Marital Problems, 574

Oct. 9, 1980: Bendix Executive Resigns Amid Rumors of an Affair, 580

Oct. 14, 1983: British Cabinet Secretary Parkinson Resigns After His Secretary Becomes Pregnant, 631

July 23, 1984: Vanessa Williams Is the First Miss America to Resign, 638

Nov. 28, 1987: Black Teenager Claims to Have Been Gang-Raped by Police Officers, 702

Mar. 30, 1991: William Kennedy Smith Is Accused of Rape, 759

Oct. 11-13, 1991: Justice Clarence Thomas's Confirmation Hearings Create a Scandal, 768

June 26, 1992: U.S. Navy Secretary Resigns in the Wake of Tailhook Sexual Assault Scandal, 784

June 23, 1993: Lorena Bobbitt Severs Her Husband's Penis, 795

Aug. 21, 1994: Sex Scandal Forces Dismissal of NAACP Chief Benjamin Chavis, 821

May 20, 1997: Air Force Prosecution of Female Officer for Adultery Reveals Double Standard, 855

Oct. 2, 2003: Newspaper Claims That Arnold Schwarzenegger Groped Women, 1016

June 2, 2004: U.N. Report Reveals That Secretary-General Kofi Annan Dismissed Sexual Harassment Charges, 1039

Oct. 13, 2004: Television Producer Files Sex Harassment Suit Against Bill O'Reilly, 1047

Mar. 14, 2006: Duke Lacrosse Players Are Accused of Gang Rape, 1086

Apr. 26, 2006: Britain's Deputy Prime Minister Admits Affair with Secretary, 1089

Apr. 11, 2007: Shock Jock Don Imus Loses His Radio Show over Sexist and Racist Remarks, 1142

Indexes

PERSONAGES INDEX

Aaliyah, 1170
Abe, Shinzo, 1145-1147
Abernathy, Ralph, 740
Abetz, Otto, 210
Adams, Elmer Bragg, 4
Adams, Michael F., 968
Adams, Sherman, 320-322
Adenauer, Konrad, 349-352
Adomitis, Daniel J., 1078-1080
Aga Khan III, 254
Ağar, Mehmet, 843
Agee, William, 580-582
Agnew, Spiro T., 455; resignation
  of vice presidency, 447-450, 454
Ahlers, Conrad, 349-352
Akagi, Norihiko, 1145
Albert, Carl, 479
Albert, Laura, 424
Albert, Marv, 865-868
Alcorn, Meade, 320
Allard, Wayne, 991-994
Allen, Bob, 1153-1155
Allen, George, 989
Allen, Herbert, Jr., 509
Allen, Joseph C., 63
Allen, Woody, 773-775
Allende, Salvador, 482
Almonte, Danny, 942-944
Almonte, Felipe, 942
Ambrose, Stephen E., 951-953, 959
Ancia, Véronique, 889
Anderson, Jack, 175, 384
Anderson, Pamela, 1020
Andrews, Julie, 612-614
Angeli, Claude, 550
Annan, Kofi, 995-998, 1039-1041,
  1053-1055
Anslinger, Harry J., 251
Aquino, Benigno, Jr., 628-630
Aquino, Corazón, 628
Arafat, Yasser, 634
Arbuckle, Fatty, 79-82, 88, 100,
  186
Archer, Jeffrey, 696-698
Archibald, Robert W., 46-48
Arena, Dominick James, 395

Armitage, Richard, 1010-1013
Armstrong, Garner Ted, 525-528
Armstrong, Herbert W., 525-528
Armstrong, Lance, 1104
Armstrong, Robert, 645
Arnold, Ervin, 70-72
Aronowitz, Stanley, 837
Arvizo, Gavin, 1025-1027
Asquith, H. H., 43-46, 58-60
Astor, Mary, 184-187
Atherton, Edwin, 191-193
Atkinson, Rick, 633
Attell, Abe, 67
Augstein, Rudolf, 349-352
Aylwin, Patricio, 1121-1123

Babbitt, Bruce, 873
Bacanovic, Peter, 1031-1034
Bachelet, Michelle, 1121-1123
Backes, Ernest, 925-927
Baels, Lilian, 276-279
Bailey, Charles W., 175
Baker, Bobby, 365-368
Baker, Scott, 861
Baker, Terence, 696
Bakker, Jim, 690-693
Bakker, Tammy Faye, 690-693
Balanchine, George, 528
Baldwin, Stanley, 187-190
Ball, Edward, 521
Ball, George L., 636
Barclay, Arthur, 142
Baring, Sir Evelyn, 298-301
Barker, Frank A., 401
Barker, Lex, 317
Barnes, Fred, 951
Barnett, Marilyn, 588-591
Barrett, David M., 872-874
Barron, Clarence, 63
Barrows, Sydney, 654-657
Barry, Joan, 220, 283
Barry, Marion, 748-750
Bates, Alfred, 181
Bates, Ruby, 150
Batista y Zaldívar, Fulgencio, 560
Batlogg, Bertram J. R., 980

Battista, James, 1173
Baudouin I, 276-279
Bauman, Robert E., 577-579
Bayley, John, 852-854
Beall, George, 447-450
Beasley, Malcolm R., 980
Beaudoin, François, 898
Beck, Dave, 323-325
Bedaux, Charles, 196, 212-214
Bedaux, Fern, 212
Begelman, David, 509-511
Belichick, Bill, 1161-1163
Bell, Alexander Graham, biography
  of, 879-881
Bell, Griffin, 636
Bellesiles, Michael A., 985-988
Belloc, Hilaire, 44
Ben Barka, Mehdi, 374-376
Benedict XVI, 954
Bengzon, Cesar, 601
Bennett, Robert S., 803
Berezhnaya, Elena, 962-964
Berezovsky, Boris, 1132-1134
Bergman, Ingrid, 263-265
Bergman, Lowell, 833
Berisha, Sali, 846-849
Berlusconi, Silvio, 591, 1092-1094
Bern, Paul, 160-163
Bernanke, Ben, 1134-1138, 1175-
  1179
Bernardin, Joseph Louis, 597
Bernhard, Prince of Lippe-
  Biesterfeld, 482
Bernstein, Carl, 425-431
Berra, Dale, 666-669
Berry, Sidney B., 488-490
Berry, William, 514
Besen, Wayne, 913
Bettman, Gary, 901-903
Biden, Joe, 698-701
Bingham, Barry, Sr., 60-62
Bingham, Mary Lily Kenan, 60-62
Bingham, Robert Worth, 60-62
Birmingham, Joseph, 954
Bjelke-Petersen, Johannes, 682
Black, Eli M., 471-473

Black, Hugo L., 418
Black, Roy, 865
Blaesing, Elizabeth Ann, 124-127
Blair, Jayson, 888, 998-1001
Blair, Tony, 1089-1091
Blanco, Kathleen Babineaux, 1068-1072
Blaney, Neil, 413-415
Blix, Hans, 995-998
Bluitgen, Kåre, 1075-1077
Bobbitt, John Wayne, 795-797
Bobbitt, Lorena, 795-797
Bodkin, Archibald, 12
Boesky, Ivan, 726-729, 753-756
Bokassa, Jean-Bédel, 550-552
Boland, Kevin, 413-415
Boone, Pat, 500-502
Borer, Thomas, 858
Bork, Robert, 680
Borman, Frank, 488
Bouchard, Lucien, 892-895
Boudreaux, Lori, 1002-1004
Bowles, Andrew Parker, 745
Bowles, Camilla Parker, 745-747, 791
Bowman, Patricia, 759-762
Boyd, Gerald, 998-1001
Boyd, James, 384
Boyle, W. A., 404-406
Bradley, Anne, 22-25
Bradshaw, Berenice Jewett, 528-530
Bradshaw, Franklin James, 528-530
Brady, Matthew A., 79, 191-193
Brady, Roger, 1062
Brawley, Tawana, 702-705
Breen, Joseph, 163
Brennan, Christine, 814
Breton, André, 136, 147
Breton, Sonia Rojas, 942
Breuning, Stephen, 720-723
Bricmont, Jean, 837
Briggs, John V., 507
Brittan, Leon, 645-647
Britton, Nan, 124-127
Brodhead, Richard H., 1086
Brominski, Bernard C., 397
Bronson, Charles, 642
Brooks, Louise Cromwell, 173

Brooks, Stephen K., 401
Brown, Arthur, 22-25
Brown, David D., IV, 1050-1052
Brown, Denise, 1129
Brown, Divine, 827-829
Brown, Michael D., 1068-1072
Brown, Ronald H., 873
Brown, Walter Folger, 144-147
Brownlee, John Edward, 176-178
Bruce, Robert V., 879
Bryan, William Jennings, 1
Bryant, Anita, 506-509
Bryant, Kobe, 1008-1010
Bryant, Vanessa, 1008
Brzak, Cynthia, 1039-1041
Bucak, Sedat, 843-845
Buckey, Peggy Ann, 624
Buckey, Peggy McMartin, 624
Buckey, Raymond, 624
Buckley, Sheila, 468-470
Buffalo Child Long Lance, 130-133
Buñuel, Luis, 136-139, 147-150
Burden, William Douglas, 130-133
Burgaud, Fabrice, 922
Burke, James, 568-570
Burkett, Bill, 1044
Burns, William J., 28, 60
Burton, Joseph R., 4-6
Bush, George H. W., 208, 762, 787, 888; Iran-Contra, 678; and Clarence Thomas, 768-772
Bush, George W.; and Hurricane Katrina, 1068-1072; insider trading investigation, 762-765; and Iraq, 1011; and Trent Lott, 988-991; military service of, 1044-1046
Butcher, Cecil H., Jr., 648-650
Butcher, Sir Herbert, 431
Butcher, Jake, 648-650
Butler, Carrie, 1022-1024
Butler, Smedley, 156
Butt, Sir Alfred, 181-184
Buttafuoco, Joey, 781-784
Buttafuoco, Mary Jo, 781-784
Butterfield, Alexander, 428
Butz, Earl L., 500-502
Buxton, Peter, 437
Byrnes, Jack, 274-276

Cabey, Darrell, 641
Cabon, Christine Huguette, 651
Caldwell, John, 176
Calhoun, John, 449
Calhoun, Rory, 295-298
Calley, William, 401-404
Calvi, Roberto, 591, 606-609
Cameron, Lucille, 52
Campbell, Helen, 248
Campbell, John, 974
Campbell, Judith, 329-332
Campbell, Walter, 193
Canseco, José, 1058-1061
Capasso, Carl, 693-695
Cardin, Lucien, 377-379
Carey, Hugh Leo, 546
Carmen, Leon, 852-854
Carroll, John, 1016
Carson, Clayborne, 739-741
Carson, Rachel, 547
Carter, Billy, 571-574
Carter, Jimmy, 546; and Billy Carter, 571-574; and "Koreagate," 479-482; and Bert Lance, 511-514, 571; personal confessions, 497-500
Cary, Walter E., 104
Casement, Roger, 31-33
Casey, Eamonn, 779-781
Casey, Robert P., 684
Casey, William J., 676
Cassone, Michelle, 759
Castle, Barbara, 298
Castro, Fidel, 331, 560
Çatli, Abdullah, 843-845
Cattier, Félicien, 33
Caudle, T. Lamar, 279-282, 310-313
Ceaușescu, Nicolae, 742-745
Cecil, Robert, 142-144
Cedarbaum, Miriam Goldman, 1031
Celler, Emanuel, 380
Cerrini, Daniel, 815-818
Chagnon, Napoleon A., 910-912
Chamberlain, Neville, 182
Chambers, Whittaker, 259-262
Chandler, Happy, 242-244
Chandra, Ranjit Kumar, 977-979

Chaplin, Charles, 108, 283-285; paternity suit, 220-222
Chaplin, Oona O'Neill, 220, 283-285
Charles, Count of Flanders, 277
Charles, Prince of Wales, 745-747, 789-792
Charles, Suzette, 638
Chautemps, Camille, 170-172
Chavis, Benjamin, 821-823
Cheney, Dick, 1012
Cherkashin, Victor, 931
Cherkasky, Michael G., 1050
Cheshire, Maxine, 453
Chesterton, Cecil, 43-46
Chiapel, Tom, 638
Chiappe, Jean, 170-172
Childers, Thomas, 951
Chomsky, Noam, 1156
Choynski, Joe, 53
Chrétien, Jean, 898-901
Christensen, Hayden, 888
Christy, Cuthbert, 142
Chung Un-chan, 1094-1097
Church, Frank, 482
Churchill, Ward, 1155-1158
Cicotte, Eddie, 66-70
Ciller, Tansu, 843
Cinquanta, Ottavio, 962
Cisneros, Henry, 872-874
Civiletti, Benjamin, 571
Claes, Willy, 889-890
Clark, Dick, 332-335
Clark, Helen, 974-977, 1112-1114
Clark, Joe, 898-901
Clark, Taliaferro, 437-440
Clark, Thomas C., 279-282
Clements, Bill, 687-689
Clinton, Bill; and Henry Cisneros, 872-873; impeachment, 874-878, 988; and Jesse Jackson, 896; and Monica Lewinsky, 126, 820, 874-878, 896, 1168; Lewinsky affair confession, 876; pardons of, 452, 805; and Tuskegee Syphilis Study, 439; and Whitewater investigation, 818-821
Clinton, Hillary Rodham, 874, 904-

905, 1114; and Eliot Spitzer, 1169; and Whitewater investigation, 818-821
Cobb, Ernie, 568
Cobb, Ty, 118-121
Cochran, Johnnie, 808
Cochran, W. E., 5
Cody, John Patrick, 597-599
Cody, Lew, 102
Cody, Richard, 1140
Coelho, Tony, 732
Coghlan, Monica, 696-698
Coleman, Milton, 633
Collingsworth, Terry, 1078-1080
Colosio, Luis Donaldo, 824-826
Comiskey, Charles, 66-70
Concepcion, Roberto, 601
Condit, Gary, 933-936
Connelly, Matthew J., 281, 310-313
Connolly, Cyril, 136
Conrad, Joseph, 32
Constable, Anne, 465
Conte, Victor, 1164-1166
Cooke, Janet, 585-588
Coolidge, Calvin, 104, 200; and Teapot Dome scandal, 95-99
Cools, André, 889-892
Cooper, Isabel, 173-175
Copp, Harley, 594
Cornell, Julien, 236
Cortelyou, George B., 1
Cosby, Bill, 703
Cosgrave, Liam, 413
Coughlin, Paula, 785
Courlander, Harold, 520-522, 525-528
Cox, Archibald, 428
Cox, Tricia Nixon, 453
Crader, Bo, 959
Cramer, Clayton E., 985
Crane, Cheryl, 317-319
Crane, Daniel, 621-624
Crane, Stephen, 317
Crane, Stephen G., 641
Crawford, Christina, 517-519
Crawford, Joan, 517-519
Creighton, Joanne V., 936-938
Cunningham, Mary, 580-582

Cunningham, Randall, 1064-1067
Curie, Marie, 37-39
Curley, James Michael, 6-9
Curley, Thomas, 6
Curnin, Tom, 636-638
Currie, Edwina, 983-985
Curzon, George Nathaniel, 25
Cushing, Richard, 397

Dacko, David, 550
Dalí, Salvador, 136-139, 147-150
Dalton, John H., 800
Daly, Augustin, 34
Daniélou, Alain, 456-459
Daniélou, Jean, 456-459
Daniels, Josephus, 70
Darden, Christopher, 808
Dardenne, Sabine, 840
Dassault, Serge, 889-892
Daugherty, Harry M., 92-95
Davenport, Dorothy, 86-89
Davies, Arthur B., 49-52
Davies, Marion, 108-111
Davis, Gray, 1017
Davis, Hugh J., 459-462
Davis, John W., 46
Davis, Oscar, 313
Davis, Peter, 1112-1114
Dawson, Charles, 292
Day, Laraine, 242
Deakin, George, 531
Dean, John W., 425-431, 500-502
DeBartolo, Edward J., Jr., 907-909
DeFreeze, Donald, 450
DeLauro, Rosa L., 1097-1100
Delay, Myriam, 922-924
Delay, Thierry, 922-924
Delhez, Laetitia, 840
Delmont, Margaret Maude, 79
De Lorean, John, 609-612
Delpey, Roger, 550
Delplanque, David, 922
Dennis, Hugh C., 5
Derrida, Jacques, 705
DeWitt, John L., 205
DeWolf, L. Harold, 739
Diana, Princess of Wales, 745-747, 789-792, 861-865
Dickie, Phil, 681

V

Diefenbaker, John G., 377-379
Dies, Martin, 248
DiFederico, Mario A., 534
Dines, Courtland S., 100-102
Dingell, John, 615-617
Dinis, Edmund S., 395
DiStefano, Phil, 1155
Dobson, James, 913
Dockweiler, John F., 202
Doctorow, E. L., 18
Dodd, Thomas J., 384-386
Doerfer, John C., 335-337
Doheny, Laurence E., 95-99
Dole, Bob, 1141
Donaghy, Tim, 1172-1175
Donaldson, Liam, 927
Doren, Charles Van, 326-329
Douglas, William O., 382
Dowd, John M., 735
Doyle, Arthur Conan, 33
Dresnick, Ronald, 765
Dreyfus, Alfred, 19-22
Du Bois, W. E. B., 142
Duhaime, Yvon, 898-901
Dukakis, Michael, 698-701
Dunaway, Faye, 518
Duncan, Isadora, 34-36
Dunleavy, Richard M., 784
Dunn, John, 341
Dunn, Patricia, 1114-1118
Duplessis, Maurice, 892-895
Dupré, Ashley Alexandra, 1167-1170
Duranty, Walter, 167-169
Durbin, Richard J., 1097-1100
Durocher, Leo, 242-244
Dutroux, Marc, 840-842
Dwyer, Budd, 684-686

Eagleton, Thomas F., 440-443
Ebbers, Bernard, 764, 909, 1074
Ebert, Roger, 1004-1007
Eckardt, Shawn, 812
Edward II, 1107
Edwards, Blake, 612-614
Edwards, Edwin, 907-909
Eisenhower, Dwight D.; and Sherman Adams, 320-322; and John Doerfer, 336; film

censorship, 252; and Joseph McCarthy, 266-270; and Richard Nixon, 286-288
Eisenhower, Julie Nixon, 453
Eisenstein, Serge, 149
Eisler, Hanns, 284
Eizenstat, Stuart, 858
Elliott, Brian Robinson, 223
Ellis, Joseph J., 936-938
Ellsberg, Daniel, 416-419
Elsner, Edward, 122
Éluard, Paul, 148
Endo, Mitsuye, 205
Enright, Dan, 326-329
Enrile, Juan Ponce, 629
Erben, Hermann F., 559
Ericta, Vicente, 600
Errichetti, Angelo, 561-564
Esenin, Sergei, 36
Espy, Mike, 873
Estes, Billie Sol, 341-343
Estevez, Emilio, 718
Estrich, Susan, 1017
Eulenburg-Hertefeld, Philipp, Prince of, 9-12
Eustachy, Larry, 950
Evans, David, 1086
Evers-Williams, Myrlie, 823
Exner, Dan, 331
Ezoe, Hiromasa, 714-717

Faber, Katelyn, 1008-1010
Fahd, 453
Fairfoul, Tom, 55
Faisal, 453
Fall, Albert B., 95-99, 125
Falwell, Jerry, 506-509, 690, 709
Faneuil, Douglas, 1031-1034
Fard, Wallace Dodd, 359
Farian, Frank, 756
Farmer, Frances, 214-217
Farmer, Lillian Van Ornum, 214
Farrakhan, Louis, 361, 633, 635
Farrow, Mia, 773-775
Fastow, Andrew, 909
Fayed, Dodi al-, 861-865
Fayed, Mohamed al-, 861
Feleppa, Anselmo, 881
Felt, W. Mark, 425

Fenjves, Pablo F., 1129-1131
Fennell, Jim, 948
Fernando, Enrique, 600
Fields, William J., 104
Finnerty, Collin, 1086
Fiorina, Carly, 1115
Fischer, Bobby, 525
Fish, Stanley, 838
Fisher, Amy, 781-784
Fiske, Robert B., 818
Fitzgerald, Patrick, 1011
Fitzgerald, Tony, 681
Fitzsimmons, Jeanette, 974
Fleischmann, Martin, 723-726
Flinn, Kelly, 855-858
Flynn, Errol, 202-205, 559-561
Flynn, Maurice, 280
Fogel, Moshe, 860
Foggo, Kyle Dustin, 1064
Foley, Mark, 1118-1120
Fomon, Robert M., 636-638
Fonda, Jane, 434-436
Forbes, Charles R., 89-92
Ford, Betty, 454
Ford, Frederick W., 337
Ford, Gerald R., 449, 497-498; and Earl Butz, 500-502; pardon of Dave Beck, 324; pardon of Richard Nixon, 429, 455, 499; and Nelson Rockefeller, 537; and Watergate, 429, 455
Ford, Harold E., Sr., 649
Ford, Harrison, 524
Ford, Robin, 251-253
Forlani, Arnaldo, 591-593
Fortas, Abe, 367, 371, 389-394
Fowler, Tillie, 991-994
Foxe, Fanne, 462-465
France, Anatole, 33
Francis, Ted, 696-698
Franke, Karl Heinz, 503-505
Fraser, Donald M., 479
Fraser, John, 660-662
Freed, Alan, 332-335
Freedman, Albert, 326-329
Freeh, Louis, 931
Freeman, Helene, 638
French, John, 58-60
Freud, Sigmund, 13, 74, 137

Frey, James, 424
Frist, Bill, 988-989
Frohnmayer, David, 662
Fualaau, Vili, 605, 849-852
Fujimura, Shinichi, 919-921
Furesz, John, 868

Gabel, Hortense W., 693-695
Gailey, Samantha, 522-524
Gaines, James R., 810
Gaines, Kevin, 884-886
Galbraith, T. G. D., 347
Galeen, Henrik, 111
Gallagher, Willie, 182
Gallo, Vincent, 1004-1007
Galman, Rolando, 628
Gandil, Chick, 66-70
Garabedian, Mitchell, 954
García Lorca, Federico, 136
Gardner, Deborah, 476-478
Gargan, Joseph F., 394
Garrett, H. Lawrence, III, 784-788
Garvey, Cyndy, 574-577
Garvey, Steve, 574-577
Gates, Henry Louis, Jr., 521
Gates, Robert, 1138
Gaulle, Charles de, 209, 232
Geller, Uri, 674
Gelli, Licio, 591
Genovese, Kitty, 369-371
Geoghan, John, 954-958
George, Mary, 476
George V, 84
George VI, 187
Gerard, Mark, 514-516
Gerbert, Elkin B., 389
Getty, J. Paul, 220
Giamatti, A. Bartlett, 735-738
Giancana, Sam, 330
Gibbs, David Charles, 1123
Gibbs, Lois, 546-550
Gibson, Mel, 1106-1109
Giesler, Jerry, 202-205
Gilbey, James, 789-792
Gillars, Mildred, 435
Gillooly, Jeff, 812
Gingrich, Newt, 731, 989
Giraudo, Antonio, 1092-1094

Giscard d'Estaing, Valéry, 550-552
Giuliani, Donna Hanover, 904
Giuliani, Judith Nathan, 904-906
Giuliani, Rudy, 726, 904-906
Glass, Stephen, 887-889
Glassford, Pelham D., 158
Glyn, Elinor, 25-27
Goebbels, Josef, 197, 231
Goerlitzer, Artur, 197
Goetz, Bernhard, 641-644
Goldfine, Bernard, 320-322
Goldman, Fred, 1129
Goldman, Judy, 765-768
Goldman, Larry, 765
Goldman, Ronald, 806-809
Goldwater, Barry, 371, 386
Golitsin, Anatoli, 347
Goodell, Roger, 1160-1163
Goodpaster, Andrew J., 488
Goodwin, Doris Kearns, 959-961
Goossens, Eugène, 304-306
Gore, Al, 988
Göring, Hermann, 196-197
Gorman, Marvin, 711-714
Gorsuch, Anne, 615-617
Graef, Ortwin de, 705
Graham, Philip, 270
Grant, Hugh, 827-829
Grass, Günter, 1109-1112
Grau, Albin, 111
Gravel, Mike, 416
Gray, Fred, 437
Gray, L. Patrick, III, 428
Gray, Lily, 594-596
Graziano, Rocky, 243
Greeley, Andrew M., 597-599
Greenberg, Jeffrey W., 1050-1052
Gregory, Wilton D., 954
Grenon, Aurelie, 922
Grimshaw, Richard, 594-596
Gronen, Jimmy, 444-446
Grozier, Richard, 63
Gruenberger, Peter, 509
Guagenti, Peter, 781
Guccione, Bob, 638-641
Guest, Frederick, 83-86
Gun, Katharine, 995-998
Gundlach, James, 1101-1103

Hager, Nicky, 974-977
Haggard, Ted, 1126-1129
Hahn, Jessica, 690
Haig, Alexander, 416
Halberstam, David, 362
Haley, Alex, 520-522
Hall, Camilla, 450
Hamburger, Christian, 289-291
Hamilton, David F., 1078-1080
Hammerman, I. H., 447
Hamsun, Knut, 229-232
Hamsun, Marie, 229
Han Hak-soo, 1094
Hanna, Richard T., 479
Hanover, Donna, 904
Hansen, Betty, 202-205
Hanssen, Robert, 931-933
Harden, Maximilian, 9-12
Harding, Florence, 89
Harding, Tonya, 812-815
Harding, Warren G., 89-95, 124-127, 200; and Teapot Dome scandal, 91, 95-99, 125
Hardy, Carlos S., 117
Hargis, Billy James, 465-467
Harlow, Jean, 160-163
Harper, Samuel N., 307
Harrick, Jim, Jr., 968-970
Harrick, Jim, Sr., 950, 968-970
Harriman, E. H., 2
Harrington, Margaret, 217-219
Harris, Jean, 565-567
Harris, Maxwell Henley, 223-225
Harris, Oren, 332-335
Harrison, George, 494-497
Harrison, Rex, 245-247
Hartery, Don, 765
Harvey, Francis J., 1138
Harvey, Marilyn, 977
Hasner, Adam, 1154
Hassan II, 374
Hastert, Dennis, 1118
Haughey, Charles James, 413-415
Hayden, Tom, 434
Hays, Wayne L., 491-493
Hays, William H., 86
Hayter, William, 347
Hayworth, Rita, 254-256
Hearst, Patricia, 450-453

Hearst, William Randolph, 74, 81, 108-111, 450
Heidemann, Gerd, 618-621
Heimann, John G., 511
Hellenbroich, Heribert, 657
Heller, Jean, 437-440
Helmsley, Harry, 776
Helmsley, Leona, 776-778
Hempel, Régis, 925
Henderson, Ian, 298
Henderson, Paul, 1097-1100
Herman, Alexis M., 873
Herman, Pee-wee (Paul Reubens), 765-768, 829
Hernandez, Macarena, 998-1001
Herrera, Ameurfina Melencio, 600
Herrschaft, Daryl, 913
Hersh, Seymour, 401
Hervey, Ramon, II, 638
Heseltine, Michael, 645-647
Hess, Dean E., 252
Hess, Rudolph, 197
Hetrick, William Morgan, 610
Higham, Charles, 559-561
Hill, Anita, 768-772
Hill, Henry, 568-570
Hilton, Paris, 1019-1021
Hindemith, Paul, 76-79
Hirabayashi, Gordon Kiyoshi, 205
Hirschfield, Alan, 509-511
Hiss, Alger, 259-262; and J. Edgar Hoover, 261
Hitler, Adolf, 213, 230, 352, 503; and Charles Chaplin, 284; faked diaries, 618-621; film censorship, 164; and Errol Flynn, 560; and France, 210; and Knut Hamsun, 231; and Norway, 226-229; purges, 11; and the Windsors, 189, 196-198
Ho Chi Minh, 257
Hobbs, Marian, 974
Hochhuth, Rolf, 353-355
Hodge, Sir Rowland, 83
Hoffman, James, 609
Hoffman, Martin R., 488
Hogan, Frank, 274-276
Holland, Al, 667
Holmes, David, 531

Hons, Emile, 476
Hoover, Herbert, 94, 99, 144; and Bonus Army, 156-160
Hoover, J. Edgar; and Charles Chaplin, 220-222, 283-285; and domestic communism, 261; and John F. Kennedy, 329-332; and Profumo affair, 357
Horrigan, Aldine, 798
Hotchner, A. E., 524
Hovind, Eric, 1123
Hovind, Jo Delia, 1123
Hovind, Kent, 1123-1126
Howard, J. Daniel, 785
Hoyzer, Robert, 1055-1058
Hubbell, Webster, 819
Hubble, Ava, 852
Huddleston, Silous, 404
Hudson, Erastus, 70
Hudson, Rock, 295-298
Hughes, Howard, 160, 251-253, 422-425
Hull, Anne, 1138-1142
Humphreys, Laud, 407-409
Hunt, E. Howard, 425-431
Hunter, C. J., 1164-1166
Hurley, Elizabeth, 827
Hurley, Patrick, 158
Hussein, Saddam, 989, 995, 1035, 1039, 1053-1055
Hussey, John, 948-950
Huth, M. E., 104
Hwang Woo-suk, 1094-1097

Ikenaga, Masaaki, 398-400
Iliescu, Ion, 742
Imus, Don, 1142-1144
Ince, Thomas H., 108-111
Ingrassia, Angelo J., 704
Insull, Samuel, 154-156
Irving, Clifford, 422-425
Irving, David, 619
Irving, Edith, 422-425
Isaacs, Godfrey, 43
Isaacs, Rufus, 43
Isorni, Jacques, 232

Jackson, Ashley, 895
Jackson, Jesse, 633-636, 640, 699, 895-897, 990

Jackson, Michael, 1025-1027
Jackson, Shoeless Joe, 66-70, 399
Jackson, Vernon L., 1148
Jameson, J. Franklin, 307
Janszen, Paul, 735
Jefferson, Thomas, 200, 936
Jefferson, William J., 1147-1150
Jenkins, Walter, 371-374
Jenks, Anton Shrewsbury, 125
Jenrette, John W., Jr., 561-562, 582-585
Jenrette, Rita, 582-585
John Paul I, 606
John Paul II, 606-609, 954
Johnson, Charles, 521
Johnson, Charles S., 142
Johnson, Frank, 739
Johnson, Jack, 52-55
Johnson, Judy, 624-627
Johnson, Lyndon B.; and Bobby Baker, 365-368; T. Lamar Caudle, 281, 312; and Billie Sol Estes, 341-343; and Abe Fortas, 392; and Doris Kearns Goodwin, 959; and Walter Jenkins, 371-374; and Vietnam, 364
Jones, Ernest, 12-15
Jones, Gareth, 167-169
Jones, Marion, 1164-1166
Jones, Michael, 1126-1129
Jones, Paula, 875
Jones, Steven E., 723
Jordan, Everett, 367
Jordan, Pat, 574-577
Jorgensen, Christine, 289-291
Jung Myung Seok, 939-941

Kamata, Toshiaki, 919-921
Kamenev, Leo, 106
Kanaly, John J., 296
Kaplan, David A., 1114
Karpinski, Janis, 1034
Kaufman, George S., 184-187
Kavanaugh, Daniel, 1153
Kawamoto, Dawn, 1116
Keally, Charles, 919-921
Kearney, Nancy, 810
Keating, Frank, 954

Keays, Sara, 631-633
Keeler, Christine, 355-358
Kefauver, Estes, 270-273
Keith, Minor C., 472
Kelley, Joe, 100-102
Kelly, James, 413
Kelly, John, 413
Kelly, R., 1170-1172
Kelly, Richard, 561-562
Kelsey, Frances Oldham, 193, 301-304
Kelso, Frank B., Jr., 784, 800
Kennan, George F., 307-310
Kennedy, Charles, 1084-1085
Kennedy, Edward M., 364, 439-440; and Chappaquiddick, 367, 394-398; and William Kennedy Smith, 759
Kennedy, John F.; assassination of, 343; and Bobby Baker, 367; and Judith Campbell, 329-332; and Matthew J. Connelly, 281, 312; extramarital affairs, 126; and J. Edgar Hoover, 329-332; and Marilyn Monroe, 344-346; and Ellen Rometsch, 367; and Vietnam, 362
Kennedy, Joseph P., 127-130
Kennedy, Mildred Pearce, 115
Kennedy, Patrick, 759
Kennedy, Robert F., 329, 700; and Dave Beck, 323-325; and Marilyn Monroe, 344
Kennedy, Rose Fitzgerald, 127
Kent, Samuel Neal, 70-72
Kenyatta, Jomo, 298
Kerr, James, 12
Kerr, Robert S., 365-368
Kerrigan, Nancy, 812-815
Kershaw, Elinor, 108-111
Keyworth, George A., II, 1114-1118
Khan, Prince Aly, 254-256
Khrushchev, Nikita S., 330, 373
Kiley, Kevin C., 1138
Kim Sun-jong, 1094
King, Billie Jean, 588-591
King, Cecil R., 279-282
King, Charles D. B., 142-144

King, Coretta Scott, 739
King, Don, 703
King, John, 93
King, Larry (lawyer), 588
King, Larry (talk show host), 390, 711, 828, 1130
King, Martin Luther, Jr., 381, 739-741, 822, 896
King, Wanda, 748
Kinnock, Neil, 698-701
Kinte, Kunta, 520
Kirstein, Lincoln, 528
Kissinger, Henry, 416, 538, 551
Kitchener, Lord, 58-60
Klein, Allen, 494-497
Knebel, Fletcher, 175
Knight, Bobby, 950
Knight, Suge, 884
Knox, Howard J., 290
Kocadağ, Hüseyin, 843-845
Koch, Edward I., 642, 693-695, 778
Koch, Kevin, 666
Kohl, Helmut, 1110
Koller, Arnold, 858, 860
Kontogiannis, Thomas, 1064
Koolmatrie, Wanda (Leon Carmen), 852-854
Kopechne, Mary Jo, 367, 394-398
Korematsu, Fred, 205
Kotchian, Carl, 482-485
Kovtun, Dimitri, 1133
Koza, Frank, 995-998
Krause, Allison, 410-413
Krever, Horace, 868-871
Krupinski, Walter, 503-505
Kuhlmeyer, Harry L., Jr., 626
Kuhn, Bowie, 556-558
Kuhn, Rick, 568-570
Kuhn, Walt, 49-52
Kujau, Konrad, 618-621

LaCroix, Larry, 401
Lacy, Lee, 667
La Falaise, Henri de, 127
Lagos, Ricardo, 1121-1123
Lake, Douglas, 1072-1074
Lamarr, Hedy, 163-166
Lambert, William G., 391

Lamont, Daniel, 1
Lance, Bert, 511-514, 571
Landis, Carole, 245-247
Landis, Floyd, 1103-1106
Landis, Kenesaw Mountain, 66-70, 118-121, 242, 399, 556, 737
Lane, Charles, 887
Lang, Robert Todd, 509
Lange, Robert Brookings, Sr., 444-446
Langevin, Jeanne, 37
Langevin, Paul, 37-39
Langfeldt, Gabriel, 229
Langley, John W., 103-105
Larson, Charles R., 800
Lasky, Jesse L., 86-89
Lategano, Cristyne, 904
Laval, Pierre, 209-211
Lavelle, Rita, 615-617
Law, Bernard, 954-958
Lawford, Peter, 344
Laws, Bolitha J., 236
Lay, Kenneth, 945-948, 1074
Leber, Georg, 503-505
Lederer, Raymond, 561-562
Leeds, Lila, 251-253
Le Gougne, Marie Reine, 962-964
Le Gros Clark, Wilfrid, 292
Leibowitz, Samuel, 150-153
Leisure, Peter K., 262
Le Mesurier, John, 531
Lenin, Vladimir Ilich, 106, 168, 307
Lennix, Harry, 382
Lenz, Widukind, 301
Leonard, Dutch, 118-121
Leopold II, 31-33
Leopold III, 276-279
LeRoy, J. T., 424
Leslie, Kristen, 1062
Le Thuy, Ngo Dinh, 362
Letourneau, Mary Kay, 605, 849-852
Levy, Chandra, 933-936
Levy, Susan, 933-936
Lewinsky, Monica, 818-821, 888; and Bill Clinton, 874-878, 896, 1168
Lewis, Jane Mitcham, 313

Lewis, Jerry Lee, 313-316
Lewis, John, 191
Lewis, Myra Brown, 313-316
Lewis, Terence, 682
Ley, Robert, 196
Libby, Lewis "Scooter," 1010-1013
Liddy, G. Gordon, 425-431
Lieber, Charles M., 980
Lincoln, Abraham, 443
Linderman, Lawrence, 612
Lindgren, James, 985
Lindstrom, Petter, 263
Lindstrom, Pia, 263
Lipschutz, Milton, 104
Litvinenko, Alexander, 1132-1134
Llosa, Luis Fernando, 942
Lloyd George, David, 43, 59, 83-86
Lodge, Henry Cabot, Jr., 362
Lombard, Fern, 212
Long, Russell, 384
Longet, Claudine, 485-487
López Arellano, Oswaldo, 471
Lott, Trent, 988-991
Lowe, Rob, 717-720
Lowell, Francis Cabot, 6
Lubbers, Ruud, 1039-1041
Lubonja, Fatos, 846-849
Ludwig, F. G., Jr., 786
Lugovoi, Andrei, 1132-1134
Luykx, Albert, 414
Lyga, Frank, 884-886
Lynch, Jack, 413-415
Lynch, Thomas C., 800-803
Lyons, Eugene, 167
Lyons, Jack, 753-756
Lyttleton, Oliver, 298

McAdoo, William G., 97
MacArthur, Douglas, 173-175; and
    Bonus Army, 156-160
McAuley, James, 223-225
McCain, John, 54, 906, 1153-1154
McCarthy, Joseph, 266-270; and
    Alger Hiss, 261
McClellan, John, 323
McCord, James W., Jr., 425-431
McCormack, John W., 380
MacDonald, Ramsay, 105-108
McDonough, Peter, 191

McDonough, Tom, 191
McDougal, Jim, 818
McDougal, Susan, 818
MacEachran, John W., 133
McEntee, Sean, 217
McEuen, Paul L., 980
McFarlane, Bud, 676
MacFarlane, Kee, 624
McGovern, George, 440-443, 463
McGrath, J. Howard, 279-282
McGuirk, Bernard, 1142-1144
McGwire, Mark, 1058-1061
Machatý, Gustav, 163
Mack, David Anthony, 884-886
Mackay, James A., 879-881
Mackey, Randy, 1154
Mackris, Andrea, 1047-1049
MacLeish, Archibald, 236
Macleod, Iain, 298
McMartin, Virginia, 624-627
Macmillan, Allan D., 176
Macmillan, Harold, 355
MacMillan, Vivian, 176-178
McNab, Gavin, 79
McNamara, Robert, 416
MacPhail, Larry, 242-244
McPherson, Aimee Semple, 115-
    118
McPherson, Rolf, 115
McTaggart, David, 651
McTaggart, Lynne, 959-961
Maddox, Alton H., Jr., 702
Mafart, Alain, 651
Mahaney, W. B., 5
Mahurin, Matt, 810
Main, Pamela, 304-306
Major, John, 647, 697, 983-985;
    and David Mellor, 792-794; and
    Tim Yeo, 798-800
Makalintol, Querube, 601
Malcolm X, 359
Mallick, Bill, 730-732
Malloy, Edward A., 948
Man, Paul de, 705-708
Mandel, Marvin, 447
Mandl, Fritz, 163
Mangini, Eric, 1161-1163
Mangum, Crystal Gail, 1086-1089
Manson, Charles, 523

Mantle, Mickey, 556-558
Mapes, Mary, 1044-1046
Maradona, Diego, 815-818
Marcinkus, Paul, 592, 606-609
Marconi, Guglielmo, 43-46
Marcos, Ferdinand, 600-602, 628-
    630
Marcos, Imelda, 628
Markham, Paul F., 395
Marks, Albert A., 638
Marriott, Reginald, 181
Marsh, Clara, 964-967
Marsh, Ray, 964-967
Marsh, Tommy Ray-Brent, 964-
    967
Marshak, Megan, 537-539
Martino, Thomas, 1173
Marvin, Lee, 540-542, 589
Mason, C. Vernon, 702
Masor, Mark, 977
Massengill, Samuel Evans, 193-
    195
Mast, Charles Emmanuel, 257-259
Masters, Christopher, 681
Mathias, Philip, 830-833
Matsuoka, Toshikatsu, 1145-1147
Maudling, Reginald, 431
Mauresmo, Amélie, 590
Mauroy, Pierre, 375
Mayer, Louis B., 163
Mays, Willie, 556-558
Mazzei, Paul, 568
Medina, Ernest, 401
Medlar, Linda Jones, 872-874
Mee, James, 1106-1109
Meese, Edwin, III, 669, 678
Meili, Christophe, 858-861
Meksi, Aleksander, 846-849
Mellor, David, 792-794
Menem, Carlos, 815
Menendez, Erik, 750-753
Menendez, Jose, 750-753
Menendez, Kitty, 750-753
Menendez, Lyle, 750-753
Merhige, Robert, Jr., 459-462
Merwin, W. S., 474
Meyer, Ron, 687-689
Mfume, Kweisi, 823
Michael, George, 881-883

Mikhailsky, Sigmund, 347-349
Milburn, Alan, 927-930
Milea, Vasile, 742
Milgram, Stanley, 338-340
Milk, Harvey, 507
Milken, Michael, 726-729
Miller, Jeffrey, 410-413
Miller, Thomas W., 92
Miller, Tom, 55-58
Millette, Dorothy, 160
Milligan, Maurice M., 200
Mills, Elizabeth Shown, 520
Mills, Gary, 520
Mills, Wilbur D., 462-465
Milner, Alfred, 25
Minchew, Daniel, 553
Minkow, Barry, 708-710
Minow, Newton, 335-337
Minter, Mabel Miles, 73-76
Mitchell, George J., 1058, 1162
Mitchell, John, 390-391, 425-431
Mitchell, Margaret, 521
Mitchelson, Marvin, 540-542
Mitchum, Robert, 251-253
Miyazawa, Kiichi, 714-717
Mody, Lori, 1147-1150
Mog, Aribert, 163
Moggi, Luciano, 1092-1094
Moltke, Kuno von, 9
Monckeberg, Nicolás, 1122
Monckton, Walter, 187
Monroe, Marilyn, 246, 344-346
Montgomery, Tim, 1164-1166
Moon, Sun Myung, 479
Moore, Carlos, 731
Moore, Demi, 718
Moore, Rasheeda, 748
Moores, Frank, 830-833
Morel, Edmund Dene, 31-33
Morelli, Benedict, 1047-1049
Morgan, Jack, 514
Morgenthau, Robert M., 641
Morissette, Pierre, 892
Morley, John J., 389
Morley, Thomas, 636-638
Morris, Joe, 304-306
Morrison, Toni, 521
Mortimer, Elias, 89, 104
Morton, Desmond, 105-108

Morton, Melinda, 1062
Morvan, Fab, 756-758
Morze, Mark, 708
Moseley, Winston, 369
Muggeridge, Malcolm, 167
Muhammad, Elijah, 359-361
Muhammad, Prophet, 1075-1077
Muir, Leilani, 133-136
Mulcahey, Michael, 971
Mulder, Connie, 543-545
Mulroney, Brian, 830-833; and
    "Tunagate," 660-662
Munsinger, Gerda, 377-379
Murnau, F. W., 111
Murphree, Debra, 711
Murphy, Annie, 779-781
Murphy, Frank, 281
Murphy, Peter, 779
Murray, Alexander, 43
Murtha, John, 563
Mussolini, Benito, 117, 164, 213,
    231, 592, 706; and Ezra Pound,
    237
Myers, Michael, 561-562
Myerson, Bess, 693-695

Nagayasu, Masayuki, 398-400
Nagin, Ray, 1068-1072
Nanni, Louis M., 948
Naone, Dana, 474
Nathan, Judith, 904-906
Navratilova, Martina, 590
Neel, James V., 910-912
Nelson, Judd, 718
Nesbit, Evelyn, 16-19
Newton, Andrew, 531
Ngo Dinh Diem, 362
Ngo Dinh Nhu, 362
Ngo Dinh Nhu, Madame, 362-365
Nguyen Duy Trinh, 434
Nicholson, Jack, 523
Nifong, Mike, 1086-1089
Nihoul, Michel, 840
Nixon, Pat, 453-456
Nixon, Richard, 286-288; and Spiro
    T. Agnew, 447-450; gifts
    received, 453-456; and Alger
    Hiss, 261; Nixon tapes, 428; and
    Pentagon Papers, 416-419; and

Watergate, 312, 418, 425-431,
    448-449, 455, 493, 497
Noailles, Charles de, 148
Noailles, Marie-Laure de, 148
Nobile, Philip, 520
Noebel, David A., 465
Norgrove, Jane, 789
Normand, Mabel, 73-76, 100-102
Norris, Clarence, 150-153
North, Oliver, 676-681
Norton, Rosaleen, 304-306
Nosenko, Yuri, 347
Novak, Robert, 1010-1013

Oakley, Kenneth, 292-295
Oană, Ioachim, 916-918
Oaten, Belinda, 1084-1086
Oaten, Mark, 1084-1086
Obama, Barack, 701
O'Connell, William Henry, 128
Oelrich, Ryan, 1081
Ogawa, Kentaro, 398-400
O'Leary, George, 948-950
Oliphant, Charles, 310
O'Morain, Michael, 413
Onassis, Jacqueline Kennedy, 694
O'Neill, Tip, 621-624, 730
O'Reilly, Bill, 1047-1049
O'Reilly, Bridget, 217-219
Ormiston, Kenneth G., 115
Ossendowski, Anton Martynovich,
    307
Oufkir, Mohammad, 374
Oustric, Albert, 139-141
Overholser, Winfred, 236
Owen, Richard, 494-497

Pacepa, Ion Mihai, 353
Pach, Walter, 49-52
Padgett, Tom, 708
Pagnam, Fred, 55
Pagones, Steven, 702
Palfrey, Deborah Jeane, 1150-1153
Palmer, Lilli, 245
Panny, William, 580
Panov, V. A., 309
Papon, Maurice, 375
Park, Tongsun, 479-482
Park Chung Hee, 479

Parker, Alton B., 1
Parker, Dave, 666-669
Parkinson, Cecil, 631-633
Parks, Bernard, 884
Parnes, Anthony, 753-756
Parsons, Jan, 717-720
Pass, Albert, 404
Patterson, Haywood, 150-153
Patton, George S., 156
Paul, Henri, 861
Paul VI, 606
Paulino, Rolando, 942-944
Paulk, Anne, 913
Paulk, John, 913-915
Paulson, Henry, 1134-1138, 1175-1179
Peace, Purnell A., 1158
Pearson, Drew, 173-175, 248-250, 384
Pearson, Lester B., 377-379
Pelletier, David, 962-964
Pelosi, Nancy, 623, 1148
Pelossi, Giorgio, 830
Pendergast, James, 199
Pendergast, Thomas Joseph, 199-201
Penenberg, Adam, 887
Peppiatt, Angela, 696
Pereira, Fernando, 651-654
Péret, Raoul Adolphe, 139-141
Perez, Rafael Antonio, 884
Perhach, Vanessa, 865
Perkins, Tom, 1114-1118
Perla, Anthony, 568
Perla, Rocco, 568
Perrault, Roger, 868
Perry, Nancy Ling, 450
Pétain, Philippe, 209-211, 232-236
Petee, Thomas A., 1101-1103
Petrovich Semenov, Evgeni, 307
Philbin, Regis, 574, 828
Phillips, Carrie, 124
Phillips, Jud, 313
Phillips, Quanis, 1159
Phipps, Ogden Mills, 514
Pickett, John O., 901-903
Picquart, Georges, 19
Pierce, Ponchitta, 537
Pierlot, Hubert, 277

Pilatus, Rob, 756-758
Pius XII, 164, 353-355
Plame, Valerie, 1010-1013
Poindexter, John M., 676
Polanski, Roman, 522-524
Polozola, Frank, 907
Pons, Stanley, 723-726
Ponzi, Charles, 63-66
Pope, Barbara S., 785
Popoff, Elizabeth, 673
Popoff, Peter, 673-675
Poppe, Henry, 274-276
Pottinger, George, 431
Poulson, John, 431-433
Pound, Dorothy Shakespear, 236
Pound, Ezra, 236-239
Powell, Adam Clayton, Jr., 380-383
Prescott, John, 1089-1091
Pressler, Larry, 563
Pressler, Mike, 1003, 1086
Preston, Billy, 494-497
Prevert, Jacques, 148
Previn, Soon-Yi, 773-775
Price, Mike, 1002-1004
Price, Victoria, 150
Priest, Dana, 1138-1142
Prieur, Dominique, 651
Prince, Jonas, 898
Privat, Maurice, 140
Priven, Dennis, 476-478
Profumo, John, 348, 355-358, 378
Purcell, Bob, 55-58
Purviance, Edna, 100
Putin, Vladimir, 1132-1134

Qaddafi, Muammar al-, 679
Quisling, Vidkun, 226-229

Radcliffe, Cyril, 347
Rader, Stanley, 525
Răducan, Andreea, 916-918
Rahman, Kambir Abdul, 562
Raines, Howell, 998-1001
Rajneesh, Bhagwan Shree, 662-665
Ralph, Tim, 1126-1129
Ramos, Fidel V., 629
Randi, James, 673-675
Raphael, Adam, 696

Rappe, Virginia, 79-82
Rasmussen, Anders Fogh, 1075
Rather, Dan, 1022-1024, 1044-1046
Rathom, John R., 70
Rauh, Carl, 803
Rauh, Joseph L., Jr., 404-406
Ray, Elizabeth, 491-493
Reagan, Marilyn Bradshaw, 529
Reagan, Ronald; Abscam, 563; and deregulation, 945; and Environmental Protection Agency, 615-616; Iran-Contra, 312, 676-681, 780; and Ku Klux Klan, 635; at Nazi cemetery, 1110; and Religious Right, 577
Reardon, David C., 795
Red Fox, 424
Redfern, Michael, 927-930
Reed, John, 223
Reenan, Cyril, 789
Rees-Jones, Trevor, 861
Regan, Judith, 1129-1131
Reguly, Robert, 377
Reid, Wallace, 86-89
Reilly, Sidney, 105-108
Replogle, Hartley L., 68
Reubens, Paul, 765-768, 829
Revers, Georges, 257-259
Reynaud, Paul, 233
Reynolds, Don, 365-368
Rhodes, James A., 410
Rhoodie, Eschel, 543
Ribbentrop, Joachim von, 197
Ribicoff, Abraham A., 384, 511
Rice-Davies, Mandy, 356
Richardson, Elliot, 447-450
Richie, Nicole, 1020
Ridenhour, Ronald, 401
Rigas, James, 971-973
Rigas, John, 971-973
Rigas, Michael, 971-973
Rigas, Timothy, 971-973
Riggs, Bobby, 589
Rivers, Eunice, 437
Riza, Iqbal, 1053-1055
Roach, Hal, 178-181
Robbins, Bruce, 837
Robert, Denis, 925-927

Roberts, Jim, 1000
Roberts, Seth, 978
Robertson, Cliff, 509-511
Robertson, Pat, 713
Robertson, Thomas A., 534
Robins, E. Claiborne, Sr., 459
Robinson, Jackie, 639
Robinson, Sir Joseph, 83
Robinson, Walter V., 936-938
Roche, James G., 991
Rockefeller, Nelson A., 537-539
Rodriguez, Marcelo, 881
Roe Jung-hye, 1094
Rogers, Michael, 1041-1044
Rogers, William D., 473
Rogge, Jacques, 962
Roh Sung-il, 1094
Röhm, Ernst, 11
Roman, Ed, 274
Rometsch, Ellen, 367
Ronson, Gerald, 753-756
Roosevelt, Eleanor, 159, 194, 205, 1114
Roosevelt, Franklin D., 62, 70, 128, 155, 159, 194, 200-201; and airmail scandal, 144; and Japanese American internment, 205-209; and Ezra Pound, 236
Roosevelt, Theodore, 1-3, 26, 50; and Joseph R. Burton, 4-6
Rosa, John W., 1062
Rose, Flemming, 1075-1077
Rose, Pete, 735-738
Roselli, John, 330
Rosenberg, Alfred, 226, 230
Rosoff, William L., 1050
Ross, Andrew, 837
Ross, Karl, 369
Rossellini, Roberto, 263-265
Rossellini, Roberto Ingmar, 263
Rostenkowski, Dan, 803-806
Rota, Robert V., 803
Roth, Al, 274
Rothstein, Arnold, 66-70
Rove, Karl, 1011
Ruckelshaus, William, 615
Rudel, Hans-Ulrich, 503-505
Rudge, Olga, 236
Ruef, Abraham, 28-30

Ruiz Massieu, José Francisco, 824-826
Rumsfeld, Donald, 991, 1034
Rushmore, Howard, 296
Ryan, Thomas Fortune, 2

Sabich, Vladimir, 485-487
Sachs, Irving, 310-313
Salé, Jamie, 962-964
Salinas de Gortari, Carlos, 824-826
Salinas de Gortari, Raúl, 824-826
Salomon, Rick, 1019-1021
Salter, Roberta Semple, 115
Samuel, Herbert, 43
Sancha, Antonia de, 792
Sanchez, Ricardo, 1034-1038
Santoni, Mimi, 456-459
Sapina, Ante, 1055-1058
Sarsgaard, Peter, 888
Sarti, Adolfo, 591-593
Sasso, Anthony P., 1155
Satterlee, Peggy, 202-205
Saud, Sultan bin Abdul Aziz al-, 453
Saunders, Ernest, 753-756
Sawyer, Charles E., 89
Sawyer, Steve, 651-654
Schatten, Gerald, 1094-1097
Scheer, Robert, 497
Scheuer, Sandra, 410-413
Schindel, Robert, 1109
Schledwitz, Karl A., 649
Schlesinger, James, 1034
Schmidlapp, W. Horace, 246
Schmidt, Hermann, 503-505
Schmitz, Eugene E., 28-30
Schmitz, John G., 603-605
Schmitz, Joseph E., 605
Schön, Jan Hendrik, 980-982
Schreiber, Belle, 52
Schreiber, Karlheinz, 830-833
Schreuder, Frances, 528-530
Schreuder, Marc, 528
Schrock, Edward, 1041-1044
Schroeder, William, 410-413
Schwartzkoppen, Max von, 20
Schwarzenegger, Arnold, 1016-1019
Schwebel, Stephen M., 1039

Schwimmer, Harry I., 310-313
Scott, Ian, 1112
Scott, Norman, 531-534
Secord, Richard V., 676
Selbekk, Vebjørn, 1075-1077
Seles, Monica, 814
Selig, Bud, 1058
Seligmann, Reade, 1086
Sentelle, David B., 818
Sevigny, Chloë, 1004-1007
Sévigny, Pierre, 377-379
Shalala, Donna, 1141
Shanley, Paul, 954
Sharpton, Al, 702-705, 1142
Shaw, Artie, 317
Shaw, Steven, 673
Sheehan, Neil, 416
Sheela, Ma Anand, 662-665
Sheldon, Jackie, 55-58
Sheppard, William Henry, 32
Sherwood, Carlton, 597-599
Shinto, Hisashi, 714-717
Short, Clare, 995-998
Shriver, Maria, 1016
Shuler, Robert P., 117
Siebert, Tara, 717-720
Siegelman, Don, 909
Signorini, Fernando, 816
Sikharulidze, Anton, 962-964
Sills, Beverly, 694
Silvey, Joyce, 509
Simpson, Nicole Brown, 806-809
Simpson, O. J., 806-812, 1129-1131
Simpson, Tom, 1103
Simpson, Wallis, 187-190, 196-198, 213
Sin, Jaime, 629
Sinatra, Frank, 329
Sinclair, Harry F., 95-99
Sindona, Michele, 591, 606-609
Singer, Isaac Merritt, 34
Singer, Paris, 34-36
Singer, Patrick, 34
Sisson, Edgar, 307-310
Skilling, Jeffrey, 945-948
Slaton, Lewis, 717
Slotnick, Barry, 641
Smith, Jesse W., 92-95
Smith, Lonnie, 666

Smith, Thomas Daniel, 431
Smith, William Kennedy, 759-762, 866
Smuts, Jan, 84
Snyder, John W., Jr., 785
Sohn, Lydia L., 980
Sokal, Alan, 837-840
Solomon, Paul M., 980
Soltysik, Patricia, 450
Sorensen, Larry, 667
Sosa, Sammy, 1058
Spaak, Paul-Henri, 276-279
Spano, John A., Jr., 901-903
Speaker, Tris, 118-121
Spence, Wishart, 377
Spitzer, Eliot L., 1013-1016, 1050-1052, 1167-1170
Spitzer, Silda Wall, 1167
Sprague, Richard, 404
Sprague, Robert, 720-723
Springer, Jerry, 828
Stacpoole, Michael, 696-698
Stalin, Joseph, 106, 167-169; and picture forgery, 811
Stammberger, Wolfgang, 349
Stanford, Karin, 895
Stanley, David, 687
Stanley, Henry Morton, 31-33
Stansel, Mary E., 821
Stant, Shane, 812
Stark, Ray, 509
Starr, Kenneth, 818-821, 874-878
Stavisky, Alexandre, 170-172
Stearns, Cliff, 1116
Stein, Gertrude, 51
Stempel, Herb, 326-329
Stennis, John, 384
Stent, Julia, 798-800
Stern, David, 1172-1175
Stern, Howard, 828
Sternberg, Saul, 978
Stevenson, Andrew, 852
Stewart, Harold, 223-225
Stewart, Martha, 1031-1034
Stiglitz, Joseph E., 1176
Stimson, Henry L., 205
Stoker, Bram, 111-114
Stoker, Florence, 111-114
Stokes, Louis, 621

Stompanato, Johnny, 317-319
Stonehouse, John, 468-470
Storer, George, 335-337
Stramm, August, 76-79
Strauss, Franz Josef, 349-352
Stringer, C. Vivian, 1142
Stuckle, Carla, 603-605
Studds, Gerry, 621-624
Suer, Oral, 1028-1030
Sullivan, Joseph, 66
Sullivan, Shannon, 1081-1083
Suskind, Richard, 422-425
Swaggart, Jimmy, 711-714, 1152
Swanson, Gloria, 127-130
Sweeney, Constance M., 954
Sweeney, James, 568
Sweet, Robert W., 1039
Sykes, Roberta, 852

Taft, William Howard, 46
Taguba, Antonio, 1034-1038
Takeoka, Toshiki, 919-921
Takeshita, Noboru, 714-717, 733-735
Talmadge, Betty, 553
Talmadge, Herman E., 553-555
Talmadge, Robert S., 553
Tanaka, Kakuei, 482-485
Tanaka, Tsutomu, 398-400
Tardieu, André, 139-141
Tarleton, Donald, 511
Tarnower, Herman, 565-567
Tate, Sharon, 246, 522
Taylor, Norman, 1028-1030
Taylor, Tony, 1158
Taylor, William Desmond, 73-76, 88
Teets, Peter B., 991
Teilhard de Chardin, Pierre, 293, 457
Temple, Tracey, 1089-1091
Terboven, Josef, 226
Teti, Raffaello, 889
Thamel, Pete, 1101
Thatcher, Margaret, 645-647, 696, 792, 798; and Edwina Currie, 983; and Cecil Parkinson, 631-633; and Westland Aircraft, 645-647

Thaw, Harry Kendall, 16-19
Thomas, Clarence, 768-772
Thomas, Frank, 431
Thomas, J. Parnell, 248-250, 260
Thomas, James Henry, 181-184
Thomas, Sir Leslie, 181
Thompson, Frank, 561-562
Thompson, Hugh, Jr., 401
Thompson, Margaret W., 133
Thomsen, Ian, 942
Thornburgh, Dick, 684
Thorpe, Franklyn, 184-187
Thorpe, Jeremy, 531-534
Thrasher, Donald, 1020
Thring, G. Herbert, 111
Thurmond, Strom, 384, 988-991, 1022-1024
Tiedge, Hans-Joachim, 657-659
Tierney, Patrick, 910-912
Tilden, Bill, 239-242
Tillman, Benjamin, 3
Timony, James, 122
Tiriac, Ion, 916
Tisa, Benedict, 609
Tobias, Randall L., 1151
Todd, Thelma, 178-181
Tokes, Laszlo, 742-745
Tolstoy, Ilia, 130-133
Tomasz, 1084-1086
Topping, Henry, 317
Tower, John, 384
Trandahl, Jeff, 1118-1120
Trevenar, Bert, 304-306
Trevor-Roper, Hugh, 618
Trindle, Renee, 991
Triola, Michelle, 540-542
Tripp, Linda, 874-878
Trotsky, Leon, 106, 226
Truman, Harry S., 8, 989, 1023; and T. Lamar Caudle, 280; and Matthew J. Connelly, 310-313; and Douglas MacArthur, 175; and Joseph McCarthy, 266-270; and Thomas Joseph Pendergast, 199-201
Trungpa, Chögyam, 474-476
Tryforos, Lynne, 565
Tuberville, Tommy, 1101-1103
Turcotte, Jean-Claude, 892-895

Turnbull, Sandy, 55
Turner, Lana, 317-319
Twain, Mark, 33
Tyler, Nancy Carole, 365
Tyson, Mike, 703

Ueberroth, Peter, 556, 666-669, 737
Ullman, Harlan K., 1151
Ulmer, Walter F., 488
Uno, Sosuke, 733-735
Us, Gonca, 843

Vander Schaaf, Derek, 785
Vassall, John, 347-349
Vaughn, Kia, 1142
Velzen, Dick van, 927-930, 936-938
Ver, Fabian, 628
Vermeersch, Arthur, 33
Vick, Michael, 1158-1161
Vincent, Fay, 735-738
Vitter, David, 1150-1153
Volcker, Paul, 858-861, 1053-1055
Von Eschenbach, Andrew C., 1097
Vorster, B. J., 543-545

Wade, Mitchell, 1064
Wagner, Robert F., 40-43
Wakeman, Nancy, 386-388
Wakeman, William T., 386-388
Waksal, Samuel D., 1031-1034
Waldheim, Kurt, 669-672
Wałęsa, Lech, 1111
Walker, Margaret, 520
Wallace, George, 604
Wallace, Mike, 424, 833-836
Walsh, Matt, 1161
Walsh, Thomas J., 95
Walters, Walter W., 156-160
Ward, Stephen, 355-358
Warner, Ed, 274
Warren, Earl, 380-383, 393

Washington, Claudell, 667
Washington, George, 938
Washington-Williams, Essie Mae, 1022-1024
Watkins, Harold Cole, 193-195
Watkins, Sherron, 945-948
Wehner, Herbert, 503
Wehner, John, 626
Weida, John A., 1062-1064
Weidenreich, Franz, 292-295
Weidner, Clinton, 1072-1074
Weightman, George W., 1138-1142
Weinberg, Melvin, 561
Weinberger, Caspar, 676
Weiner, Joseph, 292
Weinstein, Bernard, 840
Weinstein, Michael L., 1062-1064
Welch, Joseph Nye, 266-270
Welles, Orson, 110, 165, 254
Wesson, Marianne, 1156
West, Enoch, 55
West, James E., 1081-1083
West, Mae, 122-124
West, Roland, 178-181
Westmoreland, William, 937
Whalen, Robert P., 546
Whaley, Arthur, 55
White, Kevin, 948
White, Stanford, 16-19
Widnall, Sheila, 855-858
Wiesenthal, Simon, 669-672
Wigand, Jeffrey, 833-836
Wilcox, Breckenridge, 720
Wilkes, Brent, 1064
William II, 9-12
Williams, Edward Bennett, 365, 368
Williams, George Washington, 32
Williams, Harrison A., 561
Williams, Lefty, 66-70
Williams, Vanessa, 382, 638-641
Wills, Frank, 425

Willson, Henry, 295-298
Wilson, David, 597
Wilson, Harold, 468-470
Wilson, Helen Dolan, 597
Wilson, Howard, 898-901
Wilson, Joseph, 1010-1013
Windsor, Duke of, 187-190, 196-198, 213
Witt, Robert, 1002-1004
Wittig, David, 1072-1074
Wolf, Markus, 657
Wolfson, Louis, 389-391
Woodward, Arthur Smith, 292-295
Woodward, Bob, 425-431
Wörner, Manfred, 503
Wright, Betty, 730
Wright, Jim, 730-732
Wright, Roy, 150-153
Wronker-Flatow, Manfred, 111

Yablonski, Joseph, 404-406
Yaeger, Don, 1002-1004
Yamamoto, Taku, 1145
Yancy, Allen, 142-144
Yasui, Minoru, 205
Yellow Robe, Chauncey, 130
Yeo, Tim, 798-800
Yoshinaga, Yusuke, 714-717
Young, Andrew, 634
Younger, George, 83

Zamsky, Linda, 933
Zedillo Ponce de León, Ernesto, 824-826
Zheng Xiaoyu, 1097-1100
Zigo, Marc, 855-858
Zihlman, Frederick N., 103
Zimbardo, Philip, 420-422
Zinovyev, Grigory Yevseyevich, 106, 108-111
Zola, Émile, 19-22
Zwicker, Ralph W., 266-270

SUBJECT INDEX

A. H. Robins Company, 459-462
Aaliyah, 1170
ABA. *See* American Bar Association
Abe, Shinzo, 1145-1147
Aberdeen Proving Ground, 992
Abernathy, Ralph, 740
Abetz, Otto, 210
Abscam, 561-564
Abu Ghraib prison, 340, 421, 1034-1038
Academia. See *Category Index under Cultural and intellectual history; Education*
Adams, Elmer Bragg, 4
Adams, Michael F., 968
Adams, Sherman, 320-322
Adelphia Communications, 971-973
Adenauer, Konrad, 349-352
Adjusted Compensation Payment Act of 1936, 159
Adomitis, Daniel J., 1078-1080
Africa. See *Geographical Index*
Aga Khan III, 254
Ağar, Mehmet, 843
Agee, William, 580-582
Agnew, Spiro T., 455; resignation of vice presidency, 447-450, 454
Agrava Fact-Finding Commission, 602
Agusta scandal, 889-892
AHA. *See* American Historical Association
Ahlers, Conrad, 349-352
AIG (American International Group), 1176
Air Canada scandal, 830-833
Air Force, U.S.; and Kelly Flinn, 855-858
Air Force Academy, U.S., 802, 855, 991-994, 1062-1064; sexual harassment, 993
Air Mail Act of 1930, 144-147
Air National Guard, 1044-1046

Airbus affair, 830-833
Airmail scandal, 144-147
Akagi, Norihiko, 1145
Albania, 846-849
Albert, Carl, 479
Albert, Laura, 424
Albert, Marv, 865-868
Alberta, Canada; Brownlee scandal, 176-178; sterilization law, 133-136
Alcatraz Island, 434
Alcorn, Meade, 320
Alder Hey inquiry, 927-930
Algeria, 212-214; Sand Wars, 374
Allard, Wayne, 991-994
Allen, Bob, 1153-1155
Allen, George, 989
Allen, Herbert, Jr., 509
Allen, Joseph C., 63
Allen, Woody, 773-775
Allende, Salvador, 482
Almonte, Danny, 942-944
Almonte, Felipe, 942
al-Qaeda, 1011
AMA. *See* American Medical Association
Amazon measles epidemic, 910-912
Ambassador College, 525
Ambrose, Stephen E., 951-953, 959
American Anthropological Association, 911
American Bank and Trust Company, 637
American Bar Association, 769
American Christian College, 465-467
American Historical Association, 937, 952, 960
American Independent Party, 604
American Medical Association, 194
American Psychiatric Association, 506

American Psychological Association, 506
American Society of Composers, Authors, and Publishers, 333
Ancia, Véronique, 889
Andalusian Dog, An (film), 136-139, 147
Anderson, Jack, 175, 384
Anderson, Pamela, 1020
Andrews, Julie, 612-614
Angeli, Claude, 550
Angelus Temple, 115
Animal cruelty, 1158-1161
Annan, Kofi, 995-998, 1039-1041, 1053-1055
Anslinger, Harry J., 251
Antibiotics, 193, 438, 911
Anti-Doping Agency, U.S., 1165
Anti-Semitism, 44, 147-150, 603, 694, 705-708; at Air Force Academy, 1062; Austrian, 671; and Alfred Dreyfus, 19-22; and Errol Flynn, 560; French, 211, 235; and Mel Gibson, 1106-1109; and Jesse Jackson, 633-636; and Richard Nixon, 429; Russian, 309
Aquino, Benigno, Jr., 628-630
Aquino, Corazón, 628
Arafat, Yasser, 634
Arbuckle, Fatty, 79-82, 88, 100, 186
Archaeology, 292-295, 919-921
Archer, Jeffrey, 696-698
Archibald, Robert W., 46-48
Arena, Dominick James, 395
Argentina, 815-818
Arming America (Bellesiles), 985-988
Armitage, Richard, 1010-1013
Armory Modern Art Show, 49-52
Armstrong, Garner Ted, 525-528
Armstrong, Herbert W., 525-528
Armstrong, Lance, 1104
Armstrong, Robert, 645
Army, U.S.; military police, 1036

Arnold, Ervin, 70-72
Aronowitz, Stanley, 837
Art movements. *See Category Index*
Artists' Front to Win the War, 221
Arvizo, Gavin, 1025-1027
Asia. *See Geographical Index*
Asquith, H. H., 43-46, 58-60
Association of American Painters and Sculptors, 49
Astor, Mary, 184-187
Atherton, Edwin, 191-193
Atherton Report, 191-193
Atkinson, Rick, 633
Atrocities and war crimes. *See Category Index*
Attell, Abe, 67
Auberge Grand-Mère scandal, 898-901
Augstein, Rudolf, 349-352
Australasia. *See Geographical Index*
Australia. *See Geographical Index*
Australian Broadcasting Commission, 305
Austria, 197, 669-672
Autobiography of Malcolm X, The (Haley), 521
Automobile safety; Ford Pinto, 594-596; tires, 534-536
"Axis Sally," 435
Aylwin, Patricio, 1121-1123

Babbitt, Bruce, 873
Bacanovic, Peter, 1031-1034
Bachelet, Michelle, 1121-1123
Backes, Ernest, 925-927
Bad Newz Kennels, 1158-1161
Baels, Lilian, 276-279
Bailey, Charles W., 175
Bailouts, 1175-1179
Baker, Bobby, 365-368
Baker, Scott, 861
Baker, Terence, 696
Bakker, Jim, 690-693
Bakker, Tammy Faye, 690-693
Balanchine, George, 528
Baldwin, Stanley, 187-190

Ball, Edward, 521
Ball, George L., 636
"Bananagate," 471-473
Banco Ambrosiano, 606-609
Band of Brothers (television), 951
Bank fraud; and Adelphia Communications, 971-973; and Jake Butcher, 648-650; and Linda Jones Medlar, 873; and John Spano, 903
Bank of Albania, 846-849
Bank robbery, 450-453
Banking and finance. *See Category Index*
Banque Oustric et Cie, 139-141
Barclay, Arthur, 142
Baring, Sir Evelyn, 298-301
Barker, Frank A., 401
Barker, Lex, 317
Barnes, Fred, 951
Barnett, Marilyn, 588-591
Barrett, David M., 872-874
Barron, Clarence, 63
Barrows, Sydney, 654-657
Barry, Joan, 220, 283
Barry, Marion, 748-750
Baseball; and drugs, 666-669; and gambling, 242-244, 556-558, 735-738; game fixing, 66-70, 118-121, 398-400; Steve Garvey, 574-577; Japanese, 398-400; Little League, 942-944; Major League Baseball Players Association, 1058; and steroids, 1058-1061, 1162
Basketball, 865; Kobe Bryant, 1008-1010; college, 274-276, 950, 968-970, 1142-1144; and gambling, 243, 1003, 1172-1175; game fixing, 274-276, 568-570; professional, 1008-1010, 1172-1175
Bates, Alfred, 181
Bates, Ruby, 150
Batista y Zaldívar, Fulgencio, 560
Batlogg, Bertram J. R., 980
Battista, James, 1173
Battle Hymn (film), 252
Baudouin I, 276-279

Bauman, Robert E., 577-579
Bayley, John, 852-854
BBC. *See* British Broadcasting Corporation
Beall, George, 447-450
Bear Stearns, 1178
Beasley, Malcolm R., 980
Beasley Report, 981
Beatles, 494-497
Beaudoin, François, 898
Beck, Dave, 323-325
Bedaux, Charles, 196, 212-214
Bedaux, Fern, 212
"Begelgate," 509-511
Begelman, David, 509-511
Belgium. *See Geographical Index*
Belichick, Bill, 1161-1163
Bell, Alexander Graham, biography of, 879-881
Bell, Griffin, 636
Bellesiles, Michael A., 985-988
Belloc, Hilaire, 44
Belmont Park Raceway, 514-516
Beloved (Morrison), 521
Ben Barka, Mehdi, 374-376
Bendix Corporation, 580-582
Benedict XVI, 954
Bengzon, Cesar, 601
Bennett, Robert S., 803
Berezhnaya, Elena, 962-964
Berezovsky, Boris, 1132-1134
Bergman, Ingrid, 263-265
Bergman, Lowell, 833
Berisha, Sali, 846-849
Berlin Conference of 1884-1885, 31
Berlusconi, Silvio, 591, 1092-1094
Bern, Paul, 160-163
Bernanke, Ben, 1134-1138, 1175-1179
Bernardin, Joseph Louis, 597
Bernhard, Prince of Lippe-Biesterfeld, 482
Bernstein, Carl, 425-431
Berra, Dale, 666-669
Berry, Sidney B., 488-490
Berry, William, 514
Besen, Wayne, 913
"Bess mess," 693-695

Betting Houses Act of 1853, 56
Bettman, Gary, 901-903
Biden, Joe, 698-701
"Billygate," 573
Bingham, Barry, Sr., 60-62
Bingham, Mary Lily Kenan, 60-62
Bingham, Robert Worth, 60-62
Birmingham, Joseph, 954
Birth disorders, 135, 301-304, 434, 548
Bjelke-Petersen, Johannes, 682
Black, Eli M., 471-473
Black, Hugo L., 418
Black, Roy, 865
Black Mist scandal, 398-400
Black Sox scandal, 66-70, 120-121, 399-400, 556, 737, 1172
Blaesing, Elizabeth Ann, 124-127
Blair, Jayson, 888, 998-1001
Blair, Tony, 1089-1091
Blanco, Kathleen Babineaux, 1068-1072
Blaney, Neil, 413-415
Blix, Hans, 995-998
Blood, tainted, 868-871
Bluitgen, Kåre, 1075-1077
Bobbitt, John Wayne, 795-797
Bobbitt, Lorena, 795-797
Bodkin, Archibald, 12
Boesky, Ivan, 726-729, 753-756
Bokassa, Jean-Bédel, 550-552
Boland, Kevin, 413-415
Bolshevik revolution. *See* Russian Revolution
"Bonus Army," 156-160
Boone, Pat, 500-502
Borer, Thomas, 858
Bork, Robert, 680
Borman, Frank, 488
Borman Commission, 488-490
Boston; James Michael Curley, 6-9
Boston College, 1102; basketball scandal, 275, 568-570
Boston Globe, 936-938, 954-958, 998
Bouchard, Lucien, 892-895
Boudreaux, Lori, 1002-1004
Bowles, Andrew Parker, 745

Bowles, Camilla Parker, 745-747, 791
Bowman, Patricia, 759-762
Boxing, 52-55, 93; Tonya Harding, 814
Boyd, Gerald, 998-1001
Boyd, James, 384
Boyle, W. A., 404-406
Bradley, Anne, 22-25
Bradshaw, Berenice Jewett, 528-530
Bradshaw, Franklin James, 528-530
Brady, Matthew A., 79, 191-193
Brady, Roger, 1062
Brawley, Tawana, 702-705
Breen, Joseph, 163
Brennan, Christine, 814
Breton, André, 136, 147
Breton, Sonia Rojas, 942
Breuning, Stephen, 720-723
"Bribe menu" and Duke Cunningham, 1066
Bribery, 103, 569; Spiro T. Agnew, 447-450; Australian police, 681-683; "Bananagate," 471-473; Belgian politicians, 889-892; Joseph R. Burton, 4-6; and campaign contributions, 1; T. Lamar Caudle, 279-282; Congress members, 562, 583, 1064-1067, 1147-1150; Randall Cunningham, 1064-1067; Budd Dwyer, 684-686; Albert Fall, 125; Abe Fortas, 391-394; Valéry Giscard d'Estaing, 550-552; Iraqi government, 1039; Japanese politicians, 715; William J. Jefferson, 1147-1150; "Koreagate," 479-482; Lockheed Corporation, 482-485; Bess Myerson, 693-695; and payola, 333; John Poulson, 431-433; Eugene E. Schmitz, 28-30; Jesse W. Smith, 92-95; soccer players, 1056; and Teapot Dome scandal, 98; Harrison A. Williams, 562; Louis Wolfson, 390. *See also* Payola scandal; Point shaving in basketball

Bricmont, Jean, 837
Bridgestone Firestone, 1078-1080
Briggs, John V., 507
Bright Tunes Music v. Harrisongs Music (1976), 495
British Broadcasting Corporation, 187, 532-533, 560
Brittan, Leon, 645-647
Britton, Nan, 124-127
Broadcast Music, Inc., 333
Broadway theater, 122-124, 246, 353, 386, 434
Brodhead, Richard H., 1086
Brominski, Bernard C., 397
Bronson, Charles, 642
Brooks, Louise Cromwell, 173
Brooks, Stephen K., 401
Brown, Arthur, 22-25
Brown, David D., IV, 1050-1052
Brown, Denise, 1129
Brown, Divine, 827-829
Brown, Michael D., 1068-1072
Brown, Ronald H., 873
Brown, Walter Folger, 144-147
Brown Bunny, The (film), 1004-1007
Brown v. Board of Education (1954), 208
Brownlee, John Edward, 176-178
Bruce, Robert V., 879
Bryan, William Jennings, 1
Bryant, Anita, 506-509
Bryant, Kobe, 1008-1010
Bryant, Vanessa, 1008
Brzak, Cynthia, 1039-1041
Bucak, Sedat, 843-845
Buckey, Peggy Ann, 624
Buckey, Peggy McMartin, 624
Buckey, Raymond, 624
Buckley, Sheila, 468-470
Buddhism; and self-immolation, 362-365; and Chögyam Trungpa, 474-476; in Vietnam, 362-365
Buena Vista oil reserves, 96
Buffalo Child Long Lance, 130-133
Buffalo '66 (film), 1005
Bundesliga scandal of 2005, 1055-1058

Buñuel, Luis, 136-139, 147-150
Burden, William Douglas, 130-133
Bureau of Internal Revenue; and T. Lamar Caudle, 279-282; and Tom Pendergast, 200; and Irving Sachs, 311. *See also* Internal Revenue Service
Burgaud, Fabrice, 922
Burke, James, 568-570
Burkett, Bill, 1044
Burns, William J., 28, 60
Burton, Joseph R., 4-6
Bush, George H. W., 208, 762, 787, 888; Iran-Contra, 678; and Clarence Thomas, 768-772
Bush, George W.; and Hurricane Katrina, 1068-1072; insider trading investigation, 762-765; and Iraq, 1011; and Trent Lott, 988-991; military service of, 1044-1046
Business. *See Category Index*
Business Development Bank of Canada, 898
Butcher, Cecil H., Jr., 648-650
Butcher, Sir Herbert, 431
Butcher, Jake, 648-650
Butler, Carrie, 1022-1024
Butler, Smedley, 156
Butt, Sir Alfred, 181-184
Buttafuoco, Joey, 781-784
Buttafuoco, Mary Jo, 781-784
Butterfield, Alexander, 428
Butz, Earl L., 500-502
Buxton, Peter, 437
Byrnes, Jack, 274-276

Cabey, Darrell, 641
Cabon, Christine Huguette, 651
Cachet, 654
Caldwell, John, 176
Calhoun, John, 449
Calhoun, Rory, 295-298
Calley, William, 401-404
Calvi, Roberto, 591, 606-609
Cameron, Lucille, 52
"Camillagate," 745-747
Campaign contributions, 1, 93,

388, 482, 1167; and bribery, 1; foreign, 481, 875; illegal, 286-288, 384-386; Richard Nixon, 454; Herman E. Talmadge, 553-555. *See also* Presidential campaigns
Campbell, Helen, 248
Campbell, John, 974
Campbell, Judith, 329-332
Campbell, Walter, 193
Canada. *See Geographical Index*
Canadian Broadcasting Corporation, 378, 660-662, 978
Canary Capital Partners, 1013-1016
Canseco, José, 1058-1061
Capasso, Carl, 693-695
Capital City Bank, 1073
Cardin, Lucien, 377-379
Carey, Hugh Leo, 546
Carmen, Leon, 852-854
Carnegie Endowment for International Peace, 259
Carroll, John, 1016
Carson, Clayborne, 739-741
Carson, Rachel, 547
Carter, Billy, 571-574
Carter, Jimmy, 546; and Billy Carter, 571-574; and "Koreagate," 479-482; and Bert Lance, 511-514, 571; personal confessions, 497-500
Cartoons, 11, 140, 378, 498, 828, 1108, 1154; of Prophet Muhammad, 1075-1077
Cary, Walter E., 104
Casement, Roger, 31-33
Casey, Eamonn, 779-781
Casey, Robert P., 684
Casey, William J., 676
Cassone, Michelle, 759
Castle, Barbara, 298
Castro, Fidel, 331, 560
Catholic Church. *See* Roman Catholic Church
Catholic Youth Organization of Brooklyn, 243
Çatli, Abdullah, 843-845

Cattier, Félicien, 33
Caudle, T. Lamar, 279-282, 310-313
CBC. *See* Canadian Broadcasting Corporation
Ceauşescu, Nicolae, 742-745
Cecil, Robert, 142-144
Cedarbaum, Miriam Goldman, 1031
Cedel International, 925
Celler, Emanuel, 380
Censorship in film, 165
Central African Republic, 550
Central and South America. *See Geographical Index*
Central Intelligence Agency, Korean, 479
Central Intelligence Agency, U.S., 376, 670, 1067; and Cuba, 426; and Guatemala, 471; Robert Hanssen, 931-933; Iran-Contra scandal, 676-681; and Iraq, 1010-1013, 1035; and Italy, 592; Valerie Plame, 1010-1013
Cerrini, Daniel, 815-818
Chagnon, Napoleon A., 910-912
Chamberlain, Neville, 182
Chambers, Whittaker, 259-262
Chandler, Happy, 242-244
Chandra, Ranjit Kumar, 977-979
Chaplin, Charles, 108, 283-285; paternity suit, 220-222
Chaplin, Oona O'Neill, 220, 283-285
Chappaquiddick incident, 367, 394-398
Charles, Count of Flanders, 277
Charles, Prince of Wales, 745-747, 789-792
Charles, Suzette, 638
Chautemps, Camille, 170-172
Chavis, Benjamin, 821-823
"Checkers" speech (Nixon), 286-288
Chemical waste in Love Canal, 548
Cheney, Dick, 1012
Cherkashin, Victor, 931
Cherkasky, Michael G., 1050
Cheshire, Maxine, 453

Chesterton, Cecil, 43-46
Chiapel, Tom, 638
Chiappe, Jean, 170-172
Chicago White Sox, 66-70, 399, 557, 737
Chien Andalou, Un (film), 136-139
Child abuse, 841; and Joan Crawford, 517-519; false allegations, 625; in France, 922-924; and Michael Jackson, 1025-1027; and Ernest Jones, 12-15; at McMartin Preschool, 624-627; and Rajneesh movement, 664; and Roman Catholic priests, 954-958. *See also* Pornography, child
Child Abuse Prevention and Treatment Act of 1974, 625
Childers, Thomas, 951
Chile, 482, 1121-1123
Chiledeportes, 1121-1123
China; and Richard Nixon, 603; nuclear weapons, 373; pet food scandal, 1097
Chomsky, Noam, 1156
Choynski, Joe, 53
Chrétien, Jean, 898-901
Christensen, Hayden, 888
Christian Crusade, 465
Christian Gospel Mission, 939
Christy, Cuthbert, 142
Christy Commission, 142-144
Chung Un-chan, 1094-1097
Church, Frank, 482
Churchill, Ward, 1155-1158
CIA. *See* Central Intelligence Agency
Cicotte, Eddie, 66-70
Ciller, Tansu, 843
Cinquanta, Ottavio, 962
Cisneros, Henry, 872-874
Citigroup, 1176
Citizen Kane (film), 165
Citizenship, 283, 377-379
Citizenship Education Fund, 896
Civil Liberties Act (1988), 208
Civil Rights Act of 1964, 989
Civil rights and liberties. *See* Category Index

Civiletti, Benjamin, 571
Claes, Willy, 889-890
Clark, Dick, 332-335
Clark, Helen, 974-977, 1112-1114
Clark, Joe, 898-901
Clark, Taliaferro, 437-440
Clark, Thomas C., 279-282
Clearstream International, 925-927
Clements, Bill, 687-689
Clinton, Bill; and Henry Cisneros, 872-873; impeachment, 874-878, 988; and Jesse Jackson, 896; and Monica Lewinsky, 126, 820, 874-878, 896, 1168; Lewinsky affair confession, 876; pardons of, 452, 805; and Tuskegee Syphilis Study, 439; and Whitewater investigation, 818-821
Clinton, Hillary Rodham, 874, 904-905, 1114; and Eliot Spitzer, 1169; and Whitewater investigation, 818-821
Cloning, 1094-1097
CNET, 1116-1117
Coaches; baseball, 243, 400, 557; basketball, 968-970, 1172; football, 687-689, 948-950, 1002-1004, 1101-1103, 1161-1163; lacrosse, 1086-1089; track and field, 1165
Cobb, Ernie, 568
Cobb, Ty, 118-121
Cochran, Johnnie, 808
Cochran, W. E., 5
Cody, John Patrick, 597-599
Cody, Lew, 102
Cody, Richard, 1140
Coelho, Tony, 732
Coghlan, Monica, 696-698
Cold fusion, 723-726
Cold War; and film industry, 251; and Germany, 657-659; and McCarthyism, 266-270; and Soviet espionage, 259; and Vietnam, 258. *See also* Communism; Communist Party; Soviet Union

Coleman, Milton, 633
Collingsworth, Terry, 1078-1080
Colonialism and imperialism. *See* Category Index
Colosio, Luis Donaldo, 824-826
Comerica Bank, 902
Comiskey, Charles, 66-70
Commission on Care for America's Returning Wounded Warriors, 1141
Commission on Wartime Relocation and Internment of Civilians, 207
Committee on Public Information, 307, 309
Commodity Futures Modernization Act of 2000, 1177
Common Cause, 731
Commonwealth v. Buckley (1909), 26
Communications Act of 1934, 329, 334, 336
Communications and media. *See* Category Index
Communism; and Christian fundamentalism, 465; in Nicaragua, 676-681; in Romania, 742-745; Soviet, 167-169, 307-310; Vietnamese, 257-259, 362; "witch hunts," 266-270. *See also* Cold War; KGB; Soviet Union
Communist International, 106
Communist Party, 105-108; and Bonus Army, 158; and Charles Chaplin, 220, 284; and government infiltration, 259-262; and J. Edgar Hoover, 220; Italian, 591; outlawing of, 259; and "Scottsboro Boys," 152. *See also* Cold War
Comprehensive Environmental Response, Compensation, and Liability Act of 1980, 549, 615-617
Concepcion, Roberto, 601
Condit, Gary, 933-936
Confidential magazine, 295-298
Congo Free State, 31-33

Congo Reform Association, 32-33
Congress, U.S.; Robert E. Bauman, 577-579; Black Caucus, 1148; Joseph R. Burton, 4-6; and Bill Clinton, 874-878, 988; Randall Cunningham, 1064-1067; Thomas J. Dodd, 384-386; Mark Foley, 1118-1120; Wayne L. Hays, 491-493; William J. Jefferson, 1147-1150; and "Koreagate," 479-482; Trent Lott, 988-991; Wilbur D. Mills, 462-465; and Navy, 70-72; page sex scandal, 621-624; and payola, 332-335; Post Office scandal, 803-806; Adam Clayton Powell, Jr., 380-383; Dan Rostenkowski, 803-806; Edward Schrock, 1041-1044; Special Committee to Investigate Organized Crime in Interstate Commerce, 270-273; steroid investigation, 1058-1061; and Herman E. Talmadge, 553-555; J. Parnell Thomas, 248-250; David Vitter, 1150-1153; Jim Wright, 730-732. See also House Committee on Government Reform; House Committee on Standards of Official Conduct; House Committee on Un-American Activities
Congress of Vienna, 277
Connelly, Matthew J., 281, 310-313
Connolly, Cyril, 136
Conrad, Joseph, 32
Constable, Anne, 465
Conte, Victor, 1164-1166
Contergan (drug), 301
Continental Enterprise, 389-391
Contraceptive, 459-462
Cooke, Janet, 585-588
Coolidge, Calvin, 104, 200; and Teapot Dome scandal, 95-99
Cools, André, 889-892
Cooper, Isabel, 173-175
Copp, Harley, 594

Cornell, Julien, 236
"Corngate," 974-977
"Correcting the Record: Times Reporter Who Resigned Leaves Long Trail of Deception" (May 11, 2003), 1000
Corruption. See Category Index
Cortelyou, George B., 1
Cosby, Bill, 703
Cosgrave, Liam, 413
Costa Rica, 473
Coughlin, Paula, 785
Countess from Hong Kong, A (film), 285
Countrywide Financial Corporation, 1134-1138, 1176
Courlander, Harold, 520-522, 525-528
Cox, Archibald, 428
Cox, Tricia Nixon, 453
Crader, Bo, 959
Cramer, Clayton E., 985
Crane, Cheryl, 317-319
Crane, Daniel, 621-624
Crane, Stephen, 317
Crane, Stephen G., 641
Crawford, Christina, 517-519
Crawford, Joan, 517-519
Creation Science Evangelism, 1123-1126
Creighton, Joanne V., 936-938
Cremation, Georgia state law, 966
Crematories, 964-967
Crime and Misconduct Commission, 682
Crime of the Congo, The (Doyle), 33
Criminal Justice Commission, 682
Cuba, 4, 331, 374; and Central Intelligence Agency, 426; and Errol Flynn, 560; Guantanamo Bay, 1035, 1038
Cultural and intellectual history. See Category Index
Cunningham, Mary, 580-582
Cunningham, Randall, 1064-1067
Curie, Marie, 37-39

Curley, James Michael, 6-9
Curley, Thomas, 6
Curnin, Tom, 636-638
Currie, Edwina, 983-985
Curzon, George Nathaniel, 25
Cushing, Richard, 397
Customs Act of 1901, 305
Cycling, 1103-1106
Czechoslovakia, 163-166

Dacko, David, 550
Daily Star, 696-698
Dalí, Salvador, 136-139, 147-150
Dalkon Shield, 459-462
Dalton, John H., 800
Daly, Augustin, 34
Daniélou, Alain, 456-459
Daniélou, Jean, 456-459
Daniels, Josephus, 70
Darden, Christopher, 808
Dardenne, Sabine, 840
D.A.R.E. See Drug Abuse Resistance Education
Dassault, Serge, 889-892
Daugherty, Harry M., 92-95
Davenport, Dorothy, 86-89
Davies, Arthur B., 49-52
Davies, Marion, 108-111
Davis, Gray, 1017
Davis, Hugh J., 459-462
Davis, John W., 46
Davis, Oscar, 313
Davis, Peter, 1112-1114
Dawson, Charles, 292
Day, Laraine, 242
Deakin, George, 531
Dean, John W., 425-431, 500-502
Death Row Records, 884
Death Wish (film), 642
DeBartolo, Edward J., Jr., 907-909
Defense Base Realignment and Closure Commission, 1141
Defense Information Systems Agency, 1066
DeFreeze, Donald, 450
DeLauro, Rosa L., 1097-1100
Delay, Myriam, 922-924
Delay, Thierry, 922-924

Delhez, Laetitia, 840
Delmont, Margaret Maude, 79
De Lorean, John, 609-612
Delpey, Roger, 550
Delplanque, David, 922
Denmark, 289-291, 1075-1077
Dennis, Hugh C., 5
Department of Agriculture, 96
Department of Commerce and Labor, U.S., 1
Department of Defense, U.S.; sexual harassment, 993
Department of the Interior, U.S., 96
Department of Trade and Industry (U.K.), 754
Deputy, The (play), 353-355
Derrida, Jacques, 705
Deutsche Börse Clearing, 925
DeWitt, John L., 205
DeWolf, L. Harold, 739
Diana, Princess of Wales, 745-747, 789-792, 861-865
"Dianagate," 789-792
Diaries; Jeffrey Archer, 697; Mary Astor, 184-187; John Earl Brownlee, 177; Edwina Currie, 983; Alfred Dreyfus, 21; Elinor Glyn, 25; Adolf Hitler, 618-621; Rita Jenrette, 582-585; Claudine Longet, 486; John Prescott, 1089-1091
"Diary of a Mad Congresswife" (Jenrette), 582-585
Dickie, Phil, 681
Diefenbaker, John G., 377-379
Dies, Martin, 248
Dies Committee, 248
DiFederico, Mario A., 534
Dines, Courtland S., 100-102
Dingell, John, 615-617
Dinis, Edmund S., 395
DiStefano, Phil, 1155
Distillers Company, 750-753
Dobson, James, 913
Dockweiler, John F., 202
Doctorow, E. L., 18
Dodd, Thomas J., 384-386
Doerfer, John C., 335-337

Dogfighting, 1158-1161
Doheny, Laurence E., 95-99
Dole, Bob, 1141
Dominican Republic, 366, 942-944
Donaghy, Tim, 1172-1175
Donaldson, Liam, 927
Doren, Charles Van, 326-329
Douglas, William O., 382
Dowd, John M., 735
Downey Savings and Loan, 1177
Doyle, Arthur Conan, 33
Dracula (novel), 111-114
Drag, The (play), 122-124
Dresnick, Ronald, 765
Dreyfus, Alfred, 19-22
Drug Abuse Resistance Education, 888
Drugs; and birth disorders, 301. *See also Category Index*
Du Bois, W. E. B., 142
Duhaime, Yvon, 898-901
Dukakis, Michael, 698-701
Dunaway, Faye, 518
Duncan, Isadora, 34-36
Dunleavy, Richard M., 784
Dunn, John, 341
Dunn, Patricia, 1114-1118
Duplessis, Maurice, 892-895
Duplessis orphans, 892-895
Dupré, Ashley Alexandra, 1167-1170
Duranty, Walter, 167-169
Durbin, Richard J., 1097-1100
Durocher, Leo, 242-244
Dutroux, Marc, 840-842
Dwyer, Budd, 684-686

E. F. Hutton, 636-638
Eagleton, Thomas F., 440-443
Ebbers, Bernard, 764, 909, 1074
Ebert, Roger, 1004-1007
Eckardt, Shawn, 812
Economic bailouts, 1175-1179
Education. *See Category Index*
Edward II, 1107
Edward VIII. *See* Windsor, Duke of
Edwards, Blake, 612-614

Edwards, Edwin, 907-909
EEOC. *See* Equal Employment Opportunity Commission
Egypt, 861-865
Eisenhower, Dwight D.; and Sherman Adams, 320-322; and John Doerfer, 336; film censorship, 252; and Joseph McCarthy, 266-270; and Richard Nixon, 286-288
Eisenhower, Julie Nixon, 453
Eisenstein, Serge, 149
Eisler, Hanns, 284
Eizenstat, Stuart, 858
El Salvador, 473
Elixir sulfanilamide, 193-195
Elk Hills oil reserve, 95-99
Elliott, Brian Robinson, 223
Ellis, Joseph J., 936-938
Ellsberg, Daniel, 416-419
Elsner, Edward, 122
Éluard, Paul, 148
Emory University, 985-988
Emperors Club, 1167-1170
Endo, Mitsuye, 205
England. *See Geographical Index*
Enright, Dan, 326-329
Enrile, Juan Ponce, 629
Enron Corporation, 599, 764, 945-948
Environmental issues. *See Category Index*
Environmental Protection Agency, 547, 615-617, 964
"Environmental racism," 822
EPA. *See* Environmental Protection Agency
Equal Employment Opportunity Commission, 769
Erasmus Commission, 545
Erben, Hermann F., 559
Erbitux, 1031
Ericta, Vicente, 600
Ern Malley hoax, 223-225
Errichetti, Angelo, 561-564
Esenin, Sergei, 36
Espionage. *See Category Index*
Espy, Mike, 873
Estes, Billie Sol, 341-343

Estevez, Emilio, 718
Estrich, Susan, 1017
Ethics. *See Category Index*
Eugenics, 20, 133-136
Eulenburg-Hertefeld, Philipp,
  Prince of, 9-12
Europe. *See Geographical Index*
European Convention on Human
  Rights, 891
European Court of Human Rights,
  755
Eustachy, Larry, 950
Evangelists; at Air Force Academy,
  1062-1064; Herbert W.
  Armstrong, 525-528; Jim
  Bakker, 690-693; Ted Haggard,
  1126-1129; Billy James Hargis,
  465-467; Kent Hovind, 1123-
  1126; Aimee Semple
  McPherson, 115-118; Peter
  Popoff, 673-675; Jimmy
  Swaggart, 711-714
Evans, David, 1086
Evers-Williams, Myrlie, 823
Exclusion, U.S. Supreme Court on,
  382
Exner, Dan, 331
Exner, Judith. *See* Campbell,
  Judith
Exodus International, 913-915
"Expanded Guidance for Subprime
  Lending Programs" (2001),
  1136
Experiments; cold fusion, 723-726;
  faked, 980, 1094-1097; medical,
  134, 437-440, 894;
  pharmaceutical, 216;
  psychological, 338-340, 370,
  420-422
Expulsion, U.S. Supreme Court
  on, 382
Exstase (film), 163-166
Ezoe, Hiromasa, 714-717

Faber, Katelyn, 1008-1010
Fabulist, The (film), 888
Factory Investigating Commission,
  New York, 40-43
Fahd, 453

Fairfoul, Tom, 55
Faisal, 453
Faith healing, 673-675
Fall, Albert B., 95-99, 125
Falwell, Jerry, 506-509, 690, 709
Families and children. *See
  Category Index*
Family Protection Act of 1977,
  578
Faneuil, Douglas, 1031-1034
Fannie Mae, 1175
Fard, Wallace Dodd, 359
Farian, Frank, 756
Farmer, Frances, 214-217
Farmer, Lillian Van Ornum, 214
Farrakhan, Louis, 361, 633, 635
Farrow, Mia, 773-775
Fastow, Andrew, 909
Fayed, Dodi al-, 861-865
Fayed, Mohamed al-, 861
FBI. *See* Federal Bureau of
  Investigation
FCC. *See* Federal Communication
  Commission
Federal Bureau of Investigation,
  30, 191, 368; and Abscam, 561-
  564; and Charles Chaplin, 220-
  222, 283-285; and John De
  Lorean, 609-612; and Billie Sol
  Estes, 342; and financial
  markets collapse of 2008, 1178;
  and Alger Hiss, 260; and Walter
  Jenkins, 372; and John F.
  Kennedy, 329-332; and Elijah
  Muhammad, 360; and Ezra
  Pound, 237; and Watergate,
  371-374
Federal Bureau of Prisons, 933
Federal Communication
  Commission, 334-337
Federal Corrupt Practices Act of
  1910, 3
Federal Election Campaign Act of
  1971, 3
Federal Emergency Management
  Agency, 1068-1072
Federal Housing Administration,
  1137
Federal Reserve, U.S., 1136, 1176

Fédération Internationale de
  Football Association, 816,
  1056
Feleppa, Anselmo, 881
Felt, W. Mark, 425
FEMA. *See* Federal Emergency
  Management Agency
Fenjves, Pablo F., 1129-1131
Fennell, Jim, 948
Fernando, Enrique, 600
Fernando Pó, 142
FHA. *See* Federal Housing
  Administration
Fields, William J., 104
FIFA. *See* Fédération Internationale
  de Football Association
Fifth Estate, The (magazine), 660-
  662
Figure skating, 812-815, 962-964
Figure Skating Association, U.S.,
  812
Film. *See Category Index*
Film production code, 165
Financial industry, collapse of,
  1175-1179
Finnerty, Collin, 1086
Fiorentina soccer club, 1092
Fiorina, Carly, 1115
Firestone, 534-536; and Liberia,
  143, 1078-1080
First Amendment, and Watergate,
  418
FISA. *See* Foreign Intelligence
  Surveillance Act of 1978
Fischer, Bobby, 525
Fish, Stanley, 838
Fisher, Amy, 781-784
Fiske, Robert B., 818
Fitch, 1176
Fitzgerald, Patrick, 1011
Fitzgerald, Tony, 681
Fitzgerald inquiry, 681-683
*Fitzgeralds and the Kennedys: An
  American Saga*, The (Goodwin),
  959-961
Fitzsimmons, Jeanette, 974
Flanders, 276-279
Fleet Bank, 902-903
Fleischmann, Martin, 723-726

Flinn, Kelly, 855-858
Flynn, Errol, 202-205, 559-561
Flynn, Maurice, 280
Focus on the Family, 913-915
Fogel, Moshe, 860
Foggo, Kyle Dustin, 1064
Foley, Mark, 1118-1120
Fomon, Robert M., 636-638
Fonda, Jane, 434-436
Food and Drug Act of 1906, 193
Food and Drug Administration,
    U.S.; and elixir scandal, 194;
    and thalidomide, 301-304
Food, Drug, and Cosmetic Act of
    1938, 195, 303; amendment of,
    461
Football, 807; college, 687-689,
    801, 948-950, 969, 1002-1004,
    1062, 1101-1103; and gambling,
    243, 1174; professional, 1158-
    1163
Football, Association. See Soccer
Forbes, Charles R., 89-92
Ford, Betty, 454
Ford, Frederick W., 337
Ford, Gerald R., 449, 497-498; and
    Earl Butz, 500-502; pardon of
    Dave Beck, 324; pardon of
    Richard Nixon, 429, 455, 499;
    and Nelson Rockefeller, 537;
    and Watergate, 429, 455
Ford, Harold E., Sr., 649
Ford, Harrison, 524
Ford, Robin, 251-253
Ford Foundation, 822
Ford Motor Company, 535, 594-
    596, 694
Ford Pinto, 594-596
Foreign Gifts and Decorations Act
    of 1881, 453
Foreign Intelligence Surveillance
    Act of 1978, 997
Forest Service, U.S., 96
Forgery. See Category Index
Forlani, Arnaldo, 591-593
Fortas, Abe, 367, 371, 389-394
Foursquare Gospel Church, 115
Fowler, Tillie, 991-994
Fox Television, 1020, 1129

Foxe, Fanne, 462-465
France. See Geographical Index
France, Anatole, 33
Francis, Ted, 696-698
Franke, Karl Heinz, 503-505
Fraser, Donald M., 479
Fraser, John, 660-662
Fraud Discovery Institute, 709
Freddie Mac, 1175
Freed, Alan, 332-335
Freedman, Albert, 326-329
Freedom of Information Act of
    1966, 283, 429, 559, 764
Freeh, Louis, 931
Freeman, Helene, 638
French, John, 58-60
French restaurants, and city
    corruption, 29
Freud, Sigmund, 13, 74, 137
Frey, James, 424
Frist, Bill, 988-989
Frohnmayer, David, 662
Fualaau, Vili, 605, 849-852
Fujimura, Shinichi, 919-921
Furesz, John, 868

Gabel, Hortense W., 693-695
Gailey, Samantha, 522-524
Gaines, James R., 810
Gaines, Kevin, 884-886
Galbraith, T. G. D., 347
Galeen, Henrik, 111
Gallagher, Willie, 182
Gallo, Vincent, 1004-1007
Galman, Rolando, 628
Gambling. See Category Index
Game shows, 326-329
Gandil, Chick, 66-70
Garabedian, Mitchell, 954
García Lorca, Federico, 136
Gardner, Deborah, 476-478
Gargan, Joseph F., 394
Garner Ted Armstrong Evangelistic
    Association, 527
Garrett, H. Lawrence, III, 784-788
Garvey, Cyndy, 574-577
Garvey, Steve, 574-577
Gates, Henry Louis, Jr., 521
Gates, Robert, 1138

Gaulle, Charles de, 209, 232
Gay and Lesbian Alliance Against
    Defamation, 590
Geishas, 483, 733-735, 1146
Geller, Uri, 674
Gelli, Licio, 591
Gender reassignment. See
    Transsexualism
General Allotment Act of 1887,
    1157
General Motors, 535, 1143
Generals' affair, 257-259
Genesee County Bank, 637
Genetic engineering, 974-977,
    1094-1097
Genovese, Kitty, 369-371
Geoghan, John, 954-958
George, Mary, 476
George V, 84
George VI, 187
Georgia Institute of Technology,
    724
Gerard, Mark, 514-516
Gerbert, Elkin B., 389
Germany. See Geographical Index
Getty, J. Paul, 220
Giamatti, A. Bartlett, 735-738
Giancana, Sam, 330
Gibbs, David Charles, 1123
Gibbs, Lois, 546-550
Gibson, Mel, 1106-1109
Giesler, Jerry, 202-205
Gilbey, James, 789-792
Gillars, Mildred, 435
Gillooly, Jeff, 812
Gingrich, Newt, 731, 989
Giraudo, Antonio, 1092-1094
Giscard d'Estaing, Valéry, 550-
    552
Giuliani, Donna Hanover, 904
Giuliani, Judith Nathan, 904-906
Giuliani, Rudy, 726, 904-906
GLAAD. See Gay and Lesbian
    Alliance Against Defamation
Glass, Stephen, 887-889
Glassford, Pelham D., 158
Glyn, Elinor, 25-27
Goebbels, Josef, 197, 231
Goerlitzer, Artur, 197

Goetz, Bernhard, 641-644
Golden Age, The (film), 147
Goldfine, Bernard, 320-322
Goldman, Fred, 1129
Goldman, Judy, 765-768
Goldman, Larry, 765
Goldman, Ronald, 806-809
Goldman Sachs, 1176
Goldwater, Barry, 371, 386
Golitsin, Anatoli, 347
Gone with the Wind (Mitchell), 521
Good Government Association, 8
Goodell, Roger, 1160-1163
Goodpaster, Andrew J., 488
Goodwin, Doris Kearns, 959-961
Goossens, Eugène, 304-306
Gore, Al, 988
Göring, Hermann, 196-197
Gorman, Marvin, 711-714
Gorsuch, Anne, 615-617
Government. *See Category Index*
Government in the Sunshine Act of 1976, 429
Graef, Ortwin de, 705
Graham, Philip, 270
Grammy Awards, 756-758
Grant, Hugh, 827-829
Grass, Günter, 1109-1112
Grau, Albin, 111
Gravel, Mike, 416
Gray, Fred, 437
Gray, L. Patrick, III, 428
Gray, Lily, 594-596
Graziano, Rocky, 243
Great Dictator, The (film), 284
Greeley, Andrew M., 597-599
Greenberg, Jeffrey W., 1050-1052
Greenpeace, 651-654
Gregory, Wilton D., 954
Grenon, Aurelie, 922
Grey Wolves, 843-845
Grimshaw, Richard, 594-596
Grimshaw v. Ford Motor Co. (1981), 594-596
Gronen, Jimmy, 444-446
"Gropegate," 1016-1019
Grozier, Richard, 63
Gruenberger, Peter, 509
Grünenthal, 301

Guagenti, Peter, 781
Guantanamo Bay, 1035, 1038
Guccione, Bob, 638-641
Guest, Frederick, 83-86
Guinness Four, 753-756
Gun, Katharine, 995-998
Gundlach, James, 1101-1103
Gymnastics, 916-918, 963

Hager, Nicky, 974-977
Haggard, Ted, 1126-1129
Hahn, Jessica, 690
Haig, Alexander, 416
Haile Selassie, 454
Halberstam, David, 362
Haley, Alex, 520-522
Hall, Camilla, 450
Hamburger, Christian, 289-291
Hamilton, David F., 1078-1080
Hammerman, I. H., 447
Hamsun, Knut, 229-232
Hamsun, Marie, 229
Han Hak-soo, 1094
Hanna, Richard T., 479
Hanover, Donna, 904
Hansen, Betty, 202-205
Hanssen, Robert, 931-933
"Happy Birthday" (song), 344-346
Harden, Maximilian, 9-12
Harding, Florence, 89
Harding, Tonya, 812-815
Harding, Warren G., 89-95, 124-127, 200; and Teapot Dome scandal, 91, 95-99, 125
Hardy, Carlos S., 117
Hargis, Billy James, 465-467
Harlow, Jean, 160-163
Harper, Samuel N., 307
Harrick, Jim, Jr., 968-970
Harrick, Jim, Sr., 950, 968-970
Harrick exam, 969
Harriman, E. H., 2
Harrington, Margaret, 217-219
Harris, Jean, 565-567
Harris, Maxwell Henley, 223-225
Harris, Oren, 332-335
Harrison, George, 494-497
Harrison, Rex, 245-247

Hartery, Don, 765
Harvey, Francis J., 1138
Harvey, Marilyn, 977
Hasner, Adam, 1154
Hassan II, 374
Hastert, Dennis, 1118
Haughey, Charles James, 413-415
Hayden, Tom, 434
Hays, Wayne L., 491-493
Hays, William H., 86
Hayter, William, 347
Hayworth, Rita, 254-256
Hazardous and Solid Waste Act of 1984, 617
Health Management Associates scandal, 868-871
Hearst, Patricia, 450-453
Hearst, William Randolph, 74, 81, 108-111, 450
Heart of Darkness (Conrad), 32
Heidemann, Gerd, 618-621
Heimann, John G., 511
Hellenbroich, Heribert, 657
Heller, Jean, 437-440
Helmsley, Harry, 776
Helmsley, Leona, 776-778
Hempel, Régis, 925
Henderson, Ian, 298
Henderson, Paul, 1097-1100
Heritage USA, 690
Herman, Alexis M., 873
Herman, Pee-wee (Paul Reubens), 765-768, 829
Hernandez, Macarena, 998-1001
Herrera, Ameurfina Melencio, 600
Herrschaft, Daryl, 913
Hersh, Seymour, 401
Hervey, Ramon, II, 638
Heseltine, Michael, 645-647
Hess, Dean E., 252
Hess, Rudolph, 197
Hetrick, William Morgan, 610
Hewlett-Packard Corporation, 1114-1118
Higham, Charles, 559-561
Hilfswerk für Behinderte Kinder, 302
Hill, Anita, 768-772

Hill, Henry, 568-570

Hilton, Paris, 1019-1021

Hindemith, Paul, 76-79

Hirabayashi, Gordon Kiyoshi, 205

Hirabayashi v. United States (1943), 206

Hirschfield, Alan, 509-511

Hiss, Alger, 259-262; and J. Edgar Hoover, 261

Hitler, Adolf, 213, 230, 352, 503; and Charles Chaplin, 284; faked diaries, 618-621; film censorship, 164; and Errol Flynn, 560; and France, 210; and Knut Hamsun, 231; and Norway, 226-229; purges, 11; and the Windsors, 189, 196-198

Hitler Youth, 1109

Ho Chi Minh, 257

Hoaxes, frauds, and charlatanism. *See Category Index*

Hobbs, Marian, 974

Hochhuth, Rolf, 353-355

Hodge, Sir Rowland, 83

Hoffman, James, 609

Hoffman, Martin R., 488

Hogan, Frank, 274-276

Hola massacre, 298-301

Holland, Al, 667

Hollywood. *See Category Index*; Los Angeles

"Hollywoodgate," 509-511

Holmes, David, 531

Holocaust, 235, 340, 1109; and Adolf Hitler, 619; and Jesse Jackson, 634; and Pius XII, 353-355; and Swiss banks, 858-861

Homosexuality; and Julie Andrews, 612-614; anonymous sex, 408; and Anita Bryant, 506-509; and Blake Edwards, 612-614; Emperor William II, 9-12; Philipp Eulenburg, 11; in opera, 1084-1086; "outing," 1041-1044, 1112-1114; and palimony, 588-591; research on, 407-409; U.S. Navy, 70-72; John Vassall, 347-349; James E. West, 1081-1083

Honduras, 471-473

Honor code, U.S. Naval Academy, 801

Hons, Emile, 476

Hooker Chemical, 546-550

Hoover, Herbert, 94, 99, 144; and Bonus Army, 156-160

Hoover, J. Edgar; and Charles Chaplin, 220-222, 283-285; and domestic communism, 261; and John F. Kennedy, 329-332; and Profumo affair, 357

Horrigan, Aldine, 798

Horse racing, 200, 390, 557, 736; fraud, 514-516

Hotchner, A. E., 524

House Committee on Government Reform, 1012

House Committee on Standards of Official Conduct, 492, 731

House Committee on Un-American Activities, 222; and Charles Chaplin, 284; and Alger Hiss, 259-262; and Thomas J. Parnell, 248-250

House of Representatives, U.S. *See* Congress, U.S.

House Un-American Activities Committee. *See* House Committee on Un-American Activities

Housing and Urban Development, U.S. Department of, 872-874

Hovind, Eric, 1123

Hovind, Jo Delia, 1123

Hovind, Kent, 1123-1126

Howard, J. Daniel, 785

Hoyzer, Robert, 1055-1058

HUAC. *See* House Committee on Un-American Activities

Hubbell, Webster, 819

Hubble, Ava, 852

Huddleston, Silous, 404

Hudson, Erastus, 70

Hudson, Rock, 295-298

Hughes, Howard, 160, 251-253, 422-425

Hull, Anne, 1138-1142

Human rights. *See Category Index*

Human Rights Campaign, 1043

Human Tissue Act of 1961, 929

Humphreys, Laud, 407-409

Hunt, E. Howard, 425-431

Hunter, C. J., 1164-1166

Hurley, Elizabeth, 827

Hurley, Patrick, 158

Hussein, Saddam, 989, 995, 1035, 1039, 1053-1055

Hussey, John, 948-950

Huth, M. E., 104

Hwang Woo-suk, 1094-1097

"Hymietown," 633-636

I Was Wrong (Bakker), 692

ICC. *See* Interstate Commerce Commission

Ice hockey, 901-903

If I Did It (Simpson), 1129-1131

Ikenaga, Masaaki, 398-400

Iliescu, Ion, 742

ILRF. *See* International Labor Rights Fund

ImClone Systems, 1031-1034

Immigration; Charles Chaplin, 283-285

Immigration and Naturalization Service, U.S., 284, 563, 664, 671

Immigration fraud, 563, 940; Bhagwan Shree Rajneesh, 662-665

Impeachment; of Bill Clinton, 820, 874-878, 988; of judges, 46, 117; Liberian cabinet, 143; and Richard Nixon, 429; and Eliot Spitzer, 1169

Imus, Don, 1142-1144

Ince, Thomas H., 108-111

Independent Committee of Eminent Persons, 859

Indian Arts and Crafts Act of 1990, 1157

Indochina Peace Campaign, 435

IndyMac, 1177

"Infogate," 543-545

Ingrassia, Angelo J., 704

Inside Sports magazine, 574-577

Insider trading; and H. H. Asquith, 43-46; and George W. Bush,

762-765; definition, 45, 763; in Japan, 714-717; and Michael Milken, 726-729; and Martha Stewart, 1031-1034
Insull, Samuel, 154-156
Insull Utilities Trusts, 154-156
Intellectual History. *See Category Index under Cultural and intellectual history*
Internal Revenue Code, 464
Internal Revenue Service, 213, 385; and Spiro T. Agnew, 449; and churches, 481, 691; and Randall Cunningham, 1066; and Billie Sol Estes, 341-343; and Billy James Hargis, 465; and Heritage USA, 691; and Kent Hovind, 1123-1126; and Lockheed Corporation, 483; and Pete Rose, 737; and Eliot Spitzer, 1168; and Herman E. Talmadge, 553. *See also* Bureau of Internal Revenue
Internal Security Act of 1950, 267
International Association of the Congo, 31
International Christian Association, 939
International Exhibition of Modern Art, 49-52
International Labor Rights Fund, 1078-1080
International Ladies' Garment Workers' Union, 42
International relations. *See Category Index*
Interstate Commerce Act of 1887, 46
Interstate Commerce Commission, 46
Investment Company Act of 1940, 1014
Iran, 676-681; hostage crisis, 573; nuclear weapons, 1012
Iran-Contra weapons scandal, 312, 481, 676-681, 780, 820
"Irangate," 430
Iraq, 481; arms purchases, 793; Kurds, 697; war with Iran, 676

Iraq War, 340, 421, 989, 994-999, 1006, 1034-1038, 1090, 1138; and Central Intelligence Agency, 1010-1013
Ireland, 106, 779-781; orphan school fire, 217-219; weapon imports, 413-415
IRS. *See* Internal Revenue Service
Irving, Clifford, 422-425
Irving, David, 619
Irving, Edith, 422-425
Isaacs, Godfrey, 43
Isaacs, Rufus, 43
Islam, 254-256, 359-361, 1075-1077
Isorni, Jacques, 232
Israel, 21, 312, 634; and Iran-Contra, 677; secret service, 376; and Kurt Waldheim, 669
Italian Football Federation, 1092-1094
Italy. *See Geographical Index*

Jackson, Ashley, 895
Jackson, Jesse, 633-636, 640, 699, 895-897, 990
Jackson, Michael, 1025-1027
Jackson, Shoeless Joe, 66-70, 399
Jackson, Vernon L., 1148
Jameson, J. Franklin, 307
Janszen, Paul, 735
Japan. *See Geographical Index*
Japanese American internment, 205-209; Roosevelt's order, 206; U.S. government apology for, 208
Japanese Archaeology Association, 920
Japanese paleolithic hoax, 919-921
Jefferson, Thomas, 200, 936
Jefferson, William J., 1147-1150
Jenkins, Walter, 371-374
Jenks, Anton Shrewsbury, 125
Jenrette, John W., Jr., 561-562, 582-585
Jenrette, Rita, 582-585
Jesus Morning Star, 939-941
Jim Bakker Show (television), 692

JMS. *See* Jesus Morning Star
John Paul I, 606
John Paul II, 606-609, 954
John Roe I et al. v. Bridgestone (2005), 1078-1080
Johnson, Charles, 521
Johnson, Charles S., 142
Johnson, Frank, 739
Johnson, Jack, 52-55
Johnson, Judy, 624-627
Johnson, Lyndon B.; and Bobby Baker, 365-368; T. Lamar Caudle, 281, 312; and Billie Sol Estes, 341-343; and Abe Fortas, 392; and Doris Kearns Goodwin, 959; and Walter Jenkins, 371-374; and Vietnam, 364
Jokes, 500-502
Jones, Ernest, 12-15
Jones, Gareth, 167-169
Jones, Marion, 1164-1166
Jones, Michael, 1126-1129
Jones, Paula, 875
Jones, Steven E., 723
Jones v. Daly (1981), 590
Jordan, Everett, 367
Jordan, Pat, 574-577
Jorgensen, Christine, 289-291
Jubilee (Walker), 520
Jung Myung Seok, 939-941
Juventus soccer club, 1092-1094
Jyllands-Posten, 1075-1077

Kamata, Toshiaki, 919-921
Kamenev, Leo, 106
Kanaly, John J., 296
Kane and Abel (Archer), 696
Kaplan, David A., 1114
Karpinski, Janis, 1034
Kaufman, George S., 184-187
Kavanaugh, Daniel, 1153
Kawamoto, Dawn, 1116
Keally, Charles, 919-921
Kearney, Nancy, 810
Keating, Frank, 954
Keays, Sara, 631-633
Keeler, Christine, 355-358
Kefauver, Estes, 270-273

Kefauver-Harris Amendment (1962), 303
Keith, Minor C., 472
Kelley, Joe, 100-102
Kelly, James, 413
Kelly, John, 413
Kelly, R., 1170-1172
Kelly, Richard, 561-562
Kelsey, Frances Oldham, 193, 301-304
Kelso, Frank B., Jr., 784, 800
Kennan, George F., 307-310
Kennedy, Charles, 1084-1085
Kennedy, Edward M., 364, 439-440; and Chappaquiddick, 367, 394-398; and William Kennedy Smith, 759
Kennedy, John F.; assassination of, 343; and Bobby Baker, 367; and Judith Campbell, 329-332; and Matthew J. Connelly, 281, 312; extramarital affairs, 126; and J. Edgar Hoover, 329-332; and Marilyn Monroe, 344-346; and Ellen Rometsch, 367; and Vietnam, 362
Kennedy, Joseph P., 127-130
Kennedy, Mildred Pearce, 115
Kennedy, Patrick, 759
Kennedy, Robert F., 329, 700; and Dave Beck, 323-325; and Marilyn Monroe, 344
Kennedy, Rose Fitzgerald, 127
Kent, Samuel Neal, 70-72
Kent State massacre, 410-413, 491
Kenya, 298-301
Kenyatta, Jomo, 298
Kerr, James, 12
Kerr, Robert S., 365-368
Kerrigan, Nancy, 812-815
Kershaw, Elinor, 108-111
Keyworth, George A., II, 1114-1118
KGB, 347-349, 353-354, 931, 1133
Khan, Prince Aly, 254-256
Khrushchev, Nikita S., 330, 373
Kidnapping; of Mehdi Ben Barka,

374-376; and Duke lacrosse team, 1088; by Marc Dutroux, 840-842; of Elinor Glyn, 27; of Patricia Hearst, 450-453; by Jack Jackson, 54; of Aimee Semple McPherson, 115-118
Kiley, Kevin C., 1138
Killian documents scandal, 1044-1046
Kim Sun-jong, 1094
Kimball Sanitarium, 215
King, Billie Jean, 588-591
King, Cecil R., 279-282
King, Charles D. B., 142-144
King, Coretta Scott, 739
King, Don, 703
King, John, 93
King, Larry (lawyer), 588
King, Larry (talk show host), 390, 711, 828, 1130
King, Martin Luther, Jr., 381, 739-741, 822, 896
King, Wanda, 748
King in New York, A (film), 285
King Leopold's Soliloquy (Twain), 33
King v. Mister Maestro, Inc. (1963), 740
Kinnock, Neil, 698-701
Kinte, Kunta, 520
Kirstein, Lincoln, 528
Kissinger, Henry, 416, 538, 551
Kitchener, Lord, 58-60
Klein, Allen, 494-497
Knebel, Fletcher, 175
Knight, Bobby, 950
Knight, Suge, 884
Knox, Howard J., 290
Kocadağ, Hüseyin, 843-845
Koch, Edward I., 642, 693-695, 778
Koch, Kevin, 666
Kohl, Helmut, 1110
Koller, Arnold, 858, 860
Kontogiannis, Thomas, 1064
Koolmatrie, Wanda (Leon Carmen), 852-854
Kopechne, Mary Jo, 367, 394-398

"Koreagate," 430, 479-482
Korean War, 175, 289
Korematsu, Fred, 205
Korematsu v. United States (1944), 207
Kotchian, Carl, 482-485
Kovtun, Dimitri, 1133
Koza, Frank, 995-998
Krause, Allison, 410-413
Krever, Horace, 868-871
Krever Commission, 868-871
Krupinski, Walter, 503-505
Kuhlmeyer, Harry L., Jr., 626
Kuhn, Bowie, 556-558
Kuhn, Rick, 568-570
Kuhn, Walt, 49-52
Kujau, Konrad, 618-621

Labor. *See Category Index*
LaCroix, Larry, 401
Lacy, Lee, 667
La Falaise, Henri de, 127
L'Âge d'or (film), 138, 147-150
Lagos, Ricardo, 1121-1123
Lake, Douglas, 1072-1074
Lamarr, Hedy, 163-166
Lambert, William G., 391
Lamont, Daniel, 1
Lance, Bert, 511-514, 571
Landis, Carole, 245-247
Landis, Floyd, 1103-1106
Landis, Kenesaw Mountain, 66-70, 118-121, 242, 399, 556, 737
Landrum-Griffin Act of 1959, 405
Lane, Charles, 887
Lang, Robert Todd, 509
Lange, Robert Brookings, Sr., 444-446
Langevin, Jeanne, 37
Langevin, Paul, 37-39
Langfeldt, Gabriel, 229
Langley, John W., 103-105
Larson, Charles R., 800
Lasky, Jesse L., 86-89
Lategano, Cristyne, 904
Laval, Pierre, 209-211
Lavelle, Rita, 615-617
Law, Bernard, 954-958

Law and the courts. *See Category Index*
Lawford, Peter, 344
Lawrence v. Texas (2003), 508
Laws, Bolitha J., 236
Lay, Kenneth, 945-948, 1074
League of Nations, 142-144, 1080
Leber, Georg, 503-505
Lederer, Raymond, 561-562
Leeds, Lila, 251-253
Le Gougne, Marie Reine, 962-964
Le Gros Clark, Wilfrid, 292
Lehman Brothers, 1176
Leibowitz, Samuel, 150-153
Leisure, Peter K., 262
Le Mesurier, John, 531
Lend-Lease Act of 1941, 248
Lenin, Vladimir Ilich, 106, 168, 307
Lennix, Harry, 382
Lenz, Widukind, 301
Leonard, Dutch, 118-121
Leopold II, 31-33
Leopold III, 276-279
LeRoy, J. T., 424
Leslie, Kristen, 1062
Le Thuy, Ngo Dinh, 362
Letourneau, Mary Kay, 605, 849-852
Levy, Chandra, 933-936
Levy, Susan, 933-936
Lewinsky, Monica, 818-821, 888; and Bill Clinton, 874-878, 896, 1168
Lewis, Jane Mitcham, 313
Lewis, Jerry Lee, 313-316
Lewis, John, 191
Lewis, Myra Brown, 313-316
Lewis, Terence, 682
Ley, Robert, 196
Libby, Lewis "Scooter," 1010-1013
Libel cases, 10, 32, 793; and Jeffrey Archer, 696-698; and Cecil Chesterton, 44; and Clearstream, 926; and Steve Garvey, 574-577; and Stephen Glass, 888; and Sara Keays, 632; and Douglas MacArthur,

173-175; and Brian Mulroney, 831; and Mabel Normand, 101; and Drew Pearson, 173-175; and Roman Polanski, 524; and John L. Poulson, 432; and Mike Price, 1003; and John G. Schmitz, 604; and Arnold Schwarzenegger, 1018; and Émile Zola, 21
Liberia, 142-144, 1078-1080
Libya, 571-574
Lichtenstein, 606
Liddy, G. Gordon, 425-431
Liebenberg circle, 9-12
Lieber, Charles M., 980
Limelight (film), 284
Lincoln, Abraham, 443
Linderman, Lawrence, 612
Lindgren, James, 985
Lindstrom, Petter, 263
Lindstrom, Pia, 263
"Lingerie Bowl," 783
Lipschutz, Milton, 104
Literature. *See Category Index*
Little League Baseball, 942-944
Litvinenko, Alexander, 1132-1134
Liverpool; children's hospital, 927-930; soccer team, 55-58
Llosa, Luis Fernando, 942
Lloyd George, David, 43, 59, 83-86
Lockheed Corporation, 482-485
Lodge, Henry Cabot, Jr., 362
Lombard, Fern, 212
Long, Russell, 384
"Long Island Lolita," 781-784
Longet, Claudine, 485-487
López Arellano, Oswaldo, 471
Los Angeles; Hugh Grant arrest, 827-829; police corruption, 884-886; Simpson/Goldman murders, 806-809
Los Angeles Lakers, 1008
Los Angeles Times, 109, 498, 576, 604, 709, 876; and Arnold Schwarzenegger, 1016-1019
Lott, Trent, 988-991
Louisiana, 1150-1153; Edwin

Edwards, 907-909; Hurricane Katrina, 1068-1072; William J. Jefferson, 1147-1150
Love Canal, 546-550
Lowe, Rob, 717-720
Lowell, Francis Cabot, 6
Lubbers, Ruud, 1039-1041
Lubonja, Fatos, 846-849
Ludwig, F. G., Jr., 786
Lugovoi, Andrei, 1132-1134
Luxembourg; banks, 606; financial scandal, 925-927
Luykx, Albert, 414
Lyga, Frank, 884-886
Lynch, Jack, 413-415
Lynch, Thomas C., 800-803
Lyons, Eugene, 167
Lyons, Jack, 753-756
Lyttleton, Oliver, 298

McAdoo, William G., 97
MacArthur, Douglas, 173-175; and Bonus Army, 156-160
McAuley, James, 223-225
McCain, John, 54, 906, 1153-1154
McCarthy, Joseph, 266-270; and Alger Hiss, 261
McClellan, John, 323
McCord, James W., Jr., 425-431
McCormack, John W., 380
MacDonald, Ramsay, 105-108
McDonough, Peter, 191
McDonough, Tom, 191
McDougal, Jim, 818
McDougal, Susan, 818
MacEachran, John W., 133
McEntee, Sean, 217
McEuen, Paul L., 980
McFarlane, Bud, 676
MacFarlane, Kee, 624
McGovern, George, 440-443, 463
McGrath, J. Howard, 279-282
McGuirk, Bernard, 1142-1144
McGwire, Mark, 1058-1061
Machatý, Gustav, 163
Mack, David Anthony, 884-886
Mackay, James A., 879-881

Mackey, Randy, 1154
Mackris, Andrea, 1047-1049
MacLeish, Archibald, 236
Macleod, Iain, 298
McMartin, Virginia, 624-627
McMartin Preschool, 624-627
Macmillan, Allan D., 176
Macmillan, Harold, 355
MacMillan, Vivian, 176-178
MacMillan v. Brownlee (1934), 176-178
McNab, Gavin, 79
McNamara, Robert, 416
McNary-Watres Act. *See* Air Mail Act of 1930
MacPhail, Larry, 242-244
McPherson, Aimee Semple, 115-118
McPherson, Rolf, 115
McTaggart, David, 651
McTaggart, Lynne, 959-961
Maddox, Alton H., Jr., 702
Mafart, Alain, 651
Mafia, 607; and Banco Ambrosiano, 606-609; Gambino family, 1174; and Jimmy Hoffa, 325; and Diego Maradona, 816; and Adolfo Sarti, 591-593; and John Stonehouse, 469
Mahaney, W. B., 5
Mahurin, Matt, 810
Mail fraud, 1149; A. Gordon Boone, 447; James Michael Curley, 8; Budd Dwyer, 684; E. F. Hutton Company, 636; Edwin Edwards, 907; Leona Helmsley, 776-777; Webster Hubbell, 819; Michael Milken, 728; Tongsun Park, 481; Dan Rostenkowski, 803-806; Karl A. Schledwitz, 649
Main, Pamela, 304-306
Mainichi Shimbum (newspaper), 733-735, 920
Major, John, 647, 697, 983-985; and David Mellor, 792-794; and Tim Yeo, 798-800
Makalintol, Querube, 601
Malcolm X, 359

Mallick, Bill, 730-732
Malloy, Edward A., 948
Mammoth Oil Company, 96
Man, Paul de, 705-708
Man/Boy Love Association, 955
Manchester United, 55-58, 1093
Mandel, Marvin, 447
Mandl, Fritz, 163
Mangini, Eric, 1161-1163
Mangum, Crystal Gail, 1086-1089
Manhattan Beach Police Department, 626
Manhattan College, 274-276
Manifesto of Surrealism (Breton), 148
Mann Act of 1910, 52-55, 221, 1167; excerpt, 53
Manson, Charles, 523
Mantle, Mickey, 556-558
Mapes, Mary, 1044-1046
Maradona, Diego, 815-818
Marcinkus, Paul, 592, 606-609
Marconi, Guglielmo, 43-46
Marcos, Ferdinand, 600-602, 628-630
Marcos, Imelda, 628
Markham, Paul F., 395
Marks, Albert A., 638
Marriage; Blake Andrews, 612-614; Ingrid Bergman, 263-265; Lorena Bobbitt, 795-797; Jimmy Carter, 497; Charles Chaplin, 283; Charles, Prince of Wales, 745; Helen Clark, 1112-1114; and community property, 540; Leo Durocher, 242-243; Edward VIII, 187-190, 213; Mia Farrow, 773; Steve Garvey, 574-577; Rudy Giuliani, 904-906; Jean Harlow, 160-163; Rita Hayworth, 254-256; and homosexuality, 122, 296, 508, 713, 913, 1042, 1127; Rock Hudson, 296; Jack Johnson, 54; Christine Jorgensen, 290; Jung Myung Seok, 940; R. Kelly, 1170; John F. Kennedy, 346; and Kennedy family, 129; Aly

Khan, 254-256; Hedy Lamarr, 165; Carole Landis, 245-247; Leopold III, 278; Mary Kay Letourneau, 850; Jerry Lee Lewis, 313-316; Amy Semple McPherson, 116; and palimony, 540-542; Cecil Parkinson, 631; Roberto Rossellini, 263-265; sham, 664; Lana Turner, 317; underage, 313-316; Nancy Wakeman, 386-388; Stanford White, 16-19
Marriott, Reginald, 181
Marsh, Clara, 964-967
Marsh, Ray, 964-967
Marsh, Tommy Ray-Brent, 964-967
Marsh & McLennan, 1050-1052
Marshak, Megan, 537-539
Martha Stewart Living (television), 1032
Martino, Thomas, 1173
Marvin, Lee, 540-542, 589
Marvin v. Marvin (1979), 540-542, 589
Mason, C. Vernon, 702
Masor, Mark, 977
Massengill, Samuel Evans, 193-195
Mast, Charles Emmanuel, 257-259
Masters, Christopher, 681
Mathias, Philip, 830-833
Matsuoka, Toshikatsu, 1145-1147
Mau Mau rebellion, 298-301
Maudling, Reginald, 431
Mauresmo, Amélie, 590
Maurice (film), 827
Mauroy, Pierre, 375
Mayer, Louis B., 163
"Mayflower Madam," 654-657
Mays, Willie, 556-558
Mazzei, Paul, 568
Measles epidemic, Amazonian, 910-912
Medicine and health care. *See Category Index*
Medina, Ernest, 401
Medlar, Linda Jones, 872-874

Mee, James, 1106-1109

Meese, Edwin, III, 669, 678

Meili, Christophe, 858-861

Meksi, Aleksander, 846-849

Mellor, David, 792-794

"Memogate," 1044-1046

Memoirs of Chief Red Fox, The (Red Fox), 424

Memorandum from Commissioner Peter V. Ueberroth to All Clubs Re: Baseball's Drug Education & Prevention Program (May 14, 1986), 668

Menem, Carlos, 815

Menendez, Erik, 750-753

Menendez, Jose, 750-753

Menendez, Kitty, 750-753

Menendez, Lyle, 750-753

Menu Foods scandal, 1097-1100

Merhige, Robert, Jr., 459-462

Merrill Lynch, 1176

Merwin, W. S., 474

Mexico, 824-826

Meyer, Ron, 687-689

Mfume, Kweisi, 823

Michael, George, 881-883

Middle East. *See Geographical Index*

Middle Passage (Johnson), 521

MI5, 348, 533, 791

Mikhailsky, Sigmund, 347-349

Milan soccer club, 1092-1094

Milburn, Alan, 927-930

Milea, Vasile, 742

Milgram, Stanley, 338-340

Milgram experiments, 338-340

Military. *See Category Index*

Military Academy, U.S. *See West Point*

Military police, U.S. Army, 1036

Milk, Harvey, 507

Milken, Michael, 726-729

Miller, Jeffrey, 410-413

Miller, Thomas W., 92

Miller, Tom, 55-58

Millette, Dorothy, 160

Milli Vanilli, 756-758

Milligan, Maurice M., 200

Mills, Elizabeth Shown, 520

Mills, Gary, 520

Mills, Wilbur D., 462-465

Milner, Alfred, 25

Minchew, Daniel, 553

Minkow, Barry, 708-710

Minow, Newton, 335-337

Minter, Mabel Miles, 73-76

Miss America; Anita Bryant, 506; Bess Myerson, 693; Vanessa Williams, 638-641

Mitchell, George J., 1058, 1162

Mitchell, John, 390-391, 425-431

Mitchell, Margaret, 521

Mitchell Report, 1060

Mitchelson, Marvin, 540-542

Mitchum, Robert, 251-253

Miyazawa, Kiichi, 714-717

Modern Times (film), 284

Mody, Lori, 1147-1150

Mog, Aribert, 163

Moggi, Luciano, 1092-1094

Moltke, Kuno von, 9

Mommie Dearest (Crawford), 517-519

Monarchy. *See Category Index under Royalty*

Monckeberg, Nicolás, 1122

Monckton, Walter, 187

Money laundering, 271, 1132, 1149, 1152, 1168; and Abscam, 562, 583; and Clearstream International, 925-927; and Randall Cunningham, 1067; and John De Lorean, 610; Edwin Edwards, 907-909; and Italian criminals, 593; and Mafia, 606; and Raúl Salinas, 825-826; and Herman E. Talmadge, 553-555; and Watergate, 427; and Westar Energy, 1073

"Monicagate," 874-878

Monroe, Marilyn, 246, 344-346

Monseigneur affair, 377-379

Monsieur Verdoux (film), 284

Montgomery, Tim, 1164-1166

Moody's, 1176

Moon, Sun Myung, 479

Moore, Carlos, 731

Moore, Demi, 718

Moore, Rasheeda, 748

Moores, Frank, 830-833

Morel, Edmund Dene, 31-33

Morelli, Benedict, 1047-1049

Morgan, Jack, 514

Morgan Stanley, 1176

Morgenthau, Robert M., 641

Morissette, Pierre, 892

Morley, John J., 389

Morley, Thomas, 636-638

Morocco, 374-376; Sand Wars, 374

Morris, Joe, 304-306

Morrison, Toni, 521

Mortgage Guaranty Insurance Company, 367

Mortgage industry, 367, 973, 1134-1138, 1175-1179

Mortimer, Elias, 89, 104

Morton, Desmond, 105-108

Morton, Melinda, 1062

Morvan, Fab, 756-758

Morze, Mark, 708

Moseley, Winston, 369

Motion Picture Association of America, 88

Motion Picture Producers and Distributors of America, 88

Motion Picture Production Code (1930), 165

MPAA. *See Motion Picture Association of America*

MTV, 756, 767, 882

Muggeridge, Malcolm, 167

Muhammad, Elijah, 359-361

Muhammad, Prophet, 1075-1077

Muir, Leilani, 133-136

Muir v. Alberta (1996), 135

Mulcahey, Michael, 971

Mulder, Connie, 543-545

"Muldergate," 543-545

Mulroney, Brian, 830-833; and "Tunagate," 660-662

Munsinger, Gerda, 377-379

Murder and suicide. *See Category Index*

Murnau, F. W., 111

Murphree, Debra, 711

Murphy, Annie, 779-781

Murphy, Frank, 281
Murphy, Peter, 779
Murray, Alexander, 43
Murtha, John, 563
Music and performing arts. *See Category Index*
Music Television. *See* MTV
Muslims. *See* Islam; Nation of Islam
Mussolini, Benito, 117, 164, 213, 231, 592, 706; and Ezra Pound, 237
My Lai massacre, 401-404, 937
My Own Sweet Time (novel), 852-854
My Wicked, Wicked Ways (Flynn), 560
Myers, Michael, 561-562
Myerson, Bess, 693-695

NAACP. *See* National Association for the Advancement of Colored People
Nagayasu, Masayuki, 398-400
Nagin, Ray, 1068-1072
Nanni, Louis M., 948
Naone, Dana, 474
Naropa Institute, 474-476
Nasjonal Samling, 226, 230
Nathan, Judith, 904-906
Nation of Islam, 635, 822-823; and Elijah Muhammad, 359-361
National Association for the Advancement of Colored People, 152, 642, 768, 821-823
National Association of Black Journalists, 810
National Association of Evangelicals, 527, 1127
National Association of Securities Dealers, 1014
National Bank of Georgia, 511-514, 571
National Basketball Association, 275, 867, 901; Kobe Bryant, 1008-1010; Tim Donaghy, 1172-1175
National Basketball Referees Association, 1175

National Broadcasting Company, 326
National Collegiate Athletic Association; academic standards, 1101; basketball, 274, 569, 968; "death penalty," 687-689; football, 687-689, 949; and gambling, 1003
National Enquirer, 895-897, 1017, 1130
National Football League, 949, 1003; New England Patriots, 1161-1163; Michael Vick, 1158-1161
National Guard; and Hurricane Katrina, 1069-1070; Kent State shootings, 410-413, 491; and "Scottsboro Boys," 151
National Hockey League, 901-903
National Labor Relations Act of 1935, 42
National Press Photographers Association, 811
National Research Act of 1974, 439
National Security Agency, 932, 995-998
Native Americans, 130-133, 434, 1155-1158
NATO. *See* North Atlantic Treaty Organization
Naval Academy, U.S., 1102; cheating scandal, 800-803; honor code, 801; sexual harassment at, 788
Navratilova, Martina, 590
Navy, U.S.; homosexuality investigation, 70-72; Tailhook scandal, 784-788; and Teapot Dome scandal, 96
Nazi collaborators and sympathizers; Charles Bedaux, 212-214; Errol Flynn, 559-561; Günter Grass, 1109-1112; Knut Hamsun, 229-232; Pierre Laval, 209-211; Philippe Pétain, 232-236; Vidkun Quisling, 226-229; Kurt Waldheim, 669-672
NBA. *See* National Basketball Association

NCAA. *See* National Collegiate Athletic Association
Neel, James V., 910-912
Nelson, Judd, 718
Nesbit, Evelyn, 16-19
New England Patriots, 1161-1163
New Life Church, 1126-1129
New Orleans, Louisiana, 1068-1072
New Republic, The, 887-889
New South Wales Fraud Enforcement Agency, 853
New York City; Armory Modern Art Show, 49-52; Broadway theater, 122-124; called "Hymietown," 633-636; Genovese murder, 369-371; Rudy Giuliani, 904-906; Goetz shootings, 641-644; "Mayflower Madam," 654-657; Myerson scandal, 693-695; Stonewall Rebellion, 506; "Subway Vigilante," 641-644; Triangle Shirtwaist factory fire, 40-43
New York Daily News, 289
New York Islanders, 901-903
New York Racing Association, 514-515
New York Times, 8, 24, 50, 167-169, 218, 362, 488; and Abscam, 562; and Fatty Arbuckle, 81; and Auburn University, 1101-1103; and Joe Biden, 700; and Jayson Blair, 888, 998-1001; and cold fusion, 724; and Duke lacrosse team, 1088; and Doris Kearns Goodwin, 959-960; and Jesse Jackson, 896; and "Koreagate," 480; and James Mackey, 879; and Paul de Man, 705-708; and Madame Nhu, 363; and Pentagon Papers, 416-419; and Eliot Spitzer, 1167; and U.S. Air Force Academy, 1063; and U.S. Naval Academy, 801; and Kurt Waldheim, 669
New York Times Co. v. United States (1971), 417

New Zealand. *See Geographical Index*

Newport sex scandal, 70-72

News Corp, 1129-1131

News of the World, The, 696-697, 828, 1084-1086

Newsweek magazine, 576, 1114-1118; and O. J. Simpson, 810-812

Newton, Andrew, 531

NFL. *See* National Football League

Ngo Dinh Diem, 362

Ngo Dinh Nhu, 362

Ngo Dinh Nhu, Madame, 362-365

Nguyen Duy Trinh, 434

NHL. *See* National Hockey League

Nicaragua, 676-681

Nicholson, Jack, 523

Nifong, Mike, 1086-1089

Night of the Long Knives, 11

Nihoul, Michel, 840

9/11. *See* September 11, 2001, terrorist attacks

Nixon, Pat, 453-456

Nixon, Richard, 286-288; and Spiro T. Agnew, 447-450; gifts received, 453-456; and Alger Hiss, 261; Nixon tapes, 428; and Pentagon Papers, 416-419; and Watergate, 312, 418, 425-431, 448-449, 455, 493, 497

Nixon tapes, 428

Noailles, Charles de, 148

Noailles, Marie-Laure de, 148

Nobile, Philip, 520

Noebel, David A., 465

Norgrove, Jane, 789

Normand, Mabel, 73-76, 100-102

Norris, Clarence, 150-153

Norris v. Alabama (1935), 152

North, Oliver, 676-681

North Atlantic Treaty Organization, 350, 357, 490-491, 658, 744, 890

Northern Ireland, 413-415, 609

Norton, Rosaleen, 304-306

Norway, 226-232

Nosenko, Yuri, 347

Nosferatu (film), 111-114

Notre Dame University, 598; football, 948-950

Novak, Robert, 1010-1013

Nuclear weapons, 442; China, 373; Iraq, 995; testing, 651-654

Nude Descending a Staircase (Duchamp), 50

Nudity, 17, 584, 767, 774, 1027; in art, 50; Hedy Lamarr, 163-166; Vanessa Williams, 638-641

Oakley, Kenneth, 292-295

Oană, Ioachim, 916-918

Oaten, Belinda, 1084-1086

Oaten, Mark, 1084-1086

Obama, Barack, 701

Obedience to Authority (Milgram), 339

Occupational Health and Safety Administration, and 1911 Triangle fire, 42

O'Connell, William Henry, 128

Oelrich, Ryan, 1081

Office of Management and Budget, U.S., 511-514

Office of Thrift Supervision, U.S., 1177

OFFP. *See* Oil-for-Food Programme

Ogawa, Kentaro, 398-400

Oil-for-Food Programme, 481, 1053-1055

Oil reserves scandal, 95-99

O'Leary, George, 948-950

Oliphant, Charles, 310

Olympics; 1994, 812-815; 2000, 916-918, 1164-1166; 2002, 962-964; doping, 916-918, 1164-1166; figure skating, 812-815, 962-964; gymnastics, 916-918; track and field, 1164-1166

O'Morain, Michael, 413

Onassis, Jacqueline Kennedy, 694

1 Night in Paris (video), 1020

O'Neill, Tip, 621-624, 730

Opera, 76-79

Operation PUSH, 896

Operation White Snow, 479-482, 534-536

Order of internment (Roosevelt), 206

O'Reilly, Bill, 1047-1049

O'Reilly, Bridget, 217-219

O'Reilly Factor, The (television), 1047-1049

Organization of Afro-American Unity, 360

Organization of American Historians, 986

Organized crime and racketeering. *See Category Index*

Ormiston, Kenneth G., 115

Orphans; Duplessis, 892-895; Irish school fire, 217-219

Ossendowski, Anton Martynovich, 307

Oufkir, Mohammad, 374

Oustric, Albert, 139-141

Outreau affair, 922-924

Overholser, Winfred, 236

Owen, Richard, 494-497

Pacepa, Ion Mihai, 353

Pach, Walter, 49-52

Padgett, Tom, 708

Page sex scandal, 621-624

Pagnam, Fred, 55

Pagones, Steven, 702

Pakistan, 254-256, 1053-1055

Paleontology, 292-295

Palestine Liberation Organization, 634, 793

Palfrey, Deborah Jeane, 1150-1153

Palimony, 540-542, 588-591

Palmer, Lilli, 245

Panama, 473, 606

Pan-American Oil and Transport Company, 96

Panny, William, 580

Panov, V. A., 309

Paparazzi, 81, 254, 746, 861, 882, 1019; and Princess Diana, 861-865

Papon, Maurice, 375

Park, Tongsun, 479-482

Park Chung Hee, 479
Parker, Alton B., 1
Parker, Dave, 666-669
Parkinson, Cecil, 631-633
Parks, Bernard, 884
Parnes, Anthony, 753-756
Parsons, Jan, 717-720
Partnership for a Drug-Free America, 767
Pass, Albert, 404
Passion of the Christ, The (film), 1107
Paternity suits; Charles Chaplin, 220-222, 283; Steve Garvey, 574-577; Elijah Muhammad, 359-361; John G. Schmitz, 603-605
Patterson, Haywood, 150-153
Patton, George S., 156
Paul, Henri, 861
Paul VI, 606
Paulino, Rolando, 942-944
Paulk, Anne, 913
Paulk, John, 913-915
Paulson, Henry, 1134-1138, 1175-1179
Payola scandal, 332-335
Peace, Purnell A., 1158
Peace Corps, 476-478
Pearson, Drew, 173-175, 248-250, 384
Pearson, Lester B., 377-379
Pedophilia, 315, 842; and Michael Jackson, 1025-1027; and Ernest Jones, 15; and Outreau affair, 922-924; and Roman Catholic priests, 954-958
Peeling the Onion (Grass), 1111
Pee-wee's Playhouse, 765
Peking man, 292
Pelletier, David, 962-964
Pelosi, Nancy, 623, 1148
Pelossi, Giorgio, 830
Pendergast, James, 199
Pendergast, Thomas Joseph, 199-201
Penenberg, Adam, 887
Penis severing, 795-797
Pensacola Christian College, 1124

Pentagon Papers, 416-419
Penthouse magazine, 638-641, 828
People, The (newspaper), 793
People v. Goetz (1984), 641-644
Peppiatt, Angela, 696
Pereira, Fernando, 651-654
Péret, Raoul Adolphe, 139-141
Perez, Rafael Antonio, 884
Perhach, Vanessa, 865
Perjury, 885; Jeffrey Archer, 697; Hillary Clinton, 820, 876; Alger Hiss, 259-262; Lewis "Scooter" Libby, 1012; Charles Van Doren, 328; Caspar Weinberger, 679
Perkins, Tom, 1114-1118
Perla, Anthony, 568
Perla, Rocco, 568
Perrault, Roger, 868
Perry, Nancy Ling, 450
Pesticides, 547
Pet food, 661; China, 1097-1100; Chinese, 1097
Pétain, Philippe, 209-211, 232-236
Petee, Thomas A., 1101-1103
Petrovich Semenov, Evgeni, 307
Peyton Place (television), 773
Pharmaceuticals, 193
Phil Donahue Show, The (television), 583
Philbin, Regis, 574, 828
Philippines, 1, 173, 175, 600-602, 628-630
Phillips, Carrie, 124
Phillips, Jud, 313
Phillips, Quanis, 1159
Phipps, Ogden Mills, 514
Photography, Abu Ghraib prison, 1036
Pianist, The (film), 524
Pickett, John O., 901-903
Picquart, Georges, 19
Pierce, Ponchitta, 537
Pierlot, Hubert, 277
Pilatus, Rob, 756-758
Piltdown man, 292-295
Pinto, Ford, 594-596
Pius XII, 164, 353-355

Plagiarism. *See Category Index*
Plame, Valerie, 1010-1013
"Plamegate," 1010-1013
Playboy magazine, 497-500, 584, 612, 614, 639
Poetry, 474-476; Koolmatrie hoax, 223-225; Ezra Pound, 236-239
Poindexter, John M., 676
Point shaving in basketball, 274-276, 568-570, 1172
Poisoning, diethylene glycol, 194
Polanski, Roman, 522-524
Police corruption, 656, 702-705; Australia, 681-683; Belgium, 840-842; Los Angeles, 884-886; San Francisco, 191-193; Turkey, 843-845
Political contributions. *See* Campaign contributions
Politics. *See Category Index*
Polozola, Frank, 907
Pons, Stanley, 723-726
Ponzi, Charles, 63-66
Ponzi schemes, 63-66, 708-710. *See also* Pyramid schemes
Pope, Barbara S., 785
Popoff, Elizabeth, 673
Popoff, Peter, 673-675
Poppe, Henry, 274-276
Popular culture. *See Category Index*
Pornography, 640; and Adelphia Communications, 971; and Mary Astor, 184; and John Wayne Bobbitt, 796; and Divine Brown, 828; child, 625, 922, 1170-1172; films, 1004-1007; and Eugène Goosens, 304-306; and Paris Hilton, 1019-1021; and Michael Jackson, 1027; and Paul Reubens, 765-768; and Clarence Thomas, 770
Post Office scandal, 803-806
Pottinger, George, 431
Poulson, John, 431-433
Pound, Dorothy Shakespear, 236
Pound, Ezra, 236-239
Powell, Adam Clayton, Jr., 380-383

Powell v. Alabama (1932), 152

Powell v. McCormack (1969), 381-382

Prescott, John, 1089-1091

Presidential campaigns, U.S.; 1904, 1-3; 1920, 90, 93; 1924, 98; 1932, 159; 1948, 988-991; 1952, 271, 281, 286-288; 1956, 312, 320; 1960, 331, 344; 1964, 371-374, 386; 1968, 454; 1972, 425-431; 1976, 480, 497-501; 1980, 571-574; 1984, 633-636, 680; 1988, 680, 698-701, 713, 718; 1992, 874; 1996, 875; 2000, 764, 877; Joe Biden, 698-701; George H. W. Bush, 680; George W. Bush, 764; Jimmy Carter, 480, 497-500, 571-574; Bill Clinton, 874; Hillary Clinton, 1169; Michael Dukakis, 718; Thomas F. Eagleton, 440-443; Dwight D. Eisenhower, 312, 320; Gerald R. Ford, 501; Barry Goldwater, 371-374, 386; Warren G. Harding, 90; Herbert Hoover, 159; Jesse Jackson, 633-636; Lyndon B. Johnson, 371-374; Richard Nixon, 286-288, 425-431, 454; Ronald Reagan, 680; Pat Robertson, 713; Theodore Roosevelt, 1-3; Al Smith, 93; Strom Thurmond, 988-991. *See also* Campaign contributions

President's Commission on Campus Unrest, 412

President's Daughter, The (Britton), 124-127

Pressler, Larry, 563

Pressler, Mike, 1003, 1086

Preston, Billy, 494-497

Prevention of Abuses Act of 1925, 85

Prevert, Jacques, 148

Previn, Soon-Yi, 773-775

Price, Mike, 1002-1004

Price, Victoria, 150

Priest, Dana, 1138-1142

Prieur, Dominique, 651

Prime Time Live (television), 761

Prince, Jonas, 898

Privacy Act of 1974, 429

Privat, Maurice, 140

Priven, Dennis, 476-478

Profumo, John, 348, 355-358, 378

Prohibition, 75, 90, 93, 100, 102-105, 110

Propaganda Due, 591-593

Prostitution, 53. *See Category Index*

Psalm 51, 713

Psychology and psychiatry. *See Category Index*

PTL Television Network, 690-693

Public morals. *See Category Index*

Public Utility Holding Company Act of 1935, 155

Publishing and journalism. *See Category Index*

Purcell, Bob, 55-58

Purviance, Edna, 100

Putin, Vladimir, 1132-1134

Pyramid schemes, 846-849, 1132. *See also* Ponzi schemes

Qaddafi, Muammar al-, 679

Qaeda, al-. *See* al-Qaeda

Quebec, 898; Duplessis orphans, 892-895

Quisling, Vidkun, 226-229

Racism. *See Category Index under Social issues and reform*

Racketeer Influenced and Corrupt Organizations Act of 1970, 728

Radcliffe, Cyril, 347

Rader, Stanley, 525

Radio and television. *See Category Index*

Răducan, Andreea, 916-918

Ragtime (Doctorow), 18

Rahman, Kambir Abdul, 562

Rainbow Warrior (ship), 651-654

Raines, Howell, 998-1001

Rajneesh, Bhagwan Shree, 662-665

Ralph, Tim, 1126-1129

Ramos, Fidel V., 629

Rampart scandal, 884-886

RAND, 416

Randi, James, 673-675

Rape; and Fatty Arbuckle, 74, 79-82, 88; and Jimmy Bakker, 690; of Lorena Bobbitt, 795-797; of Tawana Brawley, 702-705; and Kobe Bryant, 1008-1010; and Joey Buttafuoco, 781-784; of children, 922-924; and Duke lacrosse team, 1086-1089; and Marc Dutroux, 840-842; of Francis Farmer, 216; of Amy Fisher, 781; and Errol Flynn, 202-205; of Kitty Genovese, 369-371; and Jung Myung Seok, 939-941; and Mary Kay Letourneau, 849-852; of Menendez brothers, 752; at My Lai massacre, 401; in opera, 77; and Roman Polanski, 522-524; and "Scottsboro Boys," 150-153; and William Kennedy Smith, 759-762; spousal, 795-797; and Stanford White, 17

Raphael, Adam, 696

Rappe, Virginia, 79-82

Rasmussen, Anders Fogh, 1075

Rather, Dan, 1022-1024, 1044-1046

Rathom, John R., 70

Rauh, Carl, 803

Rauh, Joseph L., Jr., 404-406

Ray, Elizabeth, 491-493

Reagan, Marilyn Bradshaw, 529

Reagan, Ronald; Abscam, 563; and deregulation, 945; and Environmental Protection Agency, 615-616; Iran-Contra, 312, 676-681, 780; and Ku Klux Klan, 635; at Nazi cemetery, 1110; and Religious Right, 577

Reardon, David C., 795

Recession, U.S., 1175-1179

Recruit scandal, 714-717

Red Cross, American, 778

Red Cross, Canadian, 869

Red Cross, International, 1035

Red Fox, 424

Red Rubber (Morel), 32

Red Scare, 71, 81, 285
Redfern, Michael, 927-930
Redfern Report, 927-930
Reed, John, 223
Reenan, Cyril, 789
Rees-Jones, Trevor, 861
Reflections of a Public Man
    (Wright), 731
Regan, Judith, 1129-1131
Reguly, Robert, 377
Reid, Wallace, 86-89
Reilly, Sidney, 105-108
Religion. *See Category Index*
Replogle, Hartley L., 68
Résumé falsification, 587, 948-950
Reubens, Paul, 765-768, 829
Révélation$ (Robert and Backes),
    925-927
Revers, Georges, 257-259
Revers Report, 257-259
Reynaud, Paul, 233
Reynolds, Don, 365-368
Rhodes, James A., 410
Rhoodie, Eschel, 543
"Rhoodiegate," 543-545
Rialto Grain and Securities
    Company, 4-6
Ribbentrop, Joachim von, 197
Ribicoff, Abraham A., 384, 511
Rice-Davies, Mandy, 356
Richardson, Elliot, 447-450
Richardson-Merrell, 302
Richie, Nicole, 1020
RICO Act. *See* Racketeer
    Influenced and Corrupt
    Organizations Act of 1970
Ridenhour, Ronald, 401
Rigas, James, 971-973
Rigas, John, 971-973
Rigas, Michael, 971-973
Rigas, Timothy, 971-973
Riggs, Bobby, 589
"Rinkagate," 531-534
Rise of Mr. Ponzi, The (Ponzi),
    64
Rivers, Eunice, 437
Riza, Iqbal, 1053-1055
Roach, Hal, 178-181
Robbins, Bruce, 837

Robert, Denis, 925-927
Roberts, Jim, 1000
Roberts, Seth, 978
Robertson, Cliff, 509-511
Robertson, Pat, 713
Robertson, Thomas A., 534
Robertson affair, 509-511
Robins, E. Claiborne, Sr., 459
Robinson, Jackie, 639
Robinson, Sir Joseph, 83
Robinson, Walter V., 936-938
Roche, James G., 991
Rockefeller, Nelson A., 537-539
Rodriguez, Marcelo, 881
Roe Jung-hye, 1094
Roe v. Wade (1973), 604, 769
Rogers, Michael, 1041-1044
Rogers, William D., 473
Rogge, Jacques, 962
Roh Sung-il, 1094
Röhm, Ernst, 11
Roman, Ed, 274
Roman Catholic Church, 456-459;
    and Banco Ambrosiano, 606-
    609; and Belgian Congo, 33;
    and Eamonn Casey, 779-781;
    and John Patrick Cody, 597-599;
    and film censorship, 164; and
    Rita Hayworth, 254-255; and
    Holocaust, 353-355; and
    homosexuality, 577-579; and
    Ireland, 413-415; and orphans,
    892-895; priests scandal, 954-
    958; and *Sancta Susanna*, 78
Romania, 742-745, 916-918
Rometsch, Ellen, 367
Ronson, Gerald, 753-756
Roosevelt, Eleanor, 159, 194, 205,
    1114
Roosevelt, Franklin D., 62, 70, 128,
    155, 159, 194, 200-201; and
    airmail scandal, 144; and
    Japanese American internment,
    205-209; and Ezra Pound, 236
Roosevelt, Theodore, 1-3, 26, 50;
    and Joseph R. Burton, 4-6
Roots (Haley), 520-522
Rosa, John W., 1062
Rose, Flemming, 1075-1077

Rose, Pete, 735-738
Roselli, John, 330
Rosenberg, Alfred, 226, 230
Rosoff, William L., 1050
Ross, Andrew, 837
Ross, Karl, 369
Rossellini, Roberto, 263-265
Rossellini, Roberto Ingmar, 263
Rostenkowski, Dan, 803-806
Rota, Robert V., 803
Roth, Al, 274
Rothstein, Arnold, 66-70
Rove, Karl, 1011
Royal Commission of Inquiry on
    the Blood System, 868-871
Royal Institute of British
    Architects, 431
Royalty. *See Category Index*
Rubber; automobile tires, 534-536;
    in Congo Free State, 31-33; in
    Liberia, 143, 1078-1080
Ruckelshaus, William, 615
Rudel, Hans-Ulrich, 503-505
Rudge, Olga, 236
Ruef, Abraham, 28-30
Ruiz Massieu, José Francisco, 824-
    826
Rumsfeld, Donald, 991, 1034
Rural Electrification Act of 1936,
    155
Rushmore, Howard, 296
Russia. *See Geographical Index*;
    Soviet Union
Russian Civil War, 106, 226
Russian Revolution, 75, 106, 167;
    and Sisson documents, 307-310
Rutgers University women's
    basketball team, 1142-1144
Ryan, Thomas Fortune, 2

S. E. Massengill Company, 193-
    195
Sabich, Vladimir, 485-487
Sachs, Irving, 310-313
Safe Drinking Water Act of 1986,
    617
Salé, Jamie, 962-964
Salinas de Gortari, Carlos, 824-826
Salinas de Gortari, Raúl, 824-826

Salmonella, 664, 983
Salomon, Rick, 1019-1021
Salter, Roberta Semple, 115
Samuel, Herbert, 43
San Antonio Express-News, 1000
San Francisco; Fatty Arbuckle trial, 79-82; city graft, 28-30; Warren Harding's death, 125; police corruption, 191-193; SLA bank robbery, 450-453
Sancha, Antonia de, 792
Sanchez, Ricardo, 1034-1038
Sancta Susanna (opera), 76-79
Santoni, Mimi, 456-459
Sapina, Ante, 1055-1058
Sarbanes-Oxley Act of 2002, 1115
Sarsgaard, Peter, 888
Sarti, Adolfo, 591-593
Sasso, Anthony P., 1155
Satterlee, Peggy, 202-205
Saud, Sultan bin Abdul Aziz al-, 453
Saunders, Ernest, 753-756
Save Our Children, 506
Saving Private Ryan (film), 951
Sawyer, Charles E., 89
Sawyer, Steve, 651-654
Scarsdale diet, 565-567
Schatten, Gerald, 1094-1097
Scheer, Robert, 497
Scheuer, Sandra, 410-413
Schindel, Robert, 1109
Schledwitz, Karl A., 649
Schlesinger, James, 1034
Schmidlapp, W. Horace, 246
Schmidt, Hermann, 503-505
Schmitz, Eugene E., 28-30
Schmitz, John G., 603-605
Schmitz, Joseph E., 605
Schön, Jan Hendrik, 980-982
Schreiber, Belle, 52
Schreiber, Karlheinz, 830-833
Schreuder, Frances, 528-530
Schreuder, Marc, 528
Schrock, Edward, 1041-1044
Schroeder, William, 410-413
Schwartzkoppen, Max von, 20
Schwarzenegger, Arnold, 1016-1019

Schwebel, Stephen M., 1039
Schwimmer, Harry I., 310-313
Science and technology. *See Category Index*
Scotland, 879-881; Distillers Co., 754
Scott, Ian, 1112
Scott, Norman, 531-534
"Scottsboro Boys," 150-153
SEC. *See* Securities and Exchange Commission
Secord, Richard V., 676
Securities Act of 1933, 155, 389
Securities and Exchange Commission, U.S., 320-322, 483, 510, 649; and Eli M. Black, 471-473; and George W. Bush, 762-765; Enron investigation, 945-948; and financial markets collapse of 2008, 1178; and Hewlett-Packard, 1117; and Michael Milken, 726-729; mutual fund investigation, 1013-1016; and Martha Stewart, 1031-1034; and Westar Energy, 1072-1074; and Louis Wolfson, 389-391
Security Outsourcing Solutions, 1115
Seduction Act of 1922 (Alberta), 176
Seeds of Distrust (Hager), 974-977
Selbekk, Vebjørn, 1075-1077
Seles, Monica, 814
Selig, Bud, 1058
Seligmann, Reade, 1086
Senate, U.S. *See* Congress, U.S.
Sentelle, David B., 818
September 11, 2001, terrorist attacks, 778, 906, 995, 1065, 1075, 1155-1158
Seven Days in May (Knebel and Bailey), 175
Sevigny, Chloë, 1004-1007
Sévigny, Pierre, 377-379
Sex. *See Category Index*
Sex change. *See* Transsexualism
Sex crimes. *See Category Index*

Sexism. *See Category Index under Social issues and reform*
Sexual harassment; and Kofi Annan, 1039-1041; and Benjamin Chavis, 821-823; and Bill Clinton, 820, 875; at military academies, 801-802, 991-994; in Navy, 784-788; and Bill O'Reilly, 1047-1049; and John Prescott, 1089-1091; and Arnold Schwarzenegger, 1016-1019; and Clarence Thomas, 768-772; in workplaces, 502
Sexual Sterilization Act of 1928 (Alberta), 133-136
Sexuality in film, 165
Shalala, Donna, 1141
Shanley, Paul, 954
Sharpton, Al, 702-705, 1142
Shattered Glass (film), 888
Shaw, Artie, 317
Shaw, Steven, 673
"Shawinigate," 898-901
Sheehan, Neil, 416
Sheela, Ma Anand, 662-665
Sheldon, Jackie, 55-58
Shell crisis of 1915, 58-60
Sheppard, William Henry, 32
Sherwood, Carlton, 597-599
Shinto, Hisashi, 714-717
Short, Clare, 995-998
Shriver, Maria, 1016
Shuler, Robert P., 117
Siebert, Tara, 717-720
Siegelman, Don, 909
Signorini, Fernando, 816
Sikharulidze, Anton, 962-964
Silent Spring (Carson), 547
Sills, Beverly, 694
Silvey, Joyce, 509
Simple Life, The (television), 1020
Simpson, Nicole Brown, 806-809
Simpson, O. J., 806-812, 1129-1131
Simpson, Tom, 1103
Simpson, Wallis, 187-190, 196-198, 213
Sin, Jaime, 629

Sinatra, Frank, 329
Sinclair, Harry F., 95-99
Sindona, Michele, 591, 606-609
Singer, Isaac Merritt, 34
Singer, Paris, 34-36
Singer, Patrick, 34
Sirens (film), 827
Sisson, Edgar, 307-310
Sisson documents, 307-310
Six Crises (Nixon), 261
60 Minutes, 424, 436, 835, 888; Abu Ghraib prison, 1034-1038; Strom Thurmond, 1022-1024; Tobacco industry corruption, 833-836
60 Minutes II, 1063; George W. Bush, 1044-1046
Sixty-ninth Regiment Armory, 49
"Skategate," 962-964
Skilling, Jeffrey, 945-948
SLA. *See* Symbionese Liberation Army
Slaton, Lewis, 717
Slavery; African slave trade, 31; in Congo, 32; Jesse Jackson on, 634; in Liberia, 142-144, 1078-1080; and orphans, 893
Slaves in the Family (Ball), 521
Slotnick, Barry, 641
Smith, Jesse W., 92-95
Smith, Lonnie, 666
Smith, Thomas Daniel, 431
Smith, William Kennedy, 759-762, 866
SMU. *See* Southern Methodist University
Smuts, Jan, 84
Snyder, John W., Jr., 785
Soap Box Derby, 444-446
Soccer, 815-818; game fixing, 55-58, 1055-1058, 1092-1094
Social issues and reform. *See Category Index*
Social Text (journal), 837-840
Society for the Suppression of Vice, 122
Sohn, Lydia L., 980
Sokal, Alan, 837-840
"Soldiers Face Neglect, Frustration

at Army's Top Medical Facility" (February 18, 2007), 1139
Solomon, Paul M., 980
Soltysik, Patricia, 450
"Some People Push Back" (Ward Churchill), 1157
Sonderbund Exhibition, 49
Song My massacre, 401-404
Sorensen, Larry, 667
Sosa, Sammy, 1058
South Africa, 84, 543-545
South Korea. *See Geographical Index*
Southern Methodist University football, 687-689
Soviet Union, 105-108, 167-169, 266, 307; atheism in, 465, 673; espionage, 347-349, 355-358, 377-379, 931-933; and space race, 320-321; and the Vatican, 353; wheat purchases, 501; World War II, 210
Spaak, Paul-Henri, 276-279
Space and aviation. *See Category Index*
Spain, 136-139
Spanish Civil War, 559
Spano, John A., Jr., 901-903
Speak Out (television), 605
Speaker, Tris, 118-121
Special Committee on Un-American Activities, 248
Special Committee to Investigate Organized Crime in Interstate Commerce, 270-273
Spence, Wishart, 377
Spiegel, Der (magazine), 349-352, 504, 658, 1111
Spitzer, Eliot L., 1013-1016, 1050-1052, 1167-1170
Spitzer, Silda Wall, 1167
Spokane, Washington, 1081-1083
Sports. *See Category Index; individual sports*
Sports Illustrated (magazine), 736, 942-943, 1002-1004
Sprague, Richard, 404
Sprague, Robert, 720-723
Springer, Jerry, 828

"Spygate," 1161-1163
Spying. *See Category Index under Espionage*
"Squidgygate," 789-792
Stacpoole, Michael, 696-698
Stalin, Joseph, 106, 167-169; and picture forgery, 811
Stammberger, Wolfgang, 349
Standard and Poor's, 1176
Standard Oil; campaign contributions, 1
Stanford, Karin, 895
Stanford University, 1102; King Papers Project, 739; prison experiment, 420-422
Stanley, David, 687
Stanley, Henry Morton, 31-33
Stansel, Mary E., 821
Stant, Shane, 812
Stark, Ray, 509
StarKist Canada, 660
Starr, Kenneth, 818-821, 874-878
State Department, U.S., 455; and "Bananagate," 471-473; and Alger Hiss, 259-262; and "Koreagate," 479, 481; and Joseph McCarthy, 266-270; and Peace Corps murder, 476-478
Stavisky, Alexandre, 170-172
Stearns, Cliff, 1116
Stein, Gertrude, 51
Stem cell research, 1094-1097
Stempel, Herb, 326-329
Stennis, John, 384
Stent, Julia, 798-800
Stern, David, 1172-1175
Stern, Der (magazine), 618-621
Stern, Howard, 828
Sternberg, Saul, 978
Stevenson, Andrew, 852
Stewart, Harold, 223-225
Stewart, Martha, 1031-1034
Stiglitz, Joseph E., 1176
Stimson, Henry L., 205
Stoker, Bram, 111-114
Stoker, Florence, 111-114
Stokes, Louis, 621
Stompanato, Johnny, 317-319
Stonehouse, John, 468-470

Stonewall Rebellion, 506
Storer, George, 335-337
Stramm, August, 76-79
Strauss, Franz Josef, 349-352
Street Betting Act of 1906, 56
Stringer, C. Vivian, 1142
Stuckle, Carla, 603-605
Studds, Gerry, 621-624
Subprime, definition of, 1136
Subprime mortgage industry, 1134-1138
"Subway Vigilante," 641-644
Suer, Oral, 1028-1030
Suicide. *See Category Index under Murder and suicide*
Sulfanilamide, 193-195
Sullivan, Joseph, 66
Sullivan, Shannon, 1081-1083
Superfund Act. *See* Comprehensive Environmental Response, Compensation, and Liability Act of 1980
Superfund Act of 1986, 617
Supreme Court, U.S., 47; Clinton impeachment, 877; Abe Fortas, 390-394; and Japanese American internment, 206; and Pentagon Papers, 417; and Adam Clayton Powell, Jr., 381; and "Scottsboro Boys," 152-153; and Teapot Dome scandal, 98; Clarence Thomas, 768-772; and Watergate scandal, 429, 448. *See also* individual cases
Supreme Court of Canada, 176, 378, 870
Supreme Court of the Philippines, 600-602
Surreal Life, The (television), 692
Surrealism, definition of, 148
Surrealist films, 136-139, 147-150
Surrealist painting, 138
Suskind, Richard, 422-425
Swaggart, Jimmy, 711-714, 1152
Swanson, Gloria, 127-130
Sweden, 263-265
Sweeney, Constance M., 954
Sweeney, James, 568
Sweet, Robert W., 1039

Swiss Bankers Association, 859
Switzerland. *See Geographical Index*
Sykes, Roberta, 852
Symbionese Liberation Army, 450-453

Taft, William Howard, 46
Taguba, Antonio, 1034-1038
Taguba Report, 1036
Tailhook Association, 785, 991
Tailhook sexual assault scandal, 784-788
Takeoka, Toshiki, 919-921
Takeshita, Noboru, 714-717, 733-735
Talk shows, 583, 828, 1032; Don Imus, 1142-1144
Talmadge, Betty, 553
Talmadge, Herman E., 553-555
Talmadge, Robert S., 553
Tanaka, Kakuei, 482-485
Tanaka, Tsutomu, 398-400
Tardieu, André, 139-141
Tarleton, Donald, 511
Tarnower, Herman, 565-567
Tariff Act of 1930, 164
Task Force Barker, 401
Tate, Sharon, 246, 522
Taung child, 292
Tax conspiracy, 310-313
Tax evasion, 84; Sherman Adams, 322; Adelphia Communications, 972; Spiro T. Agnew, 447, 449; Bobby Baker, 368; Dave Beck, 324; Earl Butz, 502; Cal Caprasso, 694; Clearstream Financial Clearinghouse, 925; Randall Cunningham, 1066; John De Lorean, 611; Leona Helmsley, 776-778; Kent Hovind, 1123-1126; Webster Hubbell, 819; Michael Milken, 728; Sun Myung Moon, 481; Tom Pendergast, 199-201; Pete Rose, 737; Irving Sachs, 312; Karlheinz Schreiber, 832
Taylor, Norman, 1028-1030
Taylor, Tony, 1158

Taylor, William Desmond, 73-76, 88
"Tea-rooming," 407
Teamsters Union, 323-325
Teapot Dome scandal, 91, 95-99, 125
Tearoom Trade (Humphreys), 407-409
Teets, Peter B., 991
Teilhard de Chardin, Pierre, 293, 457
Television; game shows, 326-329
Temple, Tracey, 1089-1091
Tennis, 239-242, 588-591
Terboven, Josef, 226
Teti, Raffaello, 889
Thalidomide, 301-304
Thamel, Pete, 1101
Thatcher, Margaret, 645-647, 696, 792, 798; and Edwina Currie, 983; and Cecil Parkinson, 631-633; and Westland Aircraft, 645-647
Thaw, Harry Kendall, 16-19
Thomas, Clarence, 768-772
Thomas, Frank, 431
Thomas, J. Parnell, 248-250, 260
Thomas, James Henry, 181-184
Thomas, Sir Leslie, 181
Thompson, Frank, 561-562
Thompson, Hugh, Jr., 401
Thompson, Margaret W., 133
Thomsen, Ian, 942
Thornburgh, Dick, 684
Thorpe, Franklyn, 184-187
Thorpe, Jeremy, 531-534
Thrasher, Donald, 1020
Three Weeks (Glyn), 25-27
Thring, G. Herbert, 111
Thurmond, Strom, 384, 988-991, 1022-1024
Tidal Basin incident, 462-465
Tiedge, Hans-Joachim, 657-659
Tierney, Patrick, 910-912
Tilden, Bill, 239-242
Tillman, Benjamin, 3
Tillman Act of 1907, 3
Time magazine, 154, 289, 376, 526, 569, 740, 757; and Ted

Haggard, 1127; "Man of the Year," 209; and O. J. Simpson, 810-812; and Eliot Spitzer, 1050; and Whitewater investigation, 811

Times of London, 59, 293, 618, 983

Timony, James, 122

Tiriac, Ion, 916

Tisa, Benedict, 609

Tobacco industry corruption, 833-836

Tobias, Randall L., 1151

Todd, Thelma, 178-181

Tohoku Paleolithic Institute, 919-921

Tokes, Laszlo, 742-745

Tolstoy, Ilia, 130-133

Tomasz, 1084-1086

Tonga, 476-478

Tonight Show, The (television), 673-675, 828, 1017

Topping, Henry, 317

Torture, 340, 840, 922; Abu Ghraib prison, 1034-1038

Tour de France, 1103-1106

Tower, John, 384

Tower Commission, 678

Trade and commerce. *See Category Index*

Trandahl, Jeff, 1118-1120

Transsexualism, 289-291

Treason; Charles and Fern Bedaux, 212-214; Alfred Dreyfus, 19-22; Errol Flynn, 559-561; Jane Fonda, 434-436; Knut Hamsun, 229-232; Robert Hanssen, 931-933; Pierre Laval, 209-211; Philippe Pétain, 232-236; Ezra Pound, 236-239; Vidkun Quisling, 226-229; and *Der Spiegel*, 349-352; Hans-Joachim Tiedge, 657-659

Treasury Department, U.S., 1176

Trevenar, Bert, 304-306

Trevor-Roper, Hugh, 618

Triangle Shirtwaist factory fire, 40-43, 219

Trindle, Renee, 991

Triola, Michelle, 540-542

Tripp, Linda, 874-878

Tri-State Crematory, 964-967

Trotsky, Leon, 106, 226

Truman, Harry S., 8, 989, 1023; and T. Lamar Caudle, 280; and Matthew J. Connelly, 310-313; and Douglas MacArthur, 175; and Joseph McCarthy, 266-270; and Thomas Joseph Pendergast, 199-201

Truman Committee, 311

Trungpa, Chögyam, 474-476

Tryforos, Lynne, 565

Tuberville, Tommy, 1101-1103

"Tunagate," 660-662

Turcotte, Jean-Claude, 892-895

Turkey, 843-845

Turnbull, Sandy, 55

Turner, Lana, 317-319

Tuskegee Syphilis Study, 437-440

Twain, Mark, 33

Twenty-One (television), 326-329

291 Gallery, 49

Tyler, Nancy Carole, 365

Tyson, Mike, 703

Ueberroth, Peter, 556, 666-669, 737

Ullman, Harlan K., 1151

Ulmer, Walter F., 488

UMWA. *See* United Mine Workers of America

U.N. *See* United Nations

Uncle Tom's Cabin (Stowe), 521

Unification Church, 479, 939

Union of European Football Associations, 1093

United American Bank, 648-650

United Fruit Company, 471

United Mine Workers of America, 404-406

United Nations; Kofi Annan, 1039-1041; Convention Against Torture, 1037; and Liberia, 1080; Oil-for-Food Programme, 481, 1053-1055; and South Korea, 479; spying on, 995-998; Kurt Waldheim, 669-672

United Nations War Crimes Commission, 670

United Penn Bank, 637

United States. *See Geographical Index*

United Way, 1028-1030

University of Alabama football, 1002-1004

University of Colorado, 1155-1158

University of Georgia, 389; basketball, 950, 968-970

University of Pittsburgh, 720-723

Uno, Sosuke, 733-735

Upton and the Army (Ambrose), 952

Us, Gonca, 843

Vander Schaaf, Derek, 785

Vassall, John, 347-349

Vatican Bank, 606-609

Vatican City, 353-355, 606-609

Vaughn, Kia, 1142

Velzen, Dick van, 927-930, 936-938

Venezuela measles epidemic, 910-912

Ver, Fabian, 628

Vermeersch, Arthur, 33

Veterans Bureau, 89-92, 95, 103

Vick, Michael, 1158-1161

Victor/Victoria (film), 612

Video evidence, 527, 562, 583, 674, 715, 920, 1008, 1077, 1088; and Marion Barry, 748-750; and Joe Biden, 698-701; and Paris Hilton, 1019-1021; and Michael Jackson, 1026; and William J. Jefferson, 1147-1150; and R. Kelly, 1170-1172; and Rob Lowe, 717-720; and McMartin Preschool, 625-626; and New England Patriots, 1161-1163; and Paul Reubens, 766

Viet Minh, 257-259

Vietnam. *See Geographical Index*

Vietnam War, 257, 269, 362-365, 442, 490, 936, 1065; and Jane

Fonda, 434-436; My Lai massacre, 401-404, 937; and Pentagon Papers, 416-419; protests against, 410-413
Vigilantism, 641-644
Vincent, Fay, 735-738
Violence. *See also Category Index*; *types of violence*
Viridiana (film), 138, 149
Vitter, David, 1150-1153
Volcker, Paul, 858-861, 1053-1055
Volcker Commission, 858-861
Volkswagen, 860
Volstead Act of 1919, 93, 103-105
Von Eschenbach, Andrew C., 1097
Vorster, B. J., 543-545

Wade, Mitchell, 1064
Wagner, Robert F., 40-43
Wagner Act. *See* National Labor Relations Act of 1935
Wakeman, Nancy, 386-388
Wakeman, William T., 386-388
Waksal, Samuel D., 1031-1034
Waldheim, Kurt, 669-672
Wałęsa, Lech, 1111
Walker, Margaret, 520
Wall Street investment banks, 1176
Wallace, George, 604
Wallace, Mike, 424, 833-836
Wallonia, 276-279
Walsh, Matt, 1161
Walsh, Thomas J., 95
Walter Reed Army Hospital, 249, 1138-1142
Walters, Walter W., 156-160
Wanda Koolmatrie hoax, 852-854
Ward, Stephen, 355-358
Warner, Ed, 274
Warren, Earl, 380-383, 393
Washington, Claudell, 667
Washington, D.C.; Marion Barry, 748-750; Bonus Army, 156-160
Washington, George, 938
Washington Merry-Go-Round, 174, 248-250, 384-386

Washington Mutual, 1177
Washington Post, 97, 385, 463, 733, 801, 998, 1028; and Janet Cooke, 585-588; and Wayne L. Hays, 491-493; and Jesse Jackson, 633-636; and Rita Jenrette, 583; and Richard Nixon, 286, 425-431, 453-456; and organized crime, 271; Pentagon Papers, 417; and J. Parnell Thomas, 248-250; and Walter Reed Army Hospital, 1138-1142; and Watergate, 425-431; and Whitewater investigation, 818; and Jim Wright, 732
Washington-Williams, Essie Mae, 1022-1024
Watch and Ward Society, 26
Water Quality Act of 1987, 617
Watergate scandal, 312, 418-419, 425-431, 448, 482, 497; and Spiro T. Agnew, 449; and First Amendment, 418; and later reforms, 553
Watkins, Harold Cole, 193-195
Watkins, Sherron, 945-948
Wehner, Herbert, 503
Wehner, John, 626
Weida, John A., 1062-1064
Weidenreich, Franz, 292-295
Weidner, Clinton, 1072-1074
Weightman, George W., 1138-1142
Weinberg, Melvin, 561
Weinberger, Caspar, 676
Weiner, Joseph, 292
Weinstein, Bernard, 840
Weinstein, Michael L., 1062-1064
Welch, Joseph Nye, 266-270
Welles, Orson, 110, 165, 254
Wesson, Marianne, 1156
West, Enoch, 55
West, James E., 1081-1083
West, Mae, 122-124
West, Roland, 178-181
West Point, 173, 937; cheating scandal, 488-490
Westar Energy, 1072-1074

Western Defense Command, 205
Western State Hospital, 216
Westland Aircraft, 645-647
Westmoreland, William, 937
Whalen, Robert P., 546
Whaley, Arthur, 55
White, Kevin, 948
White, Stanford, 16-19
White-Slave Traffic Act of 1910. *See* Mann Act of 1910
White slavery, 52
Whitewater investigation, 818-821, 874
WHO. *See* World Health Organization
Widnall, Sheila, 855-858
Wiesenthal, Simon, 669-672
Wigand, Jeffrey, 833-836
Wilcox, Breckenridge, 720
Wild Blue, The (Ambrose), 951-953
Wilhelm II. *See* William II
Wilkes, Brent, 1064
William II, 9-12
Williams, Edward Bennett, 365, 368
Williams, George Washington, 32
Williams, Harrison A., 561
Williams, Lefty, 66-70
Williams, Vanessa, 382, 638-641
Wills, Frank, 425
Willson, Henry, 295-298
Wilson, David, 597
Wilson, Harold, 468-470
Wilson, Helen Dolan, 597
Wilson, Howard, 898-901
Wilson, Joseph, 1010-1013
Windsor, Duke of, 187-190, 196-198, 213
Witch hunts, 9, 627, 900
Witt, Robert, 1002-1004
Wittig, David, 1072-1074
WJC. *See* World Jewish Congress
Wolf, Markus, 657
Wolfson, Louis, 389-391
Women's issues. *See Category Index*
Woodward, Arthur Smith, 292-295
Woodward, Bob, 425-431

Works Progress Administration, 248

World Cup, 815-818, 1055-1057, 1093

World Health Organization, 910

World Jewish Congress, 669, 858-861

World Jewish Restitution Organization, 859

World Trade Center, 1157

World War I, 84, 90, 93, 103, 139; and British royal family, 196-198; Canadian Expeditionary Force, 131; and Marie Curie, 38; and Alfred Dreyfus, 21; and European currencies, 64; and Leopold III, 277; and Douglas MacArthur, 173; and oil reserves, 96; and Russia, 309; Shell crisis, 58-60; veterans, 156-160, 174, 188; and William II, 9-12

World War II, 503-505; and British royal family, 189; and France, 209-211; German atrocities, 338; and Germany, 209-211; Japanese American internment, 205-209; and Carole Landis, 245; and Leopold III, 276; and Douglas MacArthur, 175; Nazi collaborators, 209-214, 226-236, 559-561, 1109-1112; and Pius XII, 353-355; and Ezra Pound, 236-239; in Southeast Asia, 257; Truman Committee, 311. *See also* Holocaust; Nazi collaborators and sympathizers

Worldwide Church of God, 525-528

Wörner, Manfred, 503

"Wounded warriors," 1140

Wright, Betty, 730

Wright, Jim, 730-732

Wright, Roy, 150-153

Wronker-Flatow, Manfred, 111

Yablonski, Joseph, 404-406

Yaeger, Don, 1002-1004

Yale University, 338, 705-708

Yamamoto, Taku, 1145

Yancy, Allen, 142-144

Yasui, Minoru, 205

Yasui v. United States (1943), 206

Yellow Robe, Chauncey, 130

Yeo, Tim, 798-800

Yoshinaga, Yusuke, 714-717

Young, Andrew, 634

Younger, George, 83

Zamsky, Linda, 933

Zedillo Ponce de Léon, Ernesto, 824-826

Zheng Xiaoyu, 1097-1100

Zigo, Marc, 855-858

Zihlman, Frederick N., 103

Zimbardo, Philip, 420-422

Zinovyev, Grigory Yevseyevich, 106, 108-111

Zinovyev letter; excerpt, 107

"Zippergate," 874-878

Zola, Émile, 19-22

Zwicker, Ralph W., 266-270

ZZZZ Best Company, 708-710